# Acclaim for *The Patton Papers*

"A simply superb exposure of the Great Georgie out of his own mouth."
—**S.L.A. Marshall**

"[*The Patton Papers*] reveal a much more complicated character than his comicbook legend suggested.... Blumenson has done a superb job of editing Patton's diaries, letters, memos and speeches. He has skillfully stitched them together with explanatory narrative."
—*Time*

"Here is Patton in all his truculent glory.... Blumenson is extraordinarily evenhanded in his final assessment."
—**Christopher Lehmann-Haupt**, *New York Times*

"Blumenson brings his sharp psychological insight into the inner turmoil of George Patton.... It is Patton's often acute and unexpected humorous characterizations of men that provide the freshest perceptions in this... sympathetic and flawlessly crafted biography."
—*New York Times Book Review*

"By means of superior editing and sparing comment of his own, Blumenson has permitted George S. Patton to speak for himself through his letters and diaries, and the result is a disturbing and absorbing portrait."
—*Saturday Review*

"The only definitive work ever published on America's most controversial military figure... The multifaceted personality of Patton comes through with a force that is rare in literary works today."
—*Dallas News*

"Blumenson has produced the first picture of Patton that is more than one dimensional. He gives insights into Patton's mind and character hitherto unknown, but, as important, also gives a clear portrait of Patton's era.... This biography is unique; there is nothing in print that so clarifies this individual or provides the wealth of data between two covers. A must."
—*Choice*

"The lavish use of Patton's letters and diaries brings the general sharply to life—an intelligent, bigoted, inquisitive, generous, witty, sensitive, spiteful man, impressive and exasperating, thoroughly right or totally wrong, but never a waffler. A great soldier who just possibly should never have been a soldier at all." —**Phoebe Adams**, *New Yorker*

"A long book, but it has no dull pages . . . The most definitive biography of one our most remarkable fighting men." —*Newsday*

"The excellent and judicious selection by Blumenson has given us a self-portrait of Patton that no biographer could possibly draw. . . . Blumenson has presented the sharpest delineation of any American general in World War II. . . . One could only wish that other military leaders would be so well served." —*Library Journal*

"A masterful job." —*Christian Science Monitor*

# THE PATTON PAPERS

Books by Martin Blumenson

*Breakout and Pursuit*

*The Duel for France: 1944*

*Anzio: The Gamble That Failed*

*Kasserine Pass*

*Sicily: Whose Victory?*

*Salerno to Cassino*

*Bloody River: The Real Tragedy of the Rapido*

*Eisenhower*

*The Patton Papers: 1885–1940*

*The Patton Papers: 1940–1945*

*The Battle of the Generals: The Untold Story of the Falaise Pocket,*
*the Campaign that Should Have Won War World II*

*Patton: The Man Behind the Legend*

With James L. Stokesbury

*Masters of the Art of Command*

# THE PATTON PAPERS

## 1940-1945

MARTIN BLUMENSON

ILLUSTRATED WITH PHOTOGRAPHS
AND WITH MAPS BY SAMUEL H. BRYANT

DA CAPO PRESS

Library of Congress Cataloging in Publication Data

Blumenson, Martin.
The Patton papers, 1940-1945 / Martin Blumenson; illustrated with photographs and with maps by Samuel H. Bryant.—1st Da Capo Press ed.
p. cm.
Originally published in 1974 by Houghton Mifflin as volume 2 of The Patton papers.
Includes index.
ISBN 0-306-80717-3 (alk. paper)
1. Patton, George S. (George Smith), 1885-1945. 2. Generals—United States—Biography. 3. World War, 1939-1945—United States. 4. United States. Army—Biography. I. Title.
E745.P3B55 1996
355.3'31'092—dc20 96-15251
[B] CIP

This Da Capo Press paperback edition of *The Patton Papers, 1940-1945* is an unabridged republication of the edition first published in Boston in 1974. It is reprinted by arrangement with Houghton Mifflin Company and the author.



5 6 7 8 9 10 02

Published by Da Capo Press, Inc.
A member of the Perseus Books Group



Manufactured in the United States of America

Excerpts from Drive by Charles Codman, copyright © 1957 by Theodora Duer Codman, are reprinted by permission of Little, Brown and Co., in association with The Atlantic Monthly Press. Further acknowledgments appear on page 865.

*To my wife*

. . .

*"I have come to consider myself as a sort of chip floating down a river of destiny. So far I have asked for nothing and received a great deal more than my deserts, and I believe that perhaps the same thing works in other human relations. I believe it is essential to retain your self-confidence and do your duty, and aside from that, let nature take care of itself."*

—*George S. Patton, Jr.*

# Preface

WHILE THE FIRST VOLUME of *The Patton Papers* showed the growth of the man and the soldier, this deals with the man as a general.

During the period covered here, Patton was at his peak. He put to use all the expertise he had accumulated during a lifetime of preoccupation with his profession — not only the technical knowledge of warfare in his time, but also the psychological and emotional attributes of leadership. Prepared for World War II, he attained in these years all that he ever sought. He gained victories, recognition, and applause. Yet he was never quite aware of the place he had carved for himself in history, never quite sure of the affection he had won from people everywhere. At the end he was still trying, driving himself, striving to satisfy his insatiable lust for fame.

In this volume I have attempted to follow Vincent Sheean's precept: "Very often what the general does is less important than what he is." To present what Patton was as well as what he did has been my purpose. The question that frames this book is: what was the source of his military genius and how did he make it work? My broad conclusion is that the personality and the action, the word and the deed, the style and the substance were inseparable. So were the man and the military officer.

My focus is on the living human being who became a historical figure, and I have endeavored to let him speak for himself through his papers, particularly his diary. As in Mexico and in France, Patton started a notebook when he went off to war. His journal forms the heart of this book.

The reasons why anyone makes a permanent record of his thoughts and activities are, of course, diverse. In the mind of the journal-keeper must surely be an element of self-importance, a belief that his life is significant and interesting, especially to others. There must also be a sense of history and a certainty that the individual has an effect on — perhaps merely reflects, but truly so — his time and place. He must have a feeling of personal mission and a conviction that future generations will want to know what he did and said.

In Patton's case, he wrote or dictated his words as a nod to his own destiny, that vague but almost palpable force, like a holy grail, that he was sure led and guided him toward some great historic goal.

He also maintained a journal to amuse himself, to impress his family and close friends, and, eventually, to help his biographer understand his view and version of what happened.

Perhaps most important, the diary was his means of ridding himself of his frequent anguish, of finding comfort in moments of bitterness and discontent. It was a substitute confidant, a surrogate companion, for he sorely missed the presence of his wife who understood, supported, and stabilized him. Although he wrote to her frequently, censorship constrained his remarks. The diary allowed him to say exactly what he wished, explicitly yet privately, without compromising the public loyalty to his superiors that was one of his highest virtues.

The caustic and unflattering comments about his contemporaries were the product of impulse. He was an impetuous man, and his diary was a luxury that allowed him to unburden himself without self-restraint. It served to give him balance. The entries make clear the ambivalence he had toward his associates as well as his uncertainty toward himself. How much of what he wrote he really meant or actually believed is continually open to question.

The diary entries are occasionally self-serving, sometimes inaccurate, always perceptive and fresh. They mirror faithfully his moods, the state of his spirit at any given moment, his joys and disappointments. They often reveal the flavor rather than the fact.

I have omitted most of the tactical details or operational aspects of his battles that appear in the journal, for many excellent works of military history describe and analyze his campaigns. My interest is to show what Patton did as a general rather than what his forces accomplished and how they did so. My aim is to uncover his personal contribution to the war, how he discharged the responsibilities of a leader in combat and what influence he exerted.

From time to time I have supplemented Patton's observations with the more or less official headquarters journal maintained by Major General Hobart Gay, probably his closest friend and associate.

Hardly less valuable than Patton's diary are his letters to his wife. Some were written in a hardly decipherable longhand. A few were dictated. Most were composed on his portable typewriter. The relationship implicit in the correspondence — I have included several of Mrs. Patton's letters — presents another dimension of Patton's complex character.

In the following pages, all passages taken directly from the sources are set off in the text by quotation marks or are otherwise indicated. Brackets in quotations enclose words I have added to complete or summarize a sentence or thought, or to explain what might otherwise be obscure. A series of three periods in a quotation signals the omission of words I judged to be irrelevant. In some instances I have changed the punctuation to help the reader.

All errors of omission and commission, as well as of interpretation and judgment, are mine alone.

— MARTIN BLUMENSON

# Contents

# Illustrations

*Following page 716*



We acknowledge with thanks the assistance of Mrs. J. W. Totten, the Association of the U.S. Army, the U.S. Army Photographic Library, and the Library of Congress.

## MAPS

# I

# United States

*"May God have mercy on our enemies; they will need it."*

CHAPTER 1

# Fort Benning: Brigade

*"All that is now needed is a nice juicy war."*

*News Story, "Army Horseman to Lead Ft. Benning Tank Brigade," Washington* Evening Star, *July 24, 1940*

The first tank officer of the United States Army bade farewell today to his Fort Myer command, and after a 23-year lapse returned to the mechanized mode of warfare.

Colonel George S. Patton, Jr., commander of the 3d Cavalry since 1938, was escorted from the post by a squadron of horsemen and two armored cars after ceremonies that brought unabashed tears to the veteran of 31 years [of Army service] . . .

He will report at Fort Benning, Ga., within a week to take command of a brigade of the armored division newly organized to form this country's answer to blitzkrieg war.

FOR GEORGE S. PATTON, JR., who was sure that the power of fate governed his existence and was leading him to achievement and glory, his transfer from the polo fields of Fort Myer to the tank grounds of Fort Benning was nothing less than a manifestation of his guiding spirit. The shift in locale signaled a turning point in his career, a profound change in his life and fortunes. It promised new challenges to meet, difficult problems to overcome, and vague but dazzling intimations of future greatness.

There had been many such occurrences in the past, rather abrupt alterations in his assignments and duties. Some were unforeseen. Others he himself planned and assisted, for he believed strongly in helping to shape the destiny that he was convinced awaited him. Spurred by his vision of achievement, he always worked hard. He studied assiduously, cultivated the right people, and performed every task with enthusiasm, imagination, and efficiency. His perception of the right path to follow and his persistence in gaining access to it played their roles, but luck too was a large factor in his successes.

He had departed Virginia Military Institute after one year to attend the Military Academy at West Point. Upon graduation, he opted to join the cavalry. He managed to be assigned to the Washington, D.C., area, where he came to know Henry L. Stimson, Leonard Wood, and other men of prominence. He participated in the 1912 Olympics at Stockholm. He used his European visit to perfect his fencing so he could be named Master of the Sword. His presence at Fort Bliss brought him into contact with John J. Pershing, whom he accompanied to Mexico and to France. He chose to join the newly formed Tank Corps in World War I, and he organized the American light-tank brigade and led his men in battle.

All these situations gave him profit and pleasure, for he was ready and quick to exploit his opportunities. He drove himself to attain the highest standards of excellence, and he gained recognition. He was decorated for gallantry, awarded a medal for proficiency in a position of great responsibility, and promoted to colonel before the end of the First World War.

The interwar years were somewhat disappointing. Much of the excitement of army life vanished. Small congressional appropriations to the military, life on isolated posts, lack of interest on the part of the public tended to alienate Regular Army officers from the mainstream of American concerns and to kill the spirit of study and innovation.

With most of his colleagues, he was reduced in grade. He completed his military schooling at the Command and General Staff College and at the Army War College. He commanded, in turn, a company, a battalion, and a regiment. He served as a staff officer.

Along with a small group of dedicated professionals, Patton was confident that what was called "the next war" would come. In anticipation, he continued to read history voraciously, to train his men avidly, to search for new combat techniques, to play polo fiercely.

Military actions in Asia during the 1930s threatened to erupt into global conflict, but the German invasion of Poland in September 1939 plunged Europe into what was now indisputably World War II. For Americans, the "next war" came into sharper focus.

By then, Patton was once again a colonel of cavalry. He commanded

Fort Myer. His major task was to present the widely known horse shows that were models of precision and flair in equitation, ceremonies that delighted and impressed the influential community in Washington.

But Patton's occupation was anachronistic, out of tune with the world and the times. The German blitzkrieg in Poland was a sure indication, and, in the spring of 1940, the German lightning victories in the Low Countries and France proved exactly how outmoded the old cavalry and the old ways had become.

As the U.S. Army received increasing favor and funds, as the military stirred into an activity oriented toward modernization and growth, Patton began to fret about his job. He was in a backwater, and he was bored. Why was he being overlooked? Was he too old at fifty-five?

By experience, performance, and education, he was qualified for promotion to brigadier general. What he needed was a position that required general officer rank. What he desired was a place where he could help prepare the army for combat in case the United States entered the war.

The call finally came. His transfer to the 2d Armored Division put him squarely into the new army. Taking him back to the tanks and offering him the chance of immediate promotion, it promised opportunities for further advancement, for increasing responsibility, for greater accomplishment. It was, in short, another step to his ultimate goal, the fame and applause that he sought, the fulfillment of the destiny that he believed divine providence had reserved for him.

Patton and his wife Beatrice had the servants pack their clothes and household goods, arranged to have their boats stored, and closed Green Meadows, their home in South Hamilton, Massachusetts. Since their daughters Beatrice and Ruth Ellen were married to Regular Army officers, John K. Waters, Jr., and James W. Totten, and their sixteen-year-old son George was at preparatory school, Colonel and Mrs. Patton traveled to Columbus, Georgia, in his Packard Touring Sedan. Someone drove Mrs. Patton's 1938 Ford down. Two grooms took four horses south in the van.

Assigned quarters on the post, they slipped quickly into the social activities that still retained the flavor of the old army, the traditional calls, the custom of leaving cards. After their horses arrived, they rode regularly because it was good exercise and done in their circle.

They were well known in the army, and they were liked and admired for their charm and hospitality. If their affluent and graceful mode of living sometimes provoked envy and resentment among those less favored in material wealth, their lack of ostentation and pretension, their exquisite manners, her warm and gracious personality, his verve and exuberance in language and behavior quickly overcame first-impression reservations and misgivings.

Patton himself provoked a curiously ambivalent love-hate reaction. His children adored him, thought him the handsomest man in the world and bigger than life itself. And sometimes they came close to detesting him. Thoroughly self-centered, occasionally arrogant, he never seemed to give them all the attention and interest they wished. Undoubtedly they understood, if only unconsciously, that his cultivation of the warrior image, together with his constant pursuit of professional excellence, came first, ahead of them.

From time to time he had an odd lack of sensitivity to others. Once when he was rehearsing his young daughter for a horse show, he berated her constantly, criticizing and cussing her, finding everything wrong, her posture, the way she handled her horse, her method of taking the jumps. And finally he shouted in anger, "Get off that goddamn horse and let me show you how to do it." Meekly she climbed down, a chubby twelve-year-old, and he took her place. Resplendent and supremely self-confident in his horsemanship, he prepared to jump. As he spurred toward the obstacle, she was heard to say, "Dear God, please let that son of a bitch break his neck."

Yet he could be gentle and considerate too. When a soldier was called home on emergency leave and needed carfare, he could count on Patton for a loan.

There was something paradoxical about him. Smiling and ebullient, he could change in an instant and become cold, aloof, contemptuous. Mercurial if not exactly unstable, he was quiet, even brooding, yet capable of the unrestrained outburst. Self-contained, he was tortured.

Part of this was perhaps due to the injuries and hard knocks he sustained during his hyperactive and accident-prone life. Some physicians suspected that he suffered from a subdural haematoma that affected his behavior and mood. Once when he was playing polo in Hawaii, he had a truly spectacular fall. Everyone was sure that he was seriously hurt. He picked himself off the ground, shook his head, and continued the game. Two days later, when the family was sailing in their yacht with

Patton at the helm, he suddenly turned to his wife and asked what the hell had happened. The last thing he remembered was falling off his polo pony. A doctor confirmed that he had a concussion. After that, although he never drank heavily or to excess, he could no longer hold his liquor well. If he had a few drinks in the privacy of his home, he was likely to become tearful and maudlin, reciting poetry and reminiscing about his boyhood in California.

Yet he had a strong and authoritative personality. He had a distinctly patrician presence, an air of command. Although his self-control was usually complete, he sometimes appeared to be on the verge of hysteria. He was a bundle of contradictory and conflicting traits that made him seem to be several different persons all at once.

No matter what role he played, his will and drive dominated the image he presented to the public, and that force, that power, he directed unflaggingly toward gaining success — victory — in battle.

Would that moment come to him again as it had in 1918? He had first to prove all over again his fitness for high command.

As Patton settled into his new service home and carried out, with his usual vivacity, his troop duties and military functions at reveille and retreat, at inspections and reviews, at classrooms and training sites, at his office and in the field, he also applied himself to the problem of bringing himself up to date on tank warfare.

The first officer assigned to the Tank Corps, established by the American Expeditionary Force in France, he was the leading American tank expert in World War I. He knew more than any other American how to run, maintain, repair tanks, organize and train tank units, and employ them in combat. Since then he had kept abreast of armored developments by reading the professional military journals and by studying relevant reports from military attachés abroad.

As early as 1937, he enumerated "the very real advantages accruing from the use of motorization," but he warned that "modern marching" was quite different from "an uninterrupted pleasure journey down a ribbon of concrete." The employment of many tanks would congest narrow roads and offer lucrative targets to enemy artillery and airplanes.

In 1938, he noted from his study that commanders were frequently too far behind the fighting, reacted far too slowly to new battle information, transmitted orders much too late, and used mechanized forces timidly.

Vehicular forces tended to be too large, to have difficulty refueling, to move in a compact mass, to restrict their travel to roads, and to be vulnerable to air attack. Destroying bridges was the best way to stop and delay motorized troops. Conversely, mechanized columns had to have bridging materials with them, plus foot troops to gain and hold a bridgehead on the far side of a stream, in order to cross rivers.

These thoughts remained firmly fixed in his mind as lessons of what to avoid and what to do if ever he commanded in battle again.

An article by General Heinz Guderian, father of the German blitzkrieg forces, impressed Patton, who read carefully, early in 1939, how tanks, infantry, artillery, and close-support air coordinated their operations. He made voluminous notes, mainly messages to himself. For example, keep radios silent before contact with the enemy; use tanks for firepower rather than shock; make tanks fire their guns while moving; launch attacks on a wide front to disperse enemy fire; have commanders well forward to exercise personal leadership; use surprise to outwit antitank guns; refuel during the hours of darkness; establish many small gasoline dumps rather than a few large ones.

> The shorter a battle, the fewer men will be killed and hence the greater their self-confidence and enthusiasm. To produce a short battle, tanks must advance rapidly but not hastily . . . Mobile forces should be used in large groups and [be] vigorously led. They must attempt the impossible and dare the unknown.

Here was the old Patton at his best. Here too was the new Patton, stating in embryo form the philosophy he would implement in the coming war with such extraordinary effect.

The stunning success of the German armored forces made clear Patton's purpose: how could he transform the rudimentary American tank units into an organization that could meet the German veterans with a high degree of competence and confidence?

• • •

Patton's assignment to Fort Benning put him into the Armored Force, which came into being in July 1940, immediately after the German blitzkrieg through the Low Countries and France. Disturbed not only by the power of the panzers and the speed of their victories, but also by the lack of comparable forces in the United States, the Army Chief of Staff, General George C. Marshall, appointed Brigadier General Adna R. Chaffee, a cavalryman who was an old friend of Patton's, the first Chief of the Armored Force, gave him control of all the tank elements in the infantry, most of the mechanized formations in the cavalry, some field artillery and service units, and charged him to bring into existence a combat force to match the powerful German fighting machine.

Although a single modern armored division required more than 3000 wheel and track vehicles, Chaffee inherited less than 1000 tanks, all of them out of date, most of them of World War I vintage. A few newer tanks – 28, to be exact, 18 mediums and 10 lights – were obsolescent. Chaffee at once started a massive production effort. Because of Patton's influence, most of the early models were light tanks. This reflected Patton's experience in World War I and his cavalry background, both of which led him to emphasize mobility – movement and maneuver. Later the heavier medium tanks came into their own, as did more powerful tank guns.

Chaffee supervised the design and production of tanks and weapons, the formation and training of units, the procurement of personnel – all administrative matters. In order to employ and control the Armored Force units tactically – in training and presumably in combat – he also commanded the I Armored Corps. His corps headquarters directed two armored divisions, the 1st at Fort Knox, Kentucky, and the 2d at Fort Benning, Georgia, the only ones in the U.S. Army in 1940. Two years later there would be 14 armored divisions.

Chaffee's chief of staff was Colonel Sereno E. Brett, an infantryman who had been Patton's second in command in World War I and who had remained with tanks afterward. An experienced and extremely knowledgeable tanker, Brett unfortunately had a drinking problem.

The commander of the 1st Armored Division was John Magruder, who was considered too old for the position. Commanding the 2d Armored Division was Charles L. Scott, who was thought too colorless for the job.

The 2d Armored Brigade, which Patton commanded, was an integral part of the 2d Armored Division. The brigade was the fighting force – the iron fist, they said – and the rest of the division existed to support it. The brigade was designed to strike and penetrate weak points in the enemy's defensive line; or else to outflank and envelop the enemy's defenses. In either case, the brigade was to destroy enemy command posts, communication centers, supply dumps behind the front and thereby paralyze the enemy's ability to react.

This was precisely the blitzkrieg idea that the Germans built from J. F. C. Fuller's doctrine and B. H. Liddell Hart's notion of an "expanding torrent," and it solved the major tactical problem of World War I, how to break the enemy defensive barrier.

In March 1942, the armored division was expanded to embrace two brigades, now called combat commands. In September 1943, the armored division was given three combat commands, three tank battalions, three infantry battalions, and three artillery battalions.

All this was hardly glimpsed in mid-July 1940, when the 2d Armored Division came into being at Fort Benning with an initial complement of 99 officers and 2200 men, who were scattered from Harmony Church to Lawson Field, over a distance of eight miles, most of them living in pyramidal tents. Training sites had to be prepared, barracks built, mess halls, warehouses, repair shops established, roads improved and extended. New men were constantly arriving, and they had to be incorporated into the units. There was hardly any equipment, and wooden guns, brooms, and stovepipes served as weapons. Somehow a program got under way.

The activities of turning men into soldiers had hardly started when, early in September, Patton delivered his first formal lecture to the officers. Impeccably dressed, wearing overseas cap, khaki trousers, khaki shirt and tie, a glistening white belt, cavalry boots with a high shine, he mounted the stage of the school auditorium to present his account of the German campaign in Poland.

Confident and at ease as he addressed his audience, he was a commanding figure, and he dominated the scene. He had the knack of capturing his listeners' attention at the outset and of keeping it. The rapport, the strong bond between speaker and audience, was almost visible. The formality of his appearance and dress contrasted with his offhand manner. He was an accomplished lecturer, and he could make his hearers laugh by a scowl or a delicate movement of his eyebrows. He displayed, even exhibited, his broad knowledge of military history. Throughout his talk he impressed his officers with his vitality, his professional competence, and his masterful ability to draw them together into what they felt would eventually be a cohesive and highly effective team.

"The genesis of the armored operations in Poland," he began, could be traced to World War I. As soon as the Germans recovered from "the shock of utter defeat and dismemberment," they searched for a way to achieve prompt and decisive victory in the next war. They discovered that while the tank was a new weapon, it was being used without imagination – in "a method of warfare already demonstrated as outworn." As a consequence, while the Polish and later the French and British tankers failed in 1939 and 1940 because they persisted in the outmoded pattern of warfare, the Germans triumphed because their tactics were new.

When combining airplanes and tanks for battle, the Germans avoided falling victim to the "gadget complex." An airplane was not "a flying machine" but "primarily a cannon." A tank was not "a complicated iron box on caterpillar treads" but "a mobile squad." By "rigorous physical training and ruthless elimination" of the less hardy, the Germans produced an infantry of "unequaled marching ability." By quadrupling the accompanying weapons, they gave the foot soldiers overwhelming power. They created a balanced army so that the temporary disintegration of the enemy caused by air and armored forces could be exploited by the infantry-artillery team; or, conversely, a simple infantry victory could be converted into an annihilating success through armored and air pursuit.

The Germans rehearsed this concept in Spain during the civil war and had two "dry runs" in Austria and Czechoslovakia. In 1939, "Poland was their oyster."

> I am not going to give you a geographical account of the campaign. You all remember that west Poland sticks into Germany in much the same way that Brazil protrudes into the Atlantic. To remove this pimple, the Germans used the oldest plan in the world. It was invented by the cavemen when they surrounded the mammoth to destroy him . . . [It is called] a Cannae, a double envelopment.
>
> There is an old latin saw to the effect that, "To have a Cannae, you must have a Varro" . . . [In other words] in order to win a great victory you must have a dumb enemy commander. From what we know at the moment, the Poles qualified with such a high command.

In 216 B.C., at the battle of Cannae, 50,000 Carthaginians under Hannibal defeated 90,000 Romans under Varro. Hannibal lost 6000 men, Varro 80,000. It was normal for the defeated to have the higher losses

But since the battle of Lützen in 1632, "when gunpowder first came into its own," the reverse was true. Now the armored division might turn the equation around again, as in Poland.

> I could with great ease and apparent erudition, flash on the screen a map of Poland, thickly overlaid with intricate patterns . . . colored arrows, and dotted lines purporting to indicate the routes of the victorious German columns. But what purpose would such a picture serve?
>
> People of our rank have no choice as to the . . . higher strategy . . . Our job is to . . . [fight, and] without successful combat, all plans are bunk.

The armored divisions made the biggest headlines in Poland, but the infantry divisions broke the Polish defenses. Once a hole was opened, the armored divisions went through or took advantage of the battle confusion to get around the flank. In either case, the tanks were then employed "exactly as Murat used his cavalry corps in the days of Napoleon."

> In a former geological era when I was a boy studying latin, I had occasion to translate one of Caesar's remarks which as nearly as I can remember read something like this.
>
> "In the winter time, Caesar so trained his legions in all that became soldiers and so habituated them in the proper performance of their duties, that when in the spring he committed them to battle against the Gauls, it was not necessary to give them orders, for they knew what to do and how to do it."
>
> This quotation expresses very exactly the goal we are seeking in this division. I know that we shall attain it and when we do, may God have mercy on our enemies; they will need it.

Attaining that goal was a long way off in September 1940.

In the middle of the month, when Chaffee showed signs of failing health, Scott moved to Fort Knox and assumed temporary command of the I Armored Corps, thereby removing some of Chaffee's burdens. Patton became the acting commander of the 2d Armored Division.

Ten days later, President Franklin D. Roosevelt submitted to the Senate for approval a list of officers deemed worthy of promotion. There were 52 colonels, among them Patton, named for advancement to brigadier general. With the formality of the consent of the Senate gained on October 1, the War Department published the official order on the following day.

Patton was elated. He had already written two exuberant letters to an old polo-playing friend, who was also promoted.

*Letter, GSP, Jr., to Terry de la Mesa Allen, September 29, 1940*

My dear Terry: Congratulations! ! ! The ARMY HAS CERTAINLY GONE TO HELL when both of us are made [promoted].

I guess we must be in for some serious fighting and we are the ones who can lead the way to hell with[out] too much thinking.

There is little more I can say because you know I am tickled to death. Give my best to the lovley lady. Yours.

*Letter, GSP, Jr., to Allen, September 30, 1949*

Dear Terry: I just wrote Palmer Swift that with we three generals, the morals of the army may have shrunk, but the morale would be way up.

Haveing made us, all that is now needed is a nice juicy war.

CHAPTER 2

# Fort Benning: Division

*"I have sixteen thousand men who have never seen an officer, and twelve hundred officers who have never seen a man—so I have quite a job on my hands."*

As the Armored Force expanded in size, taking in more soldiers and creating new units, the need for experienced tankers increased, as did the opportunities for promotion. Patton thought of his friend Dwight D. Eisenhower, who was junior to him, having graduated from the Military Academy six years later, and who had been a tanker during World War I, though not overseas. When Patton brought the Tank Corps home from France in 1919, he met Eisenhower, who served under him for several months. They liked and admired each other at once, for each discovered in the other a profound interest in the military profession. They remained in contact through occasional correspondence during the interwar years. When Patton learned that Eisenhower had recently returned to the United States after service with Douglas MacArthur in the Philippines and was with the infantry at Fort Lewis, Washington, as a lieutenant colonel, Patton wrote and suggested that Eisenhower request a transfer to the Armored Force, specifically to the 2d Armored Division.

*Letter, Eisenhower to GSP, Jr., September 17, 1940*

Dear George: Thanks a lot for your recent note; I am flattered by your suggestion that I come to your outfit. It would be great to be in the tanks once more, and even better to be associated with you again . . .

I suppose it's too much to hope that I could have a regiment in your division, because I'm still almost three years away from my colonelcy. But *I think* I could do a damn good job of commanding a regiment . . .

Anyway, if there's a chance of that kind of an assignment, I'd be for it 100%. Will you write me again about it, so that I may know what you had in mind?

*Letter, GSP, Jr., to Eisenhower, October 1, 1940*

It seems highly probable that I will get one of the next two armored divisions which we firmly believe will be created in January or February, depending on [tank] production. If I do, I shall ask for you either as Chief of Staff, which I should prefer, or as a regimental commander. You can tell me which you want, for no matter how we get together we will go PLACES.

If you get a better offer in the meantime, take it, as I can't be sure, but I hope we can get together. At the moment there is nothing in the brigade good enough for you. However, if you want to take a chance, I will ask for you now . . .

Hoping we are together in a long and BLOODY war.

*Letter, GSP, Jr., to Eisenhower, November 1, 1940*

If I were you, I would apply for a transfer to the Armored Corps NOW . . .

If you apply for a transfer . . . say that you are an old tanker.

If you have any pull . . . use it for there will be 10 new generals in this corps pretty damned soon.

*Letter, Eisenhower to GSP, Jr., November 16, 1940*

I have already sent in a letter similar to the one you suggested . . .

One of the new corps commanders, down south, had asked for me as his Chief of Staff, but . . . it was turned down because I was so junior in rank . . . I am probably to be allowed to stay with troops. So I ought to be available and eligible for transfer when the time comes.

Instead of going to work for Patton, Eisenhower was assigned elsewhere. His and Patton's paths would cross briefly in 1941. Starting in 1942, they would be associated in the same endeavors, and their careers and achievements would forever be joined. Patton would be working for Eisenhower.

• • •

The battle of Britain, fought in the skies for the air supremacy that

Adolf Hitler required to invade England, sputtered to an end in the fall of 1940, with Britain triumphant but near exhaustion. Frustrated in the west, Hitler looked again to the east. Meanwhile, Benito Mussolini assembled a large, though poorly equipped, army in Libya and attacked the British forces in Egypt. Repulsed, Mussolini called upon Hitler for help. Early in 1941, Hitler sent to Libya Erwin Rommel and his Afrika Korps, which would soon be upgraded to the Italo-German Panzerarmee.

In glaring contrast with these dramatic events on the world stage, Patton was busy turning his troops into a disciplined and well-trained armored division. During the latter months of 1940, he was constantly on the go, appearing everywhere to inspect, supervise, and instruct men who were learning how to march, use their weapons, handle their equipment, first as individual soldiers, then as members of close-knit crews and teams. He insisted on perfection, driving his troops as hard as he pushed himself. How else could he bring his division up to the effectiveness of the German panzers? His tank, splendidly ringed with red, white, and blue stripes — as well as a traditional yellow cavalry stripe — around the turret, was conspicuously in evidence throughout the division area. Visitors, including Secretary of War Stimson, who came for a few days, were impressed by the energy demonstrated at all echelons, the pervading sense of purpose, and the high morale of the troops.

Patton's conception of an armored division centered on its ability to move. Addressing a lawyers' club in Columbus, Georgia, he likened its functions to those fulfilled by the horse cavalry of Napoleon, Grant, and Jeb Stuart. Armor spearheaded the attack, outflanked the enemy defenses, and probed for holes in the enemy line. Once that line was pierced, tanks poured through the penetration, widened the gap, and sought to

> give the enemy a spanking from behind. You can kill more soldiers by scaring them to death from behind with a lot of noise than you can by attacking them from the front.

To stimulate mobility, Patton decided to move the division from Columbus to Panama City, Florida, and back, a trip of about 400 miles. He wished to test and practice marching formations and procedures, discipline on the road, and other techniques. He wanted also to draw public attention to the Armored Force.

It would be the longest march made by an American armored division to that time and would involve more combat vehicles than ever before in the United States outside a military reservation — 1100 vehicles, including 101 light and 24 medium tanks, plus trucks, half-tracks (a cross between a tractor and a truck), scout cars, motorcycles, jeeps (which Patton nearly always called peeps), cannon, and other assorted pieces of equipment, even several airplanes flying over the columns.

Patton's force departed Fort Benning after breakfast on December 12, and had rolled 90 miles in parallel columns by lunchtime. In the evening the troops settled down in bivouac areas at Blakely, Georgia, and Abbeville, Alabama. Only five tanks had stopped for repairs along the way, and four of these managed to resume the march. On the following day, the division breezed into Panama City. The men then turned around and roared back to Benning.

News of the event preceded the division, and schools declared holidays so that children could see the passing columns. Field hands stared in wonder at the parade. Everyone along the way, it seemed, watched with amazement and pride the display of American military power.

The exercise attracted surprisingly wide attention from the public, which was hungry for assurance of American military prowess. Newspapers throughout the country carried long and enthusiastic accounts of the movement, exaggerating the size of the force, the tanks involved, and the miles covered. Everyone was pleased with the performance, particularly the "remarkable spirit" of the men. According to Patton, "Considering the [large] number of recruits we have in this unit, their interest and efficiency show remarkable ability for adaptation." With Americans such as these in uniform, the United States had little to fear for its national security. As he put it, his division was modeled along the lines of the German panzer division — "with improvements."

*Article, "Gen. Patton of the Cavalry Sets Fast Pace for the Tank Corps—Army Knows His Name as Synonym for Daring Action," Washington Sunday* Star, *December 15, 1940*

This always-colorful figure of the old and new Army . . . directed his force of modern American panzer troops . . .

This picturesque and dashing officer . . . can do a multitude of things and do them a bit better than most people . . .

There is something of the dash and color of Gen. J. E. B. Stuart about this many-sided officer who still has a great love for the old

cavalry although he is now launched on a career in mechanization . . .
His men swear by him and . . . he would never order men to do anything in action that he wouldn't do himself. A social lion, well known in Washington drawing rooms . . . he is, nevertheless, a hard-riding, hard-hitting "fightin' man" of the old school, with a mind to absorb and improve on new military ideas.

All this was gratifying. More to the point, as Patton told a friend, "I am glad that we have gotten some successful publicity for the Army. It was what I was trying to accomplish." What he sought was a better image for the Armored Force, the tanks, and, incidentally, himself. Most important was the 2d Armored Division. "I think this outfit now has the popular imagination, and will go far."

*Letter, GSP, Jr., to Edward E. Wilcox, Philadelphia Evening* Bulletin, *January 6, 1941*

I fear we did not do so well as the papers imagine but I do feel that the 2d Armored Division can be said to be ready and willing to fight whenever the country may need us.

*Letter, GSP, Jr., to Maj. Gen. Frank R. McCoy, Foreign Policy Association, New York, January 6, 1941*

I am certainly very fortunate to have been promoted and even more fortunate to be in temporary command of a division. With any luck I hope to get this temporary command made permanent.

*Letter, GSP, Jr., to Pershing, January 8, 1941*

As I have frequently told you, it is a great pleasure to command this division, and I hope before long to get the extra stars and have the command made permanent . . . However, as I am actually in command, there seems to be some possibility that I may get it.

*Letter, GSP, Jr., to Brig. Gen. Leonard T. Gerow, War Plans Division, War Department, January 8, 1941*

If you are ever in a position to tell us who we may be expected to fight, I would appreciate it as I think we should put more emphasis in our training in trying to meet a specific enemy.

Many members of Patton's World War I tank brigade were offering to join his division. Unfortunately, most of them were too old to return to active duty. Yet he wrote to Stimson in behalf of Captain Semmes and Lieutenant Winton, "both very gallant gentlemen who deserve well of their country," as well as many others — "because I think that the spirit of that unit was one of the finest things I have ever encountered."

*Postcard, Sgt. Earl Pattison, Cheyenne, Wyo., to GSP, Jr., January 6, 1941*

Hope you are my old Col. from the old 345 Bn. Tank Corps, Bourg, France. If so would be glad to hear from you. Sincerely

*Letter, GSP, Jr., to Pattison, January 9, 1941*

I am the man you suspect back at the old job but there is quite a difference between what you and I knew and this new armored division . . . I think that probably these armored divisions are the most powerful fighting units in the world.

"I am lucky enough to be in command of a division," he wrote Major General Kenyon A. Joyce. "I hope that should the necessity arise, I will have the opportunity of demonstrating how I feel it should be fought." But he was still seeking the proper methods of employing it. "These new armored divisions are terribly powerful instruments of destruction and on account of size difficult to handle." He gave much credit for whatever success he was having to his chief of staff, Geoffrey Keyes, who was "doing a wonderful job . . . in fact I must admit that but for his assistance I would probably be unable to run this job."

While he spent most of his time in the field, he had sufficient energy to carry out all sorts of experiments. He pondered and acted on new ideas and innovations in procedures, techniques, and equipment, in the hope of advancing his profession and the well-being of his troops.

For example, how could wounded men be removed from tanks traveling at a high rate of speed? To a medical officer he wrote:

I believe that those who are seriously hurt will have to be dumped by the roadside and picked up by the ambulance following each column. Even the question of removing a casualty from a tank is not particularly simple. One of the young doctors here is working on a sort of harness which can be rigged over the top of the turret on shears and the man hauled out with a block and tackle. It will be hard on him, but there is no other way unless we use a can opener.

Several weeks later Patton concluded that "the appalling weight of armor" perhaps made the question of handling casualties academic. "In my opinion, the wounded . . . are not going to be very numerous. Casualties will be corpses."

Patton was also designing a uniform for the tankers – "to lend class to what would otherwise be a bothersome bore." The tankers needed to be different, an elite force, and special clothing would distinguish them from other soldiers. There was no need for camouflage – "In armored combat we get so close [to the enemy] that the question of concealment through color or other device is of little moment."

He finally modeled his new suit for photographers. Of dark green gabardine, selected because the color concealed grease spots, it was a light-weight double-breasted jacket with rows of white or brass buttons running down the sides, and trousers padded in strategic places to cushion the shock of tank travel, with pockets on the legs to hold first-aid equipment, maps, and ammunition clips. The headgear, of light plastic and internally padded, resembled a football helmet except that it was far better, he believed, "than the abortion the Ordnance invented."

Newspapers everywhere carried pictures of Patton wearing his uniform, which looked ridiculous. It was never adopted.

Patton experimented with light planes that could use small and unprepared fields unsuitable for other military aircraft. Incorporating planes in all his exercises, he proved their value to transmit orders to subordinates, to locate and identify units, to transport commanders and staff officers. He liked the Piper Cub, and this light craft became a standard piece of equipment for divisions, artillery groupements, and other headquarters and units during the war.

In January 1941, the division had enough vehicles for a mounted review. As the men passed the stand, Patton's quiet but obvious pride in his organization reached out and permeated the ranks, reinforcing the men's identification with what they believed was a first-rate, unbeatable unit. "The amazing thing, from my standpoint," he wrote, "was that thirteen hundred vehicles all passed the reviewing stand without any checks or stalls. We certainly could not have done that in 1918!"

He mailed Willis D. Crittenberger, Scott's chief of staff, and Brett a picture of his division's flag, "designed, constructed, and paid for by myself" – "eight dollars of my own money." He added that he was holding his "first free maneuver we have tried" on the morrow, "and I don't know just what will happen, but something is bound to occur."

Caught up in his work with tanks, Patton nevertheless remained interested in the cavalry. "In spite of my gasoline affiliations," he wrote a friend, "I am convinced that the day of the horse is far from over and that under many circumstances horse cavalry and horse drawn artillery are more important than ever."

When the Cavalry Board solicited his comments on whether to retain the saber, he replied enthusiastically and at length. "A cold steel weapon," he said, "is not only desirable but vitally necessary." All infantry soldiers armed with the rifle had a bayonet. Yet a charge on foot was much more difficult than a cavalry charge with the saber.

> If a man on foot is hit, he thanks God for an excuse to stop and usually stops. The horse, having no imagination, does not stop unless he gets a brain or heart wound or a broken leg. If the rider is hit, his ability to pull up his horse is reduced so they both go on.
>
> The rapid approach of the horsemen has a disconcerting effect, due to the race memories of stampedes of mammoths or aurochs, who of yore trampled our hairy progenitors. The truth of this is evinced by the retention of mounted police in most large cities.
>
> The herd instinct of the horse also impells him to stick along with his fellows. General Sherman once said that if the reins could only be cut, every cavalry charge would succeed.
>
> The chief argument against the mounted charge springs from undigested memories of descriptions of battlefields in World War I; which to the mind of the fiction-fed fanatic, consisted wholly of trenches, shell holes, and barbed wire over which lunar landscape a blighting blizzard of machine gun bullets constantly eddied. Where such circumstances existed – if they ever did – no charge by tanks, infantry, cavalry or bull elephants could possibly succeed.
>
> For any charge to be successful . . . there must be no insurmountable ground obstacle between the attacker and his prey . . . The enemy must be pinned to the ground by flanking fire. The enemy must have had his morale shaken by bombing, shelling, hunger, fatigue, or fifth column activities. The enemy must be totally surprised. The enemy must be already running.
>
> Under a conjunction of the above circumstances, any charge will result in success PROVIDING THOSE EXECUTING IT HAVE THE WILL TO CLOSE [with the enemy]. Only the cold steel provides this will, for to use such a weapon, one must close.

In my opinion, the mounted pistol charge is a wholly chimerical operation . . . One has only to look at any photograph of such an attack. Less than ten percent of the troopers are in a position to fire without hitting their friends . . .

Around 1600, when the pistol was first made usable, cavalry abandoned the saber in favor of the pistol and at once went into eclipse. Conde revived the saber charge and rode over the Spanish Infantry as a result. Under Louis XIV, Marshal Saxe invented the Uhlan – at that time not a lancer but a cuirassier – because . . . the enemy [would have] to meet the charge with fire and he could then ride over him, which he did.

In domestic disturbance, the only weapons of any value are the bayonet, the rifle butt, and the saber because these are the only weapons possessing selectivity in the amount of injury to be inflicted; fire arms can only kill. Frequently, killing is not indicated.

I designed the present saber and freely admit that I did too good a job; that is, the weapon, due to lack of time to train, is better than the men who use it. To attain this superior technical ability, I made it unnecessarily heavy and long. In 1938, I made up a "cavalry bayonet." I am sending this to the Board; it speaks for itself. It can cut wire, firewood, hay, or heads with equal facility . . .

I beg leave to remind the Board that very few people have ever been killed with the bayonet or the saber, but the fear of having their guts explored with cold steel in the hands of battle maddened men has won many a fight.

This hardly diverted him from his main preoccupation.

*Letter, GSP, Jr., to Pershing, February 24, 1941*

The other day we staged a mounted review for the division which was quite impressive and to my mind a great tribute to the officers and men composing it, as without a rehearsal they did an excellent job.

We now have some three thousand draftees . . . They are a surprisingly good lot of men and will be a great credit to us.

I am apparently in permanent command, although newspapers to the contrary notwithstanding, I am not a major general, but that will probably come in time.

*Letter, GSP, Jr., to Maj. Gen. James G. Harbord, Rye, N.Y., February 24, 1941*

Things are going very well with us here, and we are getting tanks faster than we could reasonably hope. We have just received 67 mediums . . . although not all of the latest type of vehicle. Still a tank is a tank, and it makes no difference so far as the enemy is concerned which type he gets killed by.

Public interest in tanks, as well as in Patton himself, developed as newspaper reporters in increasing numbers visited the 2d Armored Division. They noted the excellent relationship between Patton and his men –

> to all of them, The Old Man was as near and real as the bark on the outer walls of their makeshift mess hall. Like God (they said) he had the damndest way of showing up when things went wrong. Unlike God, he had been known to dash headlong into a creek, get a stalled tank and its wretched crew out of the water and back into the line of march, practically by the power of his curses.

Most important, when Patton was satisfied by their performance, his men were proud.

Patton and his wife Beatrice had a series of buffet suppers for all the officers and ladies of the division. About 120 persons attended each time, and it took them nine evenings to have everyone in.

Courtney Hodges left the command of the Infantry School at Fort Benning to become the Chief of Infantry in Washington, and Omar N. Bradley took his place. Patton came to know both well, and he had a high appreciation of them as men and as officers. They would be closely associated with him later.

Keeping Stimson informed of his activities, Patton said that he hoped to be ready to fight in April. "After that our only worry will be how to get at whoever you want us to destroy."

*Letter, GSP, Jr., to General Malin Craig, Washington, D.C., March 18, 1941*

We really have a very fine division with an excellent spirit . . . The thing I try to impress on them is that all members of the Armored Force . . . must be imbued with a desprate determination to get forward and must not permit themselves to be stopped by any obstacle. If I can get this across, we will be very hard to beat.

Scott submitted an efficiency report on Patton and characterized him as "Superior" in performance.

In the event of war, I would recommend this officer to command an armored corps . . . This officer renders willing and generous support to the plans of his superiors regardless of his personal views in the matter. Of 90 general officers of his grade that are personally known to me, I would give him number 3 on the list. Further remarks: An extremely energetic ambitious officer and a natural and highly capable leader.

"There is still uncertainty," Patton wrote to a friend,

as to whether or not General Chafee will be able to resume command of the Armored Force. We all hope for the best but I honestly believe that our hopes are not well founded.

*Letter, GSP, Jr., to Chaffee, March 19, 1941*

Beatrice and myself plan to move out to the [new] Cantonment Area shortly. The house for the Commanding General (I am gambling that I will keep this division) was not large enough so we put in a little extra money and had a porch and dressing room added. I believe I will be much more efficient when I am living immediately among the troops.

*Letter, GSP, Jr., to Chaffee, March 22, 1941*

My dear Adna: If the following inquiry is unduly inquisitive, please do not answer. What I would like to know is whether I will probably remain at Benning, because in the event that I do, I shall build a stable, but if I do not, I will keep my horses at the Infantry School, as the outlay will be over a hundred dollars. I am interested not to waste the money.

He informed Chaffee of an interesting exercise he had just conducted. The troops made a combat march, went into bivouac, moved in the darkness to avoid an air bombardment, then attacked at 2 A.M.

The wet conditions were as bad as possible, as it rained hard all the time; however, the results obtained were, in my opinion, extremely satisfactory due to the good work of General Gillem [the brigade commander] and his staff and ably seconded by the regimental and unit commanders. I mention this to show that we are not resting.

Soon afterward Patton staged another maneuver that included a combat problem, an all-night bivouac, and a division review. About 11,000 men and nearly 2000 vehicles participated. It rained constantly, but the efficiency of the division was outstanding. After reviewing his troops in the downpour, he gathered them together and addressed them, expressing his pride in their reaching

> the utmost expected . . . In slightly more than eight months we have changed from an idea to a powerful fighting force . . .
>
> Should the efforts of our great president in trying to avoid war by timely preparations in peace meet with failure and the grave ordeal of battle be forced upon us, I confidently expect that you men and officers . . . will so equip yourselves that our enemies shall be utterly destroyed.

Under his tutelage, the 2d Armored Division was gaining the reputation of being perfectly able to conduct a small war all by itself. It was his message, of course, and he delivered it effectively and repeatedly to his troops and to the reporters: "The armored division can smash its way into the enemy with tremendous force."

*Letter, GSP, Jr., to Col. Charles Bridge, April 7, 1941*

I am very fortunate to have fallen into command of our 2d Armored Division. It is really quite a good show and extremely powerful. I do not know just when or how we are going to have a chance to use it in battle but trust that the future will take care of that question.

*Letter, GSP, Jr., to Lt. Col. Erle F. Cress, April 8, 1941*

At the close of this summer's maneuvers, it may be possible to write a brief Standing Operating Procedure. Up until that time I believe it is better to emulate the English constitution and not write anything . . .

The chief value of Armored forces is to develop initiative and imagination. If we tear such down with Standing Operating Procedure, we vitiate our purpose.

I am always interested in all the papers which you send me, so the fact that I do not agree, I hope, will not prevent you sending me others from time to time.

On April 10, the President nominated Patton for promotion to major general. The Senate approved, and the President so appointed him, with rank from April 4. On the same day the War Department assigned him to command, no longer temporarily, the 2d Armored Division.

Patton immediately sent off a number of letters. To Marshall: "I deeply appreciate the honor you have done me. I shall continue in my efforts to justify your confidence." To Pershing: "Whatever qualities of execution I possess are due to my service under your immediate command . . . I shall always try to live up to the ideals of military perfection of which you are the embodiment." To Stimson: "When war comes I promise that you will not be ashamed of me."

Stimson replied that he had supported Patton's candidacy not so much because of his warm regard for Patton, but rather because he expected Patton to give his division a strong fighting spirit.

Many letters of congratulation arrived, and Patton acknowledged them all. To Major General Lesley J. McNair, head of the army's training program: "There is no one in the Army whose good opinion I would rather have than yours." To retired General Harbord, one of Pershing's closest associates in World War I: "I feel sure that your personal interest in me is largely responsible for my selection." To Colonel Frank S. Besson: "It all goes to prove that my luck still holds and I happen to be at the right place at the right time."

To Beatrice's half brother, Charles F. Ayer: "I am delighted to have the rank as well as the command." To Joyce: "I shall always feel that whatever ability I may have as a General I acquired while serving under you." To Major General J. K. Herr, Chief of Cavalry: "Thank you very much for your nice letter of condolence on my promotion. You know and I certainly know that but for you I would probably never have been discovered or promoted." To General Malin Craig, retired Army Chief of Staff:

I feel that I owe most of my success to your generous effort on my behalf . . .

> I am probably the most unpopular man, not only in the 2d Armored Division, but in the Army, as I got very tired of being the only person in this outfit who makes any corrections. So, today, I had the regimental commanders in and told them that from now on I would first write them a letter of admonition, and second relieve them from command if any units under them fail to carry out standing orders.
>
> I hope I met your approval in doing this. I assure you that I did not use any profanity while making this statement.

To retired Major General André W. Brewster, a former member of Pershing's staff: "I am perfectly honest when I assure you that your influence upon me has done me more good than that of any other officer with whom I have ever served." To retired Major General George Van Horn Mosely: "Ever since I was a Lieutenant, I have known, admired, and been inspired by you. I trust that I shall succeed in particularly emulating your success."

To a closer contemporary, Major General F. M. Andrews: "I trust that your anticipation of bloody work [to be done] will come out. But I will be damned if I see how we are to get at our friends, the enemy. However, something may turn up."

*Letter, GSP, Jr., to Mrs. William L. Wills, San Marino, Cal., May 15, 1941*

> Dear Aunt Susie: You now see the wonderful good effect your careful assistance in my upbringing has produced. Knowing that you have a great drag with the Lord, I trust you will bring all your efforts to prayerful intercession that I may soon get another star and be a Lieutenant General.
>
> When that time comes, you can keep right on working for four stars for me.

Patton sent congratulations to many friends who had also been promoted. To Innis P. Swift: "With you and I both made [promoted], I feel that the world is now safe for democracy."

Despite his flippancy, Patton was touched. His accomplishments had been recognized and rewarded. Throughout the higher echelons of the army, his skill and professionalism, his dedication and energy, his success in forming the division had been noted and approved.

As a child, Patton had dreamed of being a major general at the age of twenty-seven. Now that he had attained that ambition nearly 30 years later than he had hoped, he was sure that further achievement awaited him. His fate had still to be fulfilled. Whatever it was, his destiny was appreciably closer to realization.

# CHAPTER 3

# Maneuvers

*"The important thing in any organization is the creation of a soul which is based on pride."*

IN THE SPRING of 1941, Patton learned that his division would take part in large-scale maneuvers or war games later that year. General Headquarters in Washington was planning the exercises. GHQ, as it was called, was the highest command post in the army. Officially under Marshall, it was actually headed by Marshall's chief of staff, Lesley McNair, who used the faculty and the facilities of the Army War College to supervise and administer a vast training program throughout the army. Maneuvers brought together large units and put them through war problems or mock battles to test not only the efficacy of training methods but also the proficiency of commanders, staffs, and troops. It was an important occasion, for individual and unit performances would be measured and graded.

Thinking ahead to his own participation, Patton wrote to Lieutenant Colonel W. C. Crane, a friend who was a member of McNair's staff. Some of the old rules for judging the performance of units, Patton suggested, might not apply to armored divisions in general and to his in particular; and they should not be allowed to hamper the new methods of operation being developed.

> I fully realize that unsolicited comments are not greatly valued. Nonetheless, since you and I had considerable experience in umpiring, I beg leave to call your attention to the following comments of the Umpire Manual [which are out of date] . . .
>
> I think it worthy of note that the primary function of an Armored Force is to disrupt [enemy] command, communications, and supply.

Since an armored division could do more than what was prescribed in the regulations, he believed it desirable to have a member of the Armored Force with considerable rank and, by implication, an understanding of Patton's methods present as an umpire whenever armored divisions were employed. Furthermore, commanders who failed to use imagination should be severely penalized. Units that followed routine practices were

> not playing the game. The effect of surprise as to time or direction of attack should be given tremendous weight. In reading over the rules, I find no emphasis placed upon this . . .
>
> Bombers, like artillery, depend for their effectiveness on ammunition supply. Nevertheless, bombarding aviators fly blithely . . . without taking out time to reload the bomb racks. This gives a wholly erroneous impression as to the efficiency of aviation . . .
>
> For God's sake, do not get me mixed up in this Umpire business, as I am wholly desirous to command this division, upon the successful operation of which my whole future will depend.

The value of aircraft as adjuncts to armored operations was very much on Patton's mind, and he soon wrote to Crane again. "The following letter," he said, "can be used by you in any way you see fit, provided you do not stick my neck out too far." The war in Europe, he thought, thus far demonstrated the importance of armored units supported by motorized infantry and light, tactical bombers. Yet — "now I will be particularly outspoken" — the aviators believed that strategic bombardment alone could win the war, even though strategic air forces had failed "to do anything except bomb, ineffectively, unprotected cities." The Army Air Corps had little interest in helping ground troops, but the airmen should be forming and training observation, attack, parachute, and air infantry units.

> I am personally getting so air-minded that I own an aeroplane and expect shortly to have a pilots license. Next time you come here I may be able to take you for a ride if you have sufficient insurance.

Patton left it to Crane to determine whether it was "expedient" to mention anything to McNair. Patton was "not trying to cut ahead of any of my superiors," but he believed that "new ideas are what are winning this war." However, "crusading is an expensive pastime. I do not wish to lock horns with the GHQ Air Force or anyone else." If Crane found Patton's suggestions worthwhile, he could bring them forward simply as ideas "and not mention my name even in your sleep. I leave this matter to your discretion."

*Letter, GSP, Jr., to Mrs. C. L. Scott, Fort Knox, May 13, 1941*

Since General Scott was probably wholly responsible for my promotion, it was really not necessary for you to write [congratulations], which makes it all the nicer that you did.

We moved out to our new house in the woods last night and nearly froze to death.

The new house was about ten miles from the officers' quarters on the main post and close to a cantonment area known as Sand Hill that had been specially built for his division. While his men entered into the new barracks, the Pattons left the glistening white stucco house that suggested the polish and precision of the parade ground and settled into a rough but spacious log cabin more in keeping with the spirit of field service. Built by the Army Engineers and containing several additional amenities paid for by the Pattons, the house sat in a large grove of southern pines at the top of a rise overlooking an oval driveway connecting a dozen tiny huts where the members of his staff lived. Less than three miles distant was the headquarters, several barracks-type buildings, where Patton and his staff worked.

To McNair:

The thing I believe which we must remove from the minds of the high command is that the direct charge against anti-tank guns over open country is as impracticable as is a cavalry charge against barbed wire. Trusting that you will pardon my imposing on your time.

*Letter, GSP, Jr., to Crittenberger, June 2, 1941*

My dear Crit: I enclose a copy of the address I gave to the entire 2d Armored Division . . . You are probably one of the few people with sufficient historical knowledge to recognize the opening gambit as a meticulous copy of General Bonaparte's address to the Army of Italy in the spring of 1796 . . .

As you will see from my remarks, I am obsessed with the idea that tanks should be used as quail-shooting weapons and not as buffaloes.

In other words, mobility and firepower were more important than shock action, which he compared to a buffalo stampede.

As a matter of fact, he doubted that "our chief enemy is armored divisions. In my opinion, armored divisions will avoid each other to the limit of their ability." They were simply too powerful to risk a head-on collision.

Patton sent Stimson a copy of his address, realizing "that neither your limited time nor the merits of my remarks justify your reading them, but . . . so far as I know, it is the first time a division commander ever talked to all the men in his division at one time."

*GSP, Jr., Address to officers and men of 2d Armored Division, May 17, 1941*

You men and officers are, in my opinion, magnificently disciplined . . . You cannot be disciplined in great things and undisciplined in small things . . . Brave, undisciplined men have no chance against the discipline and valor of other men. Have you ever seen a few policemen handle a crowd? . . .

The salute is the mutual greeting of respect and loyalty between members of a fighting organization . . . Pride is the greatest thing that a man can have . . . pride in demonstrated ability . . .

An armored division is the most powerful organization ever devised by the mind of men . . . An armored division is that element of the team which carries out the running plays. We straight-arm, and go around, and dodge, and go around . . .

We must find out where the enemy is, we must hold him, and we must get around him . . .

One of the greatest qualities which we have is the ability to produce in our enemy the fear of the unknown. Therefore, we must always keep moving, do not sit down, do not say "I have done enough," keep on, see what else you can do to raise the devil with the enemy . . .

You must have a desperate determination to go forward. When we beat them, we will beat them by attacking sooner and harder than they do . . .

There are no bullets in maneuvers, and things sometimes get a little dull. But play the game; don't lie in the shade, don't pretend you are manning an anti-aircraft gun or a machine gun while you are lying down. Be on your toes, if an aircraft comes over you, track it with your gun and pretend you are shooting hell out of it. If a tank or an infantryman approaches you who is an enemy, do the same thing; play the game. If you have to charge, go fast; if you have to retreat, do so, but as slowly as possible . . . The umpires have the job of representing the bullets . . . You will never get anywhere if you make them mad. Do what they tell you and do it promptly, and pretty soon you will find that they err in shading the decisions in your favor. Try, above all things, to use your imagination. Think this is war. "What would I do if that man were really shooting at me?" That is the only chance, men, that you are going to have to practice. The next time, maybe, there will be no umpires, and the bullets will be very real, both yours and the enemy's.

In closing I wish to congratulate every officer and man of the 2d Armored Division for the honest effort and enthusiastic support he has demonstrated, and I want to be able to say the same thing at the close of each of the maneuvers in which we take part. And each time, I know that we will be better, and by the time the last maneuver comes off, we will be ready and anxious to meet anything that anybody can provide for us to lick.

*GSP, Jr., Address on Orientation in Maneuvers, May 1941*

Our purpose in assembling both umpires and unit commanders here this morning is three-fold. First, I want all of you to meet each other. Second, I want to reiterate the tactical doctrines of this division so that commanders will enter the forthcoming maneuvers with our desires clear in their minds and so that the umpires will know what we are trying to do. Finally, I want to restate those duties of an umpire which my experience and observation have shown me to be ot particular importance.

So far as tactics are concerned, it is the doctrine of this division to attack weakness rather than strength . . .

I can conceive of nothing more futile than to send expensive tanks against a prepared position. The doctrine for so doing was originally written by me and was based on the fact that in 1918 tanks were invincible, but a careful analysis of what the Germans have done leads me to a totally different solution for present day armored forces . . .

There is an old Chinese saying . . . "a look is worth a thousand words." This means that the commanders of each element in rear of the reconnaissance must be close up to attain full knowledge of what has transpired in front of them . . .

By attacking, you induce the enemy to think you are stronger than he is . . .

I wish to assure all officers and all men that I shall never criticize them or go back on them for having done too much but that I shall certainly relieve them if they do nothing. You must keep moving . . .

I am very insistant that all commanders who have an umpire take him absolutely into their confidence. He is not a stool pigeon or a hostile spy. If he knows what you are trying to do he can be useful and be at the point of combat. If he does not know what is going to happen, he is simply unnecessary baggage . . .

I want to bring to the attention of every officer here the professional significance which will attach to the success or failure of the 2d Armored Division in the Tennessee maneuvers. There are a large number of officers, some of them in high places in our country, who through lack of knowledge as to the capability of an armored division are opposed to them and who would prefer to see us organize a large number of old-fashioned divisions about whose ability the officers in question have more information. It is my considered opinion that the creation of too many old type divisions will be distinctly detremental and that the future of our country may well depend on the organization of a considerably larger number of armored divisions than are at present visualized. Therefore it behooves everyone of us to do his uttermost to see that in these forthcoming maneuvers we are not only a success but such an outstanding success that there could be no possible doubt in the minds of anyone as to the effectiveness of the armored divisions. Bear this in mind every moment.

By this time the soldiers in Patton's division were thinking of themselves as "trained blitzmen," "blitztroopers," "tops" among the nation's military men. They considered themselves "the most powerful striking force ever evolved," possessed of "terrifying strength," the "juggernaut of the battlefield," and "ready for the real thing." How good they were would soon be tested in the maneuvers.

In mid-June, the division traveled to Camp Forrest, Tennessee, its movements, according to the newspapers, "shrouded in secrecy." Reporters speculated that the "much vaunted" outfit, "America's answer to the panzer division," would take part in the games. Patton advertised his division's nickname, "Hell on Wheels," described his organization as "the most powerful striking force the human mind has ever developed," and characterized his tactics as "Hold 'em by the nose and kick 'em in the pants."

In its first contest, the division was unimpressive. Infantry denied the tankers freedom of movement and blunted their drive. It was a setback, perhaps due to stage fright, maybe overconfidence, and Patton was officially criticized for failing to coordinate his operations.

The criticism stung, then spurred him to greater effort. After the units shifted and realigned for the next game, the division reconnoitered during the day and attacked during the night. In a four-pronged drive from Lynchburg to Manchester, Patton's men captured the "enemy" command post at 9 A.M. on the following morning and took the commanding general and his staff "prisoner." Two hours later, long before the scheduled end of the game, the maneuver was over.

By slashing and unorthodox tactics, Patton redeemed himself and proved the validity of his training and operational methods. The fact that McNair was present to witness the swift movements of the armored division stimulated Patton to even greater daring.

In the next maneuver, Patton employed blitzkrieg tactics, knifed through the "enemy" defenses, and compelled the opposing force to surrender. Again the maneuver was over ahead of time. By virtue of Patton's speed, the entire action took nine hours instead of the allocated two days.

Finally, with Stimson on hand, Patton's division swept around the opposing defenders, cut their lines of communication, disrupted the "enemy" rear area, and captured the town of Tullahoma, the objective of the operation. Once again, the unexpected movements of the division terminated the game several hours ahead of schedule.

The highlight of the games was the performance of the 2d Armored Division. No unit was more aggressive. Patton had made his men believe they were first-rate soldiers and fighters, and their confidence in themselves, their military skills, and their efficiency were apparent to all.

For the inhabitants of the area, the maneuvers spread a panorama that brought wonder and delight over things they had never seen before—military machines and equipment in profusion, the tanks, trucks, artillery pieces, and airplanes that soon became commonplace; troops building bridges, pitching tents, or taking cover in ditches against simulated air attack; soldiers on weekend pass congesting the sidewalks and filling the restaurants in Tullahoma, Shelbyville, Manchester, and Chattanooga. What people remembered best of all was General Patton, whose exploits soon became legend.

*Letter, GSP, Jr., to Mrs. Hancock Banning, July 2, 1941*

We just got back from a very pleasant maneuver in Tennessee where I think the division covered itself with credit, in fact, it established so high a standard that we will have difficulty in maintaining it but nevertheless we shall do so.

*Letter, GSP, Jr., to Stimson, July 8, 1941*

In spite of the long march, in some cases over 110 miles, every fighting vehicle in the division, except two tanks and a scout car, got to the place it was supposed to be in time to deliver the attack . . . It was a great performance on the part of the men and I was very proud of it.

This morning I gave an illustrative talk to all the men and officers trying to show them the big picture so that they would know not only what they individually had done in each problem but also what the division as a whole had accomplished. I further took occasion to point out many errors which I made and which we will correct before the next maneuver – or war – whichever the case may be.

I trust that you enjoyed what you did see of the maneuvers. Your presence was a great stimulus to the men and officers.

Scott submitted an efficiency report on Patton and called him "Superior."

Of 60 general officers of his grade that are personally known to me, I would give him number 5 on this list. Further remarks: A most energetic and capable commander who is quick in his decisions and vigorous in their execution.

Lieutenant Colonel Thomas T. Handy, commander of an artillery unit in Patton's division, was transferred to Marshall's office in Washington, and Patton expressed his "real regret" over losing Handy, who would become one of Marshall's closest subordinates and would eventually gain the four stars of a full general.

The criticism Patton received during the Tennessee maneuvers annoyed him, and he sought to explain his actions. Writing to Floyd Parks, a member of McNair's staff, Patton said that he was "not making excuses but rather pointing out what I consider to be misconceptions . . . as to the principal functions of an armored division." He had read most of the umpire reports, and he took exception to many of them.

For example, coordination was a "fine old military word" and could be applied to describe the operations of Alexander the Great, Napoleon, or Allenby. It was not quite the same for armored divisions.

> When you are using a sabre or a bayonet, you can to a degree control (coordinate) the weapon during the lunge. When you are throwing hand grenades, you can only give them initial impetus and direction. You cannot control (coordinate) these missils during flight. Armored divisions are of the nature of such missils.
>
> It is none the less noteworthy that in every operation in which this division took part, the several elements (grenades) composing it arrived at the place intended at the time desired.

By saying repeatedly that the armored division failed to launch concentrated or mass attacks, the umpires gave the "greatest compliment possible." The desire for mass action came from "undigested memories" of the teachings at Leavenworth and the War College or from reading about the tank battle of Cambrai in World War I, when tanks were invincible and invulnerable. That condition no longer existed, "and hence the use of tanks in mass is futile and suicidal."

The widespread belief that the function of an armored division was to attack and destroy the enemy was "erroneous." The correct role was to get astride the enemy's lines of communication in the enemy's rear and disrupt his command and supply systems, thereby immobilizing him and making him vulnerable to destruction by the infantry.

"Several Umpires criticized me" for leaving his command post. A commander could sit there during an old-time infantry fight without particular harm because information arrived slowly and there was no need for a commander's instantaneous reaction. "Were the commanding general of an armored division to sit anywhere with information three hours old, his units might well be from 15 to 25 miles from the point indicated on the map." In other words, the rapidity of battle, he thought, made it necessary for the modern commander to operate away from his command post and closer to the fighting troops, a notion he had exercised in World War I – he made no mention of this in his letter – to the discomfiture of his superiors.

Furthermore, a division commander at maneuvers had a dual mission. Not only did he exercise command but he had to be in position to see how well the troops were carrying out what they had learned in training. "He cannot get this knowledge at a desk."

> We just finished three days of intensive training, beginning with the squad and ending with the reinforced battalion . . . I am convinced that this method of instruction, which I believe I invented, is the best and quickest possible. I believe that as a result of it we have provided means which will make it very difficult for the ever increasingly effective anti-tank weapons to halt us or cause us serious casualties.

"You would be surprised," he wrote a friend, "at the profound ignorance in higher places as to the use of tanks. People are still obsessed with the belief that tanks are invulnerable and try to send them head-on into prepared positions." Instead, tanks tried "to avoid a fight and put their energy into disrupting the rear areas of the opposition."

When Patton received a phone call from Parks, who suggested that it might be better for Patton's future if he curbed his flamboyance, Patton replied:

> I shall try to follow your precepts, but I do not intend to be colorless in spite of the fact that pure white, which as I remember is a lack of all color, is the popular color at present among aspirants to military preferment.

No one could have been more colorful than Patton, who appeared on the cover of *Life* magazine's "Defense" issue of July 7, which featured stories and photographs of the armed forces and lauded the work of the division in the maneuvers. Standing in the turret of his tank, holding binoculars, wearing a 2d Division patch over his left pocket, a shoulder holster and pistol, a helmet with chin strap, rings on the third and fourth fingers of his left hand, and an appropriate scowl, Patton epitomized the tough, solid professional soldier with more than a touch of personality.

A letter from the editor told him how much the division had done for the magazine. Replying, Patton said,

> Remember that the article in Life did as much for the 2d Armored Division as the 2d Armored Division could possibly have done for Life. The important thing in any organization is the creation of a soul which is based on pride, and no member of the division reading your magazine could fail to be filled with pride.

On July 8, he assembled all members of the division and, using four very large maps, showed what the organization had done during the Tennessee manuvers. He then made these remarks:

> The purpose of what I have just said is to show each of you the big picture, the picture of what the whole division did, not just what you individually accomplished. My personal opinion is that you accomplished every task set with remarkable efficiency and with minute exaction as to time . . .
>
> Certain instances require correction.
>
> Owing to the fact that all of us have been, so to speak, going to school for almost a year, we have to a degree acquired the student complex, that is, we have a tendency to wait instructions rather than proceed on our own initiative . . .
>
> People must try to use their imagination and when orders fail to come, must act on their own best judgment. A very safe rule to follow is that in case of doubt, push on just a little further and then keep on pushing . . .
>
> The issuance of an order is the simplest thing in the world. The important and difficult thing is to see: first, that the order is transmitted; and, second, that it is obeyed . . .
>
> There is still a tendency in each separate unit . . . to be a one-handed puncher. By that I mean that the rifleman wants to shoot, the tanker to charge, the artilleryman to fire . . . That is not the way to win battles. If the band played a piece first with the piccolo, then with the brass horn, then with the clarinet, and then with the trumpet, there would be a hell of a lot of noise but no music. To get

harmony in music each instrument must support the others. To get harmony in battle, each weapon must support the other. Team play wins. You musicians of Mars must not wait for the band leader to signal you . . . You must each of your own volition see to it that you come into this concert at the proper place and at the proper time . . .

There is a growing instance in this division of a disease common to the motorized age. It is called waffle-ass, and results from sitting down too much . . .

When we went on the maneuvers, I told you that I wanted you to wear the shoulder patch so that people would know that you were members of the 2d Armored Division. As it turned out, the shoulder patch was not necessary because your soldierly bearing, meticulous attention to military courtesy, and your neatness in dress told the world to what unit you belonged. You should be very proud of the impression you made on everyone who saw you, from the Secretary of War . . . and General McNair, on down. If you will but keep up the good work, and I know that you will, you will make your shoulder patch something which will cause as much dread to the enemies of your country as it causes pride among your friends.

In closing, I wish to congratulate every man and every officer for his individual effort in proving to the world that the 2d Armored Division is as good as they come.

On August 5, he called all his officers together and lectured them in preparation for the Louisiana maneuvers:

If brevity is the soul of wit, repetition is the heart of instruction. Hence, what I am about to say will have a familiar ring . . . but I want you to pay the strictest attention so that the points which I will emphasize shall become ingrained into the very depths of your minds.

He concluded: "If you do your part as leaders, the men of the 2d Armored Division will make it utterly irresistible in maneuvers or in war."

Chaffee, the first chief of the Armored Force, propelled the U.S. armored and mechanized units into modernity. In the process he overworked himself. In the summer of 1941, he was diagnosed as suffering from terminal cancer. He died in August.

Scott, who commanded the I Armored Corps, was the most likely candidate to replace Chaffee. Patton would then probably move up to succeed Scott in command of the corps.

Instead, Marshall selected as Chaffee's successor Jacob L. Devers, a West Point classmate of Patton's and an enthusiastic polo player. Devers was solid and a hard worker. He had the quality of persistence, and enjoyed the reputation of having accomplished successfully every task he was assigned. An artilleryman, he represented a compromise between the infantry and cavalry interests in the Armored Force. Furthermore, since Patton was stressing the mobility of armor and tending to use the light tank as the horse had been used, Devers would supply balance by making sure that the firepower of the armored divisions received proper attention.

Devers had trained troops in the United States during World War I. He completed his military schooling at Leavenworth and at the Army War College. He served in Panama, commanded the Provisional Brigade of Washington, D.C., where Marshall used him as a troubleshooter, and then headed the 9th Infantry Division, which he activated and trained with a sure hand. Marshall saw him as a dedicated, dependable officer who eschewed publicity and flamboyance and who projected a quiet air of authority and no-nonsense.

Appointed to the position on August 1, Devers revitalized the Armored Force headquarters. He stimulated the improvement of guns, particularly self-propelled pieces to support mobile tanks. He devoted much attention to obtaining better tank engines, suspension systems, and designs, as well as better communications and ammunition. He also attracted young and vigorous officers to the Force and facilitated the dissemination and discussion of new ideas.

*Letter, GSP, Jr., to Devers, July 28, 1941*

My dear Jake, I was very glad to get your letter . . . and learn that you got my belated wire of congratulations.

I am looking forward to having you stay with me at Benning when you come.

*Letter, GSP, Jr., to his wife Beatrice, August 9, 1941*

I was very much impressed with Devers, he has developed a lot and is a very fine leader. It is easy to see how any one comparing him to Scotty would be inclined toward Devers unless he knew how realy smart Scotty is inspite of his chipmunk expression. So far

as I am concerned, I think the change will not be to my disadvantage.
Devers is so sure of himself that I am certain he has a drag with the President and Pa Wat. [Watson, the President's military secretary] both, but the final decision of the high man in the Army will be the result of war and not friendship.

The Louisiana and Texas maneuvers in August and September involved about 400,000 men, including, for the first time, the I Armored Corps. Scott directed the operations of the 1st and 2d Armored Divisions working together, plus about 100 supporting aircraft. According to the umpires and the observers, Patton and his division rode "roughshod" over the "enemy" and distinguished themselves. Scott received some criticism for lacking firm control.

*Letter, Lt. Gen. Walter Krueger, Third Army commander, to GSP, Jr., October 9, 1941*

I was constantly impressed by the high morale, technical proficiency, and devotion to duty of the personnel of the 2d Armored Division . . . Your leadership has produced a fighting organization.

The Patton mythology continued to grow, and many letters complimenting him and the division arrived. His division, he wrote Pershing, had been in ten maneuver attacks and in every one

we obtained our objective. I am quite sure this is a unique record both as to success and as to number of operations . . . However we are not through yet. Today we are having a combined maneuver . . . and beginning on the 30th we march to North Carolina, where we shall be on maneuvers until the first of December. I hope that our luck will continue and that at the completion of this last bunch of maneuvers we shall still have been universally successful.

*Letter, GSP, Jr., to his sister Nita, October 23, 1941*

I was very much pleased with the maneuvers and believe that unquestionably our present army is better in every category than that with which we fought in 1917–18. We have the same trouble now that we had then, namely that the young officers are not sufficiently indoctrinated with basic military knowledge. Nothing can help this situation but time. I think that in another eight months we will see a great improvement. We are getting rid of a lot of older officers, both regular and national guard, who were either too old or too worthless for the jobs they held.

*Letter, GSP, Jr., to Devers, October 23, 1941*

My dear Jake, I read with great interest the release of your address to the Society of Metals. I believe it is the best summation of the purpose and present organization of the Armored Force that I have seen . . .

The combined operation . . . was very satisfactory . . . We were able to get nearly 96 guns in action and at no time were we without a powerful artillery support.

*GSP, Jr., Lecture to the 2d Armored Division, October 25, 1941*

I have showed you . . . briefly . . . the big picture of what the division did. This will enable each of you to insert yourselves into the picture and know why it was that, at that or this place on that or this day you were particularly tired, particularly hungry, or particularly choked with dust, and why the enemy invariably withdrew.

Before I tell you how good you are, I want to again emphasize certain tactical errors of which we were guilty.

We still fail to use every weapon every time . . . Each time we fight with only one weapon when we could use several weapons, we are not winning a battle; we are making fools of ourselves.

He ended by saying: "I further wish to congratulate all of you, and particularly myself, on being members of such a division; and it is my fond belief that we will get better and better."

At the end of October Patton traveled with his division to the Carolina Maneuver Area. The war games held throughout most of November proved to be another test of the 1st and 2d Armored Divisions employed as a team. Patton and his men were a sensation. His control and coordination of his units were superb, and the division figuratively ran wild. What observers noted was a drive on the part of Patton that came close to obsession, the will to win. Everything was justified – even breaking the rules – if it led to victory. Marshall, who flew down from Washington to watch the final exercises, was highly impressed with Patton's performance and behavior. The willingness to dare characterized Patton's movements, and it had considerable effect on those who pondered the unspoken question, If the United States went to war, would the American citizen-soldiers fight? Under Patton, it was evident, they would.

Those who staged and umpired the maneuvers implicitly criticized Scott's leadership, and early in December Scott relinquished command of the I Armored Corps and went to the Middle East to be the senior American military observer with the British.

*Letter, GSP, Jr., to Scott, December 3, 1941*

I want to tell you how much the 2d Armored Division appreciated serving under you, and I wish to state emphatically that we were tickled to death with all the jobs you gave us and only regret that we were not able to do more harm to the enemy [during the maneuvers]. Our failure, if any, was not for lack of trying.

The maneuvers clearly demonstrated, Patton wrote for Devers' "very private ear," that the Armored Force should have controlled the infantry rather than the reverse. "As it was, we were reduced to the speed, physical and mental, of the infantry." Under the circumstances, "General Scott performed a magnificent job."

"We all feel," Patton wrote Parks, "that General Scott . . . did a swell job, and we regret that some adverse criticism of him has been made."

There are a great many rumors around as to the future of various officers in the [Armored] Force, including myself. Personally, I have no excuses to make, and I believe that the 2d Armored Division is superior to any division in the Army . . . However, this may be only a pious hope on my part.

*Letter, Scott to GSP, Jr., subject: Commendation, December 5, 1941*

After observing the work of your division . . . I desire to commend you, the officers and all enlisted men . . . for the esprit de corps, the energy, the endurance, the initiative, and the fine fighting spirit evidenced throughout this most strenuous and exacting work [in the maneuvers].

The highest compliment that I can pay you and your command is to state that in the most difficult situations, when the enemy was pressing from all sides, when our own and the enemy's tactical dispotions were obscure, and when exacting and intricate night movements were ordered, I could always count on you and all the elements of your command being in the right place at the right time to meet effectively any hostile opposition.

By December, the array of major opponents in World War II was complete. Attacking Pearl Harbor and the Philippines, as well as Hong Kong and Malaya, Japan, which had been at war with China for a decade, brought the United States and Great Britain into the Pacific conflict. Japanese actions against French and Dutch possessions further expanded the contest. On the European side, Great Britain remained at war with Germany and Italy, while the German invasion of the Soviet Union in June 1941 broadened that struggle. German and Italian declarations of war against the United States immediately after Pearl Harbor further enlarged the scope of the fighting. France, defeated in 1940, concluded an armistice with Germany and Italy and, under the Pétain government, sat on the sidelines. Franco's Spain remained neutral.

"In view of the heightened tempo of the emergency," Patton wrote Devers several days after Pearl Harbor, he indicated the officers in his division who merited promotion. "Please do not imagine," he said,

that I am trying to over-stress the virtues of the officers of this division to the disparagement of officers of other units, but my sense of loyalty demands that I bring the long maneuver experience and loyal service of these men to your attention.

An article by Edgar Snow in the *Saturday Evening Post* lauded the division and extended further the widespread feeling that Patton had stamped his personality and drive indelibly on his men. As one officer would later say, "I shall not soon forget the 2d A.D. nor your fine example of leadership . . . I only hope that it may always keep the fine cutting edge you gave it."

Patton assembled all the members of the division on December 20, and explained the conduct of the Carolina maneuvers. He closed with the following:

Remember that war exists. Probably the next time we face opponents they will not be friendly enemies but malignant foes. Next time you will be opposed not by white flags but by hot lead. But you will be just as effective . . . and that means completely so . . .

Tactically I made mistakes, both in training and in operations, which I am now correcting through further education of myself and the officers of this division . . .

At all times we have been preparing for war . . . We are ready; and I shall be delighted to lead you against any enemy, confident in the fact that your disciplined valor and high training will bring victory . . .

Put your heart and soul into being expert killers with your weapons. The only good enemy is a dead enemy. Misses do not kill, but a bullet in the heart or a bayonet in the guts do. Let every bullet find its billet – in the body of your foes.

Many of you have not been fortunate enough to have engaged in combat, and owing to the foolish writings of sob-sisters and tear-jerkers, you may have erroneous ideas of what battle is like. You will read of men – imaginary men – who on the eve of battle sit around the camp fire and discuss their mothers, and their sisters, and their sweet-hearts, and talk regretfully of their past life and fear foolishly for their future. No one has a higher or a more respectful devotion to women than I have; but the night before battle you do not sit around a fire . . . You go to sleep and have to be kicked in the butt in the morning so as to start the war. You have not dreamed of dying or worried about your boyhood. You have slept the sleep of fighting males eager for the kill.

Battle is not a terrifying ordeal to be endured. It is a magnificent experience wherein all the elements that have made man superior to the beasts are present: courage, self-sacrifice, loyalty, help to others, devotion to duty. As you go in, you will perhaps be a little short of breath, and your knees may tremble . . . This breathlessness, this tremor, are not fear. It is simply the excitement every athlete feels just before the whistle blows – no, you will not fear for you will be borne up and exalted by the proud instinct of our conquering race. You will be inspired by magnificent hate.

Remember that these enemies, whom we shall have the honor to destroy, are good soldiers and stark fighters. To beat such men, you must not despise their ability, but you must be confident in your own superiority.

Before leaving for the Middle East, Scott submitted an efficiency report on Patton, declaring him to be "Superior." In his remarks, he noted, "Of 80 officers known personally in the same grade, I rate him number 5. A great leader – highly practical and aggressive."

*Letter, GSP, Jr., to Pershing, January 13, 1942*

Unless something happens in the next few days, I shall be in command of the I Armored Corps, which is supposed to consist of two armored divisions and a motorized division. It will be a very interesting job, and, of course, I hope to get some place where I can do a little fighting as soon as possible . . .

Our equipment is coming along splendidly and is very high class. I believe that the troops throughout the Army, and particularly in the Armored Force, have attained a very high standard of proficiency. Of course, there is still a lot of dead wood in the officer personnel. However . . . there are some men of 60 who are younger than many men of 40, and I believe that their services should be retained.

Two days later Patton received command of the I Armored Corps, the headquarters of which was transferred to Fort Benning.

From the Military Service Publishing Company, Patton ordered a book entitled *Generalship, Its Diseases and Their Cure.*

## CHAPTER 4

# Fort Benning: Corps

*"I know nothing of my immediate future, but trust that I'll have a chance to kill somebody soon."*

HIS ADVANCEMENT to the corps command prompted him to send letters to those responsible – Marshall, McNair, Devers, Stimson, and others.

Stimson assured him that he had earned his promotion on his own merits – as a result of his fine performance of duty. He thought that Patton was sure to have all the active combat service he could possibly desire.

Patton was, of course, delighted. Yet he parted from the 2d Armored Division with real regret. He had shaped the men into a reflection of his public image, the warrior. By remaining at the head of the division, he could hope to lead it one day in battle. As corps commander, he was in the ranks of the "high command," where the direction of subordinate commanders was usually more important than the personal leadership of men at war.

His farewells to the division were sentimental and sincere. He asked Crittenberger, who succeeded him, to have his personal message read to all members:

> I desire to express to all ranks my sincere appreciation of your magnificent performance. Your untiring effort in training has made you a great division. When you meet the enemy, the same spirit of devotion will make you feared and famous. I shall be very proud of you.

A letter from a mother brought him close to tears:

> We have a son in your division . . . and because of this you are no

stranger to us . . . When we are facing the reality of war with all of its demands, Russell tells us not to worry, that they are ready and anxious to "follow their General Patton into the field" – confident that you can take them through. Recognizing you, not only as a great leader but a real personality, I ask you to accept a humble tribute from a soldier's mother – who only human, cannot help but fear the future for her son. With a special prayer for my own boy, my prayers will also follow you and your men . . . I have learned that the army is not a "machine" (the average civilian conception) but is made up of fine, kind and interested human beings . . . [with] gratitude for the fine leadership and example [you] set in the armored forces.

Throwing himself into his new job, he explained his belief in automatic movements:

In order to habituate men to the orderly entrance and exit from armored vehicles, a specific drill analogous to stand to horse, prepare to mount, and mount as used in the cavalry and field artillery [ought] to be used. If this is not done, men who are surprised during a rest by air bombardment or shelling may become confused and in attempting to enter the vehicles quickly will simply produce a jam . . .

Men do in emergencies what they are habituated to do in peace time. And therefore, I believe that simple movements . . . are essential because in battles some or all of these movements will be executed under fire and the habit of doing them in peace time . . . produces in the men the idea of watching for signals and orders and instantly obeying them.

*Letter, GSP, Jr., to Eisenhower, War Plans Division, War Department, January 22, 1942*

Dear Ike: . . . After you have gotten the war plans in shape, you had better fix to get [command of] a division in the [Armored] Corps . . .

I further appreciate your advertising of the 2d Armored Division, and I am sincere in believing with you that it is ready to fight anywhere, any time.

*Letter, GSP, Jr., to Brig. Gen. Geoffrey Keyes, 3d Armored Division, Camp Polk, La., January 24, 1942*

My dear Jeff: I am enclosing for your remarks the draft of the

> memorandum which I propose to send out to division commanders . . . assigned to this corps. You will recognize most of the stuff as the result of our mutual collaboration. Are there any other points which you think should be brought out, or have I infringed on the sacred rights of division commanders? Please let me know at your convenience . . .
>
> So far I have had nothing to do except write this creed. I am also engaged in making up a note-book covering various things such as movement to ports of debarkation [for shipment overseas], combat orders, landing on hostile shores, etc . . . If you have any better ideas on this, please let me know . . .
>
> I sincerely miss you a lot.

He was happy to hear from Devers who commended him for his fine training program that stressed battle realism.

In much the same way that his father had lobbied for his appointment to the Military Academy, Patton wrote several letters in behalf of his son George. To Senator Lodge he said he supposed he could write to senators from California and congressmen from Massachusetts, but his experience with Hiram Johnson, "who never even read my letter," was discouraging. Therefore, he proposed to go to Washington and call personally on those "whom I can probably claim." His official address was San Gabriel, California,

> and all I know of my local congressmen is that one of the more recent ones is now in the penitentiary for selling an appointment for Annapolis.
>
> Please do not consider this long letter a circumlocuous request for an appointment because you have already more than done your part. The purpose of this letter is to get your ideas on the best way to proceed.

Patton went to Washington in February and called on a number of influential people. "I had very little luck," he informed Devers when he returned.

In March, Patton turned to his brother-in-law, Frederick Ayer:

> After carefully canvassing the various methods of obtaining an appointment, and having consulted three very eminent politicians,

who are also friends of mine, I am convinced that the only way . . . is to make it worth a congressman's attention, either through fear or friendship – in other words, what you have to do is called "putting on the heat."

There were several vacancies from Massachusetts, and Lodge's secretary would send Ayer a list of congressmen vulnerable to pressure.

In May, Patton had the Hill School certify George's qualifications to take the West Point entrance examination in June. And he engaged Dr. Jacob R. Silverman of New York to tutor George for the tests.

Shortly before the exam results were announced, Patton wrote a letter of thanks:

My dear Dr. Silverman: . . . I am satisfied that considering the time available, George could not have had more competent instruction nor better psychological influence [than yours]. I sincerely hope that he passes. If, however, he fails to do so, I shall attribute it to Fate, which, after all, plays a very large part in our lives.

George passed. Congressman Thomas J. Flaherty of Masschusetts appointed him.

*Letter, GSP, Jr., to his son George, July 13, 1942*

Dear George: Your mother and I are very proud of you because you have at last demonstrated to be a money rider – to come accross in a pinch. But you must realize how very close run the thing was as Lord Wellington said of Waterloo. God and Luck were on your side. Both are useful but remember the Virginia adage "That the best trainer is old Doctor Work."

As to your conduct as a CADET! ! !

You do all the getting along.

Dont talk or look smug as if it was an old story to you.

Do your damdest in an ostentatious manner all the time.

Make it a point to always be the best turned out plebe at any formation. Brass polished, trousers pressed, every thing smart. Weapons spotless and get there on time – NOT JUST ON time but WELL AHEAD OF TIME.

Never make excuses whether or not it is your fault.

If you want to be a high ranking make, you must start the first day.

You must NEVER knowingly infringe any regulation. You will get skinned but they will be accidents. No man ever walks the area [in punishment] for an accident. He walks the area for a premeditated crime.

If you truly want to be a make you must dispense with friends or "Buddies." Be friendly but let the other man make the advances. Your own classmates – the worthless ones will tease you about boning make – admit it.

I repeat to be a make you must be a man not a boy and you must never let up working. You must not be a good fellow or join in "HARMLESS LARKS." They are the result of an unstable mind.

You will probably have no choice in initial roommates or tent mates. But keep looking for a quiet studious boy or boys for roommates for the winter. The older the men you can pick, the better as roommates. It is usually best not to live with your friends – that makes you loose them. Remember you are a lone wolf.

If some little fart hases you, don't get mad, do what he says, and take it out on some one else next year. AGAIN NEVER BE LATE, ALWAYS BE WELL DRESSED, DONT BREAK THE REGULATIONS AND DONT BE CARELESS ABOUT ROOM POLICE.

Well we are realy proud of you for the first time in your life. See to it that we stay that way.

Affect [ionately],

*Letter, GSP, Jr., to Senator H. C. Lodge, Jr., July 24, 1942*

You will be glad to know that George . . . is now a New Cadet. I trust that he can stay there. Maybe, if the war gets worse, the curriculum will get easier.

• • •

Patton was becoming so prominent that *Life* magazine sent a reporter to study and interview him for a feature article. Patton said he preferred to have nothing printed about him, but asked at least to see the piece before it was published. After showing the draft article to General Surles, chief of public relations, who thought it was "a good idea to publish it," the editor sent the article to Patton, saying that no personal flattery of Patton was intended but rather that it was important for the American public to have a hero whose 2d Armored Division would soon lead the army in offensive action against the enemy.

*Letter, GSP, Jr., to Edward K. Thompson, Associate Editor,* Life *magazine, February 10, 1942*

I deeply appreciate your continued interest in me and the nice things which your great magazine has said about me. But frankly, I hope you will not publish Mr. Field's article. My reasons for making this request are:

In the first place, I do not believe it paints a just picture of me. The casual reader would think that I am one of the most profane, crude, and vulgar people on earth; because the profanity of fifty years has been compressed into a few pages.

I have always deprecated any mention of what little inherited wealth I possess because I do not believe that wealth acquired through the judicious selection of ancestors is in itself a mark of ability.

Finally, the future of an officer who has been sufficiently fortunate to arrive at the position of a corps commander, a position which, thanks to General Devers, I now hold, must depend for his future advancement upon the opinion of his military equals and superiors, not upon public sentiment. In fact, it has been my observation that untimely or excessive publicity is a great detriment to an officer's career because people are bound to believe that the publicity was asked for by the officer and that he probably dictated most of it. Now, while you and I know that this is not the case, it is none the less what other people will think.

I know that your magazine has spent quite a lot of time and money in collecting the data for this article. Therefore, when I ask you not to publish it at this time, I realize that I am asking a great favor. However, in fairness to myself I must state that when Mr. Field was here, I asked him not to write the article and only submitted to being interviewed on his promise not to publish it without my approval — a promise which you have very generously complied with. But I must repeat that it is my honest opinion that to publish this article now would not only not help me, but might very well ruin my career and bring to nothing the effort of more than 30 years.

If at some future time I should be fortunate enough to command successfully in battle, people might possibly be interested to know what manner of man I was, or most probably, I had been. Should this occur, an expurgated edition of Field's article might be appropriate. I have, therefore, gone over the manuscript and removed ninety percent of the profanity, all of the wealth, and many irrelevant statements like the one about the manure at the dinner party. This story, as is the case with several others in the article, is an old Army legend, which for reasons beyond my knowledge, has been attributed to me absolutely without foundation of fact.

*Letter, GSP, Jr., to Brig. Gen. A. D. Surles, February 10, 1942*

My dear Day: Life Magazine seems very desirous of giving me undesirable publicity. They wrote to Devers, who, of course, had to say he had no objection. But I have talked to him, and both of us think that it would be very inexpedient and very hurtful to me at this time to have the large amount of publicity that Life desires.

I, therefore, propose that you with your inimitable tact tell them that they can't do it. I am writing them to the same effect, but, of course, I have less influence than you.

I am coming up to Washington at the end of the week . . . and will come in to see if you have done anything to stop this foolishness.

Thanking you and urging you to do your damndest,

*Letter, GSP, Jr., to Devers, February 11, 1942*

My dear Jake: I am enclosing, for your information, copies of the letters which I wrote yesterday to Day and to Mr. Thompson. I agree that such an article is untimely to be published now. I was so excited about it that after mailing the letter to Surles, I called him on the telephone and asked him to do his best to stop any attempt to publish it. I think that by suggesting to them that they use it as a posthumous article, they will most likely not publish it at this time.

The story did not appear. Devers agreed that a long article in *Life* might have hurt Patton. He added that a recent piece on Patton in *Time* magazine was all to the good.

*Letter, GSP, Jr., to Walter F. Dillingham, Honolulu, February 2, 1942*

I know nothing of my immediate future, but trust that I'll have a chance to kill somebody soon.

On account of the imminence of the war and the urgings of my friends, I am not playing polo right now, and it would be sort of unfortunate to miss a war for a bad polo game.

*Letter, GSP., Jr., to Col. Harry Whitfield, Middleburg, Va., February 2, 1942*

What is going to happen to the hunting during the present emergency, it would seem to me that, if possible, it should be kept up if even on a reduced scale because I think that since most of it rests on privilege, it would be a poor idea to let the habit lapse . . .

Beatrice and I succeed in going riding about five times a week and it is absolutely necessary to do so because the history of this and all other wars shows that physical fitness is the prime requisite usually lacking in generals.

Patton made time to read and that month ordered S. L. A. Marshall's *Armies on Wheels* and *Blitzkrieg,* Phillips' *Thoughts of Strategy,* Wavell's *Generals and Generalship,* and Shirer's *Berlin Diary.*

"My famous exalted rank," he wrote Floyd Parks, "seems to be unremunerative because all I have now is a title and no job." But he was depending on Parks to see that he got a good assignment.

I should like particularly to be in a position to beat Marshal Rommel because, since no one has licked him yet, I will get more credit when I do, and I feel perfectly confident that I will. This last is not said in the spirit of boasting, but is based on the opinion that no one that has fooled with him has really wanted to fight very much. Whereas, I believe, the I Armored Corps . . . will fight like hell.

*Letter, GSP, Jr., to Maj. Gen. Omar N. Bradley, 28th Division, Camp Claiborne, La., February 18, 1942*

My dear Omar: . . . During our service together [at Fort Benning] I never was associated with anyone who more whole-heartedly and generously cooperated with everything we worked on together.

*Letter, GSP, Jr., to Eisenhower, February 20, 1942*

My dear Ike: Of all the many talks I had in Washington, none gave me so much pleasure as that with you. There were two reasons for this. In the first place, you are about my oldest friend. In the second place, your self-assurance and to me, at least, demonstrated ability, gave me a great feeling of confidence in the future. I am very glad that you hold your present position [as Chief of the Operations Division, which acted as a kind of Cabinet for Marshall] and have the

utmost confidence that through your efforts we will eventually beat the hell out of those bastards – "You name them; I'll shoot them!"
Devotedly yours,

*Letter, Eisenhower to GSP, Jr., February 25, 1942*

I don't have the slightest trouble naming the hellions I'd like to have you shoot; my problem is to figure out some way of getting you to the place you can do it.

Patton wrote to Malin Craig from time to time in behalf of his old comrades in the Tank Corps, trying to help them in their efforts to return to active duty.

Personally, I am of the opinion that older men of experience, who have smelled powder and been wounded, are of more value to the service than mere youthful exuberance, which has not yet been disciplined. However, I seem to be in the minority in this belief.

What he was worrying about was his own age. He sometimes feared that he might be considered too old for combat. As a consequence, he constantly paraded his activity and energy, driving himself as never before, to assure his associates and particularly his superiors that he still had the vitality, along with the experience, to command in battle successfully.

Having had several young officers to serve him as aides, Patton fixed upon Captain Richard N. Jenson, who was from southern California and whose family had known the Pattons, particularly his sister Nita, for many years. Jenson had a sort of shining innocence about him, and Patton appreciated and was fond of him.

Because his rank permitted him to have a second aide, Patton eventually chose one of his old tankers, Alexander C. Stiller. A sergeant in France, Stiller was a rough and unlettered man, and he would serve Patton faithfully, principally as bodyguard.

A massive reorganization of the army took place in February 1942. Immediately under the War Department, all headquarters and units were grouped into three main elements. The Army Ground Forces (AGF) under McNair became responsible for combat training. The Army Air

Forces (AAF) under H. H. Arnold directed the aviation. The Army Service Forces (ASF) under Brehon Somervell looked after the supplies and supporting services. This new structure simplified and streamlined the army establishment, abolished the Chiefs of Infantry, Cavalry, and Artillery, and placed the Armored Force, now numbering 150,000 men, under McNair.

Soon afterward, Patton received a new assignment. To a friend at the War Department, he wrote:

> I have been detailed to organize and command a Desert Training Area . . . I should deeply appreciate your sending to me . . . any and all information, pamphlets, and what-not, you may have on the minutia of desert fighting, to the end that I may duplicate, so far as is practicable, the situation which exists in the desert of North Africa . . .
>
> Pardon me for writing you such a dry letter. We will try to correct the dryness when we see each other.

It was far from clear in whose jurisdiction the new training center would reside. Would Patton remain under Devers and the Armored Force? Or would he now be directly under McNair and the AGF? It turned out to be McNair. But Patton could take no chances. He could not afford to be forgotten. He would remain in close contact with both McNair and Devers, as well as with members of their headquarters, striving always to satisfy them, giving his utmost, working hard to justify his selection for combat overseas.

CHAPTER 5

# Desert Training Center

*"When we meet the enemy, we shall be in a position to utterly destroy him."*

THE DECISION to create a training area for desert fighting had its roots in an informal understanding that American and British military officers, meeting in Washington, reached in December 1940. If the United States became involved in the war against the Axis, it would follow a Europe-first strategy, that is, hold Japan in the Pacific and defeat the European enemies first. A year later, immediately after Pearl Harbor, Prime Minister Winston Churchill and a group of his advisers traveled to Washington and confirmed the agreement. This promised an immediate allocation of American resources to aid the British. Since Libya was the only place where British ground forces were fighting, it seemed likely that American troops might be sent there. It thus became necessary for Americans to learn how to fight in the desert.

A more specific impetus for desert training occurred on January 29, 1942, when German and Italian forces under Rommel recaptured Bengasi and rolled toward Egypt, thereby threatening the Suez Canal and raising the specter of continuing eastward to a meeting with German troops in the Russian Caucasus and even with the Japanese in India. Concerned about the possible need to send American units to the Middle East, the War Department, on January 31, recommended that Americans be taught to wage war in the desert. The only suitable terrain for an installation of this sort was in the southwestern portion of the United States. Discussions on how to establish and operate it culminated in the decision to put Patton and his I Armored Corps headquarters in charge.

On March 4, Patton, accompanied by several of his staff officers, flew from Fort Benning to March Field near Riverside, California. For three days they reconnoitered, from the air and on the ground, a vast wasteland about the size of Pennsylvania that included portions of California, Nevada, and Arizona – from Indio in the west to Desert Center, from Searchlight in the north to Yuma. They were favorably impressed. There was adequate if not abundant water. Much of the land was government owned and hardly inhabited – during their inspection, Patton and his party encountered no one. Three railroads served the area. The small towns of Indio with 1600 people, Needles with 5000, Blythe with 2500, and Yuma with 5300, were on the edges. Certain military installations in the vicinity could give needed support – a field artillery training area and an ordnance section near Indio, an engineer board at Yuma, air bases at Riverside, Victorville, and Las Vegas, an air depot at San Bernardino, and others.

Patton was enchanted with the area. Desolate and remote, it was large enough for all kinds of combat exercises. There were sandy stretches, rocks, crags, dry salt-lake beds, mountains, precipitous gorges – a varied terrain with little shade and sparse vegetation. Sudden changes in weather sent temperatures climbing from below freezing during the night to over 100 degrees the next day. Sandstorms and cloudbursts were frequent occurrences. Patton was sure it was the ideal place to condition and harden troops and to train them in the rigors of realistic campaigning.

He decided there would be nothing fancy, no soft living. The men would live in tents, without electric lights, sheets for their cots, heat, or hot water. Buildings needed for administration and planning were to be primitive – single-story structures of plain wood covered with tarpaper.

Conferring with officials of the Metropolitan Water District in Los Angeles, Patton rejected the suggestion that troops build storage tanks for water. They had no time to do anything, Patton said, except learn to fight.

He met with railroad men at the Army Engineer's Office and arranged to increase the railway traffic and services. With a representative of the IX Corps Area, he worked out signal support and commercial telephone lines – he wanted no female operators at the training center.

For his base camp he chose a site 20 miles east of Indio. He selected locations near Desert Center, Iron Mountain, and Needles for division cantonments, where the men in training would live.

*Letter, GSP, Jr., to Devers, March 13, 1942*

The area possesses tremendous advantages for all forms of training, because, in addition to its climatic and geographical similitude to Libya, it also is the only place I know of where artificial restrictions are almost wholly non-existing, and where there is room to burn . . .

*Letter, GSP, Jr., to Maj. Gen. Alvan G. Gillem, II Armored Corps, Camp Polk, La., March 17, 1942*

The training area is the best that I have ever seen . . .

We are sending some officers [there] . . . this week and hope to have the show at least partially running by the middle of next month. I may be overoptimistic about this, but shall do my best to accomplish it . . . All officers and men will live in floored tents. The buildings will be limited to kitchens, latrines, mess shelters, arms storehouses, etc. The nearest railway is about twenty-one miles over a good road, and there are in the area three other localities with adequate water and public land for camping divisions . . .

I believe that you were right when you said that the job was very important, and I should do my best to make a success of it.

Endeavoring to learn everything he could about living in the desert, Patton canvassed Roy Chapman Andrews, famous explorer, who had led several expeditions into the Gobi. Patton's request:

While I have played polo and navigated ships on the Pacific, I have a limited amount of knowledge about the desert, so do not hesitate to give me the most trivial details which, from your experience, you might consider superfluous.

*Letter, GSP, Jr., to Col. Lucian K. Truscott, Fort Bliss, Tex., March 23, 1942*

I saw General Devers the other day and stated that you had hopes of getting into the Armored Force. He told me that if you would apply for a transfer, he would be more than delighted to approve it. My advice to you is to do it as fast as you can.

Early in April Patton wrote to The Adjutant General, Major General James Ulio, whom he had known in Hawaii. "My dear Jimmy: This is the third time you will have helped me with Sergeant William G. Meeks." What Patton wanted was to have his orderly transferred to his new station. "If you are unable to do this . . . I will have nothing to wear, as Meeks is about the only man who can find anything."

"My dear Jimmie," he wrote two weeks later, "Please accept my sincere thanks for your goodness . . . I trust to be able to reciprocate in time, and failing that, in spirit – you know the type of spirit."

*Letter, GSP, Jr., to Devers, April 11, 1942*

The last of the service troops got in yesterday, and the first infantry units arrived at 5 a.m. this morning. At present things are very dusty and somewhat confused, but, really, the progress made has been remarkable.

Next week I am making an initial march in the desert . . . I believe the only way to start things is to start, so next week we start. I think I shall just issue canned rations and water, and let nature take its course, taking careful notes as to different methods used by different individuals. In this way we may get some American ingenuity connected with desert cookery.

His men soon discovered a simple expedient. Patton's desert stove, as it came to be called, took several forms. One was a small tin can filled with gravel and soaked with gasoline, lighted for cooking. Another was simply a small hole dug in the sand, with gasoline poured in and set afire to heat a can of food placed on top. In an area largely devoid even of twigs, the desert stove was perfect. Newspapers and magazines gave it widespread publicity. Anything connected with Patton was colorful and newsworthy.

The first troops at the Center called it "the place that God forgot," and suggested returning the land to the Indians. Their attitude soon changed when Patton arrived. His advance party had set up the headquarters in the hotel at Indio, but Patton went at once to his base camp to live with the troops. By nightfall, the entire staff had moved, leaving only one officer at the hotel – and he was rumored to be ill; actually, he remained as liaison with all outside agencies.

*Letter, Eisenhower to GSP, Jr., April 4, 1942*

Maybe I'll finally get out of this slave seat [in Washington], so I can let loose a little lead with you. By that time you'll be the "Black Jack" [Pershing] of the dam war.

> tactical exercises . . . to show you what I have done and to secure the benefit of your tactical criticism.
>
> Unless you wish otherwise, I propose to hold the housekeeping arrangements here to the minimum, that is, to spend just as little time as possible on "prettying up" and as much time as possible on tactical and technical instruction.

To one of McNair's staff officers, Patton announced that he was going out on a three-day problem featuring the march, supply, and operations of a task force of around 200 vehicles, about the maximum number he thought could be handled as a single group. He was surprised and pleased by the progress being made. He expected soon to move into "wooden offices – which will certainly be a relief because in these tents everything which is not tied down, and many things that are, continually blows away." The spirit of the men was excellent. He had all the officers in and told them what he was trying to do and how:

> It is a common belief that this force is going to Libya, Africa, Australia, or some other desert. You are going where you are sent, and no one knows where that will be . . .
>
> If you can work successfully here in this country, it will be no difficulty at all to kill the assorted sons of bitches you will meet in any other country.
>
> I know that for a soldier it is a very boring sport to ride around in tanks . . . and not know why he is there. You are a very intelligent group of men and I am going to take some of your time to try to show you.

As soon as he got a loudspeaker, he would go over the same ground with the enlisted men.

• • •

Several things, he wrote Floyd Parks at AGF, seemed "to be in the wind which I will require your Machiavellian touch to prevent causing trouble." First, there was talk of organizing the forces at the Desert Center into a special type of armored division. He felt that an order originating in AGF would be interpreted by Devers at the Armored Force – "very naturally, although in this case, erroneously" – that Patton was the instigator. He would then be in a very embarrassing and awkward position.

Second and more important was the question of marking armored vehicles, and he wrote at length on this subject.

Finally, he was so far from the seat of power that he feared he might be forgotten.

> When any fighting of real moment starts, please remember that I have commanded troops on maneuvers, and with due modesty, commanded them successfully, for a longer period of time than any other general officer in the army and probably in the world. I have gotten to the point where I am apt to urinate in the wash basin and try to wash in the urinal, because I have forgotten what they look like.
>
> As usual, the priceless thoughts above are to be used by you according to your best judgment.

On the following day he wrote to Eisenhower on the matter of marking vehicles. He was of the "convinced opinion" that every vehicle, tank, truck, or whatever, had to be distinctly marked so that any officer could tell immediately the unit to which it belonged. At the present time, this was impossible. He guessed that the intelligence service was responsible for the secrecy – the lack of markings – and he admitted that it might be desirable every so often to prevent the enemy from knowing the opposition. But "any realist knows that when you capture a vehicle you will capture a man, and when you capture a man, there are many methods, not put down in regulations, by which he can be and will be induced to talk, both fast and fluently." Therefore, "the arguments for distinctly marking vehicles far outweighed the arguments for secrecy." There was precedent for his view:

> The very colorful uniforms, which, since the time of Gustavus Adolphus have been worn, were for the purpose of knowing who was which. The Romans and the Greeks carried specific eagles or standards to the same end. The shoulder patch invented in the World War was devised because it was a demonstrated necessity to know to which division a man belonged. Heraldry was devised and became current only when the closed helmet was invented. Prior to that, people could recognize their friends and foes by their faces because

populations were small and men knew each other, but when the closed helmet was invented, it became necessary to resort to heraldic markings to distinguish friend from foe as well as friend from friend.

My last argument might induce the thought that heraldic markings would again be useful, but this idea is erroneous. In the first place, the enemy would promptly break down our code of markings, and in the second place, staff officers, not belonging to a unit, frequently must be able to determine the nature of that unit.

I hope you will forgive this long diatribe, but it is a question, which, I believe, is vital to the success in battle. Certainly, when the Ninth Legion attacked, the fact that they were attacking scared the hell out of the enemy. They did not hide their eagles under their gunny sacks to pretend that they were the Fortieth Legion, which I recall was invariably licked . . .

Sometimes I think that your life and mine are under the protection of some supreme being or fate, because, after many years of parallel thought, we find ourselves in the situations which we now occupy. But remember that my fate largely depends on you, because in this distant locality, one can very easily be forgotten . . .

I realize that in the first part of my letter about the markings of vehicles I stick my neck out, but I trust to your great powers of discernment and persuasion to see that no one drops an ax on it.

*Letter, GSP, Jr., to McNair, May 2, 1942*

I may be overstepping the grounds of propriety but I feel the matter is so important that I would be disloyal if I failed to present my views . . .

In order to insure both administrative and tactical control of trucks and armored vehicles it is vitally necessary that they bear markings showing the company, regiment, and division to which they pertain. This should be uniform for the whole army . . .

There is a regrettable and widespread belief among civilians and in the Army that we will win this war through materiel. In my opinion we will only win this war through blood, sacrifice, and high courage. In order to get willing fighters we must develop the highest possible Esprit de Corps. Therefore, the removal of distinctive badges and insignia from the uniform is highly detrimental. To die willingly, as many of us must, we must have tremendous pride not only in our nation and in ourselves but in the unit in which we serve . . .

The Romans had distinctive standards; so had the Gauls. During the Dark Ages this practice lapsed and much confusion resulted. In fact Warrick [was] defeated by Richard III due to a mistake in an heraldic badge. When Gustavus Adolphus revitalized and modernized war, the first thing he did was to get each of his regiments a colored scarf so that the people knew that the soldiers of the yellow scarf were Montgomery's, the green Hepburn's, etc. When Napoleon organized the Young Guard, he gave it a distinctive and gaudy uniform for the sole purpose of building up morale in the new organization.

I will not bore you with further historical examples and trust that you will pardon my importunity in taking up your valuable time, but honestly, General, I believe that the two questions I have here mentioned are of vital moment to our ultimate victory.

*Letter, GSP, J., to Eisenhower, May 6, 1942*

Just the other day one of my own battalions of artillery passed me on the road and I was unable to determine whether they belonged to me or to the 35th Division which was marching through the area. I finally decided that it was mine because it had much better march discipline . . . but that is not the way troops should be identified! . . .

Things are moving very successfully here . . .

I would very much like to have you out here and get your opinion on many things which are not susceptible of being put in writing.

With best regards and a caution not to kill your damn-fool self with work,

*Letter, Eisenhower to GSP, Jr., May 11, 1942*

I talked over the insignia matter with the Chief of Staff, Ground Forces today. Fortunately, I have with me the Deputy Chief of Staff from the British Army in Egypt. I quote him as follows: "but you know, you *must* have the vehicles marked. You must have a sign on it. Yes, of course you must." I got the promise that something was going to be done about it!

• • •

*Letter, GSP, Jr., to Malin Craig, May 6, 1942*

I have been having a very interesting time here and for once in my life have gotten all the tactical work that I want. We have been here twenty-three days to date and have had thirteen major tactical exercises, including some with two nights in the desert . . .

The chief trouble here, as I suppose everywhere, is with the younger officers who haven't been at the business long enough to have any self-confidence, but I believe that the vigorous use of a polished toe against their hind ends may eventually induce them to do something besides sit on their asses!

I wish to God that we would start killing somebody, somewhere soon, and trust that if we do, you will use your best influence to see that I can take a hand in the killing. Just to keep my hand in for Marshal Rommel, I have shot one or more jackrabbits every day that I have been here, with a pistol; the best shot being a sitter at ninety paces – which was, of course, luck – but then I have usually been lucky.

*Letter, GSP, Jr., to Clarke Robinson, New York, May 16, 1942*

Please accept my sincere thanks for the interesting clippings which you sent me. Had it not been for you, I should have never seen them and would have failed to appreciate my apparent fame.

Devers complimented him on his excellent and extensive activities reports, which kept everyone up to date on developments in the desert.

Patton wanted Devers to know that he "would certainly never suggest" to AGF any change in the armored division organization unless Devers asked him to do so. "As I see it, my job is to find out how to use what we have." To that end, he was taking the entire command out for a three-day exercise terminating in a fight between two groups. He thought that the light tank ought to have a heavier gun with "more hitting power. I am not sure it needs more velocity, but I am sure it needs more explosive charge when it lands." He had learned that "the compensated compasses were to be mounted in the turret." Because of his experiences with sailboats, "Permit me to observe that if this is done, the compass will be inaccurate because the lubber line of a compass must be on the median line of the vehicle or boat in order to steer by it." Under separate cover he was sending ten sheets of diagrams showing the formations he had so far evolved. They were hardly perfect, but "viewed from the air and from the ground, and I have done this on every occasion, they certainly present targets practically invulnerable to the aviation."

A letter from Caroline Trask, a childhood friend from Pasadena, brought Patton some anguish but mostly anger. She appealed for help, saying that she needed the Army's permission to work in the internment camps to which the Japanese-Americans on the west coast had been moved immediately after Pearl Harbor.

*Letter, GSP, Jr., to Caroline Trask, May 14, 1942*

My dear Caroline: . . . I am unable to be of any assistance to you, because it is my firm conviction that I would be unpatriotic if I aided anyone in bringing aid and comfort to my country's enemies, and I consider that the coddling, visiting, and talking to Japanese by Friends' Societies or other soft-hearted and softer headed individuals is directly prejudicial to my country.

You realize how difficult it is for me to say this to you who are perhaps my oldest friend, and therefore you must realize how strongly I feel in the matter, but in such a case it is best to be honest.

Perhaps I have been what you might call "brutally frank" and if so I apologize, but I am unable to change my stand.

Mark Clark, McNair's chief of staff, indicated that everyone was pleased with Patton's energy and accomplishments. He knew that Patton could hardly wait to put his desert experiments into actual practice on the battlefield.

*Letter, GSP, Jr., to Clark, May 16, 1942*

I appreciate your kind remarks as to the job we are doing here and hope that when we meet the enemy, we shall be in a position to utterly destroy him.

*Letter, GSP, Jr., to McNair, May 20, 1942*

I am glad if my somewhat informal weekly reports are of interest. I have tried to make them short and readable but I fear the one I am sending this week will be a little long. However, since it is the first time to my knowledge that a fairly large group of armored vehicles were successfully commanded from the air by voice radio, the report may be of interest . . .

Please let me assure you that your sympathetic interest in what we are doing here is a very rich reward for whatever efforts we are putting out. The recompense that I ask is the one with which you are already familiar, namely, that when serious fighting starts I be given a chance to prove in blood what I have learned in sweat.

It was reassuring to hear from Devers on the following day: "You are certainly doing a fine job out there and doing it in a big way."

A few days later came even more gratifying approbation from Devers: "I would like to see your corps headquarters . . . sent abroad to command our armored units [when they go overseas]."

*Letter, GSP, Jr., to Devers, June 3, 1942*

When you remember my one-time aversion to the medium tank, you may be surprised at my suggestions concerning them, but you and they have certainly made a convert of me.

Patton flew to Fort Benning in June to witness a demonstration by the 2d Armored Division, then went to Fort Knox and to Washington for consultations. "From the rumors I heard," he wrote a friend, "it now seems that Eisenhower and Clark will have the big jobs."

They were going to England, apparently to prepare for an invasion of Europe. Patton returned to Indio, California.

No sooner was Patton back when he suddenly received, on June 21, an urgent order to be in Washington on the following morning. He must have immediately thought that he was going to England too. He flew to Washington and reported directly to the Chief of Staff, General Marshall.

The reason for his summons, he learned, was a deterioration of the British situation in Libya. Rommel had attacked in May and by June was pushing the British forces into Egypt. Prime Minister Churchill was in Washington conferring with President Roosevelt when news came that Tobruk, long a symbol of British strength and resistance in the area, had been lost. Marshall offered to dispatch an armored division to help the British in the Middle East. That force he intended to be under Patton.

After informing Patton of the details, Marshall sent him to the Army War College to plan the movement. Several days later, after studying the problem, Patton concluded – and proposed to Marshall – that two divisions would be more appropriate.

By this time, some of Marshall's advisers had figured that it would be October or November before the American troops could get into action. This would be far too late to help the British in their immediate hour of danger. They suggested instead that 300 tanks and 100 howitzers be rushed to the Middle East. Marshall agreed, and Churchill accepted.

Once more Patton returned to Indio. Unaware of the reason for the sudden evaporation of his potential combat mission, he believed that his proposal for additional troops had disenchanted Marshall. Instead of following Marshall's orders, Patton had presumed to suggest change. He was consequently troubled by the poor impression he feared he had made in Washington and particularly on Marshall. He also was sorry that the opportunity for combat had slipped away. "I certainly regret that we failed to get to Africa," he wrote Crittenberger, "as I am sure we would have given a splendid account of ourselves prior to our untimely demise."

The nagging thought that he had let down Marshall at a vital moment continued to bother him, and he made known his concern to his friend Floyd Parks at Army Ground Forces. When Parks assured him that such was not the case, Patton replied:

> I was very glad to get your letter and find that I had not completely destroyed my opportunities. If the question ever comes up [again], you can tell all and sundry that I am willing to take anything to any place at any time regardless of consequences.

He had learned an important lesson, and he would, in the coming years, adhere faithfully to the missions and tasks assigned to him by his superiors.

He asked Colonel E. W. Piburn, who had returned from the Middle East, to talk to the entire command and was later pleased with the performance because Piburn was "an excellent talker and a natural killer."

On July 11, Devers electrified Patton by news he stated in an offhand and indirect manner. Events were moving fast, Devers said, and, as Patton no doubt knew, the War Department was thinking of moving an armored corps overseas in September or October. The problem was to decide when to dispatch to the desert another headquarters to replace Patton's.

*Letter, GSP, Jr., to Devers, July 14, 1942*

Until getting your letter I had heard nothing of an armored corps going over seas. I appreciate your selecting me THANKS. I WONT LET YOU DOWN.

A week later Eisenhower wrote him from London. It was entirely possible, he said, that he would soon need Patton badly. When that time came, Eisenhower would have to struggle with his diffidence to request the service of someone much more senior and able than himself. As Eisenhower had often told him, Patton was his idea of a battle commander. If battles by big formations came within Eisenhower's jurisdiction, he would want Patton in the lead, wherever the fighting was most difficult. He concluded by thanking Patton for sending him congratulations on his promotion, particularly "because you and I both know that you should have been wearing additional stars long ago. Devotedly."

With Mark Clark in London, Floyd Parks took his place as AGF chief of staff, McNair's principal assistant. Parks sometimes served, purely unofficially and informally, as a conduit through whom Patton passed information or from whom he requested news. He furnished impressions he hoped Parks would make known to McNair at the right moment, and he occasionally secured from Parks an idea of the lay of the land in Washington.

In July Patton transmitted a thought to Parks – with no special request, but rather as an implicit hope. "There is an old saying," he wrote, "that 'He who tooteth not his own horn, verily the same shall not be tooted.' " Colonel E. W. Piburn, who had spent more than a year in the Middle East, believed that the terrain in the Desert Center was far worse than anything in Libya or Mesopotamia, that American troops at the Center were "more competent to go into battle today" than any unit with which he had served, including the famous British 7th Armoured Division, and that

> the junior officers of this command had more of a feeling of responsibility for impending battle than any officers, foreign or domestic, whom he had encountered. Naturally, such remarks are most pleasant to me, and knowing your interest in me and the . . . Center, I am taking the liberty of forwarding them to you.
>
> I am having my first night combat operation. I am looking forward to it with great interest and some trepidation, but I believe that the danger inherent in such operations is justified by the good that can come from their successful accomplishment.

Devers reassured him on July 27, complimenting him on the splendid work Patton was doing. He was happy that Patton was putting his emphasis on essential matters like radio communications, accuracy in shooting, air support, and mobility.

*Letter, GSP, Jr., to Devers, July 27, 1942*

This morning I went out and watched the Board work with the T-16 battlefield recovery vehicle. This machine pulled a medium tank through sand much worse than we would ever attempt to fight on, thereby demonstrating to my belief that it is the answer for battlefield recovery.

Two days later Floyd Parks sent him gratifying news. After drawing up a schedule for shipping certain armored divisions overseas, McNair had selected Patton and his headquarters to be in command of the ones at the top of the list. Patton had made a first-rate impression on both McNair and Marshall, and Parks was sure that Patton would have the honor of leading the first contingent of combat troops to leave the country.

On the following day, July 30, Patton sent a messenger from his headquarters to take a note to his wife Beatrice, who was living in Indio:

> Darling B. I have just been ordered to leave for Washington to day preparatory to going over seas on an inspection trip. I will probably be gone 2 or 3 weeks but will return here before going to war. I love you.

He would not be back, and, several weeks later, he asked Gillem, who replaced him in command of the Center, to publish the following message:

> Soldiers: Owing to circumstances beyond my control, I left you so hastily that I was unable to speak to you personally. However, I would be lacking in gratitude if, even at this late date, I failed to tell you of my sincere appreciation of the magnificent conduct of each and every one of you whom I had the honor to command.
>
> Having shared your labors, I know the extreme difficulties under which we worked and I know also how splendidly and self-sacrificingly you did your full duty.
>
> I thank you and congratulate you — it was an unparalleled honor to have commanded such men.

Before departing Indio, he managed to send McNair and Devers a paper summarizing his experience. In that mimeographed brochure he packed his observations of the training he had conducted, the performance of officers and men, the adequacy of weapons and equipment, the effectiveness of procedures and formations. All his advice was pragmatic and concrete. For example, he explicitly defined the functions of air support, stated categorically that marching was a science and susceptible to dogmatic rules, and warned that the exercise of command in battle was an art and "he who tries to define it closely is a fool." He would go only so far as to block out roughly the probable successive phases and movements of a combat action involving tanks, infantry, artillery, and air support – the elements of German blitzkrieg – and he left much to the imagination and initiative of commanders, whom he expected to cope flexibly with the unexpected.

> *GSP, Jr., Notes on Tactics and Techniques of Desert Warfare (Provisional), July 30, 1942*
> Formation and material are of very secondary importance compared to discipline, the ability to shoot rapidly and accurately with the proper weapon at the proper target, and the irresistible desire to close with the enemy with the purpose of killing and destroying him.
> The commander can exercise command from the air in a liaison plane by the use of the two-way radio. He should remain in the plane until contact [with the enemy] is gained, after which one of his staff officers should be in the plane and he himself on the ground to lead the attack . . .
> Sitting on a tank watching the show is fatuous – killing wins wars.

He departed the Center around noon and went home to the Whittier ranch they were renting. Beatrice drove him to the Palm Springs airport, where a plane was waiting to fly him to Washington.

She went on to his sister Nita's in San Marino, left her car, and took the first available flight to Washington from Los Angeles.

• • •

An innovation and an experiment, the Desert Training Center was Patton's creation. He brought it into existence swiftly, without long and precise planning, and that too suggested his manner of operation.

His ability to impart high enthusiasm and morale to men working in unusually rugged field conditions stemmed from his leadership, that was called "uncompromising but understanding." He participated in every exercise, activity, and training task. A driver and disciplinarian, he was hard on his troops. Within two weeks after his arrival, he placed several officers under arrest and ordered investigations for their failure to perform routine duties.

He taught his men, supervised them, exhorted them, scolded them, and complimented them. The officers and soldiers never knew what approaching vehicle – jeep, Packard sedan, tank, half-track, cub plane, or tractor – might disgorge the Commanding General.

He spent much time on a hill that the troops called "The King's Throne," a lone elevation between the Crocopia and Chuckwalla Mountains. There Patton sat or stood, scrutinizing critically the line of march of tanks and motorized units below him. When he detected a mistake or discovered an improvement, he shouted instructions into his radio.

So fully did the troops identify with the Old Man that they resented the War Department order to name the base Camp Young – after Lieutenant General S. B. M. Young, who had fought Indians in the region and was the Army's first Chief of Staff. The soldiers thought of the area as Patton's.

The lasting impression he left was inadvertently recorded by a visitor who wrote:

> I know of no experience that was as interesting and even thrilling as my visit with you . . .
>
> The major factor was your own vivid and significant leadership in the whole operation . . . the experimental work you are doing, the varied equipment, the important contributions . . . that you yourself have made, the whole plan of command . . . and not the least, that box-seat ride in your own tank.

Patton never lost sight of his ultimate goal, to prepare his men for combat. He concentrated on teaching his men to kill efficiently, instinctively. He presented a speaker with these words: "Men, I want to introduce to you the noblest work of God – a killer!"

He understood machines. He would bawl out a man for getting his tank stuck, then proceed to help him pull it out. Impatient because soldiers were unloading tanks at the railroad yard too slowly, he showed them how to place the timbers, as he had in France, to allow tanks to roll down smoothly from flatcar to the ground.

He had great solicitude. "I'm a hell of a guy," he said. "I'm giving the men hell one minute and crying over them the next."

Once when he was landing in his Cub plane, he narrowly missed crashing into the telephone poles near his headquarters. Without instructions, troops took down the poles and buried the wires. They did not want their general killed.

When Patton departed, his soldiers felt a distinct loss. Most of them wanted to go with him, no matter what his destination or duty. They knew they would miss him. No one else produced the sense of excitement he generated.

# II

# North Africa

*"When I think of the greatness of my job and realize that I am what I am, I am amazed, but on reflection, who is as good as I am? I know of no one."*

CHAPTER 6

# Torch

*"I am the only true gambler in the whole outfit."*

PATTON WAS SUMMONED to Washington on July 30 because President Roosevelt decided to launch a military venture with the British. In that first large-scale Anglo-American endeavor, Patton was to have a prominent place.

American and British strategists had agreed to make an eventual cross-Channel invasion of German-occupied Europe, and already in 1942, American troops and materiel were arriving in the United Kingdom to prepare for that operation. Eisenhower and Mark Clark were in London and directing that buildup – Eisenhower as commander of the European Theater of Operations, U.S. Army (ETOUSA), Clark in command of the II Corps, under which the units were grouped.

But it soon became evident that a full-scale invasion was impractical for the immediate future because the Allies lacked sufficient means to carry it out. The landings were postponed, although the stockpiling continued.

Churchill and Roosevelt were anxious to initiate some offensive action in 1942, primarily to keep the U.S.S.R. in the war. Hitler's invasion in mid-1941 had sent the Russians reeling, and German advances in the second year of campaigning might well bring the Russians to collapse. Whatever diversion the Western Allies could create would aid the Soviet Union.

Roosevelt finally accepted Churchill's suggestion for an invasion of French North Africa, which required fewer resources, could go more quickly, and would perhaps meet little French opposition. Allied troops in Tunisia would threaten the Axis forces in Libya and assist the British army in Egypt.

Code-named Torch, the invasion of North Africa was to have two main landings. The Northern Task Force, consisting of American and British troops, was to sail from the United Kingdom and land on the northern coast of Africa, inside the Mediterranean. The Western Task Force, wholly of American composition, was to steam across the Atlantic and land on the western coast of Africa. The latter was to be under Patton's command.

There were no German or Italian troops in Morocco, Algeria, or Tunisia, for under the terms of the armistice in 1940, the French promised to defend their North African possessions against invasion. Since relations with the British had deteriorated after the evacuation from Dunkirk, the subsequent capitulation, and the British bombardment of the French fleet, the French forces in North Africa were certain to give British invaders a hostile reception. But if the French harbored thoughts of fighting the Axis to redeem their defeat, as the Allies hoped, perhaps the traditional Franco-American friendship would make them less inclined to oppose an invasion that appeared and purported to be wholly American.

Thus, Eisenhower became Commander in Chief of the Allied forces — all the participating American and British contingents, including ground, naval, and air components. He assembled a staff of British and American officers to plan the operation, and this became known as the Allied Force Headquarters (AFHQ).

In Washington, Patton and a small staff he had brought with him from the I Armored Corps headquarters — Gay, Lambert, Conklin, and Muller — were temporarily assigned to Marshall's office. Occupying a few rooms in the Munitions Building, they studied the preliminary plans already in existence, familiarizing themselves with the conditions, concepts, requirements, problems, and objectives of the operation.

Because Tunisia was close to substantial Axis air forces in Sicily and Italy, the Allies decided to land in Algeria, perhaps near Oran or Algiers; they would then drive eastward and hoped to overrun Tunisia before large numbers of Italian and German troops entered to oppose them. The Allies would also invade Morocco in case Franco's Spain entered the war on the Axis side and cut the straits of Gibraltar. A bridgehead near Casablanca would preserve a direct line of communications to the United States. The trouble was that the normally heavy swells in the sea offshore would endanger an assault, perhaps even make a landing impossible.

Since the operation was scheduled to take place in October or November, there was precious little time to prepare and coordinate what would be an extremely complicated venture. In order to facilitate the planning, Marshall sent Patton to London for discussions with Eisenhower.

As he had in the past when leaving for war, Patton started a journal.

*Diary, August 5*

Got word at 6:00 P.M. last night to fly to United Kingdom. This morning arrived Washington Airport . . . Got on four-motored stratoliner . . . all on plane going to war, but all the talk was of fishing and shooting. Very normal.

Brigadier General James H. Doolittle, Colonels Kent Lambert and Hoyt Vandenberg, Captain Lauris Norstad, and several others were in Patton's party.

*Diary, August 6*

Slept well most of the night . . . Up at dawn. We were over clouds. This was good, as we could hide in them if attacked . . . Arrived London . . . Billeted at Claridge's Hotel.

*Diary, August 7*

Reported to Ike. Spent morning working on plan. Talked to many people. London seems just half alive with very few people, even soldiers, about. All the women are very homely and wear their clothes badly.

*Diary, August 8*

Big talk for four hours. I said that Northern Task Force was being favored at expense of Western Task Force. Finally got some change. No one likes the plan, but we will do it . . .

The food is very expensive . . . All women at dinner in dining room hideous.

The major difficulty in the planning was the paucity of available troops. If the French resisted, the likelihood of getting ashore was slim.

*Diary, August 9*

Read and discussed operation all day . . .

Had supper with Ike and talked until 1:00 AM. We both feel that the operation is bad and is mostly political. However, we are told to do it and intend to succeed or die in the attempt. If the worst we can see occurs, it is an impossible show, but, with a little luck, it can be done at a high price; and it might be a cinch.

*Diary, August 11*

Raised Hell with staff . . .

Big US Navy parley . . . They are certainly not on their toes.

It is very noticeable that most of the American officers here are pro-British, even Ike . . . I am not, repeat not, pro-British.

*Letter, GSP, Jr., to Beatrice, August 11, 1942*

It looks as if my birthday [November 11] may be quite an important date.

This place is not too badly bashed in; in fact the ruins have been so well cleared that one does not notice them.

The person who drives me when I get a car, which is not often, is Pvt. Kay [Summersby], a lady whose father is a Lt. Gen. It is quite embarresing to have her get out and hold the door open for me.

Women also man or woman most of the anti-air guns and barage baloons.

London looks like a dead city in that there are no motor cars except military and a very few taxies on the streets and very few people. It is always black out and realy black. The night before last I had dinner with Ike and tried to get back here at 1:00 A.M. There were no taxies so I walked and would have been walking yet had I not run into a policeman who, by scent apparently, took me here.

All of us think that if there ever were any pretty women in England they must have died. They are hideous, with fat ankles . . .

I bought a pair of shoes for $30.00, but there is nothing else for sale. The coffee is artificial and one is always hungry. The only filling thing is mush and blue milk. You get two pieces of butter the size and thickness of a quarter and very little sugar.

The only thing they seem to have lots of is smoked salmon and decayed grouse.

On the other hand, they take long weekends and get to the office at ten. It is very funny.

I am treated with great reverence as a prospective hero. The Brit. officers too are fed up with the youth movement, and so far as I can see, the generals are about my age but less well preserved. They take two hours for lunch, at which repast there is little to eat. All the whiskey is cut and the beer is like water.

Because the Navy representatives said "that the means do not exist for a second attack," the planners decided to invade with only the Northern Task Force.

> I think this is fortunate for me, so far as a longer life goes, but it is bad for the country – very dangerous in fact. Ike is not as rugged mentally as I thought; he vacillates and is not a realist.

A single landing was soon dismissed as too risky, and the planners continued to discuss a variety of objectives inside and outside the Mediterranean, using various combinations of forces.

To maintain the fiction that Torch was wholly American and also to preserve continuity in planning in execution if Eisenhower became incapacitated, he appointed Clark his deputy.

"I doubt the wisdom of it," Patton commented. "He may be too intrusive."

This negative reaction was deceptively mild, for Patton resented Clark's increasing importance. Clark was quite junior to him. He had graduated from West Point eight years after Patton. In 1941, Patton was a major general, Clark a lieutenant colonel. A year later, Clark was also a major general. Although Eisenhower had already surpassed Patton and was now a lieutenant general, he was an old friend. Clark was relatively unknown. Patton respected his undoubted ability and energy and envied his close relationship with Eisenhower. But if something happened to Eisenhower, Clark would become Patton's boss and probably a lieutenant general as well. Patton was sure he would hate to see that take place.

A telegram from Washington raised basic questions about Torch, and Eisenhower, Clark, Patton, and Doolittle went over the possibilities and problems. All but Patton felt that the odds against the invasion were too high. "I said it was 52 to 48 against us, but I favored going on." Later all agreed that "it was better than even money we could land, but a poor bet we could get Tunis ahead of the Boches."

> I feel that we should fight, but for success we must have luck . . . We must do something now. I feel that I am the only true gambler in the whole outfit.

The nub of the problem concerned the potential French resistance. If the French contested the invasion, Eisenhower informed Marshall, they could, "in view of the slowness with which Allied forces can be accumulated . . . so delay and hamper operations that the real object of the expedition could not be achieved, namely the seizing control of the north shore of Africa before it can be substantially reinforced by the Axis." In short, the operation had more than a fair chance of success only if the French forces were "so badly divided by internal dissension and by Allied political maneuvering that effective resistance will be negligible." Hardly less important was the need for Spain to remain "absolutely neutral."

*Diary, August 17*

Things seem to be jelling and I have gotten a lot of valuable information. Supposed to go back [to Washington] tomorrow. Had a drink with Clark at his flat. I do not trust him yet but he improves on acquaintance. Ike is getting megalomania.

Summing up for Marshall the results of the conference in London, Eisenhower remarked that Patton had quickly absorbed "the essentials of his problem" and had worked in a "very businesslike, sane but enthusiastic" manner. Eisenhower was delighted that Marshall had chosen Patton to lead the American venture.

Several days later Patton and his staff left for home. They were thoroughly familiar with the operation that still had, in Eisenhower's words, "so many indefinite or undetermined factors." The plan for what was now called the Eastern Task Force was rather firmly fixed, but the plan for Patton's Western Task Force was "less firm" because it resulted from "preliminary studies" made by a "skeleton staff."

As soon as Patton returned to Washington, he would have to work up a final and detailed plan for his part of the invasion.

*Letter, GSP, Jr., to Devers, August 22, 1942*

Should you be in Washington, I would like very much to see you . . . first, because you are one of my dearest friends; second, because I think you would be interested in hearing orally what I cannot put on paper; and third, because I would like to have the opportunity of personally thanking you for all the good turns you have done for me during the thirty odd years of our service together.

He wrote a long letter to his orderly, giving him detailed instructions on how and where to send his clothes, suitcases, pistols, boots, and other personal possessions and telling him that Meeks would soon be ordered east to join Patton. He concluded: "Please give my best to Virgie" – the sergeant's wife – "and an extra bone to each of the dogs."

By now the concept of the invasion was emerging more clearly. There would be three major landings. Two forces would sail from the United Kingdom and land inside the Mediterranean, probably on the coast of Algeria, then move overland to the east and conquer Tunisia. Patton would come ashore near Casablanca.

Eisenhower wrote Patton that he felt like a circus lady riding three horses without knowing exactly where any was going to go. But he was happy that Patton was part of the act.

Devers told Patton that he was pleased with Patton's role. He was sure that Patton would do the job. His success would mean that Devers had succeeded too.

Patton remarked to Doolittle that they were getting everything they asked for in the way of men and equipment. Yes, Doolittle said, "They always give the condemned man what he wants to eat for his last meal."

Scott, returned from the Middle East and assigned to Fort Knox, sent Patton a copy of a talk he had made on his observations of combat.

"You can't imagine how delighted I was to get your letter with the enclosed speech," Patton replied. "Your speech is one of the finest military documents I have ever read, and I have practically memorized it."

His immediate job, he explained,

> envisions a landing operation in the face of enemy resistance. At first, I was somewhat worried, but after considering my luck and the high class of troops to be engaged, I am now perfectly satisfied that, so far as my part in it is concerned, the operation will be a complete success. If it is not, I always have an easy way out, and in view of my long and pleasant life, not a bad way out either. However, I do not mean to indicate that it is now time for you to start saving up for flowers for my funeral – although if you have any friends in the Axis, it might be well to contemplate fitting floral tributes for their demise.

A week or so later, when Scott mailed Patton some notes, Patton responded by saying:

> I believe that they are practically a bible for the operations intended.
>
> The more I dig into this thing, the more I am sure that the only thing that will win it will be leadership, speed, and drive, plus sound tactics. I have secured Gaffey and Truscott . . . with the belief that their leadership will assure the success of two operations. I shall be in the middle one myself. I have also secured Geoffrey Keyes as deputy commanding general, so that when I pass into the beyond, there will be somebody to carry on.
>
> Spiritually, I have complete confidence, in fact certainty that we shall succeed, although when studied logically it looks almost impossible. However, wars are only won by risking the impossible. If you have any inside track with the Lord, please use it in my behalf.

> *Diary, September 24, 1942*
>
> The plan has finally [been] settled, and I feel very calm and contented. It still can be a very desperate venture if the enemy does everything he should, and we make a few mistakes. I have a sure feeling we will win.

Yet he was well aware of the uncertainties ahead. He told Eisenhower that the picture was still "gloomy," but that Eisenhower could

> rest assured that when we start for the beach we shall stay there either dead or alive, and if alive we will not surrender. When I have made everyone else share this opinion, as I shall certainly do before we start, I shall have complete confidence in the success of the operation.

The invasion was now definitely to consist of three major landings. The Eastern and Central Task Forces, both sailing from the United Kingdom, were to come ashore, respectively, near Algiers and Oran, Algeria. The assault landings would be carried out mainly by American troops. After the initial forces were safely ashore, British troops under Kenneth Anderson were to land and strike eastward into Tunisia, to seize Bizerte and Tunis and prevent Axis forces from coming into the country. Patton's Western Task Force would sail from Hampton Roads, Virginia, land near Casablanca, and be ready to move, if necessary, into Spanish Morocco.

Patton divided his own task force into three task groups. One under Truscott was to touch down near Mehdia and capture Port Lyautey. The other two – under Jonathan W. Anderson and Ernest N. Harmon – after going ashore near Fédala and Safi, were to converge on and take Casablanca from the landward side.

The major dangers came from the prospect of bitter French resistance and high seas off the coast. If the surf was rough, the Navy might be unable to carry the assault forces in small craft to the landing beaches.

Clark arrived in Washington to coordinate the final arrangements and to make sure that the planners in Washington and London were working on the same assumptions and toward the same objectives. On the same day Keyes reported as Patton's deputy commander.

*Diary, September 28*

As far as I am concerned, General Clark has explained nothing. He seems to me more preoccupied with bettering his own future than in winning the war. He seems to me slightly ill at ease . . .

Our Navy is certainly very pessimistic as to the possibility of effecting a landing at Casablanca. I feel that in spite of all, we will succeed there.

Keyes' . . . firm character and level head have been very comforting to me.

Major General Daniel I. Sultan came to talk about an invasion of the Dodecanese Islands he expected to lead from the Middle East. He was unaware that "his bogus plan," as Patton called it, was part of a deception to draw Axis attention away from North Africa. To deepen the credibility of the operation, Patton "lied to him . . . I hated to do it."

A few days later Major General Lloyd R. Fredendall stopped for a brief visit. He had headed the II Corps before relinquishing it to Clark, who took the corps headquarters to England. With Clark now Eisenhower's deputy for Torch, Fredendall again received command of the corps. On his way to London, he would head the Central Task Force, which would land near Oran. "I am glad he has a job as I feel he has been badly used."

On October 4, Patton went to West Point to say farewell to his son. Marshall sent for Patton to ask about Harmon. "I said Harmon was all right. The future will show, but I think he is."

Patton spent a night aboard the cruiser *Augusta,* flagship of Rear Admiral H. Kent Hewitt, who commanded the naval elements of the Western Task Force. A landing rehearsal the next morning at Solomon's Island, Maryland, was less than satisfactory. "The timing of the landing by the Navy was very bad, over 40 minutes late to start with, but all we can hope is that they do better next time."

The joint planning carried out by Patton's and Hewitt's staffs was often stormy. For example, army officers wished the ships loaded so that items needed on the beach first would be stored last. Navy officers had their own ideas and regulations on how to utilize space, insure safety, and the like. Patton was frequently enraged, and his high, squeaky voice, shrilling with profanity, could often be heard in the corridors of the Munitions Building. He resented what he thought was the Navy's "attempt to issue orders to me." At one point the Navy considered asking the army to replace Patton with someone easier to work with. When tempers frayed and debate seemed at an impasse, Handy, John E. Hull, and Albert C. Wedemeyer of Marshall's office and Charles M. Cooke of Ernest J. King's Office of the Chief of Naval Operations smoothed out the difficulties and restored calm and order if not always amity.

*Letter, GSP, Jr., to Walter Dillingham, Honolulu, October 9, 1942*

Dearest Walter: . . . I am writing you not a goodby but an aloha . . .

Of all the men I have met in a long life, I have liked you best . . .

You gave me the best advice and incidentally the most unselfish advice I ever had. We were having our last practice game before the Inter Island [polo championship tournament] and my team was doing badly and I was cussing hell out of them. After the game you took me up to the house, soothed my spirit with a long drink and told me what an ass I had been . . . You simply suggested that when men were doing their best, it was foolish and useless to cuss them. I have never forgotten nor have I repeated my error. As a result I am eledged to have trained the best division in the army and as a result of that I have my present job . . .

Little B's husband is in Europe as a Lt. Col. and Ruth-Ellen's is soon to go. George is a plebe at West Point and I have only two polo ponies left, so why should I linger too long . . .

This seems a very poor letter as a vehicle for really deep emotions but under the circumstances it is the best I can do.

Give my love to the family and the horses . . .

If you write me [a letter] it may, unless my number is up, reach me.

*Letter, GSP, Jr., to Devers, October 14, 1942*

I have now reached the situation which you and I have felt many times before — after the ponies have been shipped for an important match, one's worries seem to disappear. I believe that we have done everything humanly possible and that this expedition contains the best trained troops of all arms this country can produce . . .

While I expect to write you many more letters, it is humanly possible that this may be the last one. Therefore, in closing, I want to thank you from the bottom of my heart for the many good turns and magnificent backing you have given me during my entire career, and particularly since I have been serving under you.

With affectionate regards to Georgia, I am your devoted friend and admirer.

Charles P. Summerall, who had commanded the 1st Division and V Corps in combat in World War I, who later became Army Chief of Staff, and who in retirement was President of The Citadel, a military college in Charleston, had great affection for Patton, whom he had known at West Point and in France. He wrote to Beatrice to praise her husband. "We shall hear great things of him," Summerall predicted, "for he is one of our [nation's] chief assets."

Patton was in Norfolk to inspect the loading. "While things were not perfect, they were satisfactory . . . I am just a little worried about ability of Truscott. It may be [my] nerves."

There were so many regulations, he noted, on how to deal with the civilian population of Morocco that "if I do all the things set out, there will be no [time for] war."

He and Beatrice "called to pay respects to Secretary of War. Met General Marshall, Field Marshall Dill, and a British lieutenant general dining there. Interesting but felt out of place."

Stimson too was sorry he had been unable to have a word in private, and he wrote to tell Patton so and to give his blessing. Patton had won his assignment, Stimson said, because he could guarantee the leadership, courage, and fighting qualities needed for success. The only advice that Stimson extended was to ask Patton to avoid the impulse to sacrifice himself. He was needed, not only for the landings but also for the subsequent operations in what was sure to be a long war. He was confident that Patton would get ashore and stay. "Go to it," he concluded, "and may God bless you and care for you and bring you back safe!"

Patton was well aware that success in the North African endeavor was badly needed. In the Pacific the Air Forces were gaining triumphs by their raids against Japanese bases, a campaign capped by Doolittle's bombardment of Tokyo in April; the Navy achieved momentous victories at Coral Sea and Midway in May and June; the Marine Corps fought ashore at Guadalcanal in August; but the army surrendered in the Philippines in May after Douglas MacArthur was ordered to Australia, and many Americans, including Patton's friend, Jonathan M. Wainwright, were prisoners. On the European side of the conflict, large fleets of bombers were striking the German-occupied Continent, but the war at sea was going badly, the Dieppe raid in August, by a force largely Canadian in composition, had been disappointing, and the Germans were driving deeply into the Soviet Union. Much of the outcome of the war seemed to depend on the courage and skill of the untried Americans who would lead the North African invasion.

That recognition added to the enormous strain of the past few weeks. Patton supervised a constant planning and scheduling process that involved the final training, feeding, and care of thousands of men scattered in camps and stations along the East Coast, some as far as Fort Bragg, North Carolina. He then had to move them to the port of embarkation for the sea voyage. He had to oversee a multitude of details connected with securing, servicing, and loading weapons and equipment, as well as items of supply. He had to be sure that everyone and everything were ready for the initial combat test of American troops in the European sector of the war.

He was consequently tired and, at the same time, exhilarated. All the preparations excited him. He loved the burden of responsibility and the power of commanding a venture where every single piece had to fit into a predetermined pattern. To be at the head of the first combat force sent from the United States to engage in operations against the European enemies made all the prior work, all the previous study, all the dedication worthwhile.

As Patton pondered the general situation and, more especially, the position he had reached, he was satisfied that his fate was being shaped toward a supreme achievement, and he became sentimental. Was Morocco to be his destiny, his final adventure? If so, he would glory in it.

He wrote a good many letters on October 20, leaving instructions that they were to be mailed only after the invasion. To Mary Scally, his nurse, who had worked for the Patton family for many years and who was living with his sister Nita:

> When Nita gives you this letter, I will either be dead or not. If I am, please put on a good Irish wake; if I am not, get busy with the Pope. In any case, please accept my sincere love and appreciation for all you have done for Nita and myself. Affectionately,

To Mrs. Francis C. Marshall, widow of Patton's first company commander:

> Now that I am about to start on a big adventure, I should be remiss if I failed to write you, because, as you well know, you and General Marshall were an inspiration and guide in the first and formative years of my service, and I believe that whatever success I have attained, I owe largely to the influence of you and the General.

To retired Major General André W. Brewster, a member of Pershing's staff in France: "Before starting on the Second World War I wish to bid goodbye to one of the men who in the First War did so much for me."

To retired Major General James G. Harbord, Pershing's chief of staff:

> Probably unknown to yourself, you have been one of the chief inspirations of my military life. Your high sense of duty, honor, and loyalty have inspired me to attempt to the best of my ability to imitate you.
>
> As you know, George is at West Point and should it be necessary for me to pass out of the picture and not return, I would appreciate

it if you could keep an eye on him and give him such help and advice as you think fit.

I cannot thank you for all you have done for me.

And to his brother-in-law Frederick Ayer:

In spite of my faults you have always treated me as a real brother and I have felt that way towards you. I do appreciate what you have been and done to me and for me. My admiration for you as a man is without limit. You also have my devoted love as have all your family.

The job I am going on is about as desperate a venture as has ever been undertaken by any force in the world's history. We will have to meet and defeat superior numbers on a coast where one can only land 60% of the time. So my proverbial luck will have to be working all out. However, I have a convinced belief that I will succeed. If I don't, I shall not survive a second Donqurque (if that is how you spell it). Of course there is the off chance that political interests may help and we shall have, at least initially, a pushover. Personally I would rather have to fight — it would be good practice. However in any event we will eventually have to fight and fight hard and probly for years. Those of us who come back will have had some interesting experiences.

And further, when we get back we will have a hell of a job on our hands [to reshape the country]. I should like to have a crack at [it] . . .

I am enclosing a sealed letter to B. which you are only to give her when and if I am definitely reported dead. I expect you to keep it a long time . . .

Letters even to me will probably be censored, so avoid political and financial statements you don't want others to read.

This all sounds very gloomy, but is not really so bad. All my life I have wanted to lead a lot of men in a desperate battle; I am going to do it; and at fifty-six, one can go with equanimity — there is nothing much one has not done. Thanks to you and B., I have had an exceptionally happy life. "Death is as light as a feather; reputation for valor is as heavy as a mountain."

*Diary, October 21*

Saw General Marshall for 45 minutes at 8:15 AM. He was very friendly and helpful. He gave me the inside on the Clark-Fredendall switch. Apparently Clark made a big impression on the Prime Minister.

He told me to influence Hewitt but not to scare him. I mentioned Admiral Hall as a fine influence for us and the General immediately asked, "How old is he?" I said, "As he was in the class of 1913, he was probably 53 or 54." His comment was, "My, how old we all are." Marshall lacks imagination but has an unusual mind.

Called on General Pershing. He did not recognize me until I spoke. Then his mind seemed quite clear. He looks very old. It is probably the last time I shall see him, but he may outlive me.

It turned out that Patton was right on both counts.

I said that when he took me to Mexico in 1916, he gave me my start.

He replied, "I can always pick a fighting man and God knows there are few of them. I am happy they are sending you to the front at once. I like generals so bold that they are dangerous. I hope they give you a free hand."

He recalled my killing the Mexicans and when I told him I was taking the same pistol, he said, "I hope you will kill some Germans with it."

He also said that he hoped I got a chance to kill someone with my sword whip.

He said that at the start of the war he was hurt because no one consulted him, but was now resigned to sit on the sidelines with his feet hanging over. He almost cried. It is pathetic how little he knows of the war.

When I left I kissed his hand and asked for his blessing. He squeezed my hand and said, "Goodbye George, God bless and keep you and give you victory."

I put on my hat and saluted when I left, and he returned it like he used to, and 25 years seemed to drop from him. He said that when he started World War I, he was just my age. A truly great soldier.

Admiral Hewitt and I reported to the President at 2:00. He greeted us with, "Come in, Skipper and Old Cavalryman, and give me the good news."

Hewitt brought up a request from the Prime Minister for an exchange of four of our destroyers for four British. This would be fatal at this late date as each vessel has a very definite gunfire support mission, and the British could not take it over.

The President said, "Hewitt, fix up a counter proposal. I never say no, but we can stall until it is too late." He then gave Hewitt a lot of advice about how to moor a ship to keep it head to wind by a stern anchor. He had done this once with a yacht.

I had fixed up the meeting with the hope that he would put some heat on Hewitt about the necessity of landing [no matter what the sea conditions]. As nothing came of it, I said, "The Admiral and I feel that we must get ashore regardless of cost, as the fate of the war hinges on our success."

He said, "Certainly you must," and that was that. A great politician is not of necessity a great military leader.

Handy and Hull came to say goodbye and we had a long talk. They are fine men and should have commands.

Wrote paper for Bea on care of horses.

He thanked Lieutenant General Brehon Somervell, Chief of the Army Service Forces, "for the courteous and splendid assistance which all persons in the Services of Supply . . . demonstrated towards us." He made known his appreciation to Handy "for the constant and magnificent support which you have given us. If we fail, it certainly will not be your fault; if we win, yours should be most of the credit."

He was glad to receive a note from Field Marshall Sir John C. Dill, the British representative in Washington to the Combined Chiefs of Staff, and a close friend of Marshall's. Dill told him that Patton's inspiring leadership was the most important ingredient for the success of the imminent operation.

*Diary, October 22*

Called on Secretary of War, Mr. McCloy, Gen. Somervell, and Admiral Cooke, all very nice.

Left War Department at 11:15. Packed tin suitcase. Had lunch. Bea went with me to airport. General [George E.] Stratemeyer asked her to ride to Norfolk, and we saw many of the ships [in the harbor from the plane].

Keyes and I inspected loading . . . all very orderly. I asked a QM [quartermaster] captain how things were going. He said, "I don't know, but my trucks are getting on all right." That is the answer;

if everyone does his part, these seemingly impossible tasks get done.

When I think of the greatness of my job and realize that I am what I am, I am amazed, but on reflection, who is as good as I am? I know of no one.

All of us are relieved that the strain is over, and the staff and all the men I have seen are cheerful and full of confidence . . . I feel that we have all done our full duty and will succeed.

To Beatrice on October 23: "It will probably be some time before you get a letter from me but I will be thinking of you and loving you."

Halfway around the globe that day, British forces in the Middle East under General Sir Harold Alexander, more specifically the Eighth Army under General Sir Bernard L. Montgomery, attacked Field Marshall Erwin Rommel's Italo-German army at El Alamein, Egypt. If the British could push Rommel's forces into Libya, and if the Anglo-Americans in Torch could seize and overrun French North Africa, particularly Tunisia, they would threaten the Axis troops on both sides.

*Letter, Summerall to GSP, Jr., October 23, 1942*

You are so eminently qualified by experience and leadership that success would never be in doubt . . . Our men must have the fighting spirit and there is no one who can instill this like you. Your method of influencing by your personality and constant presence with your troops insures their loyalty and sacrifice. Men must have forceful leaders and you measure up to their ideals.

The army and the country are in desperate need of success and you are bound to change the situation where you go to positive results.

*Diary, October 23*

Today Captain Emmett [who commanded the troop transports] talked [to the troops] for three hours and said nothing. I talked blood and guts for five minutes and got an ovation.

Came aboard the Augusta at 2:45. I have the Captain's cabin, very nice . . .

Men and officers in fine spirits . . .

Now that it is up to the Navy, we are all relaxed. [Admiral] Hall impresses me more all the while. Saw Stiller. George Meeks is much impressed and says that he is setting an example to the sailors.

This is my last night in America. "It may be for years and it may be forever." God grant that I do my full duty to my men and myself.

CHAPTER 7

# Morocco: The Landings

*"Every once in a while the tremendous responsibility of this job lands on me like a ton of bricks, but mostly I am not in the least worried."*

*Diary, October 24*

The Augusta left here at 8:10. The sortie was remarkable for its ordered and apparently faultless efficiency. We moved in column through the mine fields and out a swept and buoyed channel . . .

All elements [of the convoy] . . . will have over 100 vessels.

Admiral Hewitt impresses me better. Admiral Hall is great.

*Diary, October 25*

"General Quarters" went at 6:30. It is also called "Man Battle Stations." I got up, exercised, and took a bath as I guessed it was a drill . . .

The mess is superior. I have to watch eating too much . . .

Went to church . . . It is less than two weeks now [to battle] if all goes well.

*Diary, October 26*

The Admiral has just started zig-zagging. I like him better all the time.

I keep feeling that I should be doing something but there is nothing to do.

*Diary, October 27*

Today is Navy Day. Keyes wrote a letter to Hewitt for me to sign. It pleased him [Hewitt] . . . Keyes is a grand man, never forgets.

*Diary, October 28*

I have been giving everyone a simplified directive of war. Use steamroller strategy, that is make up your mind on a course and direction of action and stick to it. But in tactics do not steamroller. Attack weakness. Hold them by the nose and kick them in the arse.

Having nothing to do, some of my people worry. I could myself, but won't. It is hard to realize that in 10 days I shall be up to my neck in work. At the moment I have nothing at all to do . . .

So far I have read part of the Koran, finished "Three Harbors" and "The Raft." "The Sun is my Undoing" is pretty sticky.

Someone gave him "a rowing machine so I get some exercise. I also hold on to the dresser and run in place 300 steps. It is good for the wind."

*Diary, October 30*

Hewitt has certainly been fine . . .

I finished the Koran — a good book and interesting.

It begins to look like we will get ashore without a fight. I am sorry. The troops need blooding; also, it would be better for [my] future prospects.

*Letter, GSP, Jr., to Beatrice, November 2, 1942*

From some of the messages we have, it seems that there is a good chance that the French Army and Air will join us. I hope not, for it would sort of pull the cork of the men — all steamed up to fight and not have to — also it would be better for me to have a battle. Well in six days we will know . . .

This mess is the best I have ever seen. I fear I will get fat. I take lots of exercise running in place, 480 steps, 1/4 mile in my cabin.

Every night we darken ship, but there are reading lights in my cabin . . .

This afternoon Sgt. Meeks, Stiller, Jensen, Gay, Lambert, and I did a lot of shooting on the stern. The new carbine is a lovly little thing and very accurate.

*Diary, November 3*

Every once in a while the tremendous responsibility of this job lands on me like a ton of bricks, but mostly I am not in the least worried. I can't decide logically if I am a man of destiny or a lucky fool, but I think I am destined. Five more days will show. I really do very little, and have done very little, about this show. I feel that my claim to greatness hangs on an ability to lead and inspire. Perhaps when Napoleon said, "Je m'engage et puis je vois" [I start the fight and then I see], he was right. It is the only thing I can do in this case as I see it. I have no personal fear of death or failure. This may sound like junk, or prophecy, within a week.

We had a CPX [command post exercise] this morning which was very dull. I can't see how people can be so dull and lacking imagination. Compared to them I am a genius – I think I am.

*Diary, November 4*

Things were so bad last night that they are bound to get better. Subs were all around us . . . There was a high north wind, and it was very rough. All the conditions needed for high surf at Casa [blanca].

Had radio that Giraud . . . [is] on the fence and that [Robert] Murphy wants to delay [the invasion] until they [the French] make up their mind. As if 100,000 men, all at sea, can wait. It looks from the radio as if Clark has told them [the French] D-day and H-hour. The fool.

I have always been opposed to talking with the French. Also it is reported that if we attack, the Spanish will move . . . This may interfere with Truscott at Port Lyautey. On the other hand, it may bring the French in on our side. If the Spanish move . . . it probably means they are in with the Axis and that closes the straits and we must, repeat, must take Casablanca.

Something good is bound to happen.

Reports of possible collusion with the French in North Africa were unclear. Clark's secret trip by submarine to Algeria to talk with French officers willing to help the Americans ashore and Murphy's diplomatic machinations were producing an uncertainty that would be heightened by General Henri Giraud's clandestine submarine voyage from southern France to Eisenhower's temporary headquarters at Gibraltar. Would the French fight?

*Letter, Dillingham to GSP, Jr., November 5, 1942*

I have thought of you many times in the past week and knew that your silence was the best evidence of the fact that you have been all out preparing a division whose efficiency is second to none other . . . Knowing you perhaps better than any of your many loyal friends, I can appreciate how irksome delays have been to you and how anxious you have been to prove your ability to handle a mechanized outfit in actual combat. I know that you have not only the technical ability from long years of military training, but that you have the spiritual quality which makes for the highest form of leadership. You know how many able leaders of many walks of life I have been privileged to know, and I can say without hesitation that you are outstanding, in my judgment, as having that which is given to no other man of my acquaintance. I remember what one of the generals said . . . that you were a difficult officer in time of peace, but a "hell of a good soldier" in time of war . . .

If you have picked, as you must have, a staff of officers who are qualified on the polo field, you will be supported by men who are quick in making decisions and direct and intelligent in their method of attack. Wherever you are and in whatever you are undertaking to do, you have with you all the affection and loyalty that I have to give, for there is no one in whom I place greater confidence.

*Diary, November 5*

Last night it was very rough, almost a storm. This morning it is still very rough with a 40 mile wind . . . Things are bound to get better as they could not get worse. I have done some extra praying. I hope that whatever comes up, I shall be able to do my full duty. If I can do that, I have nothing more to ask. Fate will determine what success I shall attain . . .

The Navy is quite anxious to fight. The younger of them want to close in to fire. I hope they do.

*Diary, November 6*

Things are looking up. It is calmer and the wind has fallen to about 20 miles and is northeast, which is O.K. The forecast is for a possible landing condition. The intercepts [of enemy messages] indicate that the French will fight.

*Letter, GSP, Jr., to Beatrice, November 6, 1942*

Darling B. Yesterday things looked as bad as possible . . . During the night things improved and now it looks as if we could land, though it will be pretty rough . . .

It amases me how little I am excited – some times I fear that I am too calm.

I think that ones spirit enlarges with responsibility. In 40 hours I will probably be in battle and on the spur of the moment with little information I will have to make most momentus decisions, and I feel that with Gods help I shall make them and make them right. It seems to me that almost inspite of my self my whole life has been pointed to this moment. When this job is done I presume I will be pointed to the next step in the ladder of destiny.

Inspite of my over developed personal ambition, all I want to do right now is my full duty. If I do that, the rest will take care of its self.

*Letter, GSP, Jr., to Marshall, November 6, 1942*

I am writing this at sea, Friday morning. The weather conditions, while not perfect, promise to permit a landing, Sunday morning, in fair to bad surf conditions. The forecast indicates that during Sunday and Monday the weather will get worse; however, the forecasts have been relatively inaccurate.

I should like to call your attention to the fact that the relations between the Army and Navy in this convoy could not possibly be more satisfactory. Admiral Hewitt and his chief of staff, Admiral Hall, have shown the utmost cooperation and the finest spirit. I desire to bring this to your attention because prior to leaving I had some doubts. These doubts have been removed.

Finally, I wish to again thank you for the opportunity you have given me, and to again assure you that to the uttermost of my ability I shall merit your confidence.

To Major General Guy V. Henry, a former chief of cavalry:

I have, perhaps, an illogical but firmly convinced belief that we shall be completely successful. If we are not, it is not my intention to live to make excuses; however, I feel very healthy for a dead man.

To Stimson:

I can assure you that to the limit of our ability we will strive for success. If we fail, I trust that I shall not be present to make explanations. However, I have the uttermost confidence that we will land, and having landed will stay.

With affectionate regards to Mrs. Stimson, and again thanking you for the lifetime of kindness you have shown me, I am, Devotedly yours,

*Letter, GSP, Jr., to Maj. Gen. A. D. Surles, War Department, November 6, 1942*

My dear Day: I have been informed that "Life" and "Time" magazines have a story about me which they wish to publish . . . There are several very objectionable features to this story. One to the effect that I am challenging Marshall Rommel to a personal encounter, or words to that effect. I believe, also, that they mention my athletic prowess, which is really zero, and also state that I am very wealthy, and bring out the usual line about my swearing.

In the position to which good fortune has sent me, all the above remarks are highly detrimental, and give to enemies, of whom we all have plenty, ammunition. I would regret very much if this article were published, and I should appreciate your using your great influence to stop it, or at least see that the objectionable features are removed. Please do your damdest!

It is my opinion that in spite of our large conversation about the psychology of war, we utterly fail to utilize the simplest means of stimulating pride and valor in the troops. In no account of which I have read of the fighting in the South Pacific have the names of commanders or units been mentioned. I presume that this is done with the erroneous belief that mentioning names of units and commanders would aid the enemy. You and I both know that the enemy is always fully cognizant of the names of the commanders and . . . the units he is fighting. Therefore, reticense, due to aiding the enemy, is foolishness.

On the other hand, if the people at home know that the boys from Lensville, Illinois, or Junction City, Kansas are fighting and doing well, they will get a great kick out of it and will write to the soldiers with the result that the soldiers will fight harder than ever. If, on the other hand, they learn that certain units have not done well, they will also write, and these units will do better. I am so convinced of this that it seems to me a national tragedy not to utilize man's innate love of fame and fear of censure to develop a fighting spirit.

I believe that you could not possibly do a greater service to the country than by persuading the powers that be to permit pitiless publicity, giving names and units, with regards to the good and bad actions of troops in combat. Please think this over . . .

As far as I have been concerned, the current voyage has been uneventful as I did all I could do before we started . . . The performance of the Navy in this fleet, particularly Admirals Hewitt and Hall, has been of the highest order. I am amazed at their efficiency, and I am delighted at the wholehearted spirit of cooperation they have evinced. It would seem to me desirable that they receive credit . . . I believe that they will do everything humanly possible to put us ashore.

Please . . . remember to keep Beatrice informed. If this is my last letter – which I doubt – rest assured that for a would-be corpse, I feel very well.

*Letter, GSP, Jr., to his troops, issued at sea early November, 1942*

Soldiers: We are to be congratulated because we have been chosen as the units of the United States Army best trained to take part in this great American effort . . .

It is not known whether the French African army, composed of both white and colored troops, will contest our landing. It is regrettable to contemplate the necessity of fighting the gallant French who are at heart sympathetic toward us, but all resistance by whomever offered must be destroyed. However, when any of the French soldiers seek to surrender, you will accept it and treat them with the respect due a brave opponent and future ally. Remember, the French are not Nazis or Japs . . .

When the great day of battle comes, remember your training, and remember above all that speed and vigor of attack are the sure roads to success and you must succeed – for to retreat is as cowardly as it is fatal. Indeed, once landed, retreat is impossible. Americans do not surrender.

During the first few days and nights after you get ashore, you must work unceasingly, regardless of sleep, regardless of food. A pint of sweat will save a gallon of blood.

The eyes of the world are watching us; the heart of America beats for us; God is with us. On our victory depends the freedom or slavery of the human race. We shall surely win.

*Diary, November 7*

This morning it is very quiet and cool, almost too good to be true. Thank God. I hope He stays on our side.

The Safi convoy quit us at 0600. The Lyautey one will pull out at 1500 . . .

Fortunately I found a detective story, "The Cairo Garter Murders," by Van Wyck Mason. I have just finished and will start to worry, or should I feel utterly confident? . . .

In 15 hours I should be ashore. I will not write any more in this while at sea. At 2120 radar reports land . . . Went to bed dressed and slept from 1030 [P.M.]. This was hard to do.

*Letter, Eisenhower to Marshall, November 7, 1942*

If Patton encounters any real resistance, he is going to have a tough time of it because landing problems alone are enough to occupy his full attention.

In the early morning hours of November 8, members of all the task forces in Operation Torch touched down on North African soil. In every instance, near Algiers, Oran, and Casablanca, they met immediate opposition from French army, navy, and air forces.

*Letter, GSP, Jr., to Beatrice, November 8, 1942 (morning)*

Darling B. We have had a great day so far. We have been in a naval battle since 0800 and it is still going on but at the moment we are not firing.

The French, 2 cruisers and several destroyers, came out and we went after them. This ship was not hit but one shell landed so close that it splashed me. The men were fine.

We took Safi before dawn. We had pretty [bad] losses at Fedala and some losses apparently largely [from] drowning at Lautey.

I tried to go ashore at 8:00 but the blast from our rear turett smashed our landing boat on the davits so I am still aboard.

There have been, so far as I know, two air attacks. I don't think they hit anything.

There does not seem to be very hard fighting on shore. I am going in as soon as I can get a new boat.

It is a flat calm – God was with us.

Lots of love.

*Diary, November 8*

Woke at 0200, dressed and went on deck. Fedhala lights and lights at Casa burning, also lights on shore. Sea dead calm, no swell – God is with us.

H Hour was at 0400, delayed first 30, then 45 minutes . . . There were four destroyers anchored about 6,000 yards from shore, the transports were anchored at 18,000 [too far, he thought]. They had different colored lights to show right, left, and center line of de-

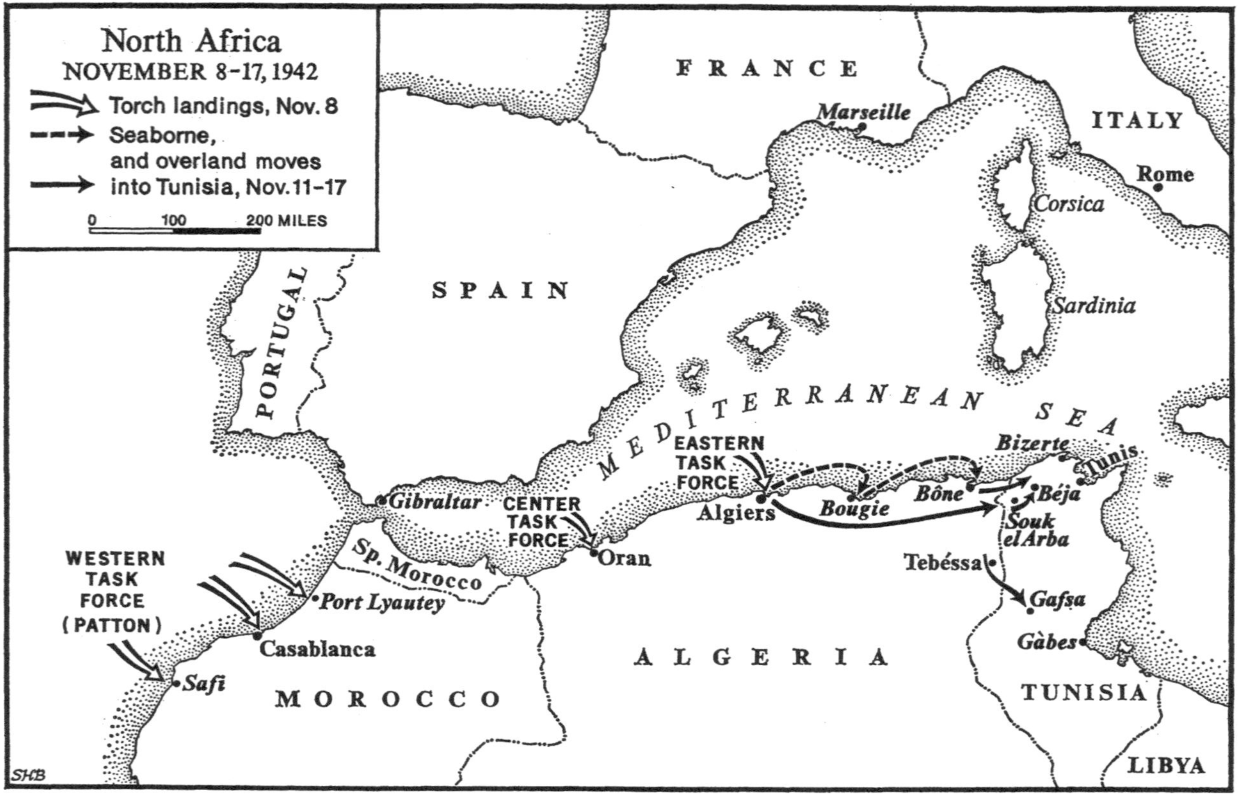
North Africa
NOVEMBER 8-17, 1942
Torch landings, Nov. 8
Seaborne,
and overland moves
into Tunisia, Nov. 11-17
0
100
200 MILES
FRANCE
ITALY
Marseille
Rome
Corsica
Sardinia
SPAIN
PORTUGAL
MEDITERRANEAN SEA
EASTERN TASK FORCE
Bizerte
Tunis
Béja
Bône
Bougie
Algiers
Souk el Arba
Gibraltar
CENTER TASK FORCE
Oran
Sp. Morocco
Tebéssa
Gafsa
Gàbes
WESTERN TASK FORCE (PATTON)
Port Lyautey
Casablanca
Safi
MOROCCO
ALGERIA
TUNISIA
LIBYA
SHB

parture. Light house went dark at 0300. We had a sub on the surface which guided the destroyers in.

At Safi we had radio "Batter up" [code for "enemy firing"] at 0455. At 0530 a search light showed apparently vertical at Fedhala, then turned on the beach. At once our destroyers opened fire with tracer. They looked like red fireflies. The light went out in about 10 minutes. At the same time a French corvette showed up from the south. She was escorting three French ships. When she refused to halt, the destroyers opened fire and shot off the mast and killed her Captain. I think she sank. The three merchant ships beat it and beached themselves to north . . .

Truscott radioed "Play ball" [code for "am fighting"] at 0713. Mississippi's batteries had been shelling battleship Jean Bart for about 30 minutes when six enemy destroyers came out of Casa at 0715. All ships in range opened on the destroyers and they went back. I was going ashore at 0800 and boat was on davits swung out with all our things in her, including my white pistols. I sent orderly to get them, and at that moment, a light cruiser and two big destroyers came out of Casa, tearing up the coast close to shore to try to get our transports. At once Augusta speeded up to 20 knots and opened fire. The first blast from the rear turret blew the leading boat to hell and we lost all our things except my pistols. At about 8:20, enemy bombers attacked transports and Augusta went to protect them. There was a hell of a racket but no damage was done. Then we went back into the fight with the French ships, about 0830, and fired hard for about three hours. Ranges ran from 18,000 to 27,000 yards. They breached us after using pink and green dyes on shells. I was on main deck just back of number two turret leaning on the rail when one [shell] hit so close that it splashed water all over me. When I was on the bridge later, one hit closer but I was too high to get wet. It was hazy and enemy used smoke well. I could just see them and make out our splashes. We had the Mississippi, the Brooklyn, the Augusta and some others all firing and going like hell in big zig-zags and curves to keep enemy from the subs . . . . The Ludlow, a destroyer, was hit and set on fire, but put it out. The Brooklyn was hit. Her 43-gun turret fired like lightning, much faster than our 8" [guns], although we fired at times two salvos (9 guns at a time) each minute. You have to put cotton in your ears. Some of the people got white but it did not seem very dangerous to me — sort of impersonal.

The French went back about 11:30. The Mississippi kept on shelling them in harbor with her 16" guns. We had lunch – naval war is nice and comfortable.

Harmon took Safi at 0515, but we did not get the message till noon. It was a complete surprise. He captured a battalion of the Foreign Legion, three tanks, and a lot of guns.

Admiral Hall, Gay, Johnson, Ely, Jenson, Stiller, George Meeks, and I went ashore at 1242, hit the beach at 1320, and got very wet in the surf. There was still quite a fight going on but I had no bullets [come my way].

At 1340, Anderson met me with a French colonel, who suggested I send to Casa to demand a surrender. He said that the French [army] did not want to fight. I sent Gay and [Colonel W. H.] Wilbur. The Admiral refused to see them. The army general said he could do nothing, as Admiral Michelier was senior [to him]. His staff, on the side, gave us all the dope and even suggested that Casa could be taken more easily from the rear . . .

Anderson is good but lacks drive – however, he did well. Captured eight of German Armistice Commission . . . They only heard of the landing at 0600, so it was a complete surprise.

I inspected the town and port and all the French soldiers except the marines saluted and grinned. We put on mixed Military Police, half American and half French, with a First Lieutenant of *chasseurs a cheval*, Moroccan, as assistant Provost Marshal.

Spent night at Hotel Miramar, very nice, but it had been hit several times so there was no water nor light and only cheese and fish to eat and champagne to drink . . .

God was very good to me today.

*Letter, Beatrice to GSP, Jr., November 8, 1942*

Darling Georgie, You have landed in Africa and I will tell you the story from this end, play by play, without trimmings.

I . . . got into Washington yesterday morning. Since Thursday, despatches . . . had been coming in; first of a big concentration of war vessels at Gibraltar and later of a great convoy steaming thru the Mediterranean.

Yesterday morning Mrs. Stimson called up and asked me to supper. At about 7:30, just as I left for Woodley [the Stimson residence], Day Surles called and told me to get on the radio by nine [o'clock]. At dinner, nothing was said about D day but as it got on for 9, I asked about some news. We went into the library and the Secretary called up Day at the office. The news was just being released and he took it on the phone and repeated it as he heard it. We got the whole thing and then hung up and heard it over the radio. I cannot describe my feelings nor their looks as the news came in that all the entire operation had come off as planned. The news that you made your landing . . . showed that you did exactly what you wanted to . . .

I came home at ten thirty and sat up . . . listening to the broadcasts . . . This A.M. I was called by Mrs. Marshall saying that you had made a successful landing . . . The Secretary has just called me now at 2:15 to tell me that all your landings have been made though no personal word has come from you. He says he will call me at intervals all day as soon as he has anything to report . . .

The names of the officers and principal generals in command of the show were given out on Army hour this afternoon and before it was over I had a call from the Times Herald asking for an interview. I gave a very nice one, saying nothing, by telephone, right then. I had no more than come upstairs to go on with this letter than the doorbell rang and a reporter from the same paper was at the door to get my picture. I sent word that I was out, as I am too busy answering the phone and writing to you to bother with anything like that this afternoon . . .

I realize that there are months and perhaps years of waiting and anxiety ahead of me, yet today all I can think of is your triumph, and the thought that rings thru my mind like a peal of bells is that the first jump is taken and you will never have to take it again. And I know that it is a success. God with us . . .

I finally broke down and let the Paramount News take my picture because they asked me to say something. They suggested I say something about army wives but I fooled them and they were tickled. When they had got the mike [microphone] ready, I said, "This is America's hour of triumph. Safely our men have crossed the sea to fight our battle. The spirit of Victory is in their hearts. They will not fail." The man's eyes were full of tears when I finished. They are doing one of Mamie [Eisenhower] and both will be in the news this week . . .

[I will] make a speech at a bond rally at Harrisonburg where there are a great many Mennonites and other conscientious objectors. I will begin with our young Virginian objector who killed a sergeant and three soldiers because he didnt want to leave his Mama, and go on from there. I bet I sell a lot of bonds.

At Gibraltar, Eisenhower was receiving garbled messages of Patton's activities. There seemed to be a battle, and one report had Patton re-embarking under a flag of truce. That Eisenhower rejected – "Unless my opinion of Georgie is 100% wrong."

*Diary, November 9*

I got out of the Hotel before dawn and went to see Anderson, who was in bed. He should have been up.

The beach was a mess and the officers were doing nothing. We had tried since the previous day to have the lighters use the harbor, but Emmitt never told them to. As a result they were beached half the time, and whenever they got off, it took half an hour. I cursed, and at last got a launch off to catch the boats and show them into the harbor. Had Anderson showed proper push, this would have been done earlier. Just as I got the launch out, a boat turned end for end and drowned 16 men. We only found three – they were a nasty blue color. I was sorry. I got one of them.

The French bombed the beach and later strafed it. One soldier who was pushing a boat got scared and ran onto the beach and assumed the Fields [foetal or prenatal] position and jibbered. I kicked him in the arse with all my might and he jumped right up and went to work. Some way to boost morale.

As a whole the men were poor, the officers worse; no drive. It is very sad. I saw one lieutenant let his men hesitate to jump into the water. I gave him hell. I hit another man who was too lazy to push a boat. We also kicked a lot of Arabs . . .

Things were going so slow that I came back to see the Admiral. He ordered the doctor to give me a drink as I had had no food. I needed it. Got back to ship at 1310.

Sent Keyes and all staff ashore at 1500.

Truscott has Lyautey but not the airport. Had a tank fight with 15 Renaults. Semmes must have had a good time.

The derrick on the sea-train broke, so there will be a delay. I may attack Casa with the 3d Infantry Division only, and with a naval bombardment and the air.

Harmon has a small airport, and I am sending one squadron of P-40's to him at dawn . . . Again God has been good.

*Diary, November 10*

Today has been bad. Could get no news from either Truscott or Harmon except that Truscott wanted help. I had none to give. Anderson closed in on Casa and one battalion . . . broke badly under shell fire. Keyes, who was on the spot as usual, stopped them. I decided to take Casa anyway with only the 3d Division and an armored battalion. It took some doing, as we were outnumbered but I felt we should hold the initiative.

An important Frenchman came and suggested that I write the Sultan [of Morocco]. I did. Doubt if it does any good.

At 2200 Admiral Hall came in to arrange naval support [for the attack on Casablanca]. He brought fine news. The airport at Lyautey was taken and 42 P-40's were on it. Harmon had defeated an enemy column, destroying 19 trucks and 6 tanks. He is marching on Casa. All this shows that we should push in. "God favors the bold, victory is to the audacious."

*Letter, Mrs. Ralph Menzing, Chicago, to GSP, Jr., November 10, 1942*

My husband and I read with joy of your arrival in Africa, not only because my nephew . . . is a Sgt and M.P. in 2d Armored Division, but because you are a "grand" general. We have your pictures in our apt [apartment], say special prayers for you and your unit . . . My husband saves all your photos in papers.

*Telegram, Eisenhower to GSP, Jr., November 10, 1942*

Algiers has been ours for two days. Oran defense crumbling rapidly . . . The only tough nut left is in your hands. Crack it open quickly and ask for what you want.

*Telegram, Eisenhower to Walter Bedell Smith, chief of staff, AFHQ, November 10, 1942*

Reports from Patton still meager but . . . information indicates he is progressing steadily. If he captures Casablanca by noon tomorrow, I will recommend both him and Fredendall for third stars.

*Diary, November 11*

Lambert woke me up at 0420 to say . . . that the French at Rabat and Lyautey had ceased firing. Staff wanted me to call off attack [against Casablanca] but I would not [do so] yet. It was too late, and besides it is bad to change plans.

Anderson wanted to attack at dawn, but I chose 0730 so as to give him a chance to form up by daylight. I also warned Admiral Hewitt to be ready to call off his air and gun fire on my signal "Cease firing." Actually the French quit at 6:40, so had we attacked 0600 as planned, many needless lives would have been lost. Again the hand of God. I said I would take Casa by D plus 3, and I did. A nice birthday present [to himself]. Keyes gave me a letter from Bea . . .

General Nogues and Admiral Michelier came to discuss terms at 1400. I had a guard of honor [for them]. No use kicking a man when he is down. I had written a set of terms along the lines Ike had sent me. They were so different from those used in Algeria that I decided to have a gentlemen's agreement [with the French] until I found out what Ike had done. The French don't want to fight [us]. I felt that most of the time they bombed the ocean rather than the beach . . .

We are in Casa and have the harbor and airport . . .

To God be the praise.

*Letter, GSP, Jr., to Beatrice, November 11, 1942*

The last time I wrote you we had just finished a naval battle . . . Afterwards we had another. And since we left the Augusta she has had two more fights . . . I missed both . . .

We spent the night at the Miramar hotel and I slept in the bed of the Chief of the German Armistice Commission . . .

Monday morning I spent on the beach. Things were pretty bad and we got bombed and straffed by French air . . .

The transports were so far out [from shore] that I went out to the Augusta to see the Admiral – the ships came closer.

This made for shorter voyages between ships and shore in the smaller landings boats and facilitated unloading men and supplies.

I sent Keyes and staff ashore and stayed on the ship . . .

In the morning Tuesday I heard that Truscott had air port at Fedala . . . I ordered Army planes to fly ashore . . .

I decided to attack Casa on the 11th [the next day] . . . it took some nerve as at the moment both Truscott and Harmon seemed in a bad way . . .

[When] the enemy quit, it was a near thing, for the bombers were over their targets and the battle ships were in position to fire.

I ordered Anderson to move in to the town and if any one stopped him to attack. No one stopped him. But the hours from 7:30 to 11:00 were the longest in my life.

Gen Nogues and Adm. Michelier came to treat for terms . . . Nogues is a crook – a handsome one. Michelier is a man and a very mad one at the moment . . .

I opened the conference by congratulating the French on their gallantry – the Navy did fight to the end. The army realy quit but keep it dark [quiet].

I closed the conference with champagne and many toasts . . .

I loved your birthday letter which Keyes gave me at 5:00 to day.

*Letter, GSP, Jr., to Stimson, December 7, 1942*

We had a fairly hard fight and lost some good men, but we inflicted very severe casualties on our late enemies . . .

Of course, as a Christian I was very glad to avoid the further fusion of blood, but as a soldier I would have given a good deal to have the fight go on because we had a very pretty scheme of maneuver, and all the troops were in position . . .

When the French came in to make terms, my sporting sense of not wishing to triumph over a gallant enemy induced me to have a guard of honor to receive the French officers. This made a very happy impression upon them and was, I believe, a precursor of the excellent entente which has existed ever since.

Before the meeting started it was very evident to me that the two sets of terms, one of which we were to apply, were not applicable to the case because French Morocco is a protectorate and not a province, and its local security therefore depends on retaining the prestige of the French Army. I . . . decided that the best way to avoid an Arab uprising was to allow the French to retain their arms and man all their works. Fortunately my guess was correct and was subsequently approved by General Eisenhower.

With these thoughts in mind, I opened the meeting by paying a high compliment to the valor and effectiveness of the French resistance, mentioning the Army, the Navy, and the Air Force. This also eased the situation.

At the end when he had reached an agreement, in fact the French agreed to what I asked them, I played a very nasty trick on them. I said, "Gentlemen, we have now settled everything, but there is one disagreeable formality which we should go through." They all looked very worried. I then produced some champagne and suggested a toast to the happy termination of a fratricidal strife and to the resumption of the age-old friendship between France and America.

They drank $40.00 worth of champagne, but it was worth it.

The fortuitous presence in Algiers on November 8 of Pétain's second in command, Admiral Darlan, made possible rapid armistice arrangements. Darlan was in Algiers to visit his son, stricken with polio, in the hospital. A commanding figure in his own right as well as representing the authority of the Pétain government, Darlan – despite Pétain's insistence that the armistice of 1940 be honored and that French forces continue to resist – had sufficient stature to conclude a cease-fire for Algiers at the end of the first day of the invasion. Fredendall's men took Oran by military action, and at the end of November 10, as Patton was preparing to attack Casablanca, Darlan agreed to terminate hostilities in all of French North Africa.

Germany and Italy reacted swiftly. In metropolitan France, starting at midnight, November 10, ten German divisions crossed the demarcation line into unoccupied France and six Italian divisions marched into the southeastern part of the country. Overrunning the free zone governed by Vichy, they occupied all of France and took Corsica.

Beatrice was writing her husband another birthday letter on November 11:

> Happy Birthday, and I know you are having one if things are going as I hear they are . . .
>
> That must have been a splendid birthday for you: Casablanca taken and an armistice over the whole of North Africa . . . How I wish I could have seen your triumph. I expect you will go for Rommel now . . .
>
> For myself, I went to communion and spent the rest of the day answering the phone. This afternoon I took an African violet to Mrs. Stimson with a message from you that you had captured it at Casablanca. The Secretary told me that you had made a speech at Lyate's tomb and that he had sent you a birthday telegram. As soon as he saw me, he called out, "Well, George had the toughest job of them all and he has got Casablanca for his birthday."
>
> The newspaper has just said that you took it at 3 am our time. Funnily enough, I woke up in the night for no reason and looked at the clock. It was just three. I thought, what is G. doing, I won-

der . . . I did not feel worried, but just lay thinking about you for some time. This has happened to me so many times in my life.

Fairfax Ayres, a friend, wrote to tell Patton that when he was asked what kind of person Patton was, he replied always, "You bet your boots he will fight."

Truscott informed him that his operation had been difficult because the Navy had landed his troops late and in some confusion, then had taken "station about half way to Bermuda," which slowed unloading. He was conducting his affairs in accordance with what he believed Patton would wish. He toasted the Patton luck.

*Diary, November 12*

Got up early and went to dock. Nothing was going right . . . Six French trucks ready to help were standing idle because no one took hold. Found a lieutenant and put him to work with the trucks . . .

Chief of Civil Staff for General Nogues came in and tried to get me committed on politics.

Just after supper four transports were torpedoed in harbor. It was really terrible to see them burn. One . . . was full of ammunition and air bombs, also 400,000 pounds of frozen beef. Scout car with my things was last vehicle to get off. God is still for me . . .

A bunch from Ike's staff tried to put me on the spot for not disarming the French. I assumed the offensive, showing them that to disarm or discredit the French meant an Arab war which would demobilize 60,000 [American military] men as a starter. All agreed with me at last.

Got only three hours' sleep today. We moved to Casa, office third floor Shell building, former manager's office, very handsome. He gave me some roses.

We had over 2,000 Navy ashore from sunk boats and clothed all, but hope to get clothes back as we have no reserves. My men gave blankets to the wounded and slept cold.

Called on French Admiral and General. They had Guards of Honor for me. So did I for them when they called back. The honor regiment of Moroccan Infantry had a goat as mascot with the band. When we first landed in England in 1917, the Welsh Fusillers had their goat. I wonder if this is a significant circumstance.

Very tired, going to bed . . .

Clark was made a lieutenant general.

We came into Casa at 1530. The citizens were quiet but certainly not moved [to enthusiasm because] the Guard of Honor . . . was poor. No music.

When I left the "Augusta" for keeps today, the entire crew lined the side of the ship and cheered. I was later told that this was spontaneous and seldom, if ever, accorded a non-naval person.

*Letter, GSP, Jr., to Eisenhower, November 14, 1942*

The following is a discoursive account of the operations . . .

[When] the radar on the flagship picked up land . . . the Commanding General [Patton] went to bed, and by the exercise of great strength of character went to sleep . . .

A naval battle is not particularly impressive, as it is too impersonal . . .

It took considerable mental energy on my part to attack [Casablanca] . . .

It is of interest I think to note that if you adhere to your plan, things usually work for you . . .

The landing at Safi . . . went as planned . . . Harmon, showing tremendous drive and initiative, captured the harbor at 0515.

He immediately landed a light armored battalion and moved it out on the Marrakech road where enemy forces of about 40 trucks and a number of armored cars were advancing. Our navy dive bombers engaged this force, and it lasted long enough to allow the light armored battalion to build up sufficient strength to check the French advance . . .

On the 10th . . . he attacked Marrakech column and destroyed a large number of trucks and armored cars . . . [then] started to march on Casablanca at 1900, completing a night march of 90 miles without lights and arriving at Mazagan at dawn.

The bridge across the river north of Mazagan . . . was defended. Harmon was just deploying to attack when he received my message that the French had ceased firing in the Casablanca area.

With great personal courage he went forward with one scout car, waving a dirty white towel, across the bridge and informed the French officers on the far side that the war was over. They immediately withdrew to their barracks.

He will pass through here enroute to Rabat about noon. His losses amounted to about 200 men killed and wounded.

Anderson's losses ran between three and five hundred, including about fifty drowned.

Harmon's forces captured around 1,000 French, who have been liberated, and killed an unknown but probably very large number of French...

The initial attack at Port Lyautey went according to plan except that . . . Truscott was unable to capture the airport.

By daylight on the 11th, he had only eight tanks and two or three armored vehicles . . . unloaded. With these Colonel Semmes attacked 18 French tanks with their accompanying infantry, destroying 6 and driving the others back about 8 kilometers with heavy losses to the infantry.

During this fight Colonel Semmes' tank was hit three times in the first five minutes, and Colonel Semmes, himself, using his M .37 [gun] accounted for four French tanks . . .

The harbor of Port Lyautey and the airfield had been captured . . . when hostilities in this area ceased. Truscott captured over 1,500 French troops with a loss of 100 [Americans] killed and two to three hundred wounded. In the fight here every soldier, including airplane mechanics, went into action, and the airport was held by air-ground and anti-aircraft personnel armed with rifles.

The unloading at Port Lyautey is proceeding very slowly. I have asked Admiral Hewitt to send some barges from Casablanca. If this is not done, it will take several weeks to complete the unloading due to bad surf conditions, and the destruction of numerous landing boats...

French Morocco is a protectorate, nominally governed by the Sultan, and owing its existence and tranquility to the prestige of the French Army and Navy. Had I insisted on disarming the army and removing the navy from the ships and shore batteries, I would have dealt such a blow to the prestige of the French that I am personally convinced a revolution would have eventuated . . .

I realize that I am taking a chance but feel convinced that the end justifies the means. We do not wish to occupy this country and pacify it...

The French Army is, in my opinion, split between its allegiance to General Nogues and . . . to General Giraud. Owing to this fact, I believe that at the present time it has no combat ability. General Nogues' adherents are of the opinion that the Germans will soon run us out of Morocco and that they therefore do not wish to commit themselves. There are some disturbing rumors from Marrakech, but I will not bother you with them until I know more about them . . .

Please accept my sincere congratulations on the success of your operations as a whole.

*Letter, GSP, Jr., to Beatrice, November 14, 1942*

Unfortunately I did not get a chance to distinguish my self [during the fighting] except not to lay down a couple of times when we got straffed.

John Waters was one of five officers whom Fredendall mentioned in orders . . .

This town (Casa) is a cross between the ultra modern and the Arabian nights but is quite clean. We took over the Shell Building and I am writing at the director's desk. The room is all panneled and very ornate . . .

We live at the Majestic Hotel which is fine except that the water is cut off.

The political situation is not too hot and the subs are bad but we have made such a good start that I think we will surely go on.

It must have occurred to him that his combat experience in Morocco equaled exactly the duration of all his actual battle time in World War I — little more than three days. Would he have more in World War II?

CHAPTER 8

# Morocco: The Letdown

*"Apparently I should have been a statesman."*

AS THE SENIOR AMERICAN COMMANDER in French Morocco, Patton became involved in political and diplomatic problems. The issues were interesting, and the situation in the country was potentially explosive. But he pined for battle.

There was little chance of combat – unless the Spanish launched an invasion out of Spanish Morocco, or the Axis landed in French Morocco. Patton had to be ready to parry these military threats.

He also had to be prepared to meet the danger of internal disturbance, a revolt by an Arab faction against the Sultan or a Moroccan uprising against the French. In this case, he saw his role as a stabilizer. He tried to uphold the authority of the French and the traditional Franco-Arab relationship, because maintenance of the status quo and continuation of civil order in Morocco left his military forces free for military action.

Although Patton enjoyed the official receptions and luncheons and ceremonies, and although he performed his duties with zest, he would have preferred to be elsewhere. Basically he resented the circumstances that compelled him to fulfill a non-combat role.

Gruenther and Doolittle flew in from Algiers and told Patton that Darlan now headed the "civil side," Giraud the military, and Nogues remained the governor of Morocco. "The first and last are crooks" was Patton's first reaction, and "Nogues is right now trying to stir up trouble."

Nogues was the most important official with whom Patton had to deal, and it was hard to figure him out. He

> gave the general impression that he is most anxious to cooperate [with us] in every way possible. General Nogues agreed in principle

> to all proposals made in my name; in fact, he agreed too readily. I am convinced that he is a man who agrees readily but may not always carry out his agreements.

Nevertheless, Nogues was ready to commit French forces to oppose a Spanish invasion of French Morocco and to use French personnel in anti-aircraft defenses, to protect Casablanca against German air attacks.

According to Nogues, the country "was completely calm except for a stirring of the Jewish population." Nogues said that "the Jews in Morocco are of the lowest order . . . They expected to take over the country . . . and are now agitating against French authorities" — actually against the Pétainist anti-Jewish laws still in force. But Nogues stated "that they were being controlled without difficulty," and that the French "would guarantee calm in the country."

Nogues had arrested and put into prison Major General R. M. Bethouard of the French Army and several other officers who had tried "to insure that our forces would be received in a friendly manner." The French held that Bethouard "and his adherents" had disobeyed orders and had to be punished. Patton felt that these men were "our friends" and had to be protected. He suggested that "any trial or similar action . . . be indefinitely deferred in order to permit existing animosities to cool." When Wilbur, at Patton's suggestion, recommended that Bethouard's trial be postponed and eventually forgotten, Nogues seemed to assent.

Eisenhower sent a letter to Nogues through Patton to define the Franco-American relationship. It was worded in fairly strong terms, but it instructed Nogues to report to Eisenhower if Patton, as Patton remarked, "failed to play ball. Probably a political move, but a mistake. As I see it, an American [here and now] can do no wrong."

But he was glad to know that Eisenhower approved Patton's policy toward the French who, he believed, feared above all that they might "lose face with the Arabs."

"While I am convinced that Nogues is a crook," Patton informed Eisenhower, "I believe that I can handle him." As evidence for his feeling, the French were guarding all the road and railway bridges from Casablanca to the Algerian border as he had requested.

More to his liking were the military matters he occasionally discussed with Eisenhower through correspondence. For example, the Western

Task Force had "achieved the impossible." Had the normal offshore conditions prevailed during the invasion, "the fifty per cent chances you and I figured out in London would have been over-optimistic." He was forced to believe that his "proverbial luck or more probably the direct intervention of the Lord was responsible."

He was sorry he was unable to communicate during the landings, but "I cannot control interstellar space, and our radio simply would not work. The only person who lost by it was myself, since" – he was making a joke – "the press was probably unable to recount my heroic deeds."

The Navy had left some landing boats on the shore, and Patton was having them repaired and floated, for they were too valuable to waste. He had also had the amphibious tractors put "in shape and am holding them," for they might come in handy in Spanish Morocco.

*Letter, GSP, Jr., to all subordinate commanders, November 15, 1942*

The following memorandum will be read to all troops:

I fully appreciate the danger and hardships you have been through and the lack of conveniences and clothing which you face. On the other hand, you, each one of you, is a representative of a great and victorious army. To be respected, you must inspire respect. Stand up, keep your clothes buttoned, and your chin straps fastened. Salute your officers and the French officers, now our allies. Keep your weapons clean and with you. Your deeds have proven that you are fine soldiers. Look the part.

*Letter, GSP, Jr., to all commanding officers, November 15, 1942*

It is my firm conviction that the great success attending the hazardous operations carried out on sea and on land by the Western Task Force could only have been possible through the intervention of Divine Providence manifested in many ways. Therefore, I should be pleased if, in so far as circumstances and conditions permit, our grateful thanks be expressed today in appropriate religious services.

"Please accept," he wrote Clark, "my sincere congratulations on your promotion and also on the magnificent work you have been doing in connection with this operation."

"We really had a splendid fight," he wrote Handy, "and the men . . . outdid themselves."

He thanked Hewitt "for the magnificent and wholehearted way in which you conducted us safely through a submarine infested ocean and landed us at exactly the proper place and time on a hostile shore." He hoped that if there were to be additional landings, "we may be so fortunate as to do so under your guidance."

*Letter, GSP, Jr., to Devers, 18 November 1942*

> I feel that what you have done for the Armored Force has been magnificently justified by the performances of that force. So far as I am personally concerned, the operations of this task force went exactly as planned with a minimum of loss and a maximum of success . . .
>
> At Port Lyautey one of the self-propelled 105's moved up to 200 yards of a stone fort and blew holes in the wall, which permitted the infantry to enter and storm the fort with hand grenades. This incident will show you that the fighting was of a first class nature.

It also showed Patton's alertness to Devers' interest in artillery.

His visit to Nogues' Residency and especially to the Sultan's Palace on November 16 delighted him. The colors, sounds, and trappings were enchanting, and he wrote long descriptions in his diary and letters.

He and Keyes drove from Casablanca, "a city which combines Hollywood and the Bible," to Rabat. At the edge of town was an escort provided by Harmon, several scout cars and tanks, to take Patton to Nogues' home. Patton felt "it would just rub it in on the French" – later he said, "such a force would appear boastful on my part" – so he dismissed the escort.

The Residency was a beautiful marble structure built by Marshal Lyautey. Nogues had two guards of honor waiting, both very impressive,

> a squadron of Spahis and a company of Goumiers, with two sets of field music, including a brass umbrella with bells around the edge, much tooting and saluting.

Patton

> inspected both guards and complimented the French officers commanding them on their appearance, which was truly soldierly in the 1914 meaning of the word. It was rather pathetic to think that one

of the light tanks in the escort could easily have destroyed all of the splendid creatures standing at salute.

Nogues and Patton, together with Keyes, then rode to the Sultan's Palace, "a tremendous three story building of Moorish design, which you enter through a gate just wide enough to permit the passing of an auto." There was a guard of about 400 Nubians wearing

red fezzes, red bolero jackets, red bloomers, white spats, red Moroccan leather equipment. The officers, white men, wore French model uniforms of red cloth. The green flag of the prophet, made of velvet with arabic letters in the middle and gold fringe, with the lance banded in gold, was held by a huge Negro with a white turban. They had a band with horns, drums, cymbals, and the brass umbrella.

As Patton "entered an inner court full of white robed men in biblical dress," he felt he was back in the Old Testament.

The Grand Vizier, "in white, with enormous gold-filled teeth, met us and we went up three flights of stairs to see the Sultan."

The throne room was

long and narrow with magnificent red rugs. On the left in stocking feet were the pashas, on the right a line of Louis XV chairs. One bowed from the hips on entering, again in the middle of the room, and again at the dais. The Sultan, a handsome, frail young man, rose and shook hands. We sat down, and he made a little speech of welcome.

The Sultan, talking in Arabic, although he has a perfect command of French, told the Grand Vizier to tell me in French, how glad he was to see me. I then talked to him through two interpreters, expressing contentment that his people and the French and ourselves were again reunited, and assured him that our one desire was to unite with his people and the French in making common head against the enemy.

The Sultan said he hoped the American soldiers would show proper respect for Mohammedan institutions. I told him that such an order had been issued in forceful language prior to our departure from the United States and was going to be enforced. I further stated that since in all armies, including the American Army, there might be some foolish persons, I hoped that he would report to me any incidents of sacrilege, which some individual soldier might commit . . . I finished by complimenting him on the beauty of his country, the discipline of his citizens, and the splendid looking cities.

Patton later thought that he had laid down the law to the Sultan "with due respect." His speech "pleased the French and Keyes thought it was good."

Nogues, Patton, and Keyes then proceeded to the Residency,

where we were entertained by Madame Nogues and her niece and treated to a most sumptious lunch in the best of taste. General Nogues impressed on me that at no time during the German occupation had any German occupied his house or sat at his table.

Later that afternoon, a "deputation from General Clark arrived with a letter for the Sultan from the President. It was patently not apropos" – it did not, in his opinion, mention the French in strong enough terms – "so I took the liberty of holding it. I will see Ike at Gib tomorrow [and explain]."

*Letter, GSP, Jr., to Beatrice, November 17, 1942*

I certainly wish you could have been along yesterday . . . It was the most colorful thing I have ever seen and would be worth a million in Hollywood . . . What I saw inside the palace and what Marco Polo saw did not differ except that the guards had rifles in the court but inside, the twelve apostles had long curved simaters in red leather scabbords which stuck out like tales when they moved.

I am flying . . . to see Ike. He and Clark certainly need to know the facts of life. They send some of the most foolish instructions I have ever read . . .

My French is pretty good. We have a black out so go to bed early and get up in the dark. The food is not bad . . .

I miss you and love you.

*Diary, November 17*

Flew to Gib in one hour 15 minutes 2 seconds – very low, about 150 feet over water. We had four P-40's for escort . . .

Ike lives in a cave in the middle of the rock – in great danger.

His chief of staff, G–2, and G–4 are British, and so are many of his words. I was disappointed in him. He talked of trivial things.

We wasted a lot of time at lunch with the governor of the Rock, an old fart in shorts with skinny red legs.

Ike backed me up about letter to Sultan . . .

He was nice but not enthusiastic over our war [the landings near Casablanca] – I must see to it that I make much of my generals.

He asked me if Clark was a Jew. I said at least one quarter, probably one half . . .

On the way back, the Spanish at Tangier shot at my left escort plane and possibly at me, but their aim was bad.

"Ike was fine," he wrote Beatrice, "except that he spoke of lunch as 'tiffin,' of gasoline as 'petrol,' and of antiaircraft as 'flack.' I truly fear that London has conquered Abilene."

On that day Kenneth Anderson's forces, mostly British but accompanied by several American units, having moved eastward almost 500 miles from the Algiers area into Tunisia, ran into Axis elements about 45 miles short of Bizerte. Italian and German troops had been shipped in the thousands into the country by air and by sea, and they opposed Anderson's advance. Although he would continue to drive eastward and would get to within 15 miles of Tunis at the end of the month, his attempt to overrun at least the northern portion of Tunisia would fail.

By this time, it was more than clear that the British had won a great victory at El Alamein in October. Driving Rommel out of Egypt, the British pushed him into Libya, trying to trap him and destroy his Italo-German army. Rommel withdrew slowly and skillfully, maintaining the integrity of his organization, holding up the British pursuit at a series of defensive lines, refusing to panic or give up.

*Letter, Beatrice to GSP, Jr., November 18, 1942*

I spent the weekend at West Point and between trains I bought a paper and went to the station restaurant . . . I ordered the supper and opened the paper, saw your name on the front page and was still reading it when I had to run for the train. I never knew who ate my oyster stew . . .

Yesterday the Secretary called me up . . . He is a wonderful friend and never misses a chance to do you honor. The same with Gen.

McNair. I saw him yesterday and if I should tell you some of the things he said, it would burn the paper . . .

I have told all the inquirers that I know you are too busy to write (Mrs. C. is quite boastful of her love letters and everyone in Wash. knows when she gets one) but all the same I am looking forward to your letters, even though I know you wont say half as much as I read in the papers.

On November 18, Patton flew to Rabat, then accompanied Nogues to the levee of the Sultan on the fifteenth annniversary of his accession to the throne. They were escorted from the Residency to the Palace by a squadron of cavalry "on white Arab stallions. Men had white capes, blue hoods, white turbans, and red blouses with black frogs." Inside the Palace, the Crown Prince was present, "a boy of perhaps 14."

Nogues read a long, prepared speech that lasted about ten minutes. "Then the Grand Vizier read a copy of it in Arabic to the Sultan" – even though the Sultan was a graduate of Oxford and spoke French and English fluently. "The Grand Vizier hunted around in his comona and produced the Sultan's speech and handed it to the Sultan who read it in Arabic, then the G.V. read a French translation.

"While this was going on, it occurred to me that the U.S. was getting scooped." He "felt that the U.S. should be heard.

"So when Nogues sat down, I stepped into the middle of the floor without asking any one's permission." He "made a very respectful but pointed speech which was well received by both the Arabs and French."

He said, as best he could later recall,

Your Majesty, as a humble representative of the Great President whom I had the honor of representing as the commander of a huge military force in Moracco, I wish to present the compliments of the U.S. . . . and to assure you that so long as Your Majesty's country in cooperation with the French government of Morroco continues with us and facilitates our efforts, we are sure with the help of God to achieve certain victory against our common enemy the Natzi. I feel that this accord is certain because one of Your Majesties great predecessors established friendship with our great President General Washington when he gave the beautiful building which houses the American mission in Tangier to General Washington as a token of friendship and respect. It is also fitting to remind Your Majesty that the friendship of America and France dates from the same period.

How careful he was not to undercut the French.

"I might have done better with more time," he later wrote Beatrice,

> but what I said had a profound effect and both the French and the Arabs were pleased.
>
> In fact, the Sultan said that . . . my being present and having spoken would have a profound effect on the entire Moslem world.
>
> Apparently I should have been a statesman.
>
> In any case, it is certain that every one in Morocco is playing ball to the limit of their capacity. It may be well to let Harry [Stimson] and George [Marshall] hear about this.

Flying to Lyautey, Patton saw Truscott and Semmes and went over the scene of their fighting. He was pleased to meet S. W. Sprindis, a platoon leader who, with 40 men, had held a lighthouse against 1000 French troops.

Patton said to him, "Lieutenant, what is your rank?"

He replied, "Second Lieutenant, sir."

Patton said, "You are a liar, sir, you are now a First Lieutenant."

President Roosevelt seemed to repudiate Eisenhower's deal with Darlan, and the news had a bad effect in French Morocco. Patton told Nogues "it was only a trial baloon and not to worry."

Informing Eisenhower that "the French were most cordial and helpful," he continued:

> As I see it, the French position in Morocco rests almost entirely on the mythical supremacy of France, which at the present time is represented to the Arab mind by Darlan as a direct emissary from the Marshall [Pétain]. Anything which is said in the United States to destroy this mythical French authority could have and probably will have a very adverse effect on the Arab.
>
> I am convinced that the Sultan . . . is wholly for us, but he has not the authority or the means of controlling the Arabian tribes whereas the French prestige, nebulous as it may seem to us, can and will maintain order.
>
> I am fully in accord with you as to the necessity of dealing with Darlan if for no other reason than to retain this prestige.

The Western Task Force had fired less ammunition than anticipated, had taken fewer losses than figured, and, therefore, supplies of ammunition and gasoline were more than satisfactory. On the other hand, the harbor of Casablanca was crowded and presented an attractive target for German bombardment. Could he have some additional aircraft, preferably night fighters equipped with radar?

The initial landing waves in future amphibious operations, he thought, ought to dispense with gas masks, extra ammunition, and even packs. "Our men were too heavily loaded . . . [and] should have only rifles and 100 rounds of ammunition."

> Owing to the dearth of commodities in Morocco, the Arabs have no interest in money . . . We have secured 24 hours work out of the tugboats by giving them a hundred pounds of coffee and a hundred pounds of sugar apiece . . . One or two ships loaded with sugar, tea, coffee, cotton goods, and perhaps some shoes [should be] sent here at your earliest convenience . . .
>
> Unless I am badly mistaken, I can handle the French and Arabs and assure you [of their] complete cooperation.

He was just about to send his long report when he received word that Eisenhower was on his way to Casablanca. "Keyes and I just got to the airport in time" to meet and welcome him. He was interested in what was happening in Morocco, but had no definite plan for the future employment of Patton's force because the situation in Spain was still uncertain.

> He said he had today recommended Fredendall and me for three stars. This looks as if Clark, who has never commanded a battalion, will get the Fifth Army. However, the Lord has helped me a lot and I think He will let me fulfill my destiny.

As Fifth Army commander, Clark would probably become Patton's direct superior, for the Fifth Army would no doubt take control of Fredendall's II Corps as well as Patton's I Armored Corps.

Patton was pleased that Eisenhower had recommended him for promotion to lieutenant general, but hardly elated. Eisenhower and Clark had their third stars. Devers had his. Besides, before leaving Washington,

Patton had been told – informally and unofficially, it was true – that the Fifth Army would probably be activated in North Africa and that he had a good chance of being appointed to command it.

It seemed to Patton that his third star, as well as command of an Army, was long overdue. He was sure that he had had the most difficult assignment in the invasion, he had met the greatest resistance, he had had the biggest success. Where was the recognition, the reward for achievement?

And how was he going to have another chance for glory if he remained in Morocco? The fighting was in Tunisia.

*Letter, Summerall to GSP, Jr., November 20, 1942*

You have long been a determining force in the army and now you are a leading figure in America's greatest venture. Your leadership, daring, skill, and speed and your compelling influence over tens of thousands of men are only a preliminary to far greater achievements that lie before you. I only hope and pray that your life and health may be spared to fulfill what I am sure is a great destiny for the good of the world as well as of our country. I would not have you do other than lead and share the dangers and hardships of your men, yet I must believe that fate has too much use for you to allow any evil to befall you. Your magnetic presence and irresistible resolution will always inspire your men to do what you want them to do but what they would not do without you.

If in any way, I have been an influence in shaping your convictions of duty and creating your standards of training and combat, it is the richest reward for all my labors. To feel that in you, I am in some measure sharing the conflict, fills me with gratitude. I shall follow you eagerly and shall rejoice . . . over your triumphs and rewards which must inevitably be yours.

*Diary, November 20*

Read press report intercepts [of newspaper stories]. Apparently the Western Task Force was not in the war. I feel a little hurt.

*Diary, November 21*

Admiral Hewitt made vice admiral [three stars] . . .

He reported French concern over

possible trouble between Jews and Arabs. I listened with interest and assured them that since the Sultan has been handling such questions for some thousands of years, I was going to leave it up to him. I consider it the height of inexpediency to get mixed up in politics. As a matter of fact, the Jews are not discriminated against and get on very well . . .

I have found that my knowledge of French, limited though it is, has been of inestimable value to me. First, in checking up on interpreters, and second, because I can, when I wish, talk to people quietly and without the intervention of an interpreter.

*Diary, November 22*

We have been here two weeks today. In a way it seems years or again only minutes.

Keyes and I went to mass this morning. I at least had reason to take a little time off to thank God. There were quite a lot of widows, made by us, in the church. They cried a good deal but did not glare at us. It seems strange to hear the Lord referred to as "Le Bon Dieu lui-mem."

. . . I inspected camps, the docks, and the airfield. Gave air officers hell for not saluting. Men fairly clean and in good spirits.

"Frequently," he wrote Somervell,

when we are going anywhere we complain about the Services of Supply, and then when we have arrived, we fail to thank them. I hope by this note to confute both practices.

He flew to Oran in the nose of a B-25 and found Fredendall

very gloomy. He fears that he and I will hold the bag while our troops in small bunches are shipped to the British. I fear that the British have again pulled our leg.

Patton was referring to Eisenhower's attempt to help Kenneth Anderson in Tunisia all he could. To that end, he was shipping units, as many as he could without jeopardizing security in Algeria and French Morocco, from Fredendall's and Patton's commands to Anderson's. What concerned Patton and Fredendall was that they would be stripped of most of their troops, who would go under British command, while the American commanders were left holding insignificant numbers of soldiers and insignificant jobs.

I seem to be the only one beating my wings against the cage of inaction. The others simply say how much better off we are than the people at home. I dont want to be better off — I want to be Top Dog and only battle can give me that.

Bea sent me a lot of stars but I fear that I shall have no occasion to put them on. On the other hand, from time to time the thought comes to me that I have a mission, and that so long as I do my full duty nothing can stop me. But the waiting is hard. Perhaps I am being made perfect through suffering, for I do suffer when I cannot move . . .

I am pretty low today. Wrote a Thanksgiving order in my best style.

*Letter, GSP, Jr., to the troops of Western Task Force, November 25, 1942*

The first Thanks giving Day was conceived as an occasion of rendering thanks to an ever merciful God for his divine help in aiding a band of people to cross a great ocean and successfully establish themselves on a distant and unknown shore, and for his further aid in providing them with food and shelter in their new home.

We, who have also crossed that same ocean in the face of man-made dangers, far greater than the perils which nature imposed upon our ancestors, should on this Thanksgiving Day again thank a merciful God for his manifest assistance in bringing us safely to shore, in providing us with ample food and supplies, and in placing us in the midst of a smiling land whose people are again united with us in the battle for human freedom.

It is with this thought in mind that in consonance with the Proclamation of the President . . . this Thursday . . . be dedicated as a day of praise and thanksgiving.

*Diary, November 26*

We moved to Villa Mas. It is the most ostentatiously magnificent house I have ever seen. My suite had five rooms, but I kept only the bedroom and bath.

Went to Thanksgiving dinner with American Consul and ate too much.

*Diary, November 27*

Was quite sick all day with stomachache, but had to go to a large dinner . . . I sat next to the Pasha [of Marrakech], whose French being almost as bad as mine, understood me very well. He is 68, has 20 wives, and is supposed to sleep with each one at least once a week. He is very thin.

*Letter, GSP, Jr., to Beatrice, November 27, 1942*

I have the most awful blues all day. Nothing seems to be happening and I just sit. I suppose it is because I want to go on [with the war] and having nothing to go on with. Also I heard that Clark got a M.H. [Medal of Honor] for riding on a sub-marine. I don't believe it but still it is not plesant . . .

Fredendall seems perfectly happy to just sit but I think I will go mad if we don't get some more battles . . .

At this moment I am safer than I was at home so don't worry about me.

*Diary, November 28*

I stayed in the house until three and took some pills of a very colorful sort . . .

Nogues and his staff called at 4:00 P.M. and talked for one and one half hours, saying nothing. I replied in kind. I should have been a diplomat.

The fact was, he was completely uninterested in political problems. The status of the Jews, economic measures, fiscal policy, and other like matters left him cold. The only thing he wanted to do was fight – that was where the glory and the excitement were. To keep his troops out of political and civilian involvement, to keep them ready for military action, he exerted his considerable charm and social grace to preserve calm and order and the status quo in the country. It had its pleasant moments, but, on the whole, he thought he had more important things to do.

*Diary, November 30*

Clark called me . . . and asked me to fly to Algiers . . . I hope it means fighting. I hate this organizing, and Keyes can do it better than I can. I am a fighter.

At Algiers on December 1, Patton found that "Ike is sick, has a cold, but is low too – lacks decision." He had supper with "the sacred family" – "Ike, Clark, and Davis, the Adjutant General."

At 9:30, Eisenhower had a phone call from Gibraltar, relaying a message from Washington or London, and he said, "Well, Wayne, you get the Fifth Army."

"The Fifth Army was authorized and Clark was to command it."

"I had expected this but it was a shock."

He was numb.

I sat on for half an hour and left. It means that I simply have a corps. "The best laid plans of mice and men." I felt so awful that I could not sleep for a while, but I shall pass them yet . . .

I am sorry for Geoff [Keyes] and the rest who came along with me in the opinion that I would get an Army. But c'est la guerre.

*Letter, GSP, Jr., to Beatrice, December 2, 1942*

There is a nice fight going on near Tunis and the 1st Armored Division was in the show yesterday helping pull out some British who were in trouble. John [Waters] was probably in the show . . .

I may get a chance to fly east in the morning and visit . . . and get shot at a little. Some times I think that a nice clean death . . . would be the easiest way out.

Don't worry because if any thing happens I will be dead and you will have been notified long before you get this.

CHAPTER 9

# Morocco: Watching and Waiting

*"I get fed up sitting here and seeing the war lost but it may all work out for the best."*

*Diary, December 2*

When I woke this morning, the sun was shining – it hardly seemed possible – such is the resilience of youth. Now it looks as if the Spanish would jump us, which is fine and may fix everything . . .

Flying back [from Algiers], which I did on the receipt of probably erroneous information of a German landing in Spanish Morocco, we hedge-hopped a lot . . . and stampeded Arabs, donkeys, sheep, and camels, and had a lot of fun . . .

I decided that my disappointment [over command of the Fifth Army] was but an additional act of God to temper me, so I feel fine.

*Diary, December 3*

Woke up feeling much younger. Spent some three hours on docks talking to men.

*Letter, Beatrice to GSP, Jr., December 2, 1942*

I have no plans to move [from Washington] . . . Practically every day I hear from someone or see someone with news from Africa and I would not do so in the country . . .

Your letter to Day about the Life article is too late as it has just come out, but it is so changed that even I do not object to it. In fact I think it is fine and you will like it too . . . I did not know it was coming out and when I went to lunch at Clare McNair's Friday, she rushed up to me with the picture turned toward me and said: "What do you think of this?" I said something insulting about it and a perfectly strange woman jumped up from her chair and cried, "Don't you run down our hero. Do you know him?" . . .

I went out to Walter Reed yesterday to see your wounded . . . There are 103, but I only saw about 30 as two hours visiting time is not much. Each one had got a purple heart in the morning and all but one sent you a personal message . . . "Tell the General we'll be back and meet him up the line." . . .

Actually I am so thrilled over your success that I just don't worry or do anything but shine in your reflected light. I feel, as you do, that all your life has pointed to this and that you still have many big things ahead, and that God is with you and guiding your every move. I can't even think about your personal ambition or promotion any more than you can, for I feel sure that you are marked by destiny and that I am willing to wait on God for that.

*Letter, GSP, Jr., to Beatrice, December 3, 1942*

It is delightful to see how much the marching and general looks of the troops has improved. The 2d Armored was of course perfect . . .

I went [to Rabat] in an open jeep with my flags up. The soldiers had never seen a general out of a limousine so were favorably impressed . . .

The Fifth Army under Clark . . . makes me mad but there is nothing that can be done about it. Ike and Wayne have the inside track. Their headquarters certainly is a mess and gets out contradictory orders almost daily. Some day they will be found out.

Ike is not well and is very querelous and keeps saying how hard it is to be so high and never to have heard a hostile shot. He could correct that very easily if he wanted to. I almost think he is timid. When he goes out, a peep full of armed men precedes and follows his armored limousine. Well in any case I would not want his job at the moment. I don't think that he or Clark have any idea of what they are going to do next. I should not be surprised to see the Brit First Army [in Tunisia] get driven back. The supply problem for them is most difficult and is not being well run. Army headquarters . . . is 100 miles behind the front. Too far by 95 miles.

We are getting some discipline into the troops here and they look better every day. I have very little to do except fret about getting into a battle, but unless the Spanish give trouble, I can't see where we will fight. If they will wait until the next convoy gets in [bringing additional men, equipment, and supplies], I would like nothing better than to fight them. It would be fine practice for our men.

"I hate to think of Christmas without you and the family all split up," Beatrice wrote,

> but I am going to do the best I can and have the best time I can too. I try all the time to think only of how you are doing that which you have longed for and trained for all your life, and how glad I am that you are having your chance to show what you really are . . .
>
> I went to the movies this afternoon to see General Nogues [in the newsreels], and now I hear that you are in Trans-lux [theater].

*Letter, GSP, Jr., to Stimson, December 7, 1942*

[The French] have certainly cooperated heartily, promptly, and loyally. I realize that some of them, perhaps all of them, are serving their own ends, but nevertheless they are doing so in a manner to facilitate our operations, which is really the only point of importance.

My relations with the Sultan have also been very friendly, and I believe that he is wholly on our side. I arranged to give two of his sons a ride in a tank and had difficulty in ever getting them out again . . .

The armored troops have been outstanding in maintaining their vehicles with nothing but a screw-driver and a monkey-wrench because in order to bring the maximum number of fighting troops we deliberately skimped on the maintenance which however is now arriving . . .

Colonel Semmes, whom you remember as Master of the Potomac Hunt, and thanks to your efforts is now in the army, attacked 18 French tanks . . .

All the more desperate attacks were led by field [grade] officers who advanced with reckless disregard of their own lives. I do not take entire credit for this but do state that before landing I had told all the generals that if they failed to carry out their missions, I did not wish to see them alive, and I promised them, on my part, that if I failed I would not leave Africa except in a box . . .

One childish illusion . . . has been utterly smashed. The picture of the flight into Egypt shows Mary on the burro and Joseph walking. Here on any street or road you can see them dressed in biblical costumes but invariably the man is riding the burro and the lady is walking . . .

I regret that personally I did not have an opportunity of engaging in close combat. Had the fight lasted a few hours longer, I believe that I would have achieved my ambition, but unfortunately it stopped.

*Letter, Beatrice to GSP, Jr., December 7, 1942*

Mrs. Roosevelt is after me again. She asked me to tea when I was going to Harrisonburg and could not, and now she has asked me for tomorrow, so I will go. I have never been to tea at the White House . . .

I had a perfectly lovely letter from Mrs. Nick Craw [whose husband was killed during the invasion], in which she says, "Tell General Patton how proud and glad Nick was to be with him."

*Letter, Beatrice to GSP, Jr., December 8, 1942*

These are certainly full days for me. I went to tea at the White House and Mamie and I joined a group of Countrywomen of the World who have sent a lot of canning materials to England . . .

I have just finished a broadcast for the Office of War Information, in French, to French women all over the world . . . It will be broadcast to Indo-China, Morocco, and intermediate points . . . It was a regular flag waver, Old Glory and the Oriflamme, tout ensemble.

*Letter, GSP, Jr., to Handy, December 8, 1942*

We have been here a month today, which means that for 26 days we have not had any fighting. This is regrettable . . .

From what I can hear, we are losing quite a few tanks in Tunisia, and I have gotten permission from General Eisenhower to take a private voyage to that front in order to learn at first hand how the Germans succeed in smashing our tanks . . .

It is . . . my belief . . . that the coxswains of landing boats should be army and not navy . . .

The soldiers in the first four waves should be almost all riflemen with a few mortars; and they should not carry over a 100 pounds, and possibly one day's rations. Our men were terribly overloaded . . .

In my opinion, naval gunfire support is a very weak reed on which to lean. It is too inaccurate, and they will not get close enough [to shore] . . .

In a landing operation, some heavily armored landing boats with two machine guns and some rocket guns would be very useful . . . These boats would not have to land but should be able to come within 50 yards of the beach to take out strongpoints.

In future amphibious landings, there would be army coxswains and rocket boats, and the men in the assault waves would carry less personal gear and be less burdened. The navy would improve its gunfire support and render excellent service.

Patton went to lunch at Nogues' on December 8, and saw the Grand Vizier, "a smart old Arab of 92."

> No one was paying any attention to him, so I went over and talked to him . . . In leaving and entering the dining room, I was supposed to preceed him but took particular pains not to do so, which seemed to have an excellent effect on the old man.
>
> After lunch . . . he said that . . . the whole life of Morocco depended upon maintaining peace. I assured him . . . that I intended to do so by consulting the wishes of His Majesty through General Nogues . . .
>
> He then talked about the race antipathies, Jews . . . I told him that . . . I understood perfectly about race antipathies, and therefore I would do nothing about it because . . . they were better fitted . . . to continue their management. He said . . . that no racial or tribal troubles would ever stick their heads above the surface.
>
> I then told him that it was very important for me to know what was going on in Spanish Morocco . . . The Grand Vizier replied . . . that the Sultan would make it his special task to keep me informed . . . as if I were a member of the family . . .
>
> The Grand Vizier assured me that my complaisance had given him the happiest fifteen minutes of his life, to which I replied that if I had afforded happiness for fifteen minutes, I felt that I had not lived in vain.
>
> This all sounds very funny when you write it down and must sound a good deal funnier when expressed in my French, but it is exactly the way the Arabs like to talk.
>
> He ended up by saying that it was necessary to converse with a great man to fully realize his greatness, and that there was an Arabic saying to the effect – that those who said all men were equal were either fools or liers – and that he and the Sultan were neither.

Summing up his impressions later, Patton thought that the French and Arabs were "scared to death of a Jew rising under American help. I told them to manage it and not let the thing come to a head."

He also thought that Nogues was "a clever crook only moved by self interest; but he knows I am his best interest for the moment, so that is that."

All the French at the luncheon, he wrote Beatrice, "acted just like old friends. Of course I know and they know that I know that they are only friendly through self interest but it works well."

He told her that he was "perfectly merciless with my French and talk long and fluently and this shows how smart the French are — I am understood."

*Eisenhower Notes dictated to Harry C. Butcher, December 10, 1942*

Among the American Commanders, Patton I think comes closest to meeting every requirement made on a commander. Just after him I would, at present, rate Fredendall, although I do not believe the latter has the imagination in foreseeing and preparing for possible jobs of the future that Patton possesses. Clark is an unusual individual and is particularly strong in his organizational ability and orderliness of his mind.

Flying to Algiers, Patton was thrilled because his plane was fired on by mistake. Trigger-happy Allied antiaircraft gunners put out 18 rounds. Three shells were near enough to shake the aircraft, and one piece hit the wing.

He drove to Tunisia to find out why the Americans were losing so many tanks. At British First Army headquarters in Ain Seymour, which the British called "Jane's Ass," Kenneth Anderson's chief of staff provided a map of the area and lunch. Patton went forward and inspected the front line. He visited John Waters' battalion, which had lost 39 tanks, two thirds of its original strength. Two of Waters' three captains had been killed. Waters himself had a bullet hole through his clothes. "He looked very well, had matured, and had much more self-confidence than I had seen him display, although he has always had confidence."

The men were glad to see him. They said that Patton was the only general officer they had seen in the 24 days they had been at the front. "I think this is true, and it is a sad commentary on our idea of leadership."

That and the tactical formations employed were contributing to the high losses. More to the point, the light tanks were too light and the 37 mm.-gun lacked the power to penetrate German tank hulls. Also, the ammunition on hand seemed to be rounds designed for training rather than combat.

These conditions would soon be corrected. The main remedy was the medium Sherman tank, which was about to arrive in the theater in substantial numbers.

Returned to Algiers, Patton found

> Ike and Clark were in conference as to what to do. Neither had been to the front, so showed great lack of decision. They are on way out, I think. [They] have no knowledge of men or war. Too damned slick, especially Clark.

They were interested in what Patton had seen, and all three talked until well after midnight.

On the following morning Patton wrote up some notes on how the Germans and the British were operating in Tunisia. His practiced eye had noted far more than his casual manner might have indicated.

He described in considerable detail and with considerable respect and approval the methods by which the Germans coordinated the operations of infantry, tanks, artillery, and dive bombers. He was less impressed by such British tendencies as leaving the high ground to the Germans, taking defensive positions in front of rather than behind rivers, and ignoring the benefits of air and ground reconnaissance. He thought that the truck traffic could be better regulated. He was dismayed because the work of maintaining the roads had not improved since "the time of the second dynasty in Egypt."

The report written, because "I was nervous about being away for so long," Patton wanted to fly home that afternoon. Air officers advised against it because the weather was bad and because the plane would arrive after dark and might be fired on by American antiaircraft gunners. He insisted, and the plane took off.

> The question of being shot down began to worry me more and more as darkness approached, and when I found that our radio in the plane would not work, I was very depressed. However, it was then too late to turn back . . .
>
> We struck a terrific rain and wind storm and could see nothing at all. This had the advantage of preventing the anti-aircraft from seeing us. It was violently rough, and we had to use our safety belts.

After about 30 minutes, we spotted the field and dropped a recognition flare, on which the field was lighted up promptly, but before we could land, it rained so hard that we could not see the field.

We circled over the city for about an hour and finally came to the decision that when the gasoline began to run short, we would try to make a bellylanding on any piece of ground we could find, or if we could not see the ground – which was the case most of the time – we would have to jump.

Fortunately, about 8:20 the rain let up for a minute and the pilot practically dived into the field through a hole in the clouds. He made a perfect landing.

I believe that this was probably the most dangerous part of the trip, which was not wholly devoid of excitement.

In his diary he noted that this "was the most dangerous experience I have had in this war. Again has God saved me for something."

The flight back from Algiers, he told Beatrice, "was an error in judgment on my part and nearly ended fatally. Next time I will listen to advice. It is foolish to fly at night here except in the case of utter military necessity."

He informed Beatrice that he had seen John Waters, who was fine. "Things are not so hot at the place he is. Looks like Dunkirk but he is O.K."

The more he thought about the situation in Tunisia, the less he liked it. "I am very worried about John," he wrote Beatrice on the following day, "as I fear he will be cut off and captured."

His remark was no less than prophetic.

He bought three rugs as Christmas presents.

The curator of the rug museum and the head of the merchants guild [came] to help us and see that we were not swindled. At that, I guess we were, for when we left they gave each of us a red leather bill fold.

His impressions of the Arabs in Tunisia were anything but complimentary,

. . . lower – if this is possible – than the Arabs in Morocco. Most of their dwellings look like manure piles, and I believe they are. They have no chimneys, and the smoke oozes out through the straw. In these dwellings, they take their cattle, donkeys, sheep, and goats, and apparently spend a happy night together . . .

The women are not veiled, which is unfortunate because it certainly destroys any illusions as to the beauty of Arabian women . . .

At Beja there is one of the finest medieval castles I have ever seen.

*Letter, GSP, Jr., to Frederick Ayer, December 16, 1942*

Owing to the nebulous state of things military, it is impossible to even hazard a guess as to what will happen any morning. At present it would seem that I will certainly be where I am for some time . . .

This is a great country for photography as everything is queer. You meet camels, burros, horses, and Arabs on the same road with tanks and self-propelled artillery. You see palaces and hovels side by side. Everywhere there are violent contrasts, even in the cloud effects.

Reporting to Clark at Oudja, Patton learned that there would be an Allied attack in Tunisia on the 24th. "I feel that this is most unwise, as, unless things have changed at the front, there is not enough force on our side to make a go of it. Nous Verrons [We shall see]."

Patton was right. Eisenhower would visit the front and on Christmas Eve call off the attack. Lack of Allied strength in personnel and supplies, the result of congested railroads and insufficient trucks, together with deteriorating weather — rains that turned the fields into mud flats — prompted Eisenhower to admit that the Allies had lost what he later called the "pell-mell race for Tunisia." He suspended active operations until good weather came in the spring.

Substantial German and Italian forces had arrived in what they called the Tunisian Bridgehead, the northeastern corner of the country. In December, they were constituted into the Fifth Panzer Army under Juergen von Arnim. He consolidated the defenses and prepared to extend his control south along the eastern coast.

Rommel was still being pressed by the British, and he was retiring across Libya toward southern Tunisia. It seemed probable that the Axis would soon have two strong Armies in Tunisia capable of mutual support and coordinated action.

*Diary, December 20*

Held a joint American-French parade at Rabat. Our troops made a fine impression; although they do not march as well as the French, they give an impression of more power. Our armor was especially impressive. The French had a number of new Renault tanks which they had kept hidden while the Germans were here. I am convinced of the loyalty of the French and only wish others in high places would be less impressed by half baked rumors from irresponsible persons . . .

Driving back after the ceremony I had a real ovation from both the French and Arabs, who cheered and applauded and waved their hats, and even a veiled lady waved at me, which is contrary to the rules. I hope Allah did not see her.

*Letter, GSP, Jr., to Beatrice, December 20, 1942*

I am certain that when and if Wayne [Clark] tries to run this country, it will be very differant. Still as I don't want to be elected to any thing I am ready to turn over to him . . . I have a feeling that he has no idea of ever assuming command. I cant quite fathom his game, he is very clever and very indirect.

Speaking of which reminds [me] that Jake [Devers] is in Cairo and is coming here. Of course the visit is not for his health . . .

[Manton S.] Eddy arrived yesterday and brought me two letters from you, the Life article and the clippings. I staid up till 1:30 A.M. reading them . . .

I wish I thought I was getting any where. I realy get discouraged at times. Not only on my own account but for the whole picture . . .

I am going to a near by country next week to talk to a potentate. I was specially selected by W.D. [War Department] due to my "demonstrated tact and personality." Some people seem to have changed their ideas about me — what?

In *Life* magazine he read an article entitled "Patton of the Armored Force: 'Old Blood and Guts' Leads U.S. Troops in Morocco and Pines to Challenge Rommel to Personal Tank Combat." A photograph showed him in a tank at the Desert Training Center, the caption quoting him as saying that tank warfare was like spaghetti — a general can't push it from behind but has to be up front pulling it.

A highly laudatory story of his life, career, appearance, personality, habits, eccentricities, and military philosophy, the article established him further as a national figure of prominence, boosted the growing Patton legend, noted his persistent profanity, and called him "one of the Army's most fabulous characters." His fellow officers agreed that he was a brilliant strategist, an early advocate of airpower and armored forces, and a great student of general military tactics.

One of his best friends said, "Eventually a battle gets down to blood and guts – performance only to count, as we say in a horse show. That's where Georgie Patton will shine."

According to Patton himself, a soldier fought primarily for two reasons – hero worship of his commanding officer and desire for glory. Patriotism was not enough, for patriots could defend, but glory hunters could attack. Patton was not interested in defense. His motto was: go forward.

Reading the article pleased Patton, but also gave him pause and some concern.

He was happy to receive a Christmas greeting from Marshall, who said: "The outstanding manner in which you surmounted the difficulties and hazards of the landing operation was a splendid demonstration of your leadership which we all anticipated."

*Letter, GSP, Jr., to Summerall, December 21, 1942*

I owe to you probably more than to any other man whatever military virtues I have to cultivate. It is my sincere hope that Providence may some day give me an opportunity of further demonstrating my ability to follow in your footsteps.

*Letter, GSP, Jr., to Beatrice, December 21, 1942*

Driving back from the review I had a regular ovation. It is quite thrilling to have about a hundred thousand people cheering, yelling, and clapping and shouting "Vive la Amerique." I kissed my hands to them which had the effect of arousing them still more. Even some of the veiled women waved at me which is quite unusual and I believe immoral. I feel that if the worst comes I shall run for Sultan.

Today at noon we went to a diffa given by the Pasha of Casa. I was late on principle as last time the French kept me waiting . . .

[A pasha] tried to talk politics to me but I told them to wait till the Bosches were licked. You could get up a revolution here for a dollar. The French have lost face and the Arabs are all for us – as long as we are winning . . .

I hope [son] George is wrong about my being a hero. It is too early and just makes enemies.

*Letter, GSP, Jr., to his sister Nita, December 22, 1942*

This place is very interesting and amusing, but I am tired of being a peacetime soldier, even in Africa . . .

Except for the biblical characters . . . Morocco is so reminiscent of California when you and I were children as to make me continually homesick. This applies not only to the type of country and the animals but also the houses, except the shacks and palaces.

The Moroccan psychology is very similar to that of the Mexicans, and I find my memory of dealing with Mexicans to be of inestimable value in dealing with potentates here.

On December 24, a young Frenchman assassinated Darlan, who had brought an uneasy unity to French North Africa but whose Vichy ties had made impossible a rapprochement with the supporters of General de Gaulle. Giraud, thoroughly a soldier, and, like Patton, fundamentally uninterested in politics, replaced Darlan as High Commissioner and Commander in Chief of all the French armed forces in North Africa.

*Letter, GSP, Jr., to Beatrice, December 26, 1942*

I dined at the Russells [Consul General] Christmas Eve and they had a tree and I got a Morroccan leather bill fold. As I already had . . . one . . . I gave it to George Meeks. So George gave me the cigars you sent him as he said he just had to give me something. He is a loyal old thing . . .

I went to church on Xmas and . . . made a great hit with the English woman I sat next to because I knew all the hymns by heart . . . Nita and I learned them as children. I remember that the day we learned "Hark the Herald Angles sing" we started to sing it every time we stood up. This woman is married to a French reserve 2 Lt. who is at the front. She is very poor. So I gave her the ring you sent me for the Sultan for her little girl and some candy for her little boy . . .

I get fed up sitting here and seeing the war lost but it may all work out for the best as some goats will have to be found soon and they are all ranker than me.

There are already rumors that one of them is on the way out. I fear it is the better of the two . . .

This morning I went to a Requiem Mass for Darlan . . . Personally I think his death is a distinct loss . . .

I . . . raised quite a lot of hell about saluting . . .

We now have 95,000 [troops, enough for an army] but are only a corps.

Well, any how I am having a lot of fun and am still young enough to learn.

*Letter, GSP, Jr., to Beatrice, December 30, 1942*

Darling B. I have had so many Christmas presents from you that I can neither count, smoke, nor eat them all – not for some time . . .

Floyd [Parks] wrote me . . . that I had my three stars . . . Something failed to click. Or rather some one else filched them. However I am not sure that it is not all for the best as I am convinced that things are not going too well with and between the "boy wonders." One will cut the others throat and then break his own neck.

I do hate to be doing nothing as I know I am expected to be on the job but am not. However, if and when I get a chance, I will do better than ever, as I am still learning and am a better commander than I have ever been.

*Letter, GSP, Jr., to Harbord, December 30, 1942*

I have been feeling rather down on my luck lately for reasons which you can possibly comprehend. But . . . [your letter] reestablishes my normal superiority complex . . .

The quiessence of my present command is not due to any lack of desire for combat on my part but to circumstances beyond my control. On the other hand, it may possibly all work out . . . because I think that eventually there will have to be a turnover in the higher brackets, in which case I might get turned up . . .

At the present time my chief preoccupation is treading the devious way between intimate association with the natives and maintenance of cordial relations with the French.

*Letter, GSP, Jr., to Handy, December 30, 1942*

Apparently for the time being I am condemned to occupy a position in readiness which is a state of affairs I deprecate but see no way of avoiding it.

*Letter, GSP, Jr., to Terry Allen, Oran, December 30, 1942*

Why in the hell don't you get into the war! Maybe if you would get up there and get in enough trouble, they would let me go up to get you out. In any case we would have a better time than sitting around.

In an attempt to influence the battlefield more directly, Eisenhower appointed Truscott his deputy chief of staff. Truscott established an advance command post in Constantine, much nearer to the fighting front than Algiers, where Eisenhower was extremely occupied with political and administrative matters. Unable to devote enough attention to military operations, he was nevertheless aware of unsatisfactory conditions. Anderson directed British, French, and American units in something less than perfect harmony. The French were loath to accept British direction. Organizations were fragmented and dispersed over a vast area. The situation was full of potential danger. By using Truscott as his personal representative for tactical affairs, Eisenhower hoped to gain cohesion among the fighting elements. A few days later, seeking still better control, Eisenhower would send Fredendall and his II Corps headquarters to lead the American units in Tunisia.

As it would turn out, Truscott was too junior in grade to have the impact that only Eisenhower himself could have exerted; and Fredendall displayed some unfortunate qualities.

Marshall too was dissatisfied with the command system in Tunisia, and he queried Eisenhower whether the command relations might be improved by promoting Patton and putting him in charge of the French and American units. Since Eisenhower had just inserted Truscott into the chain of command, he was reluctant to accept Marshall's suggestion. Furthermore, having Patton on the same level as Anderson would split the command authority. Eisenhower preferred to have the entire front under a single commander, Anderson.

Nogues, Patton recorded, thought that the British would not attack in Tunisia "before March or April. I fear he is right."

Axis planes bombed Casablanca and struck an Arab town. Patton

wrote letters to Sultan and Pasha expressing regret . . . for families of dead, 85 to date. Pasha called me to thank me and will publish my letter to him in Arab paper, also in French.

*Letter, GSP, Jr., to Beatrice, January 1943*

Not having command of an Army right now may be an advantage. Any how there is no use either guessing or grousing.

I gave 100,000 F[rancs] to the relatives of the defunct Arabs and went to the place and removed my hat. The Pasha just came to tell me what a profound effect these acts had had and I think he meant it. I went to the street door with him. This had a good effect too. I bet they will miss me when Wayne takes over the civil affairs, as he will do when the Fifth Army is hatched on the fourth [of January] . . .

I cant see that I have much future for a while but it will come.

He sent Beatrice a short story he had written of a soldier in combat.

You might try to get it published . . . If it is published, use a fake name. As if the powers that be thought I had time to write stories, it would not be good. I only write them to keep from going crazy.

He was writing all sorts of things.

*GSP, Jr., Notes on the Arab, January 1943*

Somewhere I have read that certain insects, as the ant and the dragonfly, attained their present state of development some hundreds of millions of years ago. My observation of the local Arabs makes me wonder if the same sort of arrested development does not apply to man. Certainly, between 600 and 800, the Arab race developed remarkable ability as conquerors, as scholars, and as lovers — or were they great only in comparison with the unutterable stupidity of the Dark Ages?

It were folly to pursue this line of thought, else we would inevitably shatter an idol by concluding that at Tours, Charles Martel saved Europe by beating second-rate opponents. However that may be, save it he did, and by that act insured that we of today do not exist in a world of bathrobed mendicants.

Truly, the costume of the Arab is the index of his inefficiency. In the first place, it makes him a one-armed man, for in order to retain his various garments in place, he is always using one hand as a safety pin . . . The elephant it is said would have outstripped man in the struggle for the supremacy of the earth had he possessed two trunks, but having only one he did not develop the same flexibility of mind as are acquired for the use of two arms.

For years, before coming here, I had read of the quiet dignity of the Arab. He is quiet, but his dignity, in my opinion, is pure dumbness. His aquiline face, which in the pure bred ones is quite impressive, is really the face of a dumb man . . .

As a friend of mine says, "No man can be either intelligent or proud of himself who spends his life pushing one undersized donkey up and down the road." It may well be that this donkey pace, which he has emulated for two thousand years, has reduced his mental reactions to a similar tempo . . .

Among the plains Arabs and the mountain Arabs in Morocco, there is intimate association between the sheep, the camels, the burros, and the Arabs. They all occupy one tent or straw hut, and since they are all equally illiterate, sit for hours gazing vacantly into space – perhaps the animals are thinking . . .

[They] are extremely good to their children, whom, since it is the Will of Allah, they permit to die of infantile diseases at an enormous rate.

The fatalism attributable to the Koranic Law may well be the basis for Mohammedan decadence. If a man is unsuccessful, he does not bestir himself. It is the Will of Allah. If a murder is committed, that too was preordained. It is the same with sickness; it is the same with everything – it is Kismet! . . .

But the Arab has many fine traits. He is law-abiding, he is sober, and he is a natural warrior. While not physically as husky as our men, he has more endurance. Once at a remote station, I was received by a guard of honor composed of native irregulars who had in the preceding 24 hours marched 137 kilometers (85 miles) and were still alert and very snappy.

The high caste Arabs whom I know are the most courteous, considerate, and generous gentlemen I have ever met. Should we attempt to Occidentalize the Arab, we would make a mistake. Despite the complete difference in our outlook on life, he is, in his filth and poverty, contented and perhaps happy. Our clamorous urge for a more generous life is unknown to him. Our heartaches at failure pass him by. Kismet is less exigent than ambition. After all, whether you call him God or Allah, a benign being rules the world. If the Arab way of life were completely wrong, He would not permit it – or am I, too, becoming a fatalist?

He was soon going to Spanish Morocco to pay a courtesy call on General Orgaz, the military governor. "My reputation as a diplomat," he told Beatrice, "is spreading."

On January 4, Patton, Wilbur, Stiller, and two French officers arrived at the international border at 12:05, five minutes "late on purpose," and met Orgaz. Patton's initial reaction was unexpectedly whimsical and in character. "He looked so much like Mrs. Shorb (Aunt Libby), moustache and all, that I almost kissed him."

Patton explained that he was representing Eisenhower and the President and paying nothing more than a military visit of courtesy. At Larache they drank the health of Franco, Roosevelt,

> and to the immemorial friendship between Spain, France, and America. The rest of the conversation consisted of reminiscences of the Spanish Revolution and of the Riff War.

After lunch, as they returned to the border, Orgaz "asked me not to look at his anti-aircraft defenses because they were so feeble. I had already looked at them, and they . . . certainly were feeble." Patton invited him to send his military representative in French Morocco to inspect American equipment, and Orgaz said he was "sure it would make him very envious." He admired Patton's whip with the concealed dagger so much that Patton gave it to him.

The significance of the trip, Patton advised Eisenhower, was that any movement made by Americans in French or Spanish Morocco would be known to both French and Spanish. Thus it seemed preferable to take the French, who were Allies, fully into "our confidence." The visit, the result of a unilateral American decision, might have alienated the French for no justifiable cause or gain, since success with the Spanish was doubtful and of little value.

*Letter, Beatrice to GSP, Jr., January 4, 1943*

> Next time you are in the news reel, try and give me a smile. I saw you twice yesterday . . .
>
> I subscribed to a clipping bureau which sent me 1,300 clippings [of you] in less than a month after you landed . . .
>
> Colonel C. P. Smith . . . says you are unbeatable, that no one will ever whip you or your men. I say so too, to him, and to you, and to the whole world.

Eisenhower rated Patton as a "Superior" officer — superior in physical activity, physical endurance, and knowledge of profession. He recommended that he be employed in command of a corps.

He does render willing and generous support to the plans of his superiors regardless of his personal views in the matter. Of the approximately 150 general officers of his grade personally known to me, I would rate General Patton number 5. Additional remarks: This officer is energetic, courageous, well informed, impulsive; definitely a leader type; devoted to the service.

*Diary, January 5*

[With Harmon] went to Volubilis. This was a Roman city founded in 42 B.C. and was the capital of the Roman province of West Africa, which was a triangle made by Tangiers, Volubilis, and Salle . . . The ruins are very impressive . . . Harmon and I could not but think that we, the modern equivalent of a Legate, were walking the very streets where our predecessors had walked in shining brass 2,000 years ago.

Making an inspection trip of North Africa and the United Kingdom at the behest of Marshall, Devers arrived at Patton's headquarters. "Jake," Patton remarked privately in his diary,

who has at last heard a gun go off in anger, talked in a big way till [late] . . . He has now become a great strategical expert, but he believes everything he is told until someone tells him different.

*Letter, GSP, Jr., to Beatrice, January 9, 1943*

Jake has been with both the First and Eighth British Armies and is much impressed with them. It amuses me how our country boys fall for tea and titles.

Jake is now – in his own opinion – a master of strategy. He orated till 0100 the night he was here. I often wonder what people who have seen war the easy way and for the first time think of us few professionals – they must believe we are fools not to have learned all they think they know. However he was much impressed with the discipline and order he saw here and compared it most favorably to conditions else where which are bad – in my opinion very bad . . .

I seem to be more and more in a back wash but possibly it is a good thing as the old sawdust basket is bound to collect a few heads soon. One for sure and possibly two.

Beatrice wrote to say she believed, from what she heard in Washington, that the current command setup in North Africa was "on the cards" ever since Clark got his third star. "Without experience nor background things are pretty well apt to get badly snarled," and she thought that her husband was very well off as he was

> for the nonce. You are better than you have ever been and are learning all the time the ways of the dove as well as those of the serpent and the fire dragon.

> *Diary, January 10*
>
> Clark arrived . . . I met him and had a guard of honor . . . took him on inspection of all local troops and installations. He was not in the least interested. His whole mind is on Clark. We went to the house and for one hour he spent his time cutting Ike's throat. And Ike, poor fool, sent him here. Of course Clark came so that if, as is most likely, the new attack [in Tunisia] fails, he can crawl out from under and land it on Fredendal.
>
> Kenner . . . and I talked till 1:00 AM. He too feels that Ike is not commanding and that Clark is an s.o.b. It is most discouraging.

He wrote Beatrice to say that John Waters would probably soon be in action and Patton hardly liked "the looks of the thing." There was "a growing volume of cryticism and every one for him self." He thought he was "lucky to be in my now unwanted position of a side line sitter for a while. It is very boring but it looks to me as if pretty soon they will have to put in a second team." Devers might go to the United Kingdom or become Chief of Staff in Washington, and Marshall might go to the United Kingdom to take command of the cross-Channel attack being talked about.

> I worry a lot about things. I try to do my full duty but it is hard to know just what it is. There is so much back bighting between soldiers and also politicians or between soldiers who are primarily politicians. We have many commanders but no leaders. And if one does well it is taken for granted, and every one looks for little things to find fault with.
>
> I took W. [Clark] all over the place yesterday and he was not in the least interested in the docks, the camp, or the men. All the con-

versation was on what he had done or hoped to do and the latter was pattently insincere . . .

Some times I wish I was retired but I guess I would not like that either. Probably I would only be content if I was god and probably some one [out] ranks him.

He had a display of weapons and transportation for the Sultan and had him ride in his armored car. "He insisted that I sit beside him . . . the first time that a Sultan has ever let any foreigner ride with him."

Since Clark had not had time to come to the show, the Sultan could not ask him to lunch. When Clark heard this, he was childishly provoked. Kenner, Keyes, and I were really shocked at his attitude.

Lunching with the Sultan on the following day, Patton talked French incessantly for three hours. The Prince "told me that when he is Sultan, I am to be his Grand Vizier and we will go everywhere in a tank."

The Sultan gave him "the Grand Cross of Morracco," which he had never seen a Frenchman wear.

Patton informed Nogues that Clark's Fifth Army had taken command of all the American troops in Morocco. Communications from Nogues were now to go to Clark.

Beatrice was writing to her brother Frederick Ayer about her husband:

I don't worry about him at all. I am so full of his triumph . . . that I just glow with pride . . . He is twice the man and twice the commander he has ever been . . . and I don't even worry for fear he'll be killed, though I know it might happen any minute. He feels, and I do, that he has a mission to perform, and — if a bullet gets him, we'll just have been wrong, that's all.

## CHAPTER 10

# Casablanca Conference

*"My guest book, had I kept one, would be an envy to all lion hunters."*

THE ALLIES had expected to have all of French North Africa in hand by the end of 1942, but now they looked forward to finishing the Tunisian campaign in the spring of '43. After that, what was to be done? Where should they make their next move in Europe? Should they continue their efforts in the Mediterranean area or launch a cross-Channel invasion? What about the conflicting claims of Giraud and De Gaulle and the future of France in the postwar world? How was the war on the European side of the conflict to be related to military endeavors elsewhere? How should the available resources in men and material be allocated among the various theaters of operation?

These were only some of the questions that required resolution. In order to find answers agreeable to both Allied partners – for the decisions would determine the course of Allied global strategy – Roosevelt and Churchill would meet in Casablanca with their military advisers in January 1943. They invited Joseph Stalin to attend, but he said he was too busy. The battle of Stalingrad had started in November and was reaching its climactic close.

The Casablanca Conference was code-named Symbol. Because the delegations from the United States and Great Britain were to be lodged in a suburb called Anfa, the meetings were sometimes called the Anfa Conference. As the local commander, Patton would be responsible for the billeting and feeding of the visitors, their security, and their comfort. He would take no part in the formal discussions of strategy.

*Diary, January 8*

Everett Hughes arrived this PM. I took him all around and he was most interested and complimentary. We had a long talk about the glamour boys. He fears that the senior partner is on his way out due to the knife work of the other, concerning whom he has the same ideas as I have. According to Everett, the General Staff at [Allied Force] Headquarters is purely theoretical and never inspects anything, the British are incompetent, the French mad, and no one commands anything. Devers had same idea.

A classmate of Patton's, Brigadier General Hughes was a logistical expert on the ETOUSA staff in London who would soon be brought to North Africa. The North African Theater of Operations, U.S. Army (NATOUSA) was about to be established to deal with purely American rather than Allied matters. Eisenhower would be in nominal command of NATOUSA, and Hughes would be his deputy. Since Eisenhower was involved in Allied affairs, Hughes would in fact administer the ports, the receipt and distribution of supplies, and other like concerns. He would eventually be promoted to major general.

Hughes' trip to Casablanca was perhaps connected with arrangements for the forthcoming Allied conference.

*Diary, January 9*

Geoff [Keyes] and I inspected the Anpha area in connection with Symbol. Everything is O.K. except that no arrangement has been made to take the French in. Gruenther is agreed with us that this should be done, but says that FDR and the PM [Prime Minister] both consider this as a conquered country – which it is not. The French have been told nothing and when they find out, as they will, it is going to take a hell of a lot of talk to restore their confidence. This is too bad and so terribly foolish. The British are pulling hell out of our leg and no one knows it. I believe they want to discredit the French with the Arabs so that after this war they can "acquire" French West and North Africa. The tragedy to me is that we will let them do it.

When Patton learned that Clark was going to put American troops at the port to make sure that the French guns "did not fire on Anpha," he went to see Clark

and argued him out of the idea. I had to state that if it were done,

I would request to be relieved. It would have been the crowning insult to the French and would have given the Nazis a wonderful propaganda weapon and roused the Arabs.

He had all the local unit commanders in and talked on the troop discipline to be maintained during the conference. He inspected the guard battalion.

"There is a great and very hush hush conference going on here, which I am not in – thank God," he wrote Beatrice. "I think it is a mess as are many other things."

*Diary, January 14*

Called on General G. C. Marshall and asked him to dinner . . . F.D.R. arrived by plane, met only by Secret Service. General Marshall came to dinner. Never asked a question and talked steadily about South Pacific. At dinner he got message to dine same night with A number 1 [the President], so left at 8:10.

*Diary, January 15*

Ike and [Harry] Butcher arrived at 11:30. I took them to Anpha and met Admiral King, who, when off duty, is most affable.

General Marshall asked me to have himself, King, Sir John Dill, and Mountbatten to dinner. All came but Marshall. I also had Somervell and Wedemeyer. We had a most interesting time and Lord Louis [Mountbatten] stayed late, talking combined operations. He is charming but not impressive. I think he got more from us than we got from him.

After I took him to hotel, Ike asked me to take him back to house, and he and I talked till 0130. He and Clarke are at outs, and he thinks his thread is about to be cut. Ike was his old self and listened. I told him he had to go "to the front." He feels that he cannot, due to politics, [and] said he had suggested to Gen. Marshall that I be made deputy commanding general AFHQ and run the war [in Tunsia] while he runs the politics. Keyes will get a corps [if this arrangement came to be]. I doubt if it comes out and am not sure I want [the] job.

*Diary, January 16*

Ike pinned second DSM on me at plane and repeated ideas on my being deputy commanding general.

Actually, Marshall had suggested this arrangement to Eisenhower, and as he flew back to Algiers, Eisenhower turned the idea over in his mind. He then discussed the matter with his staff, and on January 17, he told Marshall he was tentatively thinking of making the appointment. This would "allow me to use his great mental and physical energy in helping me through a critical period." Eventually he decided against it.

*Diary, January 16*

Called on General Marshall who told me to see A-1 [the President] about Nogues and Sultan . . .

Saw Harry Hopkins and A-1 and two sons for one and one half hours. A-1 most affable and interested. We got on fine. [Am] taking Nogues to see him at noon tomorrow.

Sir Dudley Pound [First Sea Lord — Admiral King's British counterpart] and General Lord Brooke [Chief of the Imperial General Staff — Marshall's counterpart], General Marshall and aide, Lieutenant Colonel [Frank] McCarthy, came to dinner. I walked home with Gen. Marshall . . .

Brooke is nothing but a clerk. Pound slept most of the time. The more I see of the so-called great the less they impress me — I am better.

Pound was already suffering the effects of a brain tumor, discovered somewhat later, and he would die that year.

*Letter, Beatrice to GSP, Jr., January 17, 1943*

Georgie [Devers] is in town while her beau is flying around the [Nile] River . . . rumoring that he is to be made [Army] chief of staff. This could not be true — just wishful thinking on their parts . . .

Last night I was invited to supper at Renie [Clark]'s to hear some more of her love letters and meet the Fifth Army staff wives . . . I thought the wives were very good class and very nice.

*Diary, January 17*

Wilbur and I took Nogues to see A-1 and we all talked for about one and one-quarter hours, then went to see B-1 [Churchill]. B-1 took Nogues off by himself and later called us in. B-1 speaks the worst French I have ever heard, his eyes run, and he is not at all impressive. Nogues said he would much rather play with US as B-1 wanted the whole world run his way.

Clark had Giraud at house for lunch with Nogues et al. I hate lunch. Giraud is an old type Gaul with blue eyes and limited brains. [British] Admiral [Andrew B.] Cunningham [commanding the Allied naval forces under Eisenhower] is to stay with me. Clark will be there tonight – I am fed up.

*Diary, January 18*

We had special lunch for General Marshall and General Giraud, Clark, Keyes, Wilbur and I . . . General Marshall was very well pleased and said so. I saw Clark off at plane . . .

I was walking when Elliot Roosevelt called me to ride in car with A-1. Many pictures taken. A-1 was very affable. When I took him home, the P.M. holed me, and I told him I would get him for dinner. Two Scotland Yard men asked if they could guard the house – they did.

For dinner we had the P.M., Hopkins, General Marshall, Admiral Cunningham, Commander Thompson [aide to the Prime Minister]. General Marshall made me talk to the P.M. and we got on well. He strikes me as cunning rather than brilliant but with great tenacity . . . He is easily flattered – all of them are. Hopkins is very clever and intuitive – like a pilot fish for a shark. He did not drink excessively and smoked my last three good cigars. The putting of me so obviously with the P.M. may have some meaning.

Hopkins asked me how I would like to be an Ambassador. I said I would resign if I got such a job. He said I had shown such ability that they needed me. I still said I would resign and go fishing rather than take such a job.

*Letter, GSP, Jr., to Sen. Henry Cabot Lodge, January 18, 1943*

I am very busily engaged in non-military activities . . .

I don't know what the future holds in store for me, but I would rather be commanding the corps in Africa than be anything except a senator in the United States (you will note my tact in the foregoing remark, and you will further note that I have been accused of not having it. Spread the news.)

The other day His Majesty the Sultan presented me with the Grand Cross of the Order of Ouissam Alaouite, which is the top flight order in this country. For formal evening wear you have a pumpkin-colored sash going across your manly bosom from right to left, with a large rosette and medal hanging from your left hip. For less formal occasions, you have a sunburst similar to that worn by Theda Bara, except that she had to wear two. This is worn on the left side in the vicinity of the naval . . .

The citation has something about the fact that when I walk about in the evening, the lions are so frightened that they cower in the rear of their dens.

*Diary, January 19*

General Marshall . . . was very complimentary about lunch and also about appearance of command. Took Hopkins and Elliott Roosevelt shopping. F.D.R., Admiral Cooke, Generals Wedemeyer and Hull, Captain McCray, self, Keyes, Wilbur, and Gay had dinner at our house, very informal. They stayed till 11:30. Then F.D.R. talked to me in car while P.M. waited, for about 30 minutes. He really appeared as a great statesman.

*Diary, January 20*

F.D.R. wanted to visit harbor but Secret Service would not let him. They are a bunch of cheap detectives always smelling of drink.

Saw Hull, Wedemeyer, and Sir John Dill at hotel at breakfast. A new plan is being concocted. The chief idea seems to get a new staff — there are too many now . . .

General Marshall, [Maj. Gen. Frank M.] Andrews, Clark for dinner . . . General Marshall gave monologue for two hours — Clark was very quiet.

*Diary, January 21*

Rode to Lyautey with Mr. Hopkins. He is extremely intelligent and very well informed. To my surprise he is quite war-like and is in favor of discipline. When we saw all the wounded and decorated men he called my attention to the similarity of the set of the mouth. I had known this for years but was surprised that he did.

Hopkins, Clark, F.D.R., and I had lunch alfresco . . . The pilot fish noted to me that nearly all the men killed were Anglo-Saxon. Clark left and had me ride back with F.D.R. Clark is trying to be nice but it makes my flesh creep to be with him.

Coming back we talked history and armor about which he knows a lot. F.D.R. says that in Georgia [Russia] there are Crusaders' Castles intact and that hundreds of suits of armor exist. Then he got on to politics. He said that the only two men who could succeed him if he died were Hopkins and the Vice President and neither of them had any personality. He also discussed the P.M. to his disadvantage. Says India is lost and that Germany and Japan must be destroyed. He is worried about the American Legion after the war, and should be . . .

Millions of pictures were taken and none for the glory of the troops, all for the glory of F.D.R., and for Clark when he could get a chance. It was very disgusting.

Must remember to get Chief Flat Foot Riley [head of the Secret Service] when time comes. Also F.B.I. needs to be slapped down. The country and army are in a hell of a fix and nothing is being done about it. People speak of Germany and Japan as defeated, and we have never even attacked them with more than a division.

Our troops put up a really fine appearance. I have never seen so many troops so well turned out or looking so fit. Will write a letter of congratulations to each unit.

*Diary, January 22*

Wilbur and I called for Nogues and took him to Grand Vizier's house at Anpha where we met the Sultan, Prince Imperial, and Grand Vizier, and [Chief of] Protocol. Wilbur took Sultan, Grand Vizier, and Protocol to see President at 1940. Sultan had especially asked to see him before Churchill arrived. Crown Prince, Nogues, and I arrived at 2000. Churchill was there in a very bad temper.

At dinner . . . President, Sultan, Protocol, self, Crown Prince, Elliott Roosevelt, Nogues, Hopkins, Murphy, Grand Vizier, Churchill. No wine, only orange juice and water. Churchill was very rude, the President was great, talking volubly in bad French and really doing his stuff. After dinner we had [motion] pictures and more talk . . .

I rode with Sultan and Grand Vizier to house of latter. On way Sultan said, "Truly your President is a very great man and a true friend of myself and of my people. He shines by comparison with the other one" . . .

Nogues was delighted that the P.M. was such a boor.

*Letter, Beatrice to GSP, Jr., January 23, 1943*

I heard the most wonderful lecture at the Geographic by Commander S. E. Morison . . . The movies with it were of the actual landings, and the whole thing was as fine as could be. It was entirely from the Navy point of view . . .

I went out to the back room . . . to congratulate him, and he said he had enjoyed meeting you . . .

He introduced me to a lot of people . . . as Mrs. General Patton, among whom was Mr. Berle.

He is an objectionable little Jew, with a strong accent. He said: "Mrs. Patton, your husband is doing a fine job over dere in spite of de newspapers."

I said, "Mr. Berle, the papers have not mentioned General Patton at all in connection with the African political situation. He is in Morocco, and I understand that the situation there is a most happy one."

Believe me, no one is going to get you mixed up with anyone else if they ask me. "Not while Tildy Ann has two shots left." . . .

The enclosed article about you is in today's [Washington] Post . . . Renie Clark just called me up about it; she says it shows a sweet side she didn't know you possessed, and that she is crazier about you than ever. Tut, tut . . .

Now I will do up my little package and some love, which takes no room, and requires no extra postage, but you will feel it there.

*Diary, January 23*

I talked to General Marshall about the Legion of Merit. He told me to see Hopkins about it. I did. Hopkins is quite a man and very understanding. I think he will get the President to remove the stipulation that the President must approve all Legion of Merit awards, certainly in so far as the Army is concerned. This will be a great thing, as at present we have no means of rewarding merit except with the DSM, which only applies to great responsibility and not to the good work of juniors . . .

The Roosevelt boy who is in the Navy came in drunk and slapped an admiral on the back and said, "How are you, you old s.o.b." Hopkins saw it and told the admiral to send the young Roosevelt to his ship in arrest and confine him there . . .

The Grand Vizier asked me to get him an interview with Mr. Hopkins, provided that the British did not know about the points [to be] discussed, i.e., future of French and Spanish Morocco, Jews, trade, and immediate help.

Wilbur saw DeGaul[le] and found him not helpful. He wants to be the political boss and let Giraud command the troops.

*Diary, January 24*

I took General Nogues and Admiral Michelier to call on A-1 . . . A-1 started to talk about DeGaul and was very frank, when B-1 came in without being asked and hung around, started to leave, and then came back. The whole thing was so patent a fear on the part of the British to have the French and Americans alone together, that it was laughable. The two Frenchmen saw and commented on it. I hope A-1 did too . . .

Giraud came after lunch to . . . say goodby. I fear he is too much a soldier to run his job as dictator – at least he wants to fight . . .

I met the new British Consul to Rabat, who began to tell me how to win a war, so I disagreed with him to draw him out, but he just got mad. He is a typical State Department fool.

*Letter, GSP, Jr., to Hopkins, January 24, 1943*

It is my present intention to give myself the honor of seeing you off, but in view of the fact you may be too busy at the last moment, I am writing this note to tell you how much I enjoyed our conversations together, and how much I appreciate the deep and sincere interest you demonstrated for the troops.

I hope you will tell the people at home how really fine they are. I also hope that something can be done to facilitate the issuance of Legion of Merit badges.

*Diary, January 25*

Admiral King, Cooke, Hall came to dinner, and I had a chance to tell how good Hall is, which is true.

*Letter, GSP, Jr., to Beatrice, January 25, 1943*

Darling B. We have had a very hectic week of social and official affairs. My guest book, had I kept one, would be an envy to all lion hunters. Keep an eye on the movies, and you may see me and be surprised.

We had a corps review . . . and for once in my life I was perfectly satisfied . . . and I am not getting less easy to please.

I only wish that after seeing this outfit, [the important] people . . . could take a look at some of the other troops. It would add to our reputation at the expense of theirs . . .

No wars in sight. I love you.

*Letter, GSP, Jr., to Malin Craig, January 25, 1943*

The state of law and order maintained here results from the prestige of the French Army, which is certainly nebulous. Therefore, it has been my study to maintain and build up in every way this prestige, because without it we might well be faced with internecine war between various Arab districts. This would not be very serious war . . . but it unquestionably would require the diversion of large numbers of our troops from their primary mission of killing Germans and chasing Italians.

Naturally, I have been criticized for being too soft with the French, but since they have done everything I have asked of them, I feel that I can stand the criticism.

The Arabs apparently like me very much and are always trying to give me indigestion by inviting me to ten-course meals, at which the smallest dish consists of a whole sheep for six people . . .

It is impossible to state just what I will do next, but I certainly would like to do something except sit around and wait for something to happen.

He told his chief of staff, Hobart Gay, to get out a training memorandum to all subordinate units. Among the points covered was the instruction that all officers and men were to be able to run one mile in ten minutes while wearing combat dress and equipment. Also, everyone was to

pay more attention to saluting U.S. Naval officers and officers of all foreign services. At the present time, the French officers and men are much more meticulous in saluting us than we are in saluting them.

*Diary, January 26*

Generals Marshall, Hull, Gailey, and Col. McCarthy came to dinner . . . We had a monologue [from Marshall]. It is most unfortunate that weather prevented General Marshall from seeing the troops [elsewhere]. He now will think they are as good as mine, which is not so. He should have especially seen the airports, which are terrible. All he did was to make excuses for the lack of discipline of the Air Force. There is no excuse – my troops are disciplined . . . Now General Marshall will fly the Atlantic with Devers and swallow all his misinformation. I wish someone would listen to me. I have something which makes people reluctant to question me; perhaps I always have an answer based on truth and not bootlick.

He saw General Marshall off the following morning.

Many of those who attended the conference wrote to thank Patton for his hospitality. Cunningham sent "a small present which I hope will do a little to relieve the Scotch shortage in your area and to which I fear I contributed." Churchill and Mountbatten were impressed by the bearing of the American troops. Air Force Lieutenant Colonel Elliott Roosevelt told him to have no hesitation to ask for a favor. Dill appreciated Patton's kindness, then added that Patton's luck had held – there had been no Axis bombing of Casablanca.

Marshall was, for him, lavish in his praise, congratulating Patton for the outstanding manner in which all the details had been handled, complimenting him on the appearance and performance of his officers and men, and thanking him for the personal entertainment, the dinners that had contributed to the informal discussions at the conference.

Devers wrote to tell Patton that he had made a splendid impression on everyone. "You have what it takes and you can dish it out."

Shortly thereafter, when Everett Hughes read a "Report on the Operations of the Western Task Force at Casablanca," written by two British officers, he passed along a passage to Patton. Dealing with the factors that contributed to the success of the operation, the authors listed the first as being:

> The personal leadership in the field of nearly all the American Commanding Generals and the spirit, emanating from Maj-General G. S. Patton and pervading the whole force, of absolute determination to stake everything on what was clearly a military gamble and either to achieve success or to face the problem of 100 per cent casualties.

Patton modestly replied:

> I do believe that the other generals were just as fully intent on winning or staying in Africa as I was.

To Helen Sprigg, a secretary who had worked with the Western Task Force in Washington, Patton wrote:

> You will probably have read in the papers and seen on the movie screen that for the last ten days we have been very busy entertaining the leading lights of the world. It was very amusing but was not war. Personally, I wish I could get out and kill someone.

# CHAPTER 11

# Kasserine Pass Offstage

*"I have nothing to do and don't seem to be getting anywhere."*

THE BATTLE of Kasserine Pass in Tunisia would develop in February, and this American disaster would threaten to disrupt the plans so carefully laid at Casablanca.

To learn what decisions reached at Casablanca pertained to North Africa, Patton flew to Oudja "in my B-25" on January 28. He saw Clark, who had just returned from talking with Eisenhower in Algiers. Clark "was too friendly and I feared a stab in the back at any moment, but none came. He told me the damnedest thing I have ever heard."

The final attack in Tunisia, Clark said, was to be launched by a group of Armies consisting of Anderson's First and Montgomery's Eighth, both British and both to be commanded by another British officer, Alexander. The American troops were to be under the II Corps, which, together with the British V Corps and the French XIX Corps, was to be in Anderson's Army.

Patton exploded. "Shades of J. J. Pershing! We have sold our birthright and the mess of pottage is, in my opinion, the title of Allied Commander to General Marshall" for the cross-Channel attack. "I am shocked and distressed."

The command arrangement in Tunisia seemed "so absurd" that he doubted whether the attack would ever come off. There were too many "boches in Tunisia now, with Rommel yet to come in," and he thought that the Allied forces would be unable to evict that many men by May 1, "as hopefully planned."

"I truly think that the whole set up is the result of clever politics by the British and selfish ambition on our part . . . Ike will be a sort of War Department" — that is, detached from the battlefield.

The next operation in the Mediterranean was to be an invasion of Sicily. It was to be carried out by a force half British and half American, both commanded by a British officer, probably Alexander, "though Clark," he thought, "is trying to get hold of it. It would be safe physically, and, if successful, would give him great credit."

> Apparently I am to command the U.S. forces . . . My luck will have to be pretty good and the Lord on the job to put it over. One is inclined to think that fighting ability is at a discount. However, I think that I was fortunate in not being Deputy Commander-in-Chief to Ike. I guess destiny is still on the job. God, I wish I could really command and lead as well as just fight.

What bothered Patton most about Sicily was the prospect of his subordination to a British commander. This seemed to be the pattern being established in Tunisia, where Alexander was eventually to take command of the Allied ground forces.

In Libya, with Montgomery still in pursuit, Rommel eluded the capture and destruction of his Army. In January 1943, he began to send units into southern Tunisia, and to improve the fortified Mareth Line, which he would use as an obstacle against the approaching British. Rommel would establish his headquarters there at the end of the month.

On January 23, three months to the day after opening the El Alamein battle and after an advance of 1400 miles across Libya, Montgomery's Army entered Tripoli, which had been destroyed by the departing Axis troops.

According to the plan formulated at Casablanca, as soon as Montgomery brought forward his forces and was ready to attack Rommel, Alexander was to fly from Cairo to Tunisia and direct the coordinated operations of Montgomery in the south and Anderson – facing Arnim – in the north. By crushing the Axis forces in Tunisia, the Allies would clear the entire north shore of Africa. Across the Mediterranean, Axis-occupied Europe, from Spain to Turkey, would then presumably be vulnerable to invasion.

What disturbed Patton was that the British seemed to be running the show. In his view, they were usurping the important positions of command, even those that rightfully belonged to him. Eisenhower was being relegated to the status of a figurehead, and British aims and methods were likely to prevail.

Still harking back to Pershing's unwavering commitment to maintaining an independent American command in World War I, Patton was not only xenophobic; he was also out of date. The appointment of Marshal Ferdinand Foch as supreme Allied commander in the latter months of that war had changed the conditions of coalition warfare in World War II — at least for the Allies if not for the Axis. But then much of Patton's resentment and indignity and hurt burst from his frustration, his enforced inactivity. A proved commander in combat, he was unemployed. It must be someone's fault, he was sure — the British, Eisenhower, Clark, Bedell Smith — and he searched for a scapegoat on whom to vent his emotions.

*Letter, GSP, Jr., to Beatrice, January 30, 1943*

I saw Wayne [Clark] day before yesterday and he gave me the picture of what is to come. If he is right, and I believe he is, we, that is Dwight, Wayne, and me, and every one else have been sold for a dish of potage. It is truly dreadful. I just can't believe it will come off. If it does come off, it will be one hell of a bloody mess with no credit to us [Americans] . . .

Don't talk to the Secretary [Stimson] or the people who live at [Fort] Myer [including Marshall] about what I have just said but listen if they talk to you . . .

The President was truly great. Another high person was really horrid.

On that day, in Tunisia, at an obscure mountain trail called the Faid Pass, German troops attacked and defeated the small French garrison guarding this opening through the mountain range known as the Eastern Dorsale. No one knew it, but this was the initial blow of what would develop into the battle of Kasserine Pass.

The engagement would affect Patton, but not at once. For the moment he seemed doomed to suffer while he watched others fight.

*Letter, GSP, Jr., to Handy, January 31, 1943*

I am firmly of the opinion that the discipline, military bearing, and neatness of the troops trained in America is not up to the standard necessary. Every time a new convoy arrives, I am impressed with this fact. The soldiers are sloppily dressed, they do not salute, they do not take care of themselves, and their officers do not insist that they correct these defects. It takes us about a month after they get here to get them up to anywhere the standard of the 2d Armored Division . . .

In the training of the troops to make a landing, viciousness and speed must be stressed. They must hit the beach running and continue to run until they are shot down . . . Languorously meandering over the sand hills will not get anyone anything but a grave.

His idleness continued to bother him. Hoping that Sir John Dill would casually mention his boredom to Marshall, Patton wrote: "I am not getting much fighting. However, I hope that this will be corrected in the not too distant future."

*Diary, February 1*

The Arab idea of hospitality is profusion. Mama must have been part Arab.

*Letter, GSP, Jr., to Beatrice, February 1, 1943*

While I hate to be idle here, I too rather think it is a good place to be for the nonce. I think that the current arrangements may make a hell of an explosion at home, and I will be on the outside looking in.

This P.M. I am . . . to spend the night in the Palace so I told George [Meeks] to put in lots of clothes and dressing gowns etc as I feel sure all my things will be inspected while I am at dinner.

When the air-raid signal sounded during the night, Patton conformed to the regulations, got up and dressed. It was a false alarm, so he returned to bed. Unable to fall asleep, he began to think about events in the past. He recalled the dangerous blood clot that had been removed from his lung in 1937. Had he then died, who would have directed the landings near Casablanca? The thought prompted him to write Doctor P. P. Johnson, the surgeon at the Beverly Hospital in Massachusetts, who had performed the operation. "I expect," he said, "that there are many other people who could have done the job [in French Morocco] as well or better," but he was grateful for Johnson's skill and devotion, and he thanked Johnson "for giving me a chance to be here."

He also described the sinking of several transports and the rescue of

400 men, some of them badly burned by oil. Only four died. "I was up with them most of the night," and the remarkable technique of treating burns amazed him.

> People that looked like pieces of bacon would be carried in and after a little . . . spraying with some kind of drug and the use of blood plasma, they seemed perfectly comfortable . . . You would have certainly enjoyed the evening as it was, I believe, a great demonstration of what modern surgery can and does do.

> *Diary, February 3*
>
> Clark called me to meet him at Oudja and go with him to Algiers . . .
>
> Ike talked in glittering generalities and then said as nearly as I can remember, "George, you are my oldest friend, but if you or anyone else criticizes the British, by God I will reduce him to his permanent grade and send him home. The reason that I have not promoted you is that I want to promote three of you, and one of the others [Fredendall] is reported to have talked against the British. If he has, by God I'll bust him. In any case you will get promoted in less than a month."
>
> Later I asked Clark if I had been accused. Clark said no, and that Ike had talked to him the same way. Clark thinks General Marshall told Ike to do it to all of us. "Cromwell, beware ambition, by it the angels fell."

Patton told all the heads of his staff sections and all his major subordinate commanders that there was to be "no criticism of Russians, British, French or any others."

Fearing that Patton might misconstrue his remarks, Eisenhower wrote to assure him that the Allies would always need fighting generals. Yet Patton sometimes made a bad impression because he was "quick-witted," had "a ready and facile tongue," and seemed to act on impulse rather than on "study and reflection." Friends of Patton knew that much of what Patton said was "a smoke-screen," but others in authority lacked that knowledge. Eisenhower therefore advised him to count to ten before speaking. His "intense desire" was to see Patton advance as rapidly as possible, for no one in the theater was a more loyal and devoted friend than Patton.

*Diary, February 5*

Got a secret letter from Ike in which he advises me to be more circumspect and less flip in my conversation on military matters. He means well and I certainly have thus far failed to sell myself in a big way to my seniors.

*Letter, GSP, Jr., to Eisenhower, no date*

Let me start by assuring you that I do want your advice . . .

For years I have been accused of indulging in snap judgments. Honestly, this is not the case because, like yourself, I am a profound military student and the thoughts I express, perhaps too flippantly, are the result of years of thought and study.

Again, both you and I have been fortunate in long and intimate associations with many eminent men . . . It may be that I am not sufficiently over-awed in the presence of high personages and therefore speak too freely, whereas others less used to associating with the great speak with more reticence and in consequence give the impression of considered thought, whereas their hesitation is really due to embarrassment . . .

Again please accept my sincere thanks for your thoughtful consideration of my interests, and your repeated efforts to have me promoted. I shall never let you down.

*Diary, February 6*

Wrote a reply to Ike but will sleep on it.

He never mailed the letter.

*Diary, February 8*

Had the cafard [blues] all day because I have nothing to do and don't seem to be getting anywhere.

*Letter, Beatrice to GSP, Jr., February 6, 1943*

Darling Georgie, George [Marshall] hadn't been home an hour when he called me from his house to tell me all about you and how fine you were at the conference and what a magnificent showing your troops made and how everyone there noticed it.

Then Malin [Craig] called me to say that he had been to a lecture in which G. [Marshall] had said the same and more of it. He especially wanted me to tell you this: Whatever propaganda may have been circulated against you in the past by your ex-classmate [Pa Watson, West Point Class of 1908, the President's military secretary] is now washed up as the person who may have listened to it has now seen for himself what you can do and apparently appreciates you as never before, and has said so.

Yesterday I had tea with the "Harrys" [Stimsons] and when he came in he said: "Well, I've been lugging this citation around in my pocket for days hoping I might see you." He then pulled out your citation from the Sultan – "Les lions dans leurs tannieres tremblent en le voyant approcher."

Oh, oh, how glad I am I am not a lion . . . [Stimson] spent yesterday afternoon with F.D.R. and said that he [the President] said the grandest things about you and your troops without knowing anything of your friendship; pretty nice, I thought . . .

Fred [Ayer] is very sore about all this "cheap publicity" you are getting, but I have written him that you made your protest . . . and if he only read the other Generals with the same interest he does you, he would see how far ahead yours is and quit worrying . . .

You are in a crossword puzzle.

*Letter, GSP, Jr., to Beatrice, February 8, 1943*

My French has gotten to a bad phase. At first I was satisfied if I could make my meaning clear. Now I try to talk correctly and I fear get on much worse unless I use some sentences I have memorized. However they all say I have improved, so I suppose I have. One can hardly talk only French for six or seven hours with people who understand no English and not get a little facility.

Worrying about what Devers would say about him when Devers reported to Marshall on his inspection trip to North Africa, Patton wrote him a flattering letter:

I certainly enjoyed the brief visit we had, and was particularly interested in your first hand view of the situation confronting us here in Africa . . . The show that the troops put on for the President . . . would have done your soldier's heart good to see the tremendous impression of force and discipline presented.

Many of the troops coming here give me the impression of lacking training in those soldierly qualities which you have always stressed . . . It generally takes me about two months to get them up to your standards.

He need not have worried. In Devers' report, his description of Patton's command was more than complimentary:

> The appearance of the camps and apparent discipline of the soldiers, particularly with regard to saluting, was outstanding in comparison with other units visited...
>
> Patton has established excellent relations with the French and the natives. Noticeable was the smartness with which French soldiers — and civilians — saluted American officers . . . . A luncheon was given for several French and native dignitaries, at which mutual self-respect was highly evident...
>
> It was the concensus of the [inspection] party that of all commands visited, General Patton's was the finest.

His West Point classmate John C. H. Lee stopped by and informed Patton that Eisenhower had his fourth star, Gruenther his second, Harmon of the Air Corps his third. Patton's reaction: "Happy day."

Devers wrote to tell Beatrice that Patton was doing an exceptional job, had the best trained and disciplined troops of any command Devers had seen, and was on top of the political situation. If Patton were in Tunisia, Devers said, he would have Rommel by the throat and throttle him.

On February 14, as the battle of Kasserine Pass opened in earnest, Patton left Algiers for Tripoli in a B-17. "On way, the crew fired their guns to see if they worked and we all got badly scared."

In Tripoli Patton met many of Britain's distinguished officers: General Sir Bernard Paget, head of home defenses who was visiting North Africa; Alexander, "very quiet and not impressive looking"; Montgomery, "small, very alert, wonderfully conceited, and the best soldier — or so it seems — I have met in this war"; Lieut. General Sir O. W. Leese, "who wore plus fours and a little coat of his own design but was and is a very able soldier" — he would command the Eighth Army later in Italy; Lieut. General Sir Miles Dempsey, who would fight in Sicily and southern Italy, then command the Second Army in Europe; Lieut. General Sir Bernard Freyberg, who "started life as a dentist in New Zealand, got the Victoria Cross at Gallipoli and in two wars has been wounded 18 times — quite a man, rather fat but with a fine mouth"; Brigadier Sir Brian Robertson, son of the field marshal in World War I; Lieut. General H. D. G. Crerar, who would command the First Canadian Army in Europe; Major General Briggs, an armored division commander "whom I liked a lot."

Briggs said that Montgomery was "the best soldier and the most disagreeable man he knew." It was also said that "Montgomery commands and Alexander supplies."

> Except for Montgomery, Freyberg, Briggs, and Robertson, I saw nothing out of the ordinary. Most of them are the same non-committal clerical type as our generals. I am about the junior [in rank] and possibly the oldest [in age], certainly the oldest looking general here.

Returned to Algiers, he had lunch with Eisenhower and talked excitedly about his visit with the British professionals.

With members of the AFHQ G-3 section he discussed the invasion of Sicily, which seemed to be "a desperate operation, especially as at least two of my divisions will not have had battle experience." The shores were mined and wired, and if German troops bolstered the Italians, the landings "will not work, but I shall do my best . . . I have always been lucky and I am going to need all I have." Yet, "What I fail to see is what real value we will achieve if we do win [in Sicily]." It was, after all, only an island. Successful operations could hardly be developed into a prolonged offensive against vital objectives.

Patton dined with Eisenhower, together with Paget and several others.

> Ike and Paget talked for a long time. Ike certainly makes a fine impression when he talks. I was proud of him. I think I could do better in the same job, but I seem to lack something which makes the politicians trust Ike.

*Letter, GSP, Jr., to Beatrice, February 19, 1943*

> D. [Eisenhower] has realy developed beyond belief and is quite a great man. He has certainly been nice to me. In fact I seem to have got more of a job than W. [Clark], but that remains to be seen.

*Diary, February 19*

> Too wet and foggy to start [for Casablanca] so I talked with Admirals Hall and Kirk on [the Sicilian] operation. Hall was fine and I felt better, but we all realize it is a damned poor bet. Still, it is an honor [for me] to be trusted with the American part of the plan. I feel I will win. I feel more and more that I have a mission; then I lose my confidence, but get it back. The real need for a man will be

after the peace in US. I could do something there, but must first demonstrate great combat leadership and have the troops with me.

Left at 3:30 in very bad visibility . . . We nearly hit several mountains and I was scared till I thought of my destiny. That calmed me. I will not be killed in a crash. Landed O.K. in about a foot of water.

Spent night with Clark. He is most polite. I think he wants to hook up with me [on the Sicilian operation].

Heard Harmon has been ordered to take over [in Tunisia].

On the following day, he stopped at Rabat "to tell Harmon goodbye. He has a very bad job, taking over a beaten and scattered division in face of the enemy."

The battle of Kasserine Pass, which had defeated and dispersed the Americans, was at its climax. On February 14, while Patton was flying to Tripoli, Axis forces had attacked French and American troops in Tunisia. Arnim struck westward from the Faid Pass and in a relatively large-scale tank engagement at Sidi bou Zid seriously hurt the 1st Armored Division. Rommel, having moved his army into the Mareth Line, sent a strong detachment to Gafsa and provoked an Allied retreat.

On February 17, Arnim's tanks drove the Americans out of Sbeitla, and Rommel's force pushed American and French units out of important airfields at Fériana and Thelepte.

Having fled in some disorder about 50 miles across the parched plain between the eastern and western mountain ranges, the Americans, aided by the British and French, tried to halt at Kasserine Pass what appeared to be an irresistible Axis march. If Tebéssa, an important supply center, and Le Kef, the key to the Allied positions, were lost, Constantine would be threatened, and the Allies might have to abandon Tunisia altogether.

With Rommel now directing the offensive, a two-pronged attack opened on February 19, one smashing from Sbeitla to Sbiba, the other penetrating Kasserine Pass. The battle raged for four days.

Meanwhile, Alexander flew from Cairo to Algiers on February 15, to prepare to take command of the ground forces in Tunisia. He spent the following three days inspecting the front. He was appalled by the confusion and doubt he discovered in the American sector. On February 19, with Eisenhower's approval, he assumed command of the Allied ground forces and directed the defense against Rommel.

Informed by Alexander that Fredendall seemed to have lost control

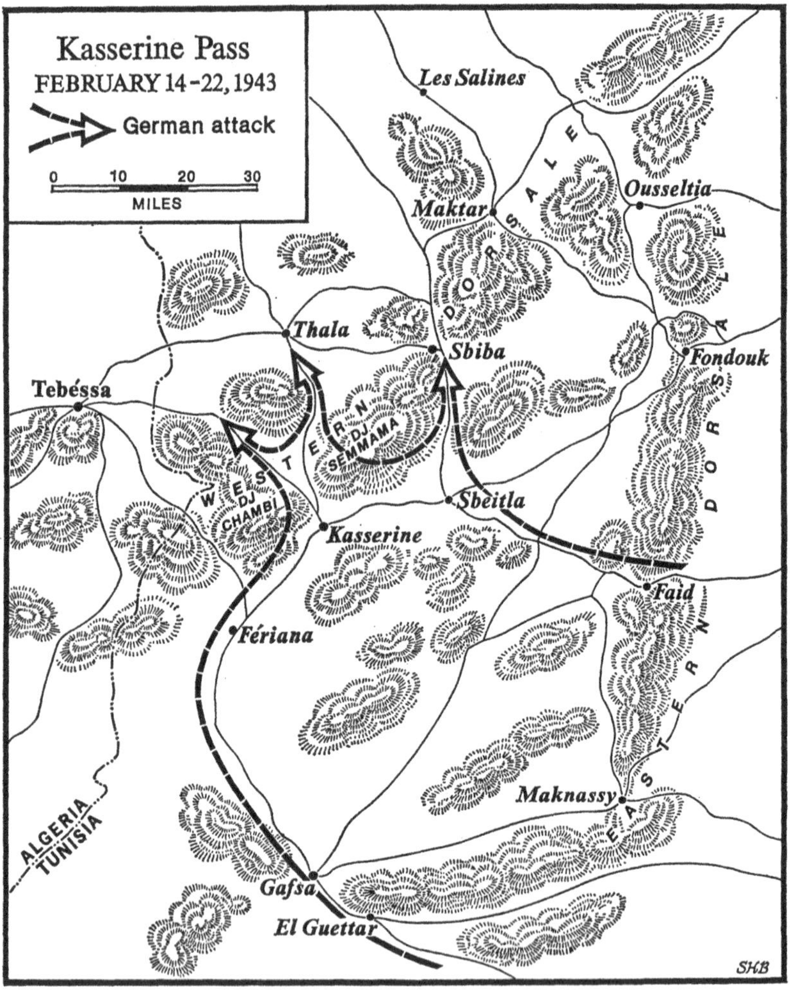


of the fighting, Eisenhower summoned Harmon to Algiers and issued him peculiar instructions. Harmon was to go to Tunisia to take command not of the II Corps or of the 1st Armored Division, but rather of the American forces in the battle.

Harmon arrived at Kasserine Pass early on February 23, a few hours after Rommel, unknown to the Allies, decided to call off his attack. Convinced that the Allies had brought too much strength to the area for him to triumph, and conscious of Montgomery's approach to the Mareth Line, Rommel broke off the offensive and sent his men marching back to southern Tunisia.

Although Rommel failed to gain a strategic victory, he nevertheless considerably damaged the Allies, and particularly American morale.

It must have occurred to both Eisenhower and Patton that if the former had appointed the latter his Deputy Commanding General as Marshall had suggested, the American rout might never have happened.

On February 22, Patton heard an account of the fighting in Tunisia. "Apparently John's [Waters'] battalion," he noted in his diary, "was destroyed. I have no news of him."

*Diary, February 23*

Long talk [with Clark] . . . He feels that Ike has sold out to British and that they talked him into not putting in the Fifth Army and [thereby creating] an American sector [in Tunisia]. He also feels that Alexander talked Ike into not attacking Gabes on January 20th, as [had been] planned, so that this could be a British victory. He may well be right. If so, it is too terrible for words. Some heads will fall if the show aborts, as it may well do.

*Letter, GSP, Jr., to Beatrice, February 23, 1943*

Jake [Devers] was here for a day, very secretive, but D. [Eisenhower] says he has passed his prime with G. [Marshall] and will fade out . . .

Montgomery (who is a sort of Stone Wall Jackson type) and I were the only ones with gray hair. I felt awfully old and looked it . . .

John's battalion was practically wiped out but he is thought to be safe. Harmon went up to take command . . . and will let me know. The show was very bad — very bad indeed.

We went to a movie called *Road to Morocco,* and found it "utterly crazy but I liked it as it was the first movie I had seen since October."

*Letter, GSP, Jr., to Summerall, February 24, 1943*

I am somewhat regretful of being so far from the scene of actual fighting, but I trust the Lord, who has always looked after me, will see that I eventually get into it again.

He moved his headquarters to Rabat.

He inspected the 2d Armored Division. "They are still playing at war. Guns not dug in and vehicles crowded. I raised hell."

"They have forgotten a lot," he told Beatrice.

> Our men are willing to die but don't yet grasp the fact that it is better to kill than be killed. It is pretty discouraging.
>
> I feel just like a bird in a room who can see the out side through the window and beats himself to death trying to get out. Some day the glass will break or the window be opened.

"I can now chin myself three times," he noted, "two days ago, I could only do it once."

*Letter, GSP, Jr., to Stimson, February 28, 1943*

> Sometimes I think that much of what happens certainly is predestined and probably my not being in this fighting in the east may turn out for my good . . .
>
> I am working very diligently to revivify the training of the troops . . . As you can readily understand, it is very hard to keep up enthusiasm and yet, very necessary, and I believe we are having considerable success . . .
>
> I just got through reading with great interest your article on what we have accomplished . . . It certainly paints in very vivid colors the amazing achievements you and General Marshal have accomplished for the Army. I do not know what we would have done without you.

He inspected the 3d Division and was displeased. "Wore helmet and pistol so as to impress men with the need of being properly equipped."

Tortured by his inactivity, Patton wrote Marshall's aide, Lieutenant Colonel Frank McCarthy, on the flimsiest sort of excuse, hoping that McCarthy would casually inform Marshall that

> We have left the palace at Casablanca and have moved to Rabat in excellent though less gorgeous guarters. I am very glad to be here as it makes it much more simple to inspect and train the troops, and gives more of an opportunity for exercise, which I am convinced is as necessary as anything else to the successful conduct of the war.

A copy of Devers' report of his inspection tour reached Patton, and he was grateful for Devers' remarks.

> You will never know how much I appreciate and value . . . the kind things that you say concerning the troops here. I am trying to follow your advice and possess my soul in patience, but it is really pretty hard . . . not [to] have a chance to fight. However, I . . . hope that eventually I may get into it.

*Letter, GSP, Jr., to his brother-in-law, Frederick Ayer, March 2, 1943*

By the time you get this you will have probably heard that John Waters is missing in action . . . However, there is still a chance that he may have escaped . . .

Personally knowing John, I do not think that he surrendered, but it is very important to make little Bea and also Bea senior believe that he did . . .

Eisenhower, with whom I just talked on the telephone, considered his action one of the finest performed in this war and has given him the Distinguished Service Cross.

*Letter, GSP, Jr., to Beatrice, March 2, 1943*

I just finished a letter to Little B. which is not a success as I am not too good a liar . . .

There is still a chance that John too may turn up . . .

D. is giving a two minute radio talk on March 14 on the occasion of the West Point dinner. All of it will hinge on John as the perfect example of a cadet and officer.

If [his son] George had been in John's place, I could not feel worse . . .

I feel terribly sorry for B.

*Diary, March 2*

Harmon just came in and told me John Waters was missing in action at Sidi-bou-Zid . . . His battalion was cut off by a German attack of 80 tanks . . .

According to Harmon, Fredendall is a physical and moral coward. Harmon did well . . . and drove the Germans from the pass of Kasserine. He said it was due to what I had told him on a fishing trip about clearing a pass by capturing the heights. That is what he did with his infantry. Fredendall never went to the front at all and tried to make Harmon the goat. Harmon won the battle . . .

I fear John is dead.

In the United States, a radio broadcast described Patton as a combination Buck Rogers, Green Hornet, and Man from Mars,

> the rootin', tootin', hip-shootin' commander of American forces in Morocco . . . If you like your military leaders on the colorful side, then you're going to like George Patton because he has enough dash and dynamite to make a Hollywood adventure-hero look like a drugstore cowboy . . . He's barking a mixture of blistering profanity and official orders . . . He's consistently out front. Every man in Patton's command knows he wouldn't ask any of them to execute an assignment which he wouldn't tackle himself . . . It's truly in character for Patton to have a strong premonition that he's going to a spectacular death in battle – in a tank, at the head of his men. He's described the death scene to his wife so often that now she believes it. Maybe that explains Patton's amazing courage . . . a flair for the dramatic . . . You grab the enemy by the nose; then you kick him in the rumble seat . . . a running blast of his usual brimstone language . . . a man whose greatest ambition is to meet Marshal Rommel in a personal tank battle, just the two of them, squared off in a duel to the death.

*Diary, March 4*

Nogues loaned me his horse . . . Wilbur and I had a nice ride.

When I got back at 4:40, Ike had phoned for me to be ready to leave tomorrow for extended field service and to pack tonight. I phoned Beedle Smith, Ike's chief of staff, and asked what it was about. He said I may relieve Fredendall. Well, it is taking over rather a mess but I will make a go of it. I think I will have more trouble with the British than with the Boches.

"God favors the brave, victory is to the audacious."

*Letter, GSP, Jr., to Beatrice, March 4, 1943*

[Ike] will call again to tell me where to go. I think I am to replace Lloyd [Fredendall] but don't know and any how it may not happen . . .

Of course I don't expect to be killed but one can never tell. If I am, I will take lots with me.

*Diary, March 5*

Am leaving in a few minutes for Algiers. Hope for the best.

His long wait had ended.

CHAPTER 12

# Tunisia: The Fight for El Guettar

*"God help me and see to it that I do my duty, but I must have Your help. I am the best there is, but of myself I am not enough."*

*Letter, GSP, Jr., to Beatrice, March 6, 1943*

Darling B. As I wrote you I got a sudden call to go to the vacinity of the place where John [Waters] was last seen. I flew to D's, leaving Rabat . . . [where] there was much tooting and band playing. The 2d Armored gave me three ruffels and played your piece [the Armored Force March].

D met me at the air port and gave me some verbal instruction and told me to go on to Constantine.

At the Maison Blanche airfield in Algiers, Eisenhower and Bedell Smith said that Patton was to replace Fredendall because the fighting in Tunisia "was primarily a tank show and I know more about tanks." Fredendall's relations with the British had been less than harmonious, and criticism of the British had to stop. Eisenhower scribbled a note in pencil and handed it to Patton as authority to assume command of the II Corps as soon as he arrived there. Fredendall had been notified of his "impending release."

Patton flew at once to Constantine and called on Alexander, "who seems competent." He later told Beatrice that Alexander was "very quiet and good looking" and impressed him "a lot."

Alexander informed Patton that the II Corps would no longer be under Anderson's First Army but would come directly under Alexander's 18th Army Group. Thus, Patton was to command a separate and wholly American sector, much like Pershing under Foch.

In his diary he noted that Alexander

> was very friendly and complimentary in his remarks, stating he wanted the best corps commander he could get and had been informed that I was the man.

Patton spent the night in Constantine. He spoke briefly to John McCloy, the Assistant Secretary of War, who was visiting the theater. His old friend W. Carey Crane, now on Alexander's staff, came to see him, "giving me a lot of dope on how to get on and we sat and talked till 1:00 [in the morning]."

Patton later remarked:

> I fear he [Eisenhower] has sold his soul to the devil on "Cooperation," which I think means we are pulling the chestnuts for our noble allies . . . It is clear that I too must "cooperate" or get out.

*Diary, March 6*

Arrived Headquarters II Corps 10:00. Gen. Fredendall still at breakfast. Very nice and conducted himself well — very well. His staff in general [is] poor. Discipline and dress poor. Lt. General Cochran, British Army, has been with Fredendall for some time. He clearly gave me the impression that he was sent to instruct me. I let him think he was doing so. He leaves in the morning.

I had Terry Allen, 1st Infantry Division, and Orlando Ward, 1st Armored Division, come in and explain the next operation . . .

Fredendall leaves in the morning.

I issued some orders on dress, saluting, etc. None have ever been issued [before]. It is absurd to believe that soldiers who cannot be made to wear the proper uniform can be induced to move forward in battle.

I think Fredendall is either a little nuts or badly scared. He won't fly to Constantine and proposes to leave at 3:30 AM by car. That is the safest time on the road.

*Letter, GSP, Jr., to Beatrice, March 6, 1943*

Fredendall is a great sport and, I feel sure, is a victim largely due to circumstances beyond his control. He says he is sure John [Waters] is alive, a prisoner, and Omar Bradley who is here feels the same. So I am much more incouraged.

> There is going to be a party [battle] here which I will be hoast of. I have Gaffey, Lambert, Koch here [from the I Armored Corps headquarters] to help pass the drinks [meaning to serve on the staff]. I hope it is a success, as it is about time. Terry Allen and Pink Ward are coming [to the party – would participate in the attack]. Also Eddy and Ryder, but as waiters [at first] not servers.
>
> By a strange coincidence the day I got the phone call to come here was a year to a day from the time we hit the desert first.
>
> Well this is one hell of a dump, cold and wet and nasty.
>
> "There is a tide in the affairs of men." I have had several but this one certainly looks like rather a high tide . . .
>
> I am wearing the woollies you sent and certainly need them. It is very hard on the men, especially the mud . . .
>
> Geoff [Keyes] is still carrying on my other party. I seem to have to double in brass as it were. I hope I live up to what seems to be expected of me as a duet player.

What he meant was that his assignment to the II Corps in Tunisia had no effect on his command of the I Armored Corps in French Morocco. Keyes was in temporary charge of the latter, and he was planning the invasion of Sicily to be carried out by Patton after the Tunisian campaign was over.

To make an official record of their conversation at the Maison Blanche airport, Eisenhower sent Patton a memo on March 6. Patton's "immediate task," he said, was to rehabilitate the American forces and prepare them for attack. He expected Patton "to respond to General Alexander's orders exactly as if they were issued by me. I want no mistake about my thorough belief in unity of command." He had brought Omar Bradley to the theater "to serve as my personal representative in a very broad capacity," and Bradley was available to Patton "for any duty you may desire." Eisenhower warned Patton about "personal recklessness." Patton had no need to prove his "personal courage" to Eisenhower, who wanted him "as corps commander – not as a casualty." He was to run his show from his command post rather than from the front line. He was to have no doubt about enjoying Eisenhower's "fullest confidence." And he was to retain no one "for one instant" who failed to measure up. "We cannot afford to throw away soldiers and equipment and . . . effectiveness" out of reluctance to hurt "the feelings of old friends." This frequently required more courage than anything else, but he expected Pat-

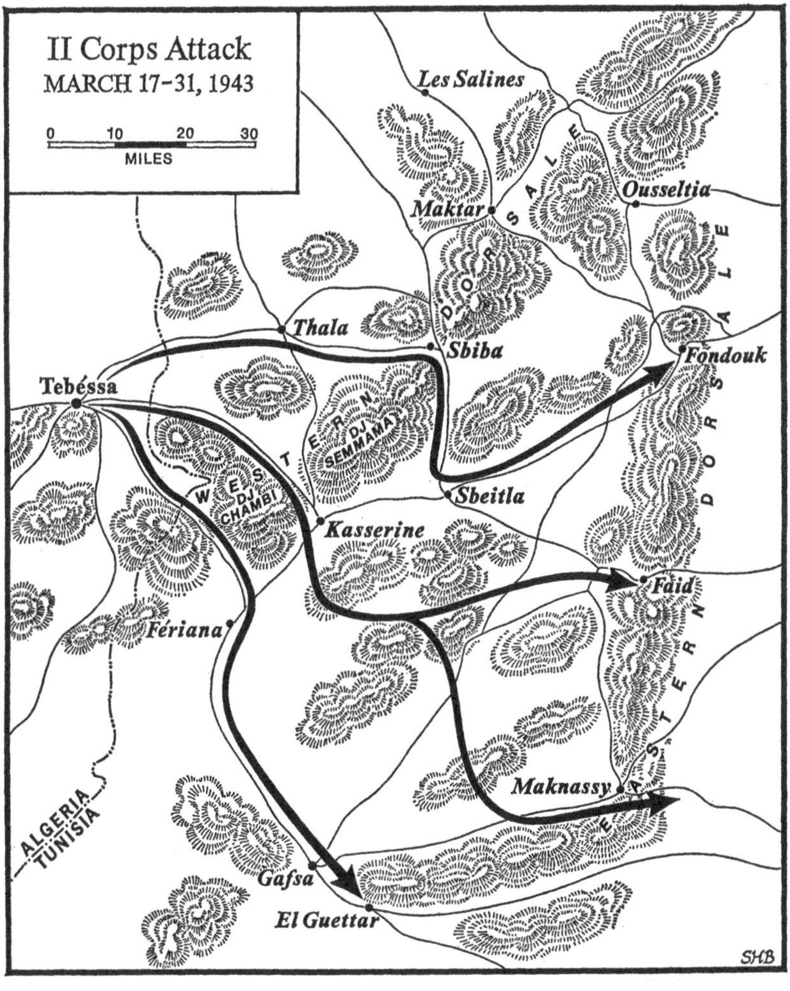


ton "to be perfectly cold-blooded about it." Patton was taking over a difficult but highly important assignment, and Eisenhower knew he could do the job.

In Tunisia Patton directed four divisions: Ward's 1st Armored, Allen's 1st Infantry, Eddy's 9th Infantry, and Ryder's 34th Infantry — altogether about 90,000 men. They occupied the southern part of the Allied front facing eastward. On their left were about 50,000 French troops. To the left of the French, in the north, were approximately 120,000 British. The Americans and the French were on the mountain range called the Western Dorsale, having been pushed there from the Eastern Dorsale by the Kasserine Pass battle.

The Allied attack being planned by Alexander had its locus in the south. Montgomery was to launch an operation to drive the Italo-Germans out of the Mareth positions and push them northward up the coastal plain, successively through Gabes, Sfax, Sousse, and Kairouan. If Montgomery compelled them to abandon the Mareth Line, so long as they held the Eastern Dorsale, which overlooks the coastal plain, they could protect a withdrawal to the north.

Patton's part in what was essentially Montgomery's show was to advance from the Western to the Eastern Dorsale. Specifically he was to retake Gafsa, thereby threatening Gabes from the flank. This, Alexander hoped, would prompt the Axis to divert troops from the Mareth Line to counter Patton and thereby weaken the defenses facing Montgomery.

Rommel, seeing no prospect of winning in Tunisia despite his victory at Kasserine, departed the country on March 9. He flew first to Italy, where he talked with Mussolini, then to Germany, where he saw Hitler. To both he urged the evacuation of the Axis forces from North Africa in order to avoid certain defeat and the loss of 200,000 men. The Axis leaders refused to heed his recommendation, and Hitler forbade him to return to Tunisia.

*Diary, March 7*

Up at 6:30, brakfast at 7:00. No one there but Gaffey. I told the cooks to close the mess at 7:30, so I believe that tomorrow people will be on time . . .

Issued an order yesterday detailing Omar N. Bradley as Deputy Corps Commander. Bradley and I inspected the 1st Armored and 9th Infantry Division command posts.

This country is really under water. Men have a terrible time, but are well and cheerful. Very cold – I damned near froze. Troops not too keen [to fight] – I hope I can pep them up.

Bradley was one of Marshall's favorites and a West Point classmate of Eisenhower's. Although Bradley had commanded a division in the

United States in a superior manner and was eligible to receive a corps command, he had no battle experience. At II Corps headquarters he would observe Patton as an understudy.

*Diary, March 8*

The discipline, dress, and condition of weapons at 34th [Division] very bad – terrible. On the other hand, elements of the division have fought well. Inspected their positions and found it weak, particularly in the emplacement of the 37 [mm.] anti-tank guns, which are on the crest instead of on the reverse slope where they belong . . .

Whole country full of ruins – great stones and pillars sticking up like ribs of wrecked ships or dead men through sand . . .

All division commanders, field artillery brigade commanders, and heads of corps staff sections came to supper . . . After dinner [II Corps] G–3 and G–2 gave plan and enemy situation. Allen and Ward gave their tentative plans. I finally approved plans, as altered, and fixed H hour . . .

My concern is for fear that the enemy will attack us first. This command post was situated . . . too far in the rear. I will change it as soon as the . . . operations start.

He was touched to receive from French Morocco a sheet of paper with a typed heading: "Good luck and God Bless you. If it isn't a private fight we would all like to go with you. From your staff." Fifty-one officers of the I Armored Corps headquarters had signed.

Kenneth Anderson sent him a nice letter. "It seems long ago since we last met at lunch at Claridge's," he wrote. "I am sorry to have lost [direction of the] II Corps just when you have taken command. I am sure you will fill it with enthusiasm and desire to kill the Boche."

"It shall be my earnest endeavour," Patton replied, "to live up to your kind thoughts concerning my ability to inspire the men of the II Corps with an adequate hatred for the Germans."

*Diary, March 9*

General Alexander and his Chief of Staff, Major General McCreery (brother of the international polo player No. 1) came . . . I had a guard of honor posted . . . and the General was very pleased . . .

I was very much taken with Alexander. He is a snob in the best sense of the word — very alert and interested in all sorts of things including genealogy . . . He seemed to agree with most of my [military] ideas. I really think he is a good soldier and much more talkative than he is supposed to be . . .

John Crane says that I am the oldest general in Africa and that he is next. I am the best anyhow.

Patton was struck with awe when he learned that Alexander had had four years in World War I, two years in Russia fighting Reds, one year on the northwestern frontier of India, and three years in World War II — altogether ten years of fighting — and had been wounded three times. "What a man," he wrote Beatrice.

*Letter, GSP, Jr., to Beatrice, March 11, 1943*

Darling B. This is the coldest damned place I have ever seen and it has rained every day since I came. To day it hailed also. As we are over 2000 feet up, that may explain it.

I was under ground in a phosphate mine for an hour to day and it was quite hot. I got several fine phosil sharks teeth which I will send if I can get them chipped out of the rock.

This whole country is covered with Roman ruins, villas, farms, rest houses. They are so common no one pays any attention. I have visited several but the arabs have played hell with most of them.

Yeterday Gen. Alexander and I . . . saw a big Arab lift a barrell of water up on the shoulders of a little woman. I said, "That is arab chivalry." Alexander said, "Let's stop and jolly well kick his ass." But we thought better of it.

I like him very much . . .

It is funny that I am not worrying at all about this next show. The only nusance will be if they attack first. Our men need an attack. They are a little too much interested in diging in.

So far I have not been straffed from the air, but it is bound to come, as I have to drive miles every day. If you see the plane in time, you stop the car and run like hell for 50 yds off the road and lay down. It seems most undignified but all do it.

Patton was to be ready by March 15, to reoccupy and reopen the Thelepte airfields, then move through Fériana and capture Gafsa. Once Gafsa was secure, he was to send other troops to Maknassy and seize a pass through the Eastern Dorsale. Meanwhile, because everyone was wary of what Rommel might do, Patton had to hold two divisions in the rear.

Eddy's 9th and Ryder's 34th Divisions would stay behind. Allen's 1st would move to Gafsa. Ward's 1st Armored Division would drive to Maknassy.

Actually, the II Corps attack was distinctly subsidiary and minor in purpose and scope. Patton was merely to mount a threat against the Axis in order to help Montgomery. Alexander had been so disappointed by the performance of the American troops during the Kasserine battle that he had little confidence in their ability to fight.

Patton preferred not to notice. "Soldiers," he announced to his men:

> All of us have been in battle. But due to circumstances beyond the control of anyone, we have heretofore fought separately. In our next battle we shall, for the first time on this continent, have many thousands of Americans united in one command . . . In union there is strength!
>
> Our duty . . . is plain. We must utterly defeat the enemy. Fortunately for our fame as soldiers, our enemy is worthy of us. The German is a war-trained veteran — confident, brave, and ruthless. We are brave. We are better-equipped, better fed, and in the place of his blood-glutted Woten, we have with us the God of Our Fathers known of Old. The justice of our cause and not the greatness of our race makes us confident. But we are not ruthless, not vicious, not aggressive, therein lies our weakness.
>
> Children of a free and sheltered people who have lived a generous life, we have not the pugnacious disposition of those oppressed beasts our enemies who must fight or starve. Our bravery is too negative. We talk too much of sacrifice, of the glory of dying that freedom may live. Of course we are willing to die but that is not enough. We must be eager to kill, to inflict on the enemy — the hated enemy — wounds, death, and destruction. If we die killing, well and good, but if we fight hard enough, viciously enough, we will kill and live. Live to return to our family and our girl as conquering heroes — men of Mars.
>
> The reputation of our army, the future of our race, your own glory rests in your hands. I know you will be worthy.

Bradley discussed with Patton several propositions Eisenhower had made with respect to Bradley's future. Bradley could go to French Morocco and take the I Armored Corps while Patton remained in command of the II Corps. Patton decided against that because he thought it was unfair to Keyes, "though possibly safer for me." Or, Bradley could stay on as Deputy Commander, work into the situation, and when the first phase of the Tunisian battle was over – whenever that happened – take the II Corps while Patton returned to the I Armored Corps.

> I accepted this as best. I am not at all sure this show [in Tunisia] will run according to plan and feel that as long as it is interesting Alexander will keep me. If it bogs down, I can get out. If Rommel attacks first, that will be something different – [and] he may.

No one on the Allied side seemed to know that Rommel had gone. Or perhaps it was more exciting to fight Rommel than anyone else.

> *Diary, March 12*
>
> We have done a lot [here] but much remains to be done. Fredendall just existed – he did not command, and with few exceptions, his staff was worthless due to youth and lack of leadership . . .
>
> Terribly cold. Took a drink to get warm.
>
> Eddy called at 2100 to tell me he had heard on radio that I am a Lieutenant General. Dick Jenson brought me a flag he had been carrying with him for a year. I am sleeping under the three stars [of Lieutenant General]. When I was a little boy at home, I used to wear a wooden sword and say to myself, "George S. Patton, Jr., Lieuenant General." At that time I did not know there were full generals. Now I want, and will get, four stars.

He had, in fact, been promoted that day.

> *Diary, March 13*
>
> Received order . . . to postpone D day to 17th. I fear Rommel will take initiative, but I shall not assume defensive. Sent Bradley to 34th Division to preach bloody war. 34th is too defensive. 9th has "Valor of Ignorance" [meaning it had yet to enter combat]. 1st is good. 1st Armored is timid . . .
>
> Having a big program on discipline. Fined several officers $25.00 a piece for improper uniform. Fined 35 men for same. Discipline consists in obeying orders. If men do not obey orders in small things,

they are incapable of being led in battle. I *will* have discipline – to do otherwise is to commit murder. Am also enforcing speed limits and intervals between trucks and demanding that maintenance [procedures] be examined [for improvement]. I cannot see what Fredendall did to justify his existence. Have never seen so little order or discipline.

I am just the same since I am a Lieutenant General.

*Letter, GSP, Jr., to Keyes, 13 March 1943*

The day and hour [of our attack] are as yet somewhat veiled and, within limits, the longer the delay the better. The situation is quite good except as to discipline which is bad, particularly with respect to vehicles. However, in the week we have been here, we have had some results and have at least got people to the point of buttoning their clothes and wearing the same kind of a hat.

*Letter, GSP, Jr., to Beatrice, March 13, 1943*

The Der Tag has been postponed but not for long.

Well at last I am a Lt. Gen. but there are so many of them that it has lost its zest. Still of course I am quite pleased . . .

It is funny how easy it is to do the things one has planned to do.

I am having a hell of a time with discipline. When I got here there was none. No salutes. Any sort of clothes and general hell.

Omar Bradley is my deputy and is good. He will get the job when I have finished this phase. If I do. I don't think it is too easy. However, it is perhaps a compliment to be used to do the fighting and still thought so important that I actually command on both coasts at the same time.

We had quite a little fight to day. We got three tanks and lost two planes. Life is never dull, but terribly cold. It is realy awful. Jimmy Doolittle is sending me a fleace lined leather coat. I guess it will be warm in two weeks . . .

Lots of love. George. *Lt.* Gen. (FIRST TIME)

*Diary, March 14*

Kasserine Pass is fierce and a sea of mud. We expected Rommel to attack today. That is why I went there, but nothing happened. McCreery met me when I got back at 1700 and brought me a bottle of Scotch, which I don't drink . . .

Think the soldiers are improving a little. Am sure it does good [for me] to be seen. Yesterday I took a walk and collected 8 soldiers and 2 lieutenants for improper uniform. Had them fall in and follow me — quite a procession . . .

It makes no difference where we fight provided we take and hold Gafsa. Whatever credit I get from this show will be due solely to personality unless, during the battle, something happens.

*Letter, GSP, Jr., to Beatrice, March 15, 1943*

I had been out in the rain all day [yesterday] . . . I was simply plastered with mud, and the mud in this part of the country is blue clay so that it sticks like cement and wont brush off.

The men here are taking an awful beating from the weather. If we can get out of these mountains onto the coastal plain, it will be warmer . . .

I have had so little time — less than ten days — [to prepare for the attack] that what ever I have done has been on the spiritual side and cooperating with the British. In fact cooperation is not the right word.

However, Alexander is o.k., though naturally selfish for his side just as I would be in his place. I do hope that I do my full duty and show the necessary guts. I rather dislike mines, and the whole damned country is full of them. We loose officers daily, mostly with legs blown off or broken. We have to have sand bags in the bottom of the cars. That helps some.

Yesterday Gen. T.R. [Teddy Roosevelt] and I got a little lost and were about six miles out side our front line. I felt scared till I came on some air listening post men who were putting up a station. I said do you know where you are, and they said no. So I told them to move to a healthier place. They had put out no sentinels — soldiers are funny.

There is a phospate mine here full of sharks teeth and things. I have one fine tooth and another fossil which the French say is the roof of a sharks mouth but which I think is the rear portion of a lobster . . .

I suppose it is an honor to be given all the hard nuts to crack. I hope my teeth hold out. The next nut after this one [the invasion of Sicily] is one I would willingly turn over to W. [Clark] but I had the chance the other day [to do so] and didn't.

Well I am always a little short of breath before a match. I wish it was the 19th [and over]. Love

*Diary, March 15*

A horrible [day] . . . Everything there was time to do has been done. Not enough, but all there is time for. Now it is up to the others [to fight] and I have not too much confidence in any of them. Wish I were triplets and could personally command two divisions and the corps. Bradley, Gaffey, and Lambert are a great comfort.

God help me and see to it that I do my duty, but I must have Your help. I am the best there is, but of myself I am not enough. "Give us the victory, Lord."

Went to bed and slept well till 0600.

*Diary, March 16*

I feel well . . . and am "radiating confidence." Actually I am quite confident and not at all worried the way I should be. The only trouble I have is a cold sore on my lip. The hardest thing a General has to do is to wait for the battle to start after all the orders are given.

Around 11 P.M., Patton heard firing north of Gafsa. "Well, the battle is on. I am taking off my shoes to go to bed."

Allen's men made an approach march during the night and on the morning of March 17, detrucked near Gafsa. Taking the town against relatively light opposition, they moved a few miles down the Gabes road toward El Guettar.

*Diary, March 17*

The great and famous battle of Gafsa has been fought and won. The show was well done . . . I went up to the OP [observation post] . . . and could see the troops moving and the shells, mostly ours, bursting . . .

I used my new scout car with the three stars and II Corps flag. At first I was nervous for fear of air attack, but soon got used to it. Courage is largely habit and self-confidence. I thank God that He has again aided me.

The battle of Gafsa was "great and famous" because it was good to see American troops, after their dismaying performance at Kasserine Pass, take the initiative and win. The triumph restored confidence and underscored Patton's ability to succeed. The capture of Gafsa received wide publicity in the United States to counter the shock of Kasserine.

A radio program on prime time, 11:15 P.M., took listeners

to a desert oasis in the wilderness of Tunisia . . . the much fought for town of Gafsa [where] . . . a hard-hitting, fast-thinking American hero is tonight planning his next move. He entered Gafsa today with his tanks and men . . .

And we can be certain that the General was at the head of the line, very likely in the very first tank . . .

General Patton is a great leader, and Mrs. Patton too was certain that he was right at the head of that column . . .

The story is making the rounds that hard-fighting General Patton is supposed to have made the promise that he would neither smoke nor drink until he had entered the city of Tunis. According to Mrs. Patton, the General is not the kind who makes promises. He does not talk about what he is or is not going to do. He simply does it . . .

The general is a man with a strong sense of discipline both of body and mind. He is hard as nails . . . He was a wonderful horseman and polo player. Still is. Still carries a small revolver we are told . . . "The idea is to hold the enemy by the nose and kick him in the rumble seat." Except that the general who has a vocabulary that is as virile as his body did not say rumble seat.

If any American officer ever had the will to win, that man is Lieutenant General George S. Patton.

He certainly won the first round today . . . Apparently the Nazis saw him coming and ran, and not a single American soldier was lost, according to reports . . .

The General, very likely, slept very little. He never sleeps much, I have been told. Another day has begun, a day on which General Patton with his irresistible spirit will inspire his American tank forces to follow him again closer to the coast . . .

Certainly the prayers and best wishes of every American are with that six foot, lean, determined American tank expert, on whose shoulders has fallen the task of helping to bring the battle of Africa to a head . . .

As the Oasis Gafsa may well become a milestone in the battle of Africa, so the name of the fighter, Patton, may well become a symbol of victory.

*Letter, GSP, Jr., to Beatrice, March 18, 1943*

I commanded in a pretty big battle . . .

We took a famous town and had practically no casualties. It was a very well run show . . .

I tried to get in, but we hit a mine field and had to stop. The Dagoes beat it and I fear we got few prisoners, but the air and artillery killed a lot of them.

I was going to attack again this morning, but it rained all night so we had to delay. It is blowing like hell now so we may have a go at them in the morning if the guns can move accross country. When I started forward, I was realy scared of an air attack but soon got used to it and stopped worrying.

Ike and Alex were both here telling me to stay back, which cramped my style, but any how this high command keeps me out of the real front line stuff, and honestly I rather resent it. But when one is fighting Erwin [Rommel], one has to be near the radio.

If you hear that I have been relieved, don't worry, there is a reason. Anyhow I will finish this show which will take some weeks. We have to go slowly to get confidence going in the troops. Terry is really good and so are his men. I am not too happy about John's outfit [1st Armored Division], but they will come back. I may have to relieve a general.

Ike and Alex seemed very well pleased. I hope they stay that way. But realy I have a hell of a job fighting with men I have not trained and with a staff I don't know. I have only Hugh G. [Gaffey], Kent L. [Lambert], and Oscar K[och] . . . with me. All the rest are boy wonders, but the G–2 [Dickson] is good.

The weather is frightful cold and wet. Jimmy Doolittle gave me a fur lined leather coat or I would freeze.

The Roman ruins are wonderful and all over one gets quite used to passing huge cities and not even knowing the names . . .

I have found out why all the pillars are broken: the Romans pinned them together with bronze pegs, and the Arabs pushed them over to get the metal. What a race!

It is hard to realize that the Romans were here [for] 700 years . . .

The great city of Thelepte is near here but I have not had time to investigate it. It is supposed to have the finest temple to Minerva in the world. I can see the columns sticking up from the road. There is a roman mile post in the yard of this building with dates and distances all over it. I could get some wonderful relics if I could move them, but they are all too big. There is a fine torso of a senator laying in the yard too. It is life size and probably weighs a ton.

I feel terribly sorry for the men in this cold . . .

Note to Censor: I am having Gen Gaffey censor this, as autograph hounds steal my letters if I sign the outside.

On March 18, the Ranger battalion, working with Allen's division, took El Guettar, ten miles east of Gafsa. The forces in that area would continue to push forward, consolidating their defenses against a possible Axis counterattack.

By then, Patton was looking to Ward's 1st Armored Division.

*Diary, March 18*

The 1st Armored Division is largely stuck in the mud.

Alexander . . . was satisfied with the situation . . . Ike left . . . He was in good form and like his old self . . .

If I can, I will start to push in on Maknassy tomorrow. All depends on the amount the ground dries . . . Of course the weather hurts the Boche as much as it does us. I feel that if we attack first we will have an advantage in making the enemy dance to our tune.

*Diary, March 19*

Left for 1st Armored Division . . . Drove over [new] road we had made, about 42 miles. Took three hours [to drive]. I never saw such mud nor such men as the Engineers who built and are maintaining it. Wet, dirty, and isolated, they keep right at it. I stopped and talked to each group and complimented them on what they had done and they seemed pleased . . .

Called on General [Paul] Robinett . . . Don't like his mental attitude — he is defensive and lacks confidence. I talked attack. Called on Ward. He is in a sea of mud, really awful . . . He fears that tanks can't move, due to mud, but I told him to do it with [his] infantry . . . I told him to use all available half-tracks to move infantry weapons. I want to hit Rommel before he hits us, also to help Eighth Army, which attacks tomorrow night . . .

When I got back, McCreary . . . was here. He explained the future plan of the campaign to us and sent outlined instructions for future operations.

Patton found these instructions galling. While holding Gafsa, the Americans were to take Maknassy and the heights immediately beyond, then stop. Just when capture of the Maknassy high ground would signify a penetration of the Eastern Dorsale, the Americans were to halt. Instead of continuing eastward to cut off the Axis facing Montgomery farther south, they were to watch the British push the Italo-Germans up the coastal corridor. As soon as Montgomery passed Maknassy, the II Corps would be out of action and have nothing to do.

It is noteworthy that these instructions definitely prohibit an American advance to the sea. In other words, we continue to threaten the enemy's right flank, but we do not participate in cutting him off.

In brief, this is to pinch us out so as to insure a British triumph. I kept my temper and agreed. There is nothing else to do, but I can't see how Ike can let them [the British] pull his leg so. It is awful. I hope I will be back in Morocco on the other job before we are pinched out . . .

Oh God, let us win in the morning! . . .

The more I think about the plan of pinching us out, the madder I get, but no one knows that except me.

Feeling, perhaps unconsciously, that if Ward's division reached and held the Maknassy heights, Alexander could hardly deny him the opportunity to enter battle on the coastal plain, Patton soon began to push Ward with a passion that verged on obsession.

*Letter, GSP, Jr., to Beatrice, March 19, 1943*

I drove about 150 miles to day visiting the two fronts [Allen's and Ward's] and past countless Roman ruins. This country is simply lousy with them . . .

We are putting on a show in the morning. The weather is awful but it cuts both ways, and I feel that if I strike first, Erwin [Rommel] will have to parry. Owing to the fact that he may also strike in the morning, I must stay here.

*Diary, March 20*

Omar Bradley woke me at midnight to read me the radio that John [Waters] is safe [captured] . . .

I had to sit at the phone all day – a hell of a way to fight a war. I hope to get in tomorrow . . . Both the 1st Infantry and the 1st Armored will attack. The Eighth Army jumped off tonight. I think that if Rommel reacts, he will do it tomorrow. I feel that I will lick him so long as the Lord stays with me.

*Letter, Jenson to Mrs. Patton, March 20, 1943*

Today all looks rosey — we got the news last night that Johnnie Waters is safe . . . It certainly lifts a dark feeling we all had . . . Next job on the calendar is to get him back, and if things keep going along as well as they are, that isn't altogether in the realm of hope or wishful thinking.

It seems that we get one bit of super news each week up here, the previous one being the third star — it didn't cause too much excitement, because all of us were just waiting, but the final recognition of the Old Man, which he should have gotten long ago, is the grandest thing that could have happened to him. Believe me, he is ten years younger in feeling and appearance, part of which is due to his having something real to do, and the strain of sitting around doing nothing is over, part to the rightful star, and now the finding that Johnny is ok tops the picture. If he gets any more good news, we will have to sit on him to keep him down. I think the hex is over.

We have had a regular epidemic of visiting firemen around here recently, but as usual most of them left when the hunting season opened up, and without going up to see what was going on. However, we make regular runs into the front areas, and it is quite a shot in the arm to the men — the General's theory of showing himself has certainly paid dividends in morale already.

*Diary, March 21*

I went to the front and sat on forward face of hill . . . Shortly after I left, the place where I had been sitting was struck by a salvo of 150's [shells] almost on the spot . . .

Things were going too slow. Wrote Ward a message to use more drive and keep his command post at the front. We were strafed twice on road but nothing hit near me.

Keyes, who was visiting in Tunisia, advised Patton to "go up personally and push Ward's attack" for the Maknassy heights. Since Patton had written Ward a strong letter the day before, he thought that a visit "might scare him to death." He sent Gaffey instead, but "Ward simply dawdled all day, finally capturing the town of Maknassy, but has not taken Maknassy Heights." Patton blamed himself for not following Keyes' advice. "If I had led the 1st Armored Division, we would have taken the heights." Patton then ordered Ward to launch a night attack against the hills. Ward did so, but failed to take the ground.

*Letter, GSP, Jr., to Malin Craig, March 22, 1943*

[I am] engaged in the third round of the battle with my old college chum Rommel. So far, since we have only fought his Italian allies, we have been quite successful. In fact, yesterday we took in 1400 of them. My aide refers to them as "additional Roman ruins."

*Diary, March 23*

The Lord helped a lot today. I visited the Surgical Hospital – it was pretty gruesome but it was strange how the men followed me with their eyes, fearing I would not speak to each one. I talked to all who were conscious. One little boy said, "Are you General Patton?" I said, "Yes," and he said, "Oh, God." Another one said, "You know *me*. You made a talk to my battalion at Casablanca." I told him I remembered him well.

I hate fighting from the rear, but today it was too complicated to leave the telephone. Ward has not done well – no drive.

On that day, at El Guettar, Allen's men stopped a German and an Italian division, both attacking up the Gabes road toward Gafsa. This was a notable American success for two reasons. Patton's advance had in fact attracted these Axis forces that would otherwise have been used against Montgomery. And the Americans manifested a strong defense without signs of hesitation or panic.

Patton made no note of this in his papers. He was hardly interested in defensive prowess. He was oriented toward the attack, and that meant Ward's 1st Armored Division.

*Diary, March 24*

After dinner I found that the 1st Armored Division had still failed to get the heights . . . so I called Ward on phone and told him to personally lead the attack on the hills and take them.

Now my conscience hurts me for fear I have ordered him to his death, but I feel that it was my duty. Vigorous leadership would have taken the hill the day before yesterday. I hope it comes out alright.

As a result of the above orders, the 1st Armored Division attacked, led by Ward, and gained a temporary foothold on top of the ridge but were unable to maintain it, due to the fact that they had wasted so much time that the position was too thoroughly organized to be held with the troops available. I, therefore, ordered the 1st Armored

Division to quit attacking and consolidate. In the course of the above attack, Ward received a slight wound. He showed good personal courage.

*Letter, GSP, Jr., to Beatrice, March 25, 1943*

I got awfully mad with Pink Ward for his slowness in taking a hill so last night I told him to lead the attack in person. He did and got hit slightly. He could not hold the hill as it was solid rock and we could not dig in. I think I have made a man of Ward . . .

This job of commanding . . . is not much personal fun because . . . I cant leave the CP due to the width of my front . . . I fear the papers are making an unnecessary hero out of me. I never felt less deserving in my life. The only way I influence things is by providing drive and keeping my temper with the B's [British]. Some times that is hard to do.

Yesterday I was down looking at a small attack and a shell hit near enough to rattle on the jeep. Luckily they were small pieces and did no harm. The day before I had to get out twice and run for cover when the air straffed me but it sounds much more thrilling than it is in fact.

I have visited the clearing station and surgical hospital daily. The men like to see me. Few of them are suffering and all but a couple are cheerful. The treatment of the wounded is much better than last war, and the food is good. They give all the men a shot in the arm before they take the ambulance ride. Every soldier has three hypos, a bottle of sulpher nilimade pills and some powder. He can give himself a shot and then takes a pill every five minutes until the bottle is empty. He dusts some of the powder on the wound.

The blood plasma is fine too. Lots of the belly wounds are curing . . .

I still get scared under fire. I guess I will never get used to it, but I still poke along. I dislike the straffing most.

I told you I think that an Arab shot at me and I missed him, worse luck.

*Diary, March 25*

Gaffey woke me to say that Allen had telephoned that his position was penetrated and that he needed the [additional] battalion . . . to defend the town. I decided to send it, then went to sleep and slept soundly. In the morning, as is usual, things looked less gloomy.

*Diary, March 27*

Visited 1st Armored Division near Maknassy and talked with Ward, explaining the ensuing operation. I also told him that he lacked drive and trusted his staff too much in that he presumed orders were carried out and did not take the trouble to find out that they were. He admitted this. I also told him that if he failed in the next operation, I would relieve him. He took it very well. I decorated him with the Silver Star for his action in leading the attack. I believe his action would have merited the DSC except for the fact that it was necessary for me to order him to do it.

*Diary, March 28*

I have little confidence in Ward or in the 1st Armored Division. Ward lacks force. The division has lost its nerve and is jumpy. I fear that all our troops want to fight without getting killed . . .

Found a chaplain who was poking around the command post while wounded were being put into ambulance close by, and gave him hell.

On March 28, with the Axis showing signs of abandoning the Mareth Line, Alexander authorized a more active role for the II Corps. Ryder's 34th Division now marched to Fondouk to seize the pass and make the Axis think he would drive to Kairouan and threaten, even more rearward, the flank of the withdrawing enemy. Eddy's 9th Division moved to Gafsa to help open a hole in the Axis defenses and make possible a drive by tanks down the road toward Gabes.

*Letter, GSP, Jr., to Marshall, March 29, 1943*

I am very remiss in writing to thank you for my promotion but I have been so busy trying to make my operations justify your choice that I have not had the time . . . At the moment, all four [of my] divisions are in action on slightly better than a one-hundred-mile front. However, this is not as bad as it sounds because three divisions are well-grouped and the fourth – the 34th – is on a sort of raiding mission to the northeast. Of course the general scope of the operations is specified by . . . [Alexander]. All I have [to do] is the actual conduct of the operation prescribed. I would like to interpolate here the fact that I find General Alexander extremely able and very fine to serve under . . .

In battle one can never tell what is going to happen, but up to the present I believe that you have cause to be satisfied. We are trying to be simple, not change our plans when once made, and keep on fighting.

*Letter, GSP, Jr., to Stimson, March 29, 1943*

Please accept my sincere thanks for my extra star. I am doing my best to justify the selection . . . The biggest fight to date is going on as I write and it is very hard for me to sit in an office. However, in order to control so many units on so large a front, it is necessary to spend some time near the telephones. Yesterday I was fortunate in getting up to a regimental command post during the fight. It really is not as dangerous as it sounds. The nearest I have come to being hit was when a shell bursted beside the road and splattered my command car. But it was only small pieces and none of them came through . . .

Unless something strange happens, we should have, I hope, quite a big success by tomorrow or the next day.

Ward shifted some of his units to El Guettar for a lightning drive toward Gabes. Patton had told him to have his troops ready to go by dawn, but the poor roads in the area delayed the movements, and the men were in place only by 7 A.M. "I am very disgusted. I would relieve Ward but fear this is the wrong time. I will send Bradley with him when he breaks out."

McCreery telephoned with orders from Alexander and later Alexander's operations officer amplified and detailed them. Patton was somewhat resentful because Alexander was telling him where to place his battalions.

> I feel that I must respectfully call General Alexander's attention to the fact that in the United States Army we tell officers what to do, not how to do it, that to do otherwise suggests lack of confidence in the officer . . . I feel that, for the honor and prestige of the U.S. Army, I must protest.

For the breakthrough down the Gabes road, Patton put the available units under Colonel C. C. Benson, who had been a tanker under Patton in France. He had great confidence in Benson's aggressiveness. Yet he recognized that if the enemy had "plenty of artillery, Benson may not get through. The worst danger is that the hole may close behind him. I feel confident that with God's help, it will work."

*Diary, March 30*

We moved all artillery forward last night to support the attack...

Ryder, 34th Division . . . wants me or Bradley to come up. I will send Brad. He is good, and I will be needed here...

Benson jumped off at noon, which was very creditable considering the amount of movement necessary [beforehand]... I watched from a hill and got shelled, then went forward over the road, which was under pretty accurate fire . . . Benson's attack was held by a mine field and we lost 3 tanks and 2 [tank] destroyers. I am not wholly satisfied with his attack. On the other hand, the conditions under which he had to operate were almost impossible for armored vehicles...

The life of a General is certainly full of thrills, but I am not worried, only cold all over. I wish I could do more personally. It is awful to have to confide everything to others, but there is no other way, and if you trust people, they seem to perform. "God show the right."

# CHAPTER 13

# Tunisia: The Fight for National Prestige

*"Ike is more British than the British and is putty in their hands. Oh God, for John J. Pershing."*

*Letter, GSP, Jr., to Beatrice, March 30, 1943*

Benson is trying to break through. I went with him part way and got shot at quite a little but not too close . . .

My old fear of fear came up again to day. There was a bad place on the road that they were shelling quite accurately. I began to find reasons why I need not go any further but of course I did and nothing happened.

I attatched Dick [Jenson] to Chauncy [Benson] for the operation to get him blooded. There will possibly be a big tank battle in the morning. We are trying to cut Rommel off and he don't like it . . .

On the defensive the Italians fight well. The Germans are very tough and well fed and cockey, especially the officers, but we are beginning to catch them . . .

The hardest thing I have to do is to do nothing. There is a terrible temptation to interfere but actually the men on the ground have to do the fighting and by and large they are doing well but there is room for improvement.

. . . I agree with Fred [Ayer] that I get a lot of cheap publicity and fear that I shall get a lot more. There are 49 correspondents and photographers here sniping at me.

Last night we had an alarm. It was air [alert] but I thought it was ground [attack] and ran out with my carbine. The old lust of close battle [is] hot as ever though I admit I hate shells and bombs.

*Diary, March 31*

This morning things look pretty bad. We seem to be stuck everywhere . . .

Benson's attack . . . broke through . . .

Eddy called me and asked that I change the plan . . . I told him it was too late. Had I listened to him, Benson would not have got through. Sometimes I earn my pay. One must be chary of ever changing a plan . . .

Beedle Smith and McCreery came . . . with a plan which I suggested the day before yesterday. It would have worked then. Now, as usual with them, it is too late.

I told Beedle about my getting orders that were too detailed. He will speak to General Alexander. I also think I got Beedle to see that battle-hardened troops are necessary for Husky [Sicily] — they are . . .

I called Ward on the phone and told him to put on an attack . . . and, if necessary, to take losses up to 25%. Our people, especially the 1st Armored Division, don't want to fight — it is disgusting.

I feel quite brutal in issuing orders to take such losses, especially when I personally am safe, but it must be done. Wars can only be won by killing, and the sooner we start the better; also an attack by the 1st Armored at Maknassy will pull the enemy off from Benson and possibly from Ryder.

I sent Bradley up to see what is the matter with Ryder. Ryder must hold on.

*Letter, GSP, Jr., to Beatrice, April 1, 1943*

Darling B. Dick Jenson was killed this morning. I have asked Beedle Smith to wire you and to notify Echo [his mother].

It was my fault in a way but this I did not tell Nita or Echo in the letters I have just written. We were putting on a tank attack under Chauncy [Benson] and were short staff officers so I sent Dick and Bradley sent his aid[e].

The attack went very well and this morning Bradley and two other generals went out to the C.P. While they were there 12 J.U. 88's bombed it. Every one jumped in a slit trench. Bradley was not ten feet from Dick. Unfortunately a 500 pound [bomb] hit right on the edge of the trench Dick was in and killed him instantly. It was concussion that got him. He never knew a thing. He was not mangled in any way.

We brought him to the cemetary here at Gafsa and will bury him at 4:00 P.M. Gaffey and I went out to see his body wrapped up in a shelter half. I knelt down and kissed him on his forehead. He was a great character and loyal long suffering friend. I shall miss him very much.

I feel very sorry for Echo. I cut a lock of his hair and sent it. I will send all his trinkets as soon as I can find them.

We are having quite a battle but are doing well. I hope we keep on. The air bombing is pretty bad but there is not much one can do about it. I may be next [to die] but doubt it. I still have a lot to do.

*Diary, April 1*

[Jenson's] watch stopped at 1012. I am terribly sorry as he was a fine boy, loyal, unselfish, and efficient. As soon as he was brought in, I went to the cemetery with Gaffey. He was on a stretcher rolled up in a shelter half. We uncovered his face and I got on my knees to say a prayer, and all the men did the same. There was some blood from his mouth, but he was not mangled, and I doubt if he was hit. There was a small stone bruise on his forehead. I kissed him on the brow and covered him up.

At 1600, Stiller, Sgt Meeks, Sgt. Mims, and I went to the cemetery. Dick was on a stretcher wrapped in a white mattress cover. We had a squad and a trumpeter, but did not fire the volleys as it would make people think an air raid was on. The corps chaplain read the Episcopal service and he was lowered in. There are no coffins here, as there is no wood. Lt. Stiller, Lt. Craig, Sgt. Meeks, and Sgt. Mims carried the stretcher. They were all his friends . . .

He was a fine man and officer. He had no vices. I can't see the reason that such fine young men get killed. I shall miss him a lot . . .

[McCreery] directed that the tank attack be called off . . . One cannot change plans in war.

The plans of the Allied High Command are all about 3 days to a week too late, and too timid. When we took Gafsa we were told to halt at El Guettar. We waited there from the 19th to the 22d and gave Boches time to bring the 10th Panzer [Division] down from the north. At the same time they told me to take Maknassy and halt on the hills just east . . . Here I failed by not personally backing the attack on the heights. Ward fooled around for 3 days and let the enemy build up and then he attacked with great personal courage but failed to take the ridge. However, I [had] asked to take the whole 9th Division in with the 1st Armored and was only allowed to take [part] . . . Not enough . . .

This morning McCreery told me to continue the attack with infantry. Now at 5:00 PM I get a note from Alexander suggesting, but not ordering, the use of armor. I will start with infantry and use armor if I get the chance.

*Letter, GSP, Jr., to Keyes, April 1, 1943*

Poor Dick Jenson went west this morning . . . I am terribly distressed . . .

I think we should bend every effort to get battle-hardened troops for the other operation [Sicily]. As you know, the 1st and 9th have both now had amphibious and mountain warfare . . . The 1st [Armored] needs discipline and training, and the 2d [Armored] needs battle experience . . .

I am really more broken up over Dick than I can express. I did not know how fond I was of him.

Several weeks later he explained to his brother-in-law in more detail what had happened at Benson's command post.

They had three big radio sets working and made the mistake of not moving the command post about every four hours. The result was, in my opinion, that the Germans intercepted on the three radios and figured that it must be something big and so deliberately sent 12 bombers — I believe they were JU 88's — to wipe it out.

They dropped about 36 500-pound bombs and only killed three men and wounded several others.

The bomb that caught Jenson was within a foot of his slit trench, and the concussion killed him. There wasn't a hole in him, but he was perfectly dead. He never knew what hit him.

General Bradley . . . was in the next trench, not five yards away, and wasn't hurt.

One man got a direct hit, and we could not find him for three days when we began to smell pieces of him, but we never found any portion of his body. Another man sitting in a tank was killed by concussion, and the tank was somewhat damaged in its electrical appliances, but was not materially injured.

*Letter, GSP, Jr., to Frederick Ayer, April 1, 1943*

This is the dirtiest place I have ever been. It was built by the Arabs and occupied by the French and then by the Italians. Every part of it smells like a very old toilet and most of it is. You cannot drink any of the water, eat any of the fruit, or use any of the latrines. If and when I get back to America, I am going to build myself a large bathroom and live in it.

In the United States, huge posters were being printed and distributed to factories. They had a few lines of text in large characters:

Old Blood & Guts attacks Rommel
"Go forward!
"Always go forward!
"Go until the last shot is fired and the last drop of gasoline is gone and then go forward on foot!"
— Lieut. General George S. Patton, Jr.
Dare we working here do less?

*Diary, April 2*

The action was very slow, due to strong enemy resistance, very difficult country, and the fatigue of our troops . . .

Had letter from Alexander asking that I relieve Ward. Radioed AFHQ for Harmon [to take Ward's place]. Photographed Dick's grave and had some flowers put on it.

Our air cannot fly at night, nor in a wind, nor support troops. The Germans do all three, and do it as the result of three years' experience in war. However, in all fairness . . . there is less wind on the German airport near the coast than there is on Thelepte airfield in the mountains.

The Situation Report, called Sitrep, was a routine paper produced every day to inform higher and adjacent headquarters of what had happened during the preceding 24 hours. The II Corps Sitrep of April 1, mentioned that front-line troops in the corps area had been "continuously bombed all morning" by German planes. The reason, according to the Sitrep, was: "Total lack of air cover for our [ground] units has allowed German air force to operate at will."

No doubt reacting to the death of Jenson, killed by German planes, Patton sent the same message out over his own signature.

When Air Marshal Conyngham, Alexander's air officer, read the Sitrep, then Patton's reiteration of the accusation, he became enraged. He immediately sent his own message to all headquarters in Tunisia, as well as to Eisenhower's AFHQ. The facts, he said, were that II Corps had lost 4 men killed and a "very small number wounded." Having at first regarded the corps Sitrep as an April Fool joke, Conyngham hoped that the II Corps was not trying to use the "air force as an alibi for lack of success on the ground." If Patton's Sitrep was "in earnest," "it can only be assumed that II Corps personnel concerned are not battleworthy in terms of the present operation." He suggested that "such inaccurate and exaggerated reports should cease" and that the II Corps Sitrep was only a "false cry of wolf."

This of course enraged Patton.

*Diary, April 8*

I got the most outrageous telegram . . . from Air Marshall Conyngham. He accused me of being a fool and of lying. He said that our calls for air support were due to the fact that American troops were not battle worthy and used the cry of wolf for lack of air support as a means of excusing our slow advance . . .

We had 15 men killed, 55 wounded, and sustained 51 air attacks, in which 161 [German] planes took part.

At noon, Chief Air Marshall Tedder, Lt. General Spaatz, and some boy wonder by the name of [Laurence] Kuter arrived, and Tedder said at once, "We did not only come about the Conyngham signal but because we wanted to see you."

I told them I was glad to see them and that I intended to take up the telegram officially [that is, make an issue of it]. They were clearly uncomfortable and talked a lot about [Allied] air superiority. At the height of this [conversation], 4 German planes flew right down the street not 50 feet from the window, firing machine guns and dropping small bombs. No one was hurt.

The appearance of the German planes could not have been more felicitous in proving Patton's contention. When the aircraft had gone, Kuter later remembered, Tedder asked Patton how he had arranged the German demonstration. Patton responded, "I'll be damned if I know, but if I could find the sonsabitches who flew those planes, I'd mail each one of them a medal."

Later that day, Conyngham's headquarters put out another message:

"Signal relating to air operations on II Corps front . . . is to be withdrawn and cancelled."

At about the same time, in a letter to Eisenhower, Patton made known his feelings. Conyngham's first telegram, he said, "naturally . . . made us quite mad and very disgusted." His second telegram, Patton said, was "an altogether inadequate apology to United States troops." He thought that Conyngham "should make a categorical apology for his specific criticisms of our soldiers."

*Diary, April 4*

Conyngham asked if he could call on me around noon. As I felt I might not want to eat with him, I had lunch early. He arrived at 1215. I asked him to come in, but made no motion to shake hands. I also asked Gaffey to be present.

Conyngham started by saying, "I am dreadfully sorry for that horrible signal. I want to apologize and do what I can to make amends."

I said, "So far as I personally am concerned, I am willing to accept your apologies and forgive you for indicating that I was a fool, etc., but I cannot accept an oral apology for your calling 60,000 American soldiers unbattleworthy and failing in their duty."

He said, "I would never have done it but I had received a barrage of requests all day. I am proud of my air force and will not have them criticized."

He spoke quite loud and I responded, equally loud, that my men had been under barrage all day due to what I considered was his fault. Then I added, "Pardon my also shouting, but I too have pride and will not stand for having Americans called cowards. I have asked for an official investigation. If I had said half what you said, I would now be a Colonel and on my way home."

He cooled down and said, "I am awfully sorry. What can I do to make amends?"

I said, "If you will send a message specifically retracting your remarks about the lack of battleworthiness of our men, and send it to the same people to whom you sent the first message, I shall consider the incident closed."

He said, "I will."

I then offered him my hand and took him to lunch. When he left, he said, "I can't thank you enough. You have been very generous."

I said, "It is always easy to be generous to a gentleman who admits his mistakes."

We parted friends, and I think we will now get better air support than ever before. I was rather proud of myself, as I was firm, but moderate. I doubt if he ever sends the telegram of retraction because Ike will tell him it is not necessary . . .

After I got through with Conyngham, I felt ill with pains in my back, so I inspected the front lines but was not fired at.

On the following day, Conyngham informed Eisenhower and Alexander that he had visited Patton to express his regret that his message had been misinterpreted

as a slight to American forces . . . I explained that a mistake in transmission had caused signal to read "Two Corps personnel concerned" instead of "Few Corps personnel concerned." I gladly renewed assurance of my regard for American forces . . . General Patton and I agreed to cancel the mutual signals which constituted the incident and to consider the matter ended.

*Letter, GSP, Jr., to Conyngham, April 5, 1943*

Please accept on the part of myself and the officers and men of II Corps our most sincere appreciation of your more than generous signal.

Personally, while I regret the misunderstanding, for which I was partially responsible, I cannot but take comfort and satisfaction from the fact that it gave me an opportunity of becoming better acquainted with you, because to me you exemplify in their most perfect form all the characteristics of the fighting gentleman.

On the file copy of this letter retained by Patton, he added in pen: "The sentence, 'for which I was partially responsible,' I put in – though a lie – to save his face. I may need his help some day in another matter."

In a message to Alexander, Patton asked that a telegram be sent to acknowledge with gratitude "the magnificent [air] support" received by the II Corps." He added, "I am sure that however unfortunate the misunderstanding may have been, it has had the effect of drawing us closer together."

"So far as I know," he wrote in pen at the bottom of the letter, "this suggested telegram was never sent."

Eisenhower assured Patton that he had taken up the "adverse criticisms" before receiving Patton's message. He realized how chagrined Patton was and understood why Patton felt that some public retraction or apology was required. However, complete Allied teamwork was all-important and there was little point in "demanding the last pound of flesh." He was certain that Conyngham appreciated the gravity of his error. There was "a certain amount of unwise distribution of your Sitrep," but he had no intention of pursuing the matter further. All senior officers had to work together to defeat the Axis, and a frank and friendly exchange of views would avoid irritations. He refused to permit criticism "couched along nationalistic lines" and hoped that Patton would fully present his views to Alexander when necessary.

He added a postscript. A copy of a telegram just received from Conyngham indicated that the incident had been entirely cleared up. Eisenhower was delighted, "but the principles I have enunciated are still applicable."

In Patton's handwriting: "It is noteworthy that had I done what Conyngham did, I would have been relieved. Ike told me later that he could not punish Conyngham because he was a NewZelander and political reasons forbad. Unfortunately I am neither a Democrat or a Republican – just a soldier."

On April 3, Alexander sent Patton his "Notes on Future Operations." There was to be a change in the Fondouk area, where the 34th Division had been in action several days. In accordance with Patton's orders, Ryder had carried out a demonstration – making noise rather than attacking seriously – since the purpose, according to Patton's understanding, was to threaten, but not actually to make, a drive through the pass toward Kairouan. The American presence alone provoked a prompt and strong reaction on the part of the Axis. Because a thrust beyond Fondouk would interfere with an Axis withdrawal up the coastal plain, German and Italian troops counterattacked and almost sent Ryder reeling back. Precisely because Fondouk had become vital to the Axis, Alexander increased the Allied strength there. He ordered Lieutenant General Sir J. T. Crocker's IX British Corps to take command and to bring in the British 6th Armoured Division and 128th Infantry Brigade. Together with the 34th Division, these units were to make a real offensive effort. Thus, Patton's II Corps would lose Ryder. With the locus of the battle shifting northward, Fondouk had first priority on troops and supplies. This meant that Patton would have to furnish artillery units and other elements from his forces in the south.

In the El Guettar area, Alexander wanted the 1st and 9th Infantry Divisions to defend against possible enemy incursions up the Gabes road and at the same time make the enemy think that an American breakthrough on that road was imminent.

At Maknassy, he wished "the most aggressive action possible when the enemy starts his withdrawal from this area." He wanted very active reconnaissance to insure early warning of any signs of enemy withdrawal.

And finally, as soon as Montgomery broke through the Axis positions in the south, the 9th Division was to move to a new front being established in the north near the Mediterranean.

Patton was outraged, but Eisenhower had given him his marching orders, and he said nothing. He confided his reaction to his diary:

> The U.S. troops get wholly separated and all chance of being in at the kill [the final battle in Tunisia] and getting some natural credit is lost. Bradley and I explained this to Ike and he said he would stop it. He has done nothing. He is completely sold out to the British. I hope the Press at home gets on to it. Brad and I have decided to saw wood and say nothing. If he [Eisenhower] falls, it is not our fault. I hope the Boches beat the complete life out of the 128th Brigade and 6th Armored Division. I am fed up with being treated like a moron by the British. There is no national honor nor prestige left to us. Ike must go. He is a typical case of a beggar on horseback — could not stand prosperity.

*Diary, April 4*

Sent Bradley to Maknassy to tell Ward he was to be relieved. While Alexander has written me a letter asking that I relieve him, I did not use this as a cloak for my act. I should have relieved him on the 22d or 23d, but did not do so as I hate to change leaders in battle, but a new leader is better than a timid one.

Alexander had made his reservations on Ward known to Eisenhower, who had insisted that Alexander inform Patton.

*Diary, April 5*

General Bull [Eisenhower's deputy, who had been visiting Tunisia] left for Algiers to see Ike. His attitude is, I think, unfortunate. He is very critical of all we do and is very prone to argue in favor of the British. Bradley and I had a long talk and decided to answer any questions Bull propounds . . . but to volunteer neither advice nor information. We feel that the U.S. is being sold out for a theory, and that the theory is bad. There is no attempt to aggrandize the American Army. We have fought continuously for 19 days and have never given ground. The Eighth Army has fought 5 days. We have pulled the 10th and 21st Panzer [Divisions] off them and it is gently – not too gently – intimated to us that we are not doing our best . . .

We asked at noon today for night reconnaissance [aircraft] tonight. Were told that it was operationally impossible, as the Air Force had other more important duties – probably sleeping. Result, we will be unable to tell whether the enemy withdrew after his feint, as we think, or whether he is still waiting to attack [us]. We have no information as to Eighth Army.

Eisenhower was writing to Patton: "Alexander has told me that your corps is *not* to be pinched out of the coming [final] campaign." The II Corps was to have "a definite sector and mission."

*Diary, April 6, 1943*

Benson . . . was very slow and put on a half-hearted attack . . . When things looked bad yesterday, I decided not to leave Gafsa alive. Bradley was with me. The decision was a comfort and did much to harden our hearts.

*Diary, April 7*

A phone message from McCreery to the effect that our tanks were timid, and that we were to push on regardless of losses. I had already ordered Benson to break through and damn the expense.

Geoff Keyes came last night to talk about "Husky" so I asked him to come with me . . . I stopped at Benson's command post and told him he must succeed or else, and that I was disgusted with his slowness yesterday. I asked him to push on until he got into a big fight or hit the ocean.

We went to the OP of Colonel [Edward] Randle. The ground is appalling. Had a good view of Benson's advance, which was meeting little resistance except from long range fire. I called Gaffey to tell him to have Benson move faster. We then drove back and headed east on the Gabes road [behind Benson]. We found Benson eating lunch — not much — so I told him to stop eating and get out in front, and he moved out. He was being delayed by a mine field. We drove through the mine field . . . At this time there was only one jeep and one scout car ahead of my jeep and everyone told me I was going to be killed. I told Benson . . . keep pushing for a fight or a bath [in the ocean] . . . Shortly after I turned back, Benson's advance guard made contact with a patrol of the . . . Eighth Army. As it was, I had no idea they [the British] were around and was simply doing my duty as I saw it. I don't think there was any danger in it.

Over a thousand prisoners were taken by Benson's force.

Patton's exploit was courageous; it was personal leadership at its finest. But meeting British instead of Axis troops meant that the Italo-Germans had escaped to the north.

How Patton would have liked to slash into the flank of the withdrawing Axis forces!

At 1940 [that evening] Brigadier Holmes, 18 Army Group, called me on the telephone and I told him that we had broken through and that Benson was going to the sea. He told me to order him back . . .

In the morning we had been ordered to push on regardless of losses. After having spent thousands of casualties making a break-through, we were not allowed to exploit it. The excuse is that we might interfere with the Eighth Army . . . One can only conclude that when the Eighth Army is in trouble, we are to expend our lives gladly; but when the Eighth is going well, we are to halt so as not to take any glory. It is an inspiring method of making war and shows rare qualities of leadership, and Ike falls for it. Oh! for a Pershing.

I must have been more tired than I realized. Went to bed at 2200 and never woke until 0600. Sic Transit Gloria Mundi.

A letter from Keyes came a few days later:

I noticed in the papers that the Eighth Army had made contact with your corps, which seemed rather odd, inasmuch as the meeting took place some fifteen miles inside their boundary.

That brought the fighting in the south around Gafsa, sometimes called the battle of El Guettar, to an end.

*GSP, Jr., II Corps General Orders 25, April 8, 1943*

Soldiers of the II Corps: after 22 days of relentless combat in mountains whose ruggedness beggars description, you have won the battle of El Guettar. Each one of you, in your sphere, has done his duty magnificently.

Not alone on the front line where death never ended his gruesome harvest, but everywhere else, all of you have demonstrated your valor and constancy.

Over countless miles of dusty, wind-swept roads, often under fire from the air or from artillery . . . under the most rigorous field conditions . . . in small, isolated groups or as individuals . . . [against] the lurking hazards of mine fields . . . [you] gave, as ever, proof of . . . untiring devotion and splendid courage . . .

Due to your united efforts and to the manifest assistance of Almighty God, the splendid record of the American Army has attained added lustre.

He sent letters of commendation to Allen and Eddy, praising them and their men, who "never faltered" and who, "undeterred by cold, lack of sleep, and by continued losses," conquered in "relentless battle," and whose "valorous exploits have brought undying fame" and "added new and imperishable laurels to the proud record of the United States Army."

*Letter, GSP, Jr., to Beatrice, April 8, 1943*

I have just won a pretty big battle . . .

Of course we lost plenty . . . Of course many are wounded and will be back soon . . .

Our job was to pull stuff away from the Eighth Army. We sure did . . .

Yesterday . . . Chauncy [Benson] with about 90 tanks . . . did not go fast enough so Geoff . . . and I went along. After a while . . . there was only a peep and a scout car in front of us . . . About a mile after I quit we made contact with the Eighth Army. It is just as well that I was not there, as it would have looked theatrical . . .

It has not been a too pleasant war. Some times I have ridden in [horse] shows when I knew the judges were hostil. Well it is the same here. D is one of them . . .

Some day the truth will come out and the sawdust baskets will be full. I do just what I am told to the best of my ability and ask no favor or make no explanations. How I wish JJP[ershing] was twins . . .

I think it likely I will soon return to Rabat to get ready for a bigger and better show. I think things will sort of peter out here, at least so far as we [Americans] are concerned, JJP being absent.

If the papers say I have been relieved, don't worry. I was only pinch hitting here. Bradley will take over the trouble. He is a swell fellow.

*Diary, April 8*

This morning a new boundary was assigned to the II Corps [now] consisting of [only] two infantry divisions . . . [and] precludes us from breaking through [the Eastern Dorsale and interfering with the Axis withdrawal]. Just what becomes of one infantry division and one armored division [remaining in the II Corps] is not said.

At lunch McCreery called, and, after his usual giggle, said that the 34th Division needed a medium artillery battalion [at Fondouk]. I replied, "I thought you would," and heard him shudder, so I added, "You see, we always think alike."

McCreery also said that he might have to ask Patton to take the Faid Pass, just above Maknassy, to help the attack at Fondouk. "I had expected that too and had already sent a medium tank battalion up."

*Diary, April 9*

I have worried a lot over the future of the II Corps and the American army, so this morning Bradley and I decided to go and have a look at the battlefield, from the enemy side . . . After seeing how strong the [enemy] position was, I don't wonder that we took so long to take it. I wonder that we ever drove them out . . .

McCreery brought Field Marshal Lord Gort [Governor of Malta] to lunch. Gort is not an inspiring type. McCreery gave us the new setup.

The II Corps, with the 9th and 34th Divisions and half of the 1st Armored, was to move to north Tunisia and deploy to attack Bizerte. The 1st Division was to be withdrawn from operations to get ready for Husky.

It may be for the best . . .

Things look pretty good but I fear the [news]papers will make too much of a play about me. I have not yet begun to fight.

*Letter, GSP, Jr., to Surles, April 10, 1943*

I was pitch-forked into this thing on one day's notice and only commanded the corps for 10 days before going into battle. Probably that accounts for not having demoralized it. As a matter of fact, I think I considerably improved it . . .

I cannot too strongly express my admiration for the unwavering and cheerful fortitude of the American soldier. He is a great fellow . . . I do not deserve or desire publicity, but I do believe that everything that can be handed to the American soldiers, whether they be in the front lines or on the lines of communication, should be handed to them.

On April 10, he left at 8:30 A.M. to see how the 1st Armored Division was preparing its attack on Faid pass.

Harmon was in his command post, and so far as I could see, nothing had been done but issue orders . . .

Went to see McQuillin, who was to lead the attack and get him started. When we got there, nothing had been done either. McQuillin told me, with evident pride, that he had just issued the orders. I asked him where the leading elements were and he did not know, so I took Harmon and went forward.

We were assured that Sidi-bou-Zid could not be entered because it was full of mines and booby traps. We drove through it with impunity and went up a dirt road toward the Pass – no mines.

At last we came to the engineers, who had just removed 10 mines. I told the recon[naissance elements] to move off the road and push on. Lost two half-tracks but saved hours of time.

We finally got to the pass south of Faid and found that mines actually existed but were pretty thin, so we walked through the minefield to encourage the others. Mines are largely a mental hazard and must not be treated too seriously. I think my walking through the minefield saved about three hours.

We sent Harmon's aide . . . to kick McQuillin along. On the way back we met two [reconnaissance] companies . . . coming up the road through some artillery, but no tanks, yet clearly tanks should have led, as we were at the pass and might be counterattacked – no flexibility of mind, no desperate desire to get forward [on the part of McQuillin].

I left Harmon at Sidi to push [the attack], and drove along the main road to Sbeitla. I was assured it was mined. I heard later that the troops were much impressed by seeing me in the minefields. There was no danger. My luck in being at the right place at the right time held.

We got home about 1900 after some 300 miles in a jeep.

*Letter, GSP, Jr., to Frederick Ayer, April 10, 1943*

It was quite a show while it lasted, and our soldiers displayed a truly remarkable fortitude. It makes you proud to be an American . . . The fact that the whole area is covered with contact mines makes walking over it very irksome.

The II Corps After Action or Operations Report for the period March 15–April 10, a detailed record of the fighting, closed with Patton's tribute to the troops:

> The conduct of our troops under the most difficult of terrain obstacles, and in the face of a crafty and experienced enemy operating from carefully prepared positions, was courageous and unfaltering. Their valorous conquests have caused the enemy to fear them. Likewise their courageous exploits have earned for them the respect of their brothers in arms of other [Allied] nations. By their deeds of the past twenty-five days they have added luster to the imperishable laurels and proud record of the United States Army.

Alexander phoned early on April 11 and asked Patton to lunch to discuss the coming operation. Conyngham was there

> and greeted me as a long lost brother. At the end of the meal he took me aside and said, "I deeply appreciate your most generous letter." I replied, "It was from the heart." And the lightning did not strike me dumb [as a result of the lie], but I think I will get plenty of air [support] from now on.

Patton asked Alexander whether the II Corps would be under the First British Army during the new attack to Bizerte.

> He was uncomfortable but said that the question of communication made it necessary. I said I preferred to be under the 18 Army

Group direct. He said that if at any time I did not get on with General Anderson, I was to call him direct. (A very improper procedure.)

He was sure that the British neither hoped nor expected the Americans to do anything in the final attack on Bizerte and Tunis. "If, by chance," Alexander said, "we [the British] are about to enter Tunis, I will send for an American and a French Combat Team to march in with us." Patton thought this was an insult, "but I failed to see it on purpose."

He said he believed that going under the British First Army was hardly right. It was not so much a question of communication or supply as of national prestige. If America were not represented as an independent force, it would be very unfortunate.

On the way home Patton became increasingly convinced that the II Corps should all be present, including the 34th Division. He wrote Alexander saying that if the 34th were withdrawn as a result of poor showing in battle – at Fondouk – it would be useless in the future. Furthermore, since it was a National Guard unit from a portion of the country where pacifism was rampant, its removal "on the say-so of a British general" would have very far-reaching political repercussions.

> God damn all British and all so-called Americans who have their legs pulled by them. I will bet that Ike does nothing about it. I would rather be commanded by an Arab. I think less than nothing of Arabs.

*Diary, April 12*

The 34th Division . . . did not do too well, but that was largely because Crocker sent it on an impossible mission with both flanks open. After we had drawn off the Germans, the British came in and took their hill. I feel all the time that there must be a showdown [with the British] and that I may be one of the victims. Ike is more British than the British and is putty in their hands. Oh, God, for John J. Pershing.

Driving home I passed a Roman mile post that must have been there 1,300 years. How young we are! Visited hospital this P.M. Some pretty sick men but all cheerful.

*Letter, GSP, Jr., to Beatrice, April 13, 1943*

On the 10th, the 1st Armored forced the pass at Faid against practically no opposition. However, they did it in a remarcably short time, for which I was personally responsible . . .

It now seems probable that I will turn over the rest of this to Omar and get back to planning my next realy big job. I hate to quit fighting, but on the other hand it may be best for my reputation, as I look ascance at some of the arrangements now pending . . .

I have spent the day writing letters of commendation to individuals and divisions. Some of the latter don't deserve them, but I have to counteract adverse criticism from other sources. Whom the gods would destroy they first make mad. It looks to me like destruction of some people was imminent . . .

The nurses are doing a swell job . . .

I saw one poor devil yesterday missing a leg. I asked him how he felt and he said fine, since you came to see me.

I suppose I do some good but it always makes me choke up. I have no personal feeling of responsibility for getting them hurt, as I took the same chances, but I hate to look at them.

*Diary, April 13*

Bradley . . . went to Hq. 18 Army Group . . . to arrange details for the transfer of the II Corps to the north flank and to repeat my urgent request that we not be put under First Army. His primary mission was to secure the participation of the 34th Division . . . He succeeded . . . [The possible political repercussions] did the trick. Our real reason was to get the maximum number of troops into the area so we could make a real effort. I feel that the British don't want us to make a success. They have asked me to come to a conference in the morning. I feel that this may be a prelude to putting a British officer on our staff. Ike will be there and I will be interested in his reaction. I think it probable that he may send me back to work on "Husky." I would like to finish this fight but shall not argue, as it seems to me that I am in the hands of fate, who is forging me for some future bigger role.

Patton wrote to Devers:

You may smile when I tell you that the confidence you expressed in me in your last letter was a constant source of comfort and inspiration to me.

*Diary, April 14*

Bradley and I left this morning in two cubs to meet Ike at Haidra . . . I got stuck in fog so landed at Thelepte and took some gas from an ambulance. Tried it again and got through. Bradley in second cub did not make it – went back to Thelepte and came on by car. Ike also landed at Thelepte and came in by car . . . When he met Bradley and me, he never mentioned our victory – some leader.

We three saw Alexander who, be it noted, did not come to the airfield to meet his alleged boss, Ike. Ike talked a lot and let Alex do just what he wanted to. Ike said that he "did not consider himself as an American but as an ally." And he told the truth. What an ass and how tragic for us. He is all heated up about "Husky" and said that he felt that I should let Bradley carry on in Tunisia and go back to work on "Husky." I said that if I was to go, today was the best time, as it would permit Bradley to make the arrangements for the next move. Eisenhower agreed to this and wrote me an order to publish to the corps.

I hate to quit a fight but feel that I had best do so as I fear that on the north flank, where Alexander has put us, there is no future; also the II Corps will be under the First British Army. I fear the worst . . .

I have been very fortunate so far. I hope the Lord keeps helping me. Saw Clark – he was sour as a pickle. I think I have passed him, and am amused at all the envy and hatred I wasted on him and many others. Looking back, men seem less vile.

*Letter, Eisenhower to GSP, Jr., April 14, 1943*

With the successful completion of that phase of the Tunisian operations for which I placed you temporarily in command of the II Corps . . . I hope that you . . . personally will accept my sincere congratulations upon the outstanding example of leadership you have given us all.

Successful he had been – in rehabilitating the II Corps and giving the men a fighting spirit, in following his orders strictly, and in leading his troops to a victory of sorts. But he regretted the cautious mode of operation by the British which had prevented him from unleasing a smashing drive against the flank of the withdrawing Axis forces, who held the passes of the Eastern Dorsale and marched virtually undisturbed into northern Tunisia. Now a final battle would have to be fought. And the American part would be up to Bradley.

*Diary, April 15*

II Corps Headquarters starts north this morning. Stiller is taking my three radio scout cars and jeep back by road with most of my staff. Gay, Sgt. Meeks, and I are driving to Constantine via Timbad . . . (Timgabia) . . . founded by Trajan in 200 or 100 A.D. It is a wonderful sight . . . Arch of Trajan, and thousands of houses . . . The ruts made by the chariot wheels are six inches deep . . . I was tremendously impressed with this monument of a great and vanished race. Yet I have fought and won a bigger battle than Trajan ever heard of . . .

I had dinner [in Constantine] at Spaatz' mess. All his staff is British, and he and all his men are for a separate air force. This is absurd. The system of command by cooperation, which we now have in joint operations with the Navy, would simply be accentuated. There must be one commander for ground, air, and sea. The trouble is, we lack leaders with sufficient strength of character. I could do it and possibly will. As I gain in experience, I do not think more of myself but less of others. Men, even so-called great men, are wonderfully weak and timid. They are too damned polite. War is very simple, direct, and ruthless. It takes a simple, direct, and ruthless man to wage war. Some times I wonder if I will have to laugh at myself for writing things like the above. But I think not. I have developed a lot and my never small self-confidence has vastly grown. I am sure that with God's help I will succeed at "Husky" and so on to the end, which is far distant.

Before leaving Gafsa I picked some nasturtiums in the yard, and Gay, Sgt. Meeks, and I went to the cemetery to tell Dick goodbye. There are more than 700 graves there now.

*Letter, Mrs. Jenson to GSP, Jr., April 15, 1943*

My dear George. Thank you so much for your letter and also for the beautiful tribute you paid Dick. You gave him the happiest years of his life. After his Father's death, you took his place, and his admiration and affection for you was unbounded. The "old man" could do no wrong. I quite agree with you that he should not be moved from Africa. His personal belongings I would like to have . . . [With] undying gratitude to you for making it possible for Dick to do the things he wanted to do.

*II Corps Draft General Orders, April 15, 1943*

Upon the victorious completion of the operation for which I was placed in temporary command of the II Corps . . . I desire to again express my deep appreciation of the valor, loyalty, and unfaltering endurance of the officers and men . . .

It is my fondest hope that I shall again have the opportunity to command some or all of you, because I feel that you exemplify the highest type of American manhood.

I would be truly derelict in my duty and untrue to my heart if I failed at this time to pay homage to our glorious dead and valorous, uncomplaining wounded. God Bless the II Corps.

A telegram from Marshall: "You did a fine job and further strengthened confidence in your leadership."

*Diary, April 16*

Spent a while looking around Constantine . . .

Had a long talk with Spaatz on air support. I think he will do, but he lacks any idea of discipline. He flew us to Algiers in his plane. Butcher met us, and I spent the night with Ike. It appears to me that Ike is acting a part and knows he is dammed near a Benedict Arnold, and is either obeying orders (if so, he does it in a soldierly way without squealing) or else the British have got him completely fooled. In any case he is usually not telling the truth. He is nothing but a Popinjay — a stuffed doll. The British are running the show on the sea, on the land, and in the air. They are running it to their advantage and are playing us for suckers, not only in a military way but politically also.

The British dictate what troops come, what quantity and type of supplies we give the French, and how and where our troops are used.

There is no excuse for moving the II Corps to the north flank, where the ground is unsuitable for a main attack. We should have gone in at Medjez-el-Bab.

Lt. General Cocran, the s.o.b., publicly called our troops cowards. Ike says that since they were serving in his corps that was O.K. I told him that had I so spoken of the British under me, my head would have come off. He agreed, but does nothing to Cocran.

Bradley, Everett Hughes, General Rooks, and I, and probably many more, feel that America is being sold. I have been more than loyal to Ike and have talked to no one and have taken things from the British that I would never take from an American. If this trickery to America comes from above, it is utterly damnable. If it emanates from Ike, it is utterly terrible. I seriously talked to Hughes of asking to be relieved as a protest. I feel like Judas. Hughes says that he and I and some others must stick it out to save the pieces. I am not sure, but I love fighting and if I asked to be relieved, I would not even be a good martyr.

*Diary, April 17*

I talked very plainly to Ike this morning – strange to say he took it – but he has a sophist argument, probably provided by the British, for everything he has done. I told him he was the reverse of J. J. Pershing. He quoted the time in March 1918 when Pershing put every American at the disposal of Foch. I countered with the time of August in the same year when General Pershing told Foch that unless he issued orders for the concentration of an American Army, Americans would not fire a shot nor move a vehicle nor train. St. Mihiel was the result.

Had lunch with Hughes who . . . is more rabid than I am. Also, he points out, with justice, that Ike cannot even enforce discipline nor police regulations in Algiers.

Left at 1400 in a C-47 loaned by Spaatz and got in to Casablanca at 1800. Keyes and Harkins met me. I have been gone 43 days, fought several successful battles, commanded 95,800 men, lost about ten pounds, gained a third star and a hell of a lot of poise and confidence, and am otherwise the same.

*Letter, GSP, Jr., to Beatrice, April 17, 1943*

Darling B. Well the campaign or battle or what ever they call it lasted 43 days and I am back where I was and will be here or hereabouts for a while. Hewitt and Jim Hall and I are working together again.

Where the [news]papers heard of my reform in smoking and drinking, I dont know, but as a result everyone . . . wants to send me cigars and whiskey. It is very amusing. I think that is the way Grant got his cancer . . .

On the way home we drove to a place called Timgad . . . the finest ruin I have ever seen. Three public baths, a theater very well preserved, a public library with the plate giving the name of the rich man who donated it, a temple to Jupiter with columns six feet thick, a temple to Janus, a forum, a Christian church, and a whore house. The principle streets were paved in gray stone and the little streets in black stone. The sewer still works and there are several toilits with carved stone seats in which the water still runs. Right at the entrance there is a fountain still running after 1700 years.

What I cant figure out is how all these ruins got covered with earth but they all are.

I flew around quite a lot in a cub and passed many nameless ruins of villas, past houses, and ruins that I cant even place. The climate must have been much better then than now to have supported such a civilization.

I agree with you that I am too popular with the press but now I think they will take a crack at me. In a way as a cover plan [to deceive the enemy about the next operation]. It will be a good thing, so don't worry. The people who count know why what is, is. George [Marshall] sent me a wonderful telegram all by him self . . .

There was one fine thing done when the 10th Panzer attacked us. One platoon . . . died to a man. The last thing they were heard yelling was come on you hun bastards.

On the 7th I put 130 guns on two bosch battalions with 50 rounds per gun, rapid fire, the first 20 gave white phosphorus [shells], the next 25 high explosive. My idea was to make them think an attack was coming and then kill them. It worked perfectly. Hap [Gay] visited the place and he said it was a mess, just pieces of men laying around. Our infantry walked in with out a casualty. Prior to that they had assaulted five times . . . I was very proud of my little shoot.

We actually counted 800 fresh graves due to other fighting and we must have missed many as the ones counted could be seen from the main road. We had plenty too . . .

I am inclined to think that some people here are too optomistic.

*Diary, April 18*

Got up late . . . and went to church.

*Diary, April 19*

Worked on lessons from Tunisia.

His "Notes on Combat" summarized his observations of the Tunisian campaign. Some of them were:

Commanders and staff officers who spent their time "sitting in front of a map, plotting situations" were of little value; they had to "go to critical points to see that orders are being executed on time."

Plans had to be simple and never changed.

Officers had to have self-confidence and men confidence in their officers.

Officers had the "paramount duty to set the example in courage. They must be the last one to take cover and the first one to leave cover. They must not show emotion except the emotion of confidence."

"It is absurd to believe that soldiers who cannot be made to wear the proper uniform can be induced to move forward in battle. Officers who fail to perform their duty by correcting small violations and in enforcing proper conduct are incapable of leading."

In night attacks, "the more noise and light produced the better."

"Death in battle is a function of time. The longer troops remain under fire, the more men get killed. Therefore, everything must be done to speed up movement."

"During the attack, infantry must not dig in until the final objective is reached. If they do, they cannot be restarted. Furthermore, it is natural for them to think that when they are told to dig in they have accomplished their mission."

"To employ a unit smaller than a battalion against an active enemy is to invite disaster."

"Junior officers in reconnaissance units must be very inquisitive."

"Mines produce a greater effect on the mind than on the body. There is a very real danger of troops becoming too mine-conscious. When mines are encountered on a road, there is a tendency to sit still until they have been removed. In many types of terrain it is possible to avoid the mine field by moving off the road . . . Since the main purpose of the mine field is to delay, the thing to be avoided is delay. Violent and reckless methods must be used to pass mine fields."

Officers in battle had to be easily distinguished, and thus had to wear their rank. "When men see a marked helmet they know it is an officer. These markings are not visible at a range beyond 200 yards, therefore the timid excuse that they produce sniping is of no value. Sniping occurs beyond that range."

*Diary, April 20*

Completed notes on Tunisia and read up on next show.

# III
# Sicily

*"If I do my duty, I will be paid in the end."*

CHAPTER 14

# Husky: Plans

*"I gave a talk on valor and killing."*

*Diary, April 20*

So far, the invasion idea is pretty confused in my mind but I think that we are much further towards a perfect solution than we were in Torch.

As usual the Navy and the Air are not lined up. Of course, being connected with the British is bad. So far, this war is being fought for the benefit of the British Empire and for post-war considerations. No one gives a damn about winning it for itself now. No one busts a gut to get as many men as possible in. They talk about supply difficulties.

Patton had forgotten that wars are fought for political considerations. Military victory alone was never enough. The political aims of World War II and the shape of the postwar world were what the fighting was eventually all about. Whoever won the war would have his kind of postwar world, and the need to win kept the coalition together.

While Patton sorted out his impressions of the preliminary plans, he answered some mail.

"Judging from what I read in the papers," he wrote a friend,

> I fear that the public at home expect too prompt results. This is not a push-over war, and anybody who thinks it is, is making a mistake. We are in for some very serious fighting soon, but I am taking advantage of the rest period to catch up on my correspondence.

Because reports of his son George's "mathematical abilities, in which he takes after me" had him "slightly worried," he asked the Commandant of

Cadets at West Point whether he could, "if necessary get some less dumb cadet to coach him a little. It would be too bad if two successive Pattons were turned back in solid conics."

He reacted indignantly to a query from a friend:

> The picture of me covered with weapons is a profound lie. I did use two pistols during the landing, but when I went to see the French, I was completely unarmed except for a concealed pistol in my shirt which wasn't for the benefit of the French but for inquisitive Arabs who might meet me on the trip.

His sister Nita, who had never married after her disappointing friendship with Pershing, adopted two English children. They wrote to Patton from time to time. In one of his replies, he said, "Dear Peter and David, I am sure that you boys are doing your best to help Nita and are thereby aiding the war effort."

To his cousin Francis P. Graves in California:

> You have probably seen in the papers the exaggerated accounts of my reform, which have so far resulted in the unanimous offer of all the drinking men of America to provide me with liquor. Unfortunately, they are unable to do so. I have no particular brief against liquor as you know, but do feel that under the present circumstances, one has very little time for such indulgence, particularly when it is almost impossible to get any exercise except that induced by having one's hair rise on one's head when bombs drop.

To Senator Henry Cabot Lodge:

> In spite of the violent overstatements in the papers, we did have a very nice fight and were wholly successful . . . My usual luck held, first, in getting command of the show, and secondly, in winning the battle . . . As a result of this war, I have had three changes of heart – I believe in female nurses; I believe in heavy field artillery; and I am strong for telephone wires instead of radio . . .
>
> The only thing I got [out of Tunisia] . . . was the loss of some five or ten pounds. Instead of being scared stiff, I was scared thin.

Summarizing for his brother-in-law the dangers he had gone through:

My car got hit while I was in it. A 155 shell hit the spot I had been sitting on two minutes after I had left it, and another salvo threw mud all over me. An Arab just missed me – unfortunately, I missed him . . . Enemy planes pursued me down the road, which is a form of sport I am not interested in. Also, I was in the first vehicle going through a mine field. I got through all right, but the next vehicle blew up. This is enough of self-advertisement.

*Letter, GSP, Jr., to Beatrice, April 23, 1943*

I saw the swellest old book in a jewelry store to day. It was open at the picture of Montgomery spearing the King in the eye. It is a sort of a pictorial history of France with maps of each epoch. I am trying to buy it but no one is interested to find out what the owner wants . . .

We wont need any more [tanks] for a while but God knows we do need infantry and all we get is SOS [Services of Supply]. People who have not seen death should not make war, especially when they are too proud to learn. Everett Hughes feels even more strongly. I suggested that I resign but he says no, that the time will come [for me to gain glory]. I hope so.

Either D is nuts or else he is under wraps. I cant make out. He is suffering like hell and cant look at you. "Uneasy lies the head etc." . . .

While I was away I spoke no French and now speak much better than when I left. I guess one thinks in ones sleep and makes up sentences. Also I know how to change latin words into French.

His work on planning for Sicily started when he had lunch with several newcomers – Ernest Dawley, who commanded the VI Corps; Troy Middleton, who commanded the 45th Division; Fred Walker, who commanded the 36th Division; Maxwell Taylor, assistant commander of the 82d Airborne Division – as well as Truscott, who now commanded the 3d Division. They were all supposed to take part in the invasion of Sicily under Patton.

He was "most impressed with Middleton, and Dawley seems O.K. Walker is hard to size up." But he told Eisenhower that he was "very much pleased with both Middleton and Walker." He had known Middleton before, having gone to Leavenworth with him, but he "had never seen much of Walker. Both of them impressed me as being very sound, and I believe their troops will do."

After lunch they went over the invasion plans. Keyes made the general presentation "and did it very well . . . I gave a talk on valor and killing and cited a few lessons."

*Letter, GSP, Jr., to Bradley, April 23, 1943*

My dear Omar: It seems years since I last saw you and so far as news of you is concerned, you might be dead, so please let me hear from you and let me know how things are going . . .

I have continued to take your advice and say nothing . . .

I have requested authority to send Dawley up to you. Please see – and do not tell him that I said this – that he gets shot at a little . . .

I want to repeat that I never enjoyed service with anyone as much as with you and trust that some day we can complete our warlike operations.

*Letter, GSP, Jr., to Beatrice, April 24, 1943*

We left the US just six months ago to day and I have been in actual combat . . . 29 days of that time, which shows how slow war is.

*Letter, GSP, Jr., to Hopkins, April 26, 1943*

Due to your efforts, the two lower grades of the Legion of Merit have been liberated . . . I am certain that nothing so far done in the war will have a better effect on morale.

It is a splendid thing to be able to recognize merit, particularly in the lower grades, and I can assure you that in those grades we have much merit . . .

One of my pleasantest reminiscences of the Casablanca Conference is the opportunity I had of talking to you and thereby convincing myself how much the country owes to your outstanding personality.

*Letter, Marshall to GSP, Jr., May 4, 1943*

You did a masterful job in reorganizing the II Corps and joining with the Eighth Army to drive the Germans out of southern Tunisia . . . You set a stiff pace for Bradley, but he seems to be following through in excellent style.

I realize that the planning you are now occupied with is a poor substitute for active combat, but it is of the utmost importance, and, as you know, your turn will come soon again.

Patton and Keyes flew to Oran, then drove to Mostaganem, "our new home." On the way, they stopped to see some of the new landing craft to be used for the first time in the invasion. They watched a landing operation rehearsal. Patton was hardly impressed.

> The Navy was one and one-half hours late getting in and missed the right beach by eight miles. The unloading was fair but there was no drive at the beach, no one gave commands, no one led. The men bunched badly. It was very bad.

On the following day, they witnessed another practice landing. It was far from perfect. No single person took charge. The Navy brought the troops ashore at the wrong place. Cables and tow chains were improperly used. The assault waves failed to move across the sand and head immediately for the hills. "This will have to be corrected."

They went to see Admiral Hewitt. "He was very affable and in his usual mental fog."

Mostaganem, Patton wrote Beatrice,

> was said to be the first town in Africa occupied by the French and it is just as French as Saumur but not quite so dirty. I have gone steadily down hill in my houses, but this one is not too bad and has hot water in and out of season . . .
>
> We have a small office in an old school which has not been cleaned for some hundreds of years.
>
> It now appears that W[ayne] was given the chance to take Lloyd [Fredendall]'s place in the beginning but refused to go as a corps commander. Now he is about [next to] nothing, and I think knows it.
>
> While I hate to be where I am, it may have its silver lining, as the other side of the cloud [in Tunisia] is certainly not rosy.

He thought that two more infantry divisions were needed in North Africa, because

> the Germans are far from being driven out of Africa, and in any case, the more troops we get in Africa, the better we can train them and get used to battle conditions . . . For reasons which I do not understand . . . [we] have about 120,000 SOS troops imported over here. I can see no purpose in working ports if you lose the war.

McNair was visiting North Africa and while observing operations in Tunisia was slightly wounded. He asked Patton to come to the hospital and see him.

That same evening, Alexander's headquarters telephoned and requested Patton to be in Algiers for a conference to be held at noon the next day.

On April 28, Patton flew first to Oran, where he saw McNair. "We had a good talk, but too short," for he had to go on to Algiers.

> He asked me what I thought about combined [or Allied] command, and I told him it will not work. Allies must fight in separate theaters or they hate each other more than they do the enemy.

His flight to Algiers delayed by fog, he reached Alexander's headquarters at 1:30 P.M. He learned that Montgomery, who was to be present at the conference, was sick, and that Leese, who was to represent him, had been grounded by bad weather. The meeting was postponed until the following morning.

Patton dined with Bedell Smith, who informed him that the session had been called to hear Montgomery's objections to the invasion plan.

The existing plan of invasion grew from a suggestion made by the Combined Chiefs of Staff. They recommended seizing two major ports, Catania in the east and Palermo in the west. Through these harbors the Allies could bring the supplies needed by the invasion forces. The cities were also close to most of the airfields that had to be captured. The landing forces would then launch converging drives along the eastern and northern shores of Sicily to Messina, thereby driving the Axis out of the island.

Alexander, who would command the ground forces in Sicily, had Montgomery coming ashore in the southeastern corner of Sicily near Catania, Patton landing near Palermo.

But Montgomery was dissatisfied, and many important ground, naval, and air commanders gathered to hear his views, which Leese would present.

Actually, it was difficult for Alexander and Montgomery to plan the invasion properly, for they were still involved in the operations in Tunisia. Alexander therefore set up a special planning headquarters in Algiers under Major General Gairdner, who acted as Alexander's chief of staff for the assault on Sicily. McCreery, who had been Alexander's chief of staff in Tunisia, was posted to command a corps, and he was replaced by Brigadier Richardson, who functioned as Alexander's chief of staff for the Tunisian campaign. The lines of authority, clear on paper, were sometimes confused. Brigadier General Arthur S. Nevins, a member of Eisenhower's staff, worked with Gairdner to insure the presence of an American point of view. Eventually, staff representatives from Patton's and Montgomery's Armies would join Gairdner and coordinate the final pre-invasion arrangements.

What Patton later called "the famous meeting" started at 10 A.M., April 29. Attending were Alexander, Leese, Cunningham, Tedder, Vice Admiral Ramsey, Conyngham, Air Marshal Wigglesworth, Commodore Dick, Major General Browning, Gairdner, Richardson, who were all British officers; Patton and Nevins, the only Americans.

*Diary, April 29*

Alex started by saying that we had met to consider changes in the Husky plan proposed by Montgomery.

Cunningham said he wished to ask if it was not too late to change.

Alex said, "We will hear what the Eighth Army wants."

Leese read a paper which said that Montgomery objected to having his Army split [around the southeastern point] and wanted to attack as a united Army in the vicinity of Siracusa. Further that Leese's XXX Corps of two divisions . . . was too weak to attack near Licata and capture and hold the airports there. The whole was predicated on the possibility that the Germans could move . . . [four divisions from the mainland of Italy] to the Island. And further, in my opinion, to make a sure thing attack for the Eighth Army and its "ever victorious General," and to hell with the rest of the war.

Tedder said, "Really, gentlemen, I don't want to be difficult but I am profoundly moved. Without the capture of these airports [near Licata], the operation is impossible."

Cunningham said, "From a naval point of view, the massing of so many ships in the Siracusa area is to invite disaster, and besides, the chief merit of amphibious attack is to do so on a broad front and disperse enemy effort. I am definitely opposed to the plan."

Alexander said, "But if from our viewpoint, that is, the army, it is necessary, we must do it."

Tedder said, "We are all in it, it is not an army show, but three arms are in it. Besides, we can't support Patton unless we get these [air]fields."

I said, "I would like to stress that point because I am sure that without the airfields, while I may get ashore, I won't live long."

Leese was then asked if he could do his part if he got an extra division, which Cunningham said he could lift [that is, transport to Sicily].

Leese said that Montgomery would never consent to splitting his Army.

To me this is a small-minded attitude and very selfish. I whispered to Tedder that my force was split by more than 45 miles.

He said, "Say it out loud," and I did.

Alex said, "That the man on the ground must decide."

I said, "In view of General Alexander's remark, I withdraw mine." But [I said] that I felt sure if I refused to attack because my force was split, I would be relieved.

Leese said, "I am sure of it in your case, and there would be a file of asp[i]rants [to take your place]."

I am not sure whether he was insulting or not.

Alex said, "I think we should send a wire to the Prime Minister."

Cunningham said, "Why not ask Eisenhower? After all, he is Commander-in-Chief."

The argument got quite hot and lasted two and three quarter hours. At one point, Cunningham said, "Well, if the army can't agree, let them do the show alone. I wish to God they would."

At last it was suggested that Alex, Tedder, and Cunningham go to visit Montgomery and argue with him.

Cunningham said, "I shan't go. I also have something to do."

It was finally suggested that Conyngham go. Tedder said, "Fine, it will be good for Monty to hear his master's voice."

About then, the telephone rang and Alexander apparently got some bad news, for he and Conyngham left at once and the meeting ended in an impasse, all due, in my opinion, to lack of force on the part of Alexander, who cut a sorry figure at all times. He is a fence walker.

After the meeting broke up, I asked Cunningham if I had been too frank. He said, "Not at all. You were the only one that said anything and, in spite of your tactful retraction, what you said had a profound effect."

Tedder overheard me and said he was for me. He took me to lunch.

After lunch we were talking and Tedder said, "It is bad form for officers to criticize each other, so I shall. The other day Alex, who is very selfish, said of General Anderson, 'As a soldier, he is a good plain military cook.' The remark applies absolutely – to Montgomery. He is a little fellow of average ability who has had such a build-up that he thinks of himself as Napoleon – he is not." . . .

I believe this meeting . . . is of momentous import and may result in a complete change in the high command. I am sure that such a change must eventually take place.

Patton was probably somewhat uncomfortable at this conference dominated by British officers. It must have seemed terribly clubby to him, and the British humor made him feel like an outsider. He was aware too of undercurrents of jealousy and resentment, and he was uneasy. But most of all, it was a peculiar way to plan an operation. It was certainly not how Americans worked. As a matter of fact, the entire planning process for Sicily was unorthodox from any standpoint.

He wrote Beatrice his impressions:

Alex presided and Sir Andrew [Cunningham] protested, and dear old Monty was sick so Sir O. Leese pinch hit for him. Tedder and Conyngham were also there. In fact, I was the only foreigner. It was quite an internecine war, and all I had to do was listen and make three well chosen remarks. Strange to say I was on the side of Tedder and Andrew . . . It ended in a stalemate. It was one hell of a performance. War by committee.

If old Monty won't give in, I don't know what will happen. I should not be too surprised at a change in the top.

Bedell Smith telephoned several days later, on May 2,

and said that there are probably going to be some big changes in the Husky plan, and that Montgomery will be there to present his ideas, and that he thinks that . . . I should have a chance to be heard.

In view of the last meeting, I fancy that Monty will insist on his plan, which means that the airfields at Gela will not be taken. This situation can be solved either by our taking them or else by delaying our landings until the British eventually take them, or by using an ad hoc plan. I intend to do a hell of a lot of listening, but will not

> sacrifice American lives to save my job. I will get there as early as possible and see Cunningham and Tedder.

Patton obtained a plane for his flight to Algiers, but it was raining on May 3, and he, Muller, and Stiller had to drive. They left at 7:45. It was a "harrowing" trip. "The first 150 miles was along the coast, pretty but crooked and slippery. Then we hit a wash out and had to come back thirty miles and take the main road which was solid with trucks." They reached Algiers at 1730, "after the worst drive I have ever had."

The meeting was, of course, over.

Nevins had hastily prepared for Patton a summary of why Montgomery was unable to accept Alexander's plan. First, it provided insufficient strength to seize and protect the airfields in the southeastern part of Sicily. Secondly, it separated the landing forces. If Patton's assaults in the western part of the island were abandoned, both invading forces could be concentrated around the southeastern corner.

This concept had some disadvantages. The port capacities of Augusta, Syracuse, Catania, and other minor harbors in the southeast could hardly nourish the forces to be landed; western ports, particularly Palermo, were needed. Supply over the beaches for so large an invasion force was impractical. The Axis airfields in the west would continue to operate, and their planes would endanger the landings. Montgomery's and Patton's Armies would still be split and mutually nonsupporting. Montgomery's plan gave the impression, according to Nevins, "that U.S. participation has been completely subordinated to General Montgomery's views," and this was "likely to have serious adverse effect on morale and co-operation." Finally, much planning already in progress would have to be discarded, and the length of time needed for new plans might require a postponement of the invasion.

Nevins believed that Montgomery's plan was "practically accepted—only awaiting for a concurrence on your part."

> I reported to Ike and said, "I am sorry I am late for the meeting, but I did the best I could."
>
> He replied, "Oh, that's all right. I knew you would do what you were ordered without question and told them so. We had better get hold of Alex and Hewitt and show you the new setup."
>
> Alex, Hughes, Bedell . . . showed me on the map what had been

> done . . . Monty . . . so far as I can gather, simply refused to play ball; so Alex yielded in spite of the fact that the supply people say that the plan Monty wants is logistically impossible.

The plan now had the British hitting the eastern face of Sicily, the Americans the southern. Montgomery would go against Syracuse and Augusta. Patton would come ashore at Scoglitti and Gela, later capture the small port of Licata and three airfields near his landing beaches. Although Leese had said that the British could not take Licata and the airfields with two divisions and two parachute regiments, Patton was expected to do so with a force of the same size.

> I told them at once that I was going to land four divisions and two parachute regiments and take Licata straight off, and that the British would have to give me some supplies through Siracusa. They said they would. They promise easily, but even so it means we have to supply more than two divisions over the beaches [that is, without a port] indefinitely; yet the Navy says that after September 1st, beach supply is impossible. Well, we will do it anyway.
>
> Spent the night with Ike. Kay came to supper. Ike and I talked till 0120. He is beginning to see the light but is too full of himself. I was quite frank with him about the British and he took it.
>
> Alex told me, with great enthusiasm, how well the 34th Division had done [in the fighting after Patton departed Tunisia]. I did not remind him that I had had to force him to use it.

Since Patton seemed to have concurred in the new plan, Alexander, in Patton's presence, instructed Gairdner to telegraph Montgomery. He wanted Montgomery to send his chief of staff, Francis de Guingand, to Algiers and arrange the details that needed to be coordinated between the Western Task Force and Eighth Army.

Gairdner asked, "What if he won't send him?"

Alexander replied, "Then we will order him."

With respect to these arrangements, Patton said "that I felt in justice to all, a definite signed agreement should be reached with the binding effect of a treaty."

Bedell Smith backed him. He later told Patton "that Lord Gort, speaking of Monty, said, 'In dealing with him one must remember that he is not quite a gentleman.' "

That evening Eisenhower made a surprising remark to Patton. He said, "Perhaps Western Task Force should be an Army."

Believing that Eisenhower was talking about putting in the Fifth Army, Patton replied that he should hate to serve under Clark.

Eisenhower said, "I don't mean that."

What he meant was that he was thinking of upgrading the I Armored Corps to the status of an Army.

Tedder and Cunningham remained unhappy over the new plan of invasion. Tedder thought that the invasion and subsequent ground operations would fail unless the Axis airfields were overrun and captured at once or destroyed. Cunningham felt that his ships, now to be concentrated in the southeastern waters off Sicily, would present a grand target to Axis planes.

To overcome their objections and provide stronger Allied air support — better protection for invasion fleet and invading troops — Eisenhower ordered Pantelleria, an island 120 miles from Palermo, to be taken by massive and sustained air and naval bombardment. Pantelleria came into Allied possession several weeks before the invasion of Sicily, and its airfields permitted additional Allied planes to join those flying from Malta and Tunisia to bomb Sicily and cover the landing forces.

As Patton thought about the new plan for invading Sicily, he realized that no one had said anything about what was supposed to happen after the landings. It seemed to him that Montgomery would be in place to drive to Messina while Patton protected his flank and rear. In other words, Montgomery would make the main effort and have the chance to win a great victory while Patton had a distinctly subsidiary role. If this reflected Alexander's continuing estimate of the relative combat effectiveness of British and American troops, something would have to be done.

*Diary, May 4*

Bedell Smith . . . says that the reason everyone yields to Monty is because Monty is the national hero and writes direct to the Prime Minister; and that if Ike crossed him, Ike might get canned. Also that Monty is senior in service to Alexander [this was incorrect] and taught Alex at the staff college [this was correct], and that Alex is afraid of him . . .

Alexander's headquarters is very mad as it was their plan which was thrown out. They gave me a paper full of objections to the new plan, some of which are sound.

Nevins, Hewitt, Muller, and I went to see Gairdner.

I said, "We are on the same side and I want your help in putting up our side when Monty's chief of staff comes up. Specifically, I want all the paratroops and a definite written promise of supplies, via Siracusa, to make up the service for what we can't get in [over the beaches]; also, I want a definite boundary between Eighth Army and Western Task Force."

He said he would help, but that some one had suggested that we needed only two paratroop battalions.

I said, "While I have the highest respect for the valor of the U.S. troops, I do not feel that they are so superior to the British that an equal number of our infantry can succeed with only a third as many paratroopers in an attack which the XXX Corps considered impossible."

They saw the point.

*Diary, May 5*

I had Dawley . . . and the staff in to discuss our new attack. I initially planned to put the 45th at Scoglitti, 36th or 1st at Gela, and 3d at Licata, with 2d Armored Division split and 82d Airborne Division landing behind the beaches. Keyes suggested that we do that but hold one combat team of the 45th and one combat team of the 36th or 1st, and one combat command of the 2d Armored . . . as a reserve. This would result in little administrative change. I accepted the idea. No one present had any objection, so that plan was accepted. It all took about one hour.

Some day bemused students will try to see how we came to this decision and credit us with profound thought we never had. The thing, as I see it, is to get a detailed study of the tactical operation of the lesser units. Execution is the thing, that and leadership.

It was hardly as simple as that. Detailed planning would have to be done. But the staff would take care of that. Patton's contribution was to make the concept clear, and this was an essential part of his genius.

*Letter, GSP, Jr., to Beatrice, May 5, 1943*

The new set up is better in many ways than the old . . .

To day I had a meeting to arrange the details of the new plan. I did it in one hour. Of course I had thought about it all night . . .

Some times I fear that I do things too easily and don't worry enough. But they seem to come out. I hope they continue to do so . . .

We are fighting fanatics with non fanatics. Cromwell was faced with the same thing and in answer to it produced the "New Model Army." He used religious intolerance. That won't work now . . . God, what those 25 years of pacafism [between the wars] are going to cost us in useless deaths and lost battles.

I think D sees the light a little but he fears for his head if he stands on his feet. The other day he and Kay were out riding and a soldier yahooed at them. He told me he glared at the man ? ? ?

*Letter, GSP, Jr., to Bradley, May 5, 1943*

Please accept my most sincere congratulations on your magnificent work. I am just as tickled as if I had been there myself. Everyone tells me what a magnificent job you have done.

I spent yesterday with Ike who was loud in your praise, and I believe you will soon be promoted. I certainly hope you will, and in fact have ordered some stars for you.

*Letter, GSP, Jr., to Frederick Ayer, May 5, 1943*

The publicity I have been getting, a good deal of which is untrue, and the rest of it ill considered, has done me more harm than good. The only way you get on in this profession is to have the reputation of doing what you are told as thoroughly as possible. So far I have been able to accomplish that, and I believe have gotten quite a reputation from not kicking at peculiar assignments.

In this last show I was put in command . . . under circumstances very unfavorable . . . However, by the use of very violent and somewhat brutal methods, everything came out all right.

One thing which was tremendously impressed on me was the magnificent optimism and ability to live under horrible circumstances possessed by the American soldier . . .

I am trying to think of some method analogous to the one Cromwell used . . . of making our men more fanatical.

As an example, some of our engineers brought me in an Arab and a burro. The burro had panniers [baskets] full of German mines and covered with a little grass. I asked them why they hadn't buried him [the Arab]. They said that he was still alive. I said, "Well, go ahead and bury him," but they said, "General, he is alive." "Well," I said, "that can be corrected." It probably was. But when you think these men were being blown up by a dirty skunk like that and they had no animosity against him, it is very interesting.

The more I see of Arabs the less I think of them. By having studied them a good deal I have found out the trouble. They are the mixture of all the bad races on earth, and they get worse from west to east, because the eastern ones have had more crosses [mixture].

For instance, the Phoenicians occupied this part of the country for 1300 years. Then the Greeks came; then the Romans; then the Vandals; then the true Arabs, who were a low bunch to start with. In addition, at all times, there has been a negro infiltration so that the Arab is really something. I am getting so that they have the same effect on me as a toad.

You mention the fact that the bomb that got Jenson might have been close to me. As a matter of fact it wasn't . . .

It is rather interesting how you get used to death. I have had to go to inspect the troops in which case you run a very good chance – or I should say a reasonable chance – of being bombed or shot at from the air, and shelled or shot at from the ground.

I had the same experience every day which is for the first half-hour the palms of my hands sweat and I feel very depressed. Then, if one hits near you, it seems to break the spell and you don't notice them any more. Going back in the evenings over the same ground and at a time when the shelling and bombing is usually heavier, you become so used to it you never think about it.

It is about the same mental attitude that I have in the New York Horse-show. The first time I ride over the jumps, I am scared. By the end of the week, it is simply routine.

I think this is the reason that veteran troops have such an advantage over green ones. They think more clearly under fire. In fact, the green ones do not think at all, but our troops are getting to be considerable veterans . . .

I have appointed your friend, Charlie Codman, as Aide in place of Jenson. He possesses many qualities desirable in an Aide, including his ability with languages. In one of these big headquarters, and this is getting pretty big and will be almost three times bigger in the next show, one has to have a person of literary accomplishments to look after incoming and outgoing dispatches and see that the right things are done.

A proper Bostonian, an aviator decorated for heroism in World War I, afterward a wine buyer for S. S. Pierce – which required yearly trips to Europe – Lieutenant Colonel Codman had precisely those qualities of demonstrated courage and coolness, together with the social graces and a perceptive intelligence, that would make Patton increasingly dependent on his loyal and devoted service.

The general concept for the invasion of Sicily was now well established, and on May 7, Patton, Keyes, Harkins, and Muller drove to Algiers to meet with Montgomery and work out some of the details. Gairdner, Richardson, and Bedell Smith were also present.

> Monty had very definite ideas and avoided being pinned down as to what he would or would not do. I tried to get him to define a boundary [between British and American forces] and a phase line [showing initial objectives], but could not.
>
> Smith talked a lot and made nasty remarks . . . but really said nothing . . .
>
> Later, Monty, Keyes, and I went into a few details. It is my opinion that Monty got out of attacking Scoglitti and Gela for two reasons: the beaches are bad, and there are no harbors. I insisted that Alexander define boundary, number of paratroop objectives, and general plan of campaign, and do it in writing. I shall put a memorandum in on this in the morning.
>
> Monty is a forceful, selfish man, but still a man. I think he is a far better leader than Alexander and that he will do just what he pleases, as Alex is afraid of him.
>
> Went to see Hewitt who can only think of objections. I told him that such talk was beside the point, as we had been ordered to attack and were going to do so.
>
> Went to Alexander's headquarters and found all my staff [who were working there] confused in details and full of reasons why things cannot be done. I straightened them out by the simple method of showing a confidence which I don't feel, although I am pretty confident. I believe it my fate, and to fulfill it, this show must be a success . . .
>
> Heard a report that we are in Bizerte and Tunis. I wish Ike had let me stay on in command of the II Corps, but it is probably all for the best.
>
> Montgomery is a very forceful man. I begin to think that the new operation, from every standpoint except supply, is easier than the old [plan].

The news from Tunisia was good. Americans entered Bizerte and the

British took Tunis. Six days later, the last Axis troops would surrender, and organized resistance in North Africa would end. The Allies would take 200,000 prisoners.

*Diary, May 8*

Went to see Ike in the morning and found him much elated over his "great victory." I had bet him that we would not be in Tunis and Bizerte till after June 15th, and a second bet that we would not be in on May 8th. I lost both with great pleasure, so got a new 500 franc bill and presented it to him on a tray with a red rose and the remark "Hail Caesar."

He walked the floor for some time, orating, and then asked me to mention how hard he had worked – what great risks he had taken – and how well he had handled the British, in my next letter to General Marshall. I wrote a letter which largely overstated his merits, but I felt that I owe him a lot and must stay in with him. I lied in a good cause. As a matter of fact, I know of no one except myself who could do any better than Ike, and God knows I don't want his job.

While I was writing the letter, I heard part of his press conference. He was asked several times what had become of me. His official explanation was that at El Guettar a tank expert was needed, while in northern Tunisia an infantry expert was required. This fooled no one, and they kept on asking, so Ike finally said, "I have had to pull General Patton out to plan a bigger operation and at the moment he commands the I Armored Corps. Please lay off mentioning him."

I know my reputation will catch hell for a month or so but it is a good cover plan. Once Grant said to Sherman in the Vicksburg campaign that he would like to make a feint with Sherman's corps at a place called Cedar Bluff, but as the operation could not succeed, he did not order it, as it would hurt Sherman's reputation. Sherman replied, "Don't let my personal reputation interfere with winning the war." I feel the same way and told Ike the story. He needs a few loyal and unselfish men around him, even if he is too weak a character to be worthy of us. But if I do my duty, I will be paid in the end.

Went to Alexander's planning headquarters – it is a mess – neither Gairdner nor Nevins has the rank or character to control Monty, and Alex is just as weak. [Major General C. R.] Huebner has been put in as [Alexander's American] deputy chief of staff, but he cannot swing it either.

Monty is all set to make Americans defend his left flank and to do it by [having the Americans] landing at the most difficult beaches. From a logistical aspect it is impossible, both the landing and the supply, but I feel that by God's help, and only by His help, we will do it. I have to exude confidence I don't feel every minute.

If the Germans succeed in getting two divisions in place, I think that the operation is impossible. But the President and the Prime Minister will insist on it anyhow. Well, one cannot live forever.

Worked with the Navy all afternoon on the beaches. Our only chance is to get all the Dukws [2½-ton amphibious trucks, a new piece of equipment still unproved in operations] possible. I got 100 extra out of the British.

According to standard doctrine, a port on the far shore was deemed necessary to handle the large amount of supplies required by landing forces. But the amphibious trucks would make feasible a new technique of over-the-beach supply.

The letter he wrote to Marshall that day at Eisenhower's request:

We are getting on very well with the remodelled Husky. To save time and avoid complications in naval planning, we simply used our existing setup of sub task forces in the new locations and since there is one less beach available in the new site, we were able in this way to provide a floating reserve.

The possession of a reserve is certainly a novel experience in Africa because up to now no one, from General Eisenhower down, has ever had a reserve. Indeed, I feel that hardly anyone realizes on what a shoe string General Eisenhower has had to operate. Had it not been for his magnificent moral courage, self-confidence, and driving energy, the truly great victory of the Allies – mostly the Americans – gained yesterday would never have come off. Ever since November he has been driving relentlessly, and in so doing, has had to assume tremendous risks, incident, first, to the ever present danger of a German eruption in Spain, and, second, to the necessity of maintaining in Tunisia an impossibly attenuated line. Further, he has had to add a great deal of starch to the somewhat flexible spines of most of the Allied commanders. The results prove that, as ever, leadership and audacity bring success.

Every once in a while I am completely overcome with gratitude and appreciation to you for the opportunities you have given me. As I said when I went to Morocco, the only way I can repay you is to promise that when I get my foot on the next historic beach, I shall not leave it except as a conqueror or a corpse.

*Diary, May 9*

Saw Admiral Hewitt, who as usual cannot decide anything and is full of querolous reasons for failure.

Saw Tedder, who is a great promiser, but I don't wholly trust him. He seems to me more interested in producing an independent air force . . . than in winning the war . . .

Told Gairdner that I thought he had been unduly criticized. It cheered him up and may help us . . .

We could not get a special plane so had to come home on the courier. This is due to British influence on Spaatz. I will write a letter to Hughes asking for a plane [of his own].

*Letter, GSP, Jr., to James B. Graham, Kansas City, Mo., May 10, 1943*

I am also deeply appreciative of the fact that my sincere sympathy for the men is appreciated by at least some. This "Blood and Guts" stuff is quite distasteful to me. I am a very severe disciplinarian, because I know, and you as an old soldier know, that without discipline it is impossible to win battles, and that without discipline to send men into battle is to commit murder.

This war makes higher demands on courage and discipline than any war of which I have known. But when you see men who have demonstrated discipline and courage, killed and wounded, it naturally raises a lump in your throat and sometimes produces a tear in your eye.

*Letter, GSP, Jr., to Beatrice, May 10, 1943*

It is practicaly impossible to fly over ones own troops because they frequently shoot at you thinking you are an enemy. This is especially true if you use a cub as it has its wheels down and so has a Stuka. I did fly in the back areas very low, about ten feet from the ground, but then the Arabs take a crack.

I did not have my command tanks [in Tunisia]. I tried some ar mored cars with head cover, but they were too slow, so I just used my jeep . . .

> D is so obscessed with planning that he does not realize about doing [executing]. Also he may have wanted to get Omar a chance as G [Marshall] likes him. Any how, Omar did a swell job. So did Harmon and Doc [Ryder] . . .
>
> W. [Clark] had a chance to go in the place of Lloyd [Fredendall] but declined to go except as an Army. Now he commands an hypothesis . . .
>
> D is a strange person. I can't make him out but I begin to feel that he has an inferiority complex. Alex certainly has . . .
>
> I was the one who forced the publication of the unit names [in the newspapers]. I did it through Alex. Now every one claims the credit. All I want is the result . . .
>
> I worked it so as to get Terry in the next party. He is better than the one traded. I will also get Omar in place of Mike D[awley].

He wanted battle-hardened troops in Sicily, and he wanted tried and proved commanders. Dawley was an unknown quantity, and his VI Corps headquarters was inexperienced in war. Walker, who had an exceptionally fine combat record in World War I, was likewise new, and his 36th Division was green.

In contrast, Bradley and Allen had been in battle, and the 1st Division was combat wise, the II Corps headquarters experienced and good.

> D has a hell of a time with the civil side. There are hundreds of people here trying to give things away. From pajamas to layats for Arab babies. It is just awful. That is why I don't subscribe to the Croix rouge [Red Cross] . . .
>
> I get all sorts of funny letters, several people claiming to be cousins. Little boys pledging to enlist as soon as they are seventeen. And a copy of the Gosple according to St. John. Also lots from old soldiers . . .
>
> The plan changed because Monty would not play ball and the big brave wolf would not say no . . .
>
> I must stop and take a walk to get in shape for my next swim or run or what ever it is.
>
> Here is a memo on two months pay I sent to Riggs [Bank]. I spend no money. I love you.

*Time* magazine early in April quoted a remark, attributed to Patton, disparaging American soldiers; he supposedly said they were amateurs. The article was written in the United States, and the magazine's correspondent in the theater was so incensed by this false report that he sent a long telegram of protest to his editors.

Patton told Beatrice:

> That damned article in Time has just raised hell. Terry accused me of criticizing our troops and I hear Doc [Ryder] feels the same way. Of course I never said any of the things against Americans. I am their great advocate, but I can't help it [what the magazine prints].

"Dear Terry," he wrote on May 1,

> I should be somewhat hurt with you for writing me the letter . . . if I did not realize that you were very tired.
>
> After the amount of publicity you have personally received, you should know that any one can be quoted without ever having been seen; and if you were not tired, you would know very well that I have never at any time nor at any place criticized any American troops for anything. And certainly after the letters [of commendation] I have written you and your divisions, you must be a fool to think that I have anything but the highest opinion of their valor and efficiency.

The term "very tired" was ominous.

*Letter, GSP, Jr., to Stimson, May 10, 1943*

The nasty article . . . was most unfortunate in that it gave some of the soldiers an idea that I criticize them, whereas one of my many faults is that I am too pro-American and can see nothing wrong in anything that our soldiers do . . .

So long as you, General Marshall, and my family understand the situation, I have no complaint and look forward with considerable pleasure to the time when I will make all these all-wise analysts and newspaper correspondents eat a few words. I am mean enough to hope that this meal will give them an acute case of indigestion.

# CHAPTER 15

# Husky: Preparations

*"We must not only die gallantly; we must kill devastatingly."*

PATTON enjoyed talking with soldiers about their military tasks and duties, their martial spirit, their problems with equipment and procedures. Every time he gave a "war talk," he was amused and thrilled "to see the men pep up when they realize you have something to say and are not just talking."

*Letter, GSP, Jr., to Frederick Ayer, May 12, 1943*

For the moment I am in a state of more or less suspended animation, except that I have to spend two or three nights a week on maneuvers, in the course of which I have destroyed two pair of trousers by being caught on the barbed wire.

The training we do over here is very much more realistic than anything I have ever seen. We actually fire ball cartridges over each others heads, actually blow up wire, and actually do lots of other things along the same lines.

*Letter, GSP, Jr., to Beatrice, May 13, 1943*

I am very healthy. I take exercises in the morning, including running, eat toast for breakfast, soup for lunch, take a mile and a half walk up a steep hill in evening, have one drink, eat a realy good and well cooked dinner, and go to bed at ten. Up at six.

He and Brigadier General John W. O'Daniel ran some experiments to judge the effectiveness of certain weapons against defenses. They fired the .50-caliber machine gun, the rocket gun, the antitank grenade, the 37-mm. gun with armor-piercing shell, the 75-mm. howitzer with high explosive shell and delay fuze, the flame thrower, and the bangalore torpedo. Patton found the tests "very encouraging."

*Diary, May 14*

Did nothing all day except think about a training directive. I know what I want [to say] but find it hard to condense it enough. I guess I am mentally lazy . . .

Received a letter from General Marshall . . . Very nice, as he seldom praises . . .

I hope I get to work in the morning.

Summerall was writing to tell of his pride in Patton's past accomplishments and his confidence in Patton's even greater achievements ahead. The whole country believed that he was preparing to lead another expedition and had complete faith in him. Patton's men were fighting for him because of his personality, because he constantly visited them at the front, and because he was quick to approve and reward performances well done. Troops, he reminded Patton, needed both success and recognition, and they followed leaders who gave them both. "I do not mean to lecture," he concluded, "for you know all that I do and far more."

Eisenhower was thinking of recommending Terry Allen to command a corps in the United States, but Patton requested his retention "at least until the initial phase of the operation is consummated" because of the "critical nature" of Husky, the "conspicuous place" of the division in the invasion, and Allen's "experience as a combat leader."

When Bradley arrived from Tunisia, Patton met him at the airport "to congratulate him in person." He had already written him two letters of praise – because he was still hurt that Eisenhower had never patted him on the back for winning the battle of El Guettar. He had a guard of honor for Bradley at the headquarters, then a luncheon in his honor, a grand affair with "two bottles of champaigne and I drank to the health of the Conqueror of Bizerte."

*Diary, May 17*

Ike called me to say we will probably do Husky as an Army. I have never asked him to do this, but am glad he is going to.

Actually, Marshall had suggested that since Montgomery would command an Army in Sicily, perhaps Patton ought also to have a command of equal importance, to enhance American "national prestige." Eisenhower was "completely in favor." In Sicily, the I Armored Corps headquarters would become the Seventh Army headquarters.

Had a long talk with Bradley. He grows on me as a very sound and extremely loyal soldier. We both feel that our chances of surviving Husky are not better than 50-50, but God, or luck, will tip the beam to us . . .

Everything I have [ever] done [before] helps [in my tasks] now – it is more than a coincidence . . . I hope we land on the mainland [of Italy after we conquer Sicily].

*Letter, GSP, Jr., to Beatrice, May 17, 1943*

Inclosed are three realy nice fan letters. I am sending some more fan male in a seperate envelope.

Leadership is a funny thing and just reafirms what Nap.[Napoleon] said, "In war men are nothing, a man is everything." I remember in the last war seeing Hanson Ely completely change the 5th Division in three days. We did the same thing to four of them in ten days, and the funny thing is that I don't know how I do it . . .

I am not so keen on Alex as I was. I fear he is not too strong . . .

It seems probable that I will not have the I Armored Corps much longer, but, as our British friends say, "I am happy about it." You can guess the rest. W[ayne] will be very mad indeed, but I am not taking over his number. As a matter of fact, we get on fine. He is much chasened.

*Letter, Harbord to GSP, Jr., May 18, 1943*

Every friend of yours – and the country seems to be full of them – has watched with intense interest the dispatches and smiled every time they heard your name mentioned . . .

We saw your name . . . for a few days, then it suddenly disappeared, and we can only conjecture what has happened. My guess is that some operation is contemplated where it is expected to give you your opportunity . . . Another theory might be that you are rapidly becoming a hero, from the bulletins that are coming in, and there may be some other hero in the neighborhood who thinks his heroic qualities are obscured by yours . . . The press of the country seems to be for you. You have exactly the qualities that appeal to them.

In a demonstration of how to follow artillery bombardment closely,

Patton rode in the tank of the captain of the leading company. Some shell fragments tore up the ground all around, and a few hit his tank. Two short rounds burst within about 20 yards of him. "I took the ride because some of the men felt it was dangerous."

Eisenhower phoned to invite Patton and Bradley to attend a victory parade in Tunis to celebrate the end of the fighting in North Africa,

> probably feeling that we had something to do with its existence. If we don't go, there will be only British there, so we are going . . . AFHQ is really a British headquarters with a neuter general, if he is not pro-British. It is a hell of a note. Some day some one at home will tumble to what is going on.

Patton and Bradley flew to Tunis on May 20. They

> passed over the ruins of Carthage, which are only visible on the map — on the ground there is nothing to see. However, the mountains back of it, of which I read a description in some old book, were perfectly familiar.
>
> When we reached the [Tunis air]field, General Eisenhower had just arrived, driven by Kay. We both shook hands with him and congratulated him, but he was so busy meeting high ranking officers of the French and British Armies that we had no time to talk to him . . .
>
> After awhile the "sacred families" got into automobiles, escorted by British armored cars. We followed behind the escort . . . When we arrived near the reviewing stand, the escorted party turned off one way and we were sent to a parking lot some blocks from the stand . . .
>
> Bradley and I were put in a stand . . . largely occupied by French civilians and minor military officers . . .
>
> Mr. [Robert] Murphy and General Eisenhower were the only two Americans on the [reviewing] stand . . .
>
> In spite of their magnificent [physical] appearance, our men do not put up a good show in reviews. I think that we still lack pride in being soldiers, and we must develop it . . .
>
> About thirty of us were asked to a lunch at the French Residency . . . It was a very formal and uneatable affair, but there were no toasts. Afterwards, most of us had to leave at once in order to get back to our stations before dark.

I hope this is only the first of many such triumphal processions that I shall participate in. Bradley and I also hope that in the next one, we will have a more conspicuous role . . .

General Giraud remembered me at once and was extremely complimentary in his remarks. He is a very impressive man and looks exactly like a modernized Vercingetorix.

*Diary, May 22*

Under the present arrangement for Husky, we have a pro-British straw man at the top, a British chief admiral and senior vice admiral, Cunningham and Ramsey. This makes our Admiral Hewitt third. Tedder controls the air with Spaatz, a straw man, under him . . . Conyngham commands the tactical air force and the close support air force by another British vice air marshal. Our close support air force is commanded by a Colonel. Browning is an airborne advisor [to Eisenhower] and trying to get command of the paratroops.

Alexander commands all the ground troops. His chief of staff is British, but we have a Director of Operations in Brigadier General Nevins and a Deputy Chief of Staff in Major General Huebner, which may help. General Montgomery, a full general, commands [Eighth Army]. I command – a poor last.

I cannot see how people at home don't see it. The U.S. is getting gypped. All Seventh Army supplies come either over beaches or else through Siracusa, a British port, and I am told to arrange with Monty as to amounts [I will get]. Only an act of God or an accident can give us a run for our money. On a study of form, especially in the higher command, we are licked. Churchill runs this war and at the moment he is not interested in Husky.

The thing I must do is to retain my SELF-CONFIDENCE. I have greater ability than these other people and it comes from, for lack of a better word, what we must call greatness of soul based on a belief – an unshakable belief – in my destiny. The U.S. must win – not as an ally, but as a conqueror. If I can find my duty, I can do it. I must.

This is one of the bad days.

*Letter, GSP, Jr., to Beatrice, May 24, 1943*

You will be surprised to learn that I went swimming yesterday. As you know, I hate swimming but it is the least unplesant exercise available here. I had been doing calesthenics in the morning and walking a mile and a half up hill every evening, but walking is a bore though I did the distance in 20 minutes.

The beach is nice and I can run about half a mile and then lay in the sand . . .

My [fan] mail is getting huge.

*Diary, May 25*

We took Alexander and Richardson on an extended inspection of all the various forms of training. They were very much impressed . . . The boats came in firing mortars and under fire themselves . . . The men then land and . . . using both high explosives and white phosphorus attack up a valley and eventually capture a pillbox with the use of a flame thrower.

The tactics on the part of the infantry were perfect except that the men were too slow in getting out of the boats and did not have their bayonets fixed . . . Alex was loud in his praise . . . as he should have been. We then . . . ended up with . . . the street-fighting instruction. This is really very terrifying to watch, and he was duly impressed.

*Letter, GSP, Jr., to Marshall, May 26, 1943*

[Alexander was] really tremendously impressed . . . and kept repeating how much [he] admired the enthusiasm of the troops. There was implied criticism of their own troops in comparison with ours . . .

We also put on a street fighting demonstration with actual firing support . . . The bullets pass extremely close to the people's heads . . . When I went through it personally, it frightened me to death . . .

Everything is moving along satisfactorily, and we have great confidence in our next operation.

*Diary, May 26*

Admiral Hewitt came to spend the night. He . . . did all the things we asked him after a little patting on the back. All you have to do to get him is to tell him how great he is.

*Diary, May 28*

On inspecting the troops, I found the officers looking on, and the noncommissioned officers doing the drilling. I put a stop to this. I then gave various groups of men some pep talks with [good] effect . . .

The authorities at AFHQ and at the Fifth Army do not realize that a trained soldier and an enlisted man are two different animals. To them a man is a man.

In spite of the fact that Ike and Wayne have both cussed the other to me, there is still some sort of an unholy alliance between them. I should not worry as I seem to be doing nicely, but I do worry. I am a fool – those two cannot upset [my] destiny. Besides I owe each of them quite a lot, but of course don't know to what extent they have undercut me. The next show must be a success or a funeral.

*Letter, GSP, Jr., to Maj. Gen. W. D. Connor, Washington, D.C., May 28, 1943*

As you know, the higher one gets the easier it really becomes, as long as the digestion remains good and you can sleep through bombardments and you don't change your mind. I am also fortunate in having very good generals.

*Letter, GSP, Jr., to Beatrice, May 28, 1943*

We have plenty of good weapons now. All we need is the will and skill to use them properly . . .

I still dislike machine gun fire more than either bombs or shelling. Mines are a distinct mental hazard . . .

I will have to get rid of Stiller. He is too dumb and too crude. He tries hard but never clicks.

I hope George is still a cadet.

*Letter, GSP, Jr., to Donald M. Taylor, Peoria, Ill., May 30, 1943*

In spite of the efforts of the newspapers to paint me as a most profane and ungodly man, I am probably just as religious as you are. I am a Communicant of the Episcopal Church and attend services every Sunday.

I have received several letters from people making an earnest effort to save my soul, which, personally, I do not believe is in any great danger.

*Letter, GSP, Jr., to Pershing, May 30, 1943*

Whatever ability I have shown or shall show as a soldier is the result of a studious endeavor to copy the greatest American soldier, namely, yourself. I consider it a priceless privilege to have served with you in Mexico and in France . . .

Your ability to put away worry has been of inestimable value to me. The night we landed in Morocco I deliberately went to bed (in full pack of course) and slept for two hours after we sighted the coast in order to prove to myself that I could emulate you.

During our fighting in Tunisia, I studiously avoided worrying. One night, about 2:00 a.m., it was necessary to make a most momentous decision . . . I gave this my careful consideration, issued the orders, went back to bed, and went to sleep. I could never have done this if it had not been for the inspiring memory of what you have done under similar, although much more difficult, circumstances.

*GSP, Jr., Message to the troops, May 30, 1943 (Memorial Day)*

We must remember that victories are not gained solely by selfless devotion. To conquer, we must destroy our enemies. We must not only die gallantly; we must kill devastatingly. The faster and more effectively you kill, the longer will you live to enjoy the priceless fame of conquerors.

*Letter, GSP, Jr., to Beatrice, June 1, 1943*

I certainly have a lot of Dog. When I travel, sirens scream and motor cycles rush about. To day when I left SOS Headquarters, there was a big crowd who clapped and cheered. I kissed my hand to them which brought down the house. However, I am not sure they knew who I was, probably thought I was Ike . . .

I feel about the Arabs the way you do – the dirty bastards . . .

Here is my latest efusion [poem].

*Diary, June 1*

Ike called up late to say that "My American Boss will visit you in the morning . . ." I asked him, "When did Mamie arrive?" Man cannot serve two masters. "My American Boss."

*Diary, June 2*

Called Bradley early and told him to meet me . . . to see General Marshall. Neither Ike nor Clark had mentioned Bradley.

Patton sent Keyes to Algiers to settle several points on shipping.

I told Keyes to say that if we had to give up so many ships, we could

> not land, and then there would be no need for either air or mines. I think it is an unanswerable argument. If this show was run by one man instead of being guided by three, with a straw lay figure at the top –

Marshall, Handy, Bull, and McCarthy came to Patton's headquarters to visit, and Patton showed them the maps and plans of the impending invasion, as well as some of the training exercises.

> Clark left, at General Marshall's suggestion, right after lunch. In Clark's presence I told General Marshall how helpful Clark had been. I am getting tactful as hell, and in this case it is true. I think that if you treat a skunk nicely, he will not piss on you – as often.

Marshall was pleased by what he saw. He asked to have Harmon and Eddy to dinner, and was impressed by them and their combat experience. "I talked up Keyes to him."

> Shortly before we left the U.S. last October, General Marshall sent for me and said that he had a hunch Harmon was no good and suggested that I leave him. I said that if he ordered me to leave Harmon, I would, but not otherwise. He said, "On your head be it." Tonight he said, "Patton, I was wrong about Harmon, and you were right. Will he be made a corps commander?" I said yes.
>
> Few men in high places will admit a mistake. General Marshall went away up with me. I have never seen him more cheerful or in better health.

When Patton wrote to thank the girls of the American Red Cross Service Club at Mostaganem for entertaining officers from his headquarters, he received a warm reply from their chief, who said that none of them had ever seen a "he man" general. Could Patton please come by some time and let them "Oh!" and "Ah!" at him from a distance?

She enclosed a clipping from a magazine that told of Patton's grandson walking around the library at Green Meadows, gazing at the walls covered with trophies of his grandfather's sailing, hunting, military, and other achievements, and saying to his grandmother, "Where are we going to put Rommel when granddaddy catches him?"

Early in June, at the end of his first year, young George Patton was "found deficient in mathematics" and would have to leave the Military

Academy. The Commandant of Cadets informed Patton that he had called George in

> and had a good chat with him. Of course, he was terribly disappointed [to learn the news] . . . He has had a tendency to try too hard and, consequently, gets excited. He worked his heart out to stay here . . . and he did not want to let you down . . .
>
> George will undoubtedly take the re-examination soon and if he passes, he will come back in September [and start again].

*Letter, GSP, Jr., to Beatrice, June 9, 1943*

I wrote George a letter telling him that I was very proud of him what ever happened and that I too would have to take an exam and might fail but not for lack of trying.

*Letter, GSP, Jr., to Frederick Ayer, June 15, 1943*

I am naturally very distressed about George's failure but apparently he came by his mathematical ability very naturally, and I now feel convinced he will end up as at least a lieutenant general, that is, if he continues to follow so accurately in my footsteps.

*Letter, GSP, Jr., to Beatrice, June 20, 1943*

I am delighted that he has elected to make a go of it. Of course it seems to me utterly ridiculous to turn a boy back on one subject during war when at the same time thousands of others are being commissioned through OCS . . .

The present system is a waste of money and talent.

To Brigadier General P. E. Gallagher, Commandant of Cadets:

Of course, I am disappointed that he was turned back, but since I was turned back in the same subject, and [since] at present [I out-] rank every man in my original class [of 1908], I do not believe that the loss is irreparable.

I am sure that the spirit of self-confidence and sense of duty, which we get at West Point, is the most vital characteristic a soldier can have, and I would deeply regret any changes in our curriculum which would make it easier to learn . . .

I am not a brilliant soldier. So far I have been quite a successful one because I am always fully confident that I can do what I am told to do, and have had my sense of duty developed to the point where I let no personal interests or danger interfere.

If cadets and soldiers could be made to understand that discipline and military courtesy are an index of their alertness, they might accept it more readily. It must be patent to the dumbest plebe or soldier that a stupidity that renders him oblivious to the immediate presence of an officer would also probably render him oblivious to the immediate presence of an enemy . . .

I have never seen a sloppy soldier who was a good soldier, and I have never seen a good soldier who is a sloppy soldier . . .

Again thanking you for your interest and trusting that George will return and get to be a cadet officer, I am with renewed thanks . . .

George was once again being tutored by Dr. Silverman. He would take and pass the examination, re-enter West Point, and, like his father, graduate after spending five years at the institution.

*Letter, GSP, Jr., to Brig. Gen. H. D. Chamberlin, June 4, 1943*

The fact of having participated in athletics is of great value to a fighter . . . because in battle as in polo or football, one has to think under pressure. Also, we who have engaged in sports know that you can never win except by unremitting offensive.

People who gain a knowledge of war solely from books are apt to think that the apparent virtue of defense makes it superior to the offense, but wars are not won by apparent virtue – else I would be in a hell of a fix – but by continued optimism and a fighting spirit.

*Letter, GSP, Jr., to Frederick Ayer, June 4, 1943*

The other day one of our chaplains, a venerable and holy man, was walking down the street. An Arab woman kept following him and saying, "chocolate, chocolate." Finally, in very bad French, he said that he had no chocolate. To which she replied in very good English, "No chocolate, no fuck, go to hell!" . . .

I am getting much thinner, which I think is a good thing and is due largely to the fact that we have been training quite hard, including swimming and running on the beach at least five afternoons a week . . .

One of our officers the other day began copying the British and putting the initials of his decorations after his name, so today I wrote him a letter, adding the simple initials, S.O.B.

On June 5, Patton issued a letter of instructions to his subordinate commanders. In it he set forth the principles he wished them to follow in the approaching Sicilian campaign:

> In view of your long experience and demonstrated ability, I have certain diffidence in writing this letter; nonetheless . . . I would be remiss in my duty if I failed to express my views and outline as briefly as may be, certain points in the conduct of operations which I expect you to observe.
>
> There is only one sort of discipline – perfect discipline . . .
>
> Discipline is based on pride in the profession of arms, on meticulous attention to details, and on mutual respect and confidence. Discipline must be a habit so ingrained that it is stronger than the excitement of battle or the fear of death.
>
> Discipline can only be obtained when all officers are so imbued with the sense of their lawful obligation to their men and to their country that they cannot tolerate negligence. Officers who fail to correct errors or to praise excellence are valueless in peace and dangerous misfits in war.
>
> Officers must assert themselves by example and by voice.
>
> The history of our invariably victorious armies demonstrates that we are the best soldiers in the world. Currently, many of you defeated and destroyed the finest troops Germany possesses. This should make your men proud. This should make you proud. This should imbue your units with unconquerable self-confidence and pride in demonstrated ability . . .
>
> There is no approved solution to any tactical situation.
>
> There is only one tactical principle which is not subject to change. It is: "To so use the means at hand to inflict the maximum amount of wounds, death, and destruction on the enemy in the minimum of time."
>
> Never attack [enemy] strength [but rather his weakness] . . .
>
> You can never be too strong. Get every man and gun you can secure provided it does not delay your attack . . .
>
> Casualties vary directly with the time you are exposed to effective fire . . . Rapidity of attack shortens the time of exposure . . .
>
> If you cannot see the enemy, and you seldom can, shoot at the place he is most likely to be . . .
>
> Our mortars and our artillery are superb weapons when they are firing. When silent, they are junk – see that they fire!

Battles are won by frightening the enemy. Fear is induced by inflicting death and wounds on him. Death and wounds are produced by fire. Fire from the rear is more deadly and three times more effective than fire from the front...

Few men are killed by bayonets, but many are scared by them. Having the bayonet fixed makes our men want to close. Only the threat to close will defeat a determined enemy...

In mountain warfare, capture the heights and work downhill . . .

Never permit a unit to dig in until the final objective is reached, then dig, wire, and mine...

Never take counsel of your fears. The enemy is more worried than you are. Numerical superiority, while useful, is not vital to successful offensive action. The fact that you are attacking induces the enemy to believe that you are stronger than he is...

A good solution applied with vigor *now* is better than a perfect solution ten minutes later...

IN CASE OF DOUBT, ATTACK! . . .

Mine fields, while dangerous, are not impassable. They are far less of hazard than artillery concentrations...

Speed and ruthless violence on the beaches is vital. There must be no hesitation in debarking. To linger on the beach is fatal.

In landing operations, retreat is impossible...

Weapons will be kept in perfect working order at all times . . .

Vehicles will be properly maintained in combat as elsewhere . . .

We can conquer only by attacking...

Continued ruthless pressure by day and by night is vital . . .

We must be particularly emphatic in the ruthless destruction of the enemy.

This was the essence of Patton's method of warfare. It was important in shaping the mental outlook of his officers and, thereby, the character of the campaign.

But still some practical details had to be settled.

*Diary, June 5*

Huebner, Cannon, and a couple of British air officers came and we argued for hours as to what air-ground forces we should take . . . If we took all that the air wants, we should have no soldiers left with which to assault the beach. If we don't take some air-ground troops, the [air]fields can't be repaired [after capture]. Also, the

Navy has suddenly pulled out 4 LST's to lay mines. I suppose we will also have losses before we start and during the trip. On the other hand, I think that we will get some local surprise, at least as to the strength of our attack, as the Boches don't know about the dukws and without dukws we could not land such a big force.

Bradley, Terry Allen [and others] came over for me to settle some arguments. Terry wanted the paratroopers to land on his left instead of his right. They can't, due to terrain. Next, he wanted to open fire at 2300, D minus 1 [the evening before the assault]. No. Then he wanted some self-propelled guns. No. He thinks that the 1st Division is the only unit in the show . . .

There are a lot of starry-eyed State Department boys busting to raise the living standard of Arabs who should be all killed off . . . No State Department people should be permitted in a theater of war, nor at the peace treaty.

Major General John Lucas, an old friend who had served with Patton in Mexico, arrived in the theater. Marshall had sent him to be of help to Eisenhower in any capacity Eisenhower wished to use him. Because of Lucas' maturity and broad military experience, Eisenhower appointed him his deputy commander and charged him with keeping Eisenhower informed of general conditions and, more specifically, of the activities carried out by the combat elements. Lucas was to act as Eisenhower's eyes and ears or as a special liaison officer to the subordinate headquarters. He visited Patton and stayed the night.

*Diary, June 7*

I got Lucas well indoctrinated in what we need and told him to say it was his idea and not mine. He was particularly impressed with the necessity of having the 9th Division immediately available for reinforcement . . .

Lucas too feels that Ike is just a staff officer and not a soldier. Too bad. When Lucas came over [to Africa], General Marshall said to him, "The situation at AFHQ is not satisfactory, or I should say it is very dangerous." Myself, Bradley, or Keyes could do the job. Personally I don't want it.

*Diary, June 8*

For some reason I am, if possible, too confident, yet at times I fear I am not doing all I should. A feeling of being a chip in a river of destiny pervades me, but while it is good for my self-confidence, it is bad for my activity. Yet I can't see anything I can do except be mentally and physically alert.

He was glad to hear from Harbord who said he had received a letter from Mrs. Patton "about the intention of you two and Mrs. Jenson" — actually it was Beatrice's idea — to establish a scholarship fund as a memorial "to your gallant Aide." Harbord said he would help.

*Letter, GSP, Jr., to Frederick Ayer, June 9, 1943*

In any of these fights, a general officer who does his duty has got to expose himself. Otherwise, he cannot look himself in the face and order men to do things that he is afraid to do himself. I am sure that whatever success I have had has resulted from my adherence to this belief . . .

Save up a good drink, preferably a cocktail, of which I have only tasted three in the last eight months, to drink when and if you read about me in the paper . . .

If I should conk [out], I do not wish to be disinterred after the war. It would be more pleasant to my ghostly future to lie among my soldiers than to rest in the sanctimonious precincts of a civilian cemetary . . . However, don't worry about this because I have no idea of departing this life.

*Diary, June 9*

I am going to see Ike tomorrow. Keyes advises that I just appear happy and ask for nothing. It should have a good effect on Ike, who is run to death.

*Diary, June 10*

Went to see Ike and told him that I wanted nothing and had no complaint . . .

Ike is getting foolish and bothering about things such as who is to be head nurse; far below his dignity.

I also saw Admiral Hewitt, who is in a haze as usual.

*Diary, June 13*

Went to church and heard a most incoherent sermon. I have the trots.

"Everything is going on well," he informed Beatrice, "and I am if any thing too confident." The invasion was little more than three weeks away.

Patton, Bradley, and Keyes drove to the Oran airfield, where they met Clark and awaited the arrival of the King of England and the Secretary of State for War, Sir James Grigg. Clark rode with the King, Patton with Grigg.

> I found him very much a politician but very broad-minded. He gives you the impression of an American more than an Englishman . . . He said that Alexander had told him that the American troops would shortly be the best soldiers in the world. I said that I did not like to disagree with General Alexander, but at present the American soldiers *are* the best soldiers in the world, and will take on any soldiers of any country at any time. He hemmed a little and said, "That is what I meant," and after that we were quite friendly. Although this may sound impolite, it is the only way to talk to an Englishman . . .
>
> Relative to making a staff work, Sir James said, "Don't keep dogs and bark yourself." . . .
>
> S.M. [Sa Majesté – His Majesty] is just a grade above a moron. Poor little fellow.

He visited Eddy's 9th Division and was very much impressed.

> After supper I addressed all the officers. I told them that I had come to tell them how to fight but after seeing them, I knew I had nothing to tell them. I then stressed shooting and killing, and the use of the bayonet, and the fact that Americans are the pick of the more adventurous people of all races.

He also told them, as he wrote Beatrice, that they would soon enter another battle alongside their allies and that

> for years we had competed with them in tennis, in sailing, on the track, in shooting, and in polo. Once more we were in a competition – a competition to see who would first defeat our common foe. It would be the grandest tournament of all.

Patton was up at 1:45 A.M. to see a practice landing. "The Navy was 45 minutes late but hit the beach exactly." The troops performed as nearly perfect as I had ever seen troops do . . . They came ashore very fast, spread out at once, and proceeded with speed and determination to their objectives – the high hills two miles from the shore – and occupied their summits in about two hours . . . The shore parties were also superior, and the ship-to-shore radio seemed to be working . . . The most satisfactory night operation I have seen. I was delighted with the whole thing.

*Diary, June 19*

I started to write my order of the day . . . Went out to shoot my weapons.

*Diary, June 20*

Went to church with Gay. We had a new preacher, at my insistence, who was good. He preached on the willingness to accept responsibility, even to your own hurt. That ability is what we need and what Ike lacks. But I do feel that I don't. I pray daily to do my duty, retain my self-confidence, and accomplish my destiny. No one can live under the awful responsibility I have without Divine help. Frequently I feel that I don't rate it.

In Algiers on June 21, to attend a meeting where the final plans were to be presented, Patton first went to see Wigglesworth about the air support for Sicily. "He said that he would do his best. I doubt this . . . I still feel sure we will get double-crossed."

All the "top flight officers" were present except Montgomery, who was entertaining the King.

*Diary, June 21*

Alexander opened the proceedings . . .

Eisenhower then talked for ten minutes – rather badly I thought – acting as an associate rather than a commander.

Captain Brownrigg of the British Navy gave the general naval plan which is terribly complicated but well thought out.

Admiral Hewitt was then called on ahead of the time he thought he was going to speak, with the result that his map did not arrive until half the conference was completed. The map was then put on the board with the result that it was not properly connected. His speech was not conducive to confidence.

Ramsey gave the British naval plan with charts and spoke well . . .

Tedder slept through the entire performance. Conyngham came on for the air and talked and talked and made no definite statements . . . Air Commodore Beamish . . . talked for forty-five minutes at the rate of five words and three ah's every minute.

Tea for thirty minutes, after which [Patton's] force, for the first time denominated Seventh Army, came on. We stole the show by using the War College method at Keyes' suggestion. I made a six-minute talk on the general mission and plan, and was followed by [the principal staff members] . . . The total presentation of the group took twenty-two minutes and thirty seconds, which was thirty seconds longer than we had rehearsed it for . . . Ike was pleased and, for a change, said so.

Patton explained what the Seventh Army expected to do. His men would fight ashore and attack inland to establish a solid front, "a secure base line from which to undertake further operations for the complete subjugation of the island as may be directed." Exactly how these "further operations" were to develop had yet to be decided.

*Diary, June 22*

Commanders and staffs went to hear the very secret G-2 estimate by the British. The man who gave it knew a lot but succeeded in keeping it to himself . . .

Then we all asked questions about what the Air would do and gradually forced them to promise quite a lot. Here it was that Ike missed being great. He could have faced the issue but sat mute . . .

So ended a very momentous conference. Had it taken place six weeks earlier, it would have saved much misunderstanding and made a better attack . . .

Alex said that it was foolish to consider British and Americans as one people, as we are each foreigners to the other. I said that it was so and the sooner everyone recognized it the better. I told him that my boisterous method of command would not work with the British no matter how successful with Americans, while his cold method would never work with Americans. He agreed.

I found out that he has an exceptionally small head. That may explain things.

*Letter, GSP, Jr., to Beatrice, June 26, 1943*

Poor D is having a hell of a time with politics . . .

I had a letter . . . from a preacher . . . He hoped I thought about Jesus and reminded that I would die and go to hell if I did not.

I wrote him that I was amazed at his temerity in writing me such a letter when I was a far better Christian than he was.

*Letter GSP, Jr., to Beatrice, June 26, 1943*

I had my teeth cleaned to day and had only one small cavaty . . .

I am going out and do a little more pistol practice . . . but I have become so sacred that I wont have a chance for any personal combat, but I am ready. Everett and John Lucas and Beedle all lecture me so much against taking risks that it is making a woman of me. I suppose they are sincere, but some times I wonder if they think I will set too hot a pace.

At this stage of a party one can only wonder. Le sort en est jete [The die is cast – or, the dice are rolled].

We are moving in with Hewitt next week and will be bored and over fed for a long time . . .

I dont expect to be killed, but if I am, I hope it is a nice clean job. But I have the feeling of being a chip on the river of destiny going to a predestined place of whose location I am ignorant. My chief concern is to do my full duty, retain my self confidence and follow my star.

Speaking of stars, I don't think I need any more for a while. If all goes very well, I may [be promoted and need them] . . .

Some people say people are jealous of me but I don't see it and refuse to think about it. I can still close my mind to unpleasant things and it is a good habit as I get quite a few kicks and jabs by little foolish underlings.

I am like the nigger prisoner who said, "I am sure going to get on with the jailer, and I expect to do most of the getting on."

*Diary, June 27*

Went to communion . . . very high church but I like it.

Spoke to officers and warrant officers of the 45th Division. Had to make two speeches as the groups were about 15 miles apart. I did not repeat myself . . . I believe this division will do all right, but as in the case with every division, the first fight may find the young officers lacking in drive.

*GSP, Jr., Talk to 45th Division, June 27, 1943*

Clearly all of you must know that combat is imminent . . . You are competing with veterans, but don't let that worry you. All of them, too, fought their first battle, and all of them won their first battle just as you will win yours. Battle is far less frightening than those who have never been in it are apt to think. All this bull about thinking of your mother and your sweetheart and your wives (who should also be your sweethearts) is overemphasized by writers who describe battles, not as they are, but as the writers who have never heard a hostile shot or missed a meal think they are.

Battle is the most magnificent competition in which a human being can indulge. It brings out all that is best; it removes all that is base.

All men are afraid in battle. The coward is the one who lets his fear overcome his sense of duty . . .

Remember that the enemy is just as frightened as you are, probably more so . . . The attacker wins. You cannot win by parrying. Yet the enemy, being uncertain of our intentions, must parry . . .

Booby traps are what the name implies — boobies get trapped . . .

You have a sacred trust in your men and to your country, and you are lower than the lowest thing that lives if you are false to this trust. An officer . . . must always be willing and anxious to take the chances his men must take. He must lead, not push, and he must assert himself . . .

Pride is the greatest thing a man can have . . .

We Americans are a competitive race. We bet on anything. We love to win. In this next fight, you are entering the greatest sporting competition of all times . . . for the greatest prize of all — victory.

*Diary, June 28*

Cleaned up desk and signed many papers . . . Tomorrow we start on the first lap of the next journey. I feel very confident especially as I saw some pictures of the [hostile] beach taken recently and it looks better than I had hoped. "Man proposes but God disposes."

*Diary, June 29*

Reported to Ike about 1700. He was full of praise for the 3d Division but never mentioned the fact that I made it what it is. I fear that I was untactful . . .

Wedemeyer is an idealist. He talked to me about who will run things after the war and proposed me. I declined, being a liar, but it is much too soon to make plans to be of effect after the war; one must end as a beloved victorious leader and many men must die before I am that. And luck may not hold!

*Diary, June 30*

Came on board . . . Much piping, etc. Have very nice room with bath . . . a desk and a clothes closet . . . My name is painted on the door and I have two mess boys to serve me. Keyes eats with me.

*Diary, July 1*

The 1st Division is back on its feet and so is Terry. Teddy [Roosevelt] . . . is a problem, but I think should have the 1st Division when Allen goes. He will need a strong No. 2 as he is weak on discipline but a brave and fairly good fighter. He bootlicks me to beat Hell.

*Letter, GSP, Jr., to Beatrice, July 2, 1943*

The only thing that bores me is that I have nothing to do, just sit and wait . . .

With in the last few months there has been a great improvement in the soldiers. They are at last becoming professionals and look and act the part. Yesterday a lot of them saluted me when I was in my bathing suit. This is truly remarcable and shows that they wanted to, as they could have easily pretended not to recognize me.

*Letter, GSP, Jr., to Francis P. Graves, July 2, 1943*

I stop [smoking] regularly and as regularly start again. But when I am really busy, I find that I smoke less than when I am sitting around as I am at present.

*Diary, July 2*

Went to a movie of myself in Tunisia. I do not photograph well, or I think I look better than I do — probably the latter.

*Diary, July 3*

Bedell Smith . . . takes delight in smearing the character of everyone . . . Brigadier Strong, G–2, AFHQ . . . would agree to anything . . .

Went to see Vice Air Marshal Wigglesworth and told him that I was pleased with the Air plan — this is not wholly true, but I can now only work by seduction. He showed me the combined air and navy map room of AFHQ — not an American in it . . .

Saw Allen and told him how good he is. He is a good battle leader . . .

All the men steal looks at me — it is complimentary but a little terrible. I am their God or so they seem to think.

*Diary, July 4*

It looks as if fate were fattening me up for something. I hope I perform when the time comes. Battles take years to get ready for, and all one's life can be expressed in one little decision but that decision is the labor of uncounted years. It is not genius but memory — unconscious memory — and character, and Divine Wrath which does not hesitate nor count the cost . . . I am sending possibly thousands to death and glory and don't, or won't, think about it. The human mind is very queer — only God could have devised such a complex machine.

*Letter, GSP, Jr., to Handy, July 5, 1943*

I have a great optimism about this operation, springing largely from the heart rather than the head. However, I do feel that the training . . . is so much better than it was in Torch as to be beyond comparision . . .

There is a lot of bunk to this so-called amphibious training. The chief people that need it are the Navy, and they need it for three things — to find where they are going; to get there on time; and to handle small boats in the surf. These three things they can practice without any soldiers being around.

*Letter, GSP, Jr., to Frederick Ayer, July 5, 1943*

This letter will be mailed after D Day . . . It is not a goodbye, as the higher ranking I get, the less chance I have to do any real fighting. However, one can always take a long swim, and swimming in oily water, which is on fire, is not healthy . . .

If you read in the papers that I have been killed, wait till you get a War Department confirmation, because I have a great many lives, and at the moment do not feel at all dead. In fact, I am looking forward with a lot of pleasure to some very good excitement . . .

If we should not meet again until we get to the other side, I am assured on credible authority that the heavenly foxes are fast, the heavenly hounds keen, the fogbank fences high and soft, and the landings firm. The horses of the sun have always been celebrated. "Whoop Ho! for a kill in the open!"

*Letter, GSP, Jr., to Beatrice, July 5, 1943*

We pull out in the morning for the invasion of Sicily . . .

I think it will be a pretty bloody show . . .

I doubt that I will be killed or even wounded, but one can never tell. It is all a question of destiny.

I think we are as well prepared as it is possible to be, and the men are very anxious to go . . .

Well when you get this you will be a widow or a radio fan, I trust the latter. In either case I love you.

*Diary, July 5*

Went to say goodbye to General Ike . . . Ike started out by giving me a long lecture on the bad discipline of the 1st Division. I told him he was mistaken and that, anyhow, no one whips a dog just before putting him in a fight.

Then he talked about criticism of the Air Corps . . . I told him that, due to his efforts, we were apparently going to get [air] support. This was a fib, as I was the one who attacked them and made them come across.

At no time did Ike wish us luck and say he was back of us — fool.

After others . . . left, I told him that I was very appreciative of being selected [for Husky].

He said, "You are a great leader but a poor planner."

I replied that, except for Torch, which I had planned and which was a high success, I had never been given a chance to plan.

He said that if Husky turned into a slugging match, he might recall me to get ready for the next operation and let Bradley finish Husky.

I protested that I would like to finish one show.

I can't make out whether he thinks Bradley is a better close fighter than I am or whether he wants to keep in with General Marshall, who likes Bradley. I know that Bradley is completely loyal to me.

Ike has never asked me to a meal since I have been here, one week. However, it turns out I would not change places with anyone I know. I am leading 90,000 men in a desperate attack and eventually it [my Army] will be over 250,000 [men]. If I win, I can't be stopped! If I lose, I shall be dead.

*Letter, GSP, Jr., to Beatrice, July 5, 1943*

I have just written you and Fred letters which Hughes will mail after the day. So there is nothing much to add here . . .

I shall not be in a position to write for a while nor will I get any mail for some time. But things pass very quickly. I have no premonitions and hope to live for ever.

CHAPTER 16

# The Landings: Seventh Army

*"I have the usual shortness of breath I always have before a polo game."*

*Diary, July 6*

Monrovia [Hewitt's flagship] gave the order "Let go all lines" at 0810, and we stood out to the anchorage followed by our landing craft; [we] anchored and took them up.

Much photography of Admiral Hewitt and myself with Algiers as a backdrop . . .

At 1710 we got finally under way. It is a moving sight, but over all is the feeling that only God and the Navy can do anything until we hit the shore. I hope God and Navy do their stuff. To be stopped now would have the most adverse effect on the future of the world. We will not be stopped.

General Lucas is sharing my cabin and is most excellent company.

*GSP, Jr., Message to men at sea*

We are indeed honored in having been selected [for] . . . this new and greater attack against the Axis . . . When we land we will meet German and Italian soldiers whom it is our honor and privilege to attack and destroy . . . During the last year we Americans have met and defeated the best troops Germany, Italy, and Japan possess. Many of us have shared in these glorious victories. Those of you who have not been so fortunate now have your opportunity to gain equal fame.

In landing operations, retreat is impossible. To surrender is as ignoble as it is foolish . . . However tired and hungry you may be, the enemy will be more tired and more hungry – keep punching. No man is beaten until he thinks he is . . . Civilians who have the stupidity to fight us we will kill. Those who remain passive will not be harmed . . .

The glory of American arms, the honor of our country, the future of the whole world rests in your individual hands. See to it that you are worthy of this great trust.

*Diary, July 8*

Lots of officers . . . say that they look forward to fishing, farming, etc. after the war. I don't – I look forward to fighting, here, in Japan, or at home, for the rest of my days . . .

I have the usual shortness of breath I always have before a polo game . . .

After supper I heard more laughing and singing among the men than I have to date. I would not change places with anyone I know right now.

At a small ceremony in Patton's stateroom, the I Armored Corps flag was taken down and the Seventh Army standard put in its place.

*Diary, July 9*

Slept as much as possible . . . Some soldiers outside the door were talking and said, "When we get ashore tomorrow, the papers will report that the Marines have landed in Sicily."

Had the chaplain in after supper to say a prayer.

Alfredo Guzzoni commanded the 200,000 men of the Italian Sixth Army and about 50,000 German troops. He had four excellent Italian divisions at central locations, where they were ready for swift dispatch to threatened sectors. His two German divisions were prepared to counterattack the invasion forces wherever they might appear.

A few minutes before 2 A.M., on July 10, Patton went on deck. "We may feel anxious but I trust the Italians are scared to death."

The invasion proper started in the early hours of July 10, with an airborne drop. The wind over Sicily was so strong that it scattered the aircraft and dispersed the troops. Very few men found themselves near two vital objectives they were supposed to seize to facilitate the invasion, a bridge near Syracuse in the British zone and an important crossroads on high ground several miles inland from the American landing beaches. British and American airborne soldiers all over the southeastern part of Sicily coalesced into small groups and proceeded to cut telephone wires and to ambush and terrorize small Axis units.

More than seven Allied divisions were to land simultaneously at 2:45

A.M., along 100 miles of shore. Montgomery's Eighth Army in the somewhat sheltered Gulf of Noto landed on schedule along 30 miles of coastline. The troops gained surprise and rolled over the defenders who offered little resistance. Leese's XXX Corps turned westward to make contact with the Americans, while Dempsey's XIII Corps prepared to capture Syracuse, Augusta, and Catania in swift succession.

Along 70 miles of coast on the southern face of Sicily, Patton's Seventh Army experienced some difficulties because the wind reached near-gale proportions. The troops were buffeted by high waves, and the assault landings were delayed. Bradley's II Corps headquarters directed Middleton's 45th Division, which went ashore near the fishing village of Scoglitti, and Allen's 1st Division, which hit the beaches near the minor port of Gela. Operating somewhat independently, Truscott's 3d Division invaded near the port of Licata.

At the outset, the opposition was relatively light. Fire from shore batteries was soon silenced by naval bombardment. Axis planes would appear later that day and harass the ground troops and sink two ships, but the first part of the invasion – getting ashore – seemed successful.

Lucas and Keyes played a large part in that success. Both were on the beach early that morning, organized work parties, and sent a steady stream of units toward their objectives.

*Diary, July 10*

Things were so complicated that I did not go ashore. I feel like a cur, but I probably did better here.

Hewitt is a perfect fool, but Admiral Lewis, his chief of staff, is good. Having trouble making Hewitt take over prisoners so as to relieve [Army] guards, or move his LSTs, now empty, back for the next load.

God has again helped me. I hope He keeps on.

The fighting became more serious during the afternoon of D-day, particularly in the Seventh Army area. Guzzoni, realizing very early that he could not counter all the landings, committed his resources against the most dangerous threats. He ordered the Germans near the east coast to defend Syracuse; he instructed a German and an Italian division to strike against Gela.

Massing for a counterattack at Gela, German and Italian elements headed for the beaches. Stopped by heavy ground and naval fires, the Axis forces built up their strength for a powerful attack on the following day.

The Americans, who had Licata, Gela, and Scoglitti in hand, recognized that Axis units were terribly close and were probing for a renewed and greater effort still to come.

British troops, meanwhile, took Cassibile and other initial objectives as scheduled. That evening, a column rolled into Syracuse. But when troops went beyond and headed toward Augusta, they were halted by a hastily erected defensive line.

On July 11, the second day of the invasion, Patton, Gay, and Stiller, with several soldiers as bodyguard, departed the *Monrovia* in the admiral's barge at 9 A.M., and arrived at the beach 30 minutes later. Patton noticed that two dukws had been destroyed by mines. While his scout car was being de-waterproofed, he inspected several abandoned landing craft that had large holes in their bottoms. A few shells, he guessed from an 88-mm. or a 105-mm. gun, hit the water about 30 yards away.

Patton and his group drove along the coastal road, intending to visit the 1st Division command post. They entered Gela and

> decided to call on Colonel Darby, commanding the Rangers. This was very fortunate because, had we proceeded down the road, we would have run into seven German tanks which at that moment were advancing . . . toward the town.

The two Axis divisions launched their attack on Gela, and a battle raged all morning long. American infantrymen, paratroopers, rangers, engineers, tankers, and artillerymen fought well and coolly, and the ships gave splendid support. Several German tanks came so close to the shoreline that the Hermann Goering Division commander informed Guzzoni: "Pressure . . . has forced the enemy to reembark temporarily." The message was premature. Axis troops never quite reached the beaches. American unloading operations were halted so that everyone on the beaches could fire, for by this time, the ships were unable to shoot – the opponents were too close to each other and fighting at pointblank range. Unable to cross the coastal road, with 16 of their tanks burning on the battlefield, the Axis forces pulled back. Ships' guns again opened up and hurried them into the hills.

During the height of the action Patton and his party were with Darby in Gela, which was cut off from the 1st Division. At an observation post in the top story of a tall building, Patton "could plainly see the enemy moving across the field, perhaps 800 yards away."

As the attack seemed to stall, two Axis planes dropped bombs on Gela.

> They hit the building we were in twice and also made a hole in the roof of the building across the street, but no one was hurt, except some civilians. I have never heard so much screaming.

When ten American tanks arrived to re-establish contact, Patton sent word to Gaffey. He wanted the gap between the town and the 1st Division closed. He also told Allen to send some tanks to help Darby. Soon afterward, Darby counterattacked, broke the direct threat to Gela, and took about 500 prisoners.

That evening Gay would write in his journal:

> It appears to me that Gela was in imminent danger of falling, particularly during the hours before noon, and I personally believe that the Commanding General's presence in the front lines had a great deal to do with the enemy attacks failing.

Somewhat later, Lucas would write to Eisenhower with respect to what he considered to be "the only serious counterattack" by the enemy:

> General Patton was ashore at the time, and I am convinced that his presence had much to do with restoring the situation.

Later, Patton would say,

> I personally helped lay some 4.2's [mortars] at a range of about 900 yards on enemy infantry. The white phosphorus was remarkable in its effect and seemed to make them quite crazy as they rushed out of the ravine, shrilling like dervishes with their hands over their heads [in surrender].
>
> On that same day we used it at about 3000 yards against tanks with some effect. The enemy, both Italian and German, are terrified of white phosphorus, and I personally do not blame them.

Learning that Truscott was all right around Licata, Patton drove to the 1st Division. He met Roosevelt and

> talked to him about the failure . . . to carry its objective last night. The chief reason, as far as I can see, is that the division attacked without anti-tank guns and without moving their artillery up.

A little later he encountered Allen, and they had a roadside conference. Fourteen German bombers came over, and when American anti-aircraft gunners opened up against them,

> quite a number of the fragments from the anti-aircraft hit along the road. One piece struck within, I should think, five to ten yards of General Gay and myself.

At the 2d Armored Division headquarters, "a German battery kept shelling us but was not very accurate."

After arranging for Allen and Gaffey to attack in the morning, Patton returned to Gela

> without incident except that I think it is quite unusual for an Army Commander and his Chief of Staff to travel some six miles on a road parallel to the front of two armies and about equally distant between the two. It was quite a lonesome feeling, but not very dangerous. It is good for self-esteem.

While waiting on the beach near Gela for a boat to take him to the *Monrovia,* Patton

> saw the most stupid thing I have ever seen soldiers doing. There were about three hundred 500-pound bombs and seven tons of 20-mm. high explosive shells piled on the sand, and these soldiers dug themselves foxholes in between the bombs and boxes of ammunition. I told them that if they wanted to save the Graves Registration burials, that was a fine thing to do, but otherwise, they better dig a foxhole somewhere else. About the time we got through explaining this to them, two bombers came over and straffed the beach, and all the soldiers jumped right back in the same holes they had dug. I continued to walk up and down and soon shamed them into getting up.

Patton and his party

> got back to the Monrovia at 7:00 o'clock, completely wet. This is the first day in this campaign that I think I earned my pay. I am well satisfied with my command today. God certainly watched over me today.

He had reason to be satisfied. Middleton's 45th Division had taken Comiso and its airfield. Allen's 1st Division and Darby's Rangers had tenaciously held Gela. Truscott's 3d Division had a substantial beachhead around Licata. Most of Gaffey's 2d Armored Division was unloaded. All three landings had been linked into a solid front.

He would have been even more satisfied had he known that Guzzoni had sent the Hermann Goering Division eastward to help block the vital approaches to Messina. For from the moment that Guzzoni learned of the invasion, his overriding concern was to maintain an escape route for the Axis forces in Sicily – through Messina and across the straits to the mainland – should evacuation of the island become necessary.

Hitler was thinking otherwise. He decided to bolster his Italian allies. He instructed Albert Kesselring, his senior officer in Italy, to fly a parachute division from France to Sicily, to move a panzer grenadier division from the Italian toe to the island, and to send Hans Valentine Hube and his XIV Panzer Corps headquarters from southern Italy to direct the augmented German forces in Sicily.

• • •

In his cabin on the *Monrovia* late in the evening of July 11, Patton was writing in his diary:

> Went to office at 2000 to see if we could stop the 82d Airborne lift, as enemy air attacks were heavy [during the day] and inaccurate Army and Navy anti-air[craft gunners] were jumpy. Found we could not get contact by radio. Am terribly worried.

Early that morning, figuring that the Axis would make a serious attempt to dislodge his beachheads, Patton had ordered a regiment of airborne troops to be flown from Africa and dropped inside his front. This was the quickest way to reinforce his units, but it was also dangerous.

Matthew B. Ridgway, the 82d Airborne Division commander, had been working on this idea of Patton's long before the invasion. He tried repeatedly to get assurance from the naval authorities that they would respect a cleared corridor for the air transports that would bring the paratroopers to Sicily. Naval commanders were reluctant to guarantee this access, for antiaircraft gunners had to respond quickly to planes appearing suddenly, particularly at low altitudes.

Several days before the landings, Ridgway finally gained the promise of cooperation but only if the air transports followed a designated route, with the last leg of that route over land. He then worked out a course with the air forces and gave the final information to Patton aboard the *Monrovia* in the Algiers harbor on July 6.

John Lucas arrived aboard the *Monrovia* at 0815 that morning, and he found Patton, Ridgway, and Joseph Swing in conference – the latter commanded the 11th Airborne Division in the United States and was visiting the theater of operations. Lucas joined them. He later recalled:

> They were discussing a message which had just been received telling the route over which the paratroopers were to be brought in by the Air Corps . . . They were all disturbed as to the difficulty of getting this information to the troops who were already embarked [that is, to warn them that paratroopers would be arriving and that there was to be no antiaircraft fire against the planes transporting them]. I asked why important information such as this had been witheld until this late date, and General Patton stated that he had been trying to get it from the Air Corps and Alexander's headquarters since July 3d, but without success.

Immediately after the meeting, Patton sent a message to all his major subordinate commanders – Bradley, Middleton, Allen, Gaffey, and Truscott. "You will warn your command," he ordered, "to expect flights of friendly troops" on any of the first six nights of the invasion – for he had not decided which night he might need them. The C-47-type planes would approach the coast near Sampieri and follow a northwesterly course. "Flights will pass between 2230 and 2400 hours approximately. Length of flight approximately forty minutes. Flights will drop parachutists or release gliders. Advise respective naval commanders."

To make sure this warning had been received and disseminated, Swing carried this message ashore at 9:30 on the morning of D-day. He visited all the major headquarters and requested all commanders to notify their troops, especially their antiaircraft units.

On the morning of July 11, having decided that the time had come to bring the airborne troops into the beachhead, Patton informed Ridgway that he wanted them to jump that night on the Farello airfield, which was in American hands. Immediately afterward, at 8:45 A.M., Patton sent a message to his major subordinates: "Notify all units, especially antiaircraft, that parachutists 82d Airborne Division will drop."

The antiaircraft gunners had a busy day on July 11, for German and Italian air forces launched almost 500 sorties, most of them in the Seventh Army area. A heavy air attack struck beaches and ships at dawn. Another at 6:35 compelled ships to weigh anchor and take evasive action. Once again at 2 P.M., four planes strafed the Gela beaches. Half an hour later, four bombers appeared over Scoglitti. Around 3:30, thirty Junkers 88s attacked the Gela area. And at 9:50 P.M., a large number of German planes flew over Gela and forced the ships to disperse. The antiaircraft responses were heavy.

Hardly had the noise of the last raid died down when Allied transports carrying Reuben H. Tucker's paratroopers – 2000 men – approached Sicily and crossed the coastline near Sampieri. The leading flight flew peacefully to the Farello airstrip, and at 10:40, the first stick jumped. The second flight was just across the shoreline when a single machine gun on the ground opened fire on the formation. Within minutes a chain reaction occurred, and it seemed that every Allied antiaircraft gun in the beachhead and offshore was hysterically blasting the slow-flying transport planes.

Squadrons broke apart and scattered. Six planes took direct hits as the parachutists were trying to get out of the door to jump. Altogether, of the 144 planes that had departed Tunisia, 23 never returned. Among the paratroopers, there were 82 dead, 131 wounded, and 16 missing. Ridgway, waiting at the airfield, was thunderstruck and helpless.

On the following morning, Patton sent his major subordinate commanders another message. He warned them that the paratroopers did not know the current countersigns and paroles. "Extreme caution must be used to identify before firing on personnel. Issue necessary orders at once to reach lowest units."

A day later, on July 13, Patton received "wire from Ike, cussing me out" because of the tragedy during the night of the 11th. "He demanded an investigation and statement of punishments for those guilty of firing on them."

> It is my opinion that every possible precaution was taken by this headquarters to obviate firing on our own airborne troops and that the failure to do so was an unavoidable incident of combat . . .
>
> As far as I can see, if anyone is blameable, it must be myself, but personally I feel immune to censure.
>
> Perhaps Ike is looking for an excuse to relieve me. I am having a full report made but will not try anyone [by court martial]. If they want a goat, I am it. Fortunately, Lucas, Wedemeyer, and Swing are here and know the facts . . . Men who have been bombed all day get itchy fingers.
>
> Ike has never been subjected to air attack or any other form of death. However, he is such a straw man that his future is secure. The British will never let him go.

An ensuing investigation was inconclusive in fixing the blame for the incident. Ridgway later summed it up best. He wrote: "The responsibility for loss of life and material resulting from this operation is so divided, so difficult to fix with impartial justice that disciplinary action is of doubtful wisdom."

• • •

On July 12, Kesselring and Guzzoni, after discussing whether it might be well to evacuate the island at once, decided to fight for time, making sure to hold the vital northeastern corner. According to secret instructions from Hitler, Hube was to conduct operations with a view to saving as many Germans as possible.

> *Diary, July 12*
>
> General Ike . . . came in a light cruiser . . . The only Americans with him were Huebner and Butcher . . .
>
> When I took him to my room to show him the situation [on the map], he was not much interested but began to compare the sparsity of my reports with the almost hourly news bulletins of the Eighth Army. I have intercepts of many of them, and they are both non-essential and imaginary in the majority of cases. Furthermore, they

are not fighting, and we are. I directed Gay to send in three reports in addition to the regular 1600 situation reports.

Ike also told me that I am too prompt in my replies and should hesitate more, the way he does, before replying. I think he means well, but it is most upsetting to get only piddling criticism when one knows one has done a good job. Ike is now wearing suede shoes a la British . . .

Left Monrovia with staff in LCT at 1700 [and went ashore].

The first thing Patton did was to see Ridgway and express his regrets over the airborne tragedy.

We have an advanced command post on a nose east of Gela and are sleeping in a huge double house in town, very gorgeous, in marble, etc., with bedbugs in the bed. I had the forethought to use my bedding roll. Stiller captured some champagne and that was all we had for supper excepting a can of cheese.

On that day, in the Eighth Army area, Dempsey's XIII Corps moved into Augusta when the Germans withdrew to better defensive positions.

Recognizing that the Axis would make a determined stand in front of Catania to deny the coastal road to Messina, Montgomery conceived the idea of bringing Leese's XXX Corps into the picture. If Leese could strike northward on an interior route and go around the western slopes of Mt. Etna, he would get behind the enemy troops blocking Catania. The best way for Leese to go was along Highway 124. But this road had been reserved for the Americans.

So Montgomery wrote a note and dispatched a messenger with instructions to hand it personally to Alexander. He said he now intended to advance to Messina by two routes. He suggested that the Americans be shifted westward to Gela to give him the interior road he needed. He recommended that the Seventh U.S. Army face westward and take defensive positions.

It was an arrogant message and would disturb the American camp.

*Diary, July 13*

I am not too pleased with progress of 1st Division . . . I ordered them to keep moving . . .

Bradley wanted to get Lt. Col. Darby to command the 180th Regimental Combat Team of the 45th Division with the rank of colonel. Darby preferred to stay with the Rangers. This is the first time I ever saw a man turn down a promotion. Darby is really a great soldier. I gave him the D.S.C. [for his action at Gela].

General Wedemeyer asked to be reduced to a colonel so he could get the 180th. I sent him up to command it as a brigadier general. I have no real authority to do this, but like to help a fighting man.

Then came the blow.

Went to lunch at 1250. General Alexander . . . and members of his staff arrived at 1310, so I had to quit eating and see them. They gave us the future plan of operations, which cuts us off from any possibility of taking Messina. It is noteworthy that Alexander, the Allied commander of a British and American Army, had no Americans with him. What fools we are.

Alexander had accepted Montgomery's suggestion. The Eighth Army was now to head for Messina, the only real strategic objective in Sicily, over two routes – one directly up the coastal road through Catania by Dempsey's XIII Corps; the other, by Leese's XXX Corps, along an inland road that would take the troops around the other side of Mt. Etna. The Seventh Army was simply to protect Leese's flank and rear in order to facilitate his advance to the northern shore of the island.

Patton was outraged, but he restrained his temper and practiced cunning.

I asked General Alexander permission to advance and take Agrigento, which is beyond the line specified for the front of the Seventh Army. He stated that if this could be done through the use of limited forces, in the nature of a reconnaissance in force, he had no objection.

Rationalizing why he wanted Agrigento, 25 miles west of Licata, but concealing the germ of a more exciting idea, he added:

It is very essential to capture this port as, by so doing, we can obviate the necessity of using Siracusa as a base, thus saving a turn around of 140 miles [by trucks] over bad roads, and also obviating

> the necessity of using a port in conjunction with the Eighth Army [which could use all the supplies coming through Syracuse].
>
> If we take Agrigento, we can supply [all the Seventh Army forces through ports] . . . This will permit abandonment of [unloading at] the beaches which are difficult and distant.

Having obtained Alexander's permission to embark on a reconnaissance in force to Agrigento, Patton told Truscott to go ahead. He also instructed Bradley to hand over Highway 124 to the British, then to sideslip the 45th Division west behind the 1st Division and around the other side. He wanted Bradley to move into the interior, heading north.

Bradley was angry. He hated to lose the road. And shuffling the 45th Division into a new zone was no easy task.

Lucas was upset. He believed that Patton should have expressed his views more vigorously and more firmly to Alexander. As the British liaison officer to the Seventh Army, Colonel Henriques, explained to Lucas, Alexander had no realization that what he stated as a wish was understood by Patton as an order "which it was a point of honor to obey." A British subordinate disagreed with his superior when he thought that the latter was wrong.

Furthermore, the British failed to appreciate fully the speed with which American troops could operate. American vehicles, particularly the 2½-ton truck, were so much better than British transport that Americans could move more rapidly on roads and cross-country. British observers were constantly astonished how quickly Americans got artillery pieces into position to fire. The self-propelled mounts enabled Americans to start firing in minutes when, in the same conditions, the British would require hours.

Patton's thoughts were elsewhere.

> The tremendous effort [the Italians] put into the construction of bands of wire, pillboxes, etc. proved abortive due to the failure of the enemy to show courage in defending them. Had the Italians and the few Germans with them fought to the limit of their ability, it would have been most difficult to evict them. Mind over matter . . .
>
> Our success . . . was due to our policy of continuous and violent attack . . . We are holding the initiative and must continue to do so.
>
> The people of this country are certainly in a deplorable condition.

> While not actually starving, they are subsisting on a minimum of food . . . It would be desirable [for us] to increase this [ration] but owing to the difficulty of landing stores, no increase is at this moment possible.

On July 14, Patton worked on a plan to continue his operations westward, "as directed by General Alexander." Alexander had approved taking Agrigento if it could be done without great effort, but Patton was looking beyond, as a matter of fact, all the way to Palermo. Denied a shot at Messina, he would at least have Palermo, a large city. Its capture would produce headlines shouting the praises of the valor and efficiency of the American soldiers.

To that end, he was already thinking of forming a provisional corps under Keyes. With the 3d Division, the 82d Airborne Division, and a regiment of the 9th Division "which is due to arrive tomorrow," Keyes could go all the way. Thus, Patton, like Montgomery, would have two corps operating on two routes – Bradley moving toward the northern shore of Sicily, Keyes moving toward Palermo. For the moment, he believed he had to keep the 2d Armored Division near Licata in reserve.

Driving to Licata, he congratulated Truscott "most warmly" and talked over with him the possibility of taking Agrigento "by bluff . . . I believe this operation can be successfully carried out with practically no loss and with great advantage to our supply system." Furthermore, "eventually this place must be taken and if it can be done now, it will be cheaper than waiting."

Beyond Agrigento:

> It is my opinion that when the present line of the combined armies is secured, which will probably be around the 19th, it will be feasible to advance rapidly with the 3d Division and 2d Armored Division and take Palermo. I will bring this question up to General Alexander when the time is ripe.

The Germans, he felt, were "not fighting as well as in Tunisia." He offered no explanation, but he must have suspected that their main motive was hardly victory but rather an attempt to preserve their escape routes.

*Diary, July 14*

The Tabor of Goums [a French unit with North African soldiers] . . . landed at Licata this afternoon. As we passed them on the road, I told them in French that I was glad to see them with us. The commanding officer . . . saluted smartly and said, "Nous vous devons beaucoup, mon General, d'etre ici pour le Quatorze Juillet" [We owe you much, General, to be here on the 14th of July – Bastille Day].

The Navy shelled Agrigento and Porto Empedocle to help Truscott's attack, but his request for bombers was refused because the air authorities had no word from Alexander that the front was to be extended beyond Licata.

Bradley, "a most loyal man," arrived and reported in great excitement that a captain had apparently taken Patton's instructions to kill too literally. He had shot between 50 and 70 prisoners

in cold blood and also in ranks – an even greater error. I told Bradley that it was probably an exaggeration, but in any case to tell the officer to certify that the dead men were snipers or had attempted to escape or something, as it would make a stink in the press and also would make the civilians mad. Anyhow, they are dead, so nothing can be done about it.

Wedemeyer returned from the 45th Division, where he had commanded an infantry regiment for several days.

I bet [Vice Air Marshal] Wigglesworth a bottle of whiskey against a bottle of gin that we would take Palermo by midnight on the 23d. He was very skeptical, but I believe without logical reason, that we can do so because I am sure that the enemy, German or Italian, cannot resist our continuous attacks. One Italian prisoner, an officer, is alleged to have said in a captured letter that the Americans were strange people; they attacked all day, marched all night, and fired all the time.

On July 16, he wrote his first letter to Beatrice since the invasion.

Darling B. As you will have seen by the papers, we did it again and are attacking right now . . . and having quite a war. We have captured more thousands of prisoners than [son] George was old [fourteen] when we sailed back from Honolulu. Also a hell of a lot of guns, air planes, rifles, and destroyed a lot of tanks . . .

The enemy has been booby trapping his dead, which has made our men very mad, with the result that there are more enemy dead than usual.

Yesterday I drove over one of our local battle fields and smelled dead men for some ten miles. It is a very strong disgusting odor.

Our losses have been relatively small, but we have lost some good men.

The town I am in is probably known to you as the Germans have broadcast that they recaptured it. They damned near did, but we beat hell out of them. I was right in the middle of it and had a swell time. Some came pretty close, but I earned my pay and probably saved the situation.

Monty is trying to steal the show and with the assistance of Devine Destiny [Eisenhower] may do so but to date we have captured three times as many men as our cousins.

Of all the countries I have ever been in, this is the most utterly damned. Dust, filth, bugs, and natives.

I have a realy fine house but the toilets dont work, and it is full of bed bugs, lice, and roaches. The people are just on the verge of starving and look utterly hopeless, but dont like us and there is a lot of sniping which is bad for us but worse for the snipers.

My CP is on the site of a pagan temple. There is only one pillar left, and that fluted. I would class it as Egyptian as its capital is like a lotus pod. No one here knows any thing about it except that Pliny wrote of it.

Lucas left for Algiers. He carried with him a map showing the daily progress of the Seventh Army.

I also requested him to see that we are not pinned down to the tail of the Eighth Army but be permitted to move west and take Palermo.

Truscott had just taken Agrigento and its satellite Porto Empedocle with little difficulty.

*Diary, July 17*

General Alexander . . . directs that the Seventh Army protect the

> rear of the Eighth Army, thus putting the Americans in a secondary role, which is a continuation of such roles for the whole campaign and may find the war ending with us being overlooked. I am flying to Tunis to see General Alexander.
>
> I am sure that neither he nor any of his British staff has any conception of the power or mobility of the Seventh Army, nor are they aware of the political implications latent in such a course of action.
>
> I shall explain the situation to General Alexander on the basis that it would be inexpedient politically for the Seventh Army not to have equal glory in the final stage of the campaign. Arranged a map showing our proposed operation and attached a copy of the order we believe should be written . . .
>
> General Wedemeyer and I left . . . at 1210, arrived at Tunis at 1309, and saw General Alexander. He explained that he had planned to do just what I asked but that his chief of staff had failed to tell me when issuing the order. [Patton found this a "pretty weak" excuse.]
>
> He gave me permission to carry out my plan if I would assure him that the road net near Caltanissetta would be held . . . If I do what I am going to do, there is no need of holding anything, but "it's a mean man who won't promise," so I did.

The presence of Wedemeyer at Patton's meeting with Alexander gave added weight to Patton's argument. Wedemeyer had been visiting Sicily as Marshall's representative, and he was returning to Washington and his duties as an important member of Marshall's staff. Should he intimate that Alexander was directing the Allied ground forces in a nationalistic spirit that favored the British at the expense of the Americans, Marshall was sure to raise the issue with the Combined Chiefs of Staff.

Huebner, Alexander's deputy chief of staff, whose role was in effect to make an American point of view available at Alexander's headquarters, was also present at what must have seemed like a showdown, although everyone was extremely polite. Alexander could not help being embarrassed, and the Americans would soon shift Huebner to another assignment.

Patton gave Wedemeyer two letters to take to Washington, one for Marshall, the other for Handy.

To Marshall, Patton was positive. Everything was going well. The troops were splendid, the Air and Navy fine. If the Navy had a better fuze that would allow shells to burst closer to ground surface, naval gunfire support, he thought, would improve. "The vigor and speed of our attack," he said, "was ruthlessly pressed forward." His "box score" of prisoners taken and enemy material destroyed, which he attached to his letter, was, he believed, "quite satisfactory." Lucas and Wedemeyer had been tireless and indifferent to danger, and their suggestions had been of great value.

To Handy, he was somewhat more candid. He mentioned the defects, as he saw them, of the system for getting close air support. The fighting quality of the Germans was less impressive than in Tunisia, but "we must remember that the fighting quality of our own troops has increased so that the differential may be more apparent than real . . . Our equipment is superb," but Americans had a tendency to want too much. Finally, he thought there was "an exaggerated idea" of the proportion of SOS troops needed to support the combat troops.

Elated by his success with Alexander, he dictated, for his own amusement, a paper that he called a "Summary of Events." It was really a list of his impressions. Some of them were:

> The Italians and Germans spent tremendous effort in time, labor, and money, building defensive positions. I am sure that just as in the case of the walls of Troy and the Roman walls across Europe, the fact that they trusted to defensive positions reduced their power to fight. Had they spent one-third as much effort fighting as they did in building, we never could have taken the positions . . .
>
> The Italian troops . . . have fought very desperately. The German troops . . . have shown gallantry but bad judgment . . .
>
> The naval gunfire support, that is, naval fire put on the beaches from vessels at sea, has been outstanding. We have even called for this support at night and gotten it on the target on the third salvo.
>
> The people of this country are the most destitute and God-forgotten people I have ever seen . . .
>
> During the first two or three days . . . the inhabitants were, to say the least, not friendly, but . . . they have become quite Americanized and spend their time asking for cigarettes.

In the United States, Beatrice Patton was helping to enhance her husband's reputation and legend. Interviewed for a radio broadcast, she said:

He has always felt that wars are won, not by the best tanks or the fastest airplanes, or the most powerful guns, but by the fightingest men. When he jumped from his landing barge into the sea to lead the attack at Gela, he knew they would not let him down. As he said in his order before Morocco: "We shall attack and attack and attack until we are exhausted, and then we shall attack again. A pint of sweat will save a gallon of blood" . . .

Invariably he writes of visiting the wounded in field hospitals. He knows what it is to be wounded, for during the last war he was grievously wounded himself, and almost left for dead. During the Tunisian campaign, he visited the hospital clearing station every day, and in his letters he never ceases to marvel at the modern treatment of the wounded. "The blood plasma saves more lives than you could ever believe," he writes, "and failing the supply of plasma, the soldiers and the nurses give their own" . . .

He's always known that some day his country would need him and that he must be ready. He's not only a great student of tactics and history, but he brings the past right into the present and applies it to the situation in hand. When he was in Africa, he used to write me about Hannibal . . .

He believes that God will help him . . . He believes in himself, and he believes in his soldiers. In his battle order before Sicily, he says, "Remember that, as attackers, we have the initiative. We must retain this tremendous advantage by attacking rapidly, viciously, ruthlessly, without rest, however tired, and punching. God is with us. We shall win."

*Letter, GSP, Jr., to Beatrice, July 18, 1943*

Our battle is still going on and, as you can see from the score sheet, we have a swell bag . . .

I flew over to Carthage to see Alex yesterday as I did not like something. It was all settled in a nice way and we can keep on attacking. If we should halt, we would loose momentum . . .

I have the diahera and feel poorly, but it only lasts two days.

We will finish this show sooner than any one thinks. After that I don't know, but it would seem that they will have to keep on using me. Vet[e]ran, what?

CHAPTER 17

# Palermo and Messina

*"If I succeed, Attila will have to take a back seat."*

HUBE brought his XIV Panzer Corps headquarters to Sicily on July 15, established a good working relationship with Guzzoni, and began to prepare a meticulous plan for evacuating the island. Although Guzzoni remained in nominal command of the Axis forces in Sicily, Hube conducted the land battle. Both men agreed that their purpose in fighting was to postpone as long as possible the Allied conquest of Sicily. The four German and the four Italian divisions were to pull slowly into the northeastern corner and eventually withdraw from the island to the Italian mainland.

*Diary, July 19*

I was amazed at what our troops have accomplished over truly terrible country [for fighting] . . . At Caltanisetta, we killed at least 4,000 civilians by air alone and the place smelled to heaven as the bodies are still in the ruins. I had to feel sorry for the poor devils.

We had lunch in the Facist Palace, which, strangely enough, was not hurt much. It was truly magnificent, all velvet and brocade and gold chairs and we had lunch of C rations in the state dining room on a silk tablecloth, lovely china and silver with toilet paper [for] napkins . . .

My policy of continuous attack is correct. The farther we press, the more stuff we find abandoned that should not be abandoned. The Italians are fighting very well in face of certain defeat. They must crack soon.

I think that the British have the bear by the tail in the Messina peninsula and we may have to go in and help. Had they let us . . . take Caltagirone and Enna ourselves, instead of waiting for them, we would have saved two days and been on the north coast now.

Alex has no idea of either the power or speed of American armies. We can go twice as fast as the British and hit harder, but to save British prestige, the XXX Corps had to make the envelopment, and now I think they are stuck. They attacked Catania with a whole division yesterday and only made 400 yards . . .

Our method of attacking all the time is better than the British system of stop, build up, and start, but we must judge by the enemy reaction. I can do it here [judge the enemy reaction] — Alex can't in Tunis.

Acting on his hunch that the Seventh Army might get a crack at Messina, Patton telegraphed Alexander and suggested bringing the entire 9th Division to Sicily before the end of the month.

On his file copy of the telegram, Patton added a handwritten note: "I was quite right in this idea as events have shown. Again I had outguessed the situation."

*Diary, July 20*

We took Enna at 0943 . . . The Canadians came in from the east eight minutes later . . . I sent a dispatch to General Alexander saying that we [both] arrived at the same time. I will bet they claim to have got there first.

Decorated a large number of [men] . . . Band played Star Spangled Banner and God Save the King and then I had a concert and all the Dagos cheered and danced and asked for food. I often wonder when one of them will try to kill me, but I think that apparent lack of fear bluffs them, and it is good for the troops to see my flags flying all over the front. One dies but once and I am on a high spot. A victorious memory may be better than to achieve success and be forgotten. However, I feel that I still have much to do, so probably won't get killed, but I do hate to be shot at just as much as I ever did.

Keyes is going great, and we may get Palermo by the 23d, and I will win my bet with Wigglesworth . . .

I could have been elected Pope right after the concert.

Patton had formed a Provisional Corps with Keyes in command. From Agrigento, Keyes sent the 82d Airborne Division westward to Marsala and Trapani and the 2d Armored and 3d Divisions to Palermo.

Meanwhile, Bradley's II Corps was advancing through the middle of Sicily toward the northern shore, heading for the coastal town of Termini Imerese.

*Letter, GSP, Jr., to Beatrice, July 20, 1943*

Our men are realy grim fighters, and I would hate to be the enemy . . .

I was actually appauled at the havoc wrought in some of the towns by our air and artillery . . .

The whole country is literally strewn with smashed trucks, guns, and tanks . . . In my opinion, their so called Tiger tanks with the 88 mm's are a flop. They are too slow.

I had lunch with Troy [Middleton] in a Facist palace recently occupied by the Germans. It was so magnificent that it would have made Louis XIV blush for shame . . .

This show has changed from a battle to a campaign . . .

Back of my house is a little court yard. Yesterday I counted eleven children, eight goats, five dogs, and a horse, also a flock of chickens minus tails. The children were competing with the other animals for scraps of food . . .

I feel terribly sorry for the poor things. Wherever you pass them, they beg for food, but I suppose they are natural beggars.

My theory of keeping on attacking has certainly worked. Now I am trying to get Gaffey loose. If I succeed, Attila will have to take a back seat . . .

It is hard to be an Army commander and a hero at the same time.

*Letter, GSP, Jr., to Beatrice, July 20, 1943*

This is the second letter I have written you to day . . .

Poor things [the natives], I feel sorry for them. They make tomato catchup in the streets and let all the filth settle on it and then eat it with spagattey. All the children beg for food all the time and one could buy any woman on the island for a can of beans, but there are not many purchasers.

*Diary, July 21*

The British have a pretty bloody nose south of Catania . . . They have asked for the 78th Division [to come to Sicily from North Africa], which last week they said they did not need.

I really feel like a great general today — all my plans have so far worked. I hope God stays with me.

Keyes sent a message, "Peanuts for breakfast," which means the 2d Armored will be on the way at 0600, July 22d . . . If the attack . . . works out, it will be a classic example of the proper use of armor. I told Gaffey and Maurice Rose [who headed a combat command in the division] to take chances — to smoke the enemy and then charge him with tanks. I am sure that this will work as the enemy is jumpy and justly so, in the face of the power we can put against him.

Eisenhower found time to prepare Patton's efficiency report covering the first six months of 1943. He graded Patton "Superior," and placed him Number 3 among the lieutenant generals — "I know them all." Patton functioned best in command of a corps or an Army. He showed "outstanding leadership" and was "aggressive, loyal, energetic. Particularly suited for creating esprit and morale in a force preparing to face great risks."

*Letter, GSP, Jr., to Beatrice, July 22, 1943*

Keyes who is commanding a provisional corps just radioed "Will kick goal this evening or at latest in the morning." By the time even the censor sees this [letter] the name of the town will be in all the papers so he can fill it in here ———.

We have out blitzed the Bosch . . . It is really a great show. I am flying to the front after lunch to see the kill.

*Diary, July 22*

Left for the front . . . The road discipline was superior. Whenever I passed any of the 2d Armored Division, all the men first saluted me and then waved. It was quite cheering.

It was probably on that day, near Licata, he wrote Beatrice eight months later, that he came to "a one way bridge with half the Hell on Wheels being delayed by a mule cart and a fight [battle] going on." Patton had the mule killed and, along with the cart, pushed off the bridge to get the traffic moving. "Actually I broke my stick over the driver. Human rights are being exalted over victory."

On the way up we passed some very fine tank traps . . . and antitank ditches . . . Only killing stops good troops — defenses sap the vitality of those who make them.

I feel that future students of the Command and General Staff School will study the campaign of Palermo as a classic example of the use of tanks. I held them back far enough so that the enemy could not tell where they were to be used; then when the infantry had found the hole, the tanks went through and in large numbers and fast. Such methods assure victory and reduce losses, but it takes fine leadership to insure the execution. General Keyes provided perfect leadership and great drive. The praise should be his.

After dusk we got to the command post of the 2d Armored Division and Colonel Perry, chief of staff, told me he thought Palermo had fallen and that Generals Keyes and Gaffey had entered it. He volunteered to guide me in, so we started . . .

It is a great thrill to be driving into a captured city in the dark. We got to the Headquarters at the Royal Palace at 2200 and found Keyes and Gaffey had gone to bed, and Combat Command A and elements of the 3d Division had the town under control. I saw Keyes and Gaffey and congratulated them. We had a small flask and each took a drink.

Alex radioed, "This is a great triumph. Well done. Heartiest congratulations to you and all your splendid soldiers." I [had] told him once that Americans needed praise and here it is.

*GSP, Jr., Account of Capture of Palermo, July 23, 1943*

We went through an almost continuous village. The street was full of people shouting, "Down with Mussolini" and "Long Live America."

When we got into the town the same thing went on. Those who arrived before dark . . . had flowers thrown on the road in front of them, and lemons and watermelons given them in such profusion that they almost became lethal weapons.

The Governor had left, but we captured the two [Italian] Generals, both of whom said that they were glad to be captured because the Sicilians were not human beings but animals.

The bag in prisoners for the day must have been close to 10,000. On the morning of the 23d, when I was inspecting the harbor, I passed a group of prisoners, all of whom stood up, saluted, and then cheered.

The harbor is not too badly damaged, but the destruction around the lip is really appalling . . .

We took over the so-called Royal Palace for a headquarters and had it cleaned by prisoners for the first time since the Greek Occupation [in antiquity]. We are also having the prisoners remove the rubbish from the streets and plug the holes in the dock . . .

The Cardinal's Vicar came to call on me, and I assured him that

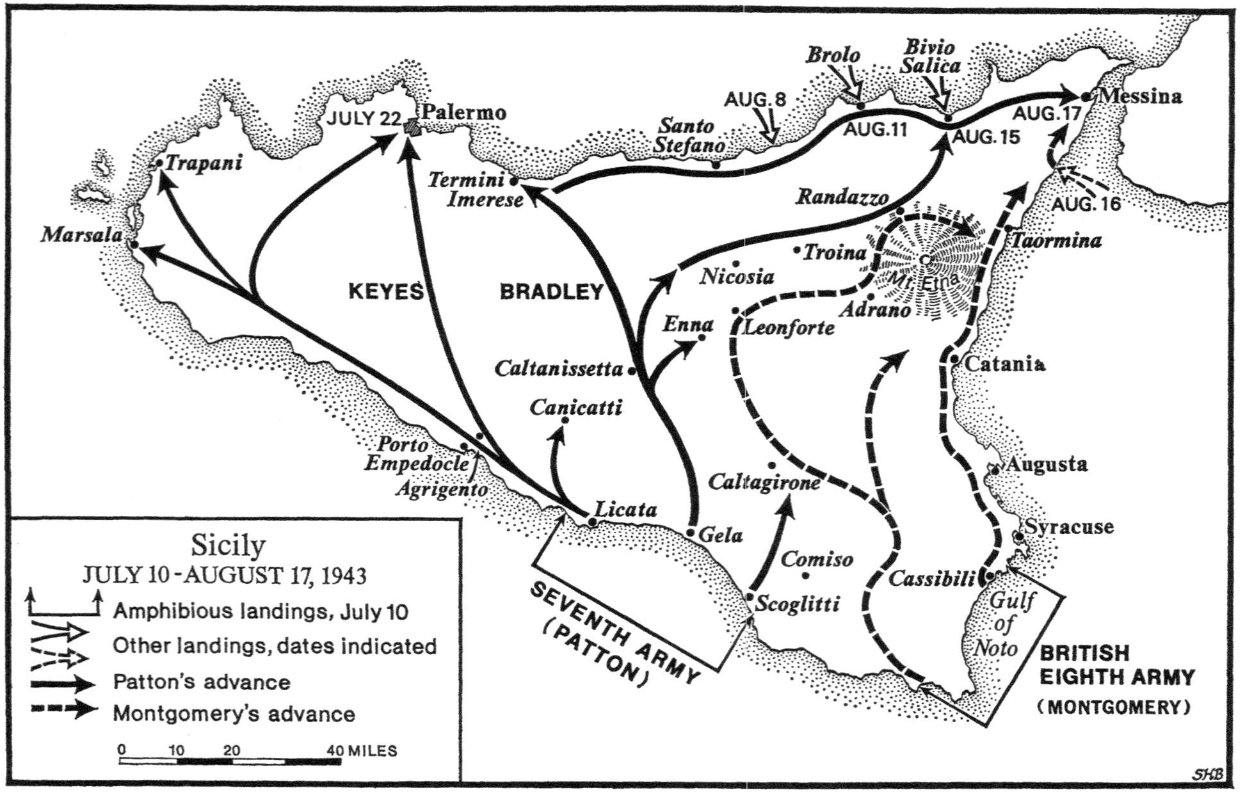
Messina
AUG. 17
AUG. 16
AUG. 15
Bivio
Salica
AUG. 11
Brolo
AUG. 8
Santo
Stefano
Palermo
JULY 22
Trapani
Marsala
Termini
Imerese
Randazzo
Taormina
Troina
Mt. Etna
Adrano
Nicosia
Enna
Leonforte
Catania
KEYES
BRADLEY
Caltanissetta
Canicatti
Porto
Empedocle
Agrigento
Licata
Gela
Caltagirone
Comiso
Scoglitti
Augusta
Syracuse
Cassibili
Gulf
of
Noto
SEVENTH ARMY
(PATTON)
BRITISH
EIGHTH ARMY
(MONTGOMERY)
Sicily
JULY 10 - AUGUST 17, 1943
Amphibious landings, July 10
Other landings, dates indicated
Patton's advance
Montgomery's advance
0
10
20
40 MILES
SHB

I was amazed at the stupidity and gallantry of the Italian army: stupid because they were fighting for a lost cause, and gallant because they were Italians. I asked him to tell them that and to spread the rumor.

I further said that we had demonstrated our ability to destroy them, and if they failed to take the hint and surrender, we would certainly do so.

As a matter of fact, I called off the air bombardment and naval bombardment which we had arranged, because I felt enough people had been killed, and felt that with the drive of the 2d Armored Division we could take the place without inflicting unproductive losses on the enemy.

I believe . . . that historical research will reveal that General Keyes' Corps moved faster against heavier resistance and over worse roads than did the Germans during their famous blitz.

We did not waste any time, however, and started this morning capturing the north road and also moving artillery to support the final effort of the II Corps which will begin in a few days.

The "final effort" to which Patton referred was to be an American drive along the northern shore toward Messina. For on July 22, the same time that Palermo fell, Bradley reached the north shore at Termini Imerese.

The British have given me [Routes] 113 and 120 [leading to the east, toward Messina] and are damned glad we are there . . . The Seventh Army has taken most of the island . . .

But the details on the use of the roads had still to be worked out.

*Letter, GSP, Jr., to Eisenhower, July 24, 1943*

It would seem . . . that the visit I paid to General Alexander . . . produced results, as it permitted us to take Palermo and thereby shorten our line of communication and facilitate unloading.

The operation of the Provisional Corps . . . is, I believe, a correct exemplification of the use of armor . . .

The performance of all the troops, infantry and armored, was outstanding, and the drive and leadership shown by General Keyes were of a superior order. I should appreciate it if his name could be released [to the press] . . .

So far as I know, out of close to 300 tanks, only 5 fell out because of mechanical trouble . . .

I have nothing but praise for all the General Officers concerned, and nothing but outstanding admiration for the endurance, hardihood, and combat efficiency of the troops . . .

The supply arrangements, both from the SOS, Navy, and our own Supply here have been very successful, and I have nothing but praise for all of those concerned . . .

I certainly appreciate your having sent the rest of the 9th Division, as I feel that we will need them in the ensuing operation which may be quite bloody. The faster we can push it, the less it will cost.

With renewed thanks for the opportunities you have always given, I am as ever, Devotedly yours,

*Letter, Col. John A. Robenson, Camp Fannin, Tex., to GSP, Jr., July 24, 1943*

Dear Georgie: I take two daily papers and saw your picture in yesterday's papers eleven times.

*Letter, GSP, Jr., to Beatrice, July 24, 1943*

So many big shots have told me how great I am that I am in danger of believing and that might cramp my style — just like it did when Gen. Craig told me I stood [number] one [in the class] at Leavenworth. But I shall try to keep proper perspective and the Leavenworth lesson will help . . .

Of course under the circumstances there is danger in too much success, but I cant help it if the cherries fall in my mouth.

So far I have heard nothing [of praise] from D, but suppose that in time it will come?

Geoff realy deserves most of the credit and I have handed it out to him via the press. I hope it gets through.

Tomorrow I go to see Alex and Monty. I hope it comes out all right. I always feel like a little lamb on such occasions but so far I have gotten by.

Some day I hope I can fight a nice war alone [without allies] but fear that it is too much to hope for. Any how I love wars and am having a fine time. When it cools off, I am going to have a close up of the Greek temples as it will be my last chance as I join Geoff tomorrow evening.

I saw a very fine statue of Charles V of Spain at Palermo. Did he

> ever own the place? It is on the front of quite a fine looking house, I should think of about 1600.

Even Gruenther, who arrived for a visit, contributed to Patton's feeling of self-importance. He was

> just snooping, trying to find out how we do things. Every time I said something, he wrote it in his notebook.

The only flaw that marred the joy was the outrageous news that Huebner was relieved as Alexander's deputy chief of staff —

> largely, I know, because he stood up for American interests . . . Bedell Smith (s.o.b.) relieved him at the request of Alexander . . . I believe the British have hurt themselves very much and have hurt the entente between themselves and the Americans . . . It is a sad commentary that a man must suffer from being an American.

Lyman L. Lemnitzer replaced Huebner.

> To report at Siracusa Airport tomorrow at 1100 to see Alex and Monty. I fear the worst, but so far have held my own with them.

While the Seventh Army headquarters started moving by road to Palermo, Patton flew in a C-47, with two Spitfires as escorts, to Syracuse. "Monty was there with several staff officers. I made the error of hurrying to meet him. He hurried a little too, but I started it. He then asked me to look at a map on the hood of his car. On this he had drawn a boundary" between the Armies.

They discussed the roads they would need in their next operations, and Patton was surprised by and somewhat suspicious of Montgomery's conciliatory attitude.

> He agreed so readily that I felt something was wrong, but have not found it yet.
>
> When this much had been arranged, Montgomery did not see why we did not take all of route 117. As it is useless to both of us, he did not have any objection to our taking it.

All this was hardly vital. What was terribly important was that Patton would have the coastal road, Highway 113, and another route, about 20 miles inland, Highway 120, for his eastward drive toward Messina.

After all this had been settled, Alex came. He looked a little mad, and, for him, was quite brusque. He told Monty to explain his plan. Monty said he and I had already decided what we were going to do, so Alex got madder and told Monty to show him the plan. He did and then Alex asked for mine and agreed, but said there were supply difficulties which General Miller [G–4, AFHQ] would explain.

All Miller wanted to do was to cut my LSTs to 35.

I held out for 45, to which Miller reluctantly agreed, but said it was up to Admiral Cunningham.

On this, Bedell Smith broke in and told Miller that AFHQ would make the division [of LSTs between the Armies] and that he, Miller, was too prone to forget the existence of AFHQ. (So is everyone else, as it never asserts itself.)

I then said I wanted LCTs for at least a reinforced battalion for small amphibious operations [along the north shore]. Alex did not think much of this but agreed to try.

I also said I needed cruisers, and Richardson said he would see that we got them. I doubt if he does.

He also asked me if I knew Huebner had been relieved, and I said I did.

He said, "I want to assure you that [Alexander's] 15th Army Group is completely Allied in mind and favors neither Army."

I know this was a lie, but said I felt that he was right — God pardon me.

Actually, by giving Patton two roads to Messina, Alexander placed the Seventh Army on an equal footing with the Eighth.

The meeting then broke up. No one was offered any lunch and I thought that Monty was ill bred both to Alexander and me. Monty gave me a 5¢ [cigarette] lighter. Some one must have sent him a box of them.

We flew back to Palermo in just one hour, arriving at 1430, at the same moment that the rest of the staff came in by motor.

Keyes met me with a Guard of Honor from the 3d Division and a band. We occupied the Royal Palace. I am in the King's room and

> there are, by count, seven ante-rooms between my room and the State dining room. My bed has three mattresses on it, but is uncomfortable, and there is a bathroom with warm water, also electric lights. Many fine oil paintings on the walls and much gold furniture, mirrors, etc. . . There is also a grand staircase — very dirty. All sorts of retainers live in holes about the place and all give the Facist salute.
>
> Stiller has no flair for history and said he was sure he could find me a nicer place in some good boarding house. I prefer the historical lift of sleeping in a royal bed and cleaning my teeth in glass etched with the Arms of Savoy.

It all enhanced his feeling of being a conqueror. He was indeed exceptionally elated.

No doubt prompted by the thought that Huebner, whom he had always admired and liked, was now available for a new assignment, Patton talked with Lucas, Bradley, and Keyes, then suggested to Eisenhower that the time had come to relieve Allen and Roosevelt — but "without prejudice on the ground that their experience will be of great value at home and that they are now battle weary." To replace them, he asked for Huebner and Norman Cota.

On July 26, Patton "heard radio broadcast that Mussolini had retired."

Mussolini's retirement was forced. He was kidnaped and imprisoned in a secret place. King Victor Emmanuel appointed Marshal Pietro Badoglio head of government and instructed him to break the alliance with Germany and make peace with the Allies. Badoglio immediately dissolved the Fascist party, declared "The war continues," and set about to see how he could negotiate with the Allies for an armistice.

Hitler was enraged by news of Mussolini's abduction. But he followed Kesselring's advice: precipitate no break with the Italians, move more German troops into Italy to prevent an Italian surrender, and fight a delaying action in Sicily to the end of conserving resources.

Eventually Hitler would rescue Mussolini and set him up as head of a puppet state in northern Italy.

*Diary, July 26*

> Called on the Cardinal. He lives in a convent as his palace was bombed. He is very small and quite intelligent. They took a lot of pictures of us in the bosom of the church. I offered to kiss his ring but Keyes said no, that only the faithful did that — he did it. We

went into a chapel and prayed. The Mother Superior is a French woman and we talked a little . . . I feel that he [the Cardinal] is on our side and this fact will have a good effect on the inhabitants.

*Letter, GSP, Jr., to Cardinal Luigi Lavitrano, July 26, 1943*

I am pleased to take under consideration your request for alleviating the condition of these prisoners of war . . .

In accordance with your further request, orders will also be issued to enable the clergy of the Diocese to visit such places of detention of prisoners . . . and to impart to them your message on the necessity of good order and discipline.

*Letter, GSP, Jr., to Beatrice, July 26, 1943*

All the towns along the coast are built on high rocky hills and have been the cites of cities since pre historic times . . . Where we are now fighting the country is the worst I have ever seen, realy terrible, hills as bare as babies bottom.

Omar, Terry, and Manton [Eddy] are having the hardest battle yet fought since last November. Of course we will win but it takes time.

The Germans are SOB but great soldiers and are sticking to the death and know it . . .

The other day . . . I apparently performed a miracle. I was at the hospital seeing the men [who had been hit] . . . I presented a lot of Purple Hearts. Finally I came to a man with an oxygen mask on, which is the last stage, so I took off my helmet, kneeled down, and pinned the PH on his pajamas – he got well.

*Time* magazine carried a photograph of Patton and a caption that quoted him as saying: "It makes no difference what part of Europe you kill Germans in."

An article describing the campaign in Sicily mentioned his brief visit to North Africa. Many stories about him had come out of Sicily, tales befitting the Patton legend, and some were rather wild. One anecdote had him "making" a two-star general go to the top of a hill "so that you can get shot at a bit," accompanying the general up the hill and waiting at the top until "a suitable number of missiles had fallen suitably near," then saying, "All right, you can go down now." Although Patton's colleagues smiled at stories such as these, they believed some of them.

Yet there was now a more balanced appreciation of Patton. "Gorgeous Georgie" and "Old Blood and Guts" – "who had once cultivated the spectacular impression" – had proved that he "was also a patient and careful and studious man, a field officer with a good staff mind."

To the correspondent with whom he talked, Patton said, "You had better come now [with me to Sicily] or my men will have killed all the bastards."

"Then he was gone, back to the places where the fighting was."

*Letter, GSP, Jr., to Beatrice, July 27, 1943*

Green Meadows and even Avalon are going to look pretty measley to me after this. To get to the royal apartment in which I sleep, you have to traverse seven anti rooms and a small dining room about forty by sixty.

Keyes lives at the other end but he has only three anti rooms – a piker.

The Palace was built in sixteen hundred but is modernized though not cleaned. I get quite a kick about using a toilet previously made maloderous by constipated royalty.

The bed has a spring matress and then three other down ones on top like the story of the Princess and the Pea, only unfortunately you are not there.

The state dining room is huge, I imagine over a hundred feet long and forty wide. We eat "K" rations on china marked with the Cross of Savoy.

Stiller who has no soul took one look at the place and said, "General, if you let me look, I can find a nice modern house much better than this old dump."

The old dump is some two blocks long. One end has offices, the middle a church, and the other end living quarters. The living part has two court yards and also a Grand Stair Case. You can either go up the stairs or else drive on a sort of circular street and get off where you like.

Me and His Eminence the Cardinal are very thick. Yesterday I called on him and to day he called on me . . . An Arch Bishop came with him . . . and a couple of other prelates. We gave them captured German champagne and bacon and had quite a time. He is of great use to me as a stabelizing agency and of course exerts great influence . . .

The war is far from over but we are going to win it in a big way. At the moment we are having a hard race with our cousins. I think we have an edge on them. I am quite curious to see what comes out at home. BBC just barely admits that we exist.

I have not the least notion what will happen next time [after Sicily] but I don't care where, when, or who I fight so long as I keep fighting. It is the greatest of all games . . .

FDR sent me a signed picture of he and I, and the PM has wired congrats, but Divine Destiny [Eisenhower] is still mute.

*Diary, July 27*

Inspected Coast Artillery Corps Anti-aircraft. The Colonel [in command] did not know where his [firing] batteries were. I told him to visit all of them at once and be able to guide me personally next time.

*Diary, July 28*

Monty, his air officer, and chief of staff arrived at noon. Codman met them at the airport with escort of scout cars and motorcycles. Keyes and I met them at the Palace with company of . . . infantry and a band. I hope Monty realized that I did this [instead of meeting him at the airport] to show him up for doing nothing for me on the 25th.

After lunch he showed me his plan . . . Monty kept repeating that the move of the 45th Division along the coast was a most significant operation. I can't decide whether he is honest or wants me to lay off [the inland route] 120. On the other hand, he said that if we got to Taormina first, we were to turn south. Previously he had insisted that we not come as far as the [east] coast . . .

I spurred both Bradley and Middleton a little today. I felt they were getting sticky, but probably I am wrong.

*Letter, GSP, Jr., to Middleton, July 28, 1943*

This is a horse race, in which the prestige of the U.S. Army is at stake. We must take Messina before the British. Please use your best efforts to facilitate the success of our race.

Still smarting from what he considered to be the condescending attitude of Alexander and Montgomery and other British officers toward American troops, whom they regarded as second-rate at worst, inexperienced at best,

Patton became obsessed with reaching Messina ahead of the British – not so much for his personal glory, although that was important, but rather to prove to the world that American soldiers were every bit as good as – indeed, better than – British troops.

*Diary, July 30*

Middleton looked tired and his attacks have lacked drive, so I said, "I think I will give the 45th a rest and use the 3d."

He said, "I would never ask for a rest."

I said, "It is my duty to see that the best interests of the United States are served, so I shall give you a rest."

He replied, "I think that is what you should do."

I thought this was an excellent example of willingness to play ball and unwillingness to ask for help. I wired Truscott to come up and talk over with Middleton the question of [division] relief . . .

Bradley called up and I told him . . . I was going to relieve the 45th, as I had talked about with him yesterday.

Drove to the command post of the leading battalion . . . just west of S. Stefano. They were attacking. I talked to the men and said, "I hope you know how good you are, for everyone else does. You are magnificent." I also told the engineers what fine work they have done. They have, but love to be told.

*Letter, Beatrice to GSP, Jr., July 30, 1943*

I think you have hit on how to make the men mad, although unwittingly. Any enemy who will booby trap their own dead deserves no mercy, and after a few hands have been blown off trying to move them, will get none from the Americans . . .

I am saving you clippings from all sorts of papers . . .

Your letter . . . written during the battle gives me the creeps and thrills. I went to Myopia [Hunt Club] to dinner last night with [half brother] Chill and [brother] Fredy and took the letter over to read to them. In the middle of dinner, John Tuckerman (himself) got up and banged for silence and suggested a standing toast to Myopia's most distinguished son – General Patton. (Pretty good for old John, as the last letter I ever got from him began, "My God, Miss Ayer, I would have tried so hard to make you perfectly happy.")

Chilly demanded that I read the letters to the company, so I did, with judicious skipture. I also read the last sentence of your . . .

jumping into the surf from the landing barge [which] has been in all the papers and when I read: "This is the first day of the campaign. I think I earned my pay," they all yelled.

Monty hardly figures at all in the papers except to compare his number of prisoners and yours, sadly to his disadvantage. Everyone wonders what he is doing and why he doesn't go ahead . . .

Your account of the fight on the 11th is great, except that you left out how you personally took command by jumping into the sea. I wish you had told about that . . .

Your visit to the Cardinal was great. I have now heard on good authority that you are a Catholic.

If I were you, I should allow the correspondents to write something of the sort you wrote me about the havoc in the towns – how you wondered, when you saw the battlefields from the enemy side, how you ever could have taken them . . . The reason I suggest this is because if any one is (or are) trying to steal your show, they might try to say it was a pushover, and a few gory details planted in the popular mind will be a good thing. You have some fine writers. I like Drew Middleton and Richard Tregaskis especially, and they are widely read. So far you are the hero; but in time of war prepare for peace, is my motto.

I do hope that you and O. won't have to change hats again. I don't believe you will. He couldn't do that to you twice . . .

The N.Y. Times tonight calls you the brilliant and mobile soldier, pretty good from them, but take my advice and have the c[orrespondent]'s put out that the resistance was bitter or people may think otherwise.

Your blitz is unheard of in its speed.

*Diary, July 31*

Ike . . . arrived . . . We had a scout car escort and Guard of Honor, the last from his old battalion of the 15th Infantry, the only unit he ever commanded. This touch was the thought of Gay, and Ike was quite pleased with the compliment. He was quite relaxed but did not compliment us . . .

He says [that after Sicily] the Eighth Army will . . . cross at Messina and the Fifth U.S. Army land at Naples with one American corps and the X British Corps. If things get serious, the Seventh Army will land later near Florence, otherwise we will go to UK for the big push [across the Channel]. I have a feeling that the UK show will never materialize [because of] the British . . .

I got Ike's permission to relieve both Allen and Roosevelt on the same terms . . . There will be a kick over Teddy but he has to go: brave, but otherwise no soldier. Huebner and [Colonel W. G.] Wyman go up in the morning [to replace them].

I telegraphed Allen's and Roosevelt's relief to Bradley and sent him a personal note suggesting that he postpone it until the 1st Division is relieved by the 9th.

*Letter, GSP, Jr., to Beatrice, August 1, 1943*

All the West is cleared up and we are pushing to the east, north of Etna. To day we made about 10 miles against very fierce resistance, but they cant stand our continuous attack . . .

Last night they bombed us for an hour . . . One bomb hit quite close to me when I was on the dock, but luckily landed in the water so did no harm.

*Diary, August 1*

We have started to move and move . . . The mountains are the worst I have ever seen. It is a miracle that our men get through them but we must keep up our steady pressure. The enemy simply can't stand it. Besides, we must beat the Eighth Army to Messina.

*Seventh Army General Orders 10, August 1, 1943*

To be read to the troops. Soldiers of the Seventh Army and XII Air Support Command: Landed and supported by the navy and air force, you have, during 21 days of ceaseless battle and unremitting toil, killed and captured more than 87,000 enemy soldiers, you have captured or destroyed 371 cannon, 172 tanks, 928 trucks, and 190 airplanes — you are magnificent soldiers! General Eisenhower . . . and General Alexander . . . have both expressed pride and satisfaction in your efforts. Now in conjunction with the British Eighth Army you are closing in for the kill. Your relentless offensive will continue to be irresistible. The end is certain and is very near. Messina is our next stop!

*Letter, GSP, Jr., to Somervell, August 2, 1943*

Some of the really important factors in successful war are not mentioned because they are so obvious, so I am taking this occasion to tell you what a wonderful thing you did in providing us with the DUKWS . . .

DUKWS permitted a strategical surprise, because no one unacquainted with the capabilities of the DUKWS – and the Germans were unacquainted – could have visualized a successful landing on the south coast where this Army landed . . .

The speed of [our] operations and the violence of attack were largely made possible by the old 2½ ton 6-wheeler [truck] and by the self-propelled artillery . . .

The cub plane has been of great assistance in maintaining communication and in permitting senior officers to inspect distant units . . .

The clothing, equipment, and weapons of the American soldiers are superior to anything that we have encountered . . . and on behalf of this Army I desire to thank you and your organization for providing us so amply and so well.

*Letter, GSP, Jr., to McNair, August 2, 1943*

The 4.2 mortar is doing a splendid job, and is spreading white phosphorus in an even more generous manner than the 105 [artillery shell] . . .

We have been very fortunate in our operations so far, and I am betting that we get to Messina first in the current horse race.

The troops have improved tremendously since Tunisia . . .

Their famous Tiger [tank] is . . . a poor piece of artillery and a bad tank.

At the moment, malaria is bothering us more than the enemy, although we are fighting pretty hard.

Already he was thinking of what he would do beyond Sicily, and his concluding remark to McNair was prophetic: "Trusting that I will not get the job of garrisoning this damn island."

*Cable, Eisenhower to Patton (through Alexander), August 2, 1943*

The Seventh Army has already made a name for itself that will live in American history. Within the next few days it will add immeasurably to the lustre of its fame. I personally assure you that if we speedily finish off the German in Sicily, you need have no fear of being left there in the backwater of the war.

*Letter, Charles F. Ayer to GSP, Jr., August 2, 1943*

I am told that in California you are considered the greatest warrior ever known and certainly in this part of the world your career is becoming an epic. In another one hundred years, and perhaps in half that time, you will, I think, be a legendary hero . . . We are watching your performance with the deepest interest and applauding in spirit, although the four thousand miles of distance prevents our making this applause audible.

*Diary, August 2*

Inspected all sick and wounded at the . . . hospital. Pinned on some 40 Purple Hearts on men hurt in air raid. One man was dying and had an oxygen mask on, so I knelt down and pinned the Purple Heart on him, and he seemed to understand although he could not speak . . .

The Monsignor who runs the chapel [at the Palace] said it was the first time that anyone but royalty had ever been there, but that from now on it is for the use of the Americans.

Alex came . . . I was very much amused at his statement that he was delighted with our ability to carry out his plans for the early capture of Palermo . . . He did everything to prevent not only its early capture but its capture at all.

*Letter, GSP, Jr., to Beatrice, August 2, 1943*

The tablet for Dick [Jenson] is not for Dick but to inspire others who will read it . . .

We have had all the hot shots to visit us, first Monty, then D, and to day Alex.

The first is much less condescending than he was — he ought to be, as a study of the map will show.

D was very nice and while not complimentary failed to criticize — first time. Apparently we have made more of a splash than we know. We have not seen a paper from home yet.

Alex is always good company and much interested in ruins. I showed him my palace . . . There is a parliament room 140 feet long by 60 broad, with all the labors of Hercules in fresco on the walls at one end and on the cealing. Someone is being roasted at the other end, Venus is having a time with some one, and in the middle there is a three headed horse and a lot of soldiers.

The middle part of the palace was built before 1000 and there is a chapel in it built by a Norman duke in 1040. The old Monsenieur who runs it told me that it was reserved for royalty but insisted on

> having a mass for me, so I went all alone. He wanted to make it a Tedium [Te Deum] mass, but I insisted on a low one as not knowing the rules, I decided to kneel all the time. It was not too bad, as I had a royal red velvet priedieu. He is a fine old man and hates Mus[solini].
>
> The walls are covered with frescoes and the part back of the alter is full of pictures made of inlaid stones. The head of Christ is the finest I have ever seen. All conquerers have made up to the priests of the conquered . . .
>
> We are going to pull a stunt on the enemy pretty soon – long before you get this, that may become quite famous.

He was referring to an amphibious end run to get troops around the mountains holding up the overland advance toward Messina. The problem was, he could get only enough landing craft to lift a battalion-sized force. This would hardly be strong enough to get behind the Germans and bottle them up.

Hube on that day completed a detailed evacuation plan, meticulously prepared, with precise defensive lines, definite ferry schedules, and exact movements specified. To get all the Axis forces off the island, he needed five nights. His problem was, could he keep the Allies from interfering with his withdrawal? Could he keep them from pushing the Axis forces out of Sicily in disorder? Moving into the corner would facilitate the evacuation, for as the front became shorter, Hube could pull units out of the line and send them to the ferries. The ground was excellent for a defensive stand.

On August 3, Patton was awarded the Oak Leaf Cluster to the Distinguished Service Cross, according to the citation, "For extraordinary heroism in action against an armed enemy" on July 11, near Gela, where he

> promptly moved to the scene of action over a road that was being constantly bombed and strafed . . . Personally directing the movement of reinforcements, he closed the gap and repulsed all counterattacks. His prompt action . . . and his presence on the front line among his troops prevented the recapture of Gela by the enemy and made possible the establishment of a secure bridgehead.

*Diary, August 3*

Stopped at an evacuation hospital and talked to 350 newly

wounded. One poor fellow who had lost his right arm cried; another had lost a leg. All were brave and cheerful. A first sergeant . . . was in for his second wound. He laughed and said that after he got his third wound he was going to ask to go home. I had told General Marshall some months ago that an enlisted man hit three times should be sent home . . .

Roosevelt came up, all perturbed about being relieved. I reassured him and also Allen.

Roosevelt's relief left him somewhat bitter. Several months later he wrote to his wife:

At El Guettar, I was in a slit trench with Terry Allen, only large enough to hold two. Patton came up. A dive bombing raid started. I got out & gave Patton my place. He took it. I never thought about it again, but a friend of mine told me two months later the story was being told.

Appointed liaison officer to the French military command, Roosevelt would serve in Italy as a member of Alphonse Juin's corps staff. Later, as assistant commander of the 4th Division, he would land in Normandy among the leading assault waves.

Allen would take command of the 104th Division in the United States, bring it to Europe in the fall of 1944, and lead it in combat with brilliance and distinction.

*Diary, August 4*

Asked General McSherry in charge of Civil Affairs to have the local civilians bury German and Italian dead found in their fields and bring us the dog tags. Also told him to put a crimp in the Facists, who are running a black market and stealing food from the poor.

Brig. Gen. [R. A.] McClure in charge of publicity was in. I told him he should take a motor trip over the country so he could see how bad it is and get proper credit for our men. He will do it tomorrow.

*Letter, President Roosevelt to GSP, Jr., August 4, 1943*

Dear George: . . . You are doing a grand job . . . It was suggested by Pa Watson and Wilson Brown and Harry Hopkins that after the war I should make you the Marquis of Mt. Etna. Don't fall into the crater!

*Letter, Everett Hughes to GSP, Jr., August 5, 1943*

Here is a quotation from a recently arrived communication which may have a moral effect on a [certain] Lieutenant General [Patton]: "It is in this follow-up [of the cross-Channel invasion] that the prestige of the Seventh Army would prove to great advantage." So once more, keep your shirt on.

Patton was worrying about where the Seventh Army would go next.

*Diary, August 5*

Inspected all the rear echelon sections and told the soldiers . . . that although they are not doing very romantic work, they are doing work of great importance and without their efforts, the more romantic aspects of war would be impossible.

Busted some pictures of Mussolini with my dagger and had one really good bust smashed at the Post Office. Told Provost Marshal to destroy all busts and pictures of him. I consider such acts a pity, but if one is not an iconoclast, one is considered unpatriotic.

We are having a good deal of trouble in getting the Navy to go in for amphibious operations east of San Stefano. They appear to have no idea of the value of time or the need for improvisation. If they can't get everything they want, they say they can't move. I think this is the result of many years during which all officers who lost a ship were tried [by court martial]. It is true that they have had two destroyers smashed by bombs and really think they should pull out, but we have had many thousands of men hit.

General Spaatz came to see me. As usual he was dirty and unshaved.

*Letter, GSP, Jr., to Frederick Ayer, August 6, 1943*

We have taken a town that we have been attacking for three days, so I feel pretty good, especially as Bernard [Montgomery] had wired me that he was coming to my assistance. Now he don't need to. We are having a horse race who will get the last big town first — it will be a close match, but I hope to beat him and so make a clean sweep.

This is a truly horrid country in climate, fleas, mosquitoes, sand bugs, mountains, and inhabitants.

Sergeant George Meeks, my colored orderly, has it sized up pretty well; he said, "When you and me commanded the 5th Cavalry, them Mexicans was mighty low; then when we got to Morocco, the Arabs was worse; then when we commanded the II Corps in Tunisia, that was worse yet, but when we got back to Algeria, that was the bottom. Now here we is, commanding a Army, and these natives is lower than the bottom!" He is about right.

The town to which Patton referred was Troina. After several days of heavy fighting and heavy Allied pressure, Hube relinquished it. He also gave up Catania to the British. By pulling back from Troina and Catania, together with Adrano, which the Canadians took, Hube abandoned what the Allies called the Etna Line and settled into a shorter line of defense.

*Diary, August 6*

I stopped to inspect the field hospital . . . and saw two men completely out from shell shock. One kept going through the motions of crawling. The doctor told me they were going to give them an injection to put them to sleep and that probably they would wake up alright.

One man had the top of his head blown off and they were just waiting for him to die. He was a horrid bloody mess and was not good to look at, or I might develop personal feelings about sending men to battle. That would be fatal for a General.

The Germans are firing at the command post regularly with a long-range gun . . . I was a little worried for a few seconds, and I felt ashamed of myself but I got over it. I have trained myself so that usually I can keep right on talking when an explosion occurs quite close. I take a sly pleasure in seeing others bat their eyes or look around.

The Navy promised Patton enough lift to move a battalion of infantry on an amphibious end run. There were plenty of good beaches for landings, and four sites, each behind a predictable defensive line, were chosen. Since Bradley feared that Patton's intense desire to get to Messina might compel him to be rash in ordering an amphibious operation, he obtained Patton's agreement to have seaborne landings closely coordinated with the overland advance. This would insure swift link-up with the landed force and prevent its isolation and destruction.

On the evening of August 6, as a battalion of infantry marched to San

Stefano for embarkation, four German aircraft bombed and strafed the area and damaged a key LST in the projected assault. Truscott postponed the operation, and the Navy rushed another vessel from Palermo.

On the following evening, as the battalion again marched to the embarkation point, another German air raid damaged the newly arrived LST. After hurried repairs, the troops were loaded, and the amphibious force, covered by two cruisers and six destroyers, sailed for Sant' Agata. The men came ashore at 3:15 A.M., August 8, and found the Germans gone.

Now Patton's Seventh Army was 75 miles from Messina; Montgomery's Eighth Army was 52 miles short of the town.

On that day, Kesselring gave Hube permission to start evacuating his forces whenever he thought it necessary.

*Diary, August 9*

Bradley . . . feels that we should try the two men responsible for the shooting of the prisoners . . . He also reports that at least three Italian [American] soldiers . . . have deserted and were caught living in civilian clothes with the natives. I shall try to have them shot. Desertion in face of the enemy – the bastards.

I am staying home today as I feel that I should not appear too often when things are going well.

*Letter, GSP, Jr., to Beatrice, August 9, 1943*

We moved our CP up the coast . . . The camp is in an ancient olive grove where Hannibal may have wandered if he ever came this way. It was full of mines, but Hap [Gay] had it deloused, and it is very nice. I have flown over it twice in a cub and cant see it. Besides, George [Meeks] has dug me a slit trench as large and deep as a grave in which I can retire.

The first afternoon they shelled us . . . and some of the fragments would howl over head. I was disgusted to find that my pulse went up – I timed it – but soon I got my self in hand.

Mostly I can have a shell hit or a mine go off quite close with out winking or ducking. This is a great assett, and besides if they were going to get you, they hit you before you hear them. One must be an actor . . .

It is the God damdest country I have ever seen. Indio looks like foot hills. The show now is more of a campaign than a battle. I am fighting on two roads with Lucien [Truscott] and Troy [Middleton] on one and Terry [Allen] and Manton [Eddy] on the other. The others are holding in the West . . .

We pulled a landing operation the other night. No opposition. When we got in an orchard, there were four hundred Germans asleep. It was butt and bayonet for a while. It was too dark to shoot. We won . . .

I tried to put an another landing to night but no soap. The sister service is a bunch of ladies. We are trying to win a horse race to the last big town. I hope we do . . . Roads more than enemy stop us.

I saw a letter taken off a German corpse the other day in which he said that this was worse than Stalingrad. He wrote his parents telling them good by – he was right . . .

I have lived a long time in the last thirty days, but I feel very humble. It was the superior fighting ability of the American soldier, the wonderful efficiency of our mechanical transport, the work of Bradley, Keyes, and the Army staff that did the trick. I just came along for the ride . . . I certainly love war . . .

This is the longest day I have ever spent. I have been at the extreme front every day for three days and decided I was being a nusance so stayed in camp all day. It was hell. I can hear the guns, and they have the damdest effect on me. I am scared but want to get up [front] . . .

P.S. It might be good to send a copy of this to Tom Handy. He would probably use it correctly. Omit the P.S.

*Letter, GSP, Jr., to McNair, August 10, 1943*

Bradley and I both feel that it is desirable to shoot over soldiers [in training], but this crawling about under fire is in our opinion, certainly in my opinion, apt to produce undue timidity rather than the reverse.

In this hot country, the composition sole of a shoe burns the men's feet . . . and thereby . . . vitiates the advantages . . . in its non-slip characteristics . . .

I am firmly of the opinion . . . that if possible the 37-mm. gun in the light tank should be replaced with the 57-mm. gun . . .

The replacements are still not as good as they should be . . .

The fire of the M-1 rifle is devastating . . .

P.S. I am perhaps presumptuous in what is to follow, but it is my opinion that an Army should consist of two infantry corps, each corps consisting of three infantry divisions . . .

In each corps, two divisions should be old and one new. In addition . . . there should be two armored divisions. Whether or not these armored divisions should be formed into a corps is open to question . . . The corps should be simply tactical and not administrative . . .

If I should be given an Army as above outlined, I should like to have General Bradley, or if General Bradley gets an Army, then General Middleton to command one of the corps and General Keyes the other corps. It is desirable I think to have different personalities for corps commanders. Keyes is very dashing; Bradley and Middleton are more methodical. All three are infinitely loyal and of superior effectiveness.

If it is desired to have an armored corps, I should recommend General Harmon . . .

My reason for suggesting three divisions to the corps is based on the absolute necessity of giving short periods of rest to battle-weary divisions.

I trust that my rather grandiloquent statements will be received by you in the spirit in which it is written. I do not consider myself a great Army commander, but do believe I have had some experience.

*Diary, August 10*

At another evacuation hospital . . . one boy with a shattered leg said, "Are you General Patton? I have read all about you." All seemed glad to see me . . . Most of them are in good shape, and I saw only two who the medical people said were going to die . . .

At 1945, Keyes called up to say that Bradley and Truscott wanted to call off the landing on the ground that 3d Division had not gotten on fast enough to support it. I told Keyes that the landings would go on. Truscott then asked to speak to me and strongly protested going on the landing. I told him it would go on. He replied, "Alright, it you order it," and I said, "I do."

I then decided to go up to see Truscott and took Gay along to see that the boats got off . . . I got to the command post, 3d Division, at 2045. The first person I met was Captain Davis, U.S. Navy, chief of staff to Admiral Davidson. He said the landing should be called off, as it had started an hour late and could not land before 0400. I told him that if it did not land until 0600, it still had to go on.

Truscott was walking up and down, holding a map and looking

futile. I said, "General Truscott, if your conscience will not let you conduct this operation, I will relieve you and put someone in command who will."

He replied, "General, it is your privilege to reduce me whenever you want to."

I said, "I don't want to. I got you the DSM and recommended you for a major general, but your own ability really gained both honors. You are too old an athlete to believe it is possible to postpone a match."

He said, "You are an old enough athlete to know that sometimes they are postponed."

I said, "This one won't be. The ships have already started."

Truscott replied, "This is a war of defile, and there is a bottleneck delaying me in getting my guns up to support the infantry. They – the infantry – will be too far west to help the landing."

I said, "Remember Frederick the Great: L'audace, toujours l'audace! I know you will win and if there is a bottleneck, you should be there and not here."

Bradley called me at this moment to see whether we were going to attack. I told him we were, and that I took full responsibility for a failure but that if things went well, he could have the credit along with Truscott.

I then told Truscott I had complete confidence in him, and, to show it, was going home and to bed, and left.

On the way back alone I worried a little, but feel I was right. I thought of Grant and Nelson and felt O.K. That is the value of history. I woke General House up to be sure we would have air cover for the Navy in the morning, as we may need their support [for the landing]. I also told him to put all his air in front of the 3d [Division].

I may have been bull-headed, but I truly feel that I did my exact and full duty and under rather heavy pressure and demonstrated that I am a great leader.

Montgomery had embarked Commando units twice for amphibious end runs on the eastern face of Sicily. He had canceled both because he thought they were too risky.

*Diary, August 11*

I am not going to the front today as I feel it would show lack of confidence in Truscott, and it is necessary to maintain the self-respect of generals in order to get the best out of them.

The infantrymen making the seaborne envelopment came ashore at Brolo at 2:30 that morning. They were behind the German front, and fortunately for them – for they were too small a force to withstand a German attack in strength – they moved across the beaches and into the high ground without being detected. When the Germans discovered their presence athwart their route of withdrawal, they mounted a strong effort to eliminate them. Dug in on good positions, helped by naval gunfire and air strikes, the men held out all day. That evening, after a massive attack on the main battle line, Truscott drove the Germans back and made contact with the Americans on the hill.

The amphibious venture had made the Germans pull back faster than they had wanted.

That evening Hube started his evacuation, sending forces across the straits by increment while still holding the Allies at bay. The withdrawal would continue during the following four nights.

*Letter, GSP, Jr., to Beatrice, August 11, 1943*

Poor old Kent [Hewitt] . . . is realy a menace. I never knew such an old lady. We have a fellow named Davidson with us here who is swell and willing to fight.

I realy did what the papers say at Gela and a lot more too, such as not taking cover etc., but mostly an Army commander is too safe. We are now about eight miles or perhaps five back of a battle. You can hear the guns clearly . . .

Yesterday I earned my pay. We were to put on a swimming operation, and it was all set. Then at 8:00 Omar and Lucien both called to say it was too risky. I told them to do it . . . It worked, and now they think they thought of it. I had to get pretty tough and ask how they would like to have stars turn out to be [colonels'] eagles.

I have a sixth sense in war as I used to have in fencing, and besides I can put myself inside the enemies head and also I am willing to take chances. Last night I remembered Frederick [the Great]'s "L'audace . . ." and Nelson putting the glass to his blind eye and saying, "Mark well, gentlemen. I have searched diligently and see no signal to withdraw. Fly the signal to continue the action." Also other acts of victorious generals.

I was coming back through a mine field alone in the dark – there was, however, a trail if you could see it – and those historic memories cheered me no end.

I was interrupted here to answer a phone call from Lucien that he was about to be counterattacked. I told him that that was one of the easiest places to kill Huns and to go to it. He was much cheered up . . .

The shooting has started up again. I think I will go and have a look.

*Telegram, Eisenhower to GSP, Jr., August 12, 1943*

All I'm doing is sending congratulations.

Patton directed that another amphibious landing be made in a few days in order "to block the enemy retrograde movement to the east."

*Diary, August 12*

Three German planes flew over. We could see the bomb bays open and the bombs drop, but as we were on a road with a wall on one side and a cliff on the other, we could do nothing about it, so . . . just stood there. The bombs did not hit too close but might well have done so.

While this bombing was going on, Truscott came up and I had a chance to congratulate him on his splendid work.

*Diary, August 13*

In bed with high fever.

*Diary, August 14*

Still quite sick, but flew late in afternoon to 3d Division CP.

*Letter, GSP, Jr., to Beatrice, August 15, 1943*

There is a disease here called locally sand fly fever, supposed to be transmitted by the bite of a tiny fly . . . You run a high fever around 104, ake all over, cant eat, and sweat all the time. It lasts four to five days, and then you are all right. I will be over it tomorrow, which is fortunate, as I think we will end the show tomorrow or next day . . .

It was funny to see our men sitting down among German corpses eating lunch . . . Our men are pretty hard . . .

I sent you a very gaudy bed spread which took the Palermo prize for embroidery in 1893. I paid $90 for it. Hope it was worth it . . .

There is no point in saying I have been sick. Too many people hope I will be. I feel pretty punk so shall go back to bed.

You will soon see me in the movies entering Messina.

*Diary, August 15*

We are going to put on a third amphibious operation tonight.

Montgomery had also decided to launch a seaborne operation, and early on August 16, British Commandos came ashore and sped toward Messina.

*Diary, August 16*

Truscott and Bradley again tried to call off the landing operation due to the fact that elements of the 3d Division had passed Falcone [the landing site]. I insisted that the landings go on because the plans had been made and also so we would get an extra regiment to the front without effort.

Early that morning a regiment of Middleton's 45th Division was lifted by sea to Bivio Salica. Men of Truscott's 3d Division had already taken the place and were pushing toward Messina.

We received a message from Truscott at about midnight that leading elements of the 3d Division entered Messina at 2200 . . . I immediately sent a message in clear [uncoded] to General Alexander and one to General Eisenhower.

Phoned Bradley at 0300 on the 17th that we would enter Messina in the morning at 1000 hours. I also phoned Truscott to make the necessary arrangements.

At daybreak, August 17, the British Commandos were two miles south of Messina and halted by a demolished bridge over a deep ravine. Herculean efforts managed to get a jeep across the gap, and the commander of the force drove for the town. When he arrived, he found, to his dismay, that Messina was in American hands.

On the hill just west of Messina, Truscott received the municipal dignitaries at 7 A.M. He sent his assistant division commander, William Eagles, into the town to organize the troops and, as Eagles later said, to see that the British did not capture the city from the Americans.

Half an hour earlier, at 6:30, Hube telegraphed Kesselring from the toe of Italy to inform him that the evacuation was complete. He had ferried across the strait 40,000 Germans, about 70,000 Italians, more than 10,000 vehicles, almost 200 guns, 47 tanks, 1000 tons of ammunition, 1000 tons of fuel, more than 15,000 tons of miscellaneous weapons and equipment.

*Diary, August 17*

Left by cub at 0850, Lucas, Gay, and self. Met Keyes at command post 3d Division . . . and drove to . . . top of hill overlooking Messina. Bradley not there — must have failed to get the message. This is a great disappointment to me, as I had telephoned him, and he certainly deserved the pleasure of entering the town.

Patton made a short talk into a dictaphone of the BBC and complimented the 3d Division, particularly the enlisted men.

We started into town about 1010. On the way, the enemy shelled the road from the Italian side [of the straits]. One of these shells hit the second car behind me, wounding all the occupants, including the G–2 of the 3d Division. The next car behind that, in which Truscott's aide was riding, had all four tires blown off without injuring the car or anyone in it.

In the town of Messina we met three British tanks and a few men who had arrived at 10:00 o'clock under the command of a general. It is very evident that Montgomery sent these men for the purpose of stealing the show. They landed from one LCT about 15 miles south and had come directly up the road. I think the general was quite sore that we had got there first, but since we had been in for 18 hours when he arrived, the race was clearly to us.

Montgomery had sent an armored column toward Messina, and the tankers made contact with the Commandos, repaired the bridge, and entered the town. The senior officer walked over to Patton, shook his hand, and said, "It was a jolly good race. I congratulate you."

We then went to the town hall and saw the Mayor, the Chief of Police, etc. I told Truscott to do the honors as he had captured Messina. The town is horribly destroyed — the worst I have seen. In one tunnel there were said to have been 5,000 civilians hiding for over a week. I do not believe that this indiscriminate bombing of towns is worth the ammunition, and it is unnecessarily cruel to civilians.

On the way back we met General Bedell Smith and General Lemnitzer. Smith had stopped back of the crest, just why I do not know, although it would be reasonable to suppose because the road beyond the crest was under fire.

*Diary, May 22, 1944*

Just heard the full story of Beedle Smith at Messina. After Keyes, Gay, and I took off to enter the town, Smith and Lemnitzer arrived and decided to follow me "if it was quite safe." Murnane [Gay's aide] took them. When they got to the top of the pass, Smith asked if we were under fire and was told it could happen. Just then one of our batteries of 155 [mm.] guns let go, firing [across the strait of Messina] into Italy. Smith thought it was enemy shells arriving and jumped from the car into the ditch in one leap, and refused to leave it, even when Lemnitzer and Murnane told him it was quite safe. When I got back he was still pale, gray, and shaky.

*Diary, August 17, 1943*

I took Smith in my car and we drove ahead to the 3d Division where we had lunch . . . I had quite a discussion with him about promotions for the staff of the Seventh Army. He said that when it was organized we were told that we would not get the makes [promotions]. I said I knew that, but now that we had demonstrated our ability, we demanded recognition, not as a favor but as a right. I feel sure he will do his best to prevent it, but I will get them anyhow. Smith is a typical s.o.b.

Well, I feel let down. The reaction from intense mental and physical activity to a status of inertia is very difficult . . .

I feel that the Lord has been most generous. If I had to fight the campaign over, I would make no change in anything I did. Few generals in history have ever been able to say as much.

So far in this war I have been a chip floating on the river of destiny. I think I had best keep on floating – I will surely be used some more, though at the worst, things look gloomy. For the moment the future of the Seventh Army does not look bright but I trust that the same fortune which has helped me before will continue to assist me. I have been very lucky.

*Letter, GSP, Jr., to Beatrice, August 18, 1943*

The Sicilian campaign has joined the countless others which this island has known and become history . . .

The attack . . . which we started on July 23 was one of the fiercest and most sustained battles in history.

We tried every thing, including three landing operations behind them. The obstacles in the way of terrain and demolitions were appauling and the valor and tenacity of the enemy was great but we were greater.

Few people, especially generals, have no regrets, but in this case, I have none . . .

Of course, had I not been interfered with . . . by a fool change of plan, I would have taken Messina in ten days. But then I would have had to turn back to get Palermo. So it all came out OK . . .

M.[essina] is the worst mess I have seen. It is realy smashed. The natives were delighted to see us.

In addition to getting M. 26 hours ahead of the British, I also got a second D.S.C. for the Gela affair.

It came as a complete surprise to me. John Lucas wrote it up. I rather feel that I did not deserve it, but wont say so.

I feel awful to day, all let down. I have no inkling what is going to happen to the Seventh Army. W[ayne Clark] will have the next job [invading southern Italy at Salerno]. I may end up with Jake [Devers] for another swimming party [invading southern France]. I hope not.

I will move back to my palace in a day or so, but at the moment we are in a fig orchard . . . It is not bad at all.

My damned fever left me very weak and with a back ake, but I am getting over it.

As I fought a perfect campaign and got a second DSC, I may have fulfilled my destiny, but hope not. Some one must win the war and also the peace.

# CHAPTER 18

# The Slapping Incident

*"I have been a passanger floating on the river of destiny. At the moment I can't see around the next bend, but I guess it will be all right."*

THE "PERFECT CAMPAIGN" was soon to be marred. For only a few days would Patton savor the bittersweet joy of the aftermath, the euphoria of success combined with the sadness of completion – the delicious consideration of achievement to be examined and cherished.

He put aside his sorrow over the losses among his men. He was always aware of the hurt of combat, but he never brooded over the inevitable costs of war. They were personally too painful for him, and besides, to be too sensitive might adversely affect his generalship.

It was good to relax and recall, to remember sailing out of the Algiers harbor toward a great adventure, to live again the fight at Gela, to think of the confrontation with Alexander, to reflect on the pressure maintained on commanders, to be grateful for winning Messina, to be proud of the American soldiers, who had proved beyond doubt their combat effectiveness.

Messages of congratulation poured in. From President Roosevelt: "All of us are thrilled . . . My thanks and enthusiastic approbation." Alexander: "My sincerest admiration for not only your recent great feat of arms in taking Messina, but for the speed and skill you have shown in the Sicilian operation. Your country will be very proud of you and so am I to have the honor of having under my command such magnificent troops." Marshall: "You have done a grand job of leadership and your corps and division commanders and their people have made Americans very proud of their army and confident of the future." Cunningham: "It has been a joy to watch the speed and dash of the Seventh Army." Montgomery: "The Eighth sends its warmest congratulations to you and your splendid Army for the way you captured Messina and so ended the campaign in Sicily." Hewitt: "The Navy is proud to have been able to participate."

Yet Patton worried about the future. Where was he next to be employed? What would happen to the Seventh Army?

Alexander said that the Seventh Army was to rest and also to train for operations in similar terrain, thereby suggesting a commitment on the mainland of Italy. Eisenhower said that the Seventh Army was to have no place in the operations on the Italian mainland. What of the Channel crossing being planned for the spring? Would Patton spearhead the amphibious assault? Would he take part in the invasion at all?

Instructions he received disturbed him. He was to retain a few essential units such as antiaircraft to garrison Sicily properly, and to send practically everything else to Clark's Fifth Army. Why would the Seventh Army be broken up – dispersed and dissipated – unless there was no further mission for it? And yet Eisenhower had promised that Patton would not remain in Sicily in the backwater of the war.

It was all rather mystifying and worrisome, particularly since he had achieved such success. He felt that he deserved to continue his exploits. Why was he being put on the shelf?

*Letter, GSP, Jr., to Marshall, August 18, 1943*

I am at a loss to find words with which to express my amazement at the ability of the American soldier to surmount obstacles . . .

Of course, this morning everyone feels considerably let down, as we do not know what the Seventh Army is going to do or when. However, I think a few weeks rest, while not vitally necessary, is desirable, both in order to let the men restore their normal resilience and also in order to perform the necessary maintenance on the Ordnance and Quartermaster equipment.

It was a great privilege to have the honor of commanding the Seventh Army, and I trust that the results we have obtained will appear satisfactory to you.

*Letter, GSP, Jr., to his sister Nita, August 19, 1943*

We are now sinking back into a state of innocuous desuetude but will probably snap out of it in about a month, although just where our next operation will be I do not know. However, my remark, quoted in the papers, that I am personally willing to kill Germans at any place at any time, still holds. We have certainly killed an awful lot of them in this show.

He wrote Bradley

to make a permanent record of my frequently expressed admiration for and appreciation of the magnificent loyalty and superior tactical ability you have evinced throughout the campaign of Sicily.

He thanked Davidson

for your constant gallant and generous assistance . . . of critical importance in the rapid and successful advance on Messina.

He wrote Eisenhower to "salute you as the Conqueror of Sicily."
He told his cousin Arvin H. Brown:

This campaign . . . will, I believe, go down in history as a damn near perfect example of how to wage war. Why I was selected as the vessel to give the illustration, I do not know, but I certainly appreciate the opportunity.

But he fretted over the uncertainty ahead even as he took pleasure in turning over in his mind his triumphs.

All this, his past accomplishments and his future usefulness, suddenly came into serious question.

The first intimation he had of impending disaster was a cable he received from Eisenhower, dated August 20:

General Lucas will arrive at Palermo airfield between five and five thirty this afternoon. It is highly important that you personally meet General Lucas and give your full attention to the message that he will bring you. In the event that it is absolutely impossible for you to meet him personally, be certain to have transportation awaiting him and leave word as to the place where he can reach you quickest.

Before Lucas arrived, Brigadier General Frederick A. Blesse, the Chief

Surgeon, AFHQ, showed up. He had come from Algiers to look into the health of the troops in Sicily, and Eisenhower ordered him to deliver a personal and secret letter from Eisenhower to Patton and also to investigate the charges made in that letter.

*Letter, Eisenhower to GSP, Jr., August 17, 1943 (delivered by Blesse)*

I am attaching a report which is shocking in its allegations against your personal conduct. I hope you can assure me that none of them is true; but the detailed circumstances communicated to me lead to the belief that some ground for the charges must exist. I am well aware of the necessity for hardness and toughness on the battlefield. I clearly understand that firm and drastic measures are at times necessary in order to secure the desired objectives. But this does not excuse brutality, abuse of the sick, nor exhibition of uncontrollable temper in front of subordinates.

In the two cases cited in the attached report, it is *not* my present intention to institute any formal investigation. Moreover, it is acutely distressing to me to have such charges as these made against you at the very moment when an American Army under your leadership has attained a success of which I am extremely proud. I feel that the personal services you have rendered the United States and the Allied cause during the past weeks are of incalculable value; but nevertheless, if there is a very considerable element of truth in the allegations accompanying this letter, I must so seriously question your good judgment and your self discipline as to raise serious doubts in my mind as to your future usefulness. I am assuming, for the moment, that the facts in the case are far less serious than appears in this report, and that whatever truth is contained in these allegations reports an act of yours when under the stress and strain of winning a victory, you were thoughtless rather than harsh. Your leadership of the past few weeks has, in my opinion, fully vindicated to the War Department and to all your associates in arms my own persistence in upholding your pre-eminent qualifications for the difficult task to which you were assigned. Nevertheless, you must give to this matter of personal deportment your instant and serious consideration to the end that no incident of this character can be reported to me in the future, and I may continue to count upon your assistance in military tasks.

In Allied Headquarters there is no record of the attached report or of my letter to you, except in my own secret files. I will expect your answer to be sent to me personally and secretly. Moreover, I strongly advise that, provided there is any semblance of truth in the allegations in the accompanying report, you make in the form of apology or other such personal amends to the individuals concerned as may be within your power, and that you do this before submitting your letter to me.

No letter that I have been called upon to write in my military career has caused me the mental anguish of this one, not only because of my long and deep personal friendship for you but because of my admiration for your military qualities, but I assure you that conduct such as described in the accompanying report will *not* be tolerated in this theater no matter who the offender may be.

The accompanying report:

*Letter, Lt. Col. Perrin H. Long, Medical Corps, to The Surgeon, NATOUSA, August 16, 1943, subject: Mistreatment of Patients in Receiving Tents of the 15th and 93d Evacuation Hospitals*

Exhibit No. 1 – Pvt. Charles H. Kuhl, L Company, 26th Infantry, 1st Division, was seen in the . . . aid station on August 2, 1943 . . . where a diagnosis of "Exhaustion" was made . . . He was evacuated to C Company, 1st Medical Battalion. There a note was made on the patient's E.M.T. [Emergency Medical Tag] that he had been admitted to Company C three times for "Exhaustion" during the Sicilian Campaign. From C Company he was evacuated to the clearing company . . . There he was put in "quarters" and was given sodium mytal . . . On 3 August '43, the following note appears on the E.M.T. "Psychoneurosis anxiety state – moderate severe (soldier has been twice before in hospital within ten days. He can't take it at the front, evidently. He is repeatedly returned.)" . . . He was evacuated to the 15th Evacuation Hospital. While he was waiting in the receiving tent . . . Lt. Gen. George S. Patton, Jr., came into the tent with the commanding officer and other medical officers . . . The General spoke to the various patients in the receiving tent and especially commended the wounded men. Then he came to Pvt. Kuhl and asked him what was the matter. The soldier replied, "I guess I can't take it." The General immediately flared up, cursed the soldier, called him all types of a coward, then slapped him across the face with his gloves and finally grabbed the soldier by the scruff of his neck and kicked him out of the tent. The soldier was immediately picked up by corpsmen and taken to a ward tent. There he was found to have a temperature of 102.2 degrees F and he gave a history of chronic diarrhea for about one month, having at times as high as ten or twelve stools a day. The next day his fever continued and a blood smear was found to be positive for malarial parasites. The final disposition diagnosis was chronic dysentery and malaria. This man had been in the Army eight months and with the 1st Division since about June 2d.

Exhibit No. 2 – Pvt. Paul G. Bennett, C Battery, 17th Field Artillery, was admitted to the 93d Evacuation Hospital . . . 10 August '43. This patient was a 21 year old boy who had served four years in the regular Army. His unit had been with II Corps since March and he had never had any difficulties until August 6th, when his buddy was wounded. He could not sleep that night and felt nervous. The shells going over him bothered him. The next day he was worried about his buddy and became more nervous. He was sent down to the rear echelon by a battery aid man and there the medical officer gave him some medicine which made him sleep, but still he was nervous and disturbed. On the next day the medical officer ordered him to be evacuated, although the boy begged not to be evacuated because he did not want to leave his unit.

Many years later, Dr. Donald E. Currier recalled that Bennett wanted to return to his unit although he "had a temperature and he was sick." Showing symptoms of dehydration, he was fatigued, confused, weak, and listless.

Lt. General George S. Patton, Jr., entered the receiving tent and spoke to all the injured men. The next patient was sitting huddled up and shivering. When asked what his trouble was, the man replied, "It's my nerves," and began to sob. The General then screamed at him, "What did you say?" The man replied, "It's my nerves, I can't stand the shelling any more." He was still sobbing. The General then yelled at him, "Your nerves, hell; you are just a Goddamned coward, you yellow son of a bitch." He then slapped the man and said, "Shut up that Goddamned crying. I won't have these brave men here who have been shot at seeing a yellow bastard sitting here crying." He then struck the man again, knocking his helmet liner off and into the next tent. He then turned to the admitting officer and yelled, "Don't admit this yellow bastard; there's nothing the matter with him. I don't have the hospitals cluttered up with these sons of bitches who haven't got the guts to fight." He then turned to the man again, who was managing to sit at attention though shaking all over and said, "You're going back to the front lines and you may get shot and killed, but you're going to fight. If you don't, I'll stand you up against a wall and have a firing squad kill you on purpose. In fact," he said, reaching for his pistol, "I ought to shoot you myself, you Goddamned whimpering coward." As he left the tent, the General was still yelling back to the receiving officer to send that yellow son of a bitch back to the front line. Nurses and patients attracted by the shouting and cursing came from adjoining tents and witnessed this disturbance.

The deleterious effects of such incidents upon the wellbeing of patients, upon the professional morale of hospital staffs, and upon the relationship of patient to physician are incalculable.

It is imperative that immediate steps be taken to prevent a recurrence of such incidents.

Demaree Bess, a correspondent for the *Saturday Evening Post,* and several of his associates heard about incidents in the hospitals, investigated the stories, found them to be true, and decided to refrain from publicizing Patton's conduct before taking up the matter with Eisenhower. They felt that Patton was subject to trial by court-martial for having struck an enlisted man. If so charged, he would have to be dismissed from his command.

Meeting with three senior correspondents, Eisenhower assured them that he would take appropriate action vis-à-vis Patton. He asked them to bury the story in the interest of preserving Patton's value as a combat leader. Should news of his actions become known to the public, he might have to be relieved. The army could ill afford to lose his driving power for the rest of the war.

The correspondents promised to withhold the story.

*Diary, August 20*

General Blesse . . . brought me a very nasty letter from Ike with reference to the two soldiers I cussed out for what I considered cowardice. Evidently I acted precipitately and on insufficient knowledge. My motive was correct because one cannot permit skulking to exist. It is just like any communicable disease. I admit freely that my method was wrong but I shall make what amends I can. I regret the incident as I hate to make Ike mad when it is my earnest study to please him.

General Lucas arrived at 1800 to further explain Ike's attitude. I feel very low.

Many years after the war, Huebner felt that he "might have precipitated the slapping incident." He recalled that Patton had asked him how things were going. Huebner said that he thought "the front lines were getting thinner." It seemed to him that among the soldiers legitimately hospitalized for wounds, injuries, and sickness were some who were malingering, had no proper reason for being in medical channels, and were avoiding their combat duties. "Well, as luck would have it," Patton went straight to a hospital.

Patton himself had recorded the incidents.

*Diary, August 3*

In the hospital I also met the only arrant coward I have ever seen in this Army. This man was sitting, trying to look as if he had been wounded. I asked him what was the matter, and he said he just couldn't take it. I gave him the devil, slapped his face with my gloves, and kicked him out of the hospital. Companies should deal with such men, and if they shirk their duty, they should be tried for cowardice and shot. I will issue an order on this subject tomorrow.

*Seventh Army Memo to corps, division, and separate unit commanders, August 5, 1943*

It has come to my attention that a very small number of soldiers are going to the hospital on the pretext that they are nervously incapable of combat. Such men are cowards and bring discredit on the army and disgrace to their comrades, whom they heartlessly leave to endure the dangers of battle while they, themselves, use the hospital as a means of escape. You will take measures to see that such cases are not sent to the hospital but are dealt with in their units. Those who are not willing to fight will be tried by Court-Martial for cowardice in the face of the enemy.

*Diary, August 10*

At another evacuation hospital . . . saw another alleged nervous patient – really a coward. I told the doctor to return him to his company and he began to cry so I cursed him well and he shut up. I may have saved his soul if he had one.

A report of the incidents from the Medical Corps came through channels to Bradley. He had two alternatives – send it forward to his immediate superior, Patton, who was certain to ignore it; or depart from military practice, violate the precept of loyalty to his immediate superior, and send it around Patton to Eisenhower. Bradley avoided both options. He put the report into his safe.

The hospital authorities then bypassed the chain of command and sent a report through technical – medical – channels.

*Diary, August 21*

I had Pvt. Paul G. Bennett . . . in and explained to him that I had cussed him out in the hope of restoring his manhood, that I was sorry, and that if he cared, I would like to shake hands with him. We shook. General John A. Crane, to whose brigade he belongs, stated to me afterwards that the man was absent without leave and had gone to the rear by falsely representing his condition to the battery surgeon. It is rather a commentary on justice when an Army commander has to soft-soap a skulker to placate the timidity of those above . . .

Bob Hope and his troupe called on me at the office later and we had them to dinner and they sang and carried on until after midnight. I put myself out to be amusing and human as I think it may help, particularly if this business about the shirkers comes up.

On August 22, Patton issued one of his most famous statements:

*Seventh Army General Orders 18*

Soldiers of the Seventh Army: Born at sea, baptized in blood, and crowned in victory, in the course of 38 days of incessant battle and unceasing labor, you have added a glorious chapter to the history of war.

Pitted against the best the Germans and Italians could offer, you have been unfailingly successful. The rapidity of your dash, which culminated in the capture of Palermo, was equalled by the dogged tenacity with which you stormed Troina and captured Messina.

Every man in the Army deserves equal credit. The enduring valor of the Infantry, and the impetuous ferocity of the tanks were matched by the tireless clamor of the destroying guns.

The Engineers . . . Maintenance and Supply . . . Signal Corps . . . Medical Department . . .

The Navy . . . our Air . . .

As a result of this combined effort, you have killed or captured 113,350 enemy troops. You have destroyed 265 of his tanks, 2,324 vehicles, and 1,162 large guns, and in addition, have collected a mass of military booty running into hundreds of tons.

But your victory has a significance above and beyond its physical aspect — you have destroyed the prestige of the enemy . . .

Your fame shall never die.

*Letter, GSP, Jr., to Beatrice, August 22, 1943*

At the moment things are pretty quiet as the natural reaction which invariably follows active operations has set in.

However personally I am quite busy visiting units and writing up notes on the operations for Lesley [McNair]. I intend to get the real dope from people who actually did the close in fighting. If I succeed, it will be the first time in history where the ideas of the little fellow will have a chance to be articulated.

As usual I seem to have made Divine Destiny a little mad but that will pass, I suppose. It [Eisenhower] has a lot of worries which it has to pass on . . .

I have had telegrams from George [Marshall] and Harry [Stimson] and a host of others, all but from D who is, I suppose, too international.

We have not the least idea of what is to happen next. In fact I think that what we do is so contingent on political reactions that any thing can happen.

We have a house on the water a fiew miles from here where we swim. It is the finest and cleanest beach I have ever seen, many times better than Waikiki with a rock about the size of Gibralta at each end.

They have a lot of latine sailed boats there that carry a huge spread of canvas. I am going out in one this afternoon . . .

Speaking in general, I find that moral courage is the most valuable and most usually absent characteristic. Much of our trouble is directly attributable to "The fear of they." Remember in the "Jungle Book" there is a poem each verse of which ends with "It is fear, O my little brother, it is fear."

*Letter, Katharine [Mrs. George C.] Marshall to GSP, Jr., August 22, 1943*

I have just been reading a copy of the message George sent to you

> and your Army on your magnificent campaign in Sicily. I am so proud of you. I had to send a note of congratulations to you for having *such* an Army as the Seventh and to them for having such a leader . . . You and your men have the admiration and gratitude of the whole country. We read of your hardships and endurance with tears in our eyes and thankfulness in our hearts that the end was so glorious . . . Remember we are with you men in spirit always.

Trying to conceal his irritation Patton was carrying out his distasteful assignment of apologizing for the slapping incident.

> *Diary, August 22*
> I had in all the doctors and nurses and enlisted men who witnessed the affairs with the skulkers. I told them about my friend in the last war who shirked, was let get by with it, and eventually killed himself. I told them that I had taken the action I had to correct such a future tragedy.

In addition, he managed, with perhaps less than complete candor and good grace, to express his regret for "my impulsive actions."

To Dr. Currier, who was summoned to Palermo along with other medical personnel and escorted into Patton's office where the general sat behind "an impressive desk," Patton's remarks sounded like "no apology at all," but rather "an attempt to justify what he had done."

> *Diary, August 23*
> I have acquired lots of fame and also sustained a great deal of mental anguish, which was, in the light of subsequent events, quite unnecessary. However, with a few brief lapses I have retained my self-confidence. I have always done my duty and have trusted to my destiny.
> At 1500, Private Charles H. Kuhl . . . came in. He was one of the two men I cussed out for skulking. I told him why I did it, namely, that I tried to make him mad with me so he would regain his manhood. I then asked him to shake hands, which he did.

Kuhl later acknowledged that Patton had apologized, saying "he didn't know that I was as sick as I was." Admittedly, Patton was "a great general." But he was also "a glory hunter. I think at the time it happened, he was pretty well worn out . . . I think he was suffering a little battle fatigue himself."

*Letter, GSP, Jr., to Beatrice, August 23, 1943*

I have been a passanger floating on the river of destiny. At the moment I can't see around the next bend, but I guess it will be all right.

Once in a while my exuberant personality gets me in a little lame with Divine Destiny, which seems to have the trait . . . of believing the worst of every one on insufficient evidence.

*Letter, Lucas to GSP, Jr., August 23, 1943*

Everything is OK. The people who were making the fuss have been told to stop yelling and have agreed to do so. Ike just read me a report to General Marshall on the campaign in which he recited your achievements in glowing terms. The situation is in hand.

In a letter to Marshall, dated August 24, Eisenhower gave brief descriptions of the senior American commanders who had been tested in battle. "First, Patton. He has conducted a campaign where the brilliant successes scored must be attributed directly to his energy, determination, and unflagging aggressiveness." The Seventh Army operations were sure to be a model of "swift conquest" for future students at the Army War College. "The prodigious marches, the incessant attacks, the refusal to be halted by appalling difficulties" were "something to enthuse about." And this came "mainly from Patton," who refused to "seize on an excuse for resting or refitting," or recuperating to bring up more strength. When an order from Alexander appeared to keep him "rather quiescent . . . he immediately jumped into a plane, went to Alexander, got the matter cleared up, and kept on driving."

In spite of all that, Patton continued "to exhibit some of those unfortunate personal traits of which you and I have always known." They caused Eisenhower several uncomfortable days. "His habit of impulsive bawling out of subordinates, extending even to personal abuse of individuals" occurred twice, and Eisenhower had to take "the most drastic steps." If he was "not cured now, there is no hope for him. Personally, I believe that he is cured — not only because of his great personal loyalty to you and to me but because fundamentally he is so avid for recognition as a great military commander that he will ruthlessly suppress any habit of his own that will tend to jeopardize it."

Aside from that, Patton had qualities that they could not "afford to lose unless he ruins himself." Therefore, Patton could be classed as an Army commander whose troops would "not be stopped by ordinary obstacles."

Still obeying Eisenhower's instructions, Patton notified all his division commanders of his intention to visit their organizations between August 24 and 30 in order to address all the officers and men. The first one he drove to was the 2d Armored Division, and Patton noted in his diary that he "gave a talk on how good they were."

It was probably significant that he chose his old division in order to make his initial apologies to the troops for his actions in the hospitals. He praised the performance of the men in the past campaign and exhorted their continued attention to and pride in military behavior. Although he failed to mention it in his diary, he also made an oblique reference to his treatment of the two men he had believed were malingerers. There was no need for him to be direct. The story had spread across the island. What he did was to make a vague statement of regret, as someone reported, "for any occasions when I may have harshly criticized individuals."

The script for his ten- or fifteen-minute speech made his main point toward the end:

> In my dealings with you I have been guilty on too many occasions, perhaps, of criticizing and of loud talking. I am sorry for this and wish to assure you that when I criticize and censure I am wholly impersonal . . . for every man I have criticized in this Army, I have probably stopped, talked to, and complimented a thousand, but people are more prone to remember ill usage than to recall compliments; therefore, I want you officers and men who are here to explain to the other soldiers, who think perhaps that I am too hard, my motives and to express to them my sincere regret . . .
>
> In the Sicilian campaign we lost some 1,500 of our comrades, killed in action. I do not grieve for their death because I thank God that such men have lived, but I do say to you all that it is our sacred duty to see that each of our dead comrades is escorted through the Pearly Gates by a large, a very large number of enemy dead. It is up to us

> now and hereafter to produce these escorts for our heroic slain.
>
> You know that I have never asked one of you to go where I feared to tread. I have been criticized for this, but there are many General Pattons and there is only one Seventh Army. I can be expended but the Seventh must and will be victorious.

The soldiers in the combat units were rather uninterested. Their activities were so regulated, their lives so circumscribed, their loyalties so localized that the slapping incidents could have happened on the moon, for all they cared. Besides, they could well understand Patton's sudden rage, his outburst, his profanity. It was all so typical of their impression of the man, so characteristic.

Those who cared and were shocked were the doctors, nurses, and medical corpsmen, who regarded combat fatigue as a legitimate symptom of psychoneurosis.

He "made a speech to the 45th Division," and again made no note in his diary of his rather circuitous explanation of what had taken place in the hospitals.

He talked with Middleton

> about Clark's operation at the Gulf of Salerno. Here again the Americans will be in the covering role; the X British Corps making the main attack. I am quite sure from my experience that the British should always do the covering and the Americans the attacking, but others do not agree with me.

Patton addressed the 9th Division, and noted: "I am more than satisfied with General Eddy every time I come in contact with him."

Alexander "came to see what he could steal" for the invasion of the Italian mainland. "If I suggest to Ike that this is the case, he will tell me I don't see the 'big picture.' I wish to God he was an American."

*Cable, Eisenhower to Marshall, August 27, 1943*

> Patton is preeminently a combat commander. Many people fail to realize that the first thing that usually slows up operations is an element of caution, fatigue or doubt on the part of a higher commander. Patton is never affected by these and, consequently, his troops are not affected. Several of his subordinate commanders turned in magnificent performances in the late show, but if they had had an example

> of pessimism, caution and delay above them, they could not possibly have acted as they did. He is a one sided individual, and particularly in his handling of individual subordinates is apt at times to display exceedingly poor judgment and unjustified temper. But his outstanding qualities must not be discounted when you are determining future assignments of senior officers.

Patton spoke "to all 1st Division" and remarked upon their improved discipline since Huebner took over.

As Huebner later recalled Patton's visit:

> I assembled 18,000 men, and Patton made a speech, a very good speech, in which he explained that he was sorry. But when he was finished, not one man clapped or said anything. There was no applause. They knew Patton was wrong, but they also knew it was something to get over with and forget as soon as possible.

*Diary, August 28*

After lunch I talked to selected officers of all grades on their battle experience. I have done this with every division and hope to get a good cross section of how wars are fought . . .

We have not solved the problem of replacements . . . The lack of replacements in all the operations so far undertaken is nothing short of scandalous . . . Divisions and Armies are not animated tables of organization but have a soul just as human beings have, and that in order to get the best results, they must be maintained at strength with men who have been in them long enough to acquire the unit soul.

Patton's letter to Eisenhower on the slapping incident was contrite and humble.

> I want to commence by thanking you for this additional illustration of your fairness and generous consideration in making your communication [of the complaint] personal [rather than official].
>
> I am at a loss to find words with which to express my chagrin and grief at having given you, a man to whom I owe everything and for whom I would gladly lay down my life, cause for displeasure with me.
>
> I assure you that I had no intention of being either harsh or cruel in my treatment of the two soldiers in question. My sole purpose was

to try and restore in them a just appreciation of their obligation as men and soldiers.

In World War I, I had a dear friend and former schoolmate who lost his nerve in an exactly analogous manner, and who, after years of mental anguish, committed suicide.

Both my friend and the medical men with whom I discussed his case assured me that had he been roundly checked at the time of his first misbehavior, he would have been restored to a normal state.

Naturally, this memory actuated me when I inaptly tried to apply the remedies suggested. After each incident I stated to officers with me that I felt I had probably saved an immortal soul.

*Diary, August 29*

To Catania. Ike had just landed and was most effusive. We had lunch with Monty, who was, I think, trying to make up for not feeding me last time. Ike decorated him with the big cross of the Legion of Merit.

Then I handed Ike my letter [of remorse] about the incidents of the two soldiers. He just put it in his pocket . . .

Well, that was a near thing, but I feel much better.

*Letter, GSP, Jr., to Beatrice, August 30, 1943*

I have been traveling so much addressing troops that I have not written for some days. Yesterday Monty, Omar, Geoff, Lucien, and I had lunch with Destiny and every thing was very fine.

Apparently I will join the Army of the unemployed for a while, so don't worry about me. I seem destined to either fight like hell or do nothing.

On that day he visited the 3d Division, the last of his units to see, the last of his talks, the last of his vague apology. It turned out to be a rather shorter speech than he intended. There was a special affection on the part of Patton for this division which had captured Agrigento, Palermo, and Messina. The men felt Patton's warmth, and they reciprocated. Truscott too was close to Patton, and he was capable of arranging or stage-managing what happened — unless the story is altogether apocryphal. Patton's audience sensed that he was about to make his statement of apology. Before he could do so, they began a spontaneous chant. "No, General, no, no; no, General, no, no," with increasing insistence, "no,

General, no, no." They would not listen, would not let him go on. He waited. Tears came to his eyes. The roar swelled in volume. "No, General, no, no." Choked with emotion, he left the speaker's stand abruptly, returned to his car, and drove away.

CHAPTER 19

# The Terrible Uncertainty

*"I have to keep working on my belief in destiny, and poor old destiny may have to put in some extra time to get me out of my present slump."*

Patton AND HIS SEVENTH ARMY headquarters would remain in Sicily and inactive for more than four months. To a large extent this stemmed from the presence in the Mediterranean theater of three American lieutenant generals, Clark, Patton, and Bradley, in that order of seniority.

The only immediate task was reserved to Clark, who, while Patton and Bradley were busy in Sicily, prepared his Fifth Army's invasion of the Italian mainland. Bradley was named his understudy and would take his place if Clark became a casualty. Bradley was also being considered for advancement to command an Army in the United Kingdom for Overlord, the cross-Channel attack scheduled for the spring of 1944. Expecting Bradley soon to go to England, Eisenhower asked Patton to fly to North Africa and become familiar with Clark's plans, particularly the landing operation near Salerno code-named Avalanche.

"I seem to be third choice," Patton noted morosely; then with a flash of spirit, "but I will end up on top."

*Diary, August 31*

To Mostaganem . . . Went to meeting for discussion of final plans for Avalanche . . . Spent night with Clark in my former villa. He left for his office after supper, so I had no chance to talk to him.

*Diary, September 1*

Went to Gruenther's office and talked to him for perhaps forty-five minutes on my experiences at Husky. He was interested in administrative matters, but not at all in tactics. However, he did ask me what I thought of the plan for Avalanche. I was very tactful, but could not help calling his attention to the fact that the plan uses the Sele River as a boundary between the British X Corps and the U.S. VI Corps, with no one actually on, or near, the river. I told him that just as sure as God lives, the Germans will attack down that river.

He said their plans provided for ample artillery to be ashore by 0630 on D Day to stop any German counterattack.

Of course plans never work [as expected], especially in a landing. I suggested this, but it did not register.

I can't see why people are so foolish. I have yet to be questioned by any planner concerning my experience at Torch, yet Torch was the biggest and most difficult landing operation attempted so far.

Patton's judgment of the Avalanche plan was incredibly perceptive. He pinpointed exactly what would happen. Neither corps making the invasion near Salerno would take hold of the Sele River, and a German counterattack down the Sele valley would threaten to reach the sea, come close to splitting the British and Americans, and prompt serious thoughts of evacuating the beachhead.

Drove to Oran to have a look at my old training area. I was impressed with the discipline of the 34th and 36th Divisions and also of the SOS troops. However, I was shocked at the number of non-employed SOS troops walking around town. There are enough men in the SOS at Oran to provide the infantry with two divisions or to provide ample replacements for all the troops in the Seventh Army, and many of these men were initially trained as infantry.

He put his finger on a chronic problem that would hamper the army throughout the war – the lack of sufficient infantry replacements for the wounded, injured, and sick.

*Letter, Arvin H. Brown to GSP, Jr., September 2, 1943*

Last Sunday I attended the services in which the memorial plaque which you gave in honor of, and to the memory of, Dick Jenson was dedicated . . . Throughout the whole service there stood out in sharp relief in my mind the two leading characters in this beautiful drama of life – the gallant young officer who has gone on before us, and his heroic general who never forgets.

*Diary, September 2*

Flew to Algiers . . . Ike sent for me . . . and lectured me . . . I realize that I acted precipitately [in the slapping incident] and accepted his remarks in the spirit intended. I feel that he likes me. Of course he should.

He told me that the Seventh Army would be dispersed, that Brad was to go to England to form a new Army and plan [the cross-Channel attack].

I told him I was a pretty good planner, but he said I did not like to do it — in that, it seems I am like him, or so he said (compliment?).

News of Bradley's departure seemed to have little effect on Patton. Perhaps he was dissimulating his disappointment. Perhaps he failed to understand the meaning of Bradley's transfer. Perhaps he felt that Eisenhower was simply alerting him to a possibility that had yet to materialize. Perhaps he hoped that Bradley's advancement to command an Army signified a similar advancement for him — to command a group of Armies. He was, after all, the only experienced American Army commander in the European theater, and he had more combat as the top American field commander than anyone.

Whatever his true reaction, he was uneasy, worried over his future, probably concerned over the extent to which the slapping incident had hurt him. He was senior to Bradley, and he felt that he should have been chosen for the job in England.

Flew back to Palermo . . . A day or two in Algiers almost kills me. No one there seems to be interested in the war, and one cannot escape the feeling that the so-called Allied Headquarters is a British headquarters commanded by an American . . . Only Hughes, Lucas, and [T. J.] Davis made any complimentary remarks concerning the activities of the Seventh Army in Sicily. It was so apparent that it is probably intentional, the most charitable assumption being that since the Seventh Army made the Eighth Army look like thirty cents, it is felt inadvisable, from an inter-Allied standpoint, to give any credit to the Seventh Army . . .

In the clippings from the U.S. . . . the fall of Messina received scant notice.

*Diary, September 3*

Recovered from Algiers.

*Diary, September 4*

Recovered some more.

Montgomery's Eighth Army crossed the straits of Messina on September 3 and, against very slight opposition, landed in the toe of Italy. This was the first Allied invasion of the European continent.

*Letter, GSP, Jr., to Beatrice, September 4, 1943*

This [operation] is the first battle since I left home that I have had to listen to on the radio, and it is quite trying. Of course Monty has a habit — a good one — of never letting out any news till it is big news. So thus far we only know that the landing was O.K. Some of our guns . . . supported it . . .

It always takes me about three days to get over a trip to Alger. One should wear chain mail to avoid the knife thrusts. It would be amusing if it were not serious.

Of course, one can never tell, for strange things happen, but I rather believe I will be out of circulation along with the ever victorious Seventh for a while. Omar is going to see Jake [Devers in London, where Devers commanded ETOUSA], and John Lucas gets his [Bradley's] outfit. I was told that I was too impetuous to do what Omar has to do. Apparently I am a man of deeds not words. Except when I talk too much . . .

Well, luck and fate have been with me thus far, so I don't worry.

I wish I could be less criptic, but if I ever return, I will keep you awake a lot talking over my experiences. Don't worry. I love you.

He was beginning to see Bradley's eventual role, to sense that Bradley was outstripping him, and to feel slighted.

Even then, two cables were on the way to him. They would reveal starkly that Clark and Bradley had the choice assignments and that Patton would remain unemployed.

The first said that the "Seventh Army will not continue as an Army." The 2d Armored, 1st, and 9th Divisions were earmarked for return to the United Kingdom. The 82d Airborne and 45th Divisions were about to go to Italy under the Fifth Army. The 3d Division would probably move to Italy too. No combat troops would stay under Patton.

The second, paraphrasing a message from Marshall, confirmed Bradley's appointment to command the First Army in England for the Normandy invasion and indicated Patton's probable – though still uncertain – role in that operation: "The prestige of Seventh Army would prove to great advantage in that follow up."

Patton did not want the follow-up role. He wanted to lead the invasion.

*Diary, September 6*

Got two radios this morning . . .

The second one ruined me . . .

It is very heartbreaking. The only time I have felt worse was the night of December 9th, 1942, when Clark got the Fifth Army . . . I feel like death but will survive – I always have.

I called in all the heads of the staff sections and had the two telegrams read.

I said, "Gentlemen, what you have heard is secret and will not be discussed nor mentioned to your assistants. I believe in destiny and that nothing can destroy the future of the Seventh Army. However, some of you may not believe in destiny, so if you can find a better job, get it and I will help you all I can. You may be backing the wrong horse or hitched your wagon to the wrong stars. In any event, we must go right on like we knew nothing, so that the enemy will fear the potential threat of the Seventh Army."

I feel that none of them will leave me.

No one did.

Ike sent two inspectors over to question soldiers about my alleged brutality to them. He said he did it in my behalf, to counteract untrue stories. I think this may be true but fear that it is to protect Ike.

And yet I believe in my star.

Patton had figured that the Seventh Army would go to England to prepare for Overlord. He and his staff were experienced in amphibious operations and in combat. They had planned and executed two successful landings in Morocco and Sicily. They were the obvious choice for the amphibious assault in Normandy, the climactic operation in Europe. That Clark's Fifth Army had been selected for the invasion of Italy, which was bound to develop into a subsidiary operation, and that Bradley had functioned in a relatively minor capacity in Tunisia and Sicily gave credence to this logic. Certainly no American had Patton's battle prestige, his record of proved success, his reputation for winning.

It seemed odd to him that Marshall and Eisenhower ignored all this. Why did they bypass him, choose others for no good reason that he could understand? Were they trying to keep him from becoming too great a hero?

What he could not know was that the image he consistently tried to project was sometimes terrifying to those above him who were responsible for expending American lives and winning the war. Eisenhower had mentioned to Marshall "those unfortunate personal traits of which you and I have always known," the tendency at times "to display exceedingly poor judgment and unjustified temper." These were the occasional flashes of instability, hardly perceptible except to those who knew him well. He had alternative periods of moodiness, almost depression, and high elation, almost hysteria. He appeared sometimes to be petulant, even childish.

All this prompted his superiors to question his capacity for self-control. That tiny doubt led to reconsideration of his fitness for higher command.

Yet it was impossible to overlook his driving power over his subordinates, his military genius, his intuitive knowledge of what the enemy was about to do, his awesome proficiency in handling combat units, his outstanding battle leadership, his ability and willingess to take risks. And that too provoked questions of his balance and judgment. For he was capable of being impetuous, so it seemed, and perhaps too ready to gamble.

The slapping incident appeared to confirm the impression. Patton was mercurial, impulsive — and so, ultimately, undependable. And perhaps he had talked too much about the British cousins.

The cross-Channel invasion was much too important to be staked on a single roll of the dice, or to be jeopardized by the slightest tinge of interallied antagonism. In a venture that required the closest Allied partnership to attain the final victory in Europe, Bradley seemed better.

Bradley was balanced, sound in judgment, and experienced. He had grown in stature. He was less apt to make mistakes. That was why he was selected for a position that was bound to increase in responsibility and authority. Marshall had already asked him to develop an Army Group headquarters "to keep pace with the British planning and requisitions."

Yet whatever faults Patton embodied, he was too valuable to discard. His prestige, reputation, proficiency, and genius would be utilized – but at a level no higher than the command of a field Army.

Unknown to Patton, Marshall informed Eisenhower that he was working on a list of recommendations for permanent – Regular Army – promotions, which governed retirement rank, and he wanted Eisenhower's advice. On Marshall's list was Patton.

*Letter, Eisenhower to Marshall, September 6, 1943*

With respect to Patton, I do not see how you could possibly submit a list . . . on combat performance to date and omit his name. His job of rehabilitating the II Corps in Tunisia was quickly and magnificently done. Beyond this, his leadership of the Seventh Army was close to the best of our classic examples. It is possible that in the future some ill-advised action of his might cause you to regret his promotion. You know his weaknesses as well as his strength, but I am confident that I have eliminated some of the former. His intense loyalty to you and to me makes it possible for me to treat him much more roughly than I could any other senior commander . . . In the last campaign he, under stress it is true, indulged his temper in certain instances toward individual subordinates who, in General Patton's opinion of the moment, were guilty of malingering. I took immediate and drastic measures, and I am quite certain this sort of thing will never happen again. You have in him a truly aggressive commander and, moreover, one with sufficient brains to do his work in splendid fashion . . . Incidentally, I think he will show up even better in an exclusively American theater than in an allied one . . .

Bradley . . . is, in my opinion, the best rounded combat leader I have yet met in our service. While he possibly lacks some of the extraordinary and ruthless driving power that Patton can exert at critical moments . . . he is among our best.

*Letter, GSP, Jr., to Beatrice, September 7, 1943*

Your saying that I learned how to make our men fight is amusing as now it is held against me, that I made the Seventh Army too bloody minded – you cant please every one . . .

I know why we [the Seventh Army] were soft pedaled [in the press]. It was in consonance with the oriental custom of face saving and possibly necessary. I hear that in London we stole the show.

Bradley, who would travel to the United States before going to England, came to tell Patton goodbye.

*Diary, September 7*

We had quite a long talk and I told him a lot of my best ideas to tell General Marshall. I suppose I should have kept them to gain reputation by springing them myself, but I am not built that way. The sooner they are put into effect, the better for our army.

Bradley has a chance to help or hurt me with General Marshall. I hope he chooses the former course, but I did not ask him to.

My resilient nature worked all right and today I am almost back to normal. But I have to keep working on my belief in destiny, and poor old destiny may have to put in some extra time to get me out of my present slump.

*Diary, September 8*

[Italian] Armistice just declared . . . I fear that as a soldier I have too little faith in political war. Suppose the Italians can't or don't capitulate? . . It [is] a great mistake to inform the troops, as has been done, of the signing of an armistice. Should they get resistance instead of friendship [during the amphibious landings at Salerno], it would have a very bad effect.

He was right again. The Italian surrender was announced on the evening of September 8, as Clark's invasion convoys were approaching their anchorages in Salerno Bay. The news was broadcast over ships' speakers, and there was an immediate letdown, even though officers tried to tell the men that Germans rather than Italians were likely to meet them on the beaches at dawn.

While Clark's Fifth Army stormed ashore, Patton worked all day on his report of operations in Sicily. He found it "a very tedious business" — perhaps because he was thinking of Clark's landings — "but necessary and, I hope, useful." He noted that he could "now chin myself five and a half times and [I] do it three times a day."

*Letter, GSP, Jr., to Beatrice, September 10, 1943*

I woke up this morning happy as a lark and started to write you a story about some imaginary ghosts I have met in the palace but at 8:30 I got a letter according to which I have done those things I ought not to have done and left undone those things I ought to have done and am a sun of a gun. So my joie de vivre left and there is no ghost story . . .

My only hope is that Waynes war may take me out of the lime light. Else I will soon be helping you cut branches off trees [at home] . . .

I guess you are the only one who loves me – I reciprocate.

The letter he referred to questioned his possible misuse of prisoners of war.

"Sometimes," Patton wrote in his diary,

I almost believe that there is a deliberate campaign to hurt me; certainly it is hard to be victimized for winning a campaign. Hap [Gay] thinks the [British] cousins are back of it because I made a fool of Monty.

Patton flew to Bizerte and accompanied Alexander to see the surrendered Italian battle fleet sail by on their way to Malta.

A great many jokes among the British officers to the effect that the ships passing us were ghost ships, since the Royal Air Force and the Royal Navy had definitely sunk them all on various occasions.

*Letter, GSP, Jr., to Arvin H. Brown, September 12, 1943*

I believe that a man can only do his best, and that if the Supreme Being wishes him to go far, his best will be useful. If He does not wish him, his best will be useless. In any case, the best must be done.

For example, no planning on the part of Napoleon or Hitler could have gotten them where they are except for fortuitous circumstances, probably injected by said Supreme Being, but the fact that two such miscreants did get as far as they got shows that we should take what we get and be thankful and not try to overdirect our affairs.

At the moment I am about completely recovered from the let-down which I have always experienced after a fight or at the end of a foot-ball or polo season. It is undoubtedly true in my experience that the pressure of high responsibility developes in one latent powers of which one had never dreamt, and that at the cessation of the extreme emergency, the neutralization of these powers produces a sort of lethargy.

*Letter, GSP, Jr., to Mrs. M. B. Horan, September 12, 1943*

So far as exercise is concerned, it is a most difficult thing to obtain. I do go swimming two or three times a week in the most lovely water that I have ever seen and on a beach that has Wakiki absolutely pushed off the map. Before taking my swim, I run about half a mile and find it quite tiresome as the sand is very soft.

I have also rented from an Italian nobleman a starboat in which I sometimes get a chance to go sailing, particularly on Sundays. I also have a horizontal bar in my room on which I chin myself before each meal.

During battle there is no incentive to eat. We all feel it . . . so we all lose weight. After battle there isn't much else to do so we all eat too much, but up to the moment I have not lost my girlish figure.

The fighting in the Salerno beachhead was touch and go.

*Letter, GSP, Jr., to Beatrice, September 13, 1943*

Waynes picture came out too soon, poor chap. He is having quite a show at this moment. I may get in yet as a relief, who knows.

*Diary, September 13*

General Dillon, Provost Marshal of AFHQ, came to tell me all my sins against the Geneva Convention. I was very nice to him . . . I suggested that he talk to the Archbishop on the treatment, said to be inhuman, of the Italian prisoners . . . Dillon talked with him and apparently the Archbishop did his stuff. He told Dillon that I had been like a father to the Italian prisoners, so that probably cleans up the allegations about my unnecessary roughness. Well, that hurdle is past.

*Diary, September 14*

Things are going worse with the Fifth Army. Last night they flew in a regimental combat team of the 82d Airborne to help out. It is noteworthy that when I asked similar assistance last month, I was told that the 82d was too valuable to be wasted as infantry. Fortunately, we won the fight without them.

Our 3d Division starts to go over to Italy tomorrow. I trust they do not arrive too late. I guess Clark needs them badly as he is on the defensive.

Truscott went over this afternoon in a torpedo boat [to prepare for the arrival of his division] . . . He told me that Ike said to him that I am the only General who can inspire men to conquer. That was very nice of Ike, but I wish he would give me a chance to do some more conquering.

Why did I not go to Italy? But perhaps my luck is still holding — I feel sure it is.

If Clark failed in Italy as Fredendall had failed in Tunisia, would Patton be called upon to rescue American prestige and gain victory?

Clark instructed his staff to prepare a plan for evacuating the VI Corps and landing it on the X Corps beaches, or the reverse.

*Diary, September 15*

Had dinner with . . . Alexander and Lemnitzer last night, on their way to investigating the situation in Italy . . . They were seriously talking about the possibility of having to withdraw. The Germans attacked . . . down the Sele River just as I told Gruenther they would, and they have apparently cut the X Corps and the VI Corps in two. The only comfort I got out of it is the fact that my military judgment was proved correct. I hope they can stop them — a withdrawal would hurt our prestige and surely prolong the war . . .

Just saw a dispatch from Navy in which it seems that Clark has re-embarked. I consider this a fatal thing to do. Think of the effect on the troops — a commander, once ashore, must conquer or die.

*Diary, September 16*

Truscott got back last night and says that situation is o.k. He feels that the British and Americans fought badly, that Clark split up units like a map problem, but that actually the Germans had very few troops and were just bluffing.

This was a perceptive remark. Although the Germans would have liked to gain a great victory and throw the Allies into the sea, they were fighting primarily to insure the withdrawal of their troops below Salerno, those opposing Montgomery. The Germans would soon start retiring slowly up the boot of Italy.

*Diary, September 17*

Ike came in by plane . . . on his way to visit Fifth Army. Clark wants to relieve Dawley from the VI Corps but needs Ike to hold his hand. I urged Ike to let Keyes have Dawley's place, or if Lucas got that, to let Keyes have II Corps. I told Ike I was willing to fight a corps under Clark. I would serve under the Devil to get a fight. He said Clark and I were not soul mates so he could not do it. When I first heard that Ike was coming, I thought it might be to relieve Clark, but no such luck.

I am to go to England and get an Army, probably under that victorious soldier, Jake Devers [who had never been in combat]. Destiny had better get busy.

*Letter, GSP, Jr., to Beatrice, September 17, 1943*

Geoff may get a. corps. If he does, I will loose him but as I have lost every thing else – at least for the moment – I can let him go . . .

Things are going fine with Fifth Army. Lucien and Troy are both over there. So the Seventh is a nebulous hypothesis, although for a while I thought I would have a chance to get my fingers singed on the chestnuts. All I can think [to console himself] is that I have been apparently out three times now and have so far bobed up . . .

I have met some nice French people so have a chance to practice my French.

*Diary, September 18*

Orders came through for Lucas to report to Fifth Army, I think in replacement for Dawley . . . and for Keyes to command the II Corps. I was delighted.

*Letter, GSP, Jr., to Beatrice, September 19, 1943*

Yesterday I felt like the Ancient Mariner: "Alone, alone, all all alone," as both Lucas and Geoff were going . . .

I am approaching an irreducable minimum but it has happened before and I have survived.

Eisenhower was writing Marshall to give him some ideas on the cross-Channel attack, which Eisenhower believed that Marshall would command. Understanding that Marshall would have two American Armies, Eisenhower felt that Patton could very well have one of them. Many generals, he said, usually thought of battle in terms of concentration, supply, maintenance, and replacement first – and only afterward of attack. This conservative type of leader was necessary because he prevented disaster.

But occasionally, under particular conditions, boldness was an overriding need. That was Patton's strength. He "thinks only in terms of attack as long as there is a single battalion that can keep advancing." Moreover, he had a "native shrewdness" that enabled him to keep his men supplied with sufficient ammunition and food, no matter what. Eisenhower doubted that he would ever consider Patton for command of an Army Group, but as an Army commander – under a sound and solid superior who could use his "good qualities" without being blinded by his love of "showmanship and histrionics" – Patton could do "as fine a job as he did in Sicily."

*Letter, Arvin H. Brown to GSP, Jr., September 21, 1943*

I suppose you know where you are, and perhaps some favored few likewise are aware of your whereabouts, but the multitude are wondering with forced calm where and when you will put in your next appearance. When you disappear, you disappear in a sort of personal blackout. It resembles black magic and recalls the fairy tales of our youth when the prince possessed the power to render himself invisible. In your case, the important thing is that you will reappear at a place and at a time that will be most inopportune for the Axis gang.

*Letter, GSP, Jr., to Beatrice, September 21, 1943*

How does the press for the ever valorous Fifth compare with that for the Seventh? The few intercepts we pick up here are very cleverly worded, but it is hard for me to judge ecuably . . .

I have met two groups of French people who got stranded here in 1940. Campy [Colonel Nicholas Campanole, who had been in Mexico with Patton, who was a linguist, and who headed the Civil Affairs staff section] and I have had two meals with them and I find that during my two months lay off from French, my language has improved. Of course these people are more at home with Italians, so speak French slowly, like the Greeks at Saumur.

*Diary, September 21*

I realize I did my duty [in Sicily] in a very tactless way, but so long as my method pleased the God of Battles, I am content.

Lucas relieved Dawley in command of the VI Corps just as the battle for Naples started. It was, he said,

Sicily over again. Same rough, rugged terrain, same mountain roads, more cover, same demolitions, but fewer mines. My experience in Sicily and especially what I learned from sitting at your feet has been worth a million dollars to me.

*Diary, September 22*

General Dawley came in this morning on his way home. He was most manly and restrained. I gather that there was constant interference [with him] and vacillation on the part of Clark, and near duplicity on the part of Gruenther. I also think that Dawley lacked drive and that McCreery of the X British Corps complained that Dawley did not keep him informed. I forgot to ask if he kept Dawley informed – I doubt it.

Took a trip . . . over the railroad . . . extremely interesting, and unnecessary precautions were taken for my safety in that we were preceded and followed by pilot trains and when we stopped for lunch, sentinels mysteriously evolved from out of the bushes. However, it is very pleasing to see that your own men think so much of you – the rest can go to hell.

*Diary, September 23*

Finally finished my notes on the Sicilian operation . . .

Went to tea with some upper middle class Italians. Women very fat.

His notes turned out to be 22 pages of single-spaced typing, arranged in four parts – amphibious operations, combat, tactical and technical observations, and notes on corps and Army. Most of the material he had already recorded in letters to McNair, Handy, and others – practical suggestions, always concrete and to the point, on functions, procedures, and equipment. Some typical comments:

The greatest importance must be placed on enthusiastic elan and self-confidence on the part of the troops making the initial assault. Battle is a violent and elemental occupation. Men to conquer in battle, particularly in a night landing, must be imbued with this elemental viciousness. A landing operation which does not continue its attack is bound to fail.

In any landing operation confusion is bound to occur. This is due to the fact that in spite of the best intentions, landing craft do not land where they are supposed to and stores get ashore regardless of categories. The main thing is to get the men and the stores ashore. If they are there, they can be used. If we waste time trying to get them ashore in some preconceived order, they will not be available.

The final note read: "The American soldier . . . is a peerless fighting man."

*Letter, GSP, Jr., to Beatrice, September 24, 1943*

I just repine and sweat, but things will change all at once. They better.

*Letter, GSP, Jr., to Kenyon Joyce, September 26, 1943*

At the moment I have not the faintest idea when, if ever, I shall be employed, but I hope for the best.

*Diary, September 26*

Campy, Codman, and I went to supper with some Italian people at a little villa by the sea. It was very pretty, and we danced to a cracked victrola and ate many horrible things. At least we killed off another day of uncertainty. I am getting awfully fed up.

*Letter, GSP, Jr., to Frederick Ayer, September 26, 1943*

Ever since I got to Sicily I have been going to Catholic Churches, largely for political reasons but also as a means of worshiping God because I think he is quite impartial as to the form in which he is approached . . .

I had all the non-Catholic chaplains in the other day and gave them hell for having uninteresting services . . . I told them that I was going to relieve any preacher who talked more than ten minutes on any subject. I will probably get slapped down by the Church union . . .

This afternoon I am going out on a picnic with an Italian banker and his family. Certainly the horrors of war have not affected the family, because the two daughters are very pretty and the mother must way at least 300 pounds. The daughters should never appear in public with her because you can see even now traces of the ability to put on the same amount of weight.

Every once in a while I become completely amused at the amount of formality accorded me, particularly when I think that within a reasonable time I will be riding a solitary bicycle from Green Meadows to Hamilton. Now when I go abroad, the sirens of motorcycles scream, armored cars pursue me, and to cap the climax, the other day I went on a private train on a private railway with a pilot train ahead of me to see that the rails were not mined, and a second pilot behind me to see that some malign influence did not jam into my sacred rear . . .

It was very amusing and I know that it accounts for the stuffiness of many generals. As long as I can see the funny side of it, perhaps I am safe.

*Letter, GSP, Jr., to McNair, September 27, 1943*

So far as the future of the Seventh Army is concerned, I am completely in the dark but trust that I shall have another chance to fight somebody somewhere.

*Letter, GSP, Jr., to Stimson, September 27, 1943*

As far as we can learn here, the Fifth Army seems to be doing a splendid job. My only regret is that I cannot be twins and be with them too.

*Diary, September 28*

Mixed armies [with British and American corps] will not work – I think they are a British scheme to gain command. All their Army commanders are four-star [generals] so they will always [out]rank us.

*Letter, GSP, Jr., to Beatrice, September 29, 1943*

Send [me] clippings on Wayne. He is doing his damdest to get a press, and I am wondering what luck he is having . . .

Things are just as dull for me as they were in Rabat last March so something may turn up. I wish I could be sent some where where I had no relations [British cousins] to bother with. I am sure that it would be better for all concerned . . .

I am certainly fed up with idleness.

*Diary, September 29*

Ike has recommended me to command an Army in UK. I knew that and can't see how he could have done otherwise. I have been very successful three times. Clark is having his first trial and to date has gone very slowly . . .

Butcher says that the British are deliberately trying to build Monty as the hero of the war. That is why they are not too fond of me. One British general said to Lemnitzer, "George is such a pushing fellow that if we don't stop him, he will have Monty surrounded." I know I can outfight the little fart any time.

*Letter, GSP, Jr., to Albert W. Kenner, September 30, 1943*

I sometimes think that it is disadvantageous to do too well, and my present lack of occupation may be traceable to this cause. On the other hand, I have been extremely lucky. This is the fourth time when I seem to have worked myself out of a job and in every case, without any activity on my part, I got a better one.

Clark took Naples on October 1, and Patton wrote him:

My dear Wayne: . . cannot refrain any longer from writing to tell you how proud we all are of the way you and your Army are getting forward. Please accept our most sincere congratulations on the capture of the biggest city ever taken by an American Army.

Early in October, President Roosevelt sent to the Senate for approval the nominations of five temporary (that is, for the duration of the war only) lieutenant generals to be advanced to the permanent rank (which would be retained in retirement) of major general – Wainwright, MacArthur's successor in the Philippines and a prisoner of war; Joseph Stilwell, commander of the U.S. forces in China, Burma, and India; Patton; Brehon Somervell, head of the Army Service Force; and Joseph McNarney, Marshall's deputy chief of staff.

Patton wrote his wife in great excitement about "a lucky day." He received "a lot of clippings" from Beatrice; a magazine story, largely her doing, on the "Life of General Patton," which was "fine"; an article in *Reader's Digest* entitled " 'Old Man Battle' which is not too bad." Then he went to dinner with Admiral Davidson who gave him a teletyped newscast about the nominations for permanent major general. "All this built up my fallen arches of self confidence quite a lot." Adding further joy was "quite a nice letter from F.D.R. him self."

However, I am still very uncertain asto where I am going to fight, if at all, and when is a mystery. I am not as jealous of Wayne as I was, for I think that his party may well be an anti-climax . . .

Must go out and exercise now.

*Letter, Hughes to GSP, Jr., October 4, 1943*

Words fail me when I start to tell you how glad I am that you have been nominated . . . There are advantages in keeping one's shirt on, are there not, even though it be a hairshirt.

*Telegram, Eisenhower to GSP, Jr., October 4, 1943*

I am highly delighted that the War Department and the President have recognized the value of your contributions by nominating you as a permanent major general. You have lived up to every one of the expectations I have held for you during the past 25 years, and I know that every job the government may give you during this war will be performed with the same dash, energy, and determination that have characterized all your action during the past 10 months.

*Letter, GSP, Jr., to Eisenhower, October 6, 1943*

Please accept my most sincere thanks . . . It is my personal conviction that you, and you alone, are responsible for the promotion, as you have been for every other promotion I have received. I have run out of proper words to thank you, so you can just put the nth power on my remarks and let it go at that.

*Letter, GSP, Jr., to Marshall, October 7, 1943*

I am very deeply appreciative of this honor and feel, as in all cases, I owe the distinction to your generosity.

Senatorial approval of nominations was usually a mere formality, and everyone assumed that the Senate would act at once. For no particular reason, the Senate delayed.

Eisenhower sent Bedell Smith to Washington to confer with Marshall on European strategy. Among the items he listed for Smith to do: "Discuss qualifications of General Patton, particularly as an assault Army commander . . . His talents should not be wasted."

*Diary, October 4*

Much mail and clippings and candy. Have to start walking again, much as I hate it.

*Letter, GSP, Jr., to Mrs. G. C. Marshall, October 4, 1943*

I really appreciate very much what you said about the men [in the Seventh Army]. They are wonderful soldiers, and we are mutually crazy about each other.

*Diary, October 5*

Went to tea with . . . about a dozen upper crust people present and it was very nice, except that a famous pianist was there who insisted on playing me things in D minor, which were terrible to hear . . . The people . . . are exactly the same sort you would meet in Boston or New York and talked about the same things.

*Diary, October 6*

Keyes . . . took off for Italy [with his II Corps headquarters]. I hate to see him go, as anyone who serves under Clark is always in danger. I told Geoff to be careful never to mention the Seventh Army and to always win.

I wish something would happen to Clark.

*Letter, GSP, Jr., to his son George, October 6, 1943*

I realize, as you well know, the difficulty of being a turn-back, and I am sure you are conducting yourself correctly in not taking advantage of your position . . .

I am sure that those turn-backs who associate with their old classmates are on the road to ruin, because as you say, neither class respects them . . .

Naturally, with the publicity I have gotten, you are a marked man, and it is a good thing to be a marked man if you live up to the reputation. More people fail through being unknown than through being known . . .

Do not try to save money on clothes. When the Cadets get found [flunk out] at Christmas, as they will, if any of them are near your size, get him to sell you the clothes and have them recut. You cannot have too many clothes, and they must be always well pressed . . .

Self-confidence is the surest way of obtaining what you want. If you know in your own heart you are going to be something, you will be it . . . Do not permit your mind to think otherwise. It is fatal . . .

So far as I am concerned, I do not know what is going to happen, but I am sure, with the same self-confidence which I am preaching to you, that something will happen, and that when it does, I will make a success of it.

*Letter, GSP, Jr., to Marshall, October 7, 1943*

I have been having great difficulty in getting exercise, as when I walk I am followed by a crowd, presumably admiring, and when I run the crowd thinks that there is a fire. The other day I discovered an abandoned riding hall in the Palace and told the Italian Carabinieri that I should like to use it. This morning they had a grand opening with 120 men in full uniform with plumes and sabers and a mounted band. This was followed by jumping and then by monkey drill. It was all very reminiscent of Fort Myer.

*Diary, October 7*

If I can ride daily, my exercise problem will be solved. I can ride during lunch and so will not have to eat.

*Letter, GSP, Jr., to Beatrice, October 7, 1943*

The other day I had tea with a very fat Bourbon Princess with a black beard which she shaves. The Chateau is realy lovely. On the Rococo side . . . built in 1710 and is very well preserved.

In some way the Princess is very rich. She talks bad French at the top of her powerful lungs. Yet when she was young, she must have been quite lovely. She has good features.

She has a girl friend who should be a wrestler but is a famous Pianoist. All she can play are Etudes and Movements, but she does that with utter abandon and great power. I have never seen such fore arms. Codman says she is not so hot, but she sounded authentic to me. I made a hit by not talking during the playing – you taught me that – so now she thinks I love music and threatens to have a musical evening "where we will just play, not eat or drink." Certainly an inexpensive system if the piano stands up.

*Letter, GSP, Jr., to Charles F. Ayer, October 8, 1943*

I am now in the position of Mr. Micawber, that is, waiting for something to turn up.

CHAPTER 20

# The Slapping Incident Again

*"I think I was luckey for more reasons than I can say."*

IT WAS PROBABLY INEVITABLE that the slapping incident, buried by the press, be brought to the surface. Too many individuals knew the story or had heard and spread the rumors. Given Patton's news value, someone was bound to capitalize on and sensationalize the event. The revelation would burst like a bombshell.

Meanwhile, Patton continued his quiet existence in Sicily, watching developments in the campaign on the mainland, awaiting word of his future employment, worrying about his future employability, and hoping that fulfillment of his destiny lay ahead of him rather than behind.

*Letter, GSP, Jr., to Beatrice, October 9, 1943*

I wrote . . . to Tom H[andy] just now urging that we speed up a little, but fear he is bogged down in dreams like the rest.

*Letter, GSP, Jr., to Beatrice, October 11, 1943*

Things are pretty slow [in Italy] due to rain and also supply difficulties. Perhaps my luck still held when I did not get that job . . .

Last evening I drove to Piano de Greco, which is an original Greek colony dating from before 450 BC. They all talk Greek, have straight noses, and smell even worse than Italians.

Commenting in his diary on the campaign in southern Italy, he thought that the nine Allied divisions could hardly advance "at any speed, if at all" against the eight German divisions because the Allies lacked sufficient superiority and were unable to rest their troops. The Germans, operating in terrain favoring the defense, could rest their men.

> There can well be a disaster but hardly an Allied victory. I don't get the picture at all. I feel that I am lucky not to be in Clark's place.

"So far as I know," he wrote to Lucas, "there is no immediate future for this [Seventh] Army."

"Still no news or even rumor," he recorded, "as to what is in store for the Seventh Army."

*Letter, GSP, Jr., to Beatrice, October 14, 1943*

> I am riding every day now and feel fine. I also walk several miles and dont smoke. When ever I get one of these yearns to be fit, it means war and has so far. At the moment I see no chance.

In September, he told Beatrice, while Monty was fighting his way north against supposedly bitter resistance from the toe of Italy to reach and help Clark at Salerno, two newspaper correspondents at the Eighth Army took a jeep, drove through enemy territory, met not a single German soldier, and arrived at Clark's headquarters safely.

> How we laughed.
>
> I was terribly disappointed not to land at Salerno instead of W., but now I think I was luckey for more reasons than I can say.

He called on Andrew B. Cunningham, who had replaced Sir Dudley Pound as First Sea Lord, and met his successor in command of the Allied naval forces in the Mediterranean, John Cunningham,

> also a fine looking man. However, it continues to rile me that all the commands go to the British. It seems to me that Hewitt should have replaced Cunningham, although far from being the same calibre of man.

*Letter, GSP, Jr., to Handy, October 18, 1943*

> I would rather be a temporary Lt. General fighting somebody than a permanent Major General with no fight on. I suppose, however, I will get some more battles before it is too late.

He, as well as the others nominated, had yet to be confirmed by the Senate for promotion to permanent major general.

Secretary of the Treasury Henry Morgenthau and his assistant, Dr. Harry Dexter White, spent a day with Patton who was "very favorably impressed" with Morgenthau, who "was charming" and who "really seemed anxious to save money for the United States." He "showed surprising historical ignorance," but was not pro-British. White impressed Patton as "very clever and a dreamer, damned near a communist."

White would, after the war, be implicated in the Alger Hiss affair.

*Letter, GSP, Jr., to Beatrice, October 22, 1943*

Last Saturday I got so nervous that I had to take sleeping pills – harmless – flew over to see Everett. He, Ike, and I had dinner together and it was like old times – almost.

Everett is very understanding of Divine Destiny and makes more allowances than I do . . .

No one including D D knows what is to become of us.

*Letter, GSP, Jr., to Arvin H. Brown, October 22, 1943*

I regret that my current disappearance from the public press is causing you so much worry. However, I assure you that I am worrying more about it than you are . . .

This you will find hard to believe. I walk two miles every day. And I know it is two miles because I get out of the automobile and have the driver go on until the speedometer has reached two miles and then wait for me.

Two weeks earlier, Patton had written to Handy to suggest how "we could kill more Germans." Admitting that he had "inadequate information of the big picture" and was "impelled by my normal desire to fight," he recommended an amphibious operation from Corsica to southern France or northern Italy – with landings at Marseilles, Toulon, Genoa, or Leghorn. Since the staff of his "somewhat emasculated Army" had little to do, he had the members making, along with his local Navy and Air Force people, "a purely academic study of the above proposition." No one except him knew that the work was "only for the purpose of practice." He felt it was "wholly immaterial where we kill the Germans, and it is very important that we keep killing them now." Yet at the end he conceded his doubt "whether anything can be done with this except throw it away, in which case, please burn it first."

The idea was designed to speed up the campaign in southern Italy and to get Patton into action again — he told Beatrice wryly, "I should prefer to winter at Monte Carlo or Nice." Although the concept essentially foreshadowed the Allied landings in southern France in August 1944, it was premature. The Allies were hoarding their resources in the United Kingdom for Overlord in the spring, and there were insufficient troops, ships, and supplies in the Mediterranean for a seaborne venture.

Yet Patton's letter gave Handy an idea that he passed to Marshall. Why not, Handy suggested, exploit Patton's presence in the Mediterranean, his reputation, and his unemployment? Marshall agreed and recommended to Eisenhower that Patton travel conspicuously to make the Germans think he was about to lead the sort of invasion he had his staff working on. Eisenhower was favorably impressed, and he directed Patton to come to Algiers when convenient, with three or four senior staff officers.

"This is a somewhat cryptic message," Patton noted in his diary, "but all my operations, starting with the creation of the Desert Training Center, have started the same way. Here's hoping."

*Diary, October 27*

[Algiers] Ike had me to lunch with Beedle Smith . . . Ike was his old self. Beedle Smith told me that I am to get an Army in England. He said he had told General Marshall that I am the greatest assault general in the world and should lead the [cross-Channel] attack. General Marshall agreed but said, "I don't trust his staff." Beedle said, "Well, they have always succeeded." General Marshall said, "I have been told that in Sicily the supply was not good. I have my own means of knowing." That means either Wedemeyer or Bradley or both [told him so].

I told Beedle that I would have to stick to my staff as they had stuck to me . . . He agreed and told me how much he admired me. He is such a liar I wonder if he ever said that to Marshall.

After lunch Smith told me that the operation on which I am to embark is a cover plan for the purpose of using the prestige of the Seventh Army to draw attention to Corsica [that is, to make the Germans believe that the Allies were preparing to use Corsica as a jump-off place for another invasion] and that in order to do the thing right, we will have to pass through Tunis because it is felt that there is a German there who will inform his people of our proposed trip.

This is the end of my hopes for war.

The Germans had departed from Corsica when they lost Sicily, and the island was again under French administration.

After stopping in Tunis, Patton and his party traveled to Corsica, where they made ostentatious inspections of the harbors, the airfields, and the terrain in order to try to deceive German intelligence agents. Patton was interested in the history of the island and in the historical monuments.

> It is quite a thrill to be in Napoleon's home town . . . Corsica is just as French as France and the people are clean and mentally alert . . . The Seventh Army staff [members with Patton], who had never before seen Frenchmen, were extremely impressed with the fact that they use the same [military] methods that we use. The answer is that we copied their methods in 1918.

Back at Palermo, Patton welcomed Courtney Hodges who arrived for a visit.

> He apparently is less dumb than I considered him . . . However, I am personally very fond of him.

He took Hodges over some of the battlefields and "had more satisfaction . . . than [with] anyone else."

Patton received fifty dollars for a poem entitled "God of Battles," published by the *Woman's Home Companion.* A reader wrote to Mrs. Patton that the lines reflected her husband's qualities:

> A God-fearing man who asks guidance from "above" – then goes into battle, fortified by that Guidance. I'd never picture him as the type who would pray to God – then sit down somewhere, and expect God to do all his work for him.
>
> Every American should be proud of the praying, fighting, poetic General Patton.

A friend of many years wrote Patton:

> You would be amazed at the many different stories that go around as to your whereabouts. You have been reported to have been in India, Burma, about to make an invasion of the Balkans, and to take part in a proposed offensive against Norway and that portion of

> Europe. So you can see that you are at least very much in the public eye and that there are many questions as to your whereabouts being asked.

Patton was in Naples. He was impressed by the "really great job of salvage" done to restore the harbor destroyed by the Germans. The methods used, he was sure, were those he had originally evolved at Casablanca and Palermo.

At the VI Corps headquarters, Lucas was "in fine spirits and delighted to see me." Lucas thought that the troops were tired and were

> asking for far too much artillery support and it is getting them into bad habits . . . I fear he is right. If troops are kept at it too long, they lose their dash and simply claw up after the guns.

Clark was "quite cordial and is evidently having trouble with the British, who simply don't fight. Their men are braver than ours, but their officers have no push." Clark's command post at Caserta was a two-and-a-half-hour drive from the divisions on the line, and Patton thought that Clark "might just as well, and it would be more comfortable, be in Naples."

He was disturbed to see that Clark's map room showed "the positions of troops down to battalions. This is bad as it tempts people [at Army level] to deal in battalions instead of . . . corps."

> Truscott . . . is fed up with the campaign and with Clark and his staff because they keep meddling with him and because both he and his men are battle weary. He is very anxious to be with me in the next show I go in. I would like to have him as a corps commander. He and Keyes would be a fine pair. Middleton could do a job in such a team, using him as a wheel-horse with two flashy players on the flanks. I hope I have the opportunity to get such a combination some day.
>
> Smith certainly is an s.o.b. of the finest type, selfish, dishonest, and very swell headed.

*Letter, GSP, Jr., to Maj. Gen. Paul B. Malone, San Francisco, November 7, 1943*

The class you conducted . . . at Fort Sheridan in 1909 was the best instruction I have ever received and certainly set me on what I believe is the road to successful war; namely, to hunt for a fight under circumstances which will permit you to kill more of the enemy than he can kill of you, and then keep on attacking.

It is just like boxing. When you get your opponent on his heels, you must keep punching hell out of him and not let him recover.

*Letter, GSP, Jr., to Mrs. Jenson, November 7, 1943*

I believe that the scholarship [in Dick Jenson's name] is going forward all right, as I have had several letters from General Harbord about it.

The Seventh Army still continues unemployed, and we are getting very much bored, but always hope for something to turn up.

*Letter, GSP, Jr., to Beatrice, November 7, 1943*

We have been at it just a year to day and in all that time I have only been in battle 72 days out of 365 – it seems a lot of time lost. We are fiddeling while Rome burns, but only in metaphor, for I doubt if she burns – not for quite a while any how.

This was a reference to the campaign in Italy, which was going very slowly. Rome, the main objective, was still distant.

I have been up in the air both actually and figuratively . . . I have seen Carthage and spent some days at Nap's old home town. Even touched the bed in which he slept. I saw Elba through the fog.

Carthage is not even a ruin. There is nothing left, first because it was destroyed the way we should destroy Berlin and Tokyo and second, because several other later towns have been built on the same site.

If you took the boldest part of the Rocky Mountains and sunk it in a lake leaving only the top, that would be Corse. No wonder they have vendetas there. There is nothing else to do . . .

Pompei . . . was bombed quite a lot – God knows why – but was not severely hurt.

Wayne has his camp in the garden of a palace after which Versailles was copied. It is very beautiful but too far to the rear.

I saw Lucien, also Mother Baehr [his classmate] and Jim [Totten, his son-in-law] . . .

Lucien has been at it more than 48 days and is tired. So are they all. I also saw John Lucas and Geoff. They are not too happy. The show is static and may get worse.

We got pretty well bombed at N[aples]. I was out in the street in a car and every one ran for cover. A lot of AA [antiaircraft] fell in the street and looked like fire flies, but I was not hit, not even a close miss. When ever the firing would stop, soldiers would run up to the car out of cellars and ask if they could carry me to shelter. They thought I must be hurt to stay in the street. I told them it was safer as if a bomb hit me it would be a clean end while in a cellar they would smother. This running for shelter is sad. It induces the thought that the enemy has something on you . . .

Well, I am still unemployed.

*Diary, November 7*

I have grown in stature, in poise, in self-confidence, and in self-control very much. Further, now I trust no one; that is, no human being. I have used every opportunity I've had to the full and see no reason to change what I did.

Had I to do it over again, in view of my present knowledge of the British, I would not have obeyed the order I got on April 4, 1943 to pull back after we broke through at El Guettar. I was too good a soldier that time. Had I told Brigadier Holmes, Alexander's G–3, to go to hell when he phoned me the order and [had I] demanded to speak to Alex, I could have stayed and America would have gotten more credit . . . As a result of that experience, I refused to stay put on July 17th, and made Alex let me start to take Palermo, though he was much opposed to my doing it. Live and learn.

In his diary of November 9, he wrote that the British "have no shame nor modesty and will take all they can get."

*Letter, GSP, Jr., to Beatrice, November 11, 1943*

Don't worry about my becoming a victim of flattery. I don't get any. Perhaps . . . I was the idle of the people. Now I may well be forgotten.

I agree with you that it was most stupid not to play up Messina. Destiny was and is leaning over backwards [in favor of the British]. Besides, Destiny has absolutely no inspirational value . . .

When I was in Napoli I got in an air rade. The driver wanted to park the car and hide. So when I made him keep right on, he has spread a great legend about me, how the "flack" fell in the street all around us etc. etc. Stiller did offer me his helmet as I was not wearing one . . .

Everett also says to "keep my shirt on and sit tight." I told him that hair shirts scratched and that I had been kicked in the tale so much I had a hard time sitting at all.

Just got back from the usual memorial service. The fool preacher . . .

Well, I am a year older. Love

*Diary, November 11*

One year ago today we took Casa. Now I command little more than my self-respect. General McNair wrote me, "You are the Seventh Army." He was more right than he knew . . .

We went to a Memorial Service at the cemetery at 1100. The Chaplain preached a sermon on sacrifice and the usual bull, so as I put the wreath at the foot of the flagpole, I said, "I consider it no sacrifice to die for my country. In my mind we came here to thank God that men like these have lived rather than to regret that they have died." When the troops marched off, I had them [the band] play quick time . . .

We had a big reception at the Grand Hotel to celebrate, not Armistice Day, but our capture of Casablanca. We had cocktails, and there was a table for me with a birthday cake.

He was fifty-eight years old.

*Letter, GSP, Jr., to son George, November 14, 1943*

It is getting pretty cold here and we have no fires in the palace, so we dress and undress fast. I wish I could find out what I am going to do and when, but so far none of us know a damned thing.

*Diary, November 14*

Hodges and I had a long talk. We both feel that viewed at face value the situation in Italy is bad. Our men are tired and fed up. They are so battle wise that they can appear to attack without doing so and only advance when there is an amazing amount of artillery support. When divisions get like that, their value, except for defense, is gone. I can't see why Ike has not asked for many more divisions . . . With the stabilized fighting Clark is having, we could blood half a dozen green divisions and have them in great shape for a real attack.

Both Clark and Gruenther are jumpy. Clark has fired several aides. I hope that he or Gruenther or both break down, but I don't want the job myself as now it is in a very bad state. Only six fresh divisions could [improve the situation] and then only provided that the British would fight. At the moment they show no intention of doing so.

There is something very phoney about all our British and American efforts. Our strategy seems to be based on votes, not victories.

*Diary, November 17*

I have seldom passed a more miserable day. I have absolutely nothing to do and hours of time in which to do it. From commanding 240,000 men, I now have less than 5,000 . . . Well, pretty soon I will hit bottom and then bounce.

That too was intuitive.

*Letter, GSP, Jr., to Maj. Gen. Sherman Miles, November 18, 1943*

Regret that I am for the moment apparently not destined to resume biting the Hun, although I have spent considerable time sharpening my teeth.

*Letter, GSP, Jr., to Beatrice, November 18, 1943*

For the last five days I have been lower than whale tracks . . .

As I have nothing pleasant to write about, I will stop.

He enclosed a poem:

Seven Up!

Once there was an Army
Then one day it died
So toll the bell and waken Hell
To give it room inside.

The story of this Army
Is very very drear
Its beginning and its ending
Were especially queer.

They made its chief a *perminent*
So he perchance could *wave*
At others hurrying past him
Their country for to save.

But now just like a skeleton
Upon the desert floor
Orders like vultures come each day
To pick away some more.

The thing has got so very bad
That now his friends suspect
That he no longer can command
Even his self respect.

Yet like the fabled Phoenix
The Seventh shall arise
Again to soar in triumph
Through flaming smoke veiled skys!

The Archbishop of Palermo informed Patton of "acts of revolt" caused by food shortages and warned, "It is of no use for an Army to achieve victory if the people are not won. The Army conquers with weapons; people are won by wise and timely provisions."

Advising Eisenhower of the near famine and widespread black market in Sicily, Patton suggested two solutions: death to black marketeers or Allied shipments of flour to undersell the hoarders.

*Letter, GSP, Jr., to Beatrice, November 20, 1943*

We went to a very heavy Italian dinner last night . . .

First we had a cordial . . .

Then we had a soup . . . Then we had a sort of pie about four inches thick. It had potatoes, calliflour, cheese, fish, beans, and other ingredients I could not determine in it. Not only was it powerful but it was copious. The hostess . . . the fat one with the good features — next to whom I sat had made it so I had to eat two helpings.

Then we had a dish that would have been a great boon to a geologist; it was stratified. On the top was lobster, then shell fish, then green assorted vegetables, then cheese, and god knows what else, all smothered in thick mayonnayse. No one near me had made it so I got by with one small helping.

For desert we had a horrid Italian cream which had been made by the lady on my right, so I had to eat all of it.

But the eating ability of the Italians is more wonderful than their cooking. I have never seen such helpings as they took and they all had at least two. One little girl of 13 ate enough to founder a horse. After dinner I examined her contour to see if she bulged, but there was no sign.

When we got home, Codman, who seldom drinks, suggested that we all take a big swig of whiskey to disinfect our insides, so we did . . .

We are all gun toating again as there seems a chance of a sort of bonus war due to lack of bread. So far there have only been minor riots . . .

At the moment I am more than on ice. I am frozen stiff like Birdseye.

My chief bother is that I don't sleep at night and feel sleepy in the day time.

He would soon have a more serious problem, real trouble. He was about to witness the distinct possibility that his career might come to an end. He was going to hit the headlines in a big and disastrous fashion, and the first intimation of personal catastrophe in Sicily was a statement picked up by the Seventh Army radio monitoring set and brought to Patton by Codman. It was a deceptively simple report that implied more than it said. In an announcement to the press, AFHQ categorically denied that Eisenhower had reprimanded Patton.

More news arrived later.

Apparently Drew Pearson has made certain allegations against me in Washington. I had been expecting something like this to happen for some time because I am sure that it would have been much better to have admitted the whole thing to start with, particularly in view of the fact that I was right [in what I did].

The slapping incident became known to the public. Pearson visited the Mediterranean theater, learned about the story, and revealed it in a radio broadcast. What would seem reprehensible to the American people was not only the event itself but also Eisenhower's failure to administer an official reprimand.

When the correspondents in Algiers clamored for a statement in the wake of Pearson's broadcast, Bedell Smith, in Eisenhower's absence, held a press conference and admitted that Eisenhower's strong letter to Patton was private rather than official. Eisenhower later considered Smith's admission to be "a bad mistake."

Pearson's broadcast created a sensation in the United States. Newspapers everywhere picked up Pearson's allegations, and a great hue and cry spread across the nation.

Many Americans wrote to their Senators and Congressmen and called for Patton's dismissal. For example, one said that Patton made his blood boil. A superior officer striking American boys

> proves he is as low and has the same heart in him as Adolph Hitler, only difference he is afraid to go quite as far as Hitler. His great progress (as I understand from men over there) is made at the cost of his men, beating, storming, and driving them as a bunch of slaves into things that will put his name in the headlines. For all, it seems too that a man that has no more heart or self control than he, is not capable of being over our boys.

Congressman Robert A. Grant of Indiana asked Secretary Stimson whether the allegations were true. Did Patton lose his temper in Sicily, slap shell-shocked soldiers in a hospital tent, "burst into rage," and employ "much profanity," calling soldiers names that hardly befitted a man of Patton's position? In the best interests of the service and of the families at home, Grant believed that a complete and thorough report on the whole matter should be sent to the Committee on Military Affairs.

Secretary of War Stimson immediately asked Eisenhower for a report.

Eisenhower replied on November 24, giving a firm and forthright account of what had happened. The mainspring of the sustained Seventh Army drive from Gela to Messina, he said, was Patton. Patton's "absolute refusal to accept any excuses for delay or procrastination" was a large factor in the early collapse of the Axis resistance in Sicily. He drove himself as hard as everyone in his Army and became "almost ruthless in his demands upon individual men."

Twice, Eisenhower admitted, while visiting the wounded in the hospitals, Patton encountered patients suffering from "nerve difficulty or what is commonly known as 'battle anxiety.'" Both times he "momentarily lost his temper and upbraided the individuals in an unseemly and indefensible manner."

Learning of these indiscretions from a medical report, which was followed by a report from "three reputable newspapermen," Eisenhower at once asked Patton about the allegations, expressed "extreme displeasure," and informed him that any repetition would result in his "instant relief." He ordered Patton to make "proper amends" to the individuals involved and to his whole Army, meanwhile reserving for himself the decision on whether to relieve Patton – until he could determine the effectiveness of Patton's "corrective action."

Eisenhower also sent two general officers to Sicily to investigate the affair, then went himself to see whether there was resentment in the Army against Patton. The problem for Eisenhower was whether the reported incidents were sufficiently damaging to Patton and to his standing in his Army to compel relief, "thus losing to the United Nations his unquestioned value as a commander of an assault force"; or whether less drastic measures would be appropriate.

Patton made his apologies to the individuals concerned, and they were accepted. He then visited every division and made known his regret over conduct that could be considered "un-American or unfair."

Eisenhower discussed the matter with the three newspapermen who had reported the incident, and they were convinced that "the measures taken were adequate in the circumstances."

Still disturbed, Eisenhower sent his Inspector General to Sicily to discover whether resentment against Patton existed. According to the report, the men felt that Patton had done "a splendid over all job and no great harm had been done."

Although Eisenhower considered Patton's conduct in the two specific slapping cases "indefensible," he knew that Patton had "in thousands of cases personally sustained, supported, and encouraged individuals." Thus, Eisenhower "took those steps that seemed to me applicable in the circumstances, because I believe that General Patton has a great . . . usefulness in any assault where gallantry, drive, and loyalty on the part of the Army commander will be essential."

He expressed his gratitude to the "American newsmen in this theater" for choosing "to regard the matter as one in which the high command acted for the best interests of the war effort."

"To sum up," it was true that Patton was guilty of "reprehensible conduct," but Eisenhower decided that the "corrective action" was "adequate and suitable in the circumstances," and he still believed so. Finally, "in every recent public appearance of Patton before any crowd composed of his own soldiers, he is greeted by thunderous applause."

Stimson presented this report to Senator Robert R. Reynolds, Chairman of the Committee on Military Affairs. In his letter of transmittal, Stimson emphasized that the basic principle followed by the War Department was to gain victory as quickly and with as little loss of life as possible. Eisenhower had weighed Patton's indefensible indiscretion against his outstanding service in World Wars I and II and had considered that the country could not afford to lose Patton for the battles still to come.

Reynolds acknowledged Stimson's letter and enclosure, which the Committee read to the Senate for printing in the *Congressional Record.*

Representative Jed Johnson of Oklahoma wrote Marshall on what he called "the despicable incident" and said he was "amazed and chagrinned" that Patton was still in command of the Seventh Army. Despite Patton's fine previous record, his "unprovoked attack" on a soldier had destroyed his usefulness. He thought that Patton should immediately be relieved of his command.

The point was, as Stimson repeated several times, keeping Patton in command of his Army was a public relations error but militarily sound. Eisenhower could not dispense with this battle-tested Army commander. Dismissing Patton would only give aid and comfort to the enemy.

By mid-December, the President, Secretary of War, and others in the executive branch of the government had received approximately 1500 letters relating to Patton. Many were vituperative, but a surprisingly large proportion favored the general, understood his reaction, and called for his promotion.

*Diary, November 23*

About 2230 I got a long wire from Beedle Smith about correspondents raising hell and about his efforts to placate them; also I was told to back up AFHQ and make no statements if I was visited by correspondents . . . I wholly concurred in his suggestion of no interview.

*Letter, Frederick Ayer to GSP, Jr., November 24, 1943*

Dear George: Apparently you are in a peck of trouble.

*Diary, November 24*

If the fate of the only successful general in this war depends on the statement of a discredited writer like Drew Pearson, we are in a bad fix. Of course I am worried, but I am quite confident that the Lord will see me through . . . I am perfectly certain that this is not the end of me.

*Letter, Eisenhower to GSP, Jr., November 24, 1943*

From Commander in Chief to General Patton for his eyes only. (Code clerk, when you have decoded this message, take it personally to General Patton and to no one else): The flood of newspaper accounts in Washington concerning incidents . . . has continued today. It is my judgment that this storm will blow over because our reporters here have generally sent forward very accurate stories including . . . my action . . . and your corrective measures. I must stress again to you the necessity for acting deliberately at all times and avoiding the giving way to impulse . . . If any inquiry is made from you by the press, I insist that you stick to the facts and give a frank exposition of what occurred. In addition, you could, I think, invite any such press men to visit units still under your command to determine for themselves the state of morale.

I do not desire that you make a formal statement for quotation at this time.

*Cable, GSP, Jr., to Eisenhower, November 25, 1943*

Regret trouble I am causing you. Will abide implicitly by your instructions.

*Diary, November 25*

Thanksgiving Day. I had nothing to be thankful for so I did not give thanks.

Patton's friends rallied around him. Summerall was "indignant about the publicity given to a trifling incident. Whatever you did, I am sure was justified by the provocation." He knew what it was to see troops disintegrate when men drifted to the rear and were "coddled" in the hospitals.

Such cowards used to be shot, but now they are encouraged . . . Only those who carry the responsibility of winning battles know the difficulty of making men fight and so far, you have excelled all others in this accomplishment . . . The country would suffer a calamity in not having your continued leadership . . . Your place is already made in history.

Unfortunately, word reached Patton that Pershing had the opposite conviction. Pershing reacted to the news by denouncing Patton's action. Badly hurt, Patton would write no more letters to the man he had idolized.

*Letter, GSP, Jr., to Beatrice, November 25, 1943*

Personally I have complete confidence that this is not my end – I feel more and more that I have a mission which is far from completed . . .

How I dislike Drew P.

I love you.

*Letter, GSP, Jr., to Bedell Smith, November 26, 1943*

Although, as you know, I have not personally known you so many years, yet I have heard so much of you from Floyd Parks and General Marshall that I feel far better acquainted than the length of time would indicate . . . I have always felt in complete accord with you since our first meeting.

Stimson was writing Beatrice to congratulate her on her superb statement to the press, which he thought would do more good than anything else that had been said. He estimated that the wave of public indignation was subsiding, and he was sure that everything would be all right.

What Beatrice Patton said appeared in the Washington *Post*. She offered no alibi for her husband but suggested that the nation try to understand him as a "tough perfectionist" and "a man fighting furiously for his country." He asked nothing of his soldiers "that he couldn't or would not do himself." He was "a man who feels deeply, and after all those days of seeing his boys blown apart," when he walked down rows of "horribly wounded soldiers," the sight of an apparently able-bodied man "sitting on a cot" probably touched off the dynamite in his personality. "He has been known to weep at his men's graves – as well as tear their hides off."

The deed is done and the mistake made, and I'm sure Georgie is sorrier and has punished himself more than anyone could possibly realize . . .

I've known George Patton for 31 years and I've never known him to be deliberately unfair. He's made mistakes — and he's paid for them. This was a big mistake, and he's paying a big price for it . . .

But don't you go writing mush about him. I won't have it. He wouldn't like it. He made a mistake — and it can't be undone — I just hope they won't kick him to death while he's down.

In the same newspaper a story quoted Representative Charles B. Hoeven, Republican of Iowa, who said in the House that the parents of "boys in the service" had no need of additional anxiety and worry over whether "hard-boiled officers" were abusing their sons. He wondered whether the army had too much "blood and guts."

Coincidentally, an article on the general appeared in *True Confessions* magazine, and Mrs. Patton was quoted there as saying — before knowledge of the slapping incident — that her husband "makes a lot of noise, but he's quite sweet really." He felt "that any man who says that he is not afraid in the face of fire is either a liar or an idiot. But that he is a coward only if he lets fear get the better of him."

Her husband, she said, was known "as the toughest, most hard-boiled general in the U.S. Army," but he had a softer side. He had recently sent her a Nazi flag "for the kids" and a "rose satin bedspread embroidered with white doves and posies" that he thought "might be pretty on the piano."

*Letter, GSP, Jr., to Stimson, November 27, 1943*

Owing to the many years during which you have shown exceptional kindness and consideration for me . . . you should have an exact statement of the incidents for which I am being criticized . . .

This letter is not intended as an excuse for obvious mistakes or as a plea for sympathy.

I believe that in war the good of the individual must be subordinated to the good of the army.

I have never asked favors or immunity for myself, and I have never granted them to those serving under me. I have, to the best of my ability, undergone all the risks of my troops.

I love and admire good soldiers and brave men. I hate and despise slackers and cowards.

I am quite tender-hearted and emotional in my dealings with wounded men.

Like all commanders I am constantly faced with the problem of malingering. If it is not checked, it spreads like a prairie fire . . .

I inspected some 300 freshly wounded men who had gallantly and unflinchingly done their duty, and who, in spite of their wounds, were cheerful and uncomplaining. The last man I came to was a forlorn individual sitting on a box, apparently waiting to have a wound dressed. I asked him where he had been hit. He replied that he had not been hit but that he "just could not take it," and had come to the hospital to avoid combat.

The contrast between this cur, who was not only skulking himself but by his cowardice was forcing other loyal and brave men to do his duty, and the heroes I had just been talking to so moved me that I slapped him across the face with the gloves I was carrying in my hand, shook him, and called him a coward, and told him to get back to his outfit and try to be a man.

When I left, I told the officer who was with me that I hoped I had made a man of that thing, and that if so, I had saved an immortal soul.

The other practically identical incident . . .

I had just talked to over a hundred wounded, the last of whom had lost his right arm and was joking about it when I came on a second of these human jackals, who also told me "He could not take it." I simply shook him, cussed him out, and told the hospital to return him to his outfit.

There is no doubt that my method was too forthright. They will not be repeated.

General Eisenhower wrote me a forceful personal letter very rightly calling my attention to the bad effects my action had on public opinion and directing me to make certain amends.

I apologized to the two men. I called in the medical personnel who witnessed the incidents, explained to them the reasons for my action, and my regret for the same. I made a speech to each of the divisions telling the men what great soldiers they were, explaining to them what they were fighting for, and emphasizing how proud I was of them. I ended by saying that if any of them felt I had been too severe, I apologized, but for every man I had corrected for his own good, I had complimented a thousand.

Any other prejudicial statements concerning me as an officer or soldier are not true.

He was reading a great deal, mainly histories of Sicily. A book on the Norman conquest of Sicily enthralled him. "When I read it," he told Beatrice,

> I feel that I may be either William Fer-a-Beas or Roger of Sicily, probably the former, as he fought his last battle at 71 . . . Any how, they are great company and inspiring fighters . . . This very wet weather and lack of heat is making my bum shoulder hurt but otherwise I am fine and taking excellent care of my self as there is nothing else to do.

*Diary, November 28*

Ike and Beedle are not at all interested in me but simply in saving their own faces. I might act the same if the case were reversed, but I doubt it . . .

Naturally I am worried but I am really more angry than uneasy. My side is not being shown and my friends must be having a hell of a time. So far as I can see, there is nothing for me to do except read the Bible and trust to destiny. I certainly do not intend to read any of the dirt published in the papers or broadcast over the radio. There is no use in giving myself indigestion for nothing.

*Letter, GSP, Jr., to Eisenhower, November 28, 1943*

For the last few days I have been reading a book called "The Greatest Norman Conquest," by Osborne.

It describes the activities of a group of twelve brothers who came from Normandy and who in the course of some sixty years conquered all of Italy south of approximately the present line held by the Fifth and Eighth Armies and who also acquired Sicily and a couple of ports in Africa.

There are many points in common with our operations. The Normans were very careful and meticulous planners. They always attacked. They were masters of landing operations, and they pursued a ruthless offensive in which the armored knights played practically the role of tanks . . .

This war . . . was as nothing, both in extent of territory and in time to what you have done in the past year . . .

One of the things for which the Normans are particularly lauded is the fact of the terrific chances they took with small forces. Here again you have them beat, because . . . you were attacking vastly superior forces; and furthermore, you never suffered any annihilating defeats, whereas the Normans were practically wiped out on two occasions.

I suppose what I have just written sounds like either bullshit or bootlick, but that is not the fact. The fact is that whereas it took some 900 years for the Normans to receive the credit due to their efforts, I trust by this letter to do my small part in handing you the credit while you are still alive and able to enjoy it.

With all good wishes for an even more successful 1943–44, I am as ever, Devotedly yours,

*Diary, November 30*

My command so far has disposed of 177,000 Germans, Italians, and French – killed, wounded, and prisoner, of which they have killed and wounded 21,000. Our average loss has been one man for 13½ of the enemy. It would be a national calamity to lose an Army commander with such a record.

Thanking him for his "very flattering letter," Eisenhower assured him that he would stand by his decision, even though he had been "more than a little annoyed" with Patton. He thought that the noise at home over the incident was dying down.

*Diary, December 1*

General Joyce, whom I talked to on the Drew Pearson incident, remarked: "George, tell them the exact truth in these words – 'I had been dealing with heroes. I saw two men whom I thought were cowards. Naturally I was not too gentle with them.' " This is exactly true, but there is no use repeating it.

Joyce was telling Beatrice how unfortunate it was to see a "sensation monger," by his "specious utterings," crucify a great soldier of incomparable value to the Allied cause. Wars were won, he said, by leaders who were "hard men." The "niceties" of life had to be left to "the softer times of peace."

*Letter, GSP, Jr., to Beatrice, December 1, 1943*

During the last few days I have not written as I have been feeling a bit anti-social . . .

The thing that hurts me is that as far as I can see, my side of the case has never been heard. It is like taxation without representation . . .

However, I am sure that my move is to make no move.

*Letter, GSP, Jr., to Keyes, December 2, 1943*

On occasion it is best to do nothing, and however repellent that is to my nature, I am doing exactly that.

CHAPTER 21

# The Terrible Wait

*"I know I am needed!"*

MEETING AT CAIRO and at Teheran in November to coordinate their global strategy and postwar policies, the Allied leaders, Roosevelt, Churchill, and Stalin, reached a number of agreements and fixed the final effort against Germany. There would be a cross-Channel invasion of northwestern Europe in the spring of 1944 and a supporting and subsidiary invasion of southern France, named Anvil, later Dragoon. Operations in France were to be the main endeavor of the Western Allies, and the campaign in Italy was to sink to secondary importance after the capture of Rome.

Patton knew vaguely that the high-level conference was in session, and he hoped that the decisions reached there might "eventuate in some action" for him.

The President and his party visited Sicily, and everyone "was most afable to me." Eisenhower "was very nice also, and said he felt sure I would soon get orders to go to UK and command an Army."

"This waiting," he wrote Beatrice, "reminds me of fishing. One always hopes for a bite but not by a shark."

He thought about "my idea" for Italy – "I feel that with our air and navy superiority we can drive the Germans completely from that country, provided we have sufficient naval lift to move one reinforced regiment" in an amphibious end run.

This was the embryonic idea for the Anzio landings, which Eisenhower, Alexander, and Clark were considering. The German defenses across southern Italy, called the Gustav Line, were firmly anchored on mountainous terrain and extremely difficult to penetrate. The positions around Cassino were particularly strong, for they blocked the entrance to the

Liri valley, which seemed, especially to Alexander, to be the best corridor for an advance to Rome. If the Allies could send an amphibious force on a seaborne hook or end run, they would go around the Gustav Line and thereby avoid the heavy fighting required to smash through the mountains. A descent in the German rear, say at Anzio, would compel the Germans to react to that threat behind their main front. They might have to release their firm hold on the Gustav Line, thereby give the Allies a better chance to break through, and make possible a quick drive to Rome.

This was the same concept that had motivated Patton in his march to Messina.

Unfortunately, even though Patton thought that a single reinforced regiment might turn the trick at Anzio, it was clear that a larger force was necessary. Unfortunately too, the Allies lacked sufficient ships to lift a force in the size deemed appropriate.

This was the problem that had confronted Patton in Sicily. The difference was that the Germans were withdrawing in Sicily but holding fast on the mainland.

It would take the power of Prime Minister Churchill – who fell ill in Tunis and who recuperated in Marrakech – to marshal the resources required for Anzio. In January, enough ships had been gathered to make the venture possible. John Lucas, VI Corps commander, would head that expedition.

*Letter, Lucas to GSP, Jr., December 3, 1943*

I am told that you have been subjected to a scurrilous attack in the United States by some SOBs who would rather vent their personal spite against a famous soldier than help the war effort by keeping their mouths shut . . .

If this is true, I know it has hurt you very much and has therefore hurt me too. I cannot believe that any harm can be done you, as your reputation is too assured for that.

I thought I had this all fixed up, but it looks like I didn't . . .

I always try to figure what you would do in my place [as VI Corps commander] but know that I fall considerably short [in my operations] of the examples you have set.

*Letter, GSP, Jr., to Beatrice, December 4, 1943*

I am now not so sure that my luck has held in view of all the bunk that seems to have appeared in the papers about me. Also if the war ends now, I hate to be out of the last act. Of course we still have Japan and that should be a nice fight . . .

I can now walk three miles in 42 minutes and never seem to get any faster, though I can make a mile in twelve and a half minutes – it is a gloomy sport.

He thought that demonstrations and unrest in Sicily came "from a too quick transition from a strong central government to our milder and more democratic system."

Patton learned on December 7 that Marshall would remain in Washington as Army Chief of Staff and that Eisenhower would go to the United Kingdom to become Supreme Allied Commander of the Overlord and later the Anvil forces. Sir Henry Maitland Wilson, commander of the British Middle East Command, would succeed Eisenhower in Algiers.

What was to become of him? Patton asked Assistant Secretary of War McCloy.

McCloy went around the mulberry bush. As Patton recorded his words, McCloy said

[I] had in my makeup certain chemicals no other General had; that I was a great fighter and an inspiring leader, though probably not a Moltke, and must be used [in battle] . . . I was not to worry about what was said about me as that would hurt my efficiency. He also said that I look and act like a general and that no one else we have does . . . You have color, personality, and size. Men like to follow a man they can respect.

Then McCloy got to the point. According to Marshall, McCloy said, Patton would have an Army.

"I should have a group of armies," Patton noted, "but that will come. I think that my luck is in again."

Harry Hopkins took him aside and said, "Don't let anything that s.o.b. Pearson said bother you," because the incident was closed.

*Letter, GSP, Jr., to Nita, December 10, 1943*

We have a very nice Episcopal minister here who holds 8:00 o'clock services in the British Church every Sunday morning. It is quite a high affair with full dress and much lighting of candels and so on but is very well done. The longer I live the more I am impressed with the fact that it is very advantageous to use a certain amount of formalism.

Your warning about the public jumping on its past heroes is apparently coming true, but . . . I am quite convinced that I will get more good out of it than harm. The American people want success and they want a fighting man, and my reputation as one who looks after soldiers is sufficiently well established to counteract any mistakes which I have made.

Further, you should remember that only half the story has been told. However, I do not want you or any other member of the family to make excuses for me or to mention anything. If I cannot stand on my record, very few people can.

*Letter, GSP, Jr., to Beatrice, December 10, 1943*

The thing for all of us to do is to do nothing and say nothing. Ike etc have been fine and so have all the others – I was unduly precipitate but . . . I picked my locality badly. But I am sure that victories still count for something . . .

The weather here is cold and nasty and as we have no fires and no heat, the only thing one can do is to shivver . . .

Send me some more pink medecin. This worry and inactivity has raised hell with my insides.

*Letter, GSP, Jr., to Frederick Ayer, December 10, 1943*

Everybody and his brother visits Sicily and I have to feed them, so am ruining my digestion . . . I am taking very good care of myself and have found a mountain . . . where Hasdrubal defied the Romans, up which I walk three miles every day and do it in less than 45 minutes. It is a beastly bore, but healthy. I also ride in the hall, and believe it or not, drink hardly at all.

"Beadle Smith has been of great assistance," he wrote Floyd Parks. "The more I see of him, the better I like him."

In part to mislead the Germans on Allied intentions and in part simply because Patton wished to see Egypt and the Holy Land, he and nine members of his staff took off on January 12 for Cairo. They stayed with Wilson, who was

large, rather fat and seems stupid but is probably a good soldier.

> I liked him and he is more impressive than either Alex or Monty. There is a very definite effort on the part of all the staff except General Wilson, to run Monty down and to try to get me to agree with them, but needless to say, I did not commit myself. Apparently the Regular Officers of the British Army do not like Montgomery at all.

Patton found Cairo "really a disgusting place . . . The Egyptian peasant who abounds in large numbers, is distinctly lower than the Sicilian whom up until that time I had considered the bottom of the human curve." The Egyptian lower classes were "unspeakably dirty in their habits and also in their dress."

He and his party flew to Jerusalem, following the line of Allenby's advance in 1918. They entered the city "through the gate which Tancred stormed." He obtained a rosary for Mary Scally and had it blessed. He believed that the sword on display at the Crusaders' Chapel was a fake because the shape of the pommel was incorrect. The walls of the city were the best he had seen, and he judged their construction to date from around 1200.

Back in Cairo, Patton was disappointed in the pyramids, "not as big nor as impressive as those around Mexico City." He made a talk on landing operations to all the officers, about 500, of the Middle East Command, and thought that it went well, "as contrary to the British custom, they applauded."

General Anders, who commanded the Polish II Corps, struck Patton as

> very much a man . . . He has been hit [wounded] seven times . . . He told me, laughing, that if his corps got in between a German and Russian army, they would have difficulty in deciding which they wanted to fight the most.

The highlight of the trip came on the last day, at Karnak, King Tut's tomb, the Temple, the Palace of Rameses II.

> Anyone who is interested in ruins should see all the non-Egyptian ones first because the Egyptian ones make the other ones look like nothing. In the courtyard at Karnak there is a Roman Forum which if viewed by itself would be quite impressive, but which you have to

have your attention called [to] in order to see on account of its being so much overshadowed.

Although most Americans regretted Patton's action in the slapping incident, Stimson informed him, they retained faith in Patton's courage, skill, and character as a battle commander. "Watch your step," Stimson cautioned, and remember that the battlefield and a hospital were hardly the same places. Patton had conducted three major operations with distinction, and Stimson expected him to have even greater success in the future.

Eisenhower wrote Marshall a long letter on December 17, to discuss the organization for the invasion. Very directly and simply he said, "I would want Patton as one of my Army commanders."

*Letter, GSP, Jr., to Beatrice, December 20, 1943*

I have had twenty odd letters of commendation from all sorts of people and only three nasty ones . . . I hear that by the Gallup pole I am 77 good to 19 bad, 4 uncertain.

*Letter, GSP, Jr., to Beatrice, December 21, 1943*

I have not had a very happy time. I could not sleep except with pills and would wake up groaning but that is all over.

It has been a good experience and I am a better general as a result of it . . . I have a destiny and I shall live to fulfil it . . .

I appreciate your loyalty and miss your aid, but your spirit is with me. I love you.

P.S. My own people have stuck like limpits. I told them I might be on the way out and that if any of them could find a better job I would try to get it for them. Not a man budged.

*Letter, GSP, Jr., to Beatrice, December 23, 1943*

The incident will still further frighten weak commanders and will even cramp my style for a while with new troops, but I have the gift of leadership and will get them on my side as I always do.

As you say, Destiny has never backed me up nor will it, but I manage some how . . .

When my turn comes, as it surely will, I will have no debts to pay. When the new set up comes out [for Overlord], you will be surprised how well our relatives have done. It is realy fantastic. How long Oh! Lord, how long? . . .

I still work on my phonograph daily [studying French] . . .

I am very well and sleeping fine. At the moment it seems that soon I shall be doing quite a lot of plan[n]ing. I will be glad to be busy again.

In a cable to Marshall on December 23, Eisenhower laid out the shape of things to come – as he wished it. He wanted Bradley to lead the assault Army in the Normandy invasion. When another American Army was committed, "probably" under Patton, Bradley was to move up and become the Army Group commander, with Hodges or William Simpson taking Bradley's place. Eisenhower suggested that Devers be transferred from London to Algiers as Wilson's deputy commander and as the senior American in the Mediterranean theater. He thought that Clark, "at the appropriate time," should take charge of Anvil and turn over the Fifth Army to Lucas.

*Diary, December 24*

I hope the war does not abort until I have a chance to put on another show in Europe so as to be the inevitable choice for Japan.

*Letter, GSP, Jr., to Beatrice, December 24, 1943*

The cardinal sent me a blessing which clears me to date and also a fruit cake which if I eat will make me need the blessing.

Things are looking up a lot and our next party will be bigger than the last.

He had a pleasant Christmas. Several members of his staff joined him that morning, and they all opened their presents "just as we would have at home, and had a lot of fun about it."

*Diary, December 25*

My men are crazy about me, and this is what makes me most angry with Drew Pearson . . . My destiny is sure and I am a fool and a coward ever to have doubted it. I don't any more. Some people are needed to do things, and they have to be tempered by adversity as well as thrilled by success. I have had both. Now for some more success.

Patton thanked Mrs. Marshall for being so nice to Beatrice "during the trying times incident to my unfortunate lack of tact." For Marshall's benefit he added:

> There is a mountain here . . . which has a very steep road, and by walking vigorously up this road for three miles, one can overcome the evil effects of a Christmas dinner as well as keep oneself in good shape for climbing to observation points.
>
> I also have a very bad horse which I ride in a very dirty riding hall, but between the horse and the mountain, I have never been healthier and have repaired my girlish figure.

Marshall questioned some of Eisenhower's recommendations and proposed certain other combinations of commanders. Replying on December 27, Eisenhower said that if Marshall wanted Devers to take part in Overlord, Eisenhower would expect Bradley to head the Army Group with Devers and Patton under him as Army commanders. If, on the other hand, Marshall saw "no place for Patton in Overlord," perhaps Clark could take the Mediterranean theater command and relinquish the Fifth Army to Patton. Or Patton could keep the Seventh Army for the invasion of southern France while Lucas took the Fifth Army. The important consideration was to be sure to use Patton as an Army commander somewhere.

*Diary, December 27*

I wish to God Ike would leave and take Smith with him. They cramp my style. Better to rule in Hell than serve in Heaven.

*Letter, GSP, Jr., to Eisenhower, December 29, 1943*

I did not know of your departure until I heard of it over the radio this morning. Had I known sooner I would have given myself the pleasure of flying to Algiers to bid you a personal farewell.

I sincerely hope that you appreciate my great admiration for you, my unlimited devotion, and my deep appreciation of the many benefits I have received at your hands, and of your unwavering loyalty to me . . . This question of loyalty is the sign of a great man. It is very easy to be loyal from the bottom up. It is more difficult to be loyal from the top down. I know you are, and I strive to be . . .

We all hate to lose you, but we are delighted that the effort on what is going to be the major theater is under your direction. I am sure that you will continue your ever victorious career.

By then, Marshall and Eisenhower seemed to be in complete accord. Devers would go to Algiers. Clark would eventually move to the Seventh Army and leave the Fifth to Lucas. For Overlord, Hodges would understudy Bradley and succeed him in command of an Army when Bradley took the army group. Patton would have the follow-up Army.

Yet this was far from settled. There would be additional question of the command setup.

*Letter, GSP, Jr., to Stimson, December 29, 1943*

Naturally I have suffered a great deal, but . . . just as iron is improved by fire so the soul of man is improved by suffering. I have also learned a great deal, and . . . I shall not again offend.

*Letter, GSP, Jr., to Beatrice, December 29, 1943*

I guess I am the only one who sees glory in war . . .

I always wear a helmet when I am with troops. It is my symbol . . .

The radio has just announced that Jake Devers is coming here as deputy to Maitland-Wilson. I never seem to break clean but it is a wonderful character builder and good for tact . . .

Ike and Tedder will be some team? I am realy sorry to loose Ike. I wrote him a fine letter . . .

Over 80% of the letters I have received are for me. Only one letter by a person of education is hostile. The rest are cranks and unsigned mostly.

*Diary, December 31*

I hope I do bigger and better fighting in 1944 . . .

Destiny will keep on floating me down the stream of fate.

Eisenhower rated him "Superior" for his performance during the preceding six months and recommended that he be utilized in command of an Army. Of 24 lieutenant generals Eisenhower knew, he would grade Patton Number 5 in effectiveness. Patton was, he concluded, "outstanding as a leader of an assault force. Impulsive and almost flamboyant in manner. Should always serve under a strong but understanding commander."

Chaplain Gerald Mygatt, compiling a "Soldiers' and Sailors' Prayer Book," asked Patton to write a prayer. Patton set out "those things for which I ask Divine assistance."

*GSP, Jr., A Soldier's Prayer*

God of our Fathers, who by land and sea has ever led us on to victory, please continue Your inspiring guidance in this the greatest of our conflicts.

Strengthen my soul so that the weakening instinct of self-preservation, which besets all of us in battle, shall not blind me to my duty to my own manhood, to the glory of my calling, and to my responsibility to my fellow soldiers.

Grant to our armed forces that disciplined valor and mutual confidence which insures success in war.

Let me not mourn for the men who have died fighting, but rather let me be glad that such heroes have lived.

If it be my lot to die, let me do so with courage and honor in a manner which will bring the greatest harm to the enemy, and please, oh Lord, protect and guide those I shall leave behind.

Give us the victory, Lord.

*Diary, January 1*

Received an "eyes only" radio from Natousa saying that I will be relieved from command of the Seventh Army today and report to Algiers for further instructions; that the Seventh Army will plan Anvil and that when Clark thinks he should quit Italy, he will . . . be assigned to command the Seventh Army . . .

I feel very badly for myself but particularly for the staff and headquarters soldiers who have stood by me all the time . . .

I suppose that I am going to England to command another Army, but if I am sent there to simply train troops which I am not to command [in battle] I shall resign . . .

I cannot conceive of anything more stupid than to change staffs on a General, nor can I conceive of anything more inconsiderate than not to notify him where he is going. It is just one more thing to remember when the time comes to pay my debts.

A Hell of a "Happy New Year."

*Diary, January 3*

On the face of it, the thing [Anvil] looks like an attempt to save Clark from the onus of his utter failure in Italy . . .

I cannot see how any normally intelligent person could inspire this fool change of staffs. It is unfair and insulting to me, but is heartbreaking for the staff of Seventh Army who have been utterly loyal, and now find that their efforts get them nowhere. It is damnable . . .

I have contemplated asking to be relieved but will stick it at least for the present . . .

Wellington . . . had many adversities. His staff also changed several times. Fate.

Field Marshal Lord Gort invited Patton to visit Malta, so on January 4, he, Codman, and Stiller took off. They flew over the old battlefields in Tunisia, and "hundreds of memories surged up and all were of success." Every trace of troops had been obliterated — nothing remained of the dumps at Tebessa, the tanks, the guns, the tents, and the command posts.

Had it been possible for me to have looked over the battlefields from an airplane . . . it would have been a distinct advantage. Certainly had either myself or Eddy been up, we would not have made the mistake of attacking the wrong half of Djebel Berda . . . The gum-tree road which penetrated our position [near El Guettar] and over which I spent many anxious hours, is not anywhere as dangerous an avenue as it shows on the map, and had I been able to look at it from the air, I might have slept better . . .

On the other hand, too intimate a knowledge of the terrain difficulties of the mountains might have made me less bold. In any case, El Guettar was a great school, both in regard as to what to do and what not to do, and also as a means of producing self-confidence.

*Letter, GSP, Jr., to Beatrice, January 7, 1944*

On the way [to Malta] we flew over a large Roman city not even shown on the map. It had a fine temple and a theater in an excellent state of preservation . . .

We stayed in a palace built in 1620, which is a realy wonderful building wholy devoid of plumbing and cold as an ice box.

The forts used by the knights in the great siege of 1528 are different from any I have ever seen. They are pre-Vauban, but are artillery forts with walls up to 16 feet thick and very high. All built by slave labor, Saracen slaves. Roger the Great Count captured it from the Saracens in 1192 . . .

I saw a cortex of 1420 on velum which was an illustrated life of St. Anthony . . .

One illustration . . . showed an armorers shop with suits of armor, helmets, etc. displayed on sorts of coat hangers. The interesting thing is that armor of all types from 1000 to 1400 was on sale. This shows that we are wrong in attributing definate dates to certain sorts of harness. The librarian did not know this and was much impressed by my wisdome.

To be a knight, one had to have 16 crosses of nobility. These records are complete for all the thousands of knights from 1100 to 1792, so they provide the greatest genealogical record in the world.

I kept thinking how you would have enjoyed it. You are one of the few people sufficiently educated to appreciate it.

*Diary, January 5*

The knights had to vow poverty, chastity, and obedience. They only kept the last vow.

*Diary, January 6*

[Palermo] I called all the chiefs of sections in . . . and had Gay read the order relieving me from Seventh Army. I told them not to worry, but to be as loyal to Clark as they have been to me, and I thanked them for their loyalty and then choked up and quit.

Patton flew to Naples, then drove to the Fifth Army headquarters at Caserta.

Both Gruenther and Clark were most condescending and treated me like an undertaker treats the family of the deceased. It was rather hard to take, especially as I am certain that they pulled the wires which got me removed from Anvil, but I had to be nice as I want my men [those staying with Seventh Army and eventually coming under Clark] promoted and decorated . . .

The left corner of Clark's mouth is slightly drawn down as if he had been paralyzed. He is quite jumpy and so is Gruenther.

After visiting Truscott and Keyes, he drove to see Lucas, who was fine but

worried. He is in charge of the Shingle operation [the landings at Anzio]. He does not think he will get the Fifth Army when Clark leaves and thinks that some hometown boy from Washington will get it . . . I hope he is successful at Shingle, but I am not sure that he has sufficient drive.

GSP, Jr., 1943

Colonel George S. Patton, Jr., upon his departure for Fort Benning, July 1940

Left: Secretary of War Stimson visiting the 2d Armored Division at Fort Benning, autumn 1940

Above: GSP, Jr., and Richard Jenson

GSP, Jr., and Adna Chaffee, 1941

GSP, Jr., commanding 2d Armored Division, 1941, one of the most publicized early photos of Patton

GSP, Jr., explaining maneuvers to his troops

GSP, Jr., Geoffrey Keyes, and Harry (Paddy) Flint during maneuvers, 1941

George and Beatrice Patton, Fort Benning, 1942

**Upper left: McNair and GSP, Jr., Desert Training Center, July 1942**

Lower left: GSP, Jr., debarking, North Africa, November 1942

Above: GSP, Jr., Hopkins, Clark, President Roosevelt, at Casablanca, February 1943

GSP, Jr., addressing troops, June 1943

GSP, Jr., and Hobart Gay arriving at beach near
Gela, Sicily, July 1943

GSP, Jr., after the Sicilian campaign

The last was a perfectly perceptive remark.

*Letter, GSP, Jr., to Beatrice, January 11, 1944*

Geoff, his aid, Codman, and I climed up to a ruined tower to have a look. At the foot of the rise was a cave with its mouth headed towards the enemy and full of ammunition and sleeping artillerymen . . .

After half way [down] one of our [artillery] batteries near by cut loose so I stopped to take a picture and then started back to the road. Just then a salvo of four German shells hit. Two were in the road where we would have [been] had I not stopped to take the picture and the other hit the place we had just been standing to take the picture . . .

Codman got a fragment or a rock on the helmet. Half the nose of a shell landed about nine inches from my toe but it must have already hit something as it had no force left and just spun around . . .

Mathematically I should be dead as none of the four craters was more than 30 feet from me, but I am not dead or even hurt. It gave me great self confidence. The Lord had a perfect cut for me and pulled his punch.

*Letter, GSP, Jr., to Beatrice, January 12, 1944*

My present status is so confused asto be unexplanable – it is confusion doubly compounded and no one has told me a thing. However I have had hints from Tom Handy and others that the future is O.K. My guess is that I will end up under Omar who will command the [army] group. Well I have been under worse people and I will surely win. You have no idea how much that near miss . . . cheered me up. I know I am needed!

Rabbi B. R. Brickner spent an hour with me just now and was much impressed with my prayer . . .

Well some day I will know what I am to do.

*Letter, GSP, Jr., to Frederick Ayer, January 14, 1944*

The Catholic Church has been very much on my side, as have the veterans and the war mothers. I think I could run for office on the strength of my misdeeds.

I am not the first General to catch hell; Wellington had plenty of it, as did Grant, Sherman, and countless others.

I am quite worried over the reaction after the war. I have already met several quite intelligent men who say "Now we will have no more wars" . . . The avowed purpose of the treaty of Vienna in 1814 was to see that that was the last war. Around 1700 B.C., the Hitites, Cretans, and Egyptians had a tri-party treaty to avert wars, and we lerned about it in 1914. Some explorers discovered the Hitite captial and in the library discovered the bricks with the treaty on them — yet before the mud had dried, the Egyptians and Cretans had ganged up and destroyed the Hitites.

If we again think that wars are over, we will surely have another one and damned quick. "Man is WAR" and we had better remember that. Also, we had better look out for ourselves and make the rest of the world look out for themselves. If we try to feed the world, we will starve and perhaps destroy America . . .

My own officers have been wonderful in their loyalty to me throughout the trouble . . . I had to loan some of them recently [to other headquarters] and they all begged me to be sure and get them back, and two of them cried. So did I.

*Diary, January 15*

No news of what will happen to me.

*Diary, January 17*

Came to office and am either coming down with some disease or else have "cafard" very badly. I simply don't feel like doing a thing, so am going home. I do wish something would eventuate about myself.

*Diary, January 18*

Feel all right this morning. Sgt Meeks told me after breakfast that he heard on the radio last night that General Bradley has been made commander of all the [American] ground troops in England. I suppose that this means that he will command the American army group. I had thought that possibly I might get this command. It is another disappointment, but so far in my life all the disappointments I have had have finally worked out to my advantage, although at the time it is hard to see how they will. If I am predestined, as I feel that I am, this too will eventually be to my advantage.

Bradley is a man of great mediocrity. At Benning in command, he failed to get discipline. At Gafsa, when it looked as though the Germans might turn our right flank . . . he suggested that we withdraw corps headquarters to Feriana. I refused to move. In Sicily, when the 45th Division approached Cefalu, he halted them for fear of a possible German landing east of Termini. I had to order him to move and told him that I would be responsible for his rear, and that his timidity had lost us one day. He tried to stop the landing operation #2 east of Cap d'Orlando because he thought it was dangerous. I told him I would take the blame if it failed and that he could have the credit if it was a success. Finally, on the night of August 16-17, he asked me to call off the landing east of Milazzo for fear our troops might shoot at each other. He also failed to get word to all units of the II Corps on the second paratroop landing.

On the other hand Bradley has many of the attributes which are considered desirable in a general. He wears glasses, has a strong jaw, talks profoundly and says little, and is a shooting companion of the Chief of Staff [Marshall]. Also a loyal man. I consider him among our better generals.

I suppose that all that has happened is calculated to get my morale so that I will say "What the Hell! Stick it up your ass, and I will go home," but I won't. I still believe [in my destiny].

Patton had no way of knowing that Devers had upset, at least temporarily, the command arrangements. Devers said he preferred to have Clark keep the Fifth Army, while Simpson, Hodges, or Middleton took the Seventh Army for Anvil.

Marshall then asked Eisenhower what he thought of keeping Patton with the Seventh for the southern France landings.

Eisenhower acknowledged on January 18 the logic of this suggestion. If Alexander and Devers wanted Clark with the Fifth Army, "then I am of the opinion that Patton would be the best man to plan and lead the Anvil affair." Patton's prestige, his excellent relations with the French, and his presence in the area favored this decision. On the other hand, Eisenhower had the impression that Devers and Patton were "not congenial," although both were "sufficiently good soldiers that possible personal antagonism should not interfere with either one doing his full duty."

What Eisenhower was doing was insuring Patton's assignment to his command. He wanted the most experienced and hardest driving Army commander for Overlord.

*Letter, GSP, Jr., to Beatrice, January 19, 1944*

I feel very much the way I did at Rabat last winter with nothing to do and no place to do it in.

Also the news about Omar was most disconcerting but I am pretty hard to beat down . . .

Sunday I felt so low that I just stayed in bed but I am all right now and just charging the batteries . . .

If I did not believe in fate . . . I would tell them all to go to Hell and put the When and If in commission and sail . . .

[At Cerami] the filth of the town was worth the trip. Gay said he did not see how the animals could live with such dirty people . . .

I am having a bronze tablet made to put up in the British [Episcopal] Church here in memory of my late Army . . . We had to melt up a broken propellor to get the material . . .

Am in fine shape but rather on the thin side.

I am not dead or buried yet by a long way.

*Diary, January 20*

Shingle [the Anzio landings] is pretty dubious as the beaches are bad and largely unknown . . . This is always a difficult operation . . . At a rehearsal some nights ago, 40 Dukws were lost [in the sea] . . . If the thing is a success, Clark will get the credit. If it fails, Lucas will get the blame.

It seems inconceivable that the Boche will not guess that we are coming [ashore at Anzio] but he has made so many foolish mistakes that we may get ashore unopposed after all.

Which was exactly what happened.

*Letter, GSP, Jr., to Beatrice, January 22, 1944*

I have had two most interesting days . . .

I have been looking for Himera, a city . . . destroyed in 405 BC by the Carthaginians. I knew where it was on the map but could see nothing of it. All that remains is the foundation of a temple built in 468 B.C. We looked at it and then went up the hills to the site of the city. There is not even a rock left. Termini was built by the survivors after they were run out of Himera . . .

Flew to Castelvetrano . . . to Silonicus . . . destroyed by the Carthaginians in 405 BC . . . There are three of the largest Greek temples I have ever seen there, simply huge . . .

> I am still getting fan mail but it is all highly favorable . . .
> I hope I am as successful in 1944 as I was in 1943 and suffer less.

On January 22, he finally received word on his future. A cable ordered him to report to the United Kingdom via Algiers. Now that it had come,

> Looking back at it in retrospect to the chain of events, this sounds logical, but . . . why have they been so slow about it and why have they taken all of my staff? It makes it most difficult for my people and for me.

He was pleased to note that the VI Corps landing at Anzio, under John Lucas, "is a success and unopposed."

The new command arrangements were finally set. Wilson replaced Eisenhower as Allied Commander in Chief of the Mediterranean theater at Algiers. Devers shifted from London to Algiers to become Wilson's deputy at AFHQ and the senior American in the theater at the head of NATOUSA.

Montgomery moved from Italy to the United Kingdom to take command of the 21 Army Group and the British troops in Overlord. Under him, Dempsey would have the Second British Army, Crerar the First Canadian Army.

Clark was supposed to depart Italy upon the capture of Rome, expected in the following month or so. But when the Anzio landings failed to dislodge the Germans holding the Gustav Line, and when the attack on the main front – to get across the Rapido River near Cassino, to penetrate the Gustav Line, and to enter the Liri valley – failed also, the seizure of Rome receded into the distant future. Upon his request, Clark would receive permission to remain in Italy at the head of the Fifth Army.

Alexander Patch, coming from the Pacific to take command of a new corps headquarters in Italy, would be assigned to the Seventh Army in Sicily. Instead of Clark, Patch would prepare and lead the invasion of southern France. Devers would subsequently take command of the Sixth Army Group and direct Patch's Seventh Army as well as De Lattre de Tassigny's First French Army.

But all this still lay far ahead.

*Letter, GSP, Jr., to son George, January 23, 1944*

Inspite of what the papers say, I do not think that this war will end soon enough to cheat you out of some of it. Besides this is not the last war, and the prestige of being a graduate [of the Military Academy] is worth a lot. Remember Ike did not get into the last war and look where he is now.

If I were you, I would cultivate the Soup [Superintendent] and especially the Mrs. Soup. I did when I was a cadet . . .

If you meet the Com.[mandant] socially, do the same for him. It is even more important.

I am about to move in the morning but I will be damned if I know where to. Cadets are not the only people who don't know everything . . .

Get as high a stand in math as you can before you hit the stuff you flunked on. In that way you will have further to retreat. It is just like war. In a delaying action, meet the enemy as far out as possible.

*Letter, GSP, Jr., to Beatrice, January 23, 1944*

I have just finished cleaning out my desk. This is the fourth time since I left home. I now feel much like we did when we quit Sheridan for Myer in 1911 – "Oh God how young we were," and started into the unknown for the first time. Well, we have done it a lot of times since and have always ended up well known. I will do it again but wish I had some definate information asto where I was headed. All I know at the moment is that I leave in the morning to visit Everett and possibly get some dope . . .

By the way Beedle Smith is now a Lt. Gen. God Bless us all . . .

When Nelly [Richardson] got three stars it almost took the pleasure out of mine. I just can't see him any more than I can Pink [Bull] . . .

I am sure that the "incident" was far harder on you than on me, as I simply did the ostrich act and would neither see nor hear any evil though I did a hell of a lot of thinking.

*Diary, January 25*

Left Algiers at 1200 in a C-54 . . . Arrived in Marrakech . . . and went to Taylor Villa, which is run by the Air Corps for visiting strangers . . .

Brigadier Dunphie who was with me in Tunisia and who was wounded the day Major Jenson was killed, happened to be in the house. I asked him why he was not wearing his Silver Star, and he told me he had never received it. I had recommended him for it on April 1, 1943, but since he went to the hospital and I left the corps shortly afterwards, the paper apparently never reached him. Colonel Codman took off his own Silver Star Ribbon, and we decorated Dunphie on the spot. I will have to see that he gets the citation when I get to England.

Left for Prestwick [Scotland] in C-54 at 2400.

The terrible time of waiting was over. There would be more waiting, but it would hardly be so terrible, for Patton had a specific job, role, and function. Additional challenges as well as additional adversities lay ahead of him. But he was moving toward his greatest adventure, his greatest success, and – he was sure of it – the fulfillment of his destiny.

# IV

# England

*"Some times I wonder if I am as good as people, including me, think."*

CHAPTER 22

# Third Army

*"I look forward with considerable pleasure to landing without the necessity of wetting my pants."*

PATTON arrived at Prestwick, Scotland, on the morning of January 26, and proceeded immediately to London.

*Diary, January 26*

Called on Ike at office and found I am to command Third Army. All [the personnel in the Army are] novices and [we are] in support of Bradley's First Army – not such a good job, but better than nothing.

Ike asked me to dinner; Kay, Butcher, a British Aide-de-Camp, and a WAC captain were present. Ike very nasty and show-offish – he always is when Kay is present – and criticized [John] Lee for his flamboyance which he – Ike – would give a million to possess.

Well, I have an Army and it is up to me. "God show the right."

As far as I can remember, this is my twenty-seventh start from zero since entering the U.S. Army. Each time I have made a success of it, and this one must be the biggest.

Patton was indeed starting from scratch. The Third Army headquarters was preparing to move from the United States to England. Courtney Hodges was in command, but as soon as he was promoted to lieutenant general, he would go to First Army and understudy Bradley, leaving the Third to Patton. There was much for Patton to do – establish the headquarters, supervise the staff plans for training in England and operating in France, keep abreast of the work on the invasion, direct the subordinate units assigned to his Army, make certain that his commanders were capable, assure himself that the supply and service systems were efficient – and a host of other matters, large and small.

Although the final details of the Overlord landings were far from fixed, the general structure was well understood. Eisenhower was the Supreme Allied Commander, and, through his Supreme Headquarters Allied Expeditionary Force (SHAEF), directed the Allied air, naval, and ground forces. Tedder was his deputy commander, Bedell Smith his chief of staff. Montgomery, at the head of the 21 Army Group and pro tem ground forces commander (until Eisenhower assumed command), directed Dempsey's Second British Army and Bradley's First U.S. Army, which were to land in Normandy side by side. When they captured a bridgehead large enough to sustain additional troops, Crerar's First Canadian Army and Patton's Third U.S. Army would join. Montgomery would then have Dempsey and Crerar under him; Bradley would relinquish the First U.S. Army to Hodges and move up to an Army Group headquarters to direct Hodges and Patton.

- Eisenhower-SHAEF
  - Tedder
    - Leigh-Mallory (Air)
    - Ramsey (Sea)
    - Montgomery-21 Army Group (Ground)
      - Dempsey Second British Army
      - Bradley First U.S. Army
        - Gerow V Corps
        - Collins VII Corps

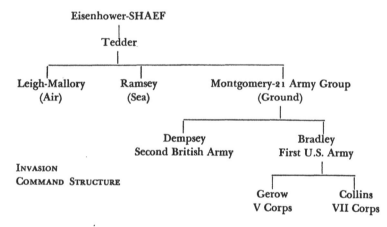

INVASION COMMAND STRUCTURE

In Morocco, Tunisia, and Sicily, Patton had been the top American field commander. He had been the star. In Europe, a much larger scene, he would be a player on the team. Montgomery for the British and Canadians, De Lattre later for the French, Bradley for the Americans (even though Devers would hold the same position in the command structure) would be the leading commanders in the field. They would make Patton less visible. Eventually, as the Allied forces were built up on the Continent, Patton would simply be one of seven Allied Army commanders. Consequently, his role was proportionately smaller, and his operations would take on the character of local ventures that were part of a larger strategy.

A cog in a vast military machine, Patton would face an even greater challenge than before. Would he be overshadowed by the sheer number of competitors? Would his military genius be smothered? How, among so many personalities, would he manage to stand out?

His answer, if he had been asked, would undoubtedly have been: work like hell and trust in destiny.

During the early months of 1944, Bradley commanded two headquarters, the 1st Army Group and the First Army. Since his primary task was to insure the success of the American landings, he concentrated his efforts on the latter organization. The Army Group remained a rather nebulous entity, run mainly by Leven C. Allen, the chief of staff, who coordinated the affairs concerning the First and Third Armies.

The Allies used the Army Group to capitalize on Patton's enormous combat reputation among the Germans. As part of a cover and deception plan designed to divert German attention away from the site of the landings, Patton became the mythical commander of the Army Group, an appointment made wholly for the consumption of the German intelligence network. For this reason his presence in England and, even more importantly, his position as Army commander were kept concealed.

Patton's actual duties revolved about his Third Army headquarters and his direction of the organizations assigned to work under him – Middleton's VIII Corps, Wade Haislip's XV Corps, Walton Walker's XX Corps, and Gilbert Cook's XII Corps. These were his immediate subordinate commanders, and they in turn would direct the divisions under them.

The planning for Overlord in all its myriad manifestations and the preparation of the troops for combat were the chief preoccupations. Little mention could be made of these secret activities. Patton was no exception, and the matters to which he alluded in his diary and letters were a small part of the efforts being made to deal with the complexities of shaping and disciplining a gigantic Allied force into an instrument of victory.

• • •

Patton spent his second day in England orienting himself to the theater, which in many respects was a new world, with its own regulations, procedures, and methods of doing business. He had a talk with his classmate John C. H. Lee, who was Eisenhower's deputy for ETOUSA and chief of the Services of Supply. He "went to see Bedell Smith, who was in rare form – s.o.b. – had just been made a Lieutenant General, and is looking better than I have ever seen him." He persuaded Smith to approve a list of fifteen Seventh Army officers he wanted transferred from Sicily to his new staff. He called on Tedder who "seemed genuinely glad to see me."

He studied Bradley's plan, "which I consider bad; the landings are so close [together] that an [enemy] attack against one [beach] affects the whole thing." The Third Army, he learned, was to take Brittany, then come up on the right of First Army and head toward the Seine.

"Well, I am off to a bad start, but am on my way."

Late that afternoon he boarded Lee's special train for an overnight trip to Greenock, on the Clyde. He went aboard the *Queen Mary* to welcome the advance party of the Third Army headquarters, 13 officers and 26 men. No doubt he recalled his own arrival in the British Isles with Pershing, 27 years earlier.

He talked to the officers, impressing on them the fact that he "was still a secret and not to be mentioned." Then he and his small group went to the train and left for Knutsford, near Chester.

Patton established the headquarters at the Toft Hall camp near Knutsford and set up his Advanced Echelon, his command group, in Peover Hall.

He rode Lee's train to Cheltenham, where the SOS had its headquarters and major facilities. Patton inspected supply installations, hospitals, ordnance shops, and the like, service units designated to support the combat units of the Third Army. At dinner with the SOS staff, Patton made a speech and warned everyone "that I am incognito."

He attended the SOS weekly staff conference, made another talk, "which was good and alive," and again cautioned everyone "that I am a myth."

Returned to London, he

> went to see Bedell Smith. We were both charming. The nurse who takes care of him . . . was present, and I had the opportunity of letting him advertise himself. I let him do all the talking and played him up. Washed mouth out later.

How real was his dislike of Bedell Smith? Was it a pose he assumed in private because he resented Smith's close working relationship with Eisenhower? Was his feeling much like his early animosity toward Clark, who had formerly been close to Eisenhower? In public, of course, Patton displayed only the most exemplary kind of loyalty to his superiors and colleagues. Yet his inner torture which he concealed through a forced ebullience, his uneasy attitude toward himself which he hid under his façade of confidence, his pathetic longing for recognition which he tried to dismiss by an assumed hardness – all this made for ambivalence on his part. The fact that he called Eisenhower Divine Destiny in his letters to his wife could hardly be coincidence, nor mere alliteration, not even allusion to Eisenhower's initials. The point was, the destiny on which he depended – his star – was, in truth and in very large measure, Eisenhower, who determined Patton's place in the scheme of things. That Bedell Smith was Eisenhower's principal instrument in carrying out his official policy, and further, that Eisenhower, who preferred to say yes and to pose as the affable good guy, used Smith as his hatchet man – to say no – only intensified Patton's sense of helplessness. He was fettered by the system, and he wished to be free to achieve the glory for which he ached so desperately. Yet he was bound by the men above him – and to a certain extent by those beneath. No wonder he reached for his diary to unburden himself of the unpleasant facts of life. For he saw himself – most of the time – as greater than any of them. And they failed to appreciate his greatness.

*Letter, GSP, Jr., to Beatrice, February 3, 1944*

My new headquarters is in a huge house last repaired in 1627 or there abouts . . .

I saw a Druid ring much bigger than Stone Henge . . . Remember the time we visited King Arthurs castle [on their honeymoon].

Omar, Monty, and I seem destined by destiny to keep on together. I hope with our usual success. Omar is most helpful. So is Spaatz. I am seeing Monty next week.

The countryside was "truly lovely." He went to the theater, his first play since October 1942, saw the Lunts, and afterward he and Codman met them backstage.

It is quite pleasant to be famous. In the theater half the audience were staring [at him] and talking [about him]. Probably bad for the soul . . .

Army commanders have not only headquarters in the country but also flats in town. Ours is very nice and right in the middle of things.

Patton had a long talk with Bradley and chatted with J. L. Collins who had commanded a division on Guadalcanal in the Pacific. The younger brother of "Wilkie," Pershing's aide in Mexico and France and a close friend of Patton's, Collins was to command the VII Corps in the invasion and land at Utah Beach; Leonard T. Gerow would take his V Corps ashore at Omaha Beach.

*Letter, GSP, Jr., to Beatrice, February 5, 1944*

[My] house . . . is quite impressive and the most inconvenient that I have so far occupied, as all the leaded windows leak and the fires dont heat and the water is scarce. However, part of it was built in 1528 and the new stable is inscribed "To my beloved son from his mother" in 1658. It is . . . half Tudor and half Georgean, and they don't blend well . . .

Monty, Omar, and the other important guests are all dining together next week. This is handy for me as I can go to the luncheon and also have my new boots and overcoat fitted. Mr. Weatherill [tailor] was charmed to see me. So was Faulkner [bootmaker]. I got an overcoat and two pair of boots, one riding and one half length for tanks. Also some trousers.

Damn the expense. This is the first time I have been in a place where I could spend money in a year and a half . . .

I could hunt here but think that with a nice battle in the offing, I wont, as I would feel such a fool if I got hurt and missed it, and it is going to be a heller too, although I shant lead off.

The other day . . . I lunched at the hotel where we stayed [on their honeymoon] with the two gentlemen from Verona. It has not changed much, if any thing is cleaner or else I am more used to dirt.

*Letter, GSP, Jr., to Beatrice, February 6, 1944*

There is a Chapel attached to this Hall . . . This morning we went to church and were put in the Lord of the Manor's seat. Right next to me was the effegy of a knight in full armor and his wife. On looking around I found two more knights, but did not have a chance to get their dates . . .

This afternoon we called on Major Leicester-Warren, who has a little place of a thousand acres completely surrounded by a brick wall. He is General Sir Oliver Leese's father in law. Leese now commands the Eighth British Army [in Italy]. They are very nice people . . . butler, gate keeper, and all . . .

I have the same job I had [in Sicily], only with a different number — a rose by any other name etc. It is going to be some job to get these new [and untried] outfits in shape, but I will do it as I have more time than usual.

He flew to northern Ireland on his first inspection trip and visited Haislip's XV Corps headquarters and the 2nd, 5th, and 8th Divisions. All impressed him favorably.

*Letter, GSP, Jr., to Beatrice, February 9, 1944*

Yesterday I made five speeches, including two one-hour orations, and today I made three more, and as I started with a cold, my voice is in a hell of a fix . . .

This thing of imitating God and creating new worlds out of thin air [a fighting army out of neophytes] is wearing, but with the help of my luck and the Lord and the staff I will do it, and I have more time than I did in Washington [before Torch] but it is a much bigger party . . .

Jake has been pretty decent about sending me my old people. Of course he feels like hell as he went up hill with quite a drop. Well, anyhow he got further than he was ever intended to go . . .

It looks now as if I may have to take Everett in some capacity. At least Destiny seems to think that some one must do something, and it will probably be me . . .

My little dictionary has not got Sycophant in it, but every division now has.

Everyone was being exceptionally nice and flattering to him.

On February 11, Patton and Bradley went to Montgomery's headquarters and, with De Guingand, Montgomery's chief of staff, and Dempsey, talked about the invasion plans. "Monty — who is an actor but not a fool" outlined the general plan of the campaign.

Calling on Eisenhower, Patton learned that Devers had declared Hughes surplus and that Eisenhower wanted Patton to take Hughes in some capacity, preferably as chief of staff. Patton had already spoken to

Gay, who said he would be glad to serve as deputy chief of staff under Hughes.

*Diary, February 12*

Ike says that Devers is .22 caliber, and I rather concur, but some others are not over .32 caliber themselves.

Ike said of me, to me, "You are fundamentally honest on the larger issues, but are too fanatical in your friendships." It is a good thing that some one is.

Patton learned that the situation at the Anzio beachhead below Rome was far from good and even

> apt to be lost . . . If we lost that beach, it will be bad, but so much sloth, or timidity, was shown at the start that the thing was doomed. Only 8 miles [gained] in 12 days. I would have been in Rome.

With more than a touch of intuition, he added, "I hope I don't have to go back and straighten things out."

*Letter, Mrs. George Frisch, Jr., Oklahoma City, to Mrs. Patton, February 12, 1944*

My husband is with your husband's army & your husband's name is George Jr. & so is mine & General Patton signs his name Georgie & so does my George & what a fine man General Patton is . . . I've always picked him as my hero.

*Letter, GSP, Jr., to Beatrice, February 14, 1944*

It sounds complacent but I think the [slapping] incident was a good thing. But for it I would probably have had Brad's job, which I certainly would not have liked, certainly not in its present form — the altitude is too great [meaning, it was too far removed from the fighting].

*Letter, GSP, Jr., to McNair, February 15, 1944*

I want to express my thanks to you for the part I am sure you had in obtaining for me my present job. I look forward with considerable pleasure to landing without the necessity of wetting my pants.

*Diary, February 16*

At 0130, Codman had a telephone call from Butcher for me to report to General Eisenhower at once . . . We started at 0600 in the pitch dark and arrived at 20 Grosvenor Square at 1045.

When I went in, Ike said, "I am afraid you will have to eat crow again for a little while."

I said, "What have I done now?"

He replied, "You may have to take command of the beachhead in Italy and straighten things out."

I replied that this was not eating crow but a great compliment because I would be willing to command anything from a platoon up in order to fight.

He then gave me a radio[gram] from Alexander.

Alexander had sent it to Brooke, Chief of the Imperial General Staff — Marshall's counterpart — who forwarded it immediately to Eisenhower, waking him up at midnight, February 15. Lucas and his VI Corps headquarters in the Anzio beachhead, Alexander said, were "negative and lack the necessary drive and enthusiasm to get things done. They appear to have become depressed by events." He was about to meet with Wilson, Devers, and Clark to see what could be done. "What we need," Alexander said, "is a thruster like George Patton."

That had prompted Eisenhower's telephone call.

Alexander said . . . that the British had sustained most of the losses (I doubt this), and, "If you cannot send me a thruster like George Patton, I recommend putting a British officer in command. I have already sent a British major general to the headquarters of the VI Corps to spur them on a little."

Ike said he would never consent to letting the British have the command, but he would loan me for a month, as the only fighting general in the army.

He also made certain remarks about Devers, wondering why the hell he hadn't got into the fight, saying, "As he was doing nothing anyway."

Ike . . . sent a telegram offering to let me go . . . They will consider it and reply.

In the meantime, one C-54 and one B-25 are waiting at the airport in London, warmed up, ready to take me to Italy, and I have telephoned for Stiller and Sgt. Meeks, and my fighting equipment.

I told Ike that I was anxious to go, but that I must be backed up by him, as otherwise I would have my throat cut. He said he would back me up and would report the whole thing to General Marshall by special messenger. I suppose I am the only person in the world who would be elated at the chance to commit personal and official suicide, but I am tickled to death and will make a go of it.

*Letter, GSP, Jr., to Beatrice, February 16, 1944*

I had the best compliment I have ever had today, given in a back handed manner . . . but I have been skipping like a gazell ever since. I guess a real love of fighting belongs to but a few people . . .

Tomorrow I'll have my new battle jacket . . . If I am to fight I like to be well dressed.

*Diary, February 17*

Went to Middlesex Hospital at 0945 to have a spot on my lip treated with x-ray. While there . . . an aide phoned to say that Ike said I could return to Knutsford. Nothing more. He did not even think it worthwhile to tell me what had happened . . .

Gay came down to see me off and warned me to get rid of the Fifth Army staff for fear that they would cut my throat. He was working on the assumption that I was to relieve Clark and take over the whole show. This is an excellent example of how much forethought and loyalty he has for me.

We were all very sorry that the show was called off — it would have been very risky, but much honor could have been gained. No man can live forever.

Truscott was elevated from the 3d Division, which was at Anzio, to replace Lucas at the VI Corps. It made good sense. Truscott was already on the scene, knew the situation, and was a winner — highly aggressive and competent. He was also, unlike Patton, sufficiently junior in rank to be no threat to Clark.

*Diary, February 18*

Called on Ike . . . He was very cavalier and told me of a General Corlett who had captured a Pacific Island in a "nearly perfect" maneuver. (He did not have to fight until after he got ashore.) Ike is going to get him for a corps commander (XIX Corps).

I told him that we had also done pretty well in landings.

This made him mad. He has an unfortunate habit of under-rating all Americans who come under him and overrates all British and all Americans who have served elsewhere.

I wish to God he was more of a soldier and less of a politician.

Called on Beedle Smith to bone (bootlick) [flatter him].

It must certainly have pained Patton that no one seemed to be taking advantage of his own considerable experience in preparing amphibious operations.

Charles Corlett too would discover, after he arrived in England, that no one was interested in his thorough knowledge of amphibious methods in the Pacific.

*Letter, GSP, Jr., to Beatrice, February 19, 1944*

George [Marshall] considers me the one fighting general . . . These remarks, together with Alex's request for me to pull the chestnuts [out of Anzio], make me feel fine.

He had dinner with Mr. and Mrs. Frank Stockdale of Alderly Edge, Cheshire, and was pleased when "Mr. Stockdale told me that he had never met such loyal and enthusiastic supporters as my staff."

His wife bosses things. We had them to supper and she ran her hand down the banesters to see if they were properly dusted and said they were not – she was right. She looked at our books [in the library] and sent over some more that she thinks are edefying.

She is really pretty and nice.

*Letter, GSP, Jr., to Beatrice, February 20, 1944*

The lack of looks of the English women has amazed all of us. They must have died out . . .

*Letter, GSP, Jr., to Beatrice, February 20, 1944*

I will have to take Everett in some capacity . . . It will be all right for me but will I fear imbarass him . . . Jake is . . . messing things up and at the same time running counter to Destiny, which is foolish . . .

I am seriously considering getting a . . . dog, and Lady Leese and Kay are both searching for one for me . . .

Jake would be a damned nusance to work under.

This house . . . is going to be quite nice after we get a few toilets etc. installed . . .

Yesterday I went into Butch[er]'s room [office] and ran into the whole press, so I just told them I was a ghost and they admitted that while every one in town had seen me, no one would admit it.

"I wish I could stop being incognito," he wrote Beatrice,

but really it makes no difference, as I am a very apparent entity.

I have a mobile loud speaker on a truck which I take around with me to exhort the troops just like a candidate for election.

Gen. Lee certainly is doing a good job in getting us what we need.

*Diary, February 23*

We suffer very much from lack of command. No one is running the show . . .

Ike has no conception of physical command, as he has never exercised it.

*Letter, GSP, Jr., to Virginia Knapp, Providence, R.I., February 24, 1944*

I am glad your troop of Girl Scouts has been praying for me, and also I am interested to learn that they have corresponded with General Eisenhower and General Clark.

I am quite sure that between the three of us – and not forgetting General Bradley – we will eventually secure the victory you want.

*Letter, GSP, Jr., to Ed Fansler, February 24, 1944*

I am taking very good care of myself. I play badminton or squash every day and also take a long walk. I eat very little and do not smoke and hardly take any drinks. I really believe that I am tougher than I was in the last war.

*Letter, GSP, Jr., to Beatrice, February 26, 1944*

I am glad you saw Mamie, as her husband in his own way is quite nice to me . . .

I am glad you have been nice to Georgie D. [Devers] as he has been pretty fair about letting me have my old men back although he is at swords points with every one else.

Here is a secret you must not divulge. I played golf yesterday and to day I bought two clubs and harrased cows all over the pasture practising up as Mrs. Stockdale beat the hell out of me. It is true of course that I have not played for 43 years so have lost some of my cunning, but I improved with the cows. Capt. [George] Murnane, Hap's aide . . . coached me . . . But what a comedown from Polo! ! !

I could hunt a little but hate to take the chance of a bad fall with a fine fight in prospect — I fear I am loosing my nerve? ?

The local relatives have certainly gone out of their way to be nice to all of us. I am having the Curate to lunch, then going to lunch my self with the Leicester-Warrens, then to tea with some one else. You see as yet we have not got all the tools here to work with so I have quite a lot of time. Besides, as there is nothing to do at night, I work after supper till about ten o'clock . . .

[Speaking of DDE], we shall miss JJP very much, but there is nothing that can be done about it . . .

I think that more and more my luck is holding. The next party is realy something and I have a chance to play the same position [end] I used to in football. If I do, I may visit some of the places we saw when we lived with the ducks [Brittany] . . .

I am pealing as a result of having gotten too friendly with my sun lamp but I look very tanned and rugged.

Bradley phoned to ask him to London to discuss improving the armored division. Quite a few people advocated reducing the American model in size to correspond with the British version,

curious added evidence of the mania to trust anyone but Americans . . . [We] are just pawns. I fear that after we get landed in France, we will be boxed in a beachhead, due to timidity and lack of drive, which is latent in Montgomery. I hope I am wrong.

He would not be so very wrong.

Everett Hughes arrived in London and became Eisenhower's personal representative — "in other words, his [private] eye."

*Diary, March 1*

Ike told me that while he would not definitely order me to replace Gay, he certainly wanted me to do so, as he felt that while Gay was an extra efficient chief of staff, he did not have the presence to represent me at other headquarters, nor to take over should I get killed. Keyes has always felt the same way.

Of course, I was originally selected for Torch through the direct action of Ike and therefore I owe him a good deal. On the other hand, I have paid my way ever since. I am very reluctant to supersede Gay, but it looks to me and to Hughes, and others with whom I have talked, that if I don't, I will be superseded myself, so I will have to make the change.

The two people I have in mind are either Gaffey or Troy Middleton. I would prefer Gaffey as I know him better, as I had him in the Desert [Training Center], and also in Tunisia. Of course if something should happen to make Keyes available, I will take him like a shot.

Ike and I dined alone and had a very pleasant time. He is drinking too much but is terribly lonely. I really feel sorry for him – I think that in his heart he knows he is not really commanding anything.

*Diary, March 2*

Hughes says I should comply with Ike's views on the chief of staff. I also went to see Beedle Smith to keep things greased, and saw Lee, who is making a fool of himself over the colored question. I fear that what he is doing is going to cause a great deal of unnecessary suffering and killing when we get back to the States.

Called on First Army Group to butter up Leven Allen.

After all the ass kissing I have to do, no wonder I have a sore lip.

Ike told me he had not decided which of us three, Hodges, Bradley, or I, should command . . . the army group. Brad will.

*Diary, March 3*

I feel very bad over this damn chief of staff business. I must do it in a way not to hurt Gay's feelings, for I truly consider him the best chief of staff in Europe, Italy, or Africa.

*Letter, GSP, Jr., to Beatrice, March 3, 1944*

I too am sorry that I was not allowed to jump the ditch [straits of Messina] . . . I would have been with His holiness long since, but family pride was injured.

At the moment I am getting a great deal of undeserved credit for invincibility by people who say (I modestly add with truth) that had I had the beach head [at Anzio] I would be in Rome. Well it is all for the best . . .

I fear that Hap will have to give place to some one with more "IT" and play deputy. I hate to do it but forces like Destiny seem bent on bringing it about and one is a fool to fly in the face of providence or destiny or what ever you choose to call the thing that shapes our ends . . .

Which one of us three will be chosen [to head the army group] is like the Bible, "Many are called etc." but realy it makes no difference. There is glory enough for all.

The pacifists are at it again. I met a visiting fireman of great eminence who told me this was the "LAST WAR." I told him that such statements since 2600 B.C. had signed the death warent of millions of young men. He replied with the stock *lie* — "Oh yes but things are different now." My God! Will they never learn?

*Letter, GSP, Jr., to Dillingham, March 4, 1944*

The greatest gift a general can have is a bad temper [under control]. A bad temper gives you a sort of divine wrath, and it is only by the use of a divine wrath that you can drive men beyond their physical ability in order to save their lives.

He bought a dog, a bull terrier, and named him Willie.

*Letter, GSP, Jr., to Beatrice, March 6, 1944*

My bull pup . . . took to me like a duck to water. He is 15 months old, pure white except for a little lemin on his tail which to a cursary glance would seem to indicate that he had not used toilet paper . . .

Troy Middleton is back on my team, also Bob Grow and Bug Oliver . . . fat Walker from the desert has a job with me too. Of course I wish I had vet[eran]s, but I haven't so that is that and these men will do all right . . .

This damned secrecy thing is rather annoying particularly as I doubt if it fools any one. Every time I make a speech I have to say now remember you have not seen me — a voice crying in the wilderness.

*Diary, March 6*

Had a long talk with Cummings on what to do about Gay. He advised telling him, so I did. It was most distasteful. I really believe I would retain more self-respect if I resigned, but I am not quite that big-hearted. Gay was fine — could not have been better. I told him the exact truth, that Ike ordered me to do it.

> Leaving for London in the morning . . . People there don't realize what a long trip it is from here.

Gaffey said he had no wish to give up the 2d Armored Division, which was in the First Army, but "since he owed me so much, he would do it, if I can get Bradley to turn him loose."

With Middleton, Patton called on Bradley who agreed to let Gaffey go. Patton then went to see Lee.

> He informed me he had phoned Beedle Smith, recommending Middleton for my chief of staff, on the alleged grounds that since General Marshall had great confidence in Middleton, it would strengthen my position. I told Lee I was quite able to take care of myself and that for the future he would not meddle. He is either a conscientious doer of good deeds or has some ulterior motive. I am rather inclined to the latter belief.
>
> I hurried back to see Bradley and asked him to come with me to see Ike . . .
>
> We went out to Widewing to see Ike. He was talking on the phone and said, "Now, listen, Arthur [Tedder], I am tired of dealing with a lot of prima donnas. By God, you tell that bunch that if they can't get together and stop quarreling like children, I will tell the Prime Minister to get someone else to run this damn war. I'll quit." . . . He talked for some time longer and repeated that he would "ask to be relieved and sent home" unless Tedder could get the British and American Air and the two Navies to agree.
>
> I was quite impressed as he showed more assurance than I have ever seen him display. But he should have had the warring factions in and jumped them himself, and not left it to his Deputy, Tedder . . .
>
> He approved all our requests . . .
>
> It is always depressing to me to see how completely Ike is under the influence of the British. He even prefers steel to rubber tracks on tanks because Monty does.

With most of the command and staff arrangements resolved, with the divisions scheduled to be in the Third Army now in the British Isles, Patton turned his attention to teaching his troops how to fight.

# CHAPTER 23

# Fighting Principles

*"All I need is another war."*

DURING MARCH AND APRIL, Patton indoctrinated his subordinates in his methods of making war. He visited, inspected, and talked with the troops, he had long conversations with his senior officers, and he issued a series of papers – letters of instruction – in which he listed his tactical or combat principles. They were his fundamental beliefs on warfare, polished and refined, the essence of his professional knowledge, reflection, work, and experience. Throughout, he stressed confidence and imagination, power and will, drive and efficiency.

His first letter of instruction, dated March 6, had the purpose of orienting the "officers of the higher echelons in the principles of command, combat procedure, and administration which obtain in this Army" and which were to "guide you in the conduct of your several commands." Among them were:

Everyone was to "lead in person." A commander who failed to obtain his objectives and who was "not dead or severely wounded has not done his full duty."

Commanders and staff members were to "visit the front daily . . . to observe, not to meddle . . . Praise is more valuable than blame . . . Your primary mission as a leader is to see with your own eyes and be seen by your troops while engaged in personal reconnaissance."

Issuing an order was worth only about 10 percent. "The remaining 90 percent consists in assuring . . . proper and vigorous execution" of the order.

Persons who did not rest did not last. When the need arose, "everyone must work all the time, but these emergencies are not frequent."

The farther forward the command posts were located, the less time was wasted in driving to and from the front.

Everyone was "too prone to believe that we acquire merit solely through the study of maps in the safe seclusion of a command post. This is an error."

Maps were necessary "in order to see the whole panorama of battle and to permit intelligent planning . . . A study of the map will indicate where critical situations exist or are apt to develop, and so indicate where the commander should be."

Plans had to be "simple and flexible . . . They should be made by the people who are going to execute them."

There could never be too much reconnaissance.

Information was "like eggs: the fresher the better."

Orders were to be short, to tell "what to do, not how." An order was "really a memorandum and an assumption of responsibility by the issuing commander."

In battle it was "always easier for the senior to go up [to the front] than for the junior to come back."

Warning orders were vital and had to be issued in time, "not only to combat units but also to the Surgeon, the Signal Officer, the Quartermaster, the Ordnance Officer, and the Engineer Officer who . . . too have plans to make and units to move. If they do not function, you do not fight."

Every means had to be used "before and after combats to tell the troops what they were going to do and what they have done."

The responsibility for supply rested equally "on the giver and the taker."

Commanders were to "visit the wounded personally" and frequently.

Decorations were to be awarded promptly.

"If you do not enforce and maintain discipline, you are potential murderers."

Walking wounded and stragglers sought "to justify themselves by painting alarming pictures."

Fatigue made "cowards of us all. Men in condition do not tire."

And finally, "Courage. DO NOT TAKE COUNSEL OF YOUR FEARS."

Disseminated throughout the Army, this guidance was widely discussed on the subordinate levels. The rules laid down by Patton began to shape the outlook, character, and personality of the Army, for they were authoritative and full of common sense, they cut through the fabric of training to the heart of combat, and — most important of all — they represented the professional thought of the Old Man, who knew what he was talking about.

• • •

Patton inspected Oliver's 5th Armored Division and was displeased. The artillery was "distinctly bad in that it was distinctly not good." The uniforms were "bad and dirty. There was no attempt to have all the men dress alike. The men were very negligent, and the condition of the quarters, kitchens, and latrines was bad." A 35-minute talk to the officers seemed to have a

> good result . . . I get the impression that the division will fight diligently but not brilliantly as it lacks finish, class, and polish — in a word it lacks a good leader.

Robert C. Grow's 6th Armored Division "had a finish entirely lacking in . . . the 5th."

Asking Walton Walker to correct Oliver "as painlessly as possible" — for the 5th "does not quite click" — Patton suggested that Walker find a pretext to take Oliver with him when he inspected the 6th, which was

> pre-eminent in all the defects I noted in the case of the 5th . . .
>
> In order to avoid individious comparisons, it might be desirable to take either Grow or Wood with you when you inspect the 5th . . .
>
> However, I do not propose to tell you how to do the job. What I want is to see the 5th . . . brought up to the level of the 6th and 4th. There is not a great deal of time to waste.

*Letter, Stiller to Mrs. Patton, March 12, 1944*

You have more reason to be proud of "your man" than even you know.

He is the real "Leader" of this war. And before it is over he will again demonstrate it in no uncertain terms.

I am very proud of the privilege to serve with him.

I will never let him down. And will do my very all to return him to you. When the job is Finished.

You can depend on it.

*Letter, GSP, Jr., to Beatrice, March 12, 1944*

All I need is another war. Of course I have become a legend and everyone says had George been at Salerno or at the [Anzio] beach, things would have been different — frankly I think they would, but in the next show they are expecting a lot from a bad start, so I will realy have to put out — I will.

Captain Basil H. Liddell Hart, Britain's foremost military historian, analyst, and publicist, called on Patton, and they had a long discussion of military procedures, weapons, and the general course, strategy, and lessons of the war.

"Liddell Hart," he told Beatrice,

has developed a great love for me. He is very well read but badly balanced and has no personal knowledge of the facts of life so far as war is concerned — in that he is not alone. He is a funny looking man, tall and skinney.

For his part, Liddell Hart found Patton stimulating and enjoyable, hardly like his photographs in the newspapers and the lurid stories circulating about him. Patton was dynamic and full of interesting ideas.

*Letter, GSP, Jr., to Beatrice, March 16, 1944*

D is having a party shortly so I will have to go back to town again. It is a most boring drive after the first few times and takes nearly five hours. Besides, they blitz the town but not here . . .

All the cousins are convinced that had Wayne and I been reversed, all would have been well — who can say?? . . .

I now have a loud speaker truck like a politician which permits me to make inspirational talks at will.

Well there is no other news I can divulge except the pronunciation of Peover — pronounced Peaver and by the process of natural evolution by the soldiers [from Pee over to] Piss over.

Putting Gaffey over Gay, he explained, was "a question of self-preservation so . . . I did it. Not too noble, I fear. However, I do feel easier in my mind, and the two get on well together."

He drove to London to attend a reception given by Eisenhower at Claridge's. All the "high" British and Americans were there except Brooke and Montgomery. "Some people were unkind enough to say that

Montgomery was absent as he could not bear to be second fiddle." Cunningham and others "took special trouble to look me up."

*Letter, GSP, Jr., to Beatrice, March 21, 1944*

I have been working for two days with pad, stenographer and glue pot on a new letter of instructions on the art of slaughter. It is most tedius as most of it is taken from former letters I have written, but one can only say a thing once and I have said most of them so often . . .

We are at the usual state in planning when every thing seems a perfect mess. But it will all smooth out in a week or so – I should be used to it but I am not.

About 1000 officers and men arrived from the United States to bring the Third Army headquarters up to strength. Patton had them form in ranks in front of Peover Hall and made a speech of welcome and of exhortation. After the men marched off, he addressed the officers. Then he had the chiefs of the staff sections and their assistants in his office and talked to them. All the talks "went over in good shape."

*Letter, GSP, Jr., to Beatrice, March 24, 1944*

I have just finished "inspiring" them . . . I reassured them asto their futures. I told them that I was just as much their father and as deeply concerned for their welfare as Courtney [Hodges] had been . . .

All my life I have abhored speach makers and now I seem fated to make them all the time. I hope I don't get the bug and rant and orate . . .

Things are shaping up pretty well now but I wish we had more of the killer instinct in our men. They are too damned complacent – willing to die but not anxious to kill.

I tell them that it is fine to be willing to die for their country but a damned sight better to make the German die for his. No one has ever told them that . . .

The B[ritish] have suffered and are mad, but our men are not . . .

Roman Civilization fell due to the loss of the will to conquer, satisfaction with the status quo, and high taxes which destroyed trade and private enterprise, and eventually forced people out of the cities. The cycle is returning . . .

I love you and your letters.

An impressionable young man was among those lined up before the steps of Peover Hall, "a half Victorian," he noted, "half Georgian manor house." He and the other new arrivals had heard rumors in New York just before sailing that Patton would replace Hodges in command of the Third Army.

> Therefore, when General Patton walked out on the little terrace, three steps above us . . . the surprise was no less exciting than it was official. Most of us had never seen him in the flesh, and when the drum, ruffles, and bugles sounded the General's march, we stood transfixed upon his appearance. Not one square inch of flesh [of everyone there was] not covered with goose pimples. It was one of the greatest thrills I shall ever know.
>
> You stood at rigid attention during the General's march, but that towering figure impeccably attired froze you in place and electrified the air. The march ended and the General took one step forward.
>
> In a somewhat boyish, shrill yet quiet voice, he said quickly, "At ease, gentlemen, I suppose you are all surprised to see me standing there in place of General Hodges. Such are the fortunes of war. But I can assure you that the Third United States Army will be the greatest Army in American history. We shall be in Berlin ahead of every one. To gain that end, we must have perfect discipline. I shall drive you until hell won't have it, but a pint of sweat is worth a gallon of blood. We are going to kill German bastards — I would prefer to skin them alive — but, gentlemen, I fear some of our people at home would accuse me of being too rough."
>
> At that point General Patton slyly smiled. Everyone chuckled enjoyably.
>
> He talked on to us for half an hour, literally hypnotizing us with his incomparable, if profane eloquence.
>
> When he had finished, you felt as if you had been given a supercharge from some divine source. Here was the man for whom you would go to hell and back.

Robert S. Allen, who would become Koch's deputy G–2, was among those assembled in front of Peover Hall. He later remembered that it was a raw, gloomy, early spring day. Patton stood on the wide manor steps dressed in a handsome, tight-fitting, brass-buttoned battle jacket, the first that Allen had seen, plus pink whipcord riding breeches and gleaming high-topped riding boots with spurs. He carried a long, hand-tooled riding crop. On his left stood Gay, on his right Willie.

As Allen recalled, Patton complimented them on their reputation as a capable and hard-working group under his predecessor. He had no doubt they would perform the same way for him. They could not afford to be damned fools because in battle damned fools became dead men. Men were inevitably killed and wounded in combat, but there was no reason for increasing losses by incompetence or carelessness. He never permitted either quality among his staff members.

They were fighting the war for three reasons – to preserve traditional liberties, to defeat the Nazis who wanted to destroy American liberties, and simply to fight – men liked to fight and always would. Only sophists and crackpots denied the latter. They were goddamned fools, cowards, or both. Whoever disliked fighting would do well to ask for a transfer now, for Patton wanted no part of him and would kick him out later.

"That's all, gentlemen, and good luck."

At Chester, the temporary home of the Royal Naval College, Patton inspected the corps of cadets ranging in age from fourteen to sixteen. He later wrote Cunningham:

> There was one Cadet standing at attention when I was inspecting him who had a fly crawling around his eye, and he never winked. I believe that this is the epitome of discipline.

On March 26, Hodges having been promoted and officially transferred to the First Army, Patton formally assumed command of the Third Army.

He flew to London and talked with John Lucas. Patton afterward thought that Lucas

> was timid at the Anzio beachhead. He said he did not feel justified in expending a corps. He did not expend it because he did not try. Had he taken the high ground, he might have been cut off, but again he might not have been. Without the high ground in his possession, the landing was useless.
>
> I feel very sorry for Lucas as I think he knows he did wrong, yet thinks he did his duty.

At a nice ceremony Field Marshal Sir Alan Brooke, representing the

King, decorated Patton, Bradley, and Eddy with the Companion of the Bath. "Don't wince, Patton," Brooke said, "I shan't kiss you." He also said that Patton had earned the decoration more than any other American. "He probably said the same thing to each one – he is of the clerical type." The decoration was "quite a large white enamel and gold cross worn around the neck and is quite pretty."

Ike said, "I wish the Americans could be as smart as the British."

Patton chatted with William Phillips, Eisenhower's political adviser, who was

> terribly worried how to prevent fraternization between Germans and Americans during the first seven months of our occupation. I told him he was crossing a bridge before he got to it and that, anyway, nothing could stop fraternization . . .
>
> Sometimes I wish people would take this war more seriously. Everett and I are the only ones that seem to give a damn.

"I am a pretty good judge of a fighting man when I see one," Mrs. Marshall wrote, "and I am expecting great things in the near future from you."

He was off to Northern Ireland to inspect the XV Corps headquarters, and the 5th and 8th Divisions.

A young officer in the 8th Division, Edward C. Williamson, had a mixed impression of Patton. By chance he was near the carefully guarded entrance to the Artillery headquarters at Fivemiletown, when Patton and his party arrived in a whirlwind of jeeps. A handful of military policemen jumped out, Tommy guns bristling, and Patton drove in.

Later that day Williamson learned from his battery commander that Patton interviewed the key artillery officers on their combat readiness. Patton maintained his severe soldierly mien and appearance, but his behavior was mild, his questions were perceptive, his statements direct and pertinent. His professional advice emerged naturally out of enormous military experience and knowledge.

Still later, on the lawn of the Enniskillen manor, came the famous Patton speech to the entire division. Williamson reflected that the show was worthy of a Latin American general or a Southern demagogue. He thought Patton's talk was mostly bombast interlarded with profanity, and he had the distinct feeling that Patton came close to advocating the killing of prisoners. It was more than apparent that the enlisted men were enthralled and thrilled, as well as moved, by the general's words.

What Patton did, Williamson decided, was to project one type of figure for the enlisted men, quite another for the officers. Both worked and worked well.

Returned to Peover Hall on April 4, Patton learned from Gaffey that a War Department inspector was in London in connection with the killing of prisoners in Italy. He was indignant.

> I tried two men, a captain and a sergeant for it, and they pleaded at the trial that I had ordered them to do it. When the question of trying these two men for what was clearly barefaced murder came up, some of my friends advised me not to do it . . . However, I did not believe then and do not believe now that I can condone murder for my own benefit.

He had forgotten his initial reaction to the news in Sicily. When Bradley had reported the incident, Patton had brushed it aside as having no consequence. It was probably Bradley, along with Middleton, who had persuaded Patton to court-martial the captain and the sergeant.

> When I addressed the 45th Division in Africa just before sailing for Sicily, I got pretty bloody, trying to get an untried division to the sticking point . . . However, I made no statements by which the wildest stretch of the imagination could be considered as directing the killing of prisoners.

*Letter, GSP, Jr., to Beatrice, April 4, 1944*

Some fair haired boys are trying to say that I killed too many prisoners. Yet the same people cheer at the far greater killing of Japs. Well, the more I killed, the fewer men I lost, but they dont think of that. Sometimes I think that I will quit and join a monestary . . .

Patton went to London to talk with Middleton about the shooting in Sicily, particularly to see whether Middleton remembered Patton's two addresses as he did. "His memory of what I said was the same as my own and was also corroborated by Stiller and Codman, who were present."

"The two men who did the murdering" did so on July 14 near the Butera airfield. The captain captured 43 Germans, five of whom were in civilian clothes, either in whole or in part, and he had them all shot without trial. The sergeant was conducting 36 prisoners to the rear and when he was well out of the battle zone halted them at the side of the road and killed them. "In my opinion both men were crazy."

But he was worried, and at Hughes' suggestion, he wrote Surles "an accurate account of the incident so that if any unscrupulous correspondents got wind of it, Surles could immediately state the facts."

He was pleased to have a report from his son-in-law's commanding general in Italy:

> I consider Jim Totten the ablest battalion commander in his sector. He is crafty and has the best eye for terrain, that I have ever seen. His battalion positions are invariably the best to be had. As a result he has been hurt least by counter battery and enemy action.

He was tickled by an amusing story about himself. Someone overheard a heated discussion between Wedemeyer and Eisenhower about Patton. Finally, Wedemeyer said, "Hell, get on to yourself, Ike; you didn't make him, he made you."

His second letter of instructions appeared on April 3. Addressed to corps, division, and separate unit commanders, it stressed

> those tactical and administrative usages which combat experience has taught myself . . . to consider vital. You will not simply mimeograph this and call it a day. You are responsible that these usages become habitual in your command.

Among the items were the following:

Formal guard mounts and retreat formations, as well as regular and supervised reveille formations, were "a great help and, in some cases, essential to prepare men and officers for battle, to give them that perfect discipline, that smartness of appearance, that alertness without which battles cannot be won."

Officers were always on duty, and their duty extended to every individual, junior to themselves, in the U.S. Army—"not only to members of their own organization."

There was "no approved solution to any tactical situation. There is only one tactical principle which is not subject to change. It is: 'To so use the means at hand to inflict the maximum amount of wounds, death, and destruction on the enemy in the minimum time.' "

Battles were won "by frightening the enemy. Fear is induced by inflicting death and wounds on him. Death and wounds are produced by fire. Fire from the rear is more deadly and three times more effective than fire from the front."

"You can never be too strong."

"Never yield ground. It is cheaper to hold what you have than to retake what you have lost. Our mortars and our artillery are superb weapons when they are firing. When silent, they are junk – see that they fire."

"A good solution applied with vigor *now* is better than a perfect solution ten minutes later."

Few men were killed by the bayonet; "many are scared by it."

The M-1 was "the most deadly rifle in the world. If you cannot see the enemy, you can at least shoot at the place where he is apt to be."

There was "no such thing as 'Tank country' in a restrictive sense. Some types of country are better than others, but tanks have and can operate anywhere."

The successful soldier won his battles cheaply so far as his own casualties were concerned, "but he must remember that violent attacks, although costly at the time, save lives in the end."

• • •

On April 7, at St. Paul's School in London, Patton attended a briefing on the invasion. Montgomery opened with a two-hour talk. Air Marshal Sir Trafford Leigh-Mallory, commanding the Allied Expeditionary Air Forces, and Admiral Sir Bertram Ramsey, commanding the Allied naval forces, followed.

> The Navy was still quite gloomy and had lots of reasons why the thing would fail. But it was interesting to note that in the talks there was much better mutual understanding between the Air, Navy, and Ground troops than there had been at a similar meeting we had in Algiers before we took off for Sicily. I think that much of this good understanding has been due to General Eisenhower's efforts.

After lunch, Bradley, Gerow, and Collins presented their plans. Then came Dempsey and his corps commanders. "As usual they were much more prolix than we are."

> The Prime Minister made the last talk and the best. He said, "Remember that this is an invasion, not a creation of a fortified beachhead."
>
> During Montgomery's lecture, it was interesting to note that I was the only Army commander of the four Army commanders involved to be mentioned by name. The other three he mentioned by number [of the Army].

At dinner with Eisenhower, McCloy, McNarney, Bradley, and Bedell Smith, Patton noted that

> McNarney jumped on Ike about the mishandling of replacements in Africa, which is correct, and they are doing a worse job here . . .
>
> I had quite a talk with them trying to justify an initial overstrength of 15 percent . . .
>
> The efficiency of a division is not measured by its shortage in personnel. A shortage of 10 percent in personnel reduces the effectiveness of a division about 20 percent, and as the losses increase, the efficiency decreases in almost geometrical ratio.
>
> I can't get anyone to realize this. That is because none of our topflight generals have ever fought.
>
> As usual, Bradley said nothing. He does all the getting along and does it to his own advantage.
>
> I expect I take chances because at heart the army is not my living and besides, I am a soldier — a simple soldier.
>
> Referring to the Inspector General incident, Ike said, "You talk too much."
>
> I said, "If you order me not to, I will stop. Otherwise I will continue to influence troops the only way I know, a way which so far has produced results."
>
> He said, "Go ahead, but watch yourself."
>
> All of them but me are scared to death. I shall certainly attempt to say nothing which can be quoted.

He told Beatrice that "the friends of freedom" were trying "to cook up another incident" on "some unnecessary killings — if killings in war are ever unnecessary." Very circumspectly, he said that plans called for the Third Army to capture Brittany in a month, but some people were wagering that Patton would do it in a week. He thought he could – "if they ever let me get started." His late start bothered him, for

> I fear the war will be over before I get loose – but who can say? Fate and the Hand of God still run most shows . . .
>
> I started my German lessons this morning. My machine has the identical conversations in both French and German so I do them both and am about to go mad.

"No doubt your colleague Gen. Clark is a very able general," Beatrice's half brother Charles F. Ayer wrote,

> but many of us here believe that if Gen. Patton had been in command of the Italian enterprise, things would have gone along more smoothly.

Patton replied that he appreciated

> your remarks concerning the relative merits of myself and certain other people, in which remarks I, with due modesty, concur. However, don't tell anybody this.

> *Letter, GSP, Jr., to Beatrice, April 12, 1944*
>
> You say that when I come back I will be so famous that we will have no private life. I doubt that. Soldiers are forgotten pretty quickly . . .
>
> There seems to have been an unwitting conspiracy to make me loose my self confidence, but so far it has failed . . .
>
> Well if I can survive till the fighting starts I will be o.k.

He called a staff meeting to discuss a new directive for employing the Third Army on the Continent. "It is pretty general," he admitted. All it meant was "that when we get to France we will fight."

> I have a feeling, probably unfounded, that neither Monty or Bradley are too anxious for me to have a command. If they knew what little respect I had for the fighting ability of either of them, they would be even less anxious for me to show them up.

*Diary, April 15*

Not a damn thing I can do. All the staff is working, and we are doing all right.

On April 15, Patton issued his third letter of instructions, this one pertaining to the separate tank battalion attached to each infantry division. Once again he enumerated the thoughts that governed his ideas of tactics. Some of them were:

Because of "a slavish adherence to the precept that 'Tanks should be used in mass,' we are not gaining the full advantage from the separate tank battalions."

"Any weapon which is not actively engaged in killing Germans is not doing its duty."

Battles were "simply an agglomeration of numerous small actions and practically never develop according to pre-conceived notions. Therefore our killing weapons must be as close as possible to the fighting zone."

Whether tanks or infantry should lead an attack was always a problem. In general, the infantry went first "against emplaced and known anti-tank guns, large anti-tank minefields, and terrestrial obstacles such as bridges and defiles."

Tanks usually preceded infantry "against scattered minefields or minefields of the new, so-called Boot type mines, against normal artillery and infantry positions, and against any type of counter-attack."

Tanks were to "keep out of villages, where they are at a tremendous disadvantage and cannot utilize their power. Block houses and strong points without anti-tank guns are duck soup for tanks."

Finally, the skillful commander used "the means at hand, all weapons, for the accomplishment of the end sought, the destruction of Germans."

He graciously added that these notes were

> based largely on the advice of Major General T. H. Middleton who has had great success in the use of tanks and infantry in the manner above described.

As a follow-up, Patton asked Walker to have an armored division put on a demonstration of how infantry and tanks should work together. "My purpose is to get these people indoctrinated with the idea of using everything they have."

Patton was reading Arthur Bryant's *The Years of Endurance* on the Napoleonic Wars, and he told Beatrice that it was a "swell book" and

> fine to buck up ones self confidence and reinstall faith in Providence but not in Destiny. The latter is not going to play much of a part [in the invasion] and it is too bad.
>
> However inspite of local and transitory discouragements, I am sure that I am needed, for no one else can do the things which must be done. It is something like fishing. You know the fish are there but you trail your hook a long time between strikes. No one I think can plan his future. Those who try fail, as Wayne did. But any one can school his mind so that if opportunity nocks, he can use it fearlessly.
>
> At the moment all the stress is on unostentatious men who are not criticized because they are colorless...
>
> As I have often said, none of us would be contented unless he were God, and God too probably has to make concessions.

Patton issued his fourth letter of instructions on April 17, this on the employment of tank-destroyer units. Some of his strictures were:

The main purpose of tank destroyers was "to knock out tanks. Secondary usages include direct or indirect fire to reinforce artillery fires; destruction of anti-tank weapons, pill boxes, permanent defensive works; and the support of infantry in defense of beach-heads and bridge-heads."

Tank-destroyer units were "not self-supporting, consequently they will be employed in close cooperation with other arms" – infantry, armor, and artillery.

The use of tank destroyers in defense "must not be stereotyped."

• • •

Patton had a long conversation with McCloy, McNarney, and Lee.

> Mr. McCloy asked me what I thought of Monty. I said first that I preferred not to answer, and then on being pressed, I said I thought Monty was too cautious and would not take calculated risks.
>
> Both McCloy and McNarney urged me to say nothing that would get me criticized, as it was possible that if I get in trouble again, someone would bring up a resolution in the Senate demanding my recall. I told them that my methods had produced men who would fight, and I would be untrue to myself if I failed to use them, re-

gardless of what happens to me. McNarney kept saying that the thing for me was to keep out of trouble so that I could lead the men. McCloy said that he would see that I command an Army in France in spite of hell.

"I liked McNarney quite well," he wrote Beatrice. "He seems ruthless but very intelligent."

I had been kicking to him about more replacements and as he left, he said, "If I were God, what beside replacements would you ask me for?" I said to fight this Army in France. That seemed to please him, as I could have asked for a lot of things . . .

I leave in the morning to visit fat Walker and his corps and to make a couple of speeches to new divisions.

*Letter, GSP, Jr., to Keyes, April 25, 1944*

We are in the clutches of the masterminds [planners] here with the inevitable result that we are changing our plans oftener than our underclothes. I have been consulted no more than I was when we went to Sicily . . .

The staff here is functioning very well but has not got the same drive which the old Seventh Army possessed to such a marked degree . . .

The new divisions which I have so far inspected are really very high class, and I am sure that if we can get them through the first shock of battle, they will be splendid. I am inclined to think, and Middleton agrees with me, that these troops will do very well even the first time . . .

I do not believe I will ever do as well without you as I have done with you, and hope that before this show is over we again have an opportunity to combine our matchless intellects.

*Letter, GSP, Jr., to Beatrice, April 25, 1944*

I had to drive over 700 miles. If one was on a vacation it would have been and in fact was a lovley drive, as spring has at last come and the country is beautiful. All the hawthorne and bracken are in bloom . . .

Lady Astor is dying to meet me. So is Lady Duff Cooper. What a life.

He was about to be in trouble again.

## CHAPTER 24

# The Knutsford Incident

*"I am destined to achieve some great thing—what, I don't know, but this last incident was so trivial in its nature, but so terrible in its effect, that it is not the result of an accident but the work of God. His Will be done."*

IT STARTED so innocently. Mr. G. Mould of the Ministry of Information invited Patton to come to Knutsford on April 25, and make a few remarks to open a Welcome Club for American soldiers.

Patton declined because he thought he might be too prominent.

His presence in England was being kept secret as part of a huge and well-organized deception plan named Fortitude. An important facet of the plan capitalized on Patton's considerable reputation among the Germans as a battle leader. The Allies hoped to convince the Germans that Patton, who had not appeared in combat since Sicily, was in England at the head of an Army Group that was preparing to cross the Channel, not in the Bay of the Seine, where Overlord was scheduled to go, but instead at the narrowest place, near Dover, to invade the Pas de Calais.

Allied intelligence had indications that the hoax was succeeding. A large and impressive German force, the Fifteenth Army, was stationed along the coast near Calais to repel landings by Patton's Group of Armies.

Having declined to speak at the opening ceremony in Knutsford, Patton consented to attend. He would thereby acknowledge his thanks to the British for helping to entertain his troops.

At 6 P.M. on the appointed day, accompanied by Campanole, Midshipman Bower, a nephew of Campanole's landlady, and the ever-present Stiller, Patton drove to Knutsford. He deliberately arrived 15 minutes late in the hope that the short ceremony would be over.

"This did no good, as they were waiting for me." Three newsmen with cameras were in the yard at the entrance to the Club. They "insisted on taking photographs." Patton said he was willing to be photographed but not for the purpose of publicity. He said he was "not there officially," and repeated several times that there was to be no mention of the Third Army.

The photographers said they understood. They took five or six pictures and promised not to publish them.

Patton then entered the Club, where he was greeted. Someone handed him a typed program, which listed four events: 1) an introduction, 2) an explanation of the purpose of the Club, 3) "General — opens the club"; the last three words were crossed out and substituted were "gives his blessing," and 4) God Save the King.

The party went upstairs to the hall, where about 50 or 60 people, mostly women, were gathered.

The honorable Mrs. Constantine Smith, chairman of the local committee, "opened the proceedings with a very laudatory address" concerning the next speaker who was Miss Foster Jeffery, Order of the British Empire, the Regular Administrator of the Women's Volunteer Services. She gave a short address and explained that the purpose of the Welcome Clubs was to "enable selected ladies of the community to meet enlisted men of the U.S. forces with the idea of making friends and eventually asking some of them to their homes for meals. It appears that this system has been very satisfactorily practiced in other parts of England." She then pronounced the club open.

"Without any warning" – so it seemed to Patton, although he had a copy of the program – Miss Jeffery turned and asked him "to say a few words."

Before he could do so, Mrs. Smith rose to introduce him. As Patton later recalled, she announced that he was not there officially and was speaking "in a purely friendly way." His "presence was not to be disclosed."

Mrs. Smith remembered having said: "I now have the pleasure of introducing someone who really is not supposed to be here, and I feel sure that if he will give this club his blessing, the club will be a success . . . I have great pleasure in introducing General Patton."

As nearly as he could tell on the following day, his remarks were as follows:

Until today, my only experience in welcoming has been to welcome

> Germans and Italians to the "Infernal Regions." In this I have been quite successful . . .
>
> I feel that such clubs as this are a very real value, because I believe with Mr. Bernard Shaw, I think it was he, that the British and Americans are two people separated by a common language, and since it is the evident destiny of the British and Americans, and, of course, the Russians, to rule the world, the better we know each other, the better job we will do.
>
> A Club like this is an ideal place for making such acquaintances and for promoting mutual understanding. Also, as soon as our soldiers meet and know the English ladies and write home and tell our women how truly lovely you are, the sooner the American ladies will get jealous and force this war to a quick termination, and I will get a chance to go and kill Japanese.

In retrospect it appeared to Patton to be "a most innocuous statement of the policy of the three great Powers as I understand it."

After his talk, Mr. F. Johnson, Chairman of the Knutsford Urban District Council, proposed a vote of thanks to Miss Jeffery and to Patton. This was seconded by Colonel Thomas Blatherwick "in a rather lengthy speech."

Mr. A. Armstrong, U.S. Consul, proposed a vote of thanks to the Chairlady and to the Women's Volunteer Service, and this was seconded by Mr. Mould of the Ministry of Information "in a lengthy speech."

"After this they played God Save the King and the Star Spangled Banner. They urged me to stay to supper, but I felt they would have a better time if I were not there, so I went home."

On the following day a great stir and a great noise arose.

> *Diary, April 26*
>
> Just before lunch the public relations people from Ike's called up to know what I had said in my talk yesterday. They got Hap Gay on the line and told him to ask what I had said about British and Americans ruling the world. I told him that I said, "Since it was the evident destiny of England and the Americans, and of course the Russians, to rule the world, the better we knew each other, the better it would be."

Despite Patton's request for no publicity, despite Mrs. Smith's announcement of a no-disclosure policy, a story of his presence at the club and of his remarks had appeared in the newspapers.

Hap told me that some papers said I mentioned the Russians and some did not . . .

It seems to have been a bad thing [for me] to do . . .

As far as I knew, no correspondents were present . . . In any case I was really trying to careful . . . I thanked everyone and went home.

When Mrs. Constantine Smith introduced me, she said, "General Patton is not here officially," which was naturally an added reason for me to think that no mention would be made of my presence or remarks in the press.

I was asked to stay to supper but felt that I did not wish that much publicity and went home.

The British Press Association released the story of what it called Patton's first public address in Great Britain to an estimated crowd of 200.

The news had little impact in Britain but created a sensation in the United States. The original report had Patton saying that only the British and Americans would be the ultimate rulers of the world, but most newspapers also carried a correction furnished by U.S. Army headquarters in London, which included the Russians.

Colonel Blatherwick distinctly remembered hearing Patton say: "Undoubtedly it is our destiny to rule the world – the Americans, the British – and then a pause – and of course the Russians."

The story appeared on the front pages of newspapers throughout the United States and provoked immediate reaction from members of Congress who sought chiefly to embarrass the Roosevelt administration. Senator Harlan J. Bushfield of South Dakota was particularly indignant. Patton, he said, had "stepped out of bounds." His job was to carry out his military duties "without discussing civilian arrangements" for the postwar world. Furthermore, because his permanent promotion was still pending, held up by the Senate Military Affairs Sub-Committee since the slapping incident in Sicily, his statement was "unwise." It placed another barrier to his advancement.

Who was to "rule the world" was the crux of the matter. Sol Bloom of New York, Chairman of the House Foreign Affairs Committee, was unconcerned. "Let God rule the world," he said, "and we'll be all right."

Others took Patton's statement more seriously or tried to use it to their advantage. Senator Ellison D. Smith of South Carolina said, "I think it's best for us to rule ourselves and treat the rest of the world as our friends."

Senator Edwin C. Johnson of Colorado, a member of the Military Affairs Committee, thought that Patton's remark "is not only nonsensical but is mischievous." Representative Jesse Sumner of Illinois found Patton's comment "as balmy as Hitler's."

Senator Allen J. Ellender of Louisiana saw Patton's words as out of place for "one so actively engaged in the war theater . . . because it is bound to cause dissatisfaction among our Allies." Senator Robert A. Taft of Ohio called it an "irresponsible" statement. Representative Hamilton Fish of New York said that the American people had no desire to rule the world and that Patton was hardly reflecting the opinion of "even a small percentage of Americans when he says so."

Others used the word "unfortunate" to describe the speech and its possible effect on Allied unity.

Marshall informed Eisenhower that newspapers were carrying lurid accounts to Patton's talk. He was sorry, for the War Department was just about to get confirmation of the permanent Regular Army promotions, among them Patton's. Marshall feared that the reported remarks had killed the possibility.

It was a tempest in a teapot, but everyone remembered the slapping incident. "If General Patton deliberately tried," one editorial writer pontificated with his tongue in his cheek, "he could hardly have produced . . . a bigger batch of propaganda for the Nazis, the Japanese, and the [anti-Roosevelt] Chicago Tribune." After all, the efforts of the United Nations to win the war and organize the peace could hardly be dislocated by an assertion that the Allies were destined to "rule the world." In Indian language, Patton was simply "Chief Foot-in-Mouth." Patton fought well and "his superiors should keep him at it."

By then, Patton knew that he was in deep trouble. Since Eisenhower was away from London observing amphibious landing rehearsals, Patton wrote to Everett Hughes and explained what had happened.

> There seems to be considerable excitement over a few remarks which I made yesterday . . .
>
> I was perfectly unaware that any reporters were present, because the meeting was so small that I had no idea that anybody would even mention it. There was a British official photographer on the outside who took a picture of me and whom I warned that he could mention my name but not my job . . .

I had no idea that anybody was going to quote anything I said.

Trusting that this information may be of service to you in seeing that I am not misrepresented.

To the letter, Patton attached the original invitation, the typed program, and affidavits from Mrs. Smith, Colonel Blatherwick, Campanole, and Midshipman Bower, all of whom corroborated Patton's explanation of the event.

*Diary, April 27*

So far as I am concerned, every effort is made to show lack of confidence in my judgment and at the same time, in every case of stress, great confidence in my fighting. None of those at Ike's headquarters ever go to bat for juniors, and in any argument between the British and the Americans, invariably favor the British. Benedict Arnold is a piker compared with them, and that includes Lee as well as Ike and Beedle.

Beedle called up at 1030 and said that he was giving me a verbal order from Ike that I am never to talk in public without first submitting what I am going to say to Ike and himself for censorship, thereby displaying great confidence in an Army commander – if I have not been relieved.

Beedle also said that due to my "unfortunate remarks," the permanent promotion of himself and me might never come off. How sad.

In consonance with this order, I am unable to talk with either the 79th, 80th, 83d, or 7th Armored Divisions, a restriction that will surely cost lives. Yet if I break it, I will get relieved, and that would mean defeat and a still larger loss.

"God show the right," and damn all reporters and gutless men.

*Letter, GSP, Jr., to Beatrice, April 27, 1944*

This has been a pretty horrid day . . .

Willie and I are going out for a long quiet walk and see what that does for our self esteem. If this sort of thing keeps up, I will be a perfect misanthrope or perhaps it would be better if I emulated the owl and just sat and thought. I love you.

Ruth Ellen Totten, Patton's daughter, wrote to her Aunt Nita:

I got the *most pitiful* letter from Daddy about his latest faux pas, which I will . . . quote:

"Apparently I am again an incident due to a three minute talk I made at a gathering of some 50 people at which, by the way, the chairman (she was a woman) said I was unofficial. I really feel pretty bad today as anything may happen, but at least I still have the When and If [his boat]. I may be using it soon.

"It is a horrid thought that one may be deprived of doing the only job one is good at due to the exercise of free speech, but that thought is always with me – it is a wonderful morale builder!?!?!

"I guess my trouble is that I can never realize that anyone should be interested in what I say . . .

"I have caught nothing but hell for nearly a year now. All I want to do is win the war and everyone seems to think that all I want is notoriety which I despise.

"When one knows one is good, it is not necessary to have people say so. I know I am. I have never asked a favor or shunned a detail or spared my neck, the soldiers think I am wonderful, but the Press??? Bah! Jesus only suffered one night but I have had months and months of it, and the cross is not yet in sight, though probably just around the corner.

"Of course, if and I say IF I get into this next show, all will be well as long as there is fighting to do. I will have to take bigger chances than usual but either you do get it or you don't, so what the hell. A nice clean grave would be better than surviving another victory, so far as I am concerned, but frankly I don't think I will be killed. I have yet a job to do and I am going to do it. I still believe in fate if not in destiny."

I think that is just awful . . . Gosh, I wish they would invade before something worse happens to him.

As soon as Eisenhower returned to London, he cabled Marshall. He was upset, he said, "that Patton had broken out again." Patton was apparently "unable to use reasonably good sense in all those matters where senior commanders must appreciate the effect of their own actions upon public opinion." This raised doubts as to "the wisdom of retaining him in high command despite his demonstrated capacity in battle leadership." Although Patton's exact remarks might have been incorrectly reported and somewhat misinterpreted, "I have grown so weary of the trouble he constantly causes you and the War Department, to say nothing of myself, that I am seriously contemplating the most drastic action." But he was deferring his decision until he heard again from Marshall. Specifically, "do you consider that his retention in high command will tend to destroy or diminish public and governmental confidence in the War Department?" If so, "stern disciplinary action must be taken."

Before receiving word from Marshall, Eisenhower cabled him again. Although he was "exceedingly weary," he said, of Patton's "habit of getting everybody into hot water through the immature character of his public actions," investigation revealed that the offense was less serious than the newspapers made out. Even so, "the fact remains that he simply does not keep his mouth shut." He repeated that he was waiting to hear from Marshall before taking final action.

In indirect extenuation of Patton, Eisenhower remarked that censorship was "quite difficult to handle." He had done much inspecting recently, and everywhere he went he normally talked for two or three minutes to officers and men. He repeatedly issued "flat orders" that nothing he said was to be quoted. Yet on several occasions he found his exact words in the papers. "This rather shakes a man."

"Like you," Marshall replied, "I have been considering the matter on a purely business basis." Patton's experience and ability could hardly be ignored and should not be wasted. But whether his capacity for combat leadership had to be dispensed with, Marshall left to Eisenhower, who had the responsibility for Overlord. If Eisenhower felt that Hodges could command the Third Army and carry out operations with the same assurance of success, Patton could be sacrificed. But if Eisenhower doubted that Hodges could do what Patton could, "then between us we can bear the burden of the present unfortunate reaction." The harm already done had been fatal for confirmation of the permanent promotion list.

Eisenhower wrote Patton that the expression of "an opinion as to the future political position of the United States, Great Britain, and Russia" had created "unfortunate repercussions both in Congress and in the public press." Eisenhower had examined all the available reports and thoroughly understood that Patton thought he was talking privately. Nevertheless, the incident was of "the utmost seriousness" and "still filled with drastic potentialities regarding yourself."

What concerned Eisenhower mainly, he said, was "that you simply will not guard your tongue" despite "the most drastic instructions and orders," and despite repeated warnings "against your impulsiveness." Reminding Patton that Eisenhower had insisted on having him as part of his command because he believed "in your fighting qualities and your ability to lead troops in battle," Eisenhower deplored Patton's "habit of dramatizing yourself" and of "committing indiscretions for no other purpose than of calling attention to yourself."

Eisenhower was beginning to doubt "your all-around judgment," and his decision would be final as soon as he heard from the War Department. Until then, any further indiscretion leading to embarrassment for the government or Eisenhower's headquarters would result in Patton's instant relief from command.

*Diary, April 29*

A company of our Military Police battalion, and a band, and a group of nurses took part in the Alderley Edge "Salute the Soldier Week." I had been asked to receive the salute there but felt that I had better keep out of the limelight, so General Gay took it. I looked on from a private automobile on a side street.

His discomfort was hardly lessened when he learned what had befallen another general officer several days earlier. Alleged to have violated military security, this officer was immediately relieved of his command and placed under arrest by Eisenhower. If the allegation was substantiated, Eisenhower made clear, further disciplinary action would follow.

It was evident that as the time of invasion approached, Eisenhower was becoming increasingly tough and hard.

When the editor of the *Coast Artillery Journal* in Washington asked Patton to do an article on the future military policy of the United States, Patton replied:

> I am highly complimented . . . However, owing to the unfortunate fact that I always attract too much notoriety, I have made it a definite rule for the future that I will not appear in print. I regret this.

*Diary, April 30*

Beedle called up and told me to report to Ike, at Ike's office, at either 1100 or 1500 tomorrow. It can be anything from a reprimand to a reduction [in grade], or a new plan of campaign. These constant pickings are a little hard on the nerves, but great training. I feel that if I get reduced and sent home, it might be quite important, as

I would get into politics as an honest and straight spoken man and would either be a great success or a dismal failure.

Gaffey was told by Hughes that, on the 28th, when Hughes went to see Ike, he was just writing a cable to General Marshall saying that he, Ike, had no further need of protecting me and would not resist my being recalled. When Hughes showed him my statements on the Knutsford speeches, he said, "Oh, hell," and tore the cable up . . .

Hughes is still worried about me – so am I.

*Letter, GSP, Jr., to Beatrice, April 30, 1944*

Just had a phone from Beedle to see him in the morning. I always get things like that on Sundays or New Years etc, so I am used to it.

Apparently much umbrage has been taken to my last, wholy casual remarks, and I may be able to go sailing sooner than I had thought, but the Chesapeake in the spring is said to be lovley.

If I have caused you added worry, I am sorry.

*Letter, GSP, Jr., to Hughes, April 30, 1944*

You probably are damn fed up with me, but certainly my last alledged escapade smells strongly of having been a frame-up in view of the fact that I was told that nothing would be said, and that the thing was under the auspices of the Ministry of Information who was present.

However . . . people are not interested in why's but in what's, and the what of this is that I raised a stink.

I have no military ambitions after the war; therefore, except from the question of a pension, my promotion to a permanent major general is not of paramount importance to me; and I hereby authorize you, if in your judgment you consider it wise, to state to the Commander-in-Chief that I am perfectly willing to have my name removed from the list of permanent generals in order to no longer defer the promotion of other officers.

Of course, you know what my ambition is – and that is to kill Germans and Japanese in the command of an Army. I cannot believe that anything I have done has in any way reduced my efficiency in this particular line of action.

With best thanks for your many services to me, and hoping to God that I do not have to call on you soon again, I am as ever, Devotedly yours,

To Marshall, Eisenhower said that he had sent for Patton to give him the opportunity "to present his case personally to me." He would probably relieve Patton from command and send him home. He had "every faith" in Hodges and was convinced that Hodges could do a "fine job" with the Third Army. "The big difference is that Patton has proved his ability to conduct a ruthless drive whereas Hodges has not."

In anticipation of sending Patton home, Eisenhower asked whether to reduce him to his regular grade of colonel or to keep him at his temporary grade of lieutenant general. Retaining him at the higher grade would give Marshall the problem of absorbing him into the training system, but it was conceivable that some situation might develop during the invasion "where this admittedly unbalanced but nevertheless aggressive fighting man should be rushed into the breach."

After working closely with Patton for a year and a half, Eisenhower despaired that he would "ever completely overcome his lifelong habit of posing," which caused him to "break out in these extraordinary ways." Although Eisenhower had been told that Patton had "completely isolated himself from any chance of contact with the press and the public," he believed that the effect of his "latest outbreak" in the United States required "disciplinary action." It was a pity but that was how Eisenhower felt. This would be his decision, "except in the unlikely circumstance that Patton can produce additional mitigating evidence."

Marshall, in reply, gave Eisenhower complete latitude to handle the case. "Do not consider War Department position in the matter. Consider only Overlord and your own heavy burden of responsibility for its success. Everything else is of minor importance." Eisenhower could do as he wished, send Patton home, in grade or reduced, relieve him from command and hold him in the theater as a surplus lieutenant general, or keep him in command "if that promises best for Overlord."

*Letter, GSP, Jr., to Beatrice, May 1, 1944*

Remember the Albetross I shot on the way home from Hawaii. Well my affinity for birds seems to haunt me and I may again break out in feathers.

Any how I fear that Destiny fears so and that Katherine's husband [Marshall] is primarily to blame . . .

Should we have a chance to put the boat in commission, remember that even if I am sea sick I hate sympathy except from you.

*Diary, May 1*

In spite of possible execution this morning, I slept well and trust my destiny. God has never let me, or the country, down yet.

Reported to Ike at 1100. He was most cordial and asked me to sit down, so I felt a little reassured.

He said, "George, you have gotten yourself into a very serious fix."

I said, "Before you go any farther, I want to say that your job is more important than mine, so if in trying to save me you are hurting yourself, throw me out."

He said, "I have now got all that the army can give me. It is not a question of hurting me but of hurting you and depriving me of a fighting Army commander."

He went on to say that General Marshall had wired him that my repeated mistakes have shaken the confidence of the country and the War Department. General Marshall even harked back to the Kent Lambert incident . . . certainly a forgiving s.o.b.

Ike said he had recommended that, if I were to be relieved and sent home, I be not reduced to a Colonel, as the relief would be sufficient punishment, and that he felt that situations might well arise where it would be necessary to put me in command of an Army.

I told Ike that I was perfectly willing to fall out on a permanent promotion so as not to hold the others back.

Ike said General Marshall had told him that my crime had destroyed all chance of my permanent promotion, as the opposition said that even if I was the best tactician and strategist in the army, my demonstrated lack of judgment made me unfit to command.

He said that he had wired General Marshall on Sunday washing his hands of me. (He did not use these words but that is what he meant.)

I told him that if I was reduced to a Colonel, I demanded the right to command one of the assault regiments; that this was not a favor but a right.

He said no, because he felt he would surely need me to command an Army.

I said, "I am not threatening, but I want to tell you that this attack is badly planned and on too narrow a front and may well result in an[other] Anzio, especially if I am not there."

He replied, "Don't I know it, but what can I do?"

That is a hell of a remark for a supreme commander. The fact is that the plan which he has approved was drawn by a group of

British in 1943. Monty changed it only by getting 5 instead of 3 divisions into the [initial] assault, but the front is too short. There should be three separate attacks on at least a 90 mile front. I have said this for nearly a year.

Ike said he had written me a "savage" letter but wanted me to know that his hand is being forced in the United States. He talked to the Prime Minister about me, and Churchill told him that he could see nothing to it, that "Patton had simply told the truth." Ike then went on to excuse General Marshall on the grounds that it was an election year, etc.

It is sad and shocking to think that victory and the lives of thousands of men are pawns to the "fear of They," and [to] the writings of a group of unprincipled reporters and weak-kneed congressmen, but so it is.

When I came out [of Ike's office], I don't think anyone could tell that I had just been killed. I have lost lots of competitions in the sporting way, but I never did better [in dissembling his hurt over the probable loss of the Third Army]. I feel like death, but I am not out yet. If they will let me fight, I will; but if not, I will resign [from the army] so as to be able to talk, and then I will tell the truth and possibly do my country more good.

All the way home, 5 hours, I recited poetry to myself...

My final thought on the matter is that I am destined to achieve some great thing – what, I don't know, but this last incident was so trivial in its nature, but so terrible in its effect, that it is not the result of an accident but the work of God. His Will be done.

*Diary, May 2*

Felt very much like a Thanks giving turkey all day, waiting for the axe to fall, but no news. I did not feel like working but luckily had little to do.

*Letter, GSP, Jr., to Beatrice, May 2, 1944*

This last incident was the "most unkindest cut of all." What I said was at a private party and I had been assured that no reporters were there, but it may be the end. At least as others see it. For me it is only a new beginning.

I have been so upset that my digestion went, but is coming back. Even I can be pushed just so far...

If I survive the next couple of days, it will be O.K. and things look

brighter. But still I get in a cold sweat when the phone rings . . .
Well we ain't dead yet. I love you and need you.

On the morning of May 3, returned from having his teeth cleaned, Patton found a telegram from Eisenhower. As Patton later recalled when he was writing in his diary, Eisenhower said: "Since the War Department has placed the decision of relieving you on me, I have decided to keep you . . . Go ahead and train your Army."

Eisenhower had reached this decision, he told Patton,

> solely because of my faith in you as an able battle leader and from no other motives . . . I expect you to . . . exercise extreme care to see that while you are developing the morale and fighting spirit, you will not be guilty of another indiscretion which can cause any further embarrassment to your superiors or to yourself.

To Marshall, Eisenhower explained that relieving Patton would "lose to us" his experience and his "demonstrated ability of getting the utmost out of soldiers in offensive operations." He was therefore retaining Patton in command "solely upon my convictions as to the effect upon Overlord."

By admitting that Patton was indispensable for the success of Overlord, Eisenhower could have extended no finer compliment.

*Diary, May 3*

I felt much better and wrote Ike, thanking him. He called up in person and was very nice. Sometimes I am very fond of him, and this is one of the times . . .

Gaffey, Gay, Codman, Stiller, and I all took a drink to celebrate.

*Letter, GSP, Jr., to Beatrice, May 3, 1944*

Every thing is again O.K. because Divine Destiny came through in a big way.

I am sorry that in some of my recent letters I sounded whiney. I don't often indulge.

I guess my trouble is that I don't realize that I am always news, but you can bet I know it now.

The whole thing was so silly and started in a perfectly harmless informal talk to a group of local ladies who . . . thought I had said such a nice thing, from their purely local point of view of course, that they quoted me.

Well the Lord came through again but I was realy badly frightened as you could gather by the letter about the feathers. I actually had a nut in my pocket [for good luck] . . .

I have youthed thirty years since my last letter.

*Diary, May 4*

I felt all tense, so took pills with a bromide, with no effect so far.

*Letter, GSP, Jr., to Beatrice, May 5, 1944*

I certainly will not say another word [in public] . . . What a stink over nothing. Poor Harry [Stimson] has a time about me. I hate to bother him so, but God knows I was inoscent that time . . .

We all feel the overriding influence of politics even here. It is rather amusing to note how many people are interested in it even more than war. I wish we could have a morotorium on it, but I suppose that is impossible . . . Well, since I have never been elected to any thing and never could be, I don't worry. After this war I am going to retire and call my self Mister Patton and cruise and fox hunt. For a few days I thought I was going to have to do it sooner than I wanted to, but now all is rosy. Nock on wood.

Later he would tell Beatrice that Stimson wrote "a, for him, quite a strong letter and gave the credit of saving my scalp to Destiny. Everett thinks so too."

"In the midst of all these great problems [of the invasion]" Eisenhower wrote Marshall, "some of my most intense irritations are caused by things that need never have arisen. For example, the Patton case . . . Such things take hours of earnest study and anxious thought."

*Diary, May 5*

Wrote a paper on the use of armored divisions . . . I have completely gotten back in the swing of things, thank God.

The invasion was exactly a month away.

CHAPTER 25

# The Approach of D-Day

*"I'm not supposed to be commanding this Army, I'm not supposed even to be in England. Let the first bastards to find out be the Goddam Germans. I want them to look up and howl, 'ACH, IT'S THE GODDAM THIRD ARMY AND THAT SON-OF-A-BITCH PATTON AGAIN!'"*

"I GUESS EVERY ONE will be surprised when the Day comes," Patton wrote Beatrice. "Of course I wish we were at it now. This waiting is hard on the nerves. I must go and exercise."

There was much more to do than exercise and wait.

He had every sort of airplane fly over all his troops so they could better identify Allied and Axis aircraft.

He attended the demonstration arranged by Walker to illustrate the combined use of infantry and tanks. At the rehearsal Patton was dissatisfied.

> The infantry advanced by rushes when defilated and failed to use their weapons. I called the officers together and explained errors to them . . .
>
> In the second rehearsal . . . the support and reserve were so far back as to be wholly useless. The tanks did better but the officers and non-coms of the infantry just went along as members of the chorus and gave no orders. It was very sad.
>
> When the tanks jumped off on the second objective, the infantry were slow [in] following. The occupation of the position was poor, and the employment of anti-tank guns awful.
>
> I again assembled the officers and gave them hell. I hope they improve . . .
>
> After dinner we had a very good conversation and I read them [18 armored officers, most of them generals] the draft of the paper

I am writing on armored divisions and asked for comments. I got very few, as none of them know anything about armored divisions. Furthermore, very few officers ever project what they do in training into battle, which is a very sad commentary on our system.

The following day was the real demonstration.

We had all the regimental and battalion commanders of infantry and the separate tank battalion commanders of the [Third] Army assembled. The demonstration was a great success except that this time the reserve company was too close.

I was delighted and feel that I have at last illustrated the use of marching fire and of tanks and infantry.

It strikes me as a sad reflection on our state of preparation for war that I had to personally conduct and drive the rehearsals, but so it is. On the other hand it was depressing to realize that had I not personally practically commanded the [demonstration] battalion on the second rehearsal, the thing would not have come off. Our officers do not realize the necessity of utilizing all the means at hand, all weapons, to accomplish victory.

*Diary, May 12*

Eisenhower had a lunch at the Officers Club at Widewing to commemorate the African campaign. As many as possible of the British and American participants in that campaign were present . . . 32 in all. Ike made an excellent speech . . .

Ike asked me to come in for a chat. We had a very pleasant few minutes together. No lecture at all.

*Letter, GSP, Jr., to Beatrice, May 13, 1944*

I have got a lot of things done and feel very satisfied with the results as a whole.

*Diary, May 15*

All the senior commanders and their chiefs of staff assembled at St. Paul's School for the final briefing for the attack. The King, the Prime Minister, and Field Marshal Smuts [of South Africa] were also present.

General Eisenhower started with a short talk emphasizing the fact that any existing disagreements between the Air, the Navy, and the Ground must be ironed out today.

Then Admiral Ramsey . . . told how difficult it was going to be to get troops ashore.

Air Marshal Leigh-Mallory followed, telling what the Air Force had done.

Then the Chief of the British Bomber Command [Air Chief Marshal Sir Arthur Harris] spoke and made what I considered very ill-timed arguments in favor of bombardment instead of attack [invasion].

Bradley and Spaatz made short and good speeches.

The King said a few words, but it was rather painful to watch the efforts he made not to stammer.

At lunch I sat opposite Mr. Churchill who asked me whether I remembered him, and when I said I did, he immediately ordered me a glass of whiskey.

After lunch there were more talks. Admiral Kirk [senior American naval commander] made a weak, stilted one, and the British opposite number made a fine fighting talk. Smuts talked a lot, but repeated himself and was not impressive. Finally the Prime Minister made a really great fighting speech, worth all that preceded it. He took a crack at overstressing Civil Government, and said that his views would hurt the feelings of his dear friend, General de Gaulle. Also that we were worrying too much about governing France before capturing it. It was a very fine fighting speech, and I intend to write him a letter about it.

It was odd that Patton made no comment on Montgomery's presentation.

*Diary, May 17*

Made a talk . . . As in all my talks, I stressed fighting and killing.

It was probably about this time, a month or so before the invasion, that he began to give his famous speech to the troops. Since he spoke extemporaneously, there were several versions. But if the words were always somewhat different, the message was always the same: the necessity to fight, the necessity to kill the enemy viciously, the necessity for everyone, no matter what his job, to do his duty. The officers were usually uncomfortable with the profanity he used. The enlisted men loved it.

Men, this stuff some sources sling around about America wanting to stay out of the war and not wanting to fight is a lot of baloney! Americans love to fight, traditionally. All real Americans love the sting and clash of battle. America loves a winner. America will not tolerate a loser. Americans despise a coward, Americans play to win. That's why America has never lost and never will lose a war.

You are not all going to die. Only two percent of you, right here today, would be killed in a major battle. Death must not be feared. Death, in time, comes to all of us. And every man is scared in his first action. If he says he's not, he's a Goddam liar. Some men are cowards, yes, but they fight just the same, or get the hell slammed out of them. The real hero is the man who fights even though he's scared. Some get over their fright in a minute, under fire, others take an hour, for some it takes days, but a real man will never let the fear of death overpower his honor, his sense of duty, to his country and to his manhood.

All through your Army careers, you've been bitching about what you call "chicken-shit drill." That, like everything else in the Army, has a definite purpose. That purpose is Instant Obedience to Orders and to create and maintain Constant Alertness! This must be bred into every soldier. A man must be alert all the time if he expects to stay alive. If not, some German son-of-a-bitch will sneak up behind him with a sock full o' shit! There are four hundred neatly marked graves somewhere in Sicily, all because ONE man went to sleep on his job . . . but they are German graves, because WE caught the bastards asleep! An Army is a team, lives, sleeps, fights, and eats as a team. This individual hero stuff is a lot of horse shit. The bilious bastards who write that kind of stuff for the *Saturday Evening Post* don't know any more about real fighting under fire than they know about fucking!

Every single man in the Army plays a vital role. Every man has his job to do and must do it. What if every truck driver decided that he didn't like the whine of a shell overhead, turned yellow and jumped headlong into a ditch? What if every man thought, "They won't miss me, just one in millions?" Where in Hell would we be now? Where would our country, our loved ones, our homes, even the world, be? No, thank God, Americans don't think like that. Every man does his job, serves the whole. Ordnance men supply and maintain the guns and vast machinery of this war, to keep us rolling. Quartermasters bring up clothes and food, for where we're going there isn't a hell of a lot to steal. Every last man on K.P. has a job to do, even the guy who boils the water to keep us from getting the G.I. shits!

Remember, men, you don't know I'm here. No mention of that is to be made in any letters. The USA is supposed to be wondering what the Hell has happened to me. I'm not supposed to be commanding this Army, I'm not supposed even to be in England. Let the first bastards to find out be the Goddam Germans. I want them to look up and howl, "ACH, IT'S THE GODDAM THIRD ARMY AND THAT SON-OF-A-BITCH PATTON AGAIN!"

We want to get this thing over and get the hell out of here, and get at those purple-pissin' Japs! ! ! The shortest road home is through Berlin and Tokyo! We'll win this war, but we'll win it only by showing the enemy we have more guts than they have or ever will have!

There's one great thing you men can say when it's all over and you're home once more. You can thank God that twenty years from now, when you're sitting around the fireside with your grandson on your knee and he asks you what you did in the war, you won't have to shift him to the other knee, cough, and say, "I shoveled shit in Louisiana."

*Letter, GSP, Jr., to son George, May 19, 1944*

Men are never beaten by any thing but their own souls when the latter curl up . . .

Before I went to Sicaly I marked on my map the places I thought I would have battles and I was 100% right – I just got through marking a map of Europe to day. I hope I come out as well both in winning and picking – I am sure I will . . . .

I am very proud of you.

*Diary, May 18*

The only worry I have about this show is how I am going to get the Army across [the Channel] and assembled on the other side. For the fighting I have no worry.

On May 20, Patton issued his fifth letter of instructions to all corps and division commanders:

Haste and speed were "not synonymous."

Hasty attacks did not "produce speedy successes or speedy advances because hasty attacks are not coordinated attacks."

When tanks advanced against the enemy, "they must use their guns for what is known as reconnaissance by fire; that is, they must shoot at any terrestrial objective behind which an anti-tank gun might be concealed."

"The quickest way to get to heaven is to advance across open ground swept by effective enemy anti-tank fire."

Great and calculated risks were necessary when using armor, "but we must not dive off the deep end without first determining whether the swimming pool is full of water."

A unit "must never halt because some other unit is stuck. If you push on, you will release the pressure on the adjacent unit, and it will accompany you."

Troops were "never defeated by casualties but by lack of resolution — of guts. Battles are won by a few brave men who refuse to fear and who push on. It should be our ambition to be members of this heroic group. More casualties occur among those who halt or go to the rear than among those who advance and advance firing. Finally, all of us must have a desperate desire and determination to close with the enemy and destroy him."

There was "a ridiculous and wide-spread fear among all our troops that they will run out of ammunition . . . In my experience this has never happened."

> In this Letter, as in those preceding it, I am not laying down inflexible rules. I am simply giving you my ideas. I must and I do trust to your military experience, courage, and loyalty to make these ideas tangible. There are many ways of fighting, all of which are good if they are successful . . .
>
> It is the duty of all commanders to see that their men are fully aware of the many vile deeds perpetrated upon civilization by Germans, and that they attack with the utmost determination, ferocity, and hate.
>
> I am sure that every man will do his duty, and I am therefore sure that victory is simply a question of when we find the enemy.

*Diary, May 22*

I memorized the map for quite a while and can almost draw it from memory now.

*Letter, GSP, Jr., to Beatrice, May 22, 1944*

Every morning I think that I have nothing to do and then around six in the evening I find I have been so busy I have not written you . . .

I will even up with some people if I live and if I die my spirit will get them. I still believe in fate and I have been pretty well tempered in the fires of adversity — I probably needed it . . .

Anger is the thing that saves souls all right, that with imagination and a sense of honor are needed and are very rare.

*Letter, GSP, Jr., to Beatrice, May 24, 1944*

My Public Relations officer . . . just came and I told him I did not want publicity except from the Germans and he was to see that I did not get it.

If I hit the Huns as hard as I hope to, they will tell the world.

Things are all so buttoned up and quiet that I realy find time hanging heavily on my hands . . .

We are still so secret that we cant sew our shoulder patches on . . .

There is a great vogue here for generals to send each other signed pictures. I have a most touching one from Beedle signed April 28, of all days [the height of the Knutsford incident]. It reminds me of the pink tree that grows in the Virginia woods [the Judas tree].

*Diary, May 25*

Just read in the Daily Mail that the Senate Military Affairs Committee has tabled my promotion. I hope they let the others through. If I get no more out of this war but a permanent Major Generalcy, I will be a failure.

On May 29, a week before the invasion, Patton had his corps commanders — Middleton, Haislip, Walker, and Cook — and their chiefs of staff, as well as Weyland, Gaffey, and Gay, to dinner. It was a family get-together, designed to promote good feeling among them, unity, solidarity, and team spirit. He noted that all were southerners. "After dinner we had quite an informal talk." He enlarged upon the policies and principles he had set out in his letters of instruction, but "The only point I tried to stress was that, in case of doubt, follow the old Confederate maxim of 'Marching to the sound of guns.' "

His classmate William H. Simpson, who commanded the Ninth Army, came for a visit. He brought his chief of staff with him.

We gave them the short briefing [on the projected invasion], and as Colonel Maddox was absent, I took the G–3 part on myself. I did this with malice aforethought because I know that Simpson trusts too much to his staff and does not know what is going on, so I thought it was a good idea for him to see what I did. It had the desired result. He was quite impressed by the fact that I could also be my own G–3 – of course, I always am.

*Diary, June 1*

Bradley went over all his final plans with me this morning. He is much more cheerful than he was, and if everything moves as planned, there will be nothing left for me to do. Naturally, I hope something turns up.

Since Montgomery had invited the four Army commanders to spend the night with him,

Bradley and I left at 1530 and flew to Portsmouth to see General Montgomery who lives at Southwick. Montgomery, Bradley, and I had tea, and then we went to his office, and without the aid of any staff officers, went over the plans.

Montgomery was especially interested in the operations of the Third Army, and it was very fortunate that, two nights ago, I had rehearsed the whole thing for Simpson, so I was very fluent.

He said twice to Bradley, "Patton should take over for the Brittany, and possibly for the Rennes operation."

This would actually happen.

After supper Dempsey and Crerar arrived.

The official meeting of the four Army commanders, and De Guingand, Montgomery's chief of staff, took place at this time.

General Dempsey had the corps in Sicily which failed to take Catania. He is not very impressive looking, and I take him to be a yes-man. The Canadian is better, but not impressive. De Guingand is very clever but is extremely nervous and continuously twists his long, black oily hair into little pigtails about the size of a match. Montgomery was very anxious to get the exact location of all command posts on D Day, and also the succession of command down to, and including, the third generation . . .

During our first conversation with General Montgomery, he called someone in London on the telephone — I think it was General Ismay [Churchill's military secretary] — and told him to dissuade the Prime Minister from visiting him on Sunday. Referring to this conversation, he said, "If Winnie comes, he'll not only be a great bore but also may well attract undue attention here. Why in hell doesn't he go and smoke his cigar at Dover Castle and be seen with the Lord Mayor? It would fix the Germans' attention to Calais."

At dinner General Montgomery produced a betting book and asked me whether or not England would be at war again in ten years after the close of the present war. He bet she would not, therefore, to be a sport, I had to bet she would. Also his Quartermaster offered to bet me $40.00 that an American horse would not win the next Grand National. In order to stick up for my country, I had to risk the $40.00 . . .

When the port was passed, General Montgomery toasted the four Army commanders. Nobody did anything about it, so I said, "As the oldest Army commander present, I would like to propose a toast to the health of General Montgomery and express our satisfaction in serving under him." The lightning did not strike me [for the lie].

After dinner we gambled in a simple way. At first I won too much but finally succeeded in finishing a slight loser. I have a better impression of Monty than I had.

*Diary, June 2*

At breakfast told Monty goodbye. He said, "I had a good time and now we understand each other."

That evening Bradley's First U.S. Army command post opened aboard the U.S.S. *Augusta.*

*Diary, June 3*

We have to provide 2,000 men for prisoner of war escort. Apparently Lee and Company were caught wholly flat-footed.

*Diary, June 4*

All of us went to church. I am awfully restless and wish I were leading the assault.

*Letter, GSP, Jr., to Beatrice, June 4, 1944*

Don't get excited when the whistle blows. I am not in the opening kick off.

*Diary, June 5*

Today might be D Day . . . but no news . . . I called Hughes and asked him to get off a radio of congratulations to Alexander, Keyes, and Clark on their success in Italy.

They had captured Rome.
Eisenhower postponed the invasion one day because of bad weather.

*Letter, GSP, Jr., to son George, June 6, 1944*

At 0700 this morning the BBC announced that the German radio had just come out with an announcement of the landing . . .

This group of unconquerable heroes whom I command are not in yet but we will be soon – I wish I was there now as it is a lovley sunny day for a battle, and I am fed up with just sitting.

I have no immediate idea of being killed but one can never tell and none of us can live for ever so if I should go, dont worry but set your self to do better than I have.

All men are timid on entering any fight. Whether it is the first fight or the last fight, all of us are timid. Cowards are those who let their timidity get the better of their manhood. You will never do that because of your blood lines on both sides . . .

There are apparently two types of successful soldiers. Those who get on by being unobtrusive and those who get on by being obtrusive. I am of the latter type and seem to be rare and unpopular; but it is my method. One has to choose a system and stick to it. People who are not them selves are nobody.

To be a successful soldier, you must know history. Read it objectively . . . You must read biography and especially autobiography . . .

In Sicily I decided as a result of my information, observations, and a sixth sense that I have that the enemy did not have another large scale attack in his system. I bet my shirt on that and I was right . . .

What success I have had results from the fact that I have always been certain that my military reactions were correct. Many people do not agree with me; they are wrong. The unerring jury of history written long after both of us are dead will prove me correct . . .

The intensity of your desire to acquire any special ability depends on character, on ambition. I think that your decision to study this summer instead of enjoying your self shows that you have character and ambition – they are wonderful possessions.

Soldiers, all men in fact, are natural hero worshipers. Officers with a flare for command realize this and emphasize in their conduct, dress, and deportment the qualities they seek to produce in their men . . .

The troops I have commanded have always been well dressed, been smart saluters, been prompt and bold in action because I have personally set the example . . . The influence one man can have on thousands is a never ending source of wonder to me . . .

Well this has been quite a sermon but dont get the idea that it is my swan song, because it is not. I have not finished my job yet.

*Letter, GSP, Jr., to Beatrice, June 6, 1944*

Ike broadcast to occupied Europe and did it well.

None of the troops of this Army are in yet and in fact I doubt if the enemy knows of its existence. We will try to give him quite a surprise . . .

I can't tell when I will go in . . . However I have had my bag packed for some time just in case.

It is Hell to be on the side lines and see all the glory eluding me, but I guess there will be enough for all . . .

I guess I will read the Bible.

CHAPTER 26

# The Invasion

*"Have been wearing my shoulder holster ever since D Day so as to get myself into the spirit of the part."*

*Diary, June 6*

I have horrible feelings that the fighting will be over before I get in, but know this is not so, as destiny means me to be in . . .

I started to pack up my clothes a little bit, always hoping, I suppose, that someone will get killed and I will have to go.

*Diary, June 7*

Began to pack seriously . . . Time certainly drags.

*Letter, GSP, Jr., to Beatrice, June 7, 1944*

This is the longest day I have ever spent as we are doing nothing but waiting . . .

Things seem to be going fine in Normandy . . . We hope to move nearer the area in about a week but I could move in ten minutes if I had the chance.

*Diary, June 8*

Facts [from France] are very meager . . . Apparently things are not going too well and one gets the impression that people are satisfied to be holding on, rather than advancing.

*Diary, June 9*

Time drags terribly.

*Letter, GSP, Jr., to Beatrice, June 9, 1944*

I feel like a slacker . . . when I am sitting at Peover just waiting. But it may all be for the best. My only fear, and it is a groundless one, is that the war may end before I get in.

I just got about 15 letters from my unknown fans condoling with me over not being promoted. One d.f. [damn fool] wants to run me for president. I hope he keeps his ideas to him self.

As a matter of fact I am amazed at the fact that after nearly ten months of inaction I am still remembered.

*Letter, Summerall to Mrs. Patton, June 9, 1944*

He is a general in the hearts of his soldiers and will be the leading figure in history by virtue of his own superiority . . . I would have wished for him an independent command in the south of France, but he will dominate wherever he is. The men will resent the treatment he has received and will fight for him all the harder . . . He stands alone in all the world in knowledge, ability, and leadership.

*Letter, GSP, Jr., to Beatrice, June 10, 1944*

I have a truck to sleep in. It is quite swell — like the cabin of a cruiser only you can stand up. There is a bed with an air mattress, a wash stand, clothes closet, desk, map board, heater, and 110 volt electric circuit with a built-in radio; also a sort of canvas porch effect. The horrors of war are fast departing and the fear of booby traps has gone. It can also black out, and has a huge map board so one can work at night. It is made out of an obsolete truck body but runs well or at least well enough.

Well, I will have to go and walk five miles and run a little so as to be ready in case of need — to run after the Germans, not from them.

*Diary, June 10*

Have been wearing my shoulder holster ever since D Day so as to get myself into the spirit of the part. I suppose I am one of the few emotional soldiers who have to build up a role, but I have always hoped to be a hero, and now may be the time to attain my ambition.

Talked to the Public Relations officers of the corps and divisions and told them how important their function is. I want credit to go to the soldiers and junior officers. To this end they are to see that the [newspaper] correspondents get news of the actual front.

Accompanied by Gay and Codman, Patton presented to the rector of the church behind Peover Hall, as he had to the English Episcopal chapels in Casablanca and Palermo, an American flag and a plaque to commemorate the fact that the Third Army headquarters "enjoyed the privilege of worshipping God in this historical chapel."

*Letter, GSP, Jr., to Beatrice, June 12, 1944*

I just read in the papers that [the Germans said] I am commanding 59 divisions in France. It was a distinct shock to me. I will probably have to explain it in the morning.

*Letter, GSP, Jr., to Beatrice, June 12, 1944*

We have not moved yet. I hope they don't win the war without us.

*Letter, GSP, Jr., to Beatrice, June 14, 1944*

Still we sit and fear that the war will be over with out us.

*Letter, GSP, Jr., to Bradley, June 15, 1944*

My dear Brad: I would have written you sooner to congratulate you on the really great success of your landing in France, but I knew that you would be pretty busy.

Having had a little experience in landings, I believe that my acclaim will have some weight with you when I say that I cannot conceive how you could have done better.

With all good wishes for your continued success, I am, Devotedly yours,

*Letter, GSP, Jr., to Beatrice, June 17, 1944*

Night before last Lady Leese took me to the theater in Manchester and at the curtain call Leslie Henson, the leading man, said he had played in Africa before the Eighth Army and that the wife of its general was in the audience. Every one clapped. Then he said that with her was the most famous American general, a man noted for blood and I will not say guts in front of ladies. Then every one cheered and yelled for a long time. After the show we went back stage and when we came out there was a huge crowd around the car and we had quite an ovation. I had a hell of a time keeping it out of the papers.

Hearing news, somewhat inaccurate, that Collins had relieved several division commanders, Patton commented:

I doubt either the expediency or justice of such wholesale beheadings [reliefs]. It creates fear and lack of self-confidence.

*Letter, GSP, Jr., to son George, June 17, 1944*

Your letter . . . found me reading about the Philipine war of

1899–1903 instead of fighting in this one. I feel like a slacker but it is all according to plan so I have to possess my soul in patience.

*Letter, GSP, Jr., to Beatrice, June 20, 1944*

Still on the side lines – still as planned – but it is an awful bore . . .

The pilotless planes [over London] are quite a nusance. I saw one and heard a lot . . . The planes sound just like a regular plane with a bad cold and look like a Spitfire only smaller. About ten seconds before they hit, the racket quits and the the explosion comes.

I think they have only nusance value . . .

I can't tell you how I hate this sitting around.

*Letter, GSP, Jr., to Beatrice, June 24, 1944*

I am sorry you worried about my being on the beaches – sorry for two reasons, first because I was not there, and second because so many people think I was . . .

Gay is over the water looking things over and picking a place for our camp . . .

Some times I wonder if I am as good as people, including me, think. I know my defects but don't know those of others and of course I have had great luck, never forgotten you as the greatest.

*Diary, June 26*

Drove to Exeter and met Ike . . . We drove all over Cornwall, stopping to inspect units . . .

Ike made an inspection by walking through the ranks and talking briefly to numerous men. He tries to find points of common interest with them and is clever at it. Then he gets the loud speaker and tells the soldiers to fall out and gather around. He talks very familiarly to them, but uses I, mine, and me too much, usually exhorting them to fight well, "So that we can end this war and I can go home and go fishing." . . The men seem to like it and usually clap and cheer a little. It is the style of an office seeker rather than that of a soldier. Two movie and two still photographers accompany him and take shots of his conversation and get the names of the men he is talking to. I presume these are later sent to the home town of that person, which, I think has a very good effect. His theory is that by this method one gets on a level with the men. A commander cannot command and be on the same level. At least that is my opinion. I try to arouse fighting emotion — he tries [for] votes — for what? However he was very plesant [to me].

*Letter, GSP, Jr., to Beatrice, June 27, 1944*

We are leaving home for a place further south . . . The idea is to get people more mobile and accustomed to tents.

*Diary, June 29*

Took my extra clothes to the Stockdales.

He made no mention of it in his diary, for he was excited by his imminent departure for France; yet he — as well as most of his men — must have felt a tug of sorrow over the thought of leaving the good friends, the lovely people of Knutsford, who had been so kind to the Americans stationed in the neighborhood.

According to Renee Stockdale, who wrote to Beatrice later, Patton — "(also Willie!!)" — had spent many evenings at her home. The door was always unlocked, and Patton knew he was welcome. Many evenings when she returned from her war job, she found Patton and her husband talking over cigars and Scotch and soda, with Willie on the rug in front of the fire.

*Letter, GSP, Jr., to Beatrice, June 29, 1944*

Still no war but we have moved our advanced C.P. south of Salisbury . . . The move has no meaning except that it puts us closer to the center of things . . .

I wish I was fighting.

On June 30, he took off in a B-26 for Breamore House, Hampshire. He dropped a blackout cover on his toe and

will probably lose the nail. Fortunately, Sgt. Meeks' feet are bigger than mine by several sizes, so I am wearing one of his boots, which keeps the pressure off my toe.

Eisenhower gave him "Superior" on his efficiency report and judged him to be, among 26 lieutenant generals that Eisenhower personally knew, Number 2 as an Army commander and Number 8 in a more general rating. He was, according to Eisenhower, "a brilliant fighter and leader, impulsive and quick tempered, likely to speak in public in an ill-considered fashion."

*Diary, July 2*

We were called up over the telephone this morning from the BUCO [Build Up Command Office] Headquarters stating that we leave for France on the 5th . . .

Wrote a paper, which Hughes will get to Ike, showing the striking similarity between the Schlieffen Plan [the opening German attack in World War I] and the situation we now occupy in Normandy. All we have to do is to change the pivot from Alsace to Caen, and you have it. By landing at Morlaix with two infantry and one armored division, we can make a rear attack on the Germans confronting the First U.S. Army, and then driving on to the line Alencon-Argentan, and thereafter on Evreux or Chartres, depending on circumstances, we will really pull a coup.

Patton was, of course, following developments in Normandy closely, and his perception of how to execute a smaller Schlieffen Plan by pivoting on Caen was remarkably intuitive. This was quite close to what would happen in August.

As for a landing at Morlaix, Eisenhower gave it careful consideration during the first two weeks in July. Even though it promised to loosen up the Continental operations, he eventually rejected the amphibious idea – it was too dangerous and would be a sideshow. Besides – and this was what ultimately decided Eisenhower – Bradley would soon come up with an interesting idea, an operation called Cobra.

*Diary, July 2*

On the other hand, if we play safe and keep on attacking with articulated [or phase] lines driving to the south [in the Cotentin], we will die of old age before we finish.

This too was a remarkable prediction of what would in fact take place. It would be better, he thought, to put

one or two armored divisions abreast and going straight down the road [toward Avranches], covering the leading elements with air bursts. I am sure that such a method, while probably expensive in tanks, due primarily to mines, would insure our breaking through to Avranches from our present position in not more than two days. This plan would have the advantage of not requiring setting up an amphibious operation [at Morlaix]. On the other hand, it is so bold that it would never be approved.

But it would indeed be approved, mainly because Patton would by then be in France and on hand to direct it.

The Allied invasion forces had, in the preceding three weeks, brought more than a million men across the Channel. They established a firm beachhead and pushed inland. Bradley's First Army was operating in the hedgerows of the Cotentin and in the bocage country around Caumont, difficult ground for offensive operations. Dempsey's Second British Army was in the Caen area.

The invasion seemed to have bogged down. It was difficult to start moving into the interior. Although Bradley's men had captured Cherbourg and were about to attack south toward Avranches, the hedgerows promised a bitter campaign that would be measured in yards. For the Germans would take advantage not only of the small fields delimited by hedgerows but also of the marshy terrain that created definite corridors of advance easy to block.

Montgomery had failed to take Caen, although he had said he would seize the town on D-day, and the relatively flat terrain to the southeast around Falaise and Argentan, the direct path to Paris and the space toward which the airmen and logisticians looked with longing, seemed a distant objective.

On July 3, Bradley opened the grinding, agonizing battle of the hedgerows, which would last two weeks and result in relatively small gains at a cost of 40,000 casualties. On July 7, Montgomery used heavy bombers in a tactical role — in close support of his ground troops — and captured half of Caen.

*Diary, July 3*

I am in . . . what is supposed to be the finest Elizabethan House in England. It is really very fine, but what people did with such enormous places, I do not know . . . There are 75 officers and about the same number of soldiers in the house, and it is not crowded, or at least not very crowded.

However, we will not have to bother with it much longer as we have some very good news and are waterproofing our vehicles at the moment.

It is funny that I have never had any doubts about licking the Germans any place I meet them. The only question in my mind is being able to survive the lapses between campaigns when I always seem to get myself in trouble.

On July 4, part of the Third Army headquarters moved to the embarkation area and started loading aboard LSTs and transports for the trip to the Continent.

*Letter, GSP, Jr., to Beatrice, July 4, 1944*

They let a lot of blood out of my toe this morning so it feels a lot better . . .

There has been a great change in the attitude of the soldiers. They realy want to fight at last.

*Diary, July 5*

Went to see Ike at 1500. He was just back from France and seemed cheerful, but a little fed up with Monty's lack of drive. He is swinging over [thinking more and more] to take personal command of the fighting, but is still temporizing. He cannot bring himself to take the plunge.

His current plan is [eventually] for four American Armies, with one small American Army for Montgomery, as the British have reached their limit of 14 divisions; Bradley to have three large American Armies with me on the southern flank. Why an American Army has to go with Montgomery, I do not see, except to save the face of the little monkey.

Since Patton would soon go to the Continent, where the Germans were bound to learn of his presence, the Fortitude cover plan would be compromised. To keep the German Fifteenth Army pinned down in the Pas de Calais and awaiting what they thought would be the main Allied invasion under Patton, Eisenhower planned to continue the 1st Army Group headquarters in existence in England as a fictitious organization. He asked Marshall to send him a well-known senior officer, like De Witt or McNair, to replace Patton in his mythical role in order to maintain the deception.

Bradley's real Army Group headquarters, now renamed the 12th Army Group, was moving to France.

*Letter, GSP, Jr., to Beatrice, July 6, 1944*

Exactly one year ago, July 6, 1943, we left Alger for Sicily. To day history repeats its self. I hope the results will be as good and be more free of incidents . . .

I don't believe that I will be doing any thing very exciting for some time as P. [Wood] and Bob Grow are not yet over, but I shall be glad to be out of here and one stage nearer the war.

My toe is much better though I still have to wear George's boots.

At 10:25 A.M., July 6, he departed England in a flight of three C-47's, each carrying a jeep, and four P-47's as escort.

His first glimpse of France, which he could barely see through the haze, was Cherbourg, where he and Beatrice had been in 1913.

Flying down the eastern side of the Cotentin peninsula, he landed, an hour after takeoff, at an airstrip near Omaha Beach.

He was exceptionally happy to be in a combat area again.

# V

# France

*"To hell with compromises."*

CHAPTER 27

# The Cotentin and Cobra

*"All that is necessary now is to take chances."*

AT THE AIRSTRIP near Omaha Beach where Patton landed,

> a great many people seemed to know me and wanted to take photographs, mostly soldiers with $5.00 Leicas, but there were some professionals present whom I warned off by assuring them I was still a secret.

News of his arrival in France spread like wildfire, and Army and Navy personnel rushed to see him. He was wearing a single pistol, no brightly polished boots, no gold helmet, no Buck Rogers uniform. When his jeep was ready, he entered the vehicle, remained standing, and delivered a short, impromptu speech to quite a few men who had gathered:

> I'm proud to be here to fight beside you. Now let's cut the guts out of those Krauts and get the hell on to Berlin. And when we get to Berlin, I am going to personally shoot that paper-hanging goddammed son of a bitch just like I would a snake.

The troops cheered.

He drove along the beaches for several miles and saw the effects of the storm that had struck in the latter days of June and destroyed one of the two prefabricated harbors towed across the Channel. There was a "tremendous pile of shipping," impressive and appalling, the "terrible sight" of "hundreds of wrecked ships," that would "certainly have shocked all honest and God-fearing taxpayers in America or England."

Also impressive was the "character of the defensive works." Some very strong pillboxes "had been taken by American infantry" – which "proves that good American troops can capture anything and that no beach can be defended if seriously attacked."

This, he was sure, was due in large measure to

> the psychological effect of concrete defenses on the defenders. If a man gets inside a concrete pillbox, ten feet thick, his first reaction is that: "The enemy must be very strong or I wouldn't have to hide." And when the line he is defending is pierced, he immediately has a creeping feeling in his spine, knowing that he is surrounded and not knowing from where an attack is coming. He must feel very much like a turtle who has been picked up on the road by small boys; and like the turtle, he is very apt to experience a fire on his back, but from a flamethrower rather than from matches.

Patton and his party drove to Bradley's headquarters south of Isigny. He was glad to find it well forward, "within 7,000 yards of the front line."

"Bradley could not have been more polite, and we had a long talk until supper." Collins of the VII Corps

> came in and showed his plans for an attack in the morning . . . It struck me as a well worked out plan, but I feel that Collins does go too far in telling divisions where to put their battalions. I told him this, but he does not agree. Bradley is required by [Montgomery's] 21 Army Group to show the positions of each battalion each day. He feels, as I do, that this is stupid.

The advance elements of the Third Army headquarters debarked and were moving into a bivouac area at Nehou, near Valognes and Cherbourg.

Patton spent the night with Bradley. It was

> extremely noisy, possibly I had forgotten about war. In any case the tent shook practically all night from the discharge of our corps and Army guns, whose firing positions were all around us.

He later told Beatrice: "Willie did not like it at all and went out of the tent several times to have a look. As a matter of fact, so did I."

At St. Sauveur le Vicomte he saw

> a sad sight, an old feudal chateau, a very large one [which] had been

nearly flattened by bombs. Too bad . . . It was a good example of a feudal defensive building.

He was in the Cotentin, sometimes called the Cherbourg peninsula, a region of vast marshy meadows, lush vegetation, tiny fields, and hedgerows everywhere.

*Diary, July 7*

I had lunch with Bradley, Montgomery, and DeGuingand. After lunch, Montgomery, Bradley, and I went to the war tent. Here Montgomery went to great length explaining why the British had done nothing. Caen was their D day objective, and they have not taken it yet.

He tried to get Bradley to state that the Third Army would not become operational until the VIII Corps had taken Avranches. Bradley refused to bite because he is using me as a means of getting out from under the 21 Army Group. I hope he succeeds.

Avranches seemed terribly distant.

According to Bradley, I will clear the Brest Peninsula with one corps and then be on the outer southern flank in the advance to the east, with most of the [Third] Army . . . He says ten infantry divisions. I doubt if I get that much . . .

Collins and Bradley are too prone to cut off heads. This will make division commanders lose their confidence. A man should not be damned for an initial failure with a new division. Had I done this with Eddy of the 9th Division in Africa, the army would have lost a potential corps commander . . . I shall be more conservative in the removal of officers and have told the corps commanders so orally.

*Letter, GSP, Jr., to Beatrice, July 8, 1944*

The whole country looks very normal and quite prosperous, lots of cattle, chickens, horses, and ducks. All the fields are cultivated . . .

The sleeping truck is realy too comfortable. I fear I will get soft.

You need not get worried about me yet, but when I do start, I will, if current plans hold, have a swell chance . . .

If you guess where I am, keep it dark as I am supposed to be some where else.

His toe hurt, and he thought it might be infected.

*Diary, July 10*

It was infected, so I had the nail pulled off after breakfast . . . It hurt like hell. I can't wear a shoe yet.

*Letter, GSP, Jr., to Beatrice, July 10, 1944*

Sunday I went to a field mass. It was quite impressive. All the men with rifles and helmets, the alter the back of a jeep. Planes on combat missions flying over and the sound of the guns all the while . . .

There is nothing to do at the moment but be a secret weapon.

Since McNair was about to arrive in London to take Patton's place at the head of the fictitious 1st U.S. Army Group, Eisenhower was preparing to leak a story to German intelligence — that Patton had lost that high command because of "displeasure at some of his indiscretions" and was now "reduced to Army command," and that the main invasion to be launched by McNair's nonexistent Army Group had been delayed by the Channel storm.

*Diary, July 11*

Stayed in the truck all day resting my toe.

*Letter, GSP, Jr., to Beatrice, July 12, 1944*

My toe is much better and I can wear a shoe.

As there is nothing I can talk about, I drew you . . . plans of the truck . . . It is quite roomy and has lots of storage space.

*Diary, July 12*

Neither Ike or Brad has the stuff. Ike is bound hand and foot by the British and does not know it. Poor fool. We actually have no Supreme Commander — no one who can take hold and say that this shall be done and that shall not be done. It is a very unfortunate situation to which I see no solution.

Toe nearly well. No pain.

*Letter, GSP, Jr., to Beatrice, July 13, 1944*

Teddy R[oosevelt] died in his sleep last night. He had made three landings with the leading wave — such is fate. I am going to the funeral tomorrow night. He was one of the bravest men I ever knew.

*Diary, July 13*

Saw hundreds of men of the First Army doing nothing. I issued orders that we keep a close check on our men and see that they are gainfully employed.

Visited the chateau at Bricquebec near here. It . . . is alleged to have originally belonged to one of Julius Caesar's officers. The tower is a transition between a square keep and a round keep, having 11 sides.

*Letter, Beatrice to GSP, Jr., July 14, 1944*

Darling Georgie, Night before last I went to Chilly's to dinner, and as I entered the room three people came up to me and cried: "He's on the way – we just heard it on N.B.C., who says that Patton's army is invading."

I listened [to the news] at 11, then at 12, and heard the same thing, without giving any location, simply quoted as a German rumor – since then, nothing. Can you imagine? I don't remember much about the dinner.

*Diary, July 14*

Went to Teddy Roosevelt's funeral at 2100. Bradley, Hodges, Collins, Barton, Huebner, and I were pall bearers. All the photographers tried to take me so I got in the rear rank.

The funeral, which should have been impressive, was a flop. Instead of the regular funeral service, two preachers of uncertain denomination made orations which they concealed under the form of prayers. The guard of honor was held far back and in column instead of in line. Towards the end of the service, our antiaircraft guns near Coutances opened on some German planes and gave an appropriate requiem to the funeral of a really gallant man.

Brad says he will put me in as soon as he can. He could do it now with much benefit to himself, if he had any backbone. Of course, Monty does not want me as he fears I will steal the show, which I will.

Bradley asked me if I objected to the 4th Armored going in on a defensive sector. I favor it – the sooner we get troops blooded the better.

The reason why Bradley asked — and it was a courtesy to Patton — was that American armored doctrine stressed the use of tanks in an offensive role, not in a defensive and static situation. Patton was right about blooding Wood's division. When it went into offensive action, it would perform brilliantly.

Sometimes I get desperate over the future. Bradley and Hodges are such nothings. Their one virtue is that they get along by doing nothing. I could break through [the enemy defenses] in three days if I commanded. They try to push all along the front and have no power anywhere. All that is necessary now is to take chances by leading with armored divisions and covering their advance with air bursts. Such an attack would have to be made on a narrow sector, whereas at present we are trying to attack all along the line. I keep worrying for fear the war will be over before I get a chance to fight.

*Letter, GSP, Jr., to Beatrice, July 15, 1944*

Paddy [Flint] is clearly nuts but fights well . . .

Hap [Gay] is not a world beater but much better than many Lt Gens and far more loyal . . .

Willie is crazy about me and almost has a fit when I come back to camp. He snores too and is company at night? . . .

Some times I think that I will go mad waiting when I know I could do a better job.

*Diary, July 16*

Half of July gone and no progress, but only casualties. The British are doing nothing in a big way, not even holding the German divisions in front of them, as two have left their front and come to ours.

On the morning of July 17, Patton drove to Cherbourg to meet Secretary Stimson who arrived accompanied by Lee, Surles, and Mr. Harvey Bundy. Stimson "told me not to criticize anyone, but let my actions speak for me."

Spending most of the day with Stimson and his party, "I let Omar do most of the talking but think that none the less it was a profitable occasion."

While Patton was out, Gay heard disturbing news. The secrecy of

Bradley's Cobra plan, which was being prepared, seemed to have been compromised. Devised to punch a hole in the enemy defenses by using the combined power of air and armor, Cobra was very hush-hush because it depended for success in large part on surprise.

William Kean, Bradley's chief of staff, telephoned to tell Gay that the newspaper correspondents assigned to First Army had complained that they had never even heard of Cobra while the reporters at Third Army appeared to know all about it.

Gay discovered that the Third Army Public Relations Officer, despite explicit instructions, had violated orders and had briefed some of the journalists, who had apparently informed some of their colleagues at First Army.

According to Patton's diary,

> On Sunday, after the usual staff conference, we had dismissed all officers and enlisted men except the heads of the staff sections and then had Colonel Maddox explain Cobra. Gay warned all present that this was Top Secret and not to be discussed. At the close, I said, "Nothing of this is to be discussed outside this tent. You are not to mention this even to other members of your sections."

Thus, the revelation was doubly serious, and when Patton returned to his headquarters at 9:30, Bradley called up and "was quite upset and so was I, as this is a very dangerous breach of security." How his Public Relations Officer could have told the journalists "after such a warning is beyond me. He will have to be relieved and probably tried."

It was 10 P.M., but Patton immediately went

> to the correspondents' camp and called them all together and told them how dangerous this slip was, and that they had violated my trust in them by divulging the fact that they had been briefed to the other correspondents who were stationed with the First Army.

According to stenographic notes, Patton said:

> I don't know whether I am more shocked or disgusted at what has happened. The transmittal to you of information on a very secret operation was a violation of orders. This is a military offense, but an offense also adheres to you because having been informed of

secret information and told that it was secret, you have violated the trust reposed in you, because within twelve hours of the time you were told, other correspondents knew that you had been so informed.

I haven't got words to express the danger which this violation of orders and of trust may have on the lives of soldiers . . .

The evil has been done, but the evil must go no further. None of you must . . . mention this thing again. I want you all to understand that. I am not threatening because it is not necessary – it is foolish to threaten – but as patriotic citizens . . . you must realize the terrible crime which has been committed.

We have tried in this Army to keep the correspondents informed. We have done it on the assumption that you would respect the trust and confidence reposed in you, yet in this case you blabbed.

The only charitable view I can take is that some of you do not realize your tremendous responsibility . . . I shall continue to trust you, but you must realize that you must not – I repeat – not, never, never, never talk about anything that you are told unless it is specifically told you that you can mention it. The information you get is for coloring, for background.

Is there anybody here who does not understand what I have just said?

All signified their understanding, a group of nearly 40 correspondents. Patton concluded the meeting by saying:

Nothing like this can ever happen again if we are to carry on. If anybody asks you whether you have been briefed on the operation, you must stand mute. I am trusting you, gentlemen.

In his diary Patton wrote: "I do not think they divulged the plan to the other correspondents, but like little boys boasted that they knew something."

On the following day he called the Public Relations Officer in

and asked him why he had told the correspondents about Operation Cobra. Apparently he did it from dumbness and from a misplaced sence of loyalty to me. I think he is honest but stupid. It would be unfortunate if I have to try him, but I may be forced to do so by

Bradley. But I will have to relieve him — I will not do it until Cobra is over, as it might cause a leak if I did it now.

*Letter, GSP, Jr., to Beatrice, July 18, 1944*

I am still waiting but it cant last for ever, and I have a lot of time in which to think . . .

There is nothing else I can write except that Bob Grow has come and so has P. [Wood]. The clans are gathering.

Cook, the XII Corps commander, was forwarding the final Third Army units from England to France and "doing a good job."

On July 20, in East Prussia at Hitler's command post near Rastenberg, Colonel Count von Stauffenberg, member of a small conspiratorial group of military officers, left a bomb in a briefcase under the table where Hitler was conferring. The blast killed several staff officers but only injured the Fuehrer, whose escape from death was regarded as miraculous. The putsch — to do away with Hitler and make peace with the Western Allies — failed. Hitler gathered even more firmly into his own hands the control and direction of civilian and military affairs in Germany. The war continued.

News of the attempted assassination was quickly picked up and disseminated in the Allied camp. It must have brought a shuddering wave of terror to Patton. Was Germany at the point of collapse? Would the war last long enough for him to get into action again?

Patton was quick to ask Stimson for the "opportunity of fighting the Japanese."

*Diary, July 22*

During the two hours trip I saluted 163 times, and people say that soldiers have a hard time saluting officers.

Put Jimmy Polk in command of the 3d Cavalry Group. He is 32 years old and seems awfully young, but I was a colonel at 31 in command of a much larger force.

To Beatrice: "Of course I was a Col. at 31, but I am sure I did not look so young as he does."

When I start, I am going to employ tanks to get the show rolling. I know it can be done if we only show guts, and select one point of attack instead of being all along the front. Fear of a flank attack is an obsession. As long as you are in depth, there is no danger, and in this congested country, you have to stay in depth.

If necessary, Gaffey and I will lead the leading companies.

*Letter, GSP, Jr., to Beatrice, July 22, 1944*

It is three weeks yesterday since I got here and still no war. But since there is nothing to do about it but look on the bright side, it may have some advantages. The troops are getting over being gun shy and other things. [They] will be better later . . .

Raining like any thing.

The rain was holding up Cobra.

*Diary, July 23*

Went to see Bradley and Hodges about operations after Cobra. Simpson was there too. Cobra . . . is really a very timid operation, but Bradley and Hodges consider themselves regular devils for having thought of it. At least it is the best operation which has been planned so far, and I hope it works.

After the Cobra operation . . . Bradley has a thought that I may utilize the XIX Corps . . . for a further advance to the southwest . . .

I am sometimes appalled at the density of human beings. I am also nauseated by the fact that Hodges and Bradley state that all human virtue depends on knowing infantry tactics. I know that no general officer and practically no colonel needs to know any tactics. The tactics belong to battalion commanders. If generals knew less tactics, they would interfere less.

A battalion of the 90th Division behaved very shamefully today . . . I talked this over with Middleton and it will be necessary to relieve the present division commander and put in [Raymond] McLain and [William G.] Weaver, as they have sufficient personality to make a go of it.

*Letter, GSP, Jr., to Beatrice, July 24, 1944*

I am awfully fed up with waiting. A year ago we started along the north coast for Messina. God what a long interlude.

Cobra, delayed for more than a week because of the rainy weather, was an effort to use heavy or strategic bombers — those normally employed to strike deep in the enemy rear — in direct and close support of the ground troops. Bradley designated a target area just south of the Periers–St. Lo road for the bombers. He hoped that a saturation or carpet bombing, as it was called, by more than 2000 aircraft attacking in waves for about two hours, would obliterate the German defenders. This would open a hole for Collins' VII Corps. Three infantry divisions were to pour through the opening and press back the sides in order to allow three mobile divisions to roll through. They would head for Coutances, on the west coast of the Cotentin, and cut off the Germans opposing the VIII Corps.

When the weather forecasters predicted a clear day for July 24, thus making it possible for aircraft to operate, the go signal was given. During the night before the scheduled bombardment, Collins pulled his men back from the Periers–St. Lo road to provide a better margin of safety against the bombs.

The planes came, but the sky was overcast. Because the pilots, navigators, and bombardiers in the initial waves had great difficulty identifying the ground features that delimited their target, Leigh-Mallory halted the bombing soon after it started. Some bombs fell north of the Periers–St. Lo road and among American soldiers, killing 25 and wounding 131.

Patton was heartsick when he learned that American soldiers had been hurt by American bombers.

To regain the ground he had given up north of the road and re-establish the front, Collins attacked after the aborted bombing. In that advance, Patton's friend Paddy Flint was killed.

*Letter, GSP, Jr., to Beatrice, July 25, 1944*

Paddy was hit in the left side of the helmet by an automatic pistol bullet . . . It must have been short range. It gouged some bone out of his head and a piece entered his brain . . . He never regained consciousness and did not suffer.

We are burying him at 10:30 tomorrow . . .

He was about at the end of his strength and would have been sent home for a rest soon. I guess it was the best end he could have had. I will write Lady [his wife] after the funeral.

A lot more will go before this show is over. Those who go as well and as bravely will be fortunate.

P. has been in several fights and has done well. He and Bob [Grow] will go in with me "if and when."

His long period of inactivity, he told Beatrice,

has been a terrible waste of brains. But things are looking up and some where between 48 hours and ten days the curtain may lift. God knows I hope it does. A big show is on at the moment but I am not in it.

The weather having improved, the bombers came again on July 25. More than 2400 planes dropped 4000 tons of high explosive, fragmentation, and napalm bombs. Several fell in error among the Americans and killed 111 men and wounded 490. Despite some disorganization among the leading units because of the casualties, Collins attacked on the heels of the bombardment. The infantrymen had great trouble moving forward. The Germans continued to resist.

"Some Germans must have survived," Patton noted in his diary. "The bombing was not a success."

Initial estimates of the effect of the bombardment were, like Patton's, pessimistic. The bombs had apparently done little to the German defenses.

That afternoon Patton was discussing plans for getting the Third Army into the battle. He proposed to enter the campaign by sending the VIII Corps to St. Malo and Brest, the XV Corps to Quiberon Bay. The Allies planned to construct a large port and supply complex at Quiberon, but the capture of other ports closer to the battlefield would later make the project unnecessary. Following the two corps initially committed to the west and southwest would be the XX Corps, which was to stop at Rennes. If additional forces were unnecessary in Brittany, the corps would head eastward toward the Seine.

On the morning of July 26, the second day of Cobra, although the German opposition seemed to be strong, Collins gambled and sent his mobile divisions forward. They discovered a hole in the German defenses. The bombing had done more good than the Americans had at first believed. Through the gap in the German front poured three divisions.

Several days later Patton flew over the battlefield in a light plane and saw where the Cobra bombs had landed. He was surprised, not at the extent of the damage but at the mildness of it. The craters were "not anywhere as great" as those in 1918.

> One of the innocent sufferers . . . was the cow. The whole countryside is covered with enormously distended cows, which will eventually be buried. Pending interment, they smell to high heaven, or at least to 300 feet high, as that was my altitude.

On July 26, Bradley phoned and asked Patton to come to dinner at 6 P.M.

> and to wear good clothes. I always do. On getting there I found that Lt. General L. J. McNair had been killed by our bombs. We buried him . . . No band. A sad ending and a useless sacrifice. He was a great friend.

Bradley, Hodges, Major General Ralph Royce, Major General Elwood Quesada, McNair's aide-de-camp, and Patton were the only ones present at the funeral.

McNair had come to the theater to perpetuate the myth that the Allies were about to make their main invasion at the Pas de Calais. Interested always in being with the combat troops — also to judge whether the training program and methods he had instituted at home were effective, he had come from London to the Cotentin to observe the Cobra attack.

*Letter, GSP, Jr., to Eisenhower, July 28, 1944*

> Bradley certainly has done a wonderful job. My only kick is that he will win the war before I get in. However, nothing can be done about that.

Operation Cobra went so well that Bradley issued new orders at noon, July 27. Instead of letting the mobile forces of the VII Corps go to Coutances and cut across the routes of advance of the VIII Corps, Bradley sent both corps down the Cotentin toward Avranches. Since the result of Cobra was a clean breakthrough of the German defenses, Bradley anticipated the relatively quick capture of Avranches, which was the doorway to Brittany.

Early that afternoon Bradley telephoned Gaffey and told him that he wished Patton to take control of the VIII Corps. Officially the Third Army would become operational four days later, at noon, August 1. Until then, Bradley wanted Patton to direct Middleton's corps unofficially and move toward the entrance into Brittany.

Gaffey immediately sent a young officer out to find Patton. He located Patton at 3:30

> at the gas dump and told me to get back to headquarters at once. I arrived at 1645 and learned that we are to take over the VIII Corps and put in the XV Corps at the left . . .
>
> I immediately visited the VIII Corps with Haislip, Gaffey, Harkins, and Hammond to arrange to take over the corps, but conducted everything very casually so as to not get people excited at the change . . .
>
> Felt much happier over the war. May get in it yet.

In the interest of continuing the cover and deception plans, Eisenhower decided to make no public announcement of Patton and his Army for the time being. "The best good luck to you," he cabled Patton. "I don't have to urge you to keep them fighting — that is one thing I know you will do."

In accordance with Patton's desire, Middleton moved Wood's 4th and Grow's 6th Armored Divisions through the infantry and to the front of the corps. In the lead and side by side, Wood and Grow drove forward. On the evening of July 28, Wood took Coutances, the objective that Middleton had been trying to get since the beginning of the month. But Coutances now had little value, and Middleton looked 30 miles beyond to Avranches.

Patton thus appeared actively on the scene when the static warfare of June and July was dissolving into the exciting and mobile warfare of what would be known as the breakout and pursuit. The beginning of that was the advance to Avranches, which lay between the See and Selune rivers. Once there, American troops would have to capture several dams on the Selune to prevent the Germans from flooding the valley; they would also have to cross the Selune near Pontaubault. That would put them into position for a plunge into Brittany.

On July 29, Patton drove through Coutances and followed in the wake of the 6th Armored Division to see how Grow was doing. On the way, he was appalled to find an infantry battalion miles behind the front digging "tomb-like slit trenches. I told them to stop it, as it was stupid to be afraid of a beaten enemy."

He caught up with the 6th Armored Division and found its advance held up by some German fire at a small stream.

> Grow was not showing any life so I built a fire under him. He was sitting on the side of the road and General Taylor, his assistant, had a large group of officers studying a map.
>
> I asked Grow what he was doing, and he said that Taylor was in charge of the advance guard and that he, personally, was doing nothing.

Grow was conforming to American doctrine – a commander told his subordinate what to do, not how. Patton accepted that, but if no results occurred in a reasonable time, something else had to be done.

> I asked him whether he had been down to look at the river, and he said, "No."
>
> So I told him that unless he did do something, he would be out of a job.
>
> I then went down and looked at the river and was not fired at, although you could see a few Germans on a hill . . . where there was a church tower or a windmill. So I directed the division to advance and cross the river. The fact that the bridge was out [destroyed] didn't matter as the river was not over a foot deep.

The division was soon rolling forward.

Patton went to church with the colored troops of a quartermaster truck battalion. The dignity of the service and the music by the choir were impressive. "The colored preacher preached the best sermon I have heard during this war."

> Bradley came up . . . at 1400 and told me his plans. They are getting more ambitious but are just what I wanted to do, as I set down the other day, so I am very happy . . . I think we can clear the Brest peninsula very fast. The thing to do is to rush them off their feet before they get set.

Speed, audacity, even recklessness were what he wanted, not meticulous advances from one set point to another. Shake up the enemy, rough him up, tear the campaign wide open. "To hell with compromises."

*GSP, Jr., Poem, July, 1944*

Absolute War

Now in war we are confronted with conditions which are strange
If we accept them we will never win.
Since by being realistic, as in mundane combats fistic
We will get a bloody nose and that's a sin.

To avoid such fell disaster; the result of fighting faster
We resort to fighting carefully and slow
We fill up terrestrial spaces with secure expensive bases
To keep our tax rate high and death rate low.

But with sadness and with sorrow we discover to our horror
That while we build the enemy gets set.
So despite our fine intentions to produce extensive pensions
We haven't licked the dirty bastard yet.

For in war just as in loving you must always keep on shoving
Or you'll never get your just reward.
For if you are dilatory in the search for lust or glory
You are up shitcreek and that's the truth, Oh! Lord.

So let us do real fighting, boring in and gouging, biting.
Let's take a chance now that we have the ball.
Let's forget those fine firm bases in the dreary shell raked spaces,
Let's shoot the works and win! yes win it all.

On the evening of July 30, a small unit of the 4th Armored Division entered Avranches and clung precariously to the town as Germans withdrawing from the Cotentin buffeted and threatened to overrun them. On the following day, Wood hurried additional elements to Avranches to make the town secure.

*Letter, GSP, Jr., to Beatrice, July 31, 1944*

I spent a gloomy evening last night arranging [Paddy Flint's papers]. It is strange how little of moment there is left to send

[home]. I got the helmet, a few letters, and a map, that's about all.

Things are realy moving this morning and so am I at long last. However you wont hear of it in the papers for a while as it is supposed to be secret . . .

P [Wood] . . . has done well. Brad has realy pulled a great show and should get credit for it.

*Diary, July 31*

I thanked the staff for their long endurance during non-employment and said I knew they would be just as good when the fighting started, and to always be audacious . . .

After supper drove to the command post of the VIII Corps . . . Middleton said he was glad to see us as he did not know what to do next and could not get hold of Bradley. His orders were to secure the line of the Selune River, which he had done, but he did not cross it. I told him that throughout history it had always been fatal not to cross a river, and that while I did not officially take over until tomorrow noon, I had actually taken over on the 28th, and therefore he was to get over now.

While we were talking about how to bridge the river at Pontaubault, a message came in saying that while the bridge had been damaged, it was still passable. This seemed to be a good omen, so I told him to get the 6th Armored Division across it. The 4th Armored Division had just captured the dams.

Wood also took the bridge at Pontaubault. There, the single road coming south from Avranches split. From there one could go west toward Brest, south toward Rennes and beyond to the Loire River, and east toward the Seine.

"On getting this news, I told Middleton to head for Brest and Rennes." Patton wanted the 6th Armored and 79th Divisions going for Brest, the 4th Armored and 8th Divisions for Rennes. "I believe that this little kick I gave him was worthwhile."

He would insert the XV Corps to head for the Seine.

The German defensive line in Normandy had been pierced, its anchor on the west coast of the Cotentin unhinged. Bradley's Operation Cobra had dislocated the Germans, and Patton was ready to exploit the victory. He was about to show the Germans — and the world — his version of blitzkrieg.

"Got to bed about 1:00 o'clock August 1st."

CHAPTER 28

# Breakout

*"The waiting was pretty bad . . . but now we are in the biggest battle I have ever fought and it is going fine except at one town we have failed to take . . . I am going there in a minute to kick some ones ass."*

*Diary, August 1*

I was very nervous all morning because it seemed impossible to get any definite news and the clock seemed to have stopped.

At noontime, the Third Army officially became operational in France.

Bradley arrived at 1500. Walker and Haislip were already here. Bradley showed us the Army boundaries. These are rather cramped so far as the Third Army is concerned, as we have to slide through a very narrow bottleneck between Avranches and St. Hilaire.

The leading elements of the 4th and 6th Armored Divisions had burst through the Avranches bottleneck and were already in Brittany and headed, respectively, to Rennes and Brest, but above Avranches all the roads were congested and everyone seemed to be on the move.

Bradley is worried about an attack west from Mortain [to Avranches]. Personally I do not give much credence to this, but by moving the 90th Division I can get it forward and also cover the exposed flank [open to Mortain]. I started this movement by truck at once.

In this case, Bradley had more intuition — or better intelligence information — than Patton.

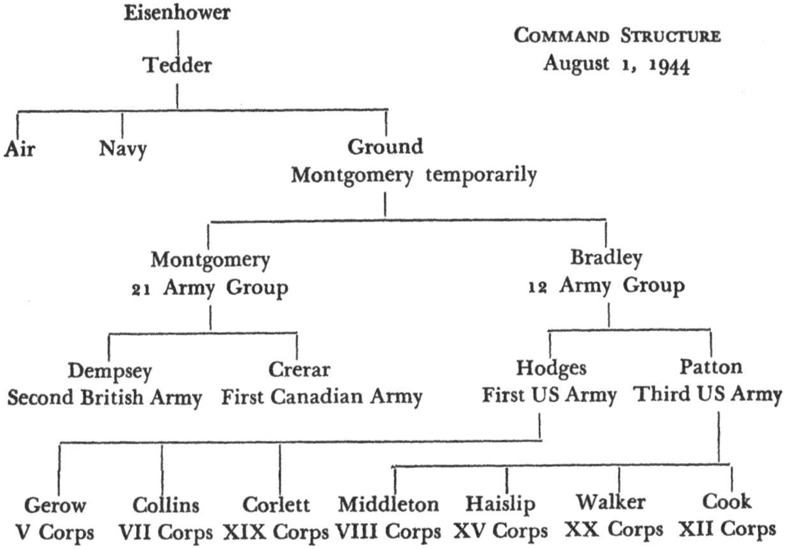


COMMAND STRUCTURE
August 1, 1944

Gaffey, Harkins, Haislip, and myself then visited the VIII Corps to coordinate the movement of the 90th Division through the rear areas. This is an operation which, at Leavenworth, would certainly give you an unsatisfactory mark, as we are cutting the 90th Division through the same town and on the same street being used by two armored and two other infantry divisions. However, there is no other way of doing it at this time.

I remained at the VIII Corps headquarters. I found that Middleton, in spite of what I had already told him, had failed to send any infantry with the 4th Armored Division but had decided to send one infantry division with the 6th Armored on Brest, and the other infantry division along the north coast behind [Brigadier General Herbert] Earnest's task force.

Middleton was concerned by a large concentration of German troops reported to be at St. Malo.

I . . . directed him to send the 8th Infantry Division behind Wood, with one regimental combat team, motorized [to follow the 4th Armored Division closely]; and to send the 79th Infantry Division behind [Grow's] 6th, similarly arranged; and to use Earnest['s Task Force A] . . . to move along the north road.

Earnest's relatively small force of about 3500 men had a special mission —

> to secure the seventeen miles of trestle on the railway in the vicinity of Morlaix, because if this piece of trestle is destroyed, the capture of Brest will have little value.

Without the railroad, the port was no good.

> I cannot make out why Middleton was so apathetic or dumb. I don't know what was the matter with him. Of course it is a little nerve-wracking to send troops straight into the middle of the enemy with front, flanks, and rear open. I had to keep repeating to myself. "Do not take counsel of your fears."
>
> Bradley simply wants a bridgehead over the Selune River. What I want and intend to get is Brest and Angers.
>
> We just had word that the 4th Armored Division is 15 kilometers north of Rennes . . .
>
> The 6th Armored Division is at Pontorson, where Beatrice and I spent a night in 1913.
>
> These truck movements of large numbers of infantry are very dangerous and might be almost fatal if the Germans should spot them [from the air], particularly if there is a traffic jam. I have all available staff officers out at critical points and have told Haislip to be personally at Avranches to see that the 90th Division gets through without a jam. I am going there myself in the morning, as I have a feeling something may happen . . .
>
> Compared to war, all [other] human activities are futile, if you like war as I do.

*Letter, Hughes to Mrs. Patton, August 2, 1944*

> I have insisted for months that George keep his shirt on. For months and months I have stood up for him and his staff against *everybody*. I have succeeded in getting George into the fight at a time when we needed fighters.
>
> I was fearful that he had been cowed by the fools who didn't realize that a fighter couldn't be a saint or a psychiatrist when the job was to kill Germans. Or cowed by those who didn't like pearl handled pistols, or fancy uniforms, or all the little idiosyncracies that are George.

And now what? All the thousands who would have torn him down will rise to cheer and shout "I told you so."

*Diary, August 2*

East of Avranches we caught up with the 90th, which is moving along the road between the See and the Selune Rivers. The division is bad, the discipline poor, the men filthy, and the officers apathetic, many of them removing their insignia and covering the markings on helmets. I saw one artillery lieutenant jump out of his peep and hide in a ditch when one plane flew over at a high altitude firing a little. I corrected these acts on the spot. I got out and walked in the column for about two miles, talking to the men. Some were getting rides on guns and the others made no comment. I called them babies and they dismounted. They seemed normal but are not in hard condition.

The 90th Division, in Eisenhower's words, had not been "well brought up," that is, not well trained in the United States and had had a particularly grueling initiation into combat in the Cotentin. But McLain and Weaver would soon turn it into a hard-hitting outfit.

I told Haislip to get the 5th Armored Division down at once and have it cross the See River east of Avranches by fording. Also to alert the 83d to follow as soon as the traffic situation permitted.

With Middleton's VIII Corps turning from Avranches westward into Brittany, Patton was starting to commit Haislip's XV Corps eastward toward the Mayenne-Laval line in anticipation of an order on the following day that would shift the bulk of the Third Army toward the Seine.

With Patton much more interested in the eastward developments, he paid little attention to Middleton.

Bradley arrived about 1600 and, with some embarrassment, stated that he had been waiting for me at the VIII Corps, and as I had not arrived there, he had taken the responsibility of telling Middleton to move the 79th Division to the east near Fougeres.

Bradley was still looking for a German counterthrust west from Mortain.

He said he knew I would concur [in his action].

I said that I would [concur], but that I did not agree with him and feared he was getting the British complex of over-caution. It is noteworthy that just about a year ago to the day I had to force him to conduct an attack in Sicily.

Patton's method was to move so rapidly that a German counterthrust would have no chance of getting started.

[Ira T.] Wyche [79th Division] was at VIII Corps headquarters, and we decided to shift him to the XV Corps and use the 83d in place of the 79th to follow the 6th Armored Division [to Brest]. I dictated the necessary orders to put these operations into effect.

*Diary, August 3*

Collins of the VII Corps is having a lot of trouble northwest of Mortain, and is also causing us trouble by using areas of this Army for his own rear echelons, particularly the road running north through Brecey.

There was actually much confusion among supply and service units of the VII and VIII Corps, caused mainly by the rapidity of the movement to Avranches and Brecey, and also by the insertion of the Third Army into the campaign. Putting the XV Corps into the battle added to the congestion.

As of 1800, things are very satisfactory. The 79th is in Fougeres; the 5th Armored . . . is between the 79th and 90th Divisions.

These three divisions formed the XV Corps, and they were headed eastward.

The 4th Armored Division has by-passed Rennes, headed on Vannes. The 6th Armored Division has passed Dinan and is being followed by one regiment of the 83d. Earnest is investing St. Malo. I did nothing.

*Letter, GSP, Jr., to Beatrice, August 3, 1944*

I was out all day yesterday but except for an air plane that straffed a little I saw nothing. I stayed in to day but will have another look in the morning. It always scares and lures me like steeplechasing.

*Diary, August 4*

Left at 1000 with Codman and Stiller. We had an L-29 armored car and a peep. I rode in the peep with Codman, and Stiller preceded us in the armored car via Avranches-Pontaubault-Pontorson-Comborg-Merdrignac.

This was a long drive to catch up with Grow's 6th Armored Division, and Patton whooped with joy every time they ran off one map and had to use the next in series.

We passed one combat command . . . and found Grow just leaving. The 6th is too careful, and so gets shot up. I told them to use more dash and keep going [all the way to Brest].

Satisfied that Grow would drive westward, Patton returned to the other front. Eisenhower had decided to swing the bulk of the Allied forces in Normandy definitely eastward toward the Seine River because of the obvious disintegration of the German defenses around Avranches. In furtherance of this concept,

Bradley wants the XV Corps . . . to attack the Mayenne River between Mayenne and Laval, direction Le Mans . . . Sent for Haislip, gave him the order, and started him.

He also began to assemble Walker's XX Corps for commitment to the campaign.

P. Wood got bull headed and turned east after passing Rennes, and we had to turn him back on his objectives, which are Vannes and Lorient, but his overenthusiasm wasted a day.

Wood wanted to go eastward too. That was where the action was, not in Brittany, which he could see was going to become a backwater of the war.

Gaffey woke me . . . to show me an order, Middleton to Wood, which gave Wood a defensive role. We changed it.

Middleton was still thinking in terms of the battle of the hedgerows in the Cotentin, meticulous advances, carefully defined boundaries, strict attention to security. It was difficult for him to adjust to the new mobile warfare in August.

*GSP, Jr., Notes on France, 1944*

This is my fourth trip to France, and each time I have been impressed with the feminine leadership. This is particularly evident even now among the little children. The girls are the leaders; the men, or little boys, simply follow in their wake. I am sure that this is a sign of decadence.

After nearly two years of being accustomed to the inarticulate shapes of the Arab women, the over-stuffed profiles of the Italians, and to the boyish figures of the British women, the obtrusive and meticulously displayed figures of the Norman and Brittan women is quite striking. In a way they remind one of a British engine with two bumpers in front and powerful driving wheels behind . . .

The road into Brittany is full of reminders of William the Conqueror and of his unwilling guest Harold, for in their campaign against Dinan they passed through Coutances where even yet the most striking cathedral I have ever seen in France stands as evidence of the uneasy conscience of William's successors.

The bridge south of Avranches undoubtedly had its predecessor in William's time, and from there the road leading to Dol and Dinan is undoubtedly the same one traversed by William and Harold, hawk on fist.

It was in the sands either south of Avranches or near Mont St. Michel that the rescue took place.

Nearly everyone of these towns has all or part of a castle, and these are more eloquent than anything else of the difference in warfare which has occurred in the last 900 years. One air bomb or salvo from our 240's would breach any castle which in those days sustained sieges measured in years . . .

In Brittany . . . the people are exactly as they were when I saw them last in 1913, except that I fail to see any old gentlemen with black sailor hats or ribbons hanging down their back. All the French people, either in Normandy or Brittany, have shown a very splendid spirit and are not feeling sorry for themselves. There is plenty of food, the only shortage being coffee and sugar. The artificial coffee is very good, tasting better than Sanka. The man who invented it may have a future after the war . . .

While thanks to our Air Force we have total air supremecy in the daytime, the Germans still come out at night and bomb us very diligently. Just what they accomplish, I do not know, but . . . on occasion their efforts are quite annoying. The motors of the German bombers are not synchronized as are ours, so you can always tell them by their throbbing hum, which has the same effect as mosquitoes. They buzz around and every once in a while you hear the coughing grunt of the bombs. On one or two occasions they came so close we could hear them whistle. There is nothing you can do about them — they either hit you or they don't, but man being a fool is prone to worry.

*Diary, August 5*

Talk over Army boundaries with Bradley and Hodges. I succeeded in getting the boundary . . . I desire as it keeps me on the outside — on the running end.

To Beatrice:

The waiting was pretty bad and lasted well after Bastile day, but now we are in the biggest battle I have ever fought and it is going fine except at one town we have failed to take . . . I am going there in a minute to kick some ones ass.

*Diary, August 6*

I went to the Headquarters VIII Corps to see what is delaying the capture of St. Malo. Apparently it is simply the fact that the people are so damn slow, mentally and physically, and lack self-confidence. Am disgusted with human frailty. However, the lambent flame of my own self-confidence burns ever brighter.

St. Malo was holding out because it was garrisoned by skillful and tenacious defenders who were more numerous than American intelligence had anticipated and who were fighting from excellent defensive positions. [Robert] Macon's 83d Division was engaged in siege warfare.

While directing this static battle, Middleton was trying to keep control of three charging commands, off, so it seemed, to the ends of the earth. Grow was on his way to Brest, and it was difficult to know where he was, what he was doing, what he was running into. Wood, driving toward Lorient, was also distant and relatively uncommunicative. Earnest had disengaged his task force from the battle at St. Malo, slipped away, and, at Patton's order, was hurrying along the north shore of Brittany to capture the vital trestle near Morlaix.

Patton, of course, was also trying to keep track of these developments in the west. In addition, he was looking after his units in the east, where Haislip's XV Corps was driving across the Mayenne River toward the LeMans-Alençon line, and where Walker's XX Corps was starting south toward Angers and the Loire River.

He wrote Kenyon Joyce that day:

> We are having one of the loveliest battles you ever saw. It is a typical cavalry action in which, to quote the words of the old story, "The soldier went out and charged in all directions at the same time, with a pistol in each hand, and a sabre in the other."

The battle was moving, and it was exciting, fast-breaking. The advances, particularly when compared with those in the Cotentin, were spectacular, dizzying.

Yet he found time on August 6 to write to his nephew Neil Ayer who had just entered West Point.

> You will catch hell [as a plebe] but . . . the best thing to do is to think about how soon it will be over and you will be an Upperclassman . . .
>
> The sure road to success at West Point, and also in life, in my opinion, is to make no excuses and to get in no arguments.
>
> When I was a Plebe, we were drilling one day and the Cadet Corporal in charge gave an order which I failed to obey, although all the other members of the squad did. He said, "Mr. Patton, why the hell didn't you do what I ordered?"
>
> I replied, "I wasn't paying attention, Sir."
>
> After that I had no more trouble but was held up as the model Plebe. That is a good tip to follow.
>
> Another good tip is never to write anything disagreeable home. They can do nothing about it except worry . . .
>
> Pay particular attention to the appearance of your clothes – see that they are pressed even if you have to sleep on them to press them.

See that they are clean, and always brace more than you are supposed to.

The people who catch hell are the people who try to get by. The ones who do their full duty are soon respected by the Upperclassmen and left alone.

Another thing, never talk to your classmates or Upperclassmen about your family. The fact that you are fortunate in coming from a wealthy family will not help you at the Military Academy, and can hurt you . . .

Stand on your own feet, which I am sure you are well capable of doing.

I should be very glad to have you drop me a line at any time.

*Letter, GSP, Jr., to Mrs. T. Taylor, Pasadena, August 6, 1944*

I should certainly consider it a great honor to be little Dick's Godfather. I am sure that he could never find a more God-fearing, God-damning Godfather than myself.

*Diary, August 7*

The bridge at Angers is intact, and as our telephone lines were blown out, I sent Gaffey . . . to pick up a combat team of the 5th Division and . . . to attack and take Angers; also directing the division to send a battalion to Nantes. I am doing this without consulting Bradley as I am sure he would think it too risky. It is slightly risky, but so is war.

We got a rumor last night from a secret source that several panzer divisions will attack west from . . . Mortain . . . on Avranches. Personally, I think it is a German bluff to cover a withdrawal, but I stopped the 80th, French 2d Armored, and 35th [Divisions] in the vicinity of St. Hilaire just in case something might happen.

This was a fine intuitive feeling. Something did happen. In the early hours of August 7, the Germans attacked with three panzer divisions, overran Mortain, and drove west toward Avranches. Fierce defensive fighting by the 30th Division and a strong Allied air effort stopped the German thrust. Because Patton had halted three divisions near the attack area in case they were needed, Bradley let him continue his sweep around the Allied right flank with Haislip's XV Corps.

Haislip took Le Mans on August 8, and Patton was thinking of sending him north to drive toward Alençon, then on Sées. This would start a gigantic encircling movement that would trap not only those German forces counterattacking from Mortain but also the bulk of the German troops in Normandy. What would eventually be known as the Argentan-Falaise pocket was taking shape.

Patton really preferred to head eastward to Chartres or Dreux before turning north, for this would be a deeper envelopment and more certain to cut off all the Germans in Normandy, "but Bradley won't let me." Even though he thought that the northward turn toward Alençon and Sées, and eventually toward Argentan, which Bradley approved, was too close in or too shallow, he was happy enough to get it started.

> Hughes and I drove to Dol to see the VIII Corps, then on to near St. Malo where the leading regiment of the 83d Division has its command post. Macon . . . is doing well . . .
>
> When Macon saw me coming with Hughes, he turned quite pale – I presume imagining that Hughes was to relieve him, so I called out, "Fine work," and he felt better. At the moment he needs more praise than blame.

> When I got back [to his headquarters] I wrote an order for the attack of the XV Corps. Hughes and Kenner said it was historic – I hope so.

This was the order sending Haislip on a 90-degree turn to the north toward Alençon.

*Letter, GSP, Jr., to Beatrice, August 8, 1944*

> This Army had a big day . . . I am quite tickled and not at all worried although I have been skating on the thin ice of self confidence for nine days.
>
> I am the only one who realizes how little the enemy can do – he is finished. We may end this in ten days.

When he had to order the destruction of a rather large city – St. Malo, "I hate to do it, but war is war. Usually I have not bombed cities."

*Letter, GSP, Jr., to Beatrice, August 9, 1944*

> We are getting on as well as in Sicily but the forces are so large – 12 divisions to me alone – that the supply system is collossal.

If I were on my own, I would take bigger chances than I am now permitted to take.

Three times I have suggested risks and been turned down and each time the risk was warranted.

*Diary, August 9*

Visited the XV Corps to see that they get going [to the north] . . . Since there is a gap, and a large one, between Mayenne and LeMans [between the First and Third Armies], we moved the 80th Division . . . into it as a precautionary measure.

On the outskirts of Brest, Grow was attacked in the rear by Germans leaving Morlaix. He turned his division around, dispersed the German movements, and captured a general, whom he sent to Patton.

Patton had him in for a talk.

I had two sentinels with fixed bayonets at my truck — usually I have more. I had one table and one chair so he had to stand. He was a good type man 58 years old and had fought well.

*Gay's Journal, August 9, 1944*

Lt. Gen. [Karl] Spang, captured near Brest was brought to the headquarters . . . Through an interpreter, Patton interviewed him as follows:

Patton: I have had the opportunity of interviewing other German generals whom I have captured, but never under circumstances so adverse to the cause of Germany.

Spang: (He saluted.)

Patton: I regret that the General, who is a professional soldier, should feel obliged to continue a useless struggle. However, I am not asking anyone to stop fighting . . . The small force of Germans in the Brittany Peninsula are opposed by an American corps of 100,000 men, and there are more than a million more Americans attacking to the east.

Spang: By orders of the Higher Command, we had to continue to fight.

Patton: As between soldiers, I have nothing but respect for your attitude.

Spang: I was personally fighting until the very last minute and had fired the last round of my pistol, but was completely surrounded by your armored wagons and had no other alternative. I didn't want to surrender, but was waiting for a round of ammunition to hit me.

Patton: I stated that I had nothing but respect, but I regret that brave men must be killed in a hopeless cause.

Spang: (He saluted.) I cannot voice a personal opinion about that.

Patton: I appreciate his feelings. You can tell the General that we will keep him here tonight and tomorrow he will be processed through normal prisoner of war channels to the States eventually.

Spang: (He saluted.)

Patton: An American officer . . . will see that he gets anything he wishes, and he will get his dinner and breakfast and be taken care of tonight – and we hope the German bombs don't get either of us.

Spang: (He saluted twice.)

*Diary, August 10*

Flew to 12th Army Group, as I am worried about the hole in our line from St. Hilaire to Mayenne, and also another gap southwest of Alencon. The people at army group headquarters did not take any interest as Bradley feels that there is no danger, but anyhow I am concentrating the 7th Armored at Fougeres just in case of trouble.

It was odd for Patton to be so conservative in his view and for Bradley to be so cavalier. Actually, the Germans were thinking of and had started planning an attack through one or the other of the two gaps. But the pressure being exerted by all the Allied armies – Crerar's First Canadian (which had become operational in the closing days of July), Dempsey's Second British, Hodges' First U.S., and Patton's Third – would prevent the Germans from launching any offensive and soon compel them to begin withdrawing from Normandy.

*Diary, August 11*

Visited XV Corps . . . I could not find LeClerc of the 2d French Armored, as he was running around the front, although I followed him further up than caution should have permitted . . .

Got home to find that Gaffey had not yet got the VIII Corps going, so we can release the 4th Armored [from Brittany]. I was quite angry.

Since Brittany had become relatively unimportant, Patton was trying to move as many units out of Brittany as he could. The 4th Armored

Division was the first one he wanted to dispatch to the more important operations oriented on the Paris-Orléans gap.

But Wood was at Lorient, holding and containing a substantial German garrison that had barricaded itself inside that fortress city. Since Grow faced a similar situation at Brest, against an even larger German force, and since the operations at St. Malo had yet to be entirely completed, Middleton felt – with Bradley's support – that no units should be withdrawn from Brittany until the business there was finished.

Meanwhile, Patton was forming in his mind possible combinations of divisions and corps he could send to the east. The planning and execution involved in these movements were enormously complicated. Each division numbered more than 15,000 men and thousands of vehicles. To get them on specific roads at appropriate times so they would not interfere with the movements of others required exceptional and ruthless scheduling and timing.

*Diary, August 12*

Decided to put the XII Corps, under Cook, southeast of the XV Corps, that is, on the right flank . . . This will permit us to retain a stranglehold on the Brest Peninsula, having two combat teams of the 6th Armored Division take over [at Lorient] from the 4th, if Bradley consents. Middleton came and I explained it to him. He was disappointed [to lose forces] but nice as usual . . .

Cook came in and we talked over his mission. He understands [what to do] . . .

Visited the Chateau Fougeres. It is one of the best, from a military point of view, that I have ever seen because the dwelling part of it was destroyed by Richelieu and people have not lived in it and improved it. It has only been taken twice until we took it, although it dates from 1100.

The XX Corps jumped off this morning.

*Editorial, "General Patton," Washington* Star, *August 12, 1944*

Ever since the invasion of Sicily, the German high command and its forces in the field have had a healthy respect for General Patton. They know a good commander when they see one and are mauled by him. The unfortunate slapping incident did not change their opinion of the man, nor did any of the intemperate criticism of him in this country. During his long absence from combat, they have been speculating a bit nervously about where he might turn up next. Now they think they have the answer. According to the Nazi news agency Transocean, they strongly suspect that he is in France commanding "the Third American Army." This news agency respectfully adds that he is "an exponent of mobile warfare."

General Eisenhower's headquarters has made no such announcement and no Allied communique has even hinted about "the Third American Army" or the whereabouts of General Patton. Nevertheless, although the Germans may be all wrong, they cannot be blamed if they suspect that something new has been added to our power in France. And since General Patton is most certainly "an exponent of mobile warfare" and since our forces are spreading and racing like a prairie fire right up to the environs of Paris, the Nazi agency's report is at least logical and may yet be confirmed as true. And if it is, all the loose things said about General Patton in the past will seem worse than childish. A great number of Americans would be happy to see this one come to pass, vindicating a man who may be short on diplomacy but whose qualities as a fighting officer are beyond dispute.

*Diary, August 13*

This morning we decided that since the XX Corps was hitting nothing, we had best send it northeast, east of Le Mans . . .

The XV Corps . . . has taken Alencon and the Sees-Argentan line and is in battle to the north. This corps could easily advance to Falaise and completely close the gap [between Argentan and Falaise and thereby encircle two German Armies], but we have been ordered to halt because the British sowed the area between with a large number of time bombs [dropped from the air]. I am sure that this halt is a great mistake, as I am certain that the British [actually the Canadians, moving fram Caen to the south] will not close on Falaise.

Three days later he added:

After I had telephonic orders to halt from Leven Allen . . . I again called him at 1215 and asked if he had any orders to permit me to advance [north beyond Argentan]. I told him . . . it was perfectly feasible to continue the operation. Allen repeated the order [from Bradley] to halt on the line and consolidate.

I believe that the order . . . emanated from the 21st Army Group, and was either due to [British] jealousy of the Americans or to utter ignorance of the situation or to a combination of the two. It is very regrettable that the XV Corps was ordered to halt, because it could have gone on to Falaise and made contact with the Canadians northwest of that point and definitely and positively closed the escape gap [through which the Germans on August 13 were starting to withdraw].

Bradley stopped the corps because it was already across the boundary separating the 21st and 12th Army Groups; Americans were operating in the British-Canadian zone. Out of consideration for coalition courtesy, Bradley halted further incursion and awaited an invitation from Montgomery to continue the advance. Under the mistaken impression that the Canadians could more easily close the pocket from the north, Montgomery made no sign for Bradley to move.

Bradley had other reasons. He was concerned about the 75-mile gap stretching between the XV Corps of the Third Army and Collins' VII Corps of the First. He felt too that the Germans, who were withdrawing from the pocket, which had yet to be closed, might stampede and overrun Patton's divisions at Argentan. As he later said, he preferred a firm shoulder at Argentan rather than a broken neck.

Restrained at Argentan, yet seeking to continue his movements, Patton had an idea of how to get into motion the deeper envelopment he had earlier suggested. He wanted to pinch off the two German Armies by sending another encircling column to the Seine River.

What he was thinking of was

getting the XX Corps moving on Dreux and the XII Corps on Chartres, the XV Corps remaining where it now is. In this formation I can turn from north to southeast without crossing columns and can shift divisions between corps at will . . .

It should be a very great success, God helping and Monty keeping hands off.

*Letter, GSP, Jr., to Beatrice, August 13, 1944*

This is better and much bigger than Sicily and so far all has gone better than I had a right to expect. L'audace, l'audace, toujours l'audace . . .

Our losses have been very light and we have killed five thousand

and captured over thirty thousand. It's a great life but very dusty.

When I eventually emerge [from the obscurity] it will be quite an explosion. I have stolen the show so far and the press is very mad that they can't write it.

Destiny is quite pleased but conceals it. Omar is fine.

A lot of bombs just fell and Willie is most unhappy. I hope they have finished [bombing] for the night.

With such interesting things happening, it is funny there is so little to say . . .

This is probably the fastest and biggest pursuit in history.

*Diary, August 14*

In exactly two weeks the Third Army has advanced farther and faster than any Army in the history of war . . .

To visit Haislip whom we found quite pepped up. I told him of my plan to move the XX Corps on Dreux and the XII Corps on Chartres.

I then flew back . . . to see Bradley and sell him the plan. He consented, and even permitted me to change it so as to move the XX Corps on Chartres, the XV Corps on Dreux, and the XII Corps on Orleans. He will also let me keep the 80th and give Middleton an infantry division from the First Army to replace the 6th Armored in Brittany.

It is really a great plan, wholly my own, and I made Bradley think he thought of it. "Oh, what a tangled web we weave when first we practice to deceive."

I am very happy and elated.

I got all the corps moving by 2030 so that if Monty tries to be careful, it will be too late.

What he did was to split Haislip's corps, leaving three divisions at Argentan and sending the other two and the corps headquarters toward Dreux. This gave him, in effect, three corps heading eastward toward the Seine River and the Paris-Orléans gap.

It was tremendously exciting. This was heady warfare fought by divisions and corps rather than by platoons, companies, and battalions as in the Cotentin. Showing an audacity bordering on the reckless, Patton was the perfect leader in exactly the right place at the right time to exploit the fast-moving and fast-changing situation.

*Diary, August 15*

Patch and the Seventh Army landed . . . [in southern France] this morning . . .

The number of cases of war-wearies (the new name for cowardice) and self-inflicted wounds have dropped materially since we got moving. People like to play on a winning team.

Leclerc of the 2d French Armored Division came in, very much excited . . . he said, among other things, that if he were not allowed to advance on Paris, he would resign. I told him in my best French that he was a baby, and I would not have division commanders tell me where they would fight, and that anyway I had left him in the most dangerous place. We parted friends.

There was every intention to let the French armored division enter Paris first. What alarmed Leclerc was that if the two American divisions of the XV Corps reached the Seine River at Mantes-Gassicourt, they would be 30 miles from the capital, much nearer than anyone else and certainly much nearer than the French at Argentan. Perhaps the march of events would dictate the entry of Americans into Paris rather than the French.

But the liberation of Paris was still in the future.

Summerall was writing to Mrs. Patton. He had just heard the news of the invasion of southern France, and he knew that Patton must be leading it. He had also learned that Senator Reynolds would now press for Patton's confirmation as permanent major general.

*Diary, August 15*

Bradley came down to see me suffering from nerves. There is a rumor, which I doubt, that there are five panzer divisions at Argentan, so Bradley wants me to halt my move to the east on the line of Chartres . . . Dreux, and Chateaudun. His motto seems to be, "In case of doubt, halt."

I am complying with the order, and by tomorrow I can probably persuade him to let me advance [farther].

I wish I were Supreme Commander.

## CHAPTER 29

# Pursuit

*"I have never given a damn what the enemy was going to do or where he was. What I have known is what I have intended to do and then have done it. By acting in this manner I have always gotten to the place he expected me to come about three days before he got there."*

THREE ESPECIALLY WELCOME PIECES of news reached Patton on August 16. The first was the capture of Châteaudun, Dreux, Chartres, and Orléans by the Third Army.

The second was his appointment to Major General, Regular Army, with date of rank from September 2, 1943.

The third was Eisenhower's public announcement that the Third Army was actively participating in the campaign and that Patton commanded it. All the achievements of the past two weeks could now be revealed in the newspapers – the marvelous breakout from the Cotentin and the subsequent pursuit of the defeated German forces, the extending right arm that had encircled the two German armies in Normandy at Argentan, the immense area of France that had been liberated, from Brest in the west more than 250 miles to the east.

Hooray, hooray, hooray! Keyes wrote him when he heard the news on the radio. The anouncement only confirmed what Keyes had felt – that Patton's Army must be responsible for the big gains.

*Letter, GSP, Jr., to Beatrice, August 16, 1944*

I supposed you had guessed it. We took Brittany, Nantes, Angers, LeMans, and Alencon and several other places still secret but just at the moment the fear of they has stopped us on what was the best run yet . . . I feel that if [I were] only unaided I could win this war. But people evolve enemy armies [out of the air] and every one ducks . . .

I visited two Evac[uation] Hospitals to day and for the first time our wounded wanted to go back and fight — on the winning team at last . . .

Well I am delighted and know that your long loving loyal confidence in me is justified.

*Letter, Harbord to GSP, Jr., August 16, 1944*

You have been patient under a good deal of misrepresentation and some adversity and you have come through as I always knew you would, and are the greatest American cavalryman of your time or any other time that I know of.

A young member of the Army headquarters was elated. He could finally tell his family how proud and lucky he was to be with Patton, "the greatest commander who ever lived."

The Reverend G. Cyril Green of Knutsford wrote to say that Patton had "changed the whole face of the war."

It was true. Patton's leverage had transformed a local breakthrough into a theater-wide triumph. He had dissolved the specter of static warfare and spread the excitement of mobile operations.

*Letter, GSP, Jr., to Stimson, August 16, 1944*

Now that I am released to the public, I can . . . write you very briefly about our operations.

It was very evident when we broke through at Avranches that the situation indicated taking calculated risks. As a matter of fact, these risks were not so great because I have — or think I have, a sixth sense as to when I think the enemy morale is shaken. It is certainly shaken now so that we could do what we did with great impunity, and the results have proved this to be a fact . . .

I have to leave now to inspect one of the corps but I could not start out without telling you on this first day which I am public property how deeply beholden I am to you for your considerate confidence in me.

*Diary, August 16*

To Chartres, which had just been taken, and met Walker at the bridge . . .

[Then to XV Corps] Haislip in the vicinity of Mantes [on the Seine River] . . .

When I returned to Third Army headquarters at 1830, Bradley called up and directed that I use the 2d French, 90th, and 80th Divisions to capture a town called Trun about halfway up in the gap [still separating the Canadians and the Americans, there to meet the Canadians and close the Argentan-Falaise pocket]. He said that Gerow of the V Corps [in the First Army] would arrive in a couple of days to take over the command of these divisions as his own corps had been pinched out.

I told him that pending the arrival of Gerow, I would make a temporary corps with Gaffey [like the Provisional Corps he had created for Keyes in Sicily].

Gaffey left [for Argentan] at 2000 with orders to attack tomorrow morning.

At 2330, Bradley called up and told me to withhold the attack [to Trun] until he, Bradley, ordered it.

I delivered this order.

Life is rather dull.

Patton could not understand the propensity to delay in the interest of orderliness. To him, it was essential to press home advantages, to keep the enemy off balance, to drive ruthlessly.

Bradley was trying to avoid a disastrous head-on collision between Canadians and Americans.

*Diary, August 17*

At 0700, Gerow called from Gaffey's headquarters north of Argentan, saying he was there with a small staff, ready to take command.

I told him that since Gaffey had arranged the attack, which might come off at any moment, Gaffey should run it and he, Gerow, could take over as the opportunity afforded.

I could not talk to Bradley on the radio as it is too dangerous, so I decided to fly up and see him.

The weather was so bad that I could not take off until 1200, arriving at headquarters 12th Army Group at 1250. Hodges was there, also under the impression that Gerow was commanding. The temporary corps [under Gaffey] . . . is attacking in conjunction with the rest of the First Army, and for this reason it is sound that Gerow should run it.

Imagining that something like this would happen, I told Gay before I left headquarters that I would call him on the radio and that if

Gerow was to take over at once, I would simply say, "Change horses."

I therefore called Gay on the phone and gave the phrase, adding that the attack should take place at once on same objectives. I doubt whether in the history of the world an attack order was ever shorter.

Gay recorded the incident as folllows. He received a phone call from 12th Army Group at 1430, and Patton came on the line.

Patton: Swap horses. Start attack. Initial objective four miles southeast of present assigned objective. When initial objective is taken, continue to original objective [Trun], thence on.

Gay: What is meant by thence on?

Patton: Another Dunkirk.

This, no doubt, was the origin of the remark attributed to Patton and later widely quoted – that in a conversation with Bradley, when he was pleading to be allowed to go beyond Argentan, he supposedly said, "Let me continue, and I'll drive the limeys into the sea."

By "another Dunkirk," he meant that if Gerow's corps reached Trun and found no Canadians there, Gerow was to continue as far as he could go.

Gay then phoned Gaffey and repeated the message. Gaffey put Gerow on, and Gay gave the message to him.

Gerow: What do you mean by swap horses?

Gay: It means you in place of Gaffey.

Gerow: Did this come from Eagle 6? [Bradley]

Gay: It came from Lucky 6 [Patton], who at that time was with Eagle 6.

Gaffey came back to the Third Army headquarters, and Gerow decided it was too late in the day to execute Gaffey's plan of attack. Gerow drew up his own plan and issued orders for the attack to start the following morning. Thus, the change in command gave the Germans 24 additional hours to extricate troops from the pocket.

To some extent this was Patton's fault. In the absence of a corps headquarters or commander at Argentan, he had asked McBride, the 80th Division commander, who was the senior officer among the three division commanders in the Argentan area, to exercise a loose sort of coordination. Had Patton sent Gaffey to Argentan immediately to take Haislip's place, Gaffey might have launched his attack to Trun 24 hours earlier than the actual jump-off.

In any event, the Canadians took Trun and the Americans Chambois and thereby closed the Argentan-Falaise pocket, where the Germans lost 50,000 troops. The considerable numbers who had escaped soon discovered they were threatened by another encirclement at the Seine River.

Haislip's corps will press the attack to secure Mantes and thereby close to the Seine ...

I will close [turn] the XX and XII Corps to the north to support this movement. We got the directive for this operation at 2210.

The XV Corps will attack in the morning.

I phoned a warning order over the radio to the XX Corps, but could not say where. However, I happened to meet Walker on the road and told him the general idea ...

I fear that Cook [XII Corps] is out of this war with bad arteries. He is a fine man and very sorry about leaving, and I am sorry to have him go ...

LeClerc cut up again today and Gaffey had to ask him categorically whether he would disobey a written order.

Leclerc, finding himself committed to attack under Gerow near Argentan, was aching to go to Paris. After the pocket was closed, Gerow's V Corps, including Leclerc's division, would be ordered to liberate the capital.

*Letter, GSP, Jr., to H. H. Arnold, August 17, 1944*

The swell job which your Air Force, particularly . . . the fighter-bombers of the XIX Tactical Air Command under General Weyland, is doing. After we got the enemy on the move, the tanks pushed him so hard he could not deploy but had to stick to the roads, and the fighter-bombers would then come down and get him. For about 250 miles I have seen the calling cards of the fighter-bombers, which are bullet marks in the pavement and burned tanks and trucks in the ditches ...

Tooey Spaatz was over here the other day and has provided me with an airplane which I deeply appreciate.

*Letter, GSP, Jr., to Marshall, August 17, 1944*

Due to the confidence reposed in me by yourself and General Eisenhower, I had the opportunity, as you know, of resuming active operations . . . Since that time we have captured about 47,000 Germans, killed some 10,000, and wounded an undetermined number. We have also been very fortunate in destroying tanks and various sorts of motor vehicles.

The cooperation between the Third Army and the XIX Tactical Air Command . . . has been the finest example of the ground and air working together that I have ever seen . . .

We are still troubled by the lack of initiative in officers, especially in the lower grades, both on the battlefield and on the march. I have seen many instances where officers were sitting in their vehicles, doing nothing, when had they been active, as they were instructed to be, and gone forward, they could have removed the temporary road block or other hindrances . . .

It is a great pleasure and privilege to work with General Bradley and General Hodges . . .

So far as I am concerned, I have made no statements or permitted any quotations, and I shall continue to follow this policy.

Again thanking you for your many acts of forebearance and confidence.

*Letter, GSP, Jr., to Maj. Gen. J. A. Crane, August 17, 1944*

I have given up wearing two pistols, at least on the outside. I now wear one on the belt and one under my arm, the latter for social purposes only. We are having a hell of a war here, out-Sicilying Sicily.

*Letter, GSP, Jr., to Beatrice, August 18, 1944*

The family [Canadians] got Falaise . . . I could have had it a week ago but modesty via destiny made me stop . . .

This Army covers so much ground that I have to fly in cubs most places. I don't like it. I feel like a clay pigeon . . .

I have no apetite. I never do when I am fighting. It is a good thing as it is hard to get exercise . . .

Courtney is realy a moron . . .

Omar is O.K. but not dashing. All that I have to do [I do] over protest. I just pushed on a lot and will be warned of over extension when the phone works. Luckily it is out for the time [being].

Omar was picked for his present job long before the slap.

*Letter, GSP, Jr., to Harbord, August 18, 1944*

The operations which the Third Army have been fortunate enough to conduct in a successful manner were largely the result of the efforts of General Bradley's Army prior to my arrival on the scene. I was simply fortunate in being able to exploit the successes he had initiated . . .

Our chief success was due to the fact that we cut the armored divisions loose and did not tie them to the infantry. However, we always kept one combat team of infantry motorized so that in the event of a serious situation, they would be available within a few hours to the armored divisions . . .

Our losses so far have been extremely small, and we have inflicted very heavy casualties on the enemy . . . His loss of materiel is something unbelievable.

I deeply appreciate the confidence which you reposed in me during the dark hours of my career and trust that I have in some measure justified this confidence.

He sent exactly the same letter to Summerall.

*Letter, GSP, Jr., to Frederick Ayer, August 18, 1944*

I have had quite a lot of fun personally . . .

We have been going so fast that our chief difficulty consists in our inability to emulate Ariadne and keep our spiderweb behind us. Our supply people, however, have really done marvels and we have always had sufficient of everything . . .

For purposes of secrecy, we are usually 48 hours ahead of where the papers say we are, because we never release our locations until the German radio has published them.

The weather has been just as good as it was for the Germans in 1940, and also for them in Poland in 1939 . . .

The part of France we are now in has suffered hardly at all except at the railroad stations where we have bombed all the tracks, but these are being repaired very rapidly.

*Diary, August 18*

In spite of the fact that I dispatched an order by armored car to the XV Corps at 2000 last night, which was an extension of the warning order sent by radio phone, the message did not reach them until 0600 today. Regardless of this fact, they jumped off and reached Mantes, meeting with small opposition . . .

I visited Cook at the hospital. His circulation is so bad that he has no feeling in his hands or legs below the elbows and knees, and his toes are turning black. It is impossible for him to walk a hundred yards. After a long conversation, in which I was very frank and honest, I told him that in justice to himself and his men, I could not retain him in command. It was a great blow to us both.

*Letter, sister Nita to GSP, Jr., August 19, 1944*

Dear Georgie: Well you are surely getting your revenge on all the slimy jealous toads who tried to do you harm. More power to you. They cannot keep a good man down and my Gosh, as I have said before, you are a natural leader of men. Papa is proud of you these days, I know, and yearning over his fair haired boy.

Time magazine had the nerve to ring up and tell me that they (of all people) had always been so sympathetic with you!!! I had to be polite but it was hard. The nerve of some magazines!!!!

That nasty Tom Trainer from the L.A. Times who is one of your correspondents dared to say when he was home and giving a speech that your men did not like you. I should be very happy if he could be made to eat his words, for never was a bigger lie!!!!

Lordy I wish I could see you going down by the Arc de Triumph in your tank. You are a modern knight in shining armour, and that is one trouble, the Toads do not like knights in shining armour, they like home town boys who sold papers on the street when the weather was cold, in other words newsmen do not LIKE GENTLEMEN.

*Diary, August 19*

I flew to Chateauneuf, then drove, via Dreux, to Mantes, and saw the Seine. I then flew to St. James, headquarters of the 12th Army Group . . .

Bradley had just returned from a visit to Monty and Ike. He now has a new plan. He thinks there are still Germans east of Argentan and in order to check up on this pocket, he wants me to move the 5th Armored Division of the XV Corps north along the west bank of the Seine to Louviers, while the XIX Corps of the First Army comes up on its left . . . The British were asked to do this but said they could not move fast enough.

This was true.

I asked if the 79th could make a bridgehead at Mantes [in other words, cross the Seine], and was given reluctant permission.

I then asked if I could take Melun-Fontainebleau and Sens. By getting these, in addition to the crossing at Mantes, the line of the Seine becomes useless to the enemy.

Bradley said it was too risky, but eventually I talked him into letting me try Monday, the 21st, if I do not receive a stop order by midnight, Sunday, the 20th.

I also asked for a plan of future operations and an inter-Army boundary, extending well to the front so I can plan supply — to the present time the boundary has always stopped at the front line.

To placate Montgomery, Eisenhower is going to put the Ninth Army between him [Montgomery] and the First Army and let them turn northeast, while the First and Third Armies go east. There is also some talk of sending the VIII Corps south over the Loire [River] at Nantes to clear up the area.

Bradley also declined to let me withdraw the 6th Armored Division from Brittany for fear of a possible [German] attack from the south [across the Loire]. In my opinion, such an attack is wholly impossible because the bridges are out, there are very few Germans [south of the Loire], and those that still exist [there] have to walk [meaning, have no transportation]. Therefore, even if they cross at the Loire, they can do no harm.

How right he was about the Germans south of the Loire would soon become apparent. About 20,000 troops stationed along the Atlantic coast south of Bordeaux started marching to the northeast to avoid the converging drives of Patton's Third Army and of Patch's Seventh Army coming up the Rhone valley. Harassed by French Forces of the Interior and by Allied aircraft, they would soon send word they were ready to surrender.

Codman flew to Vannes and brought my old friend, General Koechlin-Schwartz, French Army, of the Langres days [in World War I], up to spend the night. He said, "Had I taught 25 years ago what you are doing, I should have been put in a madhouse, but when I heard that an armored division was headed for Brest, I knew it was you."

He said that the trouble with the French army of 1940 was that for ten years they had taught, thought, and practiced defense, never attack. I reminded him that at Langres [at the staff college] he had said, "The poorer the infantry, the more artillery it needs; the American infantry needs all it can get." He was right then, and still is.

I phoned the XV Corps to attack [across the Seine as well as down the left bank] and will have the XX and XII Corps commanders in tomorrow to explain what to do.

Civil life will be mighty dull — no cheering crowds, no flowers, no private airplanes. I am convinced that the best end for an officer is the last bullet of the war. Quelle vie [What a life].

*Stiller notes, no date*

We had just finished pushing up to and against the Seine River at Mantes-Gassicourt; returned to our headquarters and on arrival were informed by the chief of staff that General B.[radley] was on his way and was "fit to be tied." He wanted to see Gen. P.[atton].

About ten minutes after our arrival, Gen. B. arrived and he immediately launched into the fact that they had had a big conference and decided that the Third Army shouldn't go beyond . . . Dreux . . . and Chartres . . . [and toward] the Seine . . . [so as to] leave an escape route . . . for the Germans in the Falaise pocket . . .

After Gen. B. had informed Gen. P. [he] was not to advance any further and that was that, Gen. P. told Gen. B. that since he was already to the Seine River, in fact had pissed in the river that morning and had just come from there, what would he want him to do — pull back . . ?

After much discussion Gen. B. told him how strong the people [Germans] were in the Falaise pocket and didn't think Gen. P. would be able to contain them, and it was his orders to leave an escape route to the east [for them].

Gen. P. asked him if he ever knew him to give up a piece of ground he had taken.

Gen. B. said, "No, but this was different."

Gen. P. said that he could and would hold it, if Gen. B. would agree.

So it was agreed that he would hold what he had, which he did, thereby closing the escape route that they had been wanting to hold open.

Gen. B. left Gen. P.'s headquarters quite cheerfully, after saying to Gen. P. — "It certainly is a pleasure to talk to someone who is sure and confident. The picture looks much different from here. But for my sake, stay put there now — don't advance any further across the river. I'll try to sell them this, but — " etc.

After Gen. B. left, I remarked to Gen. P. — "Well, you certainly charged his battery."

Gen. P. said, "I did what?"

I said, "You charged his battery. I don't think he will have any trouble starting his engine for a few days now." . . .

[Without this] crossing of the Seine . . . Montgomery might well still be sitting on his "Caen."

Stiller's recollections were somewhat jumbled, but the flavor of his description was not too far off the mark.

*Diary, August 20*

One combat team of the 79th . . . crossed the river at Mantes with little opposition.

This was the first Allied unit across the Seine.

Had in Walker of the XX Corps and Eddy [who had replaced Cook] of the XII Corps and told them to get ready to move out at daylight Monday, the XX on Melun and Montereau, and the XII on Sens. I gave them one code word, "Proset," which means "halt in place," to be used in case Bradley loses his nerve at the last moment.

I always have a funny reaction before a show like this. I think of the plan and am all for it, and then just as I give the order, I get nervous and must say to myself, "Do not take counsel of your fears," and then go ahead. It is like a steeple chase — you want to ride in it and then when the saddling bugle goes, you are scared, but when the flag drops, all is well.

*Letter, GSP, Jr., to Beatrice, August 20, 1944*

Unless I get a stop order in the next two hours, we are jumping again. On paper it looks very risky but I don't think it [really] is.

Manton Eddy who took over Doc's corps asked me when I told him his job: "How much shall I have to worry about my flank?"

I told him that depended on how nervous he was.

He has been thinking [that] a mile a day [was] good going. I told him to go fifty and he turned pale . . .

Every one in this part of the country has quit work and stand along the roads cheering, throwing kisses or apples and offering wine, all as presents. I get quite an ovation, but all soldiers get some.

It will be pretty grim after the war to drive ones self and not be cheered but one gets used to any thing.

I used to wave back but now I just smile and incline my head — very royal.

*Letter, GSP, Jr., to son George, August 21, 1944*

I believe that by now you know where I am, but if you know what I am doing, you are smarter than the Germans.

We have been having a swell time, and I trust that good fortune continues to attend our efforts.

I have used one principle in these operations . . . and this is to —

"Fill the unforgiving minute

"With sixty seconds worth of distance run."

That is the whole art of war, and when you get to be a general, remember it!

I have never given a damn what the enemy was going to do or where he was. What I have known is what I have intended to do and then have done it. By acting in this manner I have always gotten to the place he expected me to come about three days before he got there.

We are having another try this morning which is the most audacious we have yet attempted, but I am quite sure it will work. [Handwritten:] It worked! We got the bridge at Sens before he [the Germans] blew it. That is worth a week.

The great difficulty we have experienced here is that we have moved so fast and so far that we are nearly always out of communication. However . . . [the service and supply] people have done a job which will be studied for years . . .

Remember that in academics as in war the great thing is self-confidence. If you have self-confidence you have everything. Without self-confidence you have nothing.

*Diary, August 21*

We have, at this time, the greatest chance to win the war ever presented. If they will let me move on with three corps, two up and one back, on the line of Metz-Nancy-Epinal, we can be in Germany in ten days. There are plenty of roads and railroads to support the operation. It can be done with three armored and six infantry divisions . . . It is such a sure thing that I fear these blind moles don't see it.

*Letter, GSP, Jr., to Beatrice, August 21, 1944*

We jumped seventy miles to day and took Sens, Montereau, and Melun so fast the bridges were not blown. If I can keep on the way I want to go I will be quite a fellow . . .

We are going so fast that I am quite safe. My only worries are my relations not my enemies.

Well I will stop and read the Bible so asto be ready to have celestial help in my argument tomorrow to keep moving.

*Letter, Stimson to Mrs. Patton, August 21, 1944*

The attack in which he has been the commander of the leading forces bids fair to result in one of the most decisive victories the American army has ever achieved, and the daring and energy by which his work has been characterized are so dramatic that they will never be forgotten.

According to a radio broadcaster's description:

A fiction writer couldn't create him. History itself hasn't matched him. He's colorful, fabulous. He's dynamite. On a battlefield, he's a warring, roaring comet . . .

Columnists, correspondents, and troops have called him Old Blood and Guts, Hurry Up and Wait, Buck Rogers, Six Gun, Flash Gordon, the Green Hornet, the Man from Mars, Iron Pants, and that Disciplinary So and So . . .

The world knows Patton mainly as a roaring, brilliant man of battle. But General George Patton is also a devotee of Kipling, Service, and Burns. He has written two volumes of poetry . . .

Striding across a battlefield, two 45-caliber Colt revolvers strapped to his hips, or riding his tanks, with his head poking out, cased in a huge helmet, his eyes glare, and he roars encouragement, orders, advice, and oaths all at once.

As Patton has said, "You can't run an army without profanity." As his men say, "You've never lived until you have been cussed out by General Patton." Veterans of the African campaigns used to say when they heard a demolition charge explode nearby: "That's General Patton telling General Eisenhower something — in confidence."

Back in the days when Patton first started to climb in Army rank, his friends warned him to tone down his speech. As he said then: "I've got to be dignified, dammit."

The story is told that once at Fort Benning, when tanks were needed for men to train and supplies were held up, Patton bought them from Sears Roebuck on his own responsibility. And reported solemnly to Washington bigwigs that he had found "a new source of supply."

Patton understands the psychology of battle. His pep talks before and after battles are sometimes beautiful enough to be called reverent – sometimes scourging . . .

Yes, Patton will be a legend. To his men he is one of the greatest fighting generals alive.

*Diary, August 22*

Flew to 12th Army Group at 1130 to see Bradley about my plan, but found he had gone to see Eisenhower and Monty, so left my plan with Allen. It seems that Bradley has an almost identical plan, only he uses two Armies.

I told him that I feared that Middleton was through as an active commander, as he is too querulous.

Middleton was preparing to launch an all-out attack to take Brest, and he kept saying he needed more troops, more ammunition, more air support, and more time. He remembered the difficulties and hard fighting at St. Malo, and he anticipated even more at Brest. He would be right.

*Diary, August 23*

The brother of the Swedish Consul in Paris, a man named Ralph Nordling, and a group of other French individuals from Paris were in camp with a proposition. I immediately thought that this might be the asking for a surrender [on the part of Germany] . . . It turned out that these people simply wanted to get a suspension of hostilities in order to save Paris, and probably save some Germans. I sent them to Bradley.

There had been a spontaneous uprising in Paris on August 19, headed by the police, and the German commander in the city concluded an armistice with the Resistance to prevent harm to Paris and its inhabitants. In the mistaken belief that the armistice would terminate on the 23rd, Nordling and his small group traveled to the Allied forces to request that regular troops be sent to liberate Paris at once in order to prevent the

Germans from destroying the city. This spurred Eisenhower to change the Allied plans and to dispatch the 2d French Armored Division, under Gerow's V Corps, to the capital.

> [Juin] came in . . . and he was quite complimentary and said that my daring was Napoleonic. He also said that the soft place in the Siegfried Line [or West Wall, defending the German border] is through Nancy Gap. I had come to this conclusion simply by a study of the road map. It is my belief that wherever you see numbers of good roads, the going is good. I am not particularly interested in the strength of the line itself, because I believe that American troops can break any [defensive] line . . .
>
> To go east as I planned, I need two more divisions . . . so I decided to see Bradley . . . I rather hate to go east with only four divisions . . .
>
> When I got to Laval, Bradley was waiting for me on his way to see Ike and Monty. He was quite worried, as he feels that Ike won't go against Monty and that the American Armies will have to turn north in whole or in part [to support Montgomery] . . . Bradley was madder than I have ever seen him and wondered aloud "what the Supreme Commander amounted to." . . .
>
> It occurred to me that we must go north [rather than east]. The XX Corps from Melun and Montereau and the XII Corps from Sens can do it faster than anyone else. By heading on Beauvais . . . [the XV Corps can] cross at Mantes and paralleling the Seine, open that river to the British and Canadians, and have our supplies come across at Mantes, thereby reducing the present [supply] haul by 50%.
>
> This is the best strategical idea I have ever had. I sold it to Allen. If Bradley approves, he has only to wire me, "Plan A," by 1000 tomorrow. If I do not hear anything by that time, I shall then move east as already decided in "Plan B." I am having the staff put both plans in concrete form. This may well be a momentous day.

Patton's Plan A was very much like the hook he had fashioned from Le Mans to Argentan. It projected a sweep to the north to Beauvais, which would cut off and encircle the bulk of the German troops remaining in France. The disadvantage was that it would send American divisions across the projected paths of advance of the British and Canadian Armies.

> I cannot understand why Monty keeps on asking for all four Armies [to be] in the Calais area and then [move] through Belgium, where the tanks are practically useless now [because of the numerous canals] and will be wholly useless this winter. Unfortunately, he has some way of talking Ike into his own way of thinking.
>
> I told Bradley that if he, Hodges, and myself offered to resign unless we went east, Ike would have to yield, but Bradley would not agree and said we owed it to the troops to hold on, because if we left, the pickings [other jobs] were poor.
>
> I think other motives activated him. I feel that in such a showdown we would win, as Ike would not dare to relieve us.

The real issue was the shape of future operations. Montgomery had opened an argument with Eisenhower on August 19, when Eisenhower decided to cross the Seine River without pause and gave Bradley permission to do so. Plans drawn before the invasion had the British and Canadian Armies going around the Ardennes region on the north while the two American Armies moved around the Ardennes on the south. Montgomery contended that the Allied thrust beyond the Seine and toward the German border should be concentrated rather than dispersed, and further, that the most important objectives lay in the north, in his zone of operations – the V-1 and V-2 rocket-missile launching sites in the Calais area, the Rhine River, which was closer to his forces than to the Americans, the Channel ports, particularly Antwerp, required to support the growing Allied establishment on the Continent. This became known as the narrow-front approach.

Eisenhower favored a broad-front advance, with all the Armies continuing to move forward in order to stretch the German defenses and, more significantly, to preserve equal glory for the Allied forces. As Supreme Allied Commander, he had to prevent the British or the Americans alone from winning the final victory. Triumph had to be shared.

Since the speed of the advance during the breakout and pursuit was making it increasingly difficult for the Communications Zone to supply the Armies across the lengthening distance from the supply dumps near the invasion beaches, Montgomery believed that some Armies should be halted so that sufficient supplies could go to the Armies operating in the most important zone.

Bradley and Patton felt that they were responsible for the swift gains in August, Bradley by Cobra, Patton by his reckless exploitation, and they saw no reason why they should be halted in favor of British-Canadian progress.

*Diary, August 24*

BBC said this morning that Patton's Third Army had taken Paris. Poetic justice. It will be refuted, but no one will pay any attention.

The announcement was premature by one day. A small contingent of Leclerc's division, now operating under Hodges' Army, would get to the Hotel de Ville in Paris at midnight, and the entire division, reinforced by the U.S. 4th, would liberate the city on the 25th. Although it made sense, given the disposition of the troop units, to have the First Army liberate Paris, Patton resented being denied the pleasure of entering the city as a conquering hero.

*Letter, GSP, Jr., to Keyes, August 24, 1944*

You would certainly like this kind of a war, and you are the only man I know with the cold nerve to do uncomplainingly the things I have been demanding, and get them done in spite of being told that it was impossible . . .

To attack with the limited forces I have now left available – since I occupy a 300 mile front [and had lost the XV Corps to Hodges] – I am taking chances, but I am convinced that the situation in the German Army warrants the taking of such risks, and I am sure that if we drive him hard enough now, we will cause the end of the war in a very few days. I may be super-optimistic, but I don't think so.

*Diary, August 25*

Bradley called and asked me to come to his headquarters at Chartres at 1100. The cathedral is not hurt and is very lovely. All the glass has been removed; it is quite light. I said a prayer for continued success.

Hodges was at Bradley's, and we got our new directive. The First Army of nine divisions will cross the Seine at Melun and Mantes, both of which places were captured and bridgeheads erected by the Third Army. He [Hodges] will then drive in the general direction of Lille. The Third Army with seven divisions . . . will advance in the direction of the line Metz-Strasbourg. The direction is part of my plan.

*Diary, August 26*

On via Nemours to beyond Montereau to the Headquarters 5th Division under Irwin. They have done a grand job and are full of pep. I complimented them and gave them some DSC's.

Then drove back via XX Corps to Melun, where we crossed the Seine on a pontoon bridge, along with elements of the 3d Armored Division, who cheered me. Thence to Headquarters 7th Armored Division. I told Sylvester very clearly that I was not satisfied with his division, either as to looks or progress, and that he had to do better at once.

I then flew to headquarters XII Corps to see Eddy on the Sens-Troyes road. While I was there P Wood, 4th Armored, called to say he was in Troyes.

The 80th Division is to be assigned to the XII Corps today, so it will be able to carry out the new movement. Eddy asked when he should move, and I told him at 0800 on the 28th. He is not used to our speed yet, so was a little surprised.

When I got to camp [back home] I found that a flock of Red Cross doughnut girls had descended on us.

Among them was Jean Gordon, his niece, a beautiful and charming young lady from Boston, with whom he had for some time had a close relationship. Beatrice had alerted her husband to Jean's presence in Europe, and he had replied on August 3: "The first I knew about Jean's being here was in your letter. We are in the middle of a battle so [I] don't meet people. So don't worry."

*Diary, August 27*

XX Corps took Nogent last evening and will continue on Reims. XII Corps is moving on Chalons via Vitry, leaving the 35th Division to cover the right flank. I am doing this [leaving the 35th] on the order of higher authority, as personally I do not believe there is anything south of the Loire.

*Letter, GSP, Jr., to son George, August 28, 1944*

We are really having a swell time and have just captured Chateau Thierry, which, while it was fought before you were born, you probably know about . . .

At the present time, my chief difficulty is not the Germans but gasoline. If they would give me enough gas, I could go anywhere I want . . .

I know how you must feel not being in the fight, because I felt the same way for almost a year myself, but just keep your shirt on and something will happen.

*Letter, GSP, Jr., to Beatrice, August 28, 1944*

We . . . will be in the big cathedral town by dark if all goes well. At the moment it is four hundred and ten miles from one flank of this Army to the other. That is the longest swath I have yet cut but it is so big that it is a little impersonal.

*Diary, August 28*

Today was the first day that I have received letters and clippings from home which appeared subsequent to the announcement of my commanding the Third Army, and I spent a very pleasant evening reading them . . .

Bradley came in at 10:30, and I had to beg like a beggar for permission to keep on to the line of the Meuse [River]. What a life.

Bradley told Patton that the emphasis in supplies would go to the First Army, which was in support of the British and Canadians who were heading toward the more important objectives. Furthermore, higher authorities had required Bradley to turn 3000 tons of supplies daily to Paris — to nourish the civilian population — and these items would, of course, be unavailable to the Third Army.

*Diary, August 29*

Went carefully over the situation. There is no real threat against us from anywhere so long as we do not let imaginary dangers worry us . . .

I told Eddy to move on Commercy in the morning, and Gay will visit Walker and have him move on Verdun.

While at XII Corps, I found that, for unknown reasons, we had not been given our share of gas — 140,000 gallons short. This may be an attempt to stop me in a backhanded manner, but I doubt it. I will go to see Bradley in the morning and straighten the thing out. The fact that we can talk only by radio link is a great drawback because the enemy can hear this if he is listening, and I do not wish him to know we are short of gasoline.

*Diary, August 30*

To Chartres . . . Bradley, Bull (Ike's G–3) and Leven Allen were all talking when I arrived. I asked to present my case for an immediate advance to the east and a rupture of the Siegfried Line before it can be manned.

Bradley was sympathetic but Bull – and I gather the rest of Ike's staff – do not concur and are letting Montgomery overpersuade Ike to go north. It is a terrible mistake, and when it comes out in the after years, it will cause much argument.

The British have put it over again. We got no gas because, to suit Monty, the First Army must get most of it, and we are also feeding the Parisians.

When I got back . . . I found that Eddy . . . had told Gaffey during my absence that if he pushed on to Commercy, he would arrive with no gas, so Gaffey told him to halt near St. Dizier. I told Gaffey to run till his engines stop and then go on, on foot. We must and will get a crossing on the Meuse. In the last war I drained 3/4 of my tanks to keep the other 1/4 going. Eddy can do the same.

It is terrible to halt, even on the Meuse. We should cross the Rhine in the vicinity of Worms, and the faster we do it, the less lives and munitions it will take. No one realizes the terrible value of the "unforgiving minute" except me. Some way I will get on yet.

*Letter, GSP, Jr., to Beatrice, August 30, 1944*

I am headed for the Meuse, which I will get . . .

I have to battle for every yard but it is not the enemy who is trying to stop me, it is "They" . . .

No one else ever tries as hard. But they are learning. Now the infantry rides the tanks, guns, any thing that moves, to get forward. It is not pretty, but it works. Look at the map! If I could only steal some gas, I could win this war. Sad to say a colored truck company did steal some for me by careful accident. Also I captured about a million gallons [of German gasoline]; it is poor gas but runs a hot engine.

We are now in our ninth CP northeast of Sens. The woods are full of nice black berries, of which I ate too many. I hope to get to Brest tomorrow to put some pep in that show. It is 420 miles away but I have secured a big plane.

Weather very bad for flying.

In his journal Gay noted the feeling around the headquarters that the diminishing supply of gasoline available was a plot to stop the Army from continuing its successful advances.

There was no plot, no conspiracy. As a matter of fact, there was not even a shortage of gasoline on the Continent. There was plenty of fuel in supply dumps near the invasion beaches and ports. The trouble was, there was no way to get enough of it forward to the leading units. The Red Ball Express, a dramatic expedient by the Communications Zone, was no real solution, for the consumption of gasoline by the trucks on their increasingly longer round trips decreased the amounts brought to the combat units. The breakout and pursuit had simply moved too fast to allow the logisticians to set up an orderly and adequate system of support.

Even Patton in his darkest moments realized this.

*Letter, GSP, Jr., to Dill, August 31, 1944*

If you hear that we have been halted, it will be for reasons other than enemy activity, for so far we have beaten him wherever we have met him, and shall continue to do so whenever permitted.

The strain on our vehicles and our supplies has, of course, been heavy, but the supply officer of this Army has done an amazing job, and we can continue to go at any time that we are wanted.

He flew to Brittany with Bradley and talked with Middleton, who had opened his attack on Brest on August 25, with more than three divisions. The garrison of 40,000 Germans was fighting from excellent fortress positions and under first-rate leadership. It would take nearly three weeks, along with hard fighting, heavy air attacks, and a high expenditure of artillery shells, to capture the city, which by then would be demolished.

Why they persisted in this siege-type warfare to take a port city which they agreed would be useless was later explained by Bradley, as recorded by Patton:

He said to me, with reference to the Brest operation, "I would not say this to anyone but you, and have given different excuses to my staff and higher echelons, but we must take Brest in order to maintain the illusion of the fact that the U.S. Army cannot be beaten." More emotion than I thought he had. I fully concur in this view. Anytime we put our hand to a job we must finish it.

Patton spent the night with Bradley. Simpson was there, and they all arranged that he and his Ninth Army would take over Brittany and the Brest operation. He would also contain the German pocket at Lorient, using the 94th Division, which had just arrived on the continent, to relieve the 6th Armored Division, which would then move east to Troyes and rejoin the Third Army when gasoline again became plentiful.

> Bradley definitely wants us [Third Army] to go east but cannot persuade Eisenhower. This is the last day that Montgomery commands the U.S. troops, for which we all thank God!

On September 1, Eisenhower, while retaining his position as Supreme Allied Commander, replaced Montgomery in command of the Allied ground forces as had been planned long before the invasion. As Army Group commander, Montgomery continued to direct the British and Canadian Armies. In order to remove any appearance of demotion for Montgomery, he was promoted to field marshal.

*Diary, September 1*

> At 0800 we heard on the radio that Ike said Monty was the greatest living soldier and is now a Field Marshal. I then flew up to the Command Post and worked on administrative papers for the rest of the day.

Where, oh where, he wondered with real heartache, was the deserved tribute to him? He was the greatest living soldier. He had transformed Bradley's local and limited breakthrough in the Cotentin into the glorious breakout and pursuit that had carried all the Allied Armies virtually to the German border. He had pulled off a great blitzkrieg. He had given color and tone and dizzying success to the campaign. He had provided the southern jaw of the pincer encircling the German Seventh Army at Argentan and again at the Seine. He had overrun a vast part of France—from Brest to Verdun, a distance of 500 miles. All this he had done in a single month.

Eisenhower was right to have kept Patton on the Overlord team. No one but Patton could have done what he did.

He must certainly have wondered whether his brilliant feat in August was the fulfillment of his destiny. Bigger, better, faster, and more spectac-

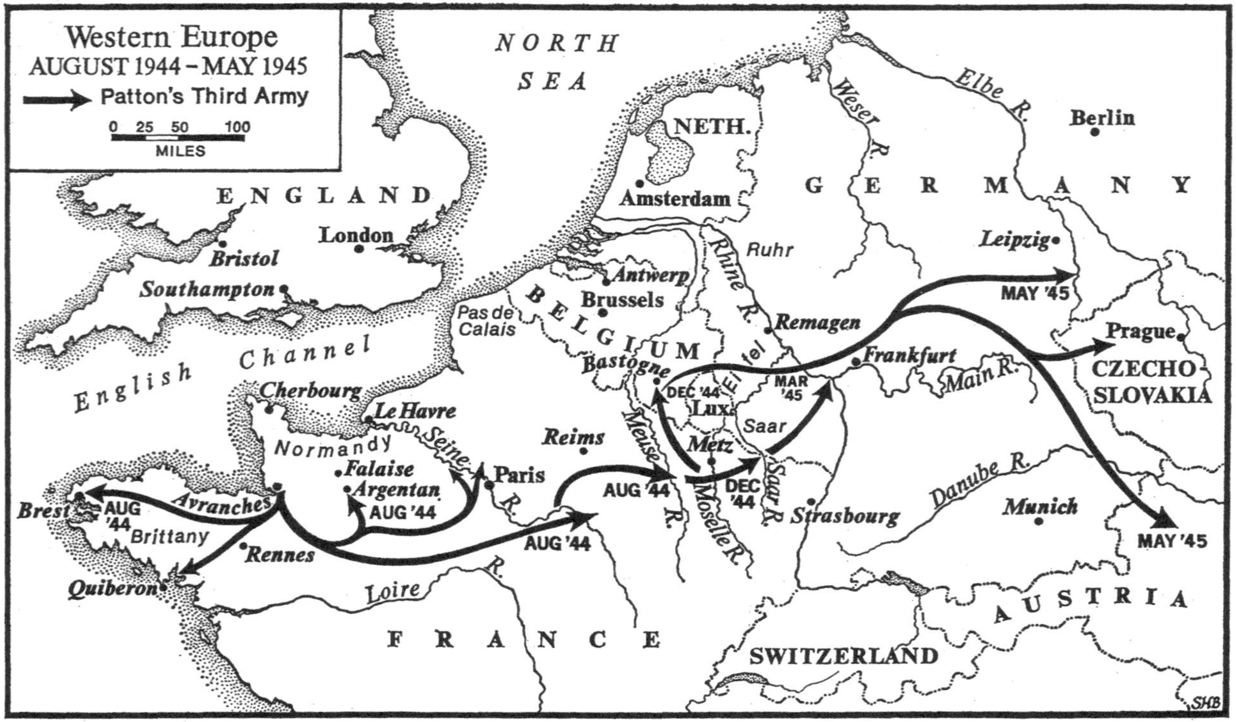
Western Europe
AUGUST 1944 – MAY 1945
Patton's Third Army
0 25 50 100
MILES
NORTH
SEA
ENGLAND
London
Bristol
Southampton
English Channel
Cherbourg
Le Havre
Normandy
Falaise
Argentan
AUG '44
Seine R.
Paris
Avranches
Brest
AUG '44
Brittany
Rennes
Quiberon
Loire R.
FRANCE
Reims
AUG '44
AUG '44
Pas de Calais
BELGIUM
Brussels
Antwerp
Bastogne
NETH.
Amsterdam
Ruhr
Rhine R.
Remagen
Eifel
DEC '44
Lux.
Metz
Meuse R.
Moselle R.
DEC '44
Saar
Saar R.
MAR '45
Strasbourg
Frankfurt
Main R.
GERMANY
Weser R.
Elbe R.
Berlin
Leipzig
MAY '45
Prague
CZECHO-SLOVAKIA
Danube R.
Munich
MAY '45
AUSTRIA
SWITZERLAND
SHB

ular than Sicily, his accomplishment in Normandy placed him squarely in the forefront of the great military leaders of all time. What else remained? How could he ever perform more spectacularly? Yet he must have decided that there was to be more. The war was not over yet. His destiny still lay ahead. There would be greater triumphs.

The press had filled its headlines with his name, and he had captivated and titillated the imagination of the world. Yet "they" were failing to award him the applause he merited; "they" were preventing him from continuing his victories. His troops had barely managed to get across the Meuse River at several places, and there his Army ran out of gasoline, sputtered, and stopped.

Hodges, along with Dempsey, continued to receive the dwindling supplies of fuel and would carry on the pursuit for almost two more weeks. No wonder Patton later became convinced that the absence of gasoline denied him the chance to end the war then and there.

*Letter, GSP, Jr., to Beatrice, September 1, 1944*

Realy I am amazed at the amount of ground the Third Army has taken, and it is chiefly due to me alone . . .

They all get scared, and then I appear and they feel better . . .

The Field Marshal thing made us sick, that is Bradley and me.

CHAPTER 30

# The Lorraine Campaign

*"God deliver us from our friends. We can handle the enemy."*

IF AUGUST had been heady, with thoughts of reaching the Rhine rampant, September and October and beyond would be, for the most part, dismal. The Communications Zone was simply unable to keep supplies – mainly gasoline and ammunition – moving to the Armies in sufficient quantities to permit them to advance. As the breakout and pursuit slowed and died, the Germans had time to man the Siegfried Line and good positions in front of these fortifications that defended the approach to the German homeland. Cold and rain came early in the fall of 1944, and added to the difficulties of the campaign. The very real optimism that the war in Europe could be ended in a matter of weeks – the Russians were crowding westward toward East Prussia, into Poland, and through the Ukraine – vanished. So did thoughts of reaching the Rhine River quickly.

*Letter, GSP, Jr., to Beatrice, September 1, 1944*

I will be stuck here for a few days waiting for supplies and due to the title of my future book, "Fear of etc."

I am delighted you know I love you.

*Letter, GSP, Jr., to Marshall, September 1, 1944*

I should like to add my request to the one Bradley has made for himself, that when this war is over, which it will shortly be, he and I get a chance to go to the Pacific. I am perfectly willing to go in any capacity so long as I can fight that particular race.

*Letter, GSP, Jr., to C. F. Ayer, September 1, 1944*

I sincerely hope that these damn fools do not blow me up so high that I will burst like an over-inflated balloon.

*Letter, GSP, Jr., to Frederick Ayer, September 1, 1944*

When you get to command several hundred thousand men, in fact nearly 450,000, you have a surprising amount of time on your hands because it is physically impossible to be at the front all the time . . .

What I usually do is to go up to the front every second day except when things are tight, in which case I go up every day. I find that people get used to you if they see too much of you.

I am impatient with my friends for not letting me go faster, as I am sure — although people do not agree with me — that the Boche has no power to resist.

Patton traveled to the 12th Army Group headquarters on September 2, to confer with Eisenhower, Bradley, Hodges, and others.

Ike was very pontifical and quoted Clausewitz to us, who have commanded larger forces than C ever heard of. He is all for cleaning up the Calais area.

This was a job for Montgomery's 21 Army Group. In order to divert Eisenhower's attention to the American front, Patton told him that the Third Army already had patrols on the Moselle River near Metz and Nancy, which was somewhat of an exaggeration.

We finally talked him into letting the V Corps of the First Army and the Third Army attack the Siegfried Line as soon as the Calais area stabilizes. Until this is done we will not be able to get gas or ammunition for a further advance.

He kept talking about the future great battle of Germany, while we assured him that the Germans have nothing left to fight with if we push on now. If we wait, there *will* be a great battle of Germany.

He also said that Lee and the Communications Zone have done a marvelous job, whereas we consider that they have failed utterly and probably lost a victory before winter through their inability to keep us supplied with gasoline.

As soon as I get sufficient gasoline, I have permission to secure crossings over the Moselle and prepare to attack the Siegfried Line.

Ike is all for caution since he has never been at the front and has no feel of actual fighting. Bradley, Hodges, and I are all for a prompt advance.

Ike did not thank or congratulate any of us for what we have done.

With the VIII Corps in Brittany about to be detached from the Third Army, Patton had three corps in Lorraine: Walker's XX facing generally Metz, Eddy's XII before Nancy, and Haislip's XV looking toward Luneville.

*Diary, September 3*

We will get crossings at Nancy and Metz by the "rock soup" method, and I gave the orders today . . . Once a tramp went to a house and asked for boiling water to make rock soup. The lady was interested and gave him the water, in which he placed two polished rocks he had in his hand. He then asked for some potatoes and carrots to put in the soup to flavor the water a little, and finally ended up by securing some meat. In other words, in order to attack, we have first to pretend to reconnoiter and then reinforce the reconnaissance and then finally attack. It is a very sad method of making war.

*Letter, GSP, Jr., to Beatrice, September 3, 1944*

We start with reconnaissance but it is hell to wage war by inadvertence [and] to conquer by deceit.

But Destiny so wills it and quotes Clausewitz — who never commanded a quarter of what I do — to prove it. Omar and Courtney were also quite ill.

What bothered the American commanders, all except Eisenhower, was that he had made Montgomery's advance the main effort of the Allied forces. That meant that Montgomery's Army Group would get more supplies than Bradley's.

When Bradley phoned to say he was coming to see him, Patton called his three corps commanders in for the meeting. Piqued by Eisenhower's decision, Bradley told them that he was giving the Third Army half of all the supplies he received. He was also assigning four additional divisions to the Third Army. Patton had permission to cross the Moselle, get through the Siegfried Line, and go as far as the Rhine.

Patton wasted no time trying to get across the Moselle, but an attempt at Pont-à-Mousson resulted in "a bloody nose," the loss of nearly 300 men.

All this comes from the fatal decision of the Supreme Commander to halt the Third Army until the Pas-de-Calais was cleared up. A fateful blunder.

*Transcript, Conference, GSP, Jr., and Third Army Correspondents, 2100, September 7, 1944*

Patton: The inquisition is now on. Before starting the inquisition, I wish to reiterate that I am not quotable, and if you want to get me sent home, quote me, God damn it.

This crossing of the Moselle River, gentlemen, is a very historic event in my opinion, because they certainly made a very definitive attempt to keep us from crossing, and I am very proud of the troops of this Army for getting across the God damn river. I like it because I like that kind of wine, but I am not quotable, God damn it. I don't drink anything but lemonade, when I can't get anything else.

Now I would appreciate it if you all could integrate in your stories the Third Army and the XIX Tactical Air Command, because the XIX Tac has done a great job with us . . .

I was at Pannes [and] Essey on the 12th of September, 1918 . . . we jumped off for the Meuse-Argonne. I was shot there that day; I ought to remember it. I was shot in the ass. There was a good story about that, but you mustn't tell it. Some fellows said, "That God damn fellow, Patton, was shot in the ass. He must have been going to the rear." My general said, "You god damn bastards, if Patton had sat in an armchair as long as you have, the bullet would have bounced." . . .

I hope to go through the Siegfried Line like shit through a goose. That is not quotable.

Question: [why was the present drive so successful?]

Patton: We have always gotten to each defensive line, not through my efforts, but through the glory of God three days before the Germans thought we would.

Question: [any comment on the holdup in gasoline?]

Patton: We mustn't talk about that . . . Off the record and not to be quoted . . . had we had the gas, which was a physical impossibility to get because we had gone much faster than we were supposed to, had we hit the Moselle four days earlier, it would have been like pissing to the wind. We would have gone on over. We are over now, so it doesn't make much difference . . . I never cared where I killed the bastards . . .

The perfectly phenomenal advance of the 21 Army Group under

Field Marshal Montgomery has just completely buggered the whole [German] show. I think that is a magnificent show, and as a result of that, it would seem to me that the German plan of defense is completely dissipated. The advance of the Guards Division and the other divisions up there has been something magnificent.

Question: [were the Germans supposed to hold along the rivers in northern France and Belgium?]

Patton: They were supposed to hold — I forget the name of the damn river — the Marne River, I think, and through here (indicating on a map), and to another God damn river up here. But they won't hold it because the British have gone through them and the American First Army . . .

Question: [anything on the Seventh Army in the south? — the forces that invaded southern France?]

Patton: They are about 90 miles from us now.

Question: [any truth in rumors of landing at Bordeaux?]

Patton: Your guess is as good as mine. I heard the same rumor. My personal opinion is that there was no such landing because as far as I know, there was no intention of any such landing.

Question: [any other big landings intended?]

Patton: No.

Question: Airborne?

Patton: No, the damn airborne can't go fast enough to keep up with us. That is off the record also.

Question: [what basis is there for your belief that you will go through the Siegfried Line quickly?]

Patton: My natural optimism.

Question: There must be something.

Patton: You can't have men retreating for 300 or 400 miles and then hold anything — the psychological result in long retreats.

Question: [the Siegfried Line may be miles in depth.]

Patton: I don't think it is. You can never tell about any of these things. My personal opinion is that I don't give a God damn where the German is; I will lick him. I mean the American or British or Canadian troops will lick him. As soon as a man gets in a concrete line, he immediately says to himself, "The other man must be damn good, or I wouldn't have to get behind this concrete."

Question: Do you still think the corporal is the most important man in the army?

Patton: The private first class.

Question: [First or Third Army going to Berlin?]

Patton: As a matter of fact, to be perfectly frank, I don't know. I am going to lick the next son-of-a-bitch in front of me, and that is as far as I can say.

Question: [how much assistance was there from the FFI?]

Patton: Better than expected and less than advertised.

Question: [what about the breakout operation at St. Lo?]

Patton: General Bradley's conception of breaking through to the south from St. Lo was a great military conception and he hasn't gotten the praise he should have for having done it.

Question: [are the Americans going to take Brest, Lorient, and St. Nazaire?]

Patton: We are going to take Brest, if we can. I will say we are going to take it . . . As soon as we get ports such as Le Havre, all through there, the importance of Brest naturally decreases, because Brest is some 600 miles from the front here, and Toulon is only 400.

Question: Have they used any buzz bombs in the Third Army yet?

Patton: No, thank God. I don't like buzz bombs; that is a damn impersonal way of going to Hell.

Question: [on artillery support]

Patton: 240-mm. is bigger than the 8-inch. 240-mm. is 9½ inches. 25-cm. is one inch. Divide and figure it out; I am not very good at mathematics.

Question: [how was breakthrough at Avranches and speed of advance achieved?]

Patton: I have always been considered a damn fool, and I still am . . . I never worried about flanks. That was probably due to my long-felt masculine virility.

Question: Can we quote you on that?

Patton: No, by God, if you do I will send you home . . . Anybody that talks about what he is going to do with the Siegfried Line is foolish until he finds the Siegfried Line. [But he spoke professionally and seriously about air bursts from artillery, air support, and the use of tanks.]

Question: Possible for British and First U.S. Army to outflank the Siegfried Line in Holland?

Patton: It will cost me $75 if they do. They may, very well.

Question: [location of the Siegfried Line]

Patton: I have never been interested in any place I was not fighting against.

Question: Was the Falaise trap part of the original plan or improvisation?

Patton: Improvisation by General Bradley. I thought we were going east and he told me to move north.

Question: Could we have closed the gap any earlier?

Patton: I can't answer that question. It is always awfully easy to say what you could have done after you haven't done it . . . As a matter of fact, gentlemen, I have the unfortunate ability to be good press for some reason or other, and as far as my military future is concerned, it is not good for me to be [good] press. So I would prefer not to be. After all, a God damn Army commander doesn't do anything but sit around and curse. As a matter of fact, I am one of the most cautious people because I have been shot [by the reporters] twice. I haven't any ambition to be shot more, and I don't take chances at all.

Question: You are public property. You are in the news.

Patton: I haven't been since last year, but it depends on the hour.

Question: Haven't you taken the last jump?

Patton: Oh, hell no. I can be accused of sodomy or anything else.

Question: They did that with Alexander the Great.

Patton: It would be a compliment, but it would still be an accusation . . . Really, I am sincere about this. It is rather a disadvantage to be large and florid and profane, because people say all kinds of things about you which are not true. For every man that I have God damned, there has been a thousand that I have patted on the back. But the patting on the back doesn't ever come out, and so I am considered to be a self-made son-of-a-bitch that goes around cursing everyone. As a matter of fact, I don't, but it is much better press to say that a man does things like that than to say he goes to the hospital and writes to the mothers, which I do. I have written more damn letters — I suppose a thousand, to the mothers of private soldiers whom I happen to know have been killed, but that never comes out, and I kick some son-of-a-bitch in the ass that doesn't do what he should, and it comes out all over the country. So, it isn't a good thing for me. After all, I have got to get some retirement pay.

Question: [possible to slow the advance?]

Patton: Whenever you slow anything down, you waste human lives. Up to the present, we have traded about between 10 or 12 [Germans] for 1 [American].

Question: [comment on the casualties of this war compared to the last?]

Patton: Well, the last war was a slow one, on a very narrow front, very great depth. In this war, there is no front. There is very little depth. It is really not comparable . . . [In this war] we cut through and wipe them out. If we hit opposition, we try not to boot into it. We try to hold and go around and then have the infantry clean it out. That is quite a nuisance, but we make time that way. If we stopped to wipe out all these people, we would be back at the Seine now.

Question: [is lack of air cover hampering operations now?]

Patton: We are using our air now at Brest. We could get it up here, but we believe it is more important to get a port which would be useful in case the war lasts so long so we can't use the beaches, which will be about the 1st of October. We have no ambition to take Brest except for that reason.

Question: [only about six more weeks of combat weather left?]

Patton: We will fight on until it [the German] quits. It is just as hard on the other fellow as it is on us. The American Army destroyed the Indian by fighting in bad weather. The American Army has always been able, due to superior equipment, clothing, and what not, to fight on in weather in which other Armies could not fight, and we would be very foolish if we failed to take advantage of that.

Question: [supplies?]

Patton: In my opinion, it has been magnificent.

Question: No criticism of the supply?

Patton: God, no. Not only no criticism, but the supply of the Armies — British Army, Canadian Army, and the First and Third Armies — has been better than any human being imagined it would be possible.

Question: [impression of war correspondents.]

Patton: . . . The intimate stories of the front-line troops are the inspirational things which make other troops go forward . . . These engineers and these signal fellows, who shovel shit and man the wires at all hours of the day and night should get all the credit that is coming to them, because they get damned little and they work like hell. I would appreciate it if you people could do something about it . . .

Question: [towns being put off limits to combat troops in reserve?]

Patton: How can you give them leave when you are short of men? I am the only officer in the last war that wasn't at Chateau-Thierry, and the only General in this war that hasn't been in Paris, and I am not going for that reason.

Question: [any indication of mass surrender by the Germans?]

Patton: I wish there was. The German is naturally, as I see him, a disciplined animal, and he does what he is told after his better sense tells him he shouldn't, but he won't admit it.

Question: [what to do with Germany to prevent another war?]

Patton: I am not a politician.

Question: [how handle the Germans as a soldier?]

Patton: I know damned well, but I decline [to answer]. Nobody can prevent another war. There will be wars as long as our great-great-grandchildren live. The only thing we can do is to produce a longer peace phase between wars.

Question: [longer occupation of Germany than last war?]

Patton: I hope to Christ I am not occupying. I want to go and fight the Japanese.

Question: [how long a war with Japan after Germany was finished?]

Patton: I don't know how long it will take to kill 17 million people, which would be my answer to that question, although that is off the record.

Question: Is China suitable for an armored attack?

Patton: Oh, lovely. If I could get myself three armored divisions in China, I would have some fun. I could do a little with one.

Question: [compare American soldier of World War I and II.]

Patton: I decline to answer. I might run for mayor some time. I have got to get some way to earn a living after the war. I do say this: that the American soldier in this war, due to length of time we have been in it, and due to the lessons learned in the last one, is much better trained. They are in fine fettle today, and they think they can beat anything, and I think they can. The relative superiority of their equipment in this war over the last one is very amazing. I want to reiterate that I try to talk to you gentlemen quite frankly, but I must not be quoted, because that is the surest way to send me home, and I don't want to go home . . . Nobody has greater admiration for General Montgomery than I have.

Question: Do operations follow outlines of a broad plan?

Patton: I don't know. An Army commander isn't told those things. You are told, "Tomorrow, you will do so and so." . . I probably overstepped the limits of caution in telling you all that, but I am quite sure you will not take advantage of it.

Question: [was gas to the Third Army cut because the Army was ahead of schedule?]

Patton: We went faster than we had planned to go. When you are planning for a couple of million men, your plans are not elastic.

Question: [if behind schedule in Normandy, much ahead of schedule now?]

Patton: What day is this?

Question: D plus 93.

Patton: We were supposed to be just short of Paris D plus 90. That mustn't come out.

Question: Where are we supposed to be on D plus 110?

Patton: Not anywhere. They didn't guess after D plus 90.

It was a magnificent performance. Patton played up to the correspondents, reinforced his image of being profane, colorful, yet thoroughly professional. And was funny too. In addition, he followed instructions, praising not only Bradley, whom he sincerely admired, but also Montgomery and the British, as well as Lee and the Communications Zone. No wonder he was good copy.

*Letter, GSP, Jr., to Beatrice, September 8, 1944*

I have always said that in bad weather officers should be out. It has been bad all day, but I went out. Via Bar-le-Duc to Toul where a fight was and is going on and not too well either.

If I only had the Germans to fight, it would be a cinch, but I have some people afraid of rumors.

Toul has been destroyed every 50 years since the dawn of history — why do people still want to live there? . .

P.S. God deliver us from our friends. We can handle the enemy.

*Diary, September 8*

P Wood has his headquarters if anything too close to the front . . . However it is refreshing to find somebody who will get up.

The people [civilians] in this part of the country are certainly pro-German and show no enthusiasm for us when we drive through.

Called Bradley to ask that the 83d and 6th Armored be moved east and let the Loire take care of itself. No supply line runs near it and any enemy who is fool enough to cross it would have to walk. As it is, we have two divisions guarding nothing [there] and our future south of Toul is in danger due to the absence of these two divisions. But Bradley said, "I can't take the risk." And by so saying takes a much worse risk.

If the weather is flyable, I will go up and try to talk him over in the morning.

On that day the XX Corps established a small bridgehead across the Moselle River. On the following day, five battalions were across the river south of Metz.

*Letter, Summerall to GSP, Jr., September 9, 1944*

The papers have more to say about your operations than of all the others . . . You have written a new chapter in open warfare and left a standard for military history. Your name will live with the great leaders and no one deserves the fame and the credit as you do . . . I know that reliance will be placed upon you in yet more campaigns there and across the Pacific.

*Diary, September 9*

Arrived headquarters 12th Army Group at 0845. Bradley, due to my telephone conversation last night, is now partially in favor of letting the 83d and 6th Armored Divisions move up [from Brittany]. He is flying to Brest to have a look at the situation and talk with Simpson.

*Letter, GSP, Jr., to Beatrice, September 10, 1944*

I am doing my damdest to get going again, but it is hard. Once people stop, they get cautious and the enemy gets set. Books will some day be written on that "Pause which did not refresh" any one but the Germans.

*Diary, September 11*

XII Corps is having a hard fight south of Nancy . . .

The XX Corps lost one bridgehead and a battalion of infantry . . . but captured a second bridgehead . . .

Elements of the 2d French Armored made contact with the 1st French Division of the Seventh Army 25 kilometers northwest of Dijon today.

Thus, the troops who had landed in southern France were in touch with those who had come ashore in Overlord. Four days later Eisenhower would extend his authority over Devers' 6th Army Group. Before long he would have 54 divisions under him along a front stretching 600 miles from the North Sea to Switzerland.

There seems to be a new plan in the offing which will place more emphasis on the First Army. I wish people would stop making plans and changing their minds, particularly when they always seem to do so at our expense. We may now lose the 83d Division.

The arrival of the 6th Armored is again delayed, so that they can help escort 20,000 Germans who surrendered south of Orleans to the border and protect them from the French Forces of the Interior. When these Germans surrendered, they said it must be specifically understood that they were not surrendering to the Ninth Army but to the Third Army.

Some way I will manage to keep going.

We fly to 12th Army Group in the morning for a conference on the whole subject.

*Diary, September 12*

It was decided that we had enough supplies to get to the Rhine and force a crossing.

Hodges had enough ammunition for five days' fighting and enough gasoline to get to the Rhine; he planned to attack near Aachen. Patton had ammunition for four days' fighting and fuel to reach the Rhine; he hoped to complete crossing the Moselle and advance from Metz to Frankfurt.

Everyone was still thinking of the deep and daring thrusts of August. No one seemed to realize that the conditions had changed — the weather, the supply situation, and the nature of the country. The Germans had recovered from their defeat in Normandy and, in what they would later call the miracle in the west, they established strong defenses along the western approaches to Germany. In the new circumstances of the campaign, they would resist in the Siegfried Line and before it with tenacity and skill. The Rhine River was still distant and on the other side of the Siegfried Line, and the Americans would have a hard time getting there.

Monty is still trying to make all the Armies attack in the Low Countries and against the Ruhr. If he does this, I shall have to hold the west bank of the Moselle defensively and put the XX Corps into Luxembourg. I persuaded Bradley to let me continue the attack until the night of the 14th, but if by that time I have not secured a bridgehead, I will move to the north [to Luxembourg] as he wishes.

Got back to camp at 1430 to find General Hughes. He brought me a pearl-handled 38 Colt.

*Letter, GSP, Jr., to Frederick Ayer, September 14, 1944*

We have been having quite severe fighting, which is still going on, but we have finally completely crossed the Moselle River which, as you know, has throughout history been a great military barrier.

*Letter, GSP, Jr., to Beatrice, September 15, 1944*

For the last week we have had a desperate battle forcing the Moselle which we could have had for the asking had we not been required to stop . . .

We may be, in fact are supposed to be, second string for a while but we may fool them yet, even if the family is jealous of us.

He had a long talk with Archbishop Spellman of New York, "a very clever little Irishman," and found him "a most interesting man — anti-Roosevelt, anti-CIO [labor], anti-Negro, Jew, and English — quite a man."

*Diary, September 15*

Monty does what he pleases and Ike says "yes, sir." Monty wants all supplies sent to him and the First U.S. Army and for me to hold. Brad thinks I can and should push on. Brad told Ike that if Monty takes control of the XIX and VII Corps of the First Army, as he wants to, he, Bradley, will ask to be relieved . . . Ike feels that we think he is selling us out but he has to, as Monty will not take orders, so we have to. Bradley said it was time for a showdown. I offered to resign with him, but he backed out.

On that day Eddy's XII Corps took Nancy.

I looked up Walker and asked him why he was so slow. He got the idea, but is having trouble with the fort west of Metz. I hope to bomb hell out of them tomorrow.

Eisenhower explained to Bradley that his whole purpose was to get substantial forces, unhampered by logistical deficiencies, across the Rhine for a sustained drive into Germany. He consequently gave precedence to Montgomery because he needed the Channel ports. Therefore, to support Montgomery, Hodges had priority over Patton, but there was "no reason why Patton should not keep acting offensively if the conditions for offensive action are right."

*Letter, GSP, Jr., to Beatrice, September 16, 1944*

My luck or the Lord still holds. I sent the XV Corps against Epinal yesterday and destroyed the troops there, including 60 tanks. On a corpse we found an order for them to attack Eddy in flank today—they wont do it now . . .

If it would only stop raining I could go faster. It is so wet that we have to winch the tanks up hill.

I wish to God I was a first priority on supply but I aint. I have fed the Army on captured food, 200,000 pounds of Argentine beef, and 100,000 gallons of [captured] gas for two days . . . We have so many indigent relatives with a great appeal that it is hard.

I was never better in my life and drink champagne instead of water. We captured 50,000 cases. I issued it to the troops.

*Diary, September 16*

Ten assorted Russians are to visit us today, so I won't be here. I decided to go to the front. I had a map prepared for them which showed exactly nothing in a big way. This is what they do to us . . .

Eddy is quite tense but doing a good job. I told him to go to bed early and take a couple of drinks. I hope he can make a rush for the Siegfried Line . . . I gave him the new boundaries and advised, but did not order, that he attack in columns of divisions . . . to secure a gap through the Siegfried Line . . . then [move] straight to the Rhine in the vicinity of Worms in the hope we may grab a bridgehead before it [the bridge] is blown up . . .

Walker was quite pessimistic as to his ability to take Metz, so that I told him that if he could not take it in a few days, I would take the 7th Armored Division away from him and give it to the XII Corps, leaving him to contain Metz with what he has. That may get him going . . .

We had a plan to use 11 groups of medium bombers on the Metz forts today but the weather prevented this. I will attempt to get it done tomorrow.

*Letter, GSP, Jr., to Beatrice, September 17, 1944*

The clippings are most interesting but I fear I am off the first page for the moment as we are not going fast. Metz is hard to take and the rain keeps us from using bombers. Still, I always feel it is just as hard on the enemy, harder, as he is less well equipped.

*Letter, GSP, Jr., to son George, September 17, 1944*

We got Nancy . . . but Metz which is one of the best fortified cities in the world is still holding out . . .

I have been going to the front so much and kicking so much about delay that I have the generals jittery so I am spending a Sunday in the truck with Willie.

*Diary, September 17*

It has rained all day and the ground is so slippery that it has adversely affected our tanks.

I sent Gaffey to the XII Corps to try to get the attack on the Siegfried Line started. The best they can do is the morning of the 19th. That is too late but we can do no better . . . I may accompany the 4th Armored in their attack on the 19th, as a little personal influence may be helpful.

Bradley called to say that Monty wants all the Americans to stop so that he, Monty, can "make a dagger-thrust with the 21st Army Group at the heart of Germany." Bradley said he thought it would be a "butter-knife thrust." To hell with Monty. I must get so involved [in operations] that they can't stop me. I told Bradley not to call me until after dark on the 19th. He agreed.

Operation Market-Garden started on that day, "the greatest airborne operation we have yet attempted," Eisenhower informed Marshall. It was Montgomery's show, an air drop by three divisions along a corridor, followed by an armored drive to link the three landings and gain a bridgehead across the lower Rhine River at Arnhem, Holland.

After Market-Garden, Eisenhower expected Montgomery to open Antwerp, the major port needed for "the final drive into Germany." Meanwhile, Hodges was coordinating his activities with Montgomery and was driving toward Cologne and Bonn to attack the Ruhr. Patton was pushing to support Hodges, and the 6th Army Group under Devers was moving up toward the Rhine River, heading generally toward Strasbourg.

*Diary, September 18*

We got a message . . . that two columns of [German] infantry and tanks were attacking Luneville . . . I told the XV Corps to move out at once on their objective . . . [Ira] Wyche happened to arrive at this moment and showed great promptitude in getting his units moving.

I left at once for Nancy to see Eddy. He was a little worried, but not badly, so he is sending a combat command of the 6th Armored Division to stop the counterattack. It is just as well that I got this unit up last night. The attack by the XII Corps against the Siegfried Line will go on as planned in the morning, [German] counterattack or not. Eddy still thinks my attack is premature – I hope that the Germans agree with him . . .

We are very short of ammunition.

The Eisenhower-Montgomery argument over broad-front versus narrow-front advances continued. On September 20, Eisenhower told Montgomery that he never considered advancing into Germany "with all Armies moving abreast." His choice of the route for the all-out offensive into Germany was from the Ruhr to Berlin. A prerequisite was the early capture of the sea approaches to Antwerp, the Schelde estuary, so that the great port could be used. With abundant supplies coming in through Antwerp and with all the Armies marshaled up along the western border, the Rhine if possible, Montgomery could drive to Berlin while Bradley supported him with the First U.S. Army. But the other forces, specifically Patton's Army, had to participate in the offensive to stretch the defenders and assure the success of the main drive.

Montgomery disagreed. He felt that, given continuing shortages of supplies, all the forces that could be adequately supplied ought to be permitted to drive forward to finish off the war, while the others halted in place.

At Verdun for a conference on September 20, Patton persuaded Bradley that he could drive through the Siegfried Line with two corps abreast and the third echeloned to the right rear – if he had two more infantry divisions, if he could take or contain Metz, and if he could get those eleven groups of bombers on Metz for three consecutive days.

This seemed like pure braggadocio, for locally, "The situation tonight is tense, but we will win out. We must."

*Diary, September 21*

Things look better today . . .

Devers was making a great deal of talk about the number of troops he is going to take from me [to bolster his 6th Army Group], so I flew to Paris for an hour this morning to see Ike and spike Devers' guns. Ike hates him. He was very nice and had me to lunch. I think my visit was a success. Devers and Patch got there shortly after I did, but were told to wait until 2:00 o'clock. We then had a meeting, but the question of stealing troops from the Third Army did not come up. However, I took the occasion to speak to Beedle Smith and ask his assistance in case it did come up. One has to fight one's friends more than the enemy.

Just called up all three corps and things seem much brighter. Ike still insists, for the present at least, the main effort must be thrown to the British and the north flank of the First Army. However, he was more peevish with Montgomery than I have ever seen him. In fact, he called him a "clever son of a bitch," which was very encouraging.

*Letter, GSP, Jr., to Beatrice, September 21, 1944*

For the last three days we have had as bitter and protracted fighting as I have ever encountered. The Huns are desperate and are attacking at half a dozen places.

Once or twice we gave ground but in all but one case got it back.

We have destroyed well over a hundred tanks and killed thousands . . .

Metz, the strongest fortress in the world, is sticky but we will get it as soon as we can get the air. However I wont be able to do an, broken field running till I cross the next river, so don't expect it.

I have done a good job in making men attack and win who wanted to halt and regroup . . .

There is one rather bad spot in my line but I don't think the huns know it. By tomorrow night I will have it plugged. Jimmy Polk is holding it now by the grace of God and a lot of guts.

At a meeting called by Eisenhower, Bradley learned that there could be no major offensive operations by American forces until Antwerp was in operation. Communications Zone could guarantee sufficient tonnage to support an attack by the First Army only if the other American Armies were on the defensive. Eisenhower consequently decided to have the 21 Army Group launch an offensive to get across the lower Rhine. Montgomery definitely had priority on supplies.

This led to be what would be known as the Third Army's October pause and the cancellation of planned river crossings south of Metz.

> [Bradley] was feeling very low because Montgomery has again put it over on Ike and demands the assistance of the First Army in a push into the Ruhr. To do this, I will have to send an armored division and also assume a defensive attitude due to lack of adequate supplies. Also, Devers told Eisenhower that since he could easily supply the XV Corps via Dijon [from the great port of Marseilles], it should go to him.
>
> Going on the defense and having our limited supplies cut still more is very discouraging. Bradley and I are depressed. We would like to go to China and serve under Admiral Nimitz.

Then Bradley phoned to say that Eisenhower was inclined to let Devers have the XV Corps permanently.

> I am not usually inclined to grumble or to think that the cards are stacked against me, but sometimes I wish that someone would get committed to do something for me. However, all my disappointments have turned out for the best. I wanted to command in Italy and that turned out badly. I wanted to command the assault on the beaches here. It also was quite a failure. I felt, and with reason, that when the XIX and VII Corps of the First Army turned north, I should have got the V Corps, which was paralleling my left. I didn't get it, and this attack [at the end of the pursuit] also soured.
>
> I should have more faith. If Jake Devers gets the XV Corps, I hope his plan goes sour. The Lord is on my side, but he has a lot of getting even to do for me.

*Letter, GSP, Jr., to Hughes, September 23, 1944*

At the moment I am being attacked on both flanks, but not by the Germans. But I may yet make my getaway.

Everyone on the Allied side was disappointed, discouraged, and even depressed. But no one was more distressed than Patton, who had to go over on the defensive.

## CHAPTER 31

# The Moselle

*"Now we are just sitting and watching the bosch dig in, but it won't be long now. Of course the weather is bad for us but it is worse for him."*

PATTON GAVE NO IMPRESSION of discouragement at a press conference held at 8 P.M., September 23. On the contrary, he was jovial.

Patton: I always feel at these meetings we should have on black hoods over our heads as in the Inquisition.

Question: [when was the Third Army going to start moving again?]

Patton: [Not] till we get supplies . . . There is no point in making a slow advance and you can't make a rapid advance because we haven't got the stuff right now. We can fight hard for five days and then we've got to throw rocks.

Question: Metz?

Patton: It is a hard nut. If we could get the supplies we need and with three good days of weather, we could take it. In fact, I am not going to get those soldiers killed until we have things on our side . . .

Question: Once through the Siegfried Line, will the advance be much like the last push?

Patton: I think we will go like shit through a tin horn.

Question: Rhine defenses formidable?

Patton: Only on account of the moat effect of the Rhine River, which has quite a rapid current.

Question: First Army on easier terrain?

Patton: Sure. How the hell do you think the son-of-a-bitches are getting along? But don't tell them that I said that.

Question: Metz tougher than the Siegfried Line?

Patton: Yes. They have larger forts. They've been building forts there since Louis XVI. Our 105's bounced off them and didn't even nick them.

Question: Are you getting your share of the supply situation?

Patton: Yes, but unfortunately we cannot make five barley loaves and three small fishes expand as they used to . . .

Question: Was Metz ever captured in history?

Patton: Not by assault. In 1871, the fort was, I think, starved out.

Question: Have you any indication of German secret weapons?

Patton: Bullshit.

Question: We making use of propaganda?

Patton: We drop about five or six leaflet bombs every day. The Psychological Warfare people make them up. I don't know what they say.

Question: What effect are they having? Any? Or much?

Patton: I don't believe so . . .

Question: Will the improvement of the supply situation make possible a limited advance or a static situation?

Patton: It is my earnest effort to keep it from becoming static because that is a poor way of fighting. The best way to defend is to attack, and the best way to attack is to attack. At Chancellorsville, Lee was asked why he attacked when he was outnumbered three to one. Lee said he was too weak to defend.

Question: Will the Nazis go underground when the Allies get to Germany?

Patton: Six feet . . .

A man was reported [at West Point] for wasting toilet paper, and he said that he could not have been more careful if he had used both sides . . .

Well, gentlemen, I repeat, whatever I said will not be used against me.

Patton drove to Nancy, met with his three corps commanders, and arranged a defensive front. He also instructed them to make limited attacks so that when the Third Army resumed the offensive, "as we will, we will have a good take-off line."

Haislip was "very depressed" by the prospect of leaving the Third Army, and Patton was "equally depressed" to think of losing him.

He formalized his orders in a letter of instruction the following day, reiterating that the acute supply situation had required Eisenhower to direct the Third Army to assume the defensive. But the change in attitude, Patton warned, had to be concealed from the enemy. Otherwise, the Germans would move troops from the Third Army front to oppose other Allied efforts. Because of that and because he wanted a suitable line of departure when offensive operations resumed, he ordered no digging in, no stringing of wires or mines. The troops on the defensive were to erect a thin outpost zone backed at suitable places by powerful mobile reserves. All artillery pieces were to be ready to take all possible avenues of enemy tank attack under heavy fire. Weyland was to be prepared to bring his fighter-bombers into action. Meanwhile, he wanted limited offensive operations

> in consonance with our reduced scale of supply. Utmost parsimony will be used in expenditures of gasoline and ammunition consistent with the economy of the lives of our troops.
>
> In closing, I desire to again compliment all of you on the magnificent dash and skill which you have shown in the operation to date. We only await the sign to resume our career of conquest.

*Diary, September 25*

> My plan for taking the defense is to . . . rectify the line, thereby maintaining the offensive spirit in the troops so that when we will attack, we will not be pacifists.

On that day Operation Market-Garden came to an end. At a cost of almost 12,000 casualties, Montgomery secured a corridor of 65 miles into the Netherlands and gained bridgeheads across the Maas and Waal rivers, but not across the Rhine.

A wire from Marshall asked Patton to make contact, when convenient, with Marshall's landlady during World War I at nearby Gondrecourt.

Taking three pounds of coffee and five pounds of sugar, Patton and Campanole departed "in the pouring rain . . . We were glad of the excuse to go," he informed Beatrice. "It was not the Germans who have stopped us, but higher strategy. Don't worry."

They learned from the mayor, who was touched by Patton's visit, that Marshall's friends no longer lived there and had moved to the south of France.

Driving to Chaumont, Patton and Campanole had a meal at the Hôtel de France where, 27 years earlier, Pershing, Harbord, Colonel de Chambrun, and Patton had lunched when they selected Chaumont to be the headquarters of the AEF.

After visiting Pershing's house and the barracks where Patton's offices had been located, they went to Langres, which "looked very natural" – apparently nothing had changed,

> but we had no time to stop and drove on to Bourg. The first man I saw in the street there was standing on the same manure pile which he undoubtedly stood on in 1918. I asked him if he had been there in the last war, and he replied, "Yes, General Patton, you were then here as a Colonel." Then we had an Old Home Week. He offered to show me around the town, which I really didn't need, but nevertheless I permitted him to do this. I visited my old office, my billet, and the chateau of Madame de Vaux and took pictures.

It was all very nostalgic.

September 27 was a "big day for visiting firemen." No less than nine generals called. Spaatz was

> all for the Third Army. I have the air force in my pocket. As usual, Lee is a glib liar. Hughes was very much depressed at having to sit at the same table with him.

The problem – "and it will be a scandal some day" – was that Lee made "no preparation at all for Line of Communication troops" and was now asking for between eight and eleven infantry battalions "to do his dirty work." He was also using all the vehicles from the newly arriving divisions "because he has failed in his supply set-up. I cannot understand why Eisenhower does not get rid of him."

A telephone call from Bradley apprised him that Devers would take the XV Corps – "May God rot his guts." He "felt very low. Must trust in God and my destiny."

He tried to get drunk. he told Beatrice, but could not, "so for the first time since Palermo am taking a green pill" – probably for his digestion or to sleep.

> If you were here, I would cry on your shoulder. Willie is no use. Some times I almost think that the fates are against me. Then I remember all the time I have "made a heap of all my winnings" . . . I took a long walk alone – not even Willie. Put two officers in arrest for speeding and felt better.

Patton visited the front to rid himself of his blues. He noted two machine guns so placed that they could hit nothing except at extreme ranges even though the ground they were supposed to cover was within 400 yards' range. The reason was that the officer who emplaced them was standing when he chose the positions, thus putting his eyes about five feet above the guns. At that elevation, one could see everything. At the muzzle of the guns, one could see nothing. "I can never understand why some officers are such fools."

On his way home a shell burst close enough to throw dirt on his jeep and a second shell struck just beside his jeep about eight feet from the side of the road. "Luckily this shell was a dud or these lines would not be written."

The hurt and the resentment remained. "As usual, Devers is a liar and, by his glibness, talked Eisenhower into giving him the [XV] Corps."

Eddy phoned early on September 29, and asked Patton to come to Nancy as soon as he could. Patton flew there and discovered that the 35th Division was being attacked by at least one German division, possibly two. He instructed Eddy to use the 6th Armored Division to help the 35th. Eddy was reluctant to do so because if they failed, they would be destroyed on the far side of the river. Patton said "that was a damn good reason why they wouldn't fail, and reminded him that Cortez burned his ships."

Patton telephoned Gaffey and told him – "unless the XX Corps was worse off than I thought" – to have Walker send Eddy a combat command of the 6th. The troops started to move toward Nancy in 15 minutes, a marvelous execution.

Returning to his headquarters because Eisenhower and Bradley were coming, Patton had a guard and a band to welcome them. After lunch Eisenhower talked to a group of officers who represented all the divisions and the two corps headquarters in the Third Army. "He explained the situation in a lucid manner and assured us that eventually we would get supplies and make a main effort."

After Eisenhower and Bradley departed, Patton had all the officers into his map room, where he explained that the Third Army would defend by attacking locally

> as and when we can get the supplies. As I see it, the Germans want both Metz and Nancy. They have Metz, so are content and will stay quiet there. Therefore, they will put all their efforts, which are not excessive, to recapturing Nancy because they realize, as I did when I captured it, that Nancy, and particularly Chateau Salins, is the doorway to . . . Germany; therefore they will keep on attacking and get killed.

He had a bad scare on September 30. He had sent Gaffey to the XII Corps, and at 3 P.M., Gaffey phoned and said that Patton "had best come to Nancy as fast as I could." He flew, arrived in 45 minutes, and found that Eddy had ordered two regiments of the 35th Division holding the woods west of Château Salins to withdraw. Gaffey had heard Eddy give the order, had not protested, but had sent for Patton.

"I was very angry." Two-thirds of the 6th Armored Division was available, and Patton had told Eddy the day before to commit the armor if the Germans attacked. "Why Eddy did not do so, I cannot make up my mind."

Eddy was at the 6th Armored Division command post, so Patton and Gaffey drove there and sent for Baade, the 35th Division commander. Patton told all three generals, Eddy, Baade, and Grow, that "I was disgusted with them." He wanted the 6th to counterattack in the morning at the latest – that evening if the troops could get across the river by then. He also ordered the generals involved to lead their troops personally "to make up for their shortcomings." Baade was to go to the front. Grow was to retake the woods "or not come back." Patton was tough because he felt that giving up the ground would be a tremendous boost to German morale – like presenting them with 100,000 men.

Patton then phoned the XX Corps and told Walker to collect trucks to be ready, on call, to move a regiment of the 90th Division, so that if the 35th broke, "as it may well do," there would be an additional unit available.

> Eddy was very manly in assuming full responsibility for the withdrawal order, but I cannot understand his frame of mind. He

worries too much. I will do all the worrying necessary. The corps commanders must fight. I would get rid of him but I do not know of any other any better except possibly Harmon, now commanding the 2d Armored Division. One explanation of Eddy's emotional failure may be that earlier in the afternoon, he, Gaffey, and Grow were all nearly killed by shell fire, and Gaffey's aide . . . and Grow's aide were hit. This may, unknown to them, have shattered their nerves.

After I got through cussing them out, I told them the same thing I told Truscott in Sicily, namely, "Now I will go home as I know you will win." I feel they will. If I stayed, it would show lack of confidence. We must remember that the German is not a superman . . .

It is now 0010, October 1, and I have heard nothing. I have called the chief of staff, XII Corps, and find that he is asleep, so things are probably all right.

*Diary, October 1*

The attack of the 6th Armored Division to restore the salient of the 35th Division west of Chateau Salins jumped off at 0600 and the situation was well restored by 1200 . . . So much for hysteria. All that was necessary was a vigorous attack. Had I let Eddy retire 5 kilometers, as he was about to do, it would have been heralded in Germany as a great victory . . . I have again earned my pay.

He and Stiller drove to Nancy on October 2, then to the woods where the fighting had taken place. He presented Bronze Stars to two regimental commanders in the 35th Division. He visited P. Wood, called on Grow, saw Baade, who had been wounded in the chin, and gave him a Bronze Star. He went to the hospitals in Nancy and talked to about 200 wounded men. "I think I did a good job. Today morale seemed high."

Wood sent Patton a paper he wrote on the employment of armored divisions, then added that he hoped "we can get a little time out for maintenance and regrouping soon." Everyone, he implied, was getting tired by the continuous commitment to combat.

Unfortunately, no relief was in sight. There were too few divisions for the front.

Mrs. Congressman [Edith Nourse] Rogers called. She was very full of venom and innuendo, and wanted to get my opinions for her political advancement. I was very careful to give her none. She is a congenitally dishonest woman but does not know it.

A battalion of the 5th Division opened an attack on Fort Driant on the morning of October 4, the beginning of what Patton hoped would eventually become a full-scale attack that would result in the capture of Metz.

*Letter, GSP, Jr., to son George, October 4, 1944*

Today, we are assaulting one of the old forts around Metz and have got two platoons of tanks inside the fort. However, this is not all you have to do because most of the defenders are under about 15 yards of concrete and the question of getting them out is difficult. I am trying an experiment of pouring gasoline down the ventilator pipes and then lighting them. I think this should at least keep the Germans from getting cold feet.

*Letter, Summerall to GSP, Jr., October 4, 1944*

While the world is amazed by your generalship, I am equally amazed and honored that you can take time to write me so generously in the midst of the burdens that you bear. It is only the great soul and the great intellect that can preserve proportion and give to the smaller things in life their niche in the vast structure of their power. This you do as no one else has done . . .

From all who write or talk to us, we hear of the devotion of your men to you.

*Letter, GSP, Jr., to Summerall, October 4, 1944*

Ever since we seized the crossings over the Moselle at Nancy we have had very severe and vicious fighting, not exactly on World War I principles but more analagous to it than anything we have had yet so far.

The other day we had a very curious psychological incident occur. One division, which had been fighting for about 60 days, suddenly came to the conclusion that it was beaten and got permission from the corps commander to withdraw . . .

The simple statement on my part that they would attack removed the nervous tension. It is really amazing what the determination on the part of one man can do to many thousands. There was no more sense in their retreating than there ever had been, yet, had I not personally intervened, they would certainly have done so. I am not saying this in a boastful way, but simply as illustration of the funny things which happen in battle . . .

Yesterday we started an assault on one of the principal forts south of Metz . . .

As you know, these forts are mostly underground, and it is very difficult to root the Germans out . . .

So far we have never failed in any operation and I can see that it is desirable to inculcate in the German mind that when the Third Army attacks, it always succeeds. If we get this fort, the problem of taking Metz will be greatly enhanced.

*Letter, GSP, Jr., to Col. Robert H. Fletcher, Leesburg, Va., October 4, 1944*

I agree with you that the press has been too good, but there is nothing I can do to stop it . . . I presume right now that since I am not advancing sixty miles a day, I am considered a failure, but, as a matter of fact, I have killed more Germans lately than I did during the whole of the fast advance.

*Letter, GSP, Jr., to Frederick Ayer, October 4, 1944*

While the papers are somewhat reticent of the valorous deeds of the Third Army, we have had up until the day before yesterday some very vicious fighting . . .

Don't mention to anyone that an American division thought about retreating . . .

Right now . . . one of the old Vauban type forts, much reinforced recently . . . We took it with tanks, which is probably the only time in the history of war that a fort has been taken with tanks. When I say taken, I am a little optimistic, because we have about a third of it, and the Germans have the rest . . .

The weather is as bad as it could be for offensive operations. It rains every morning, beginning about 5:00 o'clock and stopping about 11:00 o'clock. It then clears up and makes the ground as slippery as grease, so it is very hard to use the tanks, and it also slows up our truck movements bringing in supplies.

You will not hear anything exciting about us for some time but I think when you do, it will be quite exciting.

Patton directed the XX Corps "to completely occupy Fort Driant if it took every man in the corps." He said he could not allow an attack by the Third Army to fail.

Two days later, things were

> going very badly at Fort Driant. We may have to abandon the attack since it is not worth the cost. I was over optimistic in letting the 5th Division start, but I hate to crush initiative.

*Diary, October 7*

Generals Marshall and Bradley came in . . . The whole staff was present, and we went over the plans for the Fort Driant operation and also those for the attack by the XII Corps tomorrow. As usual, General Marshall asked very incisive questions, but we could answer them. He was more pleasant than usual and regretted that he had to go and see General Montgomery in the morning and so miss the battle.

*Letter, GSP, Jr., to Beatrice, October 8, 1944*

George [Marshall] asked me what I wanted and I said to take the Third Army and the XIX TAC to China. He seemed agreeable. So – we wont occupy Germany. I am glad as there is a rumor that Beedle will be boss there – I can stand only so much!

I had a ring side seat at quite a battle to day . . . We attacked with three divisions just to prove we were still in the ring. We could see the tanks moving and some times the infantry, three large towns were burning brightly. In one, the flames – yellow ones – were over 2,000 feet and black smoke went to 4,000. Air fighter bombers were roaring and diving into it and we had a radio over which we could hear the pilots talking, like this: "The bastards are using flack on Tom. I am going down to get him – I got him . . ." Then huge globs of black smoke and loud noises. Then you could see the tracers from the tanks and houses burst into flame and hundreds of prisoners marching in the fields . . .

It wont get much in the press, but we had close to 90,000 men in action, 20,000 bigger than Gettysburg . . .

Of course we will get a hell of a counter attack at dawn and I hope kill more Germans. Peace is going to be a hell of a let down.

*Diary, October 8*

I noticed a tendency in McBride to be content with less than perfect performance and reluctant to use all his troops. Eddy tolerates this. There was a hill held by a few Germans and no visible effort was being made to secure it before dark, so I ordered him to put in his reserve and take it . . . The hill fell readily. The whole tempo of our infantry attack is too slow.

At Verdun on October 9, Bradley explained to the three American Army commanders that Simpson's Ninth U.S. Army was to go under Montgomery's command.

Bedell Smith arrived and, as usual, was very assertive and, as usual, knew nothing. Bradley took him down quite hard, and he was better thereafter. At one point in the conversation he said to Bradley that any soldier should know so and so. Bradley replied that he thought he had more combat experience than Smith and did not care to be criticized. After that Smith was much more tolerant . . .

The Fort Driant show is going sour. We will have to pull out.

*Diary, October 10*

I believe that General Marshall and General Handy were very well pleased with what they saw. I have never known General Marshall to be so nice and human.

*Letter, GSP, Jr., to Dillingham, October 11, 1944*

You are probably busier than I am. As a matter of fact, commanding an Army is not such a very absorbing task except that one has to be ready at all hours of the day and night . . . to make some rather momentous decision, which frequently consists of telling somebody who thinks he is beaten that he is not beaten.

Patton had Walker explain to Bradley the situation at Fort Driant. Patton recommended pulling out, since "the glory of taking the fort is not worth the sacrifices in men which it would demand." Bradley concurred. The attack was definitely called off.

The ammunition allowance for the Third Army was cut drastically — "about 7 rounds per gun per day for 155's and not much better for 105's . . . This will defer our big attack until November."

For the most part, the units conducted vigorous patrolling, small-scale thrusts, and limited objective attacks, as they reinforced and strengthened their bridgeheads across the Moselle and prepared to resume the offensive.

To the key members of the newly arrived 26th Division, Patton talked about the lessons of combat, the offensive spirit, and "particularly on fire and movement. I am sure that if I could get the American infantryman to shoot his rifle, we could win the war much more cheaply."

He studied plans for his next operation, still unscheduled because of ammunition shortages. "The sooner we can start this the better, as the enemy continues to dig and mine ahead of us."

Eisenhower and Devers came for a visit. "Devers was full of himself, as usual, but is a clever man."

*Letter, GSP, Jr., to Frederick Ayer, October 18, 1944*

We have an officer of quite high rank here who is very pompous . . . One of his current hobbies is sanitation. Recently, on inspecting a company he noticed that every man had a fork in his left-hand shirt pocket. The General asked the reason for this. The soldier questioned replied that in order to carry out the General's wishes as to sanitation, they never passed the bread by hand, but if anyone wanted a piece of bread he stuck his fork in it and took it. The General said that that was excellent and complimented the man.

On going outdoors he noticed that every soldier had a string hanging out of the lower part of his fly. He asked why the string and was informed that the string was for the purpose of getting the penis out without touching it with the hand, again complying with the General's idea of sanitation.

The General was much pleased and complimented the soldier again. But suddenly an idea struck him and he said, "That is all right, but how do you get it back?" The soldier replied, "I don't know what the others do, but for myself, I use my fork."

*Letter, GSP, Jr., to Eisenhower, October 19, 1944*

I have today written General Bradley that if he can give me 2,000 tons of ammunition . . . and then guarantee a like amount daily, I can initiate an attack any time. I have learned from you to fight on a shoestring, and I realize further that the enemy is fighting on a shoestring which is more frayed than ours.

On the way back from a visit to the corps and divisions, he remarked a shell landing about 300 yards from his vehicle and duly noted it in his diary.

He wrote Beatrice some random observations. Omar "the tent maker" liked to have large discussions and took no chances. There were 65 newspaper correspondents with the Third Army. "I did not remember the lovley colors of the trees in the fall here. They are not as brilliant as ours at home but are very effective." Montgomery's airborne show was "heroic but that is all you can say for it." The only thing he wanted for Christmas was "some suspenders."

Bradley and Allen came to lunch, and Patton told them he knew there was insufficient ammunition for all three American Armies to attack, but certainly there must be enough for one. His Third Army could jump off on two days' notice.

> Bradley is too conservative — he wants to wait until we can all jump together, by which time half our men will have flu or trench foot. I argued all I could, but the best I could persuade him to do was to say I could jump off any time on or after the 5th of November . . . I wish he had a little daring.

"I nearly lost the Third Army this morning — by getting killed," he wrote Beatrice on October 24. The Germans shelled Nancy with a huge 11-inch railroad gun during the night. They seemed to be after Patton, and at 4:30, three rounds landed near his house, broke all the windows, and struck and partially demolished a dwelling across the street, trapping some people in the debris. Hearing some "hollering in French," Patton dressed, went out, and helped rescue the inhabitants.

He described the episode to his wife and son in a lighthearted way, endeavoring to be humorous, but he added: "If they start shooting to night I am going in the cellar which is bomb proof."

*Letter, GSP, Jr., to Beatrice, October 26, 1944*

> I think I got GCM [Marshall] to release the names of the officers [to the press]. When he and I were talking to Walker, I said — forgetting that George has no sense of humor — that Mrs. Walker was about to divorce him. GCM brissled up and said, no, she wont, I'll talk to her. I then said that all he had to do to save the family life was to release the fact that Walker had commanded a corps because the grounds for divorce were that Mrs. Walker thought he was a slacker . . .

I only wear the shiny helmet in the back areas and have never ridden in a tank in battle.

He made a speech at the Red Cross Doughnut Dugout, and the men there cheered for five minutes.

Truscott spent the night. He was soon to take command of the Fifth Army in Italy. "His promotion has been well deserved and he has invariably done a good, but never a brilliant job. I am very proud of him." Clark was moving up to command the Army Group in Italy, while Alexander took the place of Wilson, who was going to Washington to succeed Field Marshal Sir John Dill, who had died.

*Letter, GSP, Jr., to Beatrice, October 31, 1944*

I find it very difficult to get exercise. This locality is more German than French, and my people fear that I will get killed if I go out to walk. However I do escape sometimes . . .

You had better send me a couple of bottles of pink medicin. When I am not attacking I get bilous . . .

Willie just heard the planes and is hiding under a chair. He hates bombs.

He inspected a colored tank battalion. "They gave a very good impression but I have no confidence in the inherent fighting ability of the race." Contrary to Patton's expectation, the battalion performed exceptionally well in combat.

*Diary, November 2*

Bradley came in and explained the next plan. The First and Ninth can't go before the 10th. He asked me when I could go.

I said, "Twenty-four hours from when you say go."

He said, "Any time on or after the 8th, when you get a forecast of one good day['s weather]."

I said, "O.K., but in any case I will jump on the 8th, bombers or no."

He agreed . . .

I feel 40 years younger.

He made talks to seven divisions in turn, the subject being, according to Gay, "the honor which had been given to that Army in being allowed to make the offensive," which if conducted with dash and persistence, could end the war.

Patton was then surprised to learn that the 4th and 6th Armored Divisions, veteran troops who had no need of a pep talk, were hurt because he had not spoken to them. "I did not include them . . . as there is nothing about war I can tell them." He addressed them too.

*Diary, November 5*

Had a bad case of short breath this morning – my usual reaction to an impending fight or match.

Went to church. Devers was waiting to see me when I returned. He seemed most cooperative and said he would push the XV Corps along on our right [to help the Third Army attack].

Had Marlene Dietrich and her troupe for lunch. Later they gave us a show. Very low comedy, almost an insult to human intelligence.

Patton met with the correspondents attached to the Third Army at 4:30 P.M., November 6. "Sometime ago," he said,

I told you we were going to be stopped for a while, and I was correct. Now, we are going to start again . . . You all do some lying and say this is simply what we called in the last war "correcting a line." In other words, I do not want the Germans to start moving reserves [against the Third Army] until they have to.

In response to a question:

If you catch these bastards in Metz, you may have to kill them all, but by scaring them I hope they will have to run, in which event, there will be some very fine killing . . .

Question: Is the objective unlimited?

Patton: I don't know anything beyond Berlin.

Question: [will the immense air activity tip off the operation to the Germans?]

Patton: Personally, I don't give a good damn . . .

Question: [do the Germans have much strength in the Maginot Line?]

Patton: Yes, they have. This reminds me of years ago when we first started making armored cars. Everybody wanted to put more and more armor on them . . . The Chief of Cavalry then said, "Gentlemen, I have always feared that in the next war someone would get killed." The sooner we start, the less time the Germans will have to fix things up.

Question: Well, it's been a long time since we've gotten any real news.

Patton: Well, you gentlemen have been very patient. Now remember, I want these junior officers given breaks in this. They walk in the shit and sleep in the mud. They don't have a nice warm office like this, and you men should give them the breaks . . .

Hardly anybody below the division general staffs knows this thing, and don't even talk about it at mess because it could cost a great many thousands of lives. I know I can trust you.

*Letter, GSP, Jr., to Beatrice, November 6, 1944*

I just this morning finished one of my pre election speaking tours in which I talked to nine different divisions and drove in an open peep several hundred miles in the rain . . .

If we would only get a good day we would have the greatest air support ever, but it is raining like hell – what a country.

I am having indigestion and the heaves as I always do before a match. I suppose I would be no good if I did not; it is not fear as to the result but simply anxiety to get started.

I hope Courtney does not delay too long [to attack on his front] or I will pull the whole pack [of Germans] in on me – well all the more glory.

*Diary, November 6*

We were to have 300 heavy bombers on the Metz forts today, but the weather was so bad that it has now been postponed until tomorrow. It is useless to put any confidence in the air at this time of year.

*Letter, GSP, Jr., to Beatrice, November 7, 1944*

We jump off in the morning with ten divisions. I have commanded up to thirteen but never attacked all at once with so many. I cant see how we can loose . . .

The weather is vile so we will get no air support, but that is not too bad as the enemy will not get tipped off . . .

The plans for the show are good and the men are keen and we have plenty of ammunition and enough gas. I think we will get to the Rhine. If we do, we will cross . . .

If it is clear in the morning, I have a swell O.P. from which I can watch the kick off.

*Diary, November 7*

Two years ago today we were on the Augusta approaching Africa, and it was blowing hard. Then about 1600 it stopped. It is now 0230 and raining hard. I hope that too stops.

I know of nothing more I can do to prepare for this attack except to read the Bible and pray. The damn clock seems to have stopped. I am sure we will have a great success.

At 1900, Eddy and Grow came to the house to beg me to call off the attack due to the bad weather, heavy rains, and swollen rivers. I told them the attack would go on. I am sure it will succeed. On November 7, 1942, there was a storm but it stopped at 1600. All day the 9th of July, 1943, there was a storm but it cleared at dark.

I know the Lord will help us again. Either He will give us good weather or the bad weather will hurt the Germans more than it does us. His Will Be Done.

CHAPTER 32

# The Saar Campaign

*"The Lord came accross again."*

*Diary, November 8*

Woke up at 0300 and it was raining like hell. I actually got nervous and got up and read Rommel's book, "Infantry Attacks." It was most helpful, as he described all the rains he had in September, 1914, and also the fact that, in spite of the heavy rains, the Germans got along. Went to bed and to sleep at 0345.

At 0515, the artillery preparation woke me. The rain had stopped and the stars were out. The discharge of over 400 guns sounded like the slamming of doors in an empty house – very many doors all slamming at once. All the eastern sky glowed and trembled with the flashes of guns, and I thought how the enemy must feel, knowing that at last the attack he has dreaded has come.

I also remembered that I had always demanded the impossible, "Had dared extreme occasion and never am betrayed." How I had never taken counsel of my fears, and I thanked God for his goodness to me.

At 0745, Bradley called up to see if we were attacking. I had not told him for fear he would call off the attack, but he seemed very pleased that we were going on without any air support. Then Ike came on the line and said, "I expect a lot of you; carry the ball all the way." I wonder if he ever made a decision to take risks when his best men advised caution. I doubt if he ever has . . .

At about 1000, our fighter bombers appeared in force and attacked the known enemy command posts. The day was the brightest and best we have had in two months . . . We are doing better than we expected. Thank God.

Eddy called up after supper to say that everything was on its objective except the 35th Division, which is a little behind schedule.

It started to rain at 1700.

"The Lord came accross again," he wrote Beatrice. He observed the attack from a hill, "but we were using so much smoke to cover our bridges that the visibility was poor." All the divisions in action were doing well, even though the ground was "a bog . . . We may have won another great battle or rather won the opening period."

The purpose of the operation was to get to the Siegfried Line, some 60 miles away, and three infantry divisions in Eddy's XII Corps attacked that morning, a fourth that afternoon. Two armored divisions stood poised to pass through the infantry and exploit a penetration of the enemy defenses, while other infantry divisions were ready to reinforce success. More than 1000 prisoners of war were taken.

*Diary, November 9*

The flooded condition of the river is very bad. It is said by the local inhabitants that this is the biggest flood in the history of the Moselle valley. Many trucks, airplanes, and one hospital platoon are in the water or marooned. I am sending the Inspector General down to find out why the officers concerned did not get their stuff on high ground. Our chief trouble in this war is the inefficiency and lack of sense of responsibility on the part of company officers.

On that day Walker's XX Corps opened an attack on Metz that would continue for twelve bloody days of fighting.

Some 2,000 planes . . . came over and bombed the Metz forts and other targets on our front . . . The roar of the bombs at the observation post was quite audible, and the ground shook.

All the bridges over the Moselle south of Nancy, except at Pont-a-Mousson are out. The Seille River has increased in width from 200 to 500 feet since we started bridging it. When I crossed the Moselle at Pont-a-Mousson, I got stuck in the water and had to be pushed out by a truck . . .

I think that all the bombers we had today were really an expression of friendship to me from Spaatz and Doolittle – personality plays a tremendous part in war.

"We are doing fine," he told Beatrice.

We have gone forward every where, in some places more than 9,000 meters. It was pretty tight yesterday. We had only one bridge left standing, and the river was rising. The top has now passed, and we are O.K. Have three bridges.

The Moselle and Meurthe rivers were in the highest flood stage since 1919. Yet two armored divisions were across the Seille River, and an infantry division would soon be over too. The Germans seemed to be withdrawing, but there was no sign of German collapse or of movement out of Metz.

Eisenhower said he knew how much the floods were interfering with Patton's operations. Patton was not to be discouraged. The water would go down, and he would get on with his job, "as you always have." He wished him the best of luck and a happy birthday.

*Letter, GSP, Jr., to Eisenhower, November 11, 1944*

I am deeply appreciative of your thoughtfulness . . .

You were quite right in that the waters are a nuisance and have prevented the immediate break-through I hoped for. On the other hand, they hurt the Germans worse than they do us because they cannot get away from us, and I am quite sure we are killing a large number of them.

Bradley phoned around 5 o'clock and said he wanted the 83d Division held in reserve so it could go to the First Army if needed.

"I imagine," he wrote in his diary,

that this is one of the few times in the history of war when 1/10 of an attacking general's command was removed after the battle had been joined. I suppose that Hodges and Middleton have been working on Brad for a week and this, added to his natural timidity, caused him to make this decision. I hope history records his moral cowardice.

I am sure that it is a terrible mistake, because by using the 83d, we could take Saarbourg easily. Without it, we will not get Saarbourg and will have, therefore, to be always bothered by the triangle between the Moselle and Saar Rivers.

*Letter, GSP, Jr., to Beatrice, November 12, 1944*

I celebrated my birthday by getting up where the dead were still warm. Then I visited the wounded and made quite a hit when I removed my helmet in the presence of a man who had killed a German with a grenade and been wounded by the same weapon . . .

This may well be the crutial day of this battle. One division is over the river with no artillery and the bridge out. At the other end of the line Manton [Eddy] has made or almost made a break through . . .

I love you and wish you were here to hold my hand till the river goes down and I get some guns over.

*Diary, November 12*

Went to church where I heard the worst service yet. Sent for the Chief of Chaplains to have the offender removed and get a new chaplain . . .

The 90th and 10th Armored are still held up by the flood . . . The weather is awful and we are getting lots of trench foot . . .

I must get the XII Corps in column of divisions so as to give one division at least a chance to rest, sleep, and get hot food and dry out.

*Letter, GSP, Jr., to Beatrice, November 14, 1944*

It has rained every day since the first [of the month] and we are having a hell of a time with "imersion" [trench] feet, about as many as from enemy fire.

However the enemy must be suffering more, so it is a question of mutual crucifiction till he cracks.

There is a very slim chance that we may get Metz in 24 to 48 hours. I am going up there now.

Eisenhower came at noon, the 15th,

seemed well pleased and got copiously photographed standing in the mud talking to soldiers. After supper we talked till 2:30 A.M., and I believe I put over my ideas on getting decorations and promotions for the staff.

Writing later to thank Patton for his hospitality, Eisenhower said, "I know what a grand job you are all doing under difficult conditions. It was good to see it myself and find all the commanders in such good spirits." He was sure that Patton was "on the eve of a fine victory at Metz."

*Diary, November 17*

Eddy's allowance of shells for tomorrow is 9,000, so I told him to use 20,000. If we win now, we will not need shells later; if we do not use the shells now, we will not win the war.

*Letter, GSP, Jr., to Frederick Ayer, November 18, 1944*

For the first three days it was pretty tight, as out of nine bridges, all except two were either removed by the flood or shot out by the enemy, frequently both. Now, however, the flood has abated and things are looking up. Also, the ground is dried and so we use the tanks to better effect.

*Letter, GSP, Jr., to sister Nita, November 18, 1944*

Today I decided to stay in . . . There is nothing that I can do at the front except bother people, as they are all doing a swell job, and I believe advancing very rapidly. One of the hardest things that I have to do to – and I presume any General has to do – is not to interfere with the next echelon of command when the show is going all right.

The other day . . . I saw so many dead Germans that it actually made me sick . . . I believe about 800. They were all neatly piled like cordwood along the side of the road waiting to be buried by our Graves Registration units.

The campaign was moving too slowly, the weather was miserable, the troops were suffering from the cold and the rain, and the commanders were becoming tired and edgy.

McBride seemed fed up with Grow, Walker was dissatisfied with Irwin – "I will visit them in the morning."

*Diary, November 19*

At 0845, Eddy called to say he was having trouble with Wood and wanted to see me. He came at 0930 and stated that Wood did not drive hard yesterday and was almost insubordinate. I wrote Wood a letter which I sent him by Gaffey, telling him plainly that if things did not improve, I would have to relieve him. I hate to do this as he is one of my best friends, but war is war . . .

Walker will leave the 5th Division to clean up Metz and will attack to the east, north of Merzig. He is showing plenty of drive . . .

Called Bradley to say that while Metz has not officially surrendered, it is ours.

Wood apologized to Eddy and everything seems all right.

*Letter, GSP, Jr., to Beatrice, November 19, 1944*

We have completely surrounded Metz and are fighting in the streets. I doubt if this will be serious . . .

I think that only Attila and the Third Army have ever taken Metz by assault.

Actually the French took it in 1552. The Germans surrounded it in August 1870, and after several battles, forced the French to capitulate two months later.

Courtney [Hodges] and Charley [Simpson] are doing nothing except fight [the] weather. We beat the weather.

As things were going well yesterday, I stayed in my office. I could not but smile at how different running a battle is from the way it is told. I find that if one goes up too often, one becomes a nusance. I dont rush about the battle field sticking out of a tank the way I am painted. As it is, I get out where it is unhealthy oftener than any other general, to include division commanders.

If it only wont rain we will go places.

*Diary, December 20*

I wish things would move faster in this Army, because I fear that at the moment the French and the Seventh Army are stealing the show . . . The impetus of our attack is naturally slackening due to the fatigue of the men. I am trying to arrange to get at least one infantry division in each corps out of the line for a rest, but I doubt whether we can do it.

To Beatrice:

The Seventh Army and the First French Army [in Devers' 6th Army Group] seem to have made a monkey of me this morning, but I will get going soon.

The French Army moved through the Belfort gap and the Seventh Army through the Saverne gap, took the important cities of Belfort, Mulhouse, and Strasbourg, put the 6th Army Group at the Rhine River, and surrounded a large German force at Colmar that would hold out until February.

Patton was concerned with P. Wood, who had reached the point where he could no longer bear to see his division endure further losses. "I am trying to find some nice way of easing him out."

A German general in Metz sent word that he would not surrender but would fight to the death. "We are trying to satisfy him."

On November 22, at 2:35 P.M., Metz was officially declared clear of enemy troops, although several forts still held out. Eisenhower sent congratulations to Patton for having restored the historic city to the French.

In a hospital nearby, Patton asked a wounded soldier whether he had heard that Metz had fallen. The soldier smiled and said yes. Patton grabbed him by the hand, smiled back, and said, "Tomorrow, son, the headlines will read, 'Patton Took Metz,' which you know is a goddam lie. You and your buddies are the ones who actually took Metz."

With Gay, Koch, an interpreter, and sentries present, Patton interviewed a Nazi major general, Anton Dunckern, a member of the SS, captured in the Metz area.

> Patton: You can tell this man that naturally in my position I cannot demean myself to question him, but I can say this, that I have captured a great many German generals, and this is the first one who has been wholly untrue to everything; because he has not only been a Nazi but he is untrue to the Nazis by surrendering. If he wants to say anything he can, and I will say that unless he talks pretty well, I will turn him over to the French. They know how to make people talk.
>
> Dunckern: . . . I received orders to go in the Metz sector and defend a certain sector there, and the reason I did not perish was that I could not reach my weapons and fight back.
>
> Patton: . . . He is a liar!
>
> Dunckern: There was no possibility to continue fighting. The door was opened, and they put a gun on me.
>
> Patton: If he wanted to be a good Nazi, he could have died then and there. It would have been a pleasanter death than what he will get now.

Dunckern: . . . It was useless to do anything about it under the circumstances. (He asked permission to ask a question; it was granted.) I was fighting against American troops and captured by them, and therefore am to be considered a prisoner of war of the American forces.

Patton: He will be a prisoner of war of the French forces soon. They have a lot they want to ask him.

Dunckern: I consider myself a prisoner of war of the American forces, and I have not been captured by the French forces.

Patton: When I am dealing with vipers, I do not have to be bothered by any foolish ideas any more than he has been.

Dunckern: I consider myself a prisoner of war since I fought as a soldier and should be treated as a soldier.

Patton: You also acted as a policeman — a low type of police.

Dunckern: I acted as an officer of the police in an honorable and practical manner, and I have nothing to be ashamed of.

Patton: This is a matter of opinion — no one who is a Nazi policeman could act in an honorable manner.

Dunckern: I can only say that during every day of my life I have been honest, rightful, respectful, and humanitarian.

Patton: If this is the case, do you have anything you want to say by way of giving me information or by talking about the German people that will change my opinion?

Dunckern: No one will be able to stand up against me to testify that I did anything against the rules of humanity or human treatment.

Patton: I understand German very well, but I will not demean myself by speaking such a language. I think before I turn the General over to the French, I will send him to the Army Group who may question him or have some special investigators question him, and they can do things I can't do.

Dunckern: I am not worried about having myself investigated. Of course, there may be some mistakes I have made, which is only human, but I am not worried about inhuman acts charged against me.

Patton: . . . I have great respect for the German soldiers; they are gallant men, but not for Nazis. Have the guards take him outside and have his picture taken and then we'll see what we will do with him. Also tell him that those bayonets on the guards' guns are very sharp.

Later, Patton said that this "Gestapo General" was

> the most vicious looking human being I have ever seen, and who, after I got through talking to him, was unquestionably one of the worst scared. He is the first man I have ever brow-beaten, and I must admit I took real pleasure in doing it.

Patton immediately had Colonel Constantin Meyer, a Regular Army officer also captured in the Metz area, brought in. If he had bullied Dunckern, he was solicitous toward Meyer.

> Patton: Tell the Colonel that this SS General I had in here stood up, but I am having him [Meyer] sit down because he is a professional soldier and I have respect for him. I have great respect for the German soldier. I have read your military books and studied your army. I know the Colonel has been a gallant soldier and has shown courage and has fought for his country and army. He is not a Party man, and has fought for Germany because it is Germany. Naturally, because of the understanding which exists between members of the military profession all over, of all armies, I can't ask the Colonel to say anything he feels he shouldn't say, but I would like to have his opinion of why the Germans continue – if he wishes to so state – to fight when they are so palpably outnumbered and have so many young men killed for no purpose.
>
> Meyer: The only reason the Wehrmacht continues to fight is the hope of a possible victory, a victory based only on a specific hope [no doubt he was referring to hope for a miracle weapon that would change the course of the war].
>
> Patton: If the German army realized, as he must, the tremendous power of the American army, particularly our materiel, tanks, and guns – would they continue to fight?
>
> Meyer: They will continue to fight until such time as they will receive orders to lay down their weapons.
>
> Patton: As a humanitarian, is there anything I can do to cause them to stop this unnecessary blood shedding?
>
> Meyer: It would be very difficult for me to do anything.
>
> Patton: I am not asking the Colonel, because naturally he is a good soldier, but is there anything that can be told to the German people so they can stop getting killed for that crazy man?
>
> Meyer: If the German people and the German army could be

shown . . . in some manner that very acceptable peace terms could be established, especially with reference to the Eastern front, I believe that some means could be found to stop the war in order to preserve life . . .

I know that both the German people and the German army know that the American forces are the best equipped, the best fit, and with inestimable possibilities for replacements of any other army in Europe.

Patton: We have found that the Volks Divisions are very poor . . .

Meyer: Yes, I know that too. It is the fear of Russia that is forcing us to use every man who can carry a weapon, for we must hold on there as we fear the consequences on the Eastern front. If . . . this would be taken care of, there is no doubt that the war would be brought to a close and the American forces would be permitted to enter Germany unhampered . . .

I very respectfully request that I may be sent to the United States rather than England.

Patton: . . . General Bradley will decide that.

There are two questions I would like to ask . . . There are three forts [at Metz] holding out. Is there any way we can persuade them to surrender without killing everyone there?

Meyer: The request can be sent to General Kittle, commandant of the fortress.

Patton: He is badly wounded and is our prisoner now . . .

There is a great deal of talk from the German radio about underground movements and fighting by civilians in Germany. Do you think that will take place? It would be very sad if that happened, because many civilians would be killed.

Meyer: . . . I do not believe there will be any partisan fighting as in Russia or France . . . The German is not qualified to carry on partisan warfare . . . and if anything like this does happen to Germany, it will be an individual person, and . . . never an organized policy of warfare.

Patton: I want this Colonel treated much differently from the other man. Tell him that his treatment is much different and he should not tell that to the other one, and also he will not be with him.

Meyer: I am very grateful that I do not have to stay with the SS officer.

Patton: I don't blame you. Now about those forts holding out — they are not bothering us but they do require us to kill Germans and we also lose men . . . I could have destroyed it [Metz] but I did not want to.

Meyer: We were very much surprised about this . . .

Koch: Does the Colonel know anything about the mining of buildings?

Meyer: . . . I am almost positive that there has been no mining of buildings, or traps of any sort . . . There are naturally minefields along the fortification areas and also the bridges are prepared for blowing up, but so far as houses are concerned, there are no mines.

Patton had a guard of honor for Eddy and Walker that morning to celebrate the captures of Nancy and Metz. "Actually the band played three ruffles and three flourishes" – signifying that they were lieutenant generals. "I hope this is prophetic, as I am sure corps commanders should have three stars."

*Letter, GSP, Jr., to Beatrice, November 23, 1944*

I too hope we can have fun together again hunting and sailing, but I guess I will be hard to live with. I have been a sort of demi god too long . . .

We are continuing the attack on the Saar River line tomorrow. The weather is frightful.

Giraud called and remarked that in his opinion Patton was the "Liberator of France." Patton was glad that someone thought so – that is, someone besides himself.

Ammunition supplies were low, but Patton was determined to use what he needed until he ran out. Then he would have the troops dig in. Until then, they would go forward.

Patton felt that he was too far behind the front to visit the troops as often as he wished, and he grumbled that "the distances are terrible, and it is dark by 5:15." He wanted to move his command post forward, but there was no place except St. Avold, and he had no telephone wire laid to that point. Perhaps too, some intuitive feeling warned him against going to St. Avold.

Traveling in his private railroad car to Thionville, he decided, would give him time enough to go by jeep to the divisions; he could return home after dark by rail.

At a press conference on November 24, he had little to say.

Question: Is the German capable of many counter-offensives?

Patton: Not in my opinion.

Question: What about the SS General captured?

Patton: Oh, he is a hotshot, that bastard. He is the lowest type animal I have ever seen. I had a lot of fun with him.

Question: Would the decisive battles be fought this side of the Rhine?

Patton: In my opinion they will be fought there. The Germans will get some people, but not all.

Question: Will we have to fight all the way to Berlin?

Patton: We will have to start but we won't fight all the way . . .

Question: What was the reason for the attack on November 8?

Patton: I jumped off then because I felt that we could cross the river and I felt sure the Germans felt we couldn't, and my guess was right.

It was hardly a scintillating performance. Patton was, no doubt, disappointed that he had secured no breakthrough. The Germans were resisting well, the country was difficult for dramatic sweeps, and the weather continued to be abominable.

In his diary:

Evidently Devers talked Eisenhower out of letting me have the XV Corps. It is a very stupid decision . . . Well, it can't be helped, but I hate it, and from a military standpoint it is stupid.

I called Bradley and protested but got nowhere. His thesis is that all four American Armies should consist of 12 divisions. This is absurd. An Army should be the size necessary to accomplish its task in the theater of operations where it is committed. The First and Ninth Armies are on narrow fronts and need fewer divisions than the Third Army, which is on a wide front.

Furthermore, the First Army is making a terrible mistake in leaving the VIII Corps static, as it is highly probable that the Germans are building up east of them.

Of all the many remarkably prophetic statements made by Patton, none was more astute than this one. As he expected, the VIII Corps would be struck by the Germans in their Ardennes counteroffensive launched in December.

The only way to think about these things is to remember that "what can't be cured must be endured." Bradley is without inspiration and all for equality [among the Armies] — he may also be jealous.

Bradley came with the final arrangements for a new boundary between the Third and Seventh Armies. The VI Corps in the Seventh Army was to move along the Rhine.

We will see how this comes out. I personally believe the VI Corps should have crossed the Rhine, but it was stopped by Eisenhower the day he visited Devers.

I called up Haislip to congratulate him on his breakthrough, and he said I was the only person who had commended him — neither his Army commander [Patch] nor his Army Group commander [Devers] had said a word about it.

Averell Harriman, Ambassador to Russia, came to visit.

The ground was as bad is it could be — practically all the meadows looked like lakes.

Harriman told me that Stalin had praised the Third Army in the highest terms . . . He said to Harriman in the presence of the Chief of Staff of the Red Army, "The Red Army could not have conceived and certainly could not have executed the advance of the Third Army across France."

Harriman says that Stalin is a strong, ruthless revolutionist and therefore a very potential threat to future world conditions. He says that discipline in the Red Army is the most rigid and ruthless he has ever seen, and that the officer caste is a new nobility. This is a strange result of communism.

I think he had a very pleasant time.

*Diary, November 29*

The shortage of replacements for the Third Army is this day 9,000, and none in sight. I cannot see why Eisenhower could be caught short on both men and ammunition, because after all, these are the two elements with which wars are fought. I will have to withdraw 5% of the headquarters personnel of the Army and make infantrymen out of them.

A few days later he noted:

> It will certainly be necessary to take another 5% of the headquarters units and also to cannibalize the divisions [taking men from the rear units] to provide riflemen [replacements].

Hughes sent Patton a letter from a friend who wrote:

> Tell Georgie that all the [stock] market needs to send it into a peace panic is to learn that he is on the rampage again. The Dow-Jones average slipped three points when he started storming Metz. Patton for President clubs will be forming soon. Really, the slapping incident has helped glamourize him. However, I suggest that next time he should pick on a general. Why don't you be the victim?

"If the suggestion has any merit in your opinion," Hughes said, "please call on me. I will go as far as to let you boot me if you think it would do any good, for I am still pro Patton."

*Letter, GSP, Jr., to Hughes, November 30, 1944*

I am like Sherman – I would not run if nominated, nor serve if elected. As you know, at the close of the war, I intend to remove my insignia and wrist-watch, but will continue to wear my short coat so that everyone can kiss my ass.

In a more serious vein . . . how the hell we can fight a war without men and ammunition I don't know!

Ex-Governor Herbert Lehman of New York, Administrator of the United Nations Relief and Rehabilitation Agency, came to dinner and spent the night. Patton thought him "quite a man."

Major General Paul R. Hawley, Chief Surgeon, ETOUSA, wrote to tell Patton that his command directive on trench foot was the best that Hawley had seen and he applauded Patton for his "vigorous action."

Patton had issued a memorandum to his corps and division commanders, saying:

> If the prevention of trench foot were impossible, I would not mention it, but prevention is perfectly practicable and is a function of command . . .

If company officers and non-commissioned officers did their full duty, there would be no trench foot. The onus of their failure rests on you . . .

We are going to have weather conditions from now on until the end of the war which will be conducive to trench foot. To win the war we must conquer trench foot. You have conquered every other obstacle — I am sure you can conquer this.

Both XII Corps and XX Corps reached the Saar River around the beginning of December, and Patton sent the 90th and 95th Divisions across even though it was flooded. His troops would hit toward the strongest part of the Siegfried Line "because a straight line is the shortest distance between points and also it is so strong that it is probably not too well defended . . . All I can do is pray to beat Hell. The attack will go on." He was going up in the morning in case they needed "a little more emphasis."

To Beatrice:

It has been a long time since I saw you but the imprint of your lips on a recent letter looked pretty attractive . . . I love and miss you but this is no place for you.

To a friend on December 1:

We are pulling off the biggest gamble I have yet indulged in, but being a good gambler I am sure it will win . . . As is usual with my efforts, the Lord seems to be on my side, for the sun has come out for the first time in a week, and we will probably get fighter-bombers out this afternoon.

To his daughter Ruth Ellen Totten:

We are attacking the Siegfried Line. I know that there are many generals with my reputation who would not have dared to do it because . . . "They are more afraid of losing a battle than anxious to win one." . . . I do not believe that any of these lines are impregnable . . . If we get through, we will materially shorten the war — there is no *if* about getting through; I am sure we will!

But this was nothing more than the old Patton flash, the Patton spirit; he was really not so sure.

"It was finally necessary to ask for P. Wood's relief, as he is entirely too nervous to remain in command at the present time."

He wrote Beatrice:

> I got P sent home on a 60 day detached service. He is nearly nuts due to nerves and inability to sleep. I hope I can get him a job in the States. He is too hard to handle.

*Diary, December 3*

Wood came to say goodbye . . . I doubt that he was really sorry to go . . .

Damn the weather; it is starting to rain.

He sent Gaffey to take command of the 4th Armored Division in place of Wood.

*Letter, GSP, Jr., to Surles, December 3, 1944*

We are having one hell of a war, and the lack of ammunition and replacements is getting more and more serious. I don't know what the young manhood of America is doing, but they are certainly not appearing over here.

At the present moment, this Army is 11,000 men short and with very little apparent prospect of getting some replacements.

People do not realize that 92% of all casualties occur in the infantry rifle companies, and that when the infantry division has lost 4,000 men, it has practically no riflemen left. Therefore, with 11,000 odd short in an Army consisting of three armored and six infantry divisions, we are closely approaching a 40% shortage in each rifle company.

This is very serious. I do not know that there is anything you can do about it, but I do know that I can't talk to anyone else on the subject, so I am shooting off my head to you.

A visit to the XV Corps and Seventh Army convinced him that their supply replacement situation was much better than his own and, generally, than in the 12th Army Group. The main reason was Marseilles, through which a steady stream of supply items and replacement soldiers flowed. The 12th Army Group, as well as the 21 Army Group, had no comparable port. But this was about to be remedied. The Canadians cleared the Germans from the banks of the Schelde in hard-fought operations ending November 8, and Allied naval units swept the waters of the estuary during the following three weeks. On November 28, Antwerp was opened to shipping, and the supply situation for Montgomery's and Bradley's Army Groups would soon improve.

*Letter, Marshall to GSP, Jr., December 1944*

Since landing in France your Army has written a great page in history of which the American people will always be very proud. Your recent advances despite most adverse conditions and the bitter fighting of the enemy have given us all great encouragement.

Thanks . . . for the photographs . . . Send me another lot taken east of the Rhine.

*Letter, GSP, Jr., to Handy, December 5, 1944*

I believe that the enemy has nearly reached his breaking point. As a matter of fact, we are stretched pretty thin ourselves . . .

It will be a great help if the Ordnance Department would put another co-axial machine gun – preferably a .50[caliber] but at least a .30 – in all tanks. I have talked to [Levin] Campbell [Chief of Ordnance] about this, but as usual with the Ordnance they are making too many studies. I believe that if you would tell him to do it and be goddam, something might happen.

P. Wood got so nervously exhausted that General Eisenhower sent him home on a 60 day DS [detached service]. I know that you are one of P's greatest friends, and he is my best friend. It is my considered opinion that due to P's inability to sleep, he should, if possible, be retained in the U.S. in his present rank.

Unquestionably, in a rapid moving advance, he is the greatest division commander I have ever seen, but when things get sticky he is inclined to worry too much, which keeps him from sleeping and runs him down, and makes it difficult to control his operations.

However, if it is a question of having him reduced, I will take him back even if I have to personally command him.

The few remaining forts around Metz were surrendering because of "lack of salt, lack of water, and lack of guts." The Germans were holding out to prevent Patton from advancing, but he was using the region as a rest area and giving new units practice in firing with captured German artillery pieces using captured German artillery shells.

*Diary, December 6*

[Fourteen] Congressmen came . . . Congresswoman Luce made a very unfavorable impression on me and, I think, on everyone else. The whole crowd seemed to be below average and was looking for trouble. We had them in for lunch, gave them nothing to drink, and only fed them issue food [what the soldiers ate], as they were the type who would go home and say we ate too well.

*Letter, GSP, Jr., to Beatrice, December 7, 1944*

There is always a chance – to day it seems strong – that the fear of they may again stop me . . .

Regrouping is the curse of war and a great boon to the enemy.

*Diary, December 7*

Devers . . . promised complete cooperation, and so far seems to have given it. I am not sure that, as the lesser of two evils, it might not be better to be in his army group; he interferes less and is not as timid as Bradley. It would perhaps be a mercy if the latter were gathered [into heaven] – a fine man, but not great.

*Letter, GSP, Jr., to Beatrice, December 9, 1944*

It is still raining. The Saar usually 50 feet wide is now 300, but that wont stop us.

Willie and I have two green leather chairs in my room where we sit of evenings. When he snores too much I give him a nose drop.

Patton had by then levied 5000 men from Army and corps headquarters and from other noncombat jobs and had sent them to a training center at Metz to turn them into riflemen replacements. He thought that "additional economies will have to be made." And he wondered why Eisenhower refused to order the Com Z to give up 10 percent of its "vast army" for training and infantry replacements. "For some reason, he is reluctant to issue such an order."

To Stimson:

I hope that in the final settlement of the war, you insist that the

Germans retain Lorraine, because I can imagine no greater burden than to be the owner of this nasty country where it rains every day and where the whole wealth of the people consists in assorted manure piles...

P.S. Of course the remarks about Lorraine were intended for a joke. I label it because some of my jokes are not always appreciated.

To Cook:

The fight we are now having is less spectacular than the fight across France, but it is a damn sight harder . . . However, I believe we are breaking through – at least we are doing our damdest.

To Beatrice:

I have never seen or imagined such a hell hole of a country. There is about four inches of liquid mud over every thing and it rains all the time, not hard but steadily.

He wrote a letter of instructions on how to conduct attacks of envelopment, techniques "applicable to all combats against Germans except in fortified positions such as the Siegfried Line." Already he was looking forward to his operations beyond the West Wall. "To repeat," he said at the end,

There is no purpose in capturing these manure-filled, water logged villages. The purpose of our operations is to kill or capture the German personnel and vehicles . . . so that they cannot retreat and repeat their opposition. Straight frontal attacks against villages are prohibited unless after careful study there is no other possible solution.

*Diary, December 11*

I had the Army Chaplain direct all chaplains to pray for dry weather. I will publish this prayer with a Christmas greeting on the back of it to all members of the command.

He decided to move his command post to St. Avold, but not before the 19th, again an intuitive feeling preventing him from starting at once.

*Third Army Letter, Relations with the German People, December 12, 1944*

The friendship and cooperation of the French people will be replaced in Germany by universal hostility, which will require that we regard all Germans, soldiers and civilians, men, women, and even children, as active enemies. It is expected that we shall encounter sniping, guerrilla warfare, sabotage, and treachery. Everyone must be warned of these probabilities and prepared to take all possible protective measures . . .

Fraternizing or friendly association with any German is absolutely forbidden and will be punished. Any pretense of friendship must be viewed with the utmost suspicion. Individuals claiming to have escaped from German prisoner of war camps or to be non-German members of the German Army or forced laborers will be considered as enemies until cleared by careful investigation.

On December 13, the last fort of isolated Metz capitulated.

*Diary, December 14*

Into Saarlautern where the fighting is still going on. Nearly all the houses I inspected . . . are really forts. It was supposed to be dangerous to cross the bridge [into town], but we had only one shot hit near us . . . Walker wished to go across the bridge with me, but I decided it was not necessary to risk both an Army and a corps commander . . .

The rifle strength [in the infantry battalions] is very low, poor devils, but they are killing large numbers of Germans . . .

Drove to Luxembourg to see Bradley. Apparently Monty, with the assistance of the Prime Minister, will get the Ninth Army. Monty is bitterly opposed to the operations of both Patch and myself. He still wants all available forces massed on the north and wants to command them. He told Ike and Brad that when he commanded the war, it was a success, but since he has been relieved of the Supreme [Ground] Command, it has become a stalemate. I do not see how they stand such conversation. Montgomery still maintains that the Rhine can only be crossed at one place, namely, at Cologne, and that this must be done under one Army Group commander.

My attack will still go on with its present short means, but if it fails to break through . . . I will have to go on the defensive until more troops arrive, and pending their arrival, I will probably lose several divisions [to other Armies]. It is certainly up to me to make a breakthrough, and I feel that, God helping, it will come about.

It has certainly rained less since my prayer . . .

Had Eddy come in and spend the nights of the 13th and 14th, as he is tired and nervous and should relax.

*Letter, GSP, Jr., to Beatrice, December 15, 1944*

This is one of the days when every one but me has lost faith. I still have to push them over but it does not seem to bother me.

There was no rain on December 15, but the weather remained overcast and damp. On the following morning, concealed by a heavy fog, the Germans launched their Ardennes counteroffensive, a massive attack against the VIII Corps of the First Army, and quickly pushed a salient or a bulge into the American lines.

Although Patton's Third Army would continue for several more days their operations in the Saar, the German offensive brought to an end the long, dismal period of grim and relentless warfare.

Patton's November operations, which continued into December, won substantial gains and inflicted heavy casualties on the Germans. But he failed to penetrate the West Wall. The Third Army had advanced methodically about 35 or 40 miles through one defended town after another. Now in mid-December the troops were up against the German border guarded by the string of pillboxes and dragon's teeth that marked the Siegfried Line or West Wall.

When the Germans struck in the Ardennes and opened a dramatic turn of events, they gave Patton his greatest opportunity for professional and personal achievement.

# VI

# Belgium and Luxembourg

*"Some people call it luck, some genius.*
*I call it determination."*

# CHAPTER 33

# Bastogne

*"We have to push people beyond endurance in order to bring this war to its end."*

THE FIRST INTIMATION Patton had of the German Ardennes counteroffensive came in a telephone call from 12th Army Group, which instructed him to move an armored division from Walker's XX Corps to Middleton's VIII "to help repulse a rather strong German attack."

Unaware of the extent of the German effort, Patton protested. He said that the Third Army had paid "a very heavy price in blood in the hope of a break through at Saarlautern and Saarbrucken," and consequently his Army needed the division in case the Germans extended their attack into his area. In his opinion, he told Bradley, moving the armored division would play into the Germans' hands.

> Bradley admitted my logic but took counsel of his fears and ordered the . . . move.
>
> I wish he were less timid.

But then on reconsideration, "He probably knows more of the situation than he can say over the telephone."

He was beginning to sense the importance of the German counterattack.

> *Diary, December 17*
>
> The German attack is on a wide front and moving fast . . . This may be a feint . . . although at the moment it looks like the real thing. If the Germans . . . are intending to attack me, we will stop them as we are very well placed . . .
>
> Had the V and VIII Corps of the First Army been more aggressive, the Germans could not have prepared this attack; one must never sit still.

Everything was ready to move his headquarters to St. Avold, but he decided to wait until the tactical situation in the Ardennes cleared.

Bradley phoned and said he might have to call on Patton for two more divisions to help contain the Germans.

> *Letter, GSP, Jr., to Maj. Gen. Fox Conner, Hendersonville, N.C., December 17, 1944*
>
> Yesterday morning the Germans attacked to my north in front of the VIII Corps of the First Army. It reminds me very much of March 25, 1918 [Ludendorff's final offensive] and I think will have the same results.
>
> I have always felt that the war will be terminated east of the Rhine, and I am convinced that this attack by the Germans will be very thoroughly smashed, and they will have nothing left.

Bradley telephoned at 10:30 A.M., December 18, and asked Patton to bring his G–2, G–3, and G–4, to Luxembourg for a conference as soon as he could. He added that "what he was going to suggest would be unacceptable to me, but that he wanted to see me."

Within ten minutes after receiving the call, Patton, Koch, Maddox, and Muller departed for Luxembourg.

When Patton arrived, Bradley said,

> "I feel you won't like what we are going to do, but I fear it is necessary."
>
> He then showed [on the map] that the German penetration is much greater than I had thought.
>
> He asked me what I could do. I told him that I would halt the 4th Armored and concentrate it near Longwy, starting at midnight, and that I would start the 80th in the morning on [meaning, to] Luxembourg. I also said that I could alert the 26th to move in 24 hours if necessary. He seemed satisfied.

This was rather a large shift of units, complicated as well as risky. Yet Patton had reacted instantly.

He telephoned Gay, Third Army chief of staff since Gaffey's assumption of 4th Armored Division command, and said:

> Stop Hugh [Gaffey] and McBride [80th Division] from whatever

> they are doing. Alert them for movement [elsewhere]. They should make no retrograde movement at this time, but this is the real thing and they will undoubtedly move tomorrow. They will go under General M. [Millikin, III Corps]. Arrange to have sufficient transportation on hand to move McBride. Hugh can move on his own power. I am going to leave here and stop to see Johnnie W. [Walker]. It will probably be late when I come home.

Almost immediately Maddox telephoned and asked Gay to have John Millikin (III Corps) and his G–2, G–3, and G–4, come to the Third Army headquarters for a conference; they were to be prepared to spend the night.

While Patton was returning from Luxembourg, Bradley phoned Gay. He said that the situation was deteriorating and that

> it was practically a sure thing now we would move the 80th and 4th, and he wanted to know if Gay thought one combat command of the 4th could be moved tonight.

Gay replied he knew it could. Furthermore, he was sure that the 80th and the remainder of the 4th Armored could move early the next morning.

Bradley asked to have Patton telephone him at 8 P.M.

Patton "drove home in the dark, a very dangerous operation, which I hate."

He phoned Bradley at 8 o'clock, and Bradley said:

> The situation up there is much worse than it was when I talked to you. Move Hugh and McBride at once, one combat command of Hugh's to move tonight, if possible. Destination, Longwy. Have Millikin report to Allen at my command post at 1100 tomorrow. You and a staff officer meet me for a conference with General Eisenhower at Verdun at approximately 1100. I understand from General Eisenhower that you are to take over VIII Corps as well as the offensive to be launched by the new troops coming into the area.

At 8:15, Patton and his principal staff officers met with Millikin and his. They discussed the plan "insofar as it was known," and agreed on the routes that the 4th Armored and 80th Divisions would use to move against the Germans.

This change in plans required calling off a big air bombardment scheduled on the Siegfried Line in front of the XII Corps, which now, for a while at least, would have to assume a defensive posture.

The more Patton thought about the German bulge into the American lines, the more he thought that the best thing to do would be to let the Germans penetrate for 40 or 50 miles, and then make a bold move to cut them off in their rear and destroy their entire thrust. This might end the war altogether, but it would take great nerve and aplomb to permit the Germans to roll forward, for they had a massive force in the Ardennes.

In conformance with Hitler's bold concept, the Germans assembled 25 divisions and committed 20 to the attack along a 60-mile front between Monschau and Echternach. Taking advantage of a heavy fog on the morning of December 16, and of forecasts for bad weather during the following days, three German armies, totaling 200,000 troops, struck about 80,000 Americans of the VIII Corps — composed of newly arrived divisions breaking in and battered divisions recuperating in a quiet sector — rolled westward across northern Luxembourg and Belgium, and headed for Antwerp, about 100 miles away. Within a few days they pushed a bulge into the American lines, a salient stretching about 50 miles almost to the Meuse River.

If they crossed the Meuse, they had a good chance of taking Antwerp, thereby destroying the foundation of the Allied supply system. They would also split the Allied Armies. They would, therefore, delay the Allied drive into Germany and presumably give Hitler the opportunity to negotiate for peace in the West.

It was an ambitious vision, a stroke of genius on the part of the Fuehrer, even though his generals doubted that the German resources, that late in the war, were strong enough to attain Hitler's goal.

On December 19, at 7 A.M., Patton met with his principal staff members, as well as with Eddy, Millikin, and the VIII Corps Artillery Officer. He outlined his plan "insofar as he knew it." An hour later he met with his entire general staff and Weyland and his staff. He

> explained the change in plan and told them we would have to make rapid movements, which would depend on them. I then made a

rough plan for operations based on the assumption that I would use the VIII Corps and the III Corps on any two of three possible axes [roads] . . . I made a simple code, one copy of which I left with Gay so that if I was ordered to execute the operation, I could call him on the phone [and get it started].

He also talked with Gay about a new boundary between the XII Corps and Devers' 6th Army Group, made arrangements about which units might be attached to the III Corps in Luxembourg, and sketched possible directions of action.

At 9:15, Patton and Harkins departed for Verdun, which they reached at 10:45. Eisenhower, Bradley, Devers, Tedder

and a large number of staff officers were there. Ike had the SHAEF G–2 give the picture and then said he wanted me to get to Luxembourg and take command of the battle and make a strong counterattack with at least six divisions. The fact that three of these divisions exist only on paper did not enter his head.

These three divisions had virtually been wiped out by the Germans.

He said he was prepared to take [go over on] the defense from Saarlautern south and asked Devers how much of the line he could take over.

Devers made a long speech on strictly selfish grounds and said nothing.

Bradley said little.

I kept still, except that I said we needed replacements.

But that was an old story.

Ike said, "When can you attack?"

I said, "On December 22, with three divisions; the 4th Armored, the 26th, and the 80th."

This was the sublime moment of his career.

Later, Patton added:

When I said I could attack on the 22d, it created quite a commo-

> tion — some people seemed surprised and others pleased — however, I believe it can be done.

It was a very short time for unscrambling forces set up to operate one way and putting them together to go in a different direction.

> He [Ike] said he was afraid this was not strong enough, but I insisted that I could beat the Germans with three divisions, and if I waited [to get more divisions into the effort], I would lose surprise.
>
> Tedder urged me to get rid of the XX Corps, but I wish to hold it and use it for a possible rest area.

Patton's proposal was astonishing, technically difficult, and daring. It meant reorienting his entire Army from an eastward direction to the north, a 90-degree turn that would pose logistical nightmares — getting divisions on new roads and making sure that supplies reached them from dumps established in quite a different context, for quite a different situation. Altogether, it was an operation that only a master could think of executing.

Eisenhower approved.

In much the same way that Hitler's Mortain counterattack in August foreshadowed his much larger Ardennes counteroffensive, Patton's turn of Haislip's eastward-moving XV Corps to the north to Argentan resembled what he would now do with his Army, a wheeling movement to Bastogne. Patton would break off his attack in the Saar region, face to the north, and thrust into the German flank while Devers extended his left to cover the front that Patton was vacating in the Saar.

"Ike said in departing, 'Every time I get a new star I get attacked.' "

He had been promoted just before the battle of Kasserine Pass. And now he had recently received his fifth star to become general of the army.

"I said, 'And every time you get attacked, I pull you out.' "

> Before leaving Verdun, I directed [in a telephone call to Gay] that the 26th and 4th Armored move at once on Arlon via Longwy, and the 80th move on Luxembourg. The 4th had actually pulled out last night, and the 80th started this morning on Thionville and received instructions there to move on Luxembourg.

He drove to the XX Corps to explain the situation to Walker and "decided to spend the night there" because he hated to drive during darkness and invite the possibility of being captured. Rumor had it that the Germans were using troops who could speak English and were dressed in American uniforms in order to kidnap Eisenhower and other high-ranking Allied commanders.

He sent Codman to Nancy to get the Third Army headquarters started moving to Luxembourg.

Prince Felix of Luxembourg

> also spent the night with Walker. Obviously he is afraid to stay in Luxembourg, not from personal reasons, but because it would be a great feather in the Germans' cap to catch him.

> *Diary, December 20*
>
> In the morning I drove to Luxembourg arriving at 0900. Bradley had halted the 80th Division at Luxembourg and had also engaged one combat command of the 4th Armored Division in the vicinity east of Bastogne without letting me know, but I said nothing.
>
> While I was there, Ike called and he and Brad had a long talk. He told Bradley that he was putting in Monty in operational control of the First and Ninth Armies, due to the fact that telephonic connections between Bradley and those two Armies was difficult. As a matter of fact, telephonic communications were all right, and it is either a case of having lost confidence in Bradley or having been forced to put Montgomery in through the machinations of the Prime Minister or with the hope that if he gives Monty operational control, he will get some of the British divisions in [to the fight]. Eisenhower is unwilling or unable to command Montgomery.

Patton's speculation was interesting but beside the point. Although telephonic communications, as Patton said, were all right from Bradley's headquarters to Hodges and Simpson, the physical distances to the Army headquarters — around the deep bulge driven into the American line — made it difficult for Bradley to confer personally with his Army commanders. In a fast-changing situation, face-to-face consultation might be required, and Montgomery was closer at hand to take necessary action.

Bradley resented Eisenhower's decision precisely because it might be misinterpreted as a loss of confidence in Bradley's efficiency at a time of great emergency. Moreover, it would enable Montgomery to press for his reappointment to the Allied ground force command.

Patton

> Drove to Arlon and saw Middleton, Millikin, Gaffey, and Paul. The VIII Corps is fighting very well, but at the moment consisting of nothing but remnants, except in the case of the 101st Airborne Division, which is holding Bastogne. In Bastogne there is also one combat command of the 9th Armored Division and one of the 10th Armored, two companies of tank destroyers, and some colored artillery.
>
> I told Middleton to give ground and blow up bridges so that we can get the enemy further extended before we hit him in flank. However, on Bradley's suggestion, in which Middleton strongly concurred, we decided to hang on to Bastogne, because it is a very important road net, and I do not believe the enemy would dare pass it without reducing it.

This decision committed the airborne troops and the other units to their heroic defense of Bastogne, where Anthony McAuliffe, in temporary command of the 101st while Maxwell Taylor was in the United States, would respond to the German ultimatum to surrender with his famous "Nuts."

> Ordered up all the self-propelled tank destroyer battalions and division tank battalions I could get hold of. I ordered Eddy to move his headquarters and artillery at once to Luxembourg. I ordered the 35th to move to Metz at once and pick up replacements. I told Gay to fill the 90th and 95th Divisions [with replacements], and to put anything that was left in the 4th Infantry Division [which had been initially struck by the Germans]. I told the 9th and 10th Armored Divisions to cannibalize their anti-tank gun units and other units to fill up their infantry riflemen . . . I also got up ammunition, hospitals, and bridges [to the new area] . . . I also ordered the 5th Infantry Division to move to Luxembourg.

In a dazzling display of footwork, he rearranged the compositions of his corps.

I have no staff officers [with me] and conducted the whole thing by telephone through Gay and a fine staff at Nancy...

This has been a most wonderful move on the part of the whole Army. We will attack at 4:00 A.M., December 22d.

An important figure in the whole new situation was Gay, who remained at Nancy to coordinate the mass movement to the north.

*Letter, GSP, Jr., to Beatrice, December 21, 1944*

Though this is the shortest day of the year, to me it seems interminable. We shoot the works on a chestnut pulling expedition in the morning.

I am very confident that a great success is possible and I hope certain.

Yesterday I again earned my pay. I visited seven divisions and regrouped an Army alone. It was quite a day and I enjoyed it . . .

I have a room in a very nice hotel with heat and a bath which is fine.

The Bosch landed a lot of para troops in our uniforms for the purpose of murdering Ike, Brad, me, etc...

The situation is very reminisent of Mar. 25, 1918, and I think the results will be similar.

Remember how a tarpon always makes one big flop just before he dies.

We should get well into the guts of the enemy and cut his supply lines.

Destiny sent for me in a hurry when things got tight. Perhaps God saved me for this effort.

*Diary, December 21*

Ike and Bull are getting jittery about my attacking too soon and too weak. I have all I can get. If I wait, I will lose surprise...

The First Army could, in my opinion, attack on the 22d if they wanted (or if they were pushed), but they seem to have no ambition in that line.

The enemy may attempt to put in a spoiling attack from the vicinity of Echternach...

I had all staffs, except the VIII Corps, in for a conference. As usual on the verge of an attack, they were full of doubt. I seemed always to be the ray of sunshine, and by God, I always am. We can and will win, God helping...

I wish it were this time tomorrow night. When one attacks, it is the enemy who has to worry. Give us the victory, Lord.

*Letter, GSP, Jr., to Beatrice, December 22, 1944*

We jumped off at 0630 and have progressed on a twenty mile front to a depth of seven miles. I had hoped for more but we are in the middle of a snow storm and there were a lot of demolitions. So I should be content which of course I am not . . .

I think that this move of the Third Army is the fastest in history. We moved over a hundred miles starting on the 19th and attacked to day all ship shape and Bristol fashion.

With a little luck I will put on a more daring operation just after Xmas.

Replacements are the bottle neck. I took 8,000 out of my rear echelons and made doeboys of them. If others would do the same, we could finish this show in short order.

John Millikin is doing better than I feared. I told him he had to go up and hear them [the shells and bullets] whistle. I think he will.

In his diary he judged that the attack of the III Corps was making "fair progress." The troops would continue pushing ahead during the night.

Bastogne was still holding out, and Patton was planning to drop supplies into the town from the air.

I am satisfied but not particularly happy over the results of today. It is always hard to get an attack rolling.

I doubt if the enemy can make a serious reaction for another 36 hours. I hope by that time we will be moving.

The men are in good spirits and full of confidence . . .

We now have 108 battalions of corps and Army artillery supporting this attack – in other words, 1,296 guns of 105 or bigger. I don't see how the Boche can take this much artillery . . .

The situation at Bastogne is grave but not desperate.

*Diary, December 23*

We have not done so well today as I had hoped but have advanced from two to five miles and have beaten the enemy wherever we have met him . . . not yet reached Bastogne, but they are re-supplying it by air . . .

The weather today is fine. We had seven groups of fighter-bombers, eleven groups of medium bombers, one division of the Eighth Air Force, and some RAF planes helping us. I hope it got results.

*Diary, December 24*

This has been a very bad Christmas Eve. All along our line we have received violent counterattacks, one of which forced . . . the 4th Armored back some miles with the loss of ten tanks. This was probably my fault, because I had been insisting on day and night attacks. This is all right on the first or second day of the battle and when we had the enemy surprised, but after that the men get too tired. Furthermore, in this bad weather, it is very difficult for armored outfits to operate at night . . .

In the XX Corps all is quiet, and a very low grade of troops is opposing Colonel Polk — in fact Polk is insulted because he said, "They are nothing but Poles with ulcers."

I believe the German General Staff is running this attack and has staked all on this offensive to regain the initiative. They are far behind schedule and, I believe, beaten. If this is true, the whole army may surrender. On the other hand, in 1940 they attacked as at present, and then came over at Saarbrucken and Thionville to Metz. They may repeat — but with what?

On a wallet-size card distributed to every officer and man in the Third Army was Patton's Christmas message:

> To each officer and soldier . . . I wish a Merry Christmas. I have full confidence in your courage, devotion to duty, and skill in battle. We march in our might to complete victory. May God's blessing rest upon each of you on this Christmas Day.

On the reverse side was Patton's prayer, actually written by Chaplain James O'Neill:

> Almighty and most merciful Father, we humbly beseech Thee, of Thy great goodness, to restrain these immoderate rains with which we have to contend. Grant us fair weather for Battle. Graciously hearken to us as soldiers who call upon Thee that armed with Thy

power, we may advance from victory to victory, and crush the oppression and wickedness of our enemies, and establish Thy justice among men and nations. Amen.

*Letter, GSP, Jr., to Beatrice, December 25, 1944*

I have been unable to open any boxes except one from you with sox etc. – thanks . . .

The Lord has given us the 3 consecutive days of good weather and things are looking up but so far I am the only one attacking.

I am going out now to push it. I love you and hope for the best.

The worst of the danger was over by Christmas. Patton's prompt shift of units, the recovery of the American troops, and improvement in the weather, which allowed massive Allied air strikes, were about to turn the tide. But this was more apparent in retrospect.

*Diary, December 25*

A clear cold Christmas, lovely weather for killing Germans, which seems a bit queer, seeing Whose birthday it is. Last night Codman and I went to the Candlelight Communion at the Episcopal Church here in Luxembourg. It was very nice and we sat in the former Kaiser Wilhelm I's box.

I left early this morning to try to visit all the divisions in contact with the enemy . . . All were very cheerful. I am not, because we are not going fast enough . . . All the men . . . in most cases got hot turkey sandwiches for dinner . . . I feel that all are doing their best . . .

The 101st Airborne Division [in Bastogne] was not re-supplied by air today because the ships could not take off from the UK due to icy conditions, and nobody had the forethought to have ships take off from France . . .

After supper Brad and I had a talk. Monty says that the First Army cannot attack for three months and that the only attack that can be made is by me, but that I am too weak; hence we should fall back to the Saar-Vosges line or even to the Moselle . . .

I feel that this is disgusting and might remove the valor of our army and the confidence of our people. It will have tremendous political implications and probably condemn to death or slavery all the inhabitants of Alsace and Lorraine if we abandon them to the Germans. If ordered to fall back, I think I will ask to be relieved.

*Diary, December 26*

Today has been rather trying as in spite of our efforts, we have failed to make contact with the defenders of Bastogne . . .

At 1400 Gaffey phoned to say that if I authorized the risk, he thought that . . . Colonel Wendell Blanchard could break through to Bastogne by a rapid advance. I told him to try it. At 1845 they made contact, and Bastogne was liberated. It was a daring thing and well done. Of course they may be cut off, but I doubt it . . . The speed of our movements is amazing, even to me, and must be a constant source of surprise to the Germans.

Blanchard, a member of the 2d Armored Division during the early days of Patton's command, broke through the German line surrounding Bastogne, surged into town, and eliminated the danger of losing not only the substantial number of encircled Americans but also the excellent road net that would have facilitated the German offensive.

Why in hell the SHAEF thinkers hold the 11th Armored, 17th Airborne, and 87th Infantry Divisions at Reims is beyond me. They should be attacking.

The German has shot his wad. Prisoners have had no food for from three to five days. We should attack.

*Letter, GSP, Jr., to Beatrice, December 26, 1944*

Ever since the 22, we have been trying to relieve Bastogne. Just now at 1845 Gaffey called to say we had made contact. Of course we did not do it with much, but we did it. I hope that the troops making the advance don't get bottled up too.

My Prayer seems to be working still as we have had three days of good weather and our air has been very active. Of course they overstate [their results] at least 50% but they do scare the Huns.

For the first time since Gela the Bosch bombed and straffed me . . . I don't like it a bit better than I used to.

I have some [Christmas] boxes from you that I will open after supper.

The corridor between the 4th Armored Division and the 101st Airborne Division in Bastogne was considerably widened on December 27, and the traffic of supplies and the evacuation of wounded began.

Yet the Germans continued to menace Bastogne as they fought fiercely to hold the shoulder of the bulge and prevent their troops inside from being trapped.

*Diary, December 27*

Bradley left at 1000 to see Ike, Montgomery, and Smith. If Ike will put Bradley back in command of the First and Ninth Armies, we can bag the whole German army.

I wish Ike were more of a gambler, but he is certainly a lion compared to Montgomery, and Bradley is better than Ike as far as nerve is concerned. Of course he did make a bad mistake in being passive on the front of the VIII Corps. Monty is a tired little fart. War requires the taking of risks and he won't take them . . .

If I could get three more divisions, I could win this war now.

Hardly into Bastogne, Patton was already planning to attack from that town to Houffalize. He wanted to move the 6th Armored Division into the Bastogne area during darkness and surprise the Germans.

Bradley managed on December 28 to get two divisions released from SHAEF reserve and made available to Patton in order to strengthen the VIII Corps effort to reach Houffalize.

*Letter, GSP, Jr., to Beatrice, December 29, 1944*

The relief of Bastogne is the most brilliant operation we have thus far performed and is in my opinion the outstanding achievement of this war. Now the enemy must dance to our tune, not we to his.

In the morning we are starting on a new series of attacks which may well be decisive if I can only get Destiny to use reserves to attack and not to defend . . .

This is my biggest battle . . .

I now have 16 divisions but four have strings tied to them [meaning that he had to obtain permission before he could use them in battle].

That afternoon he dictated a letter to Beatrice "to give you a little insight into what is actually going on." Five divisions had been in action between Saarlautern and Sarreguemines and by telephone he sent three to Luxembourg to stop the Germans. The staff responsible for these complicated moves, he said in some exaggeration, "consisted of my self and [his driver] Sergeant Mims." He could have had his units jump off toward Bastogne a day earlier, "but the attack would have been a little ragged." With some legitimate boasting, he added, "if you put in such a solution at Leavenworth, you would go to the doghouse or St. Elizabeth's [mental institution in Washington]." He enclosed several copies of this "sort of thumbnail sketch of what is going on" and suggested that Beatrice might want to send them to his sister Nita, Harbord, Summerall, and Guy Henry.

The plans evolved on December 29 and approved in principle by Bradley had the VIII Corps attacking to seize high ground near Houffalize, then being ready to continue to St. Vith; the III Corps attacking directly from Bastogne to St. Vith; the XII Corps to attack to Echternach and then to Bitburg.

Middleton phoned on the afternoon of December 29, and Patton told him "he didn't care how Middleton made the attack, but he must make it, and he must take the objective."

*Diary, December 30*

The 11th Armored and 87th Infantry Divisions jumped off west of Bastogne as planned and ran right into the flank of a large German counterattack headed [toward Bastogne] . . . This lucky meeting stopped the Germans and probably corrected a bad situation.

Everyone of the generals involved urged me to postpone the attack . . . but I held to my plan, although I did not know the German attack was coming. Some people call it luck, some genius. I call it determination.

The 35th and 26th Divisions also got attacked at dawn . . . We had an inkling that it was coming and were set for it . . .

Drove to Bastogne and had to pass about a thousand yards from the Germans, but they did not fire . . . I decorated Brig. Gen. A. C. McAuliffe . . . and Lt. Col. S. A. Chappuis with the DSC . . . They were delighted and wanted me to drive slowly so the soldiers could see me.

*Editorial, "Patton Of Course," Washington* Post, *December 30, 1944*

It has become a sort of unwritten rule in this war that when there is a fire to be put out, it is Patton who jumps into his boots, slides down the pole, and starts rolling . . .

This is the same Patton who has a number of indiscretions on his record, but who has again and again demonstrated that when a jam develops, he is the one who is called upon to break it.

*Letter, GSP, Jr., to Beatrice, December 31, 1944*

Darling B. Happy New Year! I hope I am home for the next one.

He would be dead before the end of the next year.

Yesterday my luck held in a big way. I was launching two new divisions, but they were late getting to the assembly area, and every one urged that the attack be suspended. I insisted that they attack, if it was only with their advance guards. They did attack and ran right into the flank of a German attack. Had this not happened, things could have been critical. As it was, we stopped the attack in its tracks.

Historians will clame that such perfect timing was a stroke of jenius. It was just mulishness on my part. I had no idea the Germans were attacking.

On the other side of Bastogne, they also hit us hard. But we stopped them with the loss of one village to us and 55 tanks to them.

To day has been a slugging match, but I got Bob Grow['s 6th Armored Division] in and things are better. Tomorrow will be the crutial test. I think, in fact know, we will stop them and attack at once.

*Diary, December 31*

This has been a very long day for me. The Germans launched a heavy counterattack on the 26th Division . . .

It has snowed and frozen over all day, and the tractors which pull our medium and heavy artillery are perfectly useless. We either have to replace them by truck or send a truck ahead with a cable to haul them over the road . . .

Total number of [German] counterattacks for today aggregates 17 — all repulsed. On the other hand, we have not made much ground.

Bradley submitted an efficiency report on Patton's performance and characterized him as "Superior," recommended him for command of an Army or Army Group, and, among all others he knew of Patton's grade, listed him Number 1 as an Army commander in combat.

*Third Army General Orders 1, January 1, 1945*

To the officers and men of the Third Army and to our comrades of the XIX TAC:

From the bloody corridor at Avranches, to Brest, thence across France to the Saar, over the Saar into Germany, and now on to Bastogne, your record has been one of continuous victory. Not only have you invariably defeated a cunning and ruthless enemy, but also you have overcome by your indomitable fortitude every aspect of terrain and weather. Neither heat nor dust nor floods nor snow have stayed your progress. The speed and brilliancy of your achievements is unsurpassed in military history . . .

My New Year wish and sure conviction for you is that under the protection of Almighty God and the inspired leadership of our President and the High Command, you will continue your victorious course to the end that tyranny and vice shall be eliminated, our dead comrades avenged, and peace restored to a war-weary world.

In closing, I can find no fitter expression for my feelings than to apply to you the immortal words spoken by General Scott at Chapultepec when he said, "Brave soldiers, veterans, you have been baptized in fire and blood and have come out steel."

*Letter, GSP, Jr., to Middleton, January 1, 1945*

As I see the situation now, you will eventually use the 17th Airborne to augment your attack on Houffalize. When this starts, I believe that the further use of the 87th will terminate, and we can trade that for the 94th.

Looking into the future, I propose to have you . . . attack on the axis Bastogne–St. Vith. In conjunction with an attack by the XII Corps from Diekirch north on St. Vith, the VII Corps [of the First Army] will attack the day after tomorrow morning on the road Houffalize-Vaux-Chavanne. It is therefore my belief that, if the 101st feels it can do it, and the situation otherwise is satisfactory, you should move on Noville the day after tomorrow.

For the big picture, with you and Eddy moving on St. Vith, the III Corps will hold defensively on any line obtained and successively break off divisions from the west to augment the attack of the XII Corps.

This plan is subject to change without notice as all plans are. However, we must still bear in mind that the 4th Armored Division should eventually get to the XII Corps, so that the XII Corps can have one armored division and two infantry divisions. You will then have one armored division and two or three infantry divisions, which should make a very powerful pair of scissor blades.

*Diary, January 1*

The 6th Armored did well in spite of snow and icy roads. The 11th Armored yesterday fought well but stupidly and lost too many tanks. Apparently they are very green and particularly inept at fighting in the woods . . .

All my troops are just where they should be, so if we lost, it will be due to better fighting on the part of the enemy . . . not to any mistakes which I may have made.

*GSP, Jr., Press Conference, Luxembourg City, January 1, 1945*

Patton: The purpose of this operation as far as the Third Army is concerned is to hit this son-of-a-bitch — pardon me — in the flank, and we did it, with the result that he is damn well stopped and going back. If you got a monkey in a jungle hanging by his tail, it is easier to get him by cutting his tail than kicking him in the face. The same thing is true here.

I am very well pleased with the situation . . . To me it is a never ending marvel what our soldiers can do.

He outlined and discussed the movements between December 19 and 22.

Now that sounds like what a great man George Patton is, but I did not have anything to do with it. I told General Gay and the staff, and they got the movement orders out. The people who actually did it were the younger officers and soldiers. When you think of those men marching all night in the cold, over roads they had never seen, and nobody getting lost, and everybody getting to the place in time, it is a very marvelous feat; I know of no equal to it in military history . . . I take off my hat to them.

The 35th Division did a marvelous thing . . .

The day before yesterday, the 11th Armored and the 87th Infantry Divisions came up from Reims. They were supposed to close in the afternoon. The 11th got in at 2200 and attacked at 0800 the next morning, and the 87th got in at 6 A.M. and attacked at 6:30. That was a very fortunate piece of timing . . . If I were a liar, I would have said that I planned it, but actually I was lucky as hell . . .

I think yesterday was the crucial time in the operation. He [the enemy] could have done something yesterday; he can't do it now.

All this is of course off-the-record . . .

Question: Will the First Army jump soon?

Patton: I'm not my brother's keeper.

Question: . . . future plans?

Patton: . . . We want to catch as many Germans as possible, but he is pulling out.

Question: If you pinch off a lot of Germans, is there any chance of the front collapsing?

Patton: What do you think I went to church for yesterday . . .

Question: What about the [enemy] concentration of armor?

Patton: They got damn little armor left – unless they have reproductive tanks.

Question: . . . enemy capabilities in eastern Holland?

Patton: That is out of my line. I am only interested in the son-of-a-bitch where he is right now in front of me . . . We can lick the Germans any place . . . I don't care where he fights. We'll find him and kick his teeth in.

Question: Just how important was Bastogne?

Patton: It was just as important as the Battle of Gettysburg was to the Civil War. The credit for seeing that goes to General Bradley . . . You know that when you catch a carp and put him in the boat, he flips his tail just before he dies, and I think this is the German's last flip . . .

Question: [getting through the Siegfried Line?]

Patton: Never in the history of the world has there been a line that could be successfully defended. The Trojans built a big wall but the Greeks took it; Hadrian built a wall; the Chinese built a wall; the French – with due respect – built a wall upside down. We built walls in the first World War – trenches are nothing but upside down walls. The only way you can win a war is to attack and keep on attacking, and after you have done that, keep attacking some more . . .

Question: General, what do you think the over-all purpose [of the Ardennes counterattack] was?

Patton: I will be damned if I know. My private theory, which has no backing except in my vivid imagination, is that the German General Staff knew the war was lost if they remained on the defensive, and they thought there was a possibility that they could retain the initiative by attacking. I also think that they are getting ready for the third World War, and they think the prestige of the German army going down in attack is better than its going down while on the defensive. Now that is my private opinion.

*Diary, January 2*

I had in all four corps commanders before lunch to discuss the plan, so that now each one knows what all the others are doing . . .

At last the VII Corps of the First Army is attacking in the direction of Houffalize . . . I still see no reason to change my disposition. God show the right.

*Letter, GSP, Jr., to Beatrice, January 2, 1945*

The Bosch is fighting all out and so are we and doing it better . . .

Dear Courtney comes in at long last in the morning, and that will relieve the pressure. Any how I am not worried. I took a nap after lunch.

By then, even the syndicated columnists who had been hostile to Patton were giving him what one called "belated orchids." Patton, they said, might be irascible and acid, profane and hard, but no one could question his professional soundness and his ability as a fighter.

*Diary, January 3*

The new SHAEF Directive returns the First Army [from Montgomery's control] to the 12th Army Group [and Bradley] as soon as contact between the First and Third Armies is made near Houffalize. When this has occurred, the Armies drive northeast via St. Vith.

The 6th Army Group is trying to steal the XX Corps.

Montgomery got some fool Englishman in America to suggest that as Eisenhower had too much work, he (Montgomery) should be made Deputy Ground Forces Commander of all troops in Europe. If this occurs, I will ask to be relieved. I will not serve under Montgomery and neither, I think, will Bradley.

At 5 P.M., Middleton telephoned Patton and recommended that the VIII Corps attack, scheduled for the following morning, be postponed because of the enemy buildup near Bastogne. Patton refused, holding that once an attack was set to be launched, it should go. His main mission was to destroy the enemy, and this could be done better by attacking the Germans than by waiting for them to attack.

*Diary, January 4*

I want to attack to the north from Diekirch but Bradley is all for putting new divisions in the Bastogne fight. In my opinion, this is throwing good money after bad. In this weather, on the defensive, the Germans can hold us well enough so that we can never trap them there, whereas if we attack close to the base [of the Bulge], they will have to pull out and we will regain ground and probably catch just as many Germans as the other way . . .

The 11th Armored is very green and took unnecessary losses to no effect. There were also some unfortunate incidents in the shooting of prisoners (I hope we can conceal this).

The 17th Airborne, which attacked this morning, got a very bloody nose and reported the loss of 40% in some of its battalions. This is, of course, hysterical. A loss for any one day of over 8 to 10% can be put down to a damn lie, unless the people run or surrender. General Miley did not impress me when I met him at Bastogne . . . He told me he did not know where his right regiment was, yet he was not out looking for it . . .

Bastogne was being shelled when I drove in. The flashes of the shells of our guns on the snow was pretty, but I could have foregone the beauty.

It took two hours to drive home from Bastogne in the dark, and it was very cold.

We can still lose this war. However, the Germans are colder and hungrier than we are, but they fight better. I can never get over the stupidity of our green troops.

*Letter, GSP, Jr., to Beatrice, January 5, 1945*

These new units are not worth a thing in their first fight. This is the second that has gone sour in the last week.

The whole country is covered with snow and ice. How men live, much less fight, is a marvel to me. – A 280 shell just hit near here –

Those Germans are vicious fighters . . .

Some times even I get skeptical about the end of this show.

*Letter, GSP, Jr., to Frederick Ayer, January 5, 1945*

I really believe that . . . was the most brilliant operation ever performed, and was due wholly to my staff and to the tremendous efficiency of the veteran American soldiers who now compose our armies.

At the present time the fighting is very hot, but we are retaining the initiative and killing more Germans than I have ever previously accounted for . . .

I really feel that, although the German breakthrough was regrettable, it may terminate the war sooner . . . because, when they fail, as they will – or as they have – there will be nothing to look forward to. Of course they have an uncanny method of pulling new troops out of the hat, but at the moment it seems to me that they have everything in they can possibly put in, while we still have a few cards up our sleeves.

*Diary, January 5*

After talking to Bradley, we concurred that the German pocket southeast of Bastogne must be eliminated before we can attack Houffalize . . .

Walker is a very fine soldier. He has never yet complained about any order he has received. The fact that he is not complaining when I take the 90th Division [from his corps] is particularly noteworthy.

*Letter, GSP, Jr., to Summerall, January 6, 1945*

At the present moment I am attacking with an Army of 17 divisions and slowly but surely smashing a hole in the German's left flank. It has been a very violent battle under appalling weather conditions, but we are going to win.

*Diary, January 6*

Had Millikin, Van Fleet, and my general staff in the office this morning to get the plan for the attack by the 90th Division settled in all details . . .

The 90th is doing a very clever piece of work in registering its guns. As the guns come in, they register, and similar guns from the 26th Division cease firing. In this way, I believe, we can wholly deceive the enemy as to the arrival of a new unit . . .

I had to use the whip on both Middleton and Millikin today. They are too cautious. I know that their men are tired, but so are the Germans. We have to push people beyond endurance in order to bring this war to its end, because we are forced to fight it with inadequate means.

Only three small counterattacks today – all repulsed. I fear this indicates the enemy is getting away.

The weather, caution on the part of commanders, fatigue on the part of the men, lack of sufficient troops, terrain favorable to the German defense – all this was frustrating, particularly after his brilliant maneuver to bring pressure on the Germans around Bastogne. Prevented from smashing into the flank of the German bulge, trapping substantial numbers of enemy, and winning a great victory, Patton was somewhat discouraged. But only for the moment.

CHAPTER 34

# Battle of the Bulge

*"We are going to attack until the war is over."*

THE NIGHT OF JANUARY 6 was "almost too quiet" for Patton's comfort, and he began to feel ever more strongly that the Germans were going to get away – pull out all the men they had in the Bulge without getting trapped. To prevent this, he told Middleton "to push out till he bumps" into the enemy.

Eddy was worried that the Germans might strike his XII Corps through Diekirch, and so was Bradley. Patton doubted it, yet gave Eddy more protection. He alerted two armored divisions to be ready to help if Eddy was attacked, and he made sure that the road blocks and mines in front of the corps were strong and effective. "If the enemy tries to get through, he will be well stopped."

He had lunch at Bradley's headquarters with Paul McNutt and the Manpower Board.

> McNutt is a pompous fool not at all interested in manpower . . . He told me he knew all about war. I told him he knew nothing about it compared to the people fighting it, and that he and his Board were responsible for the deaths of all Americans who gave their lives due to the shortage of replacements. I doubt if he loves me; it's mutual.

During lunch he sat next to a Harvard professor,

> who remarked that apparently I did not give a damn as to what people thought of me. I told him that depended upon who the people were, but that in any case I did not give very much of a damn.

To Beatrice:

McNutt and the man power bord . . . I told them the truth about their failure to provide men and they did not like it. [They] talked about laws. I told them we were talking in blood and that it was on their heads . . .

We got 17 counter attacks from 16 German divisions yesterday and nocked them all back for losses.

To day they are too quiet, so I am convinced they are cooking something up, but [they] have not the force to hurt us except for a moment.

We are going to put on a hell of a show soon which should realy rock them. At the moment I have 17 divisions but 3 of them are pretty weak.

*Diary, January 8*

Bradley asked me if I could attack Houffalize today . . . I said I could, but felt it a mistake as all plans were made for a general attack tomorrow . . .

I met Gaffey on the road . . . When I told him that he was to attack in the morning, he made no remarks at all, but simply wanted to know when, and in what direction . . .

I passed through the last battalion of the 90th Division moving in by truck. They must have been riding in the cold, blizzard weather in open trucks for many hours, but were in splendid form and cheered and yelled as I drove past. It was a very inspiring sight.

We attack in the morning . . . [with] eight divisions. It should work . . .

The 87th and 17th Airborne got fairly well chopped up yesterday due at least in part to Middleton's reluctance to use the 11th Armored in backing them up. He is still over-worried about his left flank and rear. Too much so.

At supper Middleton called to say that the 87th and 17th Airborne could not attack tomorrow, and that the 101st Airborne and 4th Armored should, if possible, wait until the 10th. I told him everything would go on as ordered and that all units would attack on the 9th, tomorrow, with the understanding that the 87th and 17th Airborne would probably not be able to put on a very good show.

Next, Gaffey called up and made the same recommendation and got the same answer.

Then Eddy called and said he heard the 4th Armored was going into that fight, and [therefore] he couldn't count on it to support him, and that it would take nine hours for the 10th Armored to reach him. I told him that in that event, he would certainly have to hold for nine hours.

Again I earned my pay.

We continue to get a rumor of a German concentration [of troops] at Saarbrucken. The chief reason I believe it is so, is that if I were the Germans, that is what I would do . . . It would be a great feather in their caps if they recaptured Metz. I told Walker . . . to prepare all roads for demolition [as a precaution against a German attack].

*Letter, GSP, Jr., to Beatrice, January 9, 1945*

The ground and the snow and the brief period of daylight are a greater menace than the enemy . . .

We simply have to keep attacking or he [the enemy] will. I wish that great soldier Sir B. [Bernard L. Montgomery] would do a little more.

The rumors of a German counterattack through Saarbrucken continued, although Patton could hardly see how the Germans had enough troops to launch it – unless they were pulling all their armor out of the Bulge, "which they may have done."

*Letter, GSP, Jr., to Stimson, January 10, 1945*

The success which the Third Army has attained, while apparently attributed to me, should certainly be given in equal measure to all the gallant men and officers composing this Army. They have continued in the past and are now doing more than it is humanly possible to do . . .

The two things which bother us . . . are replacements and ammunition. I am sure that everything is being done, but cannot help stressing the importance of maintaining the troops at full strength and giving us all the ammunition we can shoot.

In my opinion, this present battle is a replica of Grant's "Wilderness Campaign," and we will have to fight it out on these lines if it takes all winter and all next summer.

Naturally, things would be facilitated if we had more divisions, but as far as I know, there are no more, so will have to get by with what we have.

This was as close to complaining as he dared go.

Because the Germans had launched a diversionary attack against the Seventh Army, Bradley phoned to tell Patton that Eisenhower wanted the Third Army effort in the Bastogne area and toward Houffalize to be stopped. He wanted at least an armored division freed from contact with the enemy and dispatched to the XX Corps in case the German effort against the Seventh Army spilled over into the Saarbrucken area.

Patton immediately agreed, but as he thought about it, the more he thought it would be a mistake. He asked Bradley to go with him to Arlon and look over the situation personally. Bradley consented.

At Arlon, after discussion with Middleton and Millikin, they decided to pull the 4th Armored Division out of the front. Patton then phoned and halted the attacks of the 101st Airborne and 4th Armored Divisions. He ordered the latter to assemble southeast of Luxembourg, astride a road net that would enable it to go, if necessary, to the XX or XII Corps.

For these somewhat complicated movements, "no written orders were issued." Patton, Middleton, and Millikin simply drove to Bastogne and talked with the division commanders, Taylor, Gaffey, and Grow, to arrange the details.

When Patton returned to Luxembourg, he

> actually found elements of the 4th Armored moving to their new assembly positions. The remarkable ability which Gaffey has of doing what he is told fast was well exemplified here.

It appeared to Patton that the Germans were withdrawing from the Bulge. If this were so, he could take Houffalize with what he had left in the Bastogne area; and if no great danger developed at Saarbrucken, he could attack to the north at once with the XII Corps.

But there was another rumor, "invented" he thought by the 12th Army Group, of an enemy troop concentration near Trier.

> To me it is patently impossible that the Germans can have concentrations all over the face of nature — I do not believe it. However, the position in which we have placed the 4th Armored is such that it can operate against this threat too.
>
> This is the second time I have been stopped in a successful attack due to the Germans having more nerve than we have — that is, not

me, but some of the others. The ability of American troops to maneuver when properly led is wonderful. Their ability to fight is not so good . . .

It was very cold driving, and I may have frozen my face a little.

Herbert Lehman, Director General of the United Nations Relief and Rehabilitation Agency, wrote from Washington to express his thanks for the "many courtesies" extended by Patton during Lehman's trip to Europe. He thought it might interest Patton to know that he had returned home on a ship carrying American soldiers, many of whom were wounded. A large proportion volunteered the information that they wished they were serving under Patton.

*Diary, January 11*

The III Corps . . . made good progress and are taking a lot of prisoners. The end of the Bastogne operation is in sight . . .

I would prefer to attack at once and take the German bridgehead at Saarbrucken. This could be done now. Bradley thinks we had best wait . . .

I believe that today ends the Bastogne operation. From now on it is simply a question of driving a defeated enemy.

*Diary, January 12*

The VIII and III Corps attack tomorrow to take Houffalize and should get it, as there is not much in the way. That will tidy up that job and next to the crossing of France, it is the biggest one we have done. I hope we get the credit.

When Houffalize is taken, we will have a junction between the First and Third Armies, which will put Bradley back in control of the First Army. This will be very advantageous, as Bradley is much less timid than Montgomery.

Besides, Bradley and Patton usually saw eye to eye on the issues. In addition, they felt that they were more concerned with upholding American interests than Eisenhower.

I believe that the Bastogne operation is the biggest and best the Third Army has accomplished, not excluding the battle of France, and I hope the troops get the credit for their great work . . .

Bradley came over late this afternoon to discuss long range plans . . . He wants to attack east with the First Army [directed] on Cologne, while the Third Army maintains pressure and really holds a defensive flank . . . This plan has the advantage of attacking where we have already breached the Siegfried Line and also of using the shortest road to Cologne. It is probably sound but slow . . .

Personally, I believe that an attack by the XX Corps . . . straight east through Saarlautern would bring better results and would certainly be more crippling to Germany, as it would get the whole [industrial] Saar valley.

Wherever we attack, one thing is certain, we should attack, because if we don't, the Germans will.

*GSP, Jr., Press Conference, Luxembourg, January 12, 1945*

Patton: [As in 1918], unquestionably this [German] attack was also to end this war, and they failed. There will be another one, and it too will fail. In fact, I hope to God they do attack down south, for we'll wipe their ass right off!

The operation at Bastogne is finished. The 6th Armored, 35th, and 90th all made contact yesterday. Without deprecating the great heroism of the 101st, I think you should know that one combat command of the 9th Armored, one combat command of the 10th Armored, and two tank destroyer outfits were also in Bastogne . . .

I am very much satisfied with this operation so far, and I am hopeful that these sons-of-bitches attack somewhere soon. If they do, I won't be able to hold myself, for I will attack then. We can lick them anywhere . . .

There are two things that the enemy can do. He can hit from around Metz or further down, and in either case he is shit out of luck!

Question: [will the Germans pull out and defend or attack again?]

Patton: You cannot win a war without retaining the initiative. If he pulls out and sits on his ass, he is through. You've got to keep pushing . . .

Question: . . . new role of the 4th Armored?

Patton: Just waiting to bite this fellow in the ass when he comes through.

*Letter, GSP, Jr., to Beatrice, January 12, 1945*

Personally I would attack them right now . . . but others don't like to take the chances I do. I feel that if we attack him, he cant attack us . . .

Just saw the tent maker on long range plans. I think they are too long range.

Hughes remarked in a letter to Beatrice that some people wondered in Sicily whether soldiers would serve under Patton. Now everyone wanted to be in his Army.

*Diary, January 13*

There is a distinct difference in the mental attitude of the officers and men today . . . They all feel that they are on the winning side, pursuing a beaten enemy; while yesterday . . . they were dubious as to whether we could stop the German attack. It is an interesting psychological situation. Now that all feel the enemy is licked, they are sure of themselves. Until today I was the only one sure of victory.

The fighting today has been bitter, but it is just what one would expect, as it is to the north and northeast of Bastogne where the enemy must hold in order to extricate what he has left east of the town. We will get them . . .

Wrote the Editor of the Stars and Stripes protesting against his paper as subversive of discipline. I sent a copy of my letter to general Lee . . . I stated that unless there is an improvement, I will not permit the paper to be issued in this Army, nor permit his reporters or photographers in the Army area. It is a scurrilous sheet.

What he particularly disliked were Bill Mauldin's cartoons, showing Willie and Joe, typical infantrymen, as unshaved and dirty.

*Letter, GSP, Jr., to Beatrice, January 15, 1945*

The Germans are definitely on the run . . .

I rather fear that our super planners have been scared more than the soldiers have . . .

I still have about 20 Xmas boxes to open. I gave a lot of cakes to some orphans . . .

We have had three nice clear days and hope that our air has done half as much as it says. However, they do try, especially Weyland and his fighter bombers.

*Diary, January 16*

The 11th Armored made contact with the . . . 2d Armored Division [of the First Army] at Houffalize. This restores Bradley to the command of the First Army . . . and terminates the German offensive. Now we will drive them back . . .

Devers is to liquidate the Colmar pocket . . . We have to loan him the 10th Armored Division and three battalions of artillery, which he will probably try to steal. Personally I would rather fight Germans than resist the inroads of Devers and Monty.

*Letter, GSP, Jr., to son George, January 16, 1945*

Leadership . . . is the thing that wins battles. I have it – but I'll be damned if I can define it. Probably it consists in knowing what you want to do and then doing it and getting mad if any one stepps in the way. Self confidence and leadership are twin brothers . . .

I think we accounted for some 80,000 Germans. The woods are full of corpses, and it is going to stink some in the spring.

One of these damned jet planes that goes 470 miles an hour just dropped a bomb. It shook this house . . . and scared Willie. They also shoot rockets at us, but one gets used to such things. It is like a thunder storm. You are not apt to be in the way. And if you are, what the Hell, no more buttoning and unbuttoning.

*Letter, GSP, Jr., to Beatrice, January 16, 1945*

As we are having a tidying up battle to day, there is not much to do . . .

I fear we have not got the mental equipment for one big push. From a material and personnell view point, it could be and should be done . . .

Even the tent maker admits that Courtney is dumb. He is also very jealous of me.

*Diary, January 17*

Visited Millikin and Middleton at Arlon. I had already congratulated both over the telephone and repeated it in person. They have done exceptionally well. Of course, Millikin, being a greenhorn, required considerable shoving, but I think he has done a good job . . .

I told the division and corps commanders that it will be necessary to continue the attack, and that I know they are tired; therefore, they should try to arrange to get one third of their forces out to rest up and warm up, because we are going to attack until the war is over.

*Diary, January 18*

SHAEF called and directed us to send a division to the 6th Army Group . . . We selected the 101st Airborne because we will probably lose that anyhow . . .

Walker . . . called up late and asked if he could continue a serious attack . . . I told him to go ahead. Now is the time to attack and keep it up . . .

When Hughes came yesterday, he told me with great glee that in his last interview with Eisenhower, the latter said to him, "Do you know, Everett, George is really a very great soldier, and I must get Marshall to do something for him before the war is over."

*Letter, GSP, Jr., to Beatrice, January 19, 1945*

Things are a little slow just now mostly due to utterly vile weather. Yesterday Eddy jumped off in a London fog which turned to rain and sleet. We are going forward but are mostly delayed by the ice.

Milly and Troy are starting again Sunday and Walker keeps pitching all the time . . .

I always hate not to have a desperate job on my hands. I guess I am getting too used to it.

*Letter, GSP, Jr., to Lt. Col. John A. Degen, Brookline, Mass., January 19, 1945*

Fortunately for my sanity, and possibly for my self-esteem, I do not see all the bullshit which is written in the home town papers about me.

*Letter, GSP, Jr., to Beatrice, January 20, 1945*

The 101 Air Borne call themselves the tripple B's – "Battered Bastards of Bastogne." They did well but like the Marines of the last war, they get more credit than they deserve.

The weather could not be worse. It is snowing like hell again now. But we are still going forward about a mile a day . . .

I doubt if Willie needs a sweater . . .

When I am reading in bed, he gets in with me. But as soon as I start to open the windoe he hurries into the bath room where it is warm.

Troy and Milly renew the attack in the morning. I will go up and have a look. It will not be a great sensation but will kill Germans. Really I don't see how they can stand the continued attacks on both flanks — I hope we get to Berlin first. But if we do we will have to get a move on [to beat the Russians].

*Diary, January 21*

Drove . . . to give each officer a pat on the back. They have finally found themselves and have done well. A few days ago I was on the point of relieving both Miley and Kilburn; one should not act too fast . . . At one time I was at the point of relieving [Brig. Gen. W. A.] Holbrook, but now he seems to be doing a good job.

I noticed another instance of the complete incapacity of inexperienced officers. Several ordnance trailers, each loaded with between 40 and 50 replacements . . . were stuck on a slippery hill and not moving. There were a number of officers present, but none of them had enough sense to make the men dismount and push the vehicles until Stiller and I did so. Then the trucks got moving fast.

In the Canal Zone in 1948, Mrs. Patton was halted by a sentry who inspected her pass. He was wearing the Third Army patch, and she asked whether he had ever seen General Patton. "Oh, yes," the soldier said, "I knew him, though I only saw him once. We were stuck in the snow and he came by in a jeep. His face was awful red, and he must have been about froze, riding in that open jeep. He yelled to us to get out and push, and first I knew there was General Patton pushing right alongside of me."

Devers is howling for more troops, although when he started to obliterate the Colmar Pocket, he said he could do it with one division. I fear we may lose the 8th Armored [to him]. We have already sent him the 101st Airborne and the 10th Armored.

*Letter, GSP, Jr., to Beatrice, January 22, 1945*

Saw a lot of dead Germans yesterday frozen in funny attitudes. I got some good pictures but did not have my color camera, which was a pity, as they were a pale claret color.

They are definitely on the run and have suffered more than we hoped.

*Diary, January 22*

I told Eddy not to halt on his final objective but to continue . . . There is a rumor that the enemy is withdrawing, which I doubt.

Called Bradley on the phone . . . and urged all Armies to attack in spite of fatigue or losses, as I am sure that in view of the Russian offensive, now is the time to strike.

*Diary, January 23*

In spite of strong remonstrances by Bradley and myself, SHAEF ordered the 35th Division . . . to the 6th Army Group. It is too bad that the highest levels of command have no personal knowledge of war . . .

The elimination of the Colmar pocket seems to have developed into a fiasco. I hope I don't get sent down to strike it out . . .

Called on Bradley [about] . . . future plans . . . If this plan fails, Bradley will have to give Monty a number of divisions, possibly twelve, and all the remainder of the First and Third Armies will sit on the defensive while Monty proceeds to do nothing as usual. We must succeed in our attack to avoid this, and also to maintain the prestige of the American Army.

Bradley's plan for the attack is good, and I think it will succeed. He is also trying to get Monty to temporarily take over the Ninth Army front so we can send four more divisions to Devers to clean up the Colmar pocket, and then put the 6th Army Group on the defensive.

*Diary, January 24*

Hodges . . . arrived at lunch time, and after lunch we had a meeting attended by Bradley . . . The boundaries between the Armies were worked out, very satisfactorily to us and I also believe to Hodges.

Just when everything had been satisfactorily arranged and Hodges said he could attack Sunday, the telephone rang and General Whiteley [a British officer and deputy G–3 of SHAEF] called up Bradley and wanted to withdraw additional divisions . . . to help Devers. Bradley told him that . . . we would be giving up a sure thing for a side show.

For the only time to my knowledge he lost his good humor and told Whiteley that if he wanted to destroy the whole operation, he could do so and be damned, or words to that effect, and to take *all* the corps and divisions.

It occurs to me that this patent attempt to prevent the attack of the First and Third Armies is a British effort to give Monty the leading role. If our attacks fail after a good try, we will have to give Monty troops, and the Americans simply sit on the defensive while U.S. blood aids British prestige. At the moment four British divisions are out of contact [with the enemy] and Monty says the earliest he can attack is February 8.

Bradley was very firm and even angry.

Bull [the SHAEF G–3, Whiteley's superior] got on the phone and Bradley repeated his statements, adding that much more than a tactical operation was involved, in that the prestige of the American army was at stake.

We were all very pleased with Bradley's attitude and told him so.

Gay recorded what happened this way. After everyone at the meeting had satisfactorily worked out the details of the attack by both Armies to break through the Siegfried Line, someone from SHAEF phoned Bradley. Gay remembered what Bradley said on the phone as follows:

"I want you to understand that there is more at stake than the mere moving of divisions and corps and of a certain tactical plan. The reputation and the good will of the American soldiers and the American army and its commanders are at stake. If you feel that way about it, then as far as I am concerned, you can take any goddam division and/or corps in the 12th Army Group, do with them as you see fit, and those of us that you leave back will set on our ass until hell freezes. I trust you do not think I am angry, but I want to impress upon you that I am goddam well incensed."

At that time, Gay noted,

practically every officer in the room stood up and applauded, and General Patton said in a voice that could be heard over the telephone, "Tell them to go to hell and all three of us will resign. I will lead the procession."

*Diary, January 24*

Hodges expects to jump on Sunday. I trust that I can beat him by one day.

If SHAEF insists on the Colmar pocket venture, it is playing into the enemy's hands by moving our troops from a vital area to one of very little secondary importance. Furthermore, this will be the third time such a mistake has been made, and I do not believe that people guilty of such errors in judgment can eventually avoid the censure of history.

Bradley, Hodges, and myself are determined to carry on our attack no matter how much they deplete us. Personally, I am convinced that the Germans are pulling out, probably as far as the Rhine, and if we go ahead, we will get to the Rhine, and very soon. To do otherwise at this moment would, in my opinion, be criminal.

*Diary, January 26*

Heavy local snows and intense cold . . .

Bradley leaves for his new command post at Namur today . . . I called on him . . . to say goodbye. He is a good officer but utterly lacks "it." Too bad.

*Diary, January 27*

Middleton . . . is in very good spirits and eager to attack . . .

Eddy . . . is full of offensive ardor and wants to get going.

*Letter, GSP, Jr., to Beatrice, January 28, 1945*

I have written nearly daily for inspite of what people think, an Army commander is not very very busy lots of the time . . .

Driving in a peep is not so hot, not in zero weather. However I have plenty of clothes. I have a woolen scarf that I find makes a lot of difference — if you keep your neck warm. I also have a lap robe made of a shelter half lined with a blanket and I have plastic glass doors on the side of the peep . . .

We are starting a new attack to day and it is snowing like Hell. However, I think that the Germans are in a bad way and that we will be able to get through. Unfortunately we have to storm the Siegfried line as a starter.

By that date the bulge had been eliminated. The Germans had been expelled from the salient. The front had been restored. Now everyone could get on with the old business of cracking the Siegfried Line and driving to the Rhine.

*Letter, GSP, Jr., to Beatrice, January 31, 1945*

Yesterday I drove in a peep in zero weather for about eight hours.

> When I came in I was so cold I got in a hot tub and to give a tropical aspect, turned on the sun lamp. And left it on for about 20 minutes. It was some 12 feet away, but is pretty potent. My eyes were already bad from the snow.
>
> I woke up at 1145 in great pane with my eyes running like a spigot. I got up and woke Col. Odom, the Dr. who lives with us — my personal physician? — He put cold barasic compresses on for two hours, gave me a shot of morphine and a sleeping powder.
>
> I stayed in bed till noon in a dark room, and now the eyes are well. I am like a puppy, always sticking my nose into trouble.
>
> The night of the 28 at 0130 our time, which is 5:30 your time, I dreamed I was in a boat in a muddy creek and had just started to back down stream when you came running over the mud and called "Georgie" the way you do. Were you in any trouble?

Eddy wanted to attack on the 6th, but Patton told him he would have to jump off on the 4th.

> He said I never gave him time to get ready and did not appreciate time and space factors.
>
> I told him that had I ever given a corps commander the time he asked for, we would still be on the Seine.

Shortly afterward a telephone call from 12th Army Group instructed Patton to commit nothing for the moment. He would get orders later.

> As the result of this, I told Eddy to stop his preparations. Hell and damn. This is another case of giving up a going attack in order to start one that has no promise of success except to exalt Monty, who has never won a battle since he left Africa and only El Alamein there. I won Mareth for him.

Somewhat angry, he told Harry Maloney that his 94th Division was the worst in the Army insofar as the ratio of non-battle casualties to battle casualties was concerned. If conditions did not improve, he said, Maloney himself would become a non-battle casualty. "I was intentionally rough."

Patton then talked to the field officers and representatives from each company in the division and gave them

> the usual talk. I also praised the men for what they had done, but told them very frankly that the 94th had lost more men as prisoners of war than all the other troops I had commanded during my entire military service and that they must wipe out the disgrace. I then patted General Maloney on the back, and believe that this technique will have the desired effect.

In a phone call Bradley justified Patton's "worst fears." Patton would lose the 95th Division to the Ninth Army and perhaps also five or six artillery battalions. As usual, Patton was

> quite outspoken in my objections, but Bradley said that it was not even Eisenhower's plan, but was forced on him by the Combined Chiefs of Staff.

Eisenhower had gone to Marseilles to see Marshall who was on his way to the Yalta Conference, and Marshall had passed along the instruction.

> Damn this political war. However, the mistakes of the high command have thus far turned to my personal advantage and glory. Here's hoping.

Driving to Spa, Belgium, Patton was appalled by the destruction of Houffalize, which was "completely removed. I have never seen anything like it in this war. In my opinion, it is worse than St. Vith."

> O little town of Houffalize,
> How still we see thee lie;
> Above they steep and battered streets
> The aeroplanes sail by.
>
> Yet in thy dark streets shineth
> Not any Goddamned light;
> The hopes and fears of all thy years
> Were blown to hell last night.

At Spa on February 2, Patton discovered that Hodges had his office in the room where Hindenburg decided in the fall of 1918 that the war was lost. From the windows, Patton could see the lake around which the Kaiser walked while awaiting word from Hindenburg.

> Bradley, Hodges, Simpson, and I, with a few staff offiers, met after lunch in what may be another momentous mistake. Bradley stated that after General Eisenhower had seen General Marshall . . . he had been directed on the authority of the Combined Chiefs of Staff to attack with the British 21st Army Group and the Ninth Army, all under General Montgomery.
>
> Bradley thought that part of this decision was the desire to see that the 14 British divisions, which have been sitting in northern Belgium for the last two months without fighting, were used.
>
> The purpose of the attack is to secure as rapidly as possible a wide stretch of the Rhine River so that in the event that Germany collapses, we will have a quick entry.
>
> I feel, and I believe Hodges also agrees, that our present attack, which is moving, has a better chance of getting to the Rhine first than has a new attack which will not start until February 10th, if then. Furthermore, neither of us has a very high opinion of the offensive value of British troops.

In other words, the 21 Army Group would make the main effort, and the Ninth Army, in direct support of the British, was to be built up at the expense of the First and Third Armies. The First Army was to secure the Roer River dams and protect the right flank of the Ninth.

Or, as Eisenhower later explained, the general attack in the Ardennes was to be abandoned, and the entire weight of the Allied forces was to be thrown into an attempt to reach the Rhine River below Düsseldorf.

> The First and Third Armies will be allowed to continue their present attack until the 10th, and thereafter, provided the casualties and the ammunition expenditures are not excessive . . . We have not got sufficient ammunition or replacements to maintain the attack of three [American] Armies.
>
> The 6th Army Group is to go on the defensive . . .
>
> Personally, I think that this is a foolish and ignoble way for the Americans to end the war. In my opinion, every division should be attacking, and if such an attack were made, the Germans do not have the resources to stop it.

> We were all very gloomy . . . It was further revealed to us that SHAEF is taking several divisions for a theater reserve – reserve against what? – which seems to me painting the lily, or locking the stable door after the horse is stolen.

To cheer himself up, he ordered two shotguns, one for himself, the other for his brother-in-law, Frederick Ayer.

Patton had his four corps commanders in on February 3, and explained that the Third Army had to continue its attack to prevent the Germans from moving troops against Montgomery.

*Diary, February 3*

> My plan of attack is only tenable on the assumption that the Germans have not got the power to hit back. I believe this to be the case. I tried to get an extra armored division to give to the XX Corps in order to clear up the Moselle-Saar triangle, but as usual my request was turned down.

He thought it "the height of folly, both from a political and military angle," to end the war with the 6th Army Group and the Third Army on the defensive. He expected little from the 21 Army Group attack because "Monty is so slow and timid that he will find a German build-up in front of him and will stall."

Since he felt that Bradley would stop him if he knew that Patton was starting a new attack with the XII Corps, "I shall not tell him."

Van Fleet, whose division was with the First Army, and Leclerc, whose division was with the Seventh, asked Patton to try to get them reassigned to the Third Army. "Is it bootlick or admiration?"

*Letter, GSP, Jr., to Beatrice, February 4, 1945*

> You may hear that I am on the defensive but it was not the enemy who put me there.
>
> I don't see much future for me in this war. There are too many "safety first" people running it. However, I have felt this way before and something has always turned up. I will go to church and see what can be done . . .
>
> I feel pretty low to be ending the war on the defensive.

But not even he could cope with his resilience. He expanded his notion of his attack and soon believed that "We may still . . . have an opportunity of getting to the Rhine first."

*Letter, GSP, Jr., to Beatrice, February 5, 1945*

Am going to Bastogne to meet Destiny and the tent maker . . . I hope it wont be a stop order as we are doing very nicely . . .

If I become defense, I think I will visit the Leicester-Warrens and the Stockdales for a few days. I am not tired but get bored when there is no fighting.

*Diary, February 5*

I am trying to keep the impending Bitburg offensive secret so that the powers that be will not order it stopped. Therefore I was quite worried when Bradley telephoned and asked if I could meet him and Ike at Bastogne. I trust that it is simply a desire to be photographed in that historic city, but it may be further orders. In any event, Eddy will jump off at 0100 on the 7th.

The meeting at Bastogne

was purely a social one, but I was more amused than surprised when Eisenhower failed to make any remark about my Bastogne operation; in fact, he made no reference whatever to the great successes of the Third Army.

How Patton wanted a tribute!

So far in my dealings with him, he has never mentioned in a complimentary way any action that myself or any other officer has performed. I do not believe that it is intentional, but just carelessness; however, it is poor leadership. He had on his new five stars — a very pretty insignia.

They were photographed in front of a carefully selected "junk heap," then drove to First Army headquarters. Patton carefully avoided mentioning the forthcoming XII Corps attack.

He told Eisenhower that if he had to lose a corps, he hoped it would not be Middleton's. Eisenhower said that he could see no reason why a man could not keep those whom he trusted. He added that he felt handicapped "by having to keep Devers under him, whom he distrusted. I told him I felt the same way about Devers."

Middleton was pleased when he learned of Patton's request. "While he had nothing against Hodges, he had nothing for him."

Patton awakened for no reason at 3 A.M., February 6, and it suddenly occurred to him that if he got a breakthrough in either the VIII or XII Corps area – or in both – he might be able to launch two, possibly three, armored divisions in a swift exploitation, thereby

> re-enacting the Brest Peninsula show. Whether ideas like this are the result of inspiration or insomnia, I don't know, but nearly every tactical idea I have had popped into my head like Minerva and not as historians attempt to describe generals who work things out on paper in a laborious manner.
>
> If we do launch three divisions, we will have practically nothing to hold the line defense; however, it is my considered opinion that if we launch three divisions, there will be no line left to hold. In any case, I will take a chance. The Lord will provide.

"This," he said later, "was the origin of the Palatinate Campaign."

*Letter, GSP, Jr., to Frederick Ayer, February 6, 1945*

We are having a very funny battle right now. I am taking one of the longest chances of my chancy career; in fact, almost disobeying orders in order to attack, my theory being that if I win, nobody will say anything, and I am sure I will win.

*Letter, GSP, Jr., to Beatrice, February 6, 1944*

At 0100 tomorrow I am starting my biggest gamble. You remember that when Nelson was attacking Calvi in Corsica, he learned that there were twice as many French there as he had reported to his chief, so he kept the secret and won the battle.

Yesterday, when I saw Omar and Destiny, I was in the same fix. If the thing works, I may be able to cut Hugh and Bob loose and repeat the Driant show. If I loose, I will be where I am now.

As usual I am short of men owing to the need of supporting Big Simp.

As usual Destiny never mentioned the Bastogne operation. Nor has anyone else.

Neither Patton nor Eddy was satisfied with XII Corps progress on February 7, and things continued to be gloomy on the 8th, "mostly due to weather." Patton phoned Bradley to ask whether he could postpone giving up the 17th Airborne,

> but he was no help. His success is due to his lack of backbone and subservience to those above him. I will manage without him. In fact, I always have; even in Sicily he had to be carried. Personally I fight every order that I do not like, which makes me unpopular but successful.

James F. Byrnes, who had visited Patton several weeks earlier, wrote to say that at a luncheon with about a dozen of his former colleagues in the Senate he had repeated Patton's "very generous tribute" to Bradley for his part in planning Patton's summer campaign. Everyone was pleased to know of the "affectionate regard" that the two generals had for each other.

*Letter, GSP, Jr., to Byrnes, February 7, 1945*

> The chief thing I deprecate about the unfortunate publicity I have received is the misguided remarks which have occurred in a few Southern papers connecting me with politics. I have no more gift for politics than a cow has for fox hunting, and am not interested in it. Also, I am sure it is very bad for a man's military reputation to be confounded with it. Personally I have never voted and do not intend to.

At a press conference on February 9, he said, "I think we are going to play this part of the war by ear. If we can get a breakthrough, we will be all right."

But the weather was abominable. When the Germans destroyed the Roer River dams, they flooded the ground in front of the Ninth Army and stalled Simpson before he started. Bradley then hoped that the First and Third Armies could attack to seize Cologne and Coblenz. He told Patton to give a corps headquarters to the First Army. Patton sent the III because, even though Millikin did

> a good job at Bastogne, he is very amateurish compared to the other

corps commanders. I don't like him and never have [since West Point days]. Furthermore, I would rather have three big corps than four little ones. I hope we have to go back to the old plan and keep attacking.

*Diary, February 11*

The situation in the VIII Corps is very critical due to the fact that the roads are literally disintegrating . . . I told Middleton to dismount tank crews and use them as infantry if necessary, but not to give up the bridgehead the 6th Armored Division has secured over the Sauer River. I hate to get men hurt to take a place and then give it up.

*Diary, February 12*

All troops not actually fighting are working on the roads.

I have given the XII Corps permission to stop the attack if they want to, but any such permission always acts in reverse on Eddy, so he continued the attack. They are making fine progress.

*Letter, GSP, Jr., to Beatrice, February 13, 1945*

The only army group I would like to have would be one in China without Allies. Here things are pulled in so many directions by every passing breeze of expediency that we get on slowly.

Also the thaw and our terrific traffic has almost obliterated the roads in Belgium.

*Diary, February 13*

Crossed the Sauer River into Germany and drove along the east bank . . . The men were quite surprised to see me. However, the chance of getting hit was small and worth the risk due to the effect it had on the troops . . .

I will be the first on the Rhine yet.

*Letter, GSP, Jr., to Beatrice, February 14, 1945*

Some times I get so mad with the troops for not fighting better and then they do something superb. The forcing of the crossing of the Sauer and Our Rivers . . . was an Homeric feat.

The Siegfried line runs right along the river with hundreds of pill boxes and submerged barbed wire. The river was in flood, running at ten to twelve miles an hour, and yet they crossed.

One day we lost 136 boats but not all the men. We built bridges under [enemy] fire, and even when I crossed they still had to keep them covered with smoke.

I got up closer than I intended to but nothing happened, and the soldiers were all glad to see me. If I only had one more division, I could break through, but the brains are all set on another fool move which never has and never will succeed, particularly under Sir B. L. [Montgomery].

*Diary, February 14*

I decided to visit Hughes in Paris as neither the VIII nor XII Corps will be able to resume their attack until the 17th, the day I plan to return . . .

Codman and I departed on our first leave since the 24th of October, 1942. We got on the railway car, and Hughes has secured rooms for us at the George V Hotel.

The drama and the desperation of the Battle of the Bulge were over, and the fighting once again was slow and slogging. But now at least the Rhine River was definitely in view.

# VII
# Germany

*"I do not see how they can keep it up much longer."*

CHAPTER 35

# The Palatinate

*"I will be damned if I see why we have divisions if not to use them."*

To EVERETT HUGHES, Patton looked fine, less nervous. He had stopped smoking, had a fund of funny stories, and retained his sense of humor. Everywhere he went, he was recognized.

At Versailles, where SHAEF was established,

> [Bedell] Smith was very eloquent and said, "I suppose you don't know the high strategy, but I am convinced that my northern effort [21 Army Group] cannot logistically support more than 35 divisions. As we have 83 divisions, that leaves quite a few I can use anywhere else, and I want you to be prepared to resume the old effort through Saarlautern and Saareguemines. How many divisions would you require?"
>
> I said I could make the attack with five.
>
> He said, "I think you should have twelve."
>
> I had never known how great he really is.

Smith took him hunting on one of the "old royal preserves of the Kings of France now used by the Presidents," and Patton

> killed three ducks, one phesant, and three hares, and then got ptomane and had to go in. I am all right to day.
>
> We went to the "Follies" which is perfectly naked, so much so that no one is interested. As usual there was a big going on when I got there. We had a box and drank champagne back stage with the manager and his wife. She said, "My dear General, when ever you come to Paris, make the Follies your home. You can rest here always." I can think of no place less conducive to rest.

Then he returned to the war.

*Diary, February 19*

Wrote Bradley a letter saying that all U.S. troops, except the Third Army, were doing nothing, and that while I was still attacking, I could do better with more divisions, and asked him for from one to three additional ones. I wrote this letter in order to get on record, as we will be criticized by history, and rightly so, for having sat still so long. Also, I do not wish any more of my ideas used without credit to me as happens when I give them orally.

Walker called . . . to say that he feels the 94th Division is prepared for a breakthrough in the triangle, and wanted to know if we could get him an armored division.

I phoned Bradley who, fortunately, was out, so I called Bull [SHAEF G–3], and as a result of my proselyting of the other day [in Versailles], secured the 10th Armored with a string tied on it, "only for this operation."

I will be damned if I see why we have divisions if not to use them.

He wrote to Bradley to ask for more divisions – so the XX Corps could reduce a pocket in the Saar-Moselle triangle, remove all threat to Luxembourg, and make possible the capture of Trier; so the VIII Corps could start an advance to Bonn or Coblenz; so the XII Corps could capture Bitburg, essential for movement to the Rhine.

Bradley agreed with the desirability of all of Patton's points. Unfortunately, "higher authority" had already decided to make the main effort elsewhere. "Regardless of what you and I think of this decision, we are good enough soldiers to carry out these orders." Therefore, since assuming a static posture was necessary, Bradley hoped that Patton would get all his divisions "rested, refitted, and filled up to full strength, so that when the proper time" came, he would be able to deliver "a decisive blow in conjunction with Hodges."

He came personally to explain the facts of life to Patton.

Bradley looked very tired to me and did not seem at all sure of himself. I asked definitely if there was any objection to my making a run for Coblenz ahead of time or of taking Cologne if opportunity suddenly developed. He said there was no objection.

*Letter, GSP, Jr., to Beatrice, February 21, 1945*

Well we did it again on the usual shoe string. I refer to the taking of the Saar-Moselle triangle yesterday . . . I had to use decept[ion], tears, and every other means to get one [division] . . . One would think people would like to win a war.

Now I am trying to wheedle an infantry division, seven of which are resting, so I can take a large and famous city [Trier].

Yesterday I drove all day looking at roades or rather at places where roades had been. I have never seen such mud, just miles and miles of cocoa colored goo . . .

I went inside some of their pill boxes [in the Siegfried Line]. They were stupendus . . .

I love to read about my self. The scrap books will probably be my only literature [after the war] . . .

There is much envy, hatred, and malace, and all unchareatableness. To hell with them. They have associates, I have fate.

*Diary, February 22*

Met Walker and Morris [10th Armored Division]. To my disgust, I discovered that Morris had let his bridge train get lost, so had not crossed at Saarbourg, as I had supposed, but had sat there until well after noon waiting to find the train and was still sitting, due to the fact that he was being held up by small arms and mortar fire at the far side of the river. I told him to fine the officer who got lost and to cross at once.

I feel we missed the boat on this one – just lack of drive. Walker should have been on the job too, and perhaps I am also to blame. Had I been personally present, the train would probably never have been lost, and the same thing applies to Walker and then to Morris – all three of us fell down.

Everyone was terribly tired and discouraged by the bad weather and the mud.

*GSP, Jr., Press Conference, Luxembourg, February 23, 1945*

Patton: The operations of the so-called Moselle-Saar triangle were exceedingly well timed. It was a very fine sense of touch, played by ear so to speak, and General Walker did a great job . . .

The fighting up in the VIII Corps has illustrated again the thing I keep on talking about – the utter futility of defense . . . We have to keep stressing it and preaching it even after the war. A host of people who squat and piss say this will be the last war and that you'll only need clubs, but they are responsible for the death of millions of people . . . The only thing to do when a son-of-a-bitch looks cross-eyed at you is to beat the hell out of him right then and there . . .

They now say that we've got 3,000 miles of ocean, but 20 years from now this 3,000 miles of ocean will be just a good spit. This is a very serious thing, and many people don't visualize this very grave danger . . .

Wars are won by the people who actually go out and do things . . .

The Third Army appreciates the efforts which you gentlemen have made . . .

We are prone to think too much that weapons are more important than the knowledge of soldiering . . . It takes ability to take care of yourself and live under bad conditions, and above all, it means ability to work with other men . . .

Question: The Germans are still building tank ditches?

Patton: If they would use all that energy in some other way, they might do much better, but they are still building those things, and the only thing they are good for are toilets . . .

Question: Any indication where the next line of resistance will be?

Patton: I think any time you can break through you can go straight ahead. Of course every town and every crossroad and bridge will be defended, but that is not too serious.

Question: Are we going to try to take Trier?

Patton: I fear we lost the boat on that one. We had a bridge train knocked out — but don't say that. This is the first bad luck the Army has had. Every minute you don't put this operation across, it makes it that much harder. I think it is a very feasible operation, though, and we have done well.

*Diary, February 23*

The situation in the triangle is annoying, not due to the Germans but due to the Americans. SHAEF has a new toy called SHAEF Reserve, and every time they let an Army have a division, they want one in return. Now they say that if I keep on using the 10th Armored, I will have to put the 11th, 6th, or 4th Armored in reserve — this despite the fact that all these divisions are properly placed to attack. I just hope something will turn up to prevent my having to do this. The best I could do for the moment was to settle for 48 hours more time, by which time the situation may have cleared.

Bradley called to state that I would get two new infantry divisions but would have to pull out two old ones in this so-called reserve.

*Letter, GSP, Jr., to son George, February 24, 1945*

Remember this: no set piece of tactics is of any merit in itself, unless it is executed by heroic and disciplined troops who have self-confidence and who have leaders who take care of them.

At the moment, the Third Army is on a sort of defensive job — or at least any other Army would be — but we are still managing to keep pushing and have captured or buried about 20,000 Germans in the last three weeks.

*Diary, February 24*

The Ninth Army seems to be doing all right, but the Second British has not done a thing, nor probably will it.

I sent Gay to see what is the matter with the XX Corps. Either we must get going in that sector or we will have to quit, and I will get in a jam with SHAEF for holding on to the 10th Armored Division.

*Diary, February 25*

Had Middleton, Walker, and Gaffey in for lunch. Bradley called and asked if he could also come . . . and we were delighted. I coached all three corps commanders and also Weyland what to say in order to sell the idea of continuing the attack to take Trier . . .

I personally pointed out that we have a chance of taking this town and that it will be criminal not to do so just in order to comply with the dictum of the Combined Chiefs of Staff, 4,000 miles away [in Washington], who insist on a certain number of inactive divisions in a so-called reserve.

We argued hard and at last Bradley said we could keep on till dark of the 27th, provided Ike let us call the 90th Division, at the moment out of action, a SHAEF reserve unit.

I wonder if ever before in the history of war, a winning general had to plead to be allowed to keep on winning.

*Letter, GSP, Jr., to Beatrice, February 25, 1945*

We just finished a very strange meeting. The tent maker felt that we should stop attacking, and it took me and all three corps commanders half a day to get permission to continue the attack for another 48 hours, at which time if we have not taken a certain town [Trier] we will have to stop. What a war.

Well we will do it any how. I have never been stopped either by orders or the enemy yet . . .

I wish fools in congress would stop trying to get me promoted. I fear that GCM [Marshall] will think I am back of it — I am not. They must promote Omar first or relieve him. We will all get four stars some day, and I never cared to be like the others.

I will stop now and take a walk.

*Diary, February 26*

Got a lot of clippings from home. A Congressman Brooks from Louisiana has made a move in Congress to get me four stars, and other people are writing about me as a potential political character. This is very bad publicity and might be hurtful.

The current operation for the encirclement of Trier is the result of the ability to change plans to meet opportunities developed by combat or as Napoleon said, "I attack and then I look."

The XX Corps started to take the triangle chiefly as a means of training the relatively green 94th Division. When things developed satisfactorily, Walker asked for and got the 10th Armored . . . The success of this operation was better than anticipated, so I determined to have a try at Trier . . .

When Trier is taken, I am planning to resume the attack to the east and secure the bridges over the Kyll and then attack Coblenz . . .

It may be of interest to future generals to realize that one makes plans to fit circumstances and does not try to create circumstances to fit plans. That way danger lies.

*Diary, February 27*

I called General Bradley because we were supposed to stop at dark today if we had not taken Trier. He said to keep on going . . . until higher authority steps in. He also said he would not listen for the telephone.

"Bill Morris and the 10th Armored are within 4.8 miles of Trier," he wrote Beatrice, "and I think I have won my bet."

*Diary, March 1*

Walker called . . . to announce that the 10th Armored was in Trier . . . It has been a very fine operation and has netted us over 7,000 prisoners. When he crossed at Saarbourg, the Germans thought he was going south . . . so his quick turn to the north took them completely by surprise.

Tried to get Eisenhower and Bradley on the wire to notify them, but was unable to do so and called Smith. Later Bradley called me from the Ninth Army and was very much pleased, and both Beedle and Brad were complimentary. Ike was in the room with Bradley; I heard his voice – but he did not take the trouble to speak to me.

I certainly again proved my military ideas are correct and have put them over in spite of opposition from the Americans.

*Letter, GSP, Jr., to Beatrice, March 1, 1945*

Fooled them again . . . and I had to beg, lie, and steal to get a chance to take [Trier]. Inspite of being fat, Walker is good . . .

B. [Bradley] actually congratulated me!

I was in Saarbourg yesterday. It was the home of John the blind, king of Bohemia and Duke of Luxembourg who was killed at Crecy. The Prince of Wailes uses his crest.

Yesterday while I was sight seeing, a shell came quite close. Also they shelled hell out of a town at the time I was supposed to be there – I was late – I think they tap our [telephone] wires.

In a radio broadcast to the American people, Vincent Sheean talked about Patton and generalship. Because most reporters were interested only in the common soldier, he said, civilians had a hazy notion of how the military worked. The mainspring of all action was the commander, who, at every echelon, whether junior or senior, planned operations, directed his men, and imparted confidence to all under him. The most important place where command was exercised was at the head of an Army, "the highest strictly operational field unit," the point where strategy – the ideas emanating from Washington, London, and, say, Yalta – became translated into tactics, activity on the battlefield.

During the past six weeks Sheean had been moving around in the Third Army, which had raced across France in August and had hurled itself toward Bastogne in December. The Army commander was without question the mainspring of "these phenomenal moves." Quickly apparent to any visitor was the extent to which the Army was imbued with pride and confidence in Patton. Part of that identification between the men and their commander came from the frequency with which Patton showed himself to his troops; some of it arose from stories, myths that ascribed superhuman qualities to Patton; but the most important element was the knowledge of "his masterly decisions."

A great commander, Sheean said, was made by his great accomplishments. If Patton's career were to end at once, his performance in Sicily, in France, and at Bastogne would be enough to place him among the greatest generals in history.

Well, what did he do as a general? It was difficult to be exact. Very often what a general did was of less consequence than what he was. His character and personality, sometimes his showmanship, made him real to his troops, who absorbed the confidence that he had in himself.

A general, whether great or merely good, had first to be master of the technical or professional matters of warfare. Beyond that, he had to be right in his critical decisions. And he had to animate the mind, imagination, and spirit of his men. Patton's impact on his troops came from the vigor of his unique personality, his talent for language, his exuberance and self-assurance. To call these qualities mere swashbuckling was to underrate and misunderstand Patton's genius. Everyone knew of Patton's familiarity with military history, theory, and literature, with Napoleon, Clausewitz, and others, with the command of units at every level of the Army. The combination of practical experience and theoretical preparation gave Patton the solid base, the stage, on which he played his role as a spectacular, yet sound leader.

Patton's qualities, Sheean continued, occasionally startled and outraged the public, which sometimes objected to what were irrelevant details in his makeup. Too much unfavorable talk had minimized Patton's generalship, when in fact his Army had moved faster than any other in history. The American soldiers were good and well-equipped. But they needed to be led by a bold and skillful man who had, more than most, a sharp military instinct. By his speed of action and reaction, Patton had already shortened the war and saved innumerable lives. To Sheean he seemed "the most original, the boldest, and the most modern talent" in field operations that America had produced.

*Diary, March 2*

Walker . . . told me that . . . the corps of the Third Army did better than in the other Armies because the corps commanders have had confidence that if they made a mistake, they would still be backed up.

Bradley called to ask when I can relieve the 10th Armored. He is simply hipped on the subject . . .

Drove to Bitburg . . . It was the first time I have seen the Dragon's teeth [of the Siegfried Line], a useless form of amusement.

*Diary, March 3*

All three corps are fighting to secure bridgeheads through which we can launch a combined armor and infantry attack.

Middleton called me last night to say that the 11th Armored Division would not be in position to attack this morning as planned, but would attack tomorrow. I told him that it must attack by noon today.

The Ninth Army, after a brilliant offensive, having reached the Rhine, Patton telegraphed Simpson "on your magnificent achievement."

"We are all delighted," he wrote Stimson, "with the wonderful success that the Ninth Army has achieved, and a little envious for fear they will steal our reputation."

He persuaded Bradley "with considerable difficulty to let me attack with all three corps."

To Beatrice: "I won a decisive battle just now against the tent maker, so I can now continue my 'passive defense' with renewed ardor."

To Hodges: "Please accept my hearty personal congratulations . . . for your recent magnificent successes and the capture of Cologne."

All the Armies had reached the Rhine except the Third, which had a longer distance to go, which faced massed German forces trying to keep escape routes open across the river, and which operated in awful terrain.

*Letter, GSP, Jr., to Beatrice, March 6, 1945*

I have never had any pearl handled pistols except one Hughes brought me. Also I never carry pearl. It is unluckey . . . I want ivory . . .

It looks as if Hugh has broken through. He took 2,000 PW yesterday, including a corps commander and staff complete and advanced about 24 miles.

We are in a horse race with Courtney. If he beats me [across the Rhine], I shall be ashamed.

*Diary, March 6*

Bradley called . . . and was pleased at what we were doing. I told him that now was the time to use everything, and the [newly-arrived] 89th and 65th should be used on our lines of communication. He said that would keep them from getting [combat] trained. He just fails to see war as a struggle, not as an educational course.

Patton interviewed Major General Ernst George Edwin Graf von Rothkirch und Trach, a captured corps commander, and asked why, in spite of Allied superiority in men and materiel, the German army continued to fight even though the soldiers recognized the futility of hoping to win the war. Rothkirch answered that they were under orders and would have to carry on as soldiers in spite of personal opinions and beliefs. Patton thought they were "great people but fools."

*Diary, March 7*

Bradley called . . . to congratulate us – he is learning . . .

We are making contact with the First Army . . . 4th Armored Division . . . reached the Rhine north of Coblenz, making 65 miles in about 36 hours – a very remarkable performance . . .

I feel that Kilburn is no good. He simply lacks drive. I should have relieved him after Bastogne. I am really not mean enough.

The big news that day was in the First Army.

9th Armored Division of the III Corps . . . got a bridge intact over the Rhine at Remagen. This may have a fine influence on our future movements. I hope we get one also.

By a stroke of luck, by the perspicacity and drive of William Hoge and his combat command, and by the high courage of the men who stormed across the Remagen bridge, Hodges got over the Rhine River first. Patton's admiration was unbounded and sincere.

"We got to the Rhine last night," he wrote Beatrice, "but as yet have no bridge and are again waiting for some one to decide what next to do."

*Diary, March 9*

All the Rhine bridges in my sector are out, and it will take too much time to build one. I shall not wait for the Seventh Army [to cross the river] . . .

It is essential to get the First and Third Armies so deeply involved in their present plans that they cannot be moved north to play second fiddle to the British-instilled idea of attacking with 60 divisions on the Ruhr plain.

Bradley was anxious for me to coordinate my plan with Patch, but since he cannot jump [the Rhine] until the 15th, I am going to attack as soon as possible, because at this stage of the war, time is more important than coordination . . .

The 11th Armored has reached the Rhine River at Andernach . . . We have got about 8,000 prisoners – and I had to beg to do it.

When Bradley phoned, Patton apologized for being off the front pages of the newspapers, which were giving Hodges and the First Army lots of space on the Remagen bridge. Bradley said, "Well, even you have to regroup once in a while."

*Diary, March 12*

Kilburn came in . . . at his request and talked to me for 35 minutes trying to explain his actions.

I told him that it was a considered opinion, and separate opinions of both Middleton and myself, arrived at on different occasions, that he was not suitable due to lack of offensive spirit, to the command of an armored division; but that I was willing to let him be a combat commander under Gaffey, who had expressed his willingness to take him.

He asked me for 48 hours to consider this.

I told him that was too long. The very fact that he asked for 48 hours is the index to his inability to command. I told him he would have to let the chief of staff know his decision by 5:00 o'clock.

He asked if he could call up Bedell Smith on the telephone and get another job, and I said yes.

Everyone is wrong but him. I should have relieved him in January.

A captured officer, Lieutenant Colonel Freiherr von Wangenheim, was interrogated and said:

> The greatest threat . . . was the whereabouts of the feared U.S. Third Army. General Patton is always the main topic of military discussion. Where is he? When will he attack? Where . . ? How? With what? Those are the questions which raced through the head of every German general since the famous German counteroffensive last December. The location of the U.S. First and Ninth Armies was well known, but one was not sure where the U.S. Third was . . .
>
> General Patton is the most feared general on all fronts. The successes of the U.S. Third Army are still overshadowing all other events of the war, including the campaigns in Russia . . . The tactics of General Patton are daring and unpredictable . . . He is the most modern general and the best commander of armored and infantry troops combined.

*Letter, GSP, Jr., to Marshall, March 13, 1945*

When the operations against Germany are brought to a successful conclusion, I should like to be considered for any type of combat command from a division up against the Japanese.

I am sure that my method of fighting would be successful.

I also am of such an age that this is my last war, and I would therefore like to see it through to the end.

Please pardon my bothering you with personal matters.

About this time *Cosmopolitan* magazine purchased one of Patton's poems — "Fear" — and paid him $250 for it.

Eisenhower now intended to capture or destroy all the enemy forces still west of the Rhine. He expected this "breaking through the fortified lines" to be "a nasty business," but success would "multiply the advantage" of having the Remagen bridge.

*Letter, GSP, Jr., to Beatrice, March 14, 1945*

XX Corps attacked . . . yesterday and is doing well but the going is terrible, just woods and mountains. Still they made about 4 miles. When we get a hole [in the enemy defenses], I will send Morris . . . through for a drive on Mainz . . .

We have taken 89,000 [prisoners] since Feb 1, and got 9,000 plus yesterday, the biggest single bag we have had.

When someone said that Patton's instructions were always "in a layman's language . . . easily read and understood," Patton replied:

> We can never get anything across unless we talk the language of the people we are trying to instruct. Perhaps that is why I curse.

*Diary, March 14*

> Visited Trier . . . So did Caesar . . . whose Gallic wars I am now reading. It is interesting to view in imagination the Roman legions marching down that same road. One of the few things undestroyed in Trier is the entrance to the old Roman amphitheater which still stands in its sturdy magnificence.

Driving into Trier, he followed Caesar's old road and "could smell the sweat of the legions."

> The Seventh Army attacks in the morning . . . I certainly hope we beat them to Mainz . . .
>
> Called Walker and told him to turn on the heat as I feel we are not going fast enough.

Radio news broadcasts announced the promotions of nine officers to full – four-star – general rank. On the list were Bradley, Devers, and Clark, all Army Group commanders, as well as Handy, Kenney, Krueger, McNarney, Somervell, and Spaatz. Patton phoned Bradley his congratulations and sent telegrams to Devers and Clark.

He told Beatrice that the mayor of Metz gave him a large bronze medallion, Prince Felix of Luxembourg presented him the Croix de Guerre, the French made him Grand Officer of the Legion of Honor, and he was sure that additional promotions would be announced. "I hope they dont make Courtney and I on the same list. I think I would refuse."

Marshall and Eisenhower had discussed including Patton and Hodges on the list of promotions, but to have done so would have been a slight to Bradley and Devers. Eisenhower seemed to imply regret that Patton did not command the 6th Army Group, which would have made him eligible for promotion, and he had put Patton ahead of Devers in his recommendations. Marshall replied that promoting Patton ahead of Devers would compromise the latter's usefulness.

Had Patton remained at the head of the Seventh Army and brought it ashore in southern France, he might well have moved up to command the Army Group despite the slapping incident. But Eisenhower was right to have wanted him for his own invasion, Overlord. Who else would have swept across France so swiftly and turned against the Bulge so rapidly?

Patton must surely have thought about this, perhaps discussed it with Hughes, who had sponsored Patton's retention for southern France. Yet how could mere promotion equal the fame and glory he had achieved in France and Luxembourg?

As Patton told Beatrice,

> Ike was quite apologetic about the 4-star business, but has, however, good reasons — that is, you must maintain the hierarchy of command or else relieve them, and he had no reason for relieving them. He said that George [Marshall] had promised that I would be number one Army commander on the [next] list. At the moment I am having so much fun fighting that I don't care what the rank is.

Bradley telephoned Patton around 11 o'clock on March 16, to say that Eisenhower's plane was unable to land at Bradley's headquarters and would come down at Luxembourg. Patton drove to the airfield and arrived there just in time to meet Eisenhower and Bedell Smith as they were leaving in a borrowed car. He took them to his headquarters, showed them into his map room, and discussed the situation. Eisenhower "was quite enthusiastic and complimentary, as was Smith."

After lunch Patton had a guard of honor for Smith,

> Eisenhower declining . . . on the grounds that it originally had been planned for Smith, and Smith never had had one. Smith was very much pleased and drove away immediately afterward to visit Bradley.

Patton and Eisenhower drove to Trier and found the generals there "not pushing hard enough in our opinion."

Four Red Cross girls came to dinner, and Eisenhower seemed to have a good time. He and Patton sat up talking until 2:30 in the morning.

At the morning briefing on the following day, Eisenhower spoke and paid me the first compliment he has ever vouchsafed. He stated that we of the Third Army were such veterans that we did not appreciate our own greatness and should be more cocky and boastful . . . [Eisenhower was] extremely complimentary and stated that not only was I a good general but also a lucky general and that Napoleon preferred luck to greatness.

They then flew to Seventh Army headquarters at Luneville, where they lunched with Devers and Patch, who "were extremely nice."

Eisenhower left for Reims, and Patton returned to Luxembourg.

Walker called me up . . . and stated that he was not at all satisfied with Morris and recommended that he be relieved. I told him that I was not satisfied either, but that I could think of no one better that I could get in his place . . .

I also called Eddy . . . and told him I was very much disgusted with the slowness of the 11th Armored and that they must get moving.

I then called Middleton and told him he was the only corps commander whom I had not cussed out, and congratulated him on the good work he had done in securing Coblenz.

*GSP, Jr., Press Conference, Luxembourg, March 17, 1945*

Patton: The Marines go to town by reporting the number [they have had] killed. I always try to fight without getting [our] people killed . . .

Do you know — you can put it out today — the Third Army will have been operational 230 days and we have 230,000 prisoners — that is a thousand a day. We are going to have a picture of it [the 230,000th man captured]. They wouldn't let us turn out the last picture [the 200,000th prisoner] because it was humiliating a prisoner of war by showing his face. This time we will take a picture of his ass . . .

Another bit of publicity I'm asking which is not for me — God knows I've got enough — I could go to heaven and St. Peter would recognize me right away — but it is for the officers and men. You can release any damn division in this Army. I want the Germans to know we have four armored divisions jumping on them — the 4th, 10th, 11th, and 12th. The 12th goes tomorrow morning. Of course you needn't say where . . .

Don't say that the Marines advertise casualties. I was merely trying to emphasize my point.

Question: What is more important, a bridge across the Rhine or the fighting down here?

Patton: A bridge across the Rhine.

*Letter, GSP, Jr., to Beatrice, March 19, 1945*

The Third Army is realy going to town to day in the greatest operation we have ever put on.

The 4 AD is six miles from Worms and will get there to night . . .

We are the eighth wonder of the world. And I had to beg, lie, and steal to get started – now every one says "that is what we always wanted to do."

I hope things keep smooth. It seems too good to be true.

*Diary, March 19*

The VIII Corps is holding Coblenz . . . The XII Corps is nearing Worms. The XX Corps is nearing Bad Durkeim. This is a great show.

Bradley and Hodges came to visit. Explaining that Hodges would advance to Kassel, Bradley suggested that Patton cross the Rhine, not near Coblenz, but in the Mainz-Worms area, then head for Kassel too. The result would be to close a First and Third Army pincers at Kassel.

Unless we get a crossing over the Rhine and start north on Kassel before the British jump off [across the Rhine], we may lose ten divisions to the British.

In his diary, Patton marveled once again at the "difficulties I had in getting" the past operations started.

They did not want me to take Trier nor go to the Rhine nor to cross the Moselle southwest of Coblenz, and now, if we don't cross the Rhine, we may be halted again. We have got by due to persistence and on ability to make plans fit circumstances. The other Armies try to make circumstances fit plans.

*Telegram, Marshall to Eisenhower, March 21, 1945*

Please pass on my personal and enthusiastic congratulations to Patton. I will deal more formally later with the entire effort [to get to the Rhine], Bradley, Hodges, Patton, Devers, and Patch, not to mention air.

[In longhand:] Dear George: To this I add that I continue to have reason to cheer that you came with me to this war. Always, Ike.

*Diary, March 21*

The operations in the Palatinate, namely in the Rhine and Moselle triangle, are practically completed and have been most successful; really a historic accomplishment . . .

I really believe this operation is one of the outstanding operations in the history of war. We have put on a great show, but I think we will eclipse it when we get across the Rhine.

He had already told Eddy to cross the Rhine at Oppenheim, Middleton at Boppard or near Lorch.

*Diary, March 22*

Ever since we closed on the Rhine, I have been using my utmost endeavors to get at least one battalion of infantry across the river. Eddy is going to make the attempt tonight . . . There is a strong chance that the operation will be very successful because the Germans are so used to build-ups prior to attempts to cross rivers that they will not think it feasible.

Middleton will make a crossing in his area Saturday night.

The 5th Division started across at 10 P.M.

*Diary, March 23*

The 5th Division is over the Rhine. God be praised. It was a . . . fitting climax to the preceding ten days . . .

Patch himself was very complimentary but he told me Devers was rather sore at the fact that the Third Army had stolen the thunder of the Seventh Army . . .

I am sure that the thing to do is to get as many troops across on as wide a front as possible and keep on attacking.

For reasons unknown to me, the First Army, which has seven or eight divisions across [near Remagen] is unable to continue its attack for two more days . . .

I am very grateful to the Lord for the great blessings he has heaped on me and the Third Army, not only in the success which He has granted us, but in the weather which He is now providing.

*Letter, GSP, Jr., to Beatrice, March 23, 1945*

I am realy scared by my good luck. This operation is stupendous . . .

Last night in a surprise crossing, I got a whole division . . . over the Rhine [near] . . . Oppenheim.

Jake [Devers] was supposed to cross at our right south of Worms but he was waiting for an air blitz which could not be put on for ten days. We did not wait and caught most of the 15 Panzer [Division] in bed.

The displaced persons is a problem. They are streaming back utterly forlorn. I saw one woman with a perambulator full of her worldly goods sitting by it on a hill crying. An old man with a wheel barrow and three little children wringing his hands. A woman with five children and a tin cup crying. In hundreds of villages there is not a living thing, not even a chicken. Most of the houses are heaps of stones. They brought it on them selves, but these poor pesants are not responsible.

I am getting soft? I did most of it.

*Letter, GSP, Jr., to son George, October 22, 1945*

I did not know until you told me that Napoleon crossed near Oppenheim. I had picked this when I was still in England as the place to cross the Rhine because the terrain on my side dominated that on the other side, as the former was far enough away from the Frankfurt hills to prevent direct fire on the bridges, and because, above everything else, there was a barge harbor there from which we could launch the boats unseen.

*Third Army General Orders 70, March 23, 1945*

To the officers and men of the Third Army and to our comrades of the XIX TAC:

In the period from January 29 to March 22, 1945, you have wrested 6,484 square miles of territory from the enemy. You have taken 3,072 cities, towns, and villages, including . . . Trier, Coblenz, Bingen, Worms, Mainz, Kaiserslautern, and Ludwigshafen . . .

You have captured 140,112 enemy soldiers and have killed or wounded an additional 99,000, thereby eliminating practically all of the German Seventh and First Armies. History records no greater achievement in so limited a time . . .

The world rings with your praises: better still, General Marshall,

General Eisenhower, and General Bradley have all personally commended you. The highest honor I have ever attained is that of having my name coupled with yours in these great events.

Please accept my heartfelt admiration and thanks for what you have done, and remember that your assault crossing over the Rhine . . . assures you of even greater glory to come.

*Diary, March 24*

Drove to the river and went across on the pontoon bridge, stopping in the middle to take a piss in the Rhine, and then pick up some dirt on the far side . . . in emulation of William the Conqueror.

The operation in crossing the Rhine was most remarkable in that the total casualties in killed and wounded were only 28. This does not mean that it was no fight. It means that the 5th Division, making its 23d river crossing, was very skillful, and the operation was very daringly performed. Maj. Stiller, at his own request, went in the first boat . . .

Tomorrow . . . a crossing at St. Goar, near the fabled home of the Lorelei. It would seem rather pathetic that a crossing should be made at the very site of the home of one of the heroines of German mythology . . .

I must construct the railway bridge [near Mainz] as that should be the main supply line . . .

I told each corps commander that I was betting on him to get there [to Giessen] first, so as to produce a little friendly rivalry . . .

Today the Third Army will process the 300,000 prisoner of war taken since August 1, which puts the take of this Army ahead of the First Army by over 1,000 prisoners, although he had a 59-day handicap in starting . . .

I do not see how they [the Germans] can keep it up much longer.

Montgomery's forces crossed the Rhine at 4 A.M., after a tremendous artillery bombardment of 70,000 rounds, an air bombardment, smoke screens, and an airborne landing in support — quite in contrast with Patton's virtually ad hoc crossings.

*Diary, March 25*

I decided that we should cross at Mainz north of the Main River and directed Walker to do it as soon as practicable.

It was all tremendously exciting. The German resistance was crumbling, the weather was improving, and roads were dry and good, and Patton looked ahead to the same kind of exhilarating advance through Germany that characterized his mobile operations across France.

*Letter, GSP, Jr., to Beatrice, March 25, 1945*

We are through again and are on the edge of Frankfurt right now.

The good news and the marvelous outlook were marred by an unfortunate event:

*Diary, March 26*

Col. Jack Hines, son of my old friend, Major General John L. Hines [who succeeded Pershing as U.S. Army Chief of Staff], was struck in the face by an 88 armor-piercing shell, which removed his eyes, his nose, and upper jaw, and also took off his left hand.

Apparently his wounds had a bad effect on Grow, as the division was very logey today . . . I told Grow if he did not get into Frankfurt tonight, I would relieve him . . .

I then flew to Bad Kreuznach to see Colonel Hines. When I arrived, he was on the operating table and unconscious. At least if he dies, I can tell his father I saw him.

He lived and returned to the United States, was awarded the Distinguished Service Cross – an award made personally by his father at Walter Reed Hospital in Washington at Patton's suggestion – recovered and rehabilitated himself in miraculous and courageous fashion.

*Letter, Eisenhower to GSP, Jr., March 26, 1945*

I have frequently had occasion to state, publicly, my appreciation of the great accomplishments of this Allied force during the past nine months. The purpose of this note is to express to you personally my deep appreciation of the splendid way in which you have conducted Third Army operations from the moment it entered battle last August 1. You have made your Army a fighting force that is not excelled in effectiveness by any other of equal size in the world, and I am very proud of the fact that you, as one of the fighting commanders who has been with me from the beginning of the African campaign, have performed so brilliantly throughout.

We are now fairly started on that phase of the campaign which I

> hope will be the final one. I know that Third Army will be in at the finish in the same decisive way that it has perfomed in all the preliminary battles.

Eisenhower wrote Marshall that Bradley and Patton were "extraordinarily proud" of the messages Marshall had sent them. He himself was sending each of the four Army commanders letters of "short personal commendation." Patton was

> a particularly warm friend of mine and has been so over a period of 25 years. Moreover, I think I can claim almost a proprietary interest in him because of the stand I took in several instances . . . In certain situations he has no equal, but by and large it would be difficult indeed to choose between him, Hodges, and Simpson . . . while Patch is little, if any, behind the others.

Yet at that moment, at the very time when things were going so well for Patton, another incident was about to develop, another event was to threaten his career.

## CHAPTER 36

# The Hammelburg Incident

*"I have been nervous as a cat all day as every one but me thought it too great a risk. I hope it works."*

ON THE DAY that the Third Army was across the Rhine, on March 23, Patton wrote Beatrice: "We are headed right for John's place and may get there before he is moved."

He was referring to a prisoner of war camp at Hammelburg, some 60 miles to the east, where Allied officers were rumored to be held. But he was hardly so sure as his letter indicated that John Waters, his son-in-law, was really there.

Waters had been captured in Tunisia in February 1943, transported to Italy, and eventually moved to Poland. Early in 1945, he was known to be in a camp near Szubin. When Red Army troops overran the town, they found that the German authorities had evacuated the place and marched their captives to the west to prevent their falling into Russian hands. The Russian commander had been alerted to Waters' confinement, and he notified higher headquarters that the prisoners were gone. Eventually the American Military Mission in Moscow received word, and on February 9 sent a telegram to Eisenhower for Patton passing on the Soviet report. Two weeks later, the news having reached Washington, Hull advised Patton of the Russian advance and said that there was no knowledge of Waters' new location.

Since then, Allied intelligence had established that Hammelburg was a principal camp for captured Allied officers, that it held about 4700 inmates, among them some 1500 Americans, and that many of those at Szubin had been transferred to Hammelburg. Thus, there was a good chance that Waters was there, but no certainty.

Since the Americans were approaching Hammelburg, it was likely that the Germans would move the prisoners again. Patton began to think of rescuing a large number of Allied officers.

A month earlier, in the Philippines, MacArthur had gained much publicity by taking the prison camps of Santo Tomas and Bilibid in Manila, thereby liberating 5000 military prisoners and civilian internees. Patton was reported to have said that he would make MacArthur look like a piker.

On March 25, he told Beatrice: "Hope to send an expedition tomorrow to get John."

This was shorthand of a sort. He and his wife were primarily interested in their son-in-law, but if he rescued John, he would also liberate other prisoners. In addition, Patton could hardly tell her about Hammelburg because of censorship.

On the following day, he flew to the XII Corps headquarters and, according to his diary,

> directed Eddy to send an expedition to the east about 60 miles for the purpose of recapturing some 900 American prisoners alleged to be in a stockade there.

The thrust would have to be mounted by the 4th Armored Division, now under William Hoge, whose combat command had captured the Remagen bridge and who had replaced Gaffey in command of the division. Eddy and Hoge

> were reluctant to do this because they said if I failed, I would be severely criticized. However, I do not believe that fear of criticism should prevent my getting back American prisoners, particularly as in the last death struggles of the Germans, our men might be murdered.

The corps and division commanders disliked Patton's instructions because the mission was dangerous. Sending troops independently and deeply into enemy territory invited disaster. The men going to Hammelburg could be easily surrounded and quickly destroyed.

Eddy probably objected also on the ground that the XII Corps was to advance to the north – not to the east – in order to join units of the First Army in an encirclement of the Ruhr.

If he replied, Patton probably said that the thrust to Hammelburg would serve as a feint to deceive the enemy into thinking the Third Army was going to the east rather than to the north.

But there was no mention of this in the diary at the time.

Then arose the question of the size of the force to commit. Was a larger organization more suitable for a move that was essentially deceptive in purpose and only secondarily designed to rescue the prisoners? Would a smaller force be better on a hit-and-run operation executed to liberate prisoners of war and only incidentally to mount a deception?

Thus started a long-lingering controversy. Was Waters incidental to the Hammelburg mission? Or did he motivate it? Did the action have a sound military basis? Or did Patton's personal interest dictate it?

He wrote to Beatrice on March 27:

> Last night I sent an armored column to a place 40 miles east of Frankfurt where John and some 900 prisoners are said to be. I have been nervous as a cat all day as every one but me thought it too great a risk. I hope it works. Al Stiller went along. If I loose that column, it will possibly be a new incident, but I wont loose it.

In his diary on the same date, he noted:

> I was quite nervous all morning over the task force I sent to rescue the prisoners, as we could get no information concerning them. I do not believe there is anything in that part of Germany heavy enough to hurt them, but for some reason I was nervous – probably I had indigestion.

*Diary, March 28*

We have no further information concerning the task force out after the prisoners . . .

There is still no news of the task force.

*Letter, GSP, Jr., to Frederick Ayer, March 29, 1945*

Some days ago I heard of an American prisoner of war camp . . . so I sent an armored expedition to get it. So far I have not been able to hear what they did. It is possible that John may be among the prisoners. If so, I will be very delighted to take the place.

To Beatrice on March 29:

> My rescue attempt is still unheard from though one air plane reported seeing such a column headed west with a lot of men walking and riding on the tanks.

To his son George on March 30:

> The other day I sent an armored column out to recapture a prison camp . . . I am afraid that this was a bad guess, and that the column has been destroyed. If so, I lost 225 men.

Actually, 307 men had been dispatched to Hammelburg.

> Of course, the majority of them were probably taken prisoners, but on the same day we took 22,000 Germans prisoner, so the exchange was not bad.

At a press conference that day, Patton said:

> There has been a black-out on an operation we pulled about 60 miles from this point. There was a prisoner of war camp containing at least 900 Americans – mostly officers, both ground and air . . . I felt that I could not sleep during the night if I got within 60 miles and made no attempt to get that place. I felt by hazarding a small force I would confuse the enemy completely as to where we were going. It did work, for they thought I was going to Nuremburg. I don't know whether that force has been captured or what. If they have the Third Army luck, they might get through.

Nuremburg was a Seventh Army objective, and Hammelburg now lay in the Seventh Army zone of advance.

That evening, on March 30, Patton noted in his diary:

> The German radio announced today that the American troops that had been sent on a special mission to Hammelburg had been captured or destroyed. We have no confirmation of this state, but, on the other hand, we have not been able to locate them either from the air, due to bad flying weather, or by radio. It is therefore probable that they are lost.

*Diary, March 31*

So far I have only made one mistake, and that was when I lost two companies of the 4th Armored Division in making the attack on Hammelburg. I made it with only two companies on account of the strenuous objections of General Bradley to making any [effort] at all. Had I sent a combat command as I had first intended to do, this mistake would not have occurred.

*Letter, GSP, Jr., to Beatrice, March 31, 1945*

Just got your message that J. [John] was at Hammelburg. I had known of the camp there for a week but did not know definately he was in it.

Beatrice — or, more likely, Mrs. Waters — was probably informed by the Red Cross, perhaps by army intelligence, of Waters' whereabouts.

I sent a force to capture it but fear that the force was destroyed. However, it was the proper thing to do as there were at least 900 Americans there.

What happened?

Once Patton directed that the Hammelburg mission be undertaken, Eddy and Hoge, perhaps Patton too, discussed the size of the unit and the number of men to be dispatched. A combat command, somewhere around 4000 men and about 150 tanks, with artillery and other supporting units, was well able to take care of itself on a foray deep into enemy territory. Was it foolish to send so large a force? Few German elements were in the area. Or, would a smaller group have a better chance of success in an operation designed to strike rapidly and come back? Fewer men and vehicles meant quicker movement, more surprise, and a larger possibility of escaping detection.

Stiller later recalled that Patton told him he had ordered Eddy "to send a task force on a mission behind the German lines — to create a diversion by a fast moving force to attack a prisoner of war camp" and at the same time to liberate the 400 to 500 Americans presumed to be there; but this, of course, clouded the fundamental issue.

Because Stiller knew Waters and could identify him, Patton asked him whether he would like to accompany the task force. Stiller understood this to be an order — "a request by a general is an order." When Stiller assented, Patton told him to report to Eddy who would let him know which division would do the job. Eddy instructed him to report to Hoge, who said that the task force had yet to be formed. He would call Stiller when the troops were ready to go. Since Stiller "had not even seen a bed for some 48 hours," he found a cot and slept until Hoge sent for him.

Hoge gave the job to Combat Command B, headed by Creighton W. Abrams, who instructed Harold Cohen, an infantry battalion commander, to form a task force. Cohen designated the elements to go – 10 medium tanks, 6 light tanks, 27 half-tracks, 7 jeeps, 3 motorized assault guns, and a cargo carrier called a weasel. In command was Captain Abraham J. Baum, who was to drive directly to Hammelburg, liberate the prisoners, load as many on his vehicles as he could, and return.

Summoned by Hoge, Stiller learned the composition of the task force. He was somewhat surprised when Hoge asked him what he thought of it.

According to his later recollections, Stiller said he thought it was too small for the mission. Since there were several streams to cross on the way to Hammelburg, Stiller anticipated dropping off some men to guard each bridge to keep it open when the force returned. He thought that the group was strong enough to get to Hammelburg but not strong enough to return.

Hoge said he did not expect the task force to get back. He was opposed to sending anything.

Stiller then reported to Baum, who was suspicious of why he was there. Stiller was a major and therefore outranked Baum, but Stiller assured the captain that he was along merely "for the thrills and laughs." Baum then invited him to ride in his command jeep.

Task Force Baum slipped out of the Aschaffenburg area under the cover of early morning darkness and in the confusion of an attack launched to the north. Hammelburg was only 40 miles away, and the vehicles traveled uneventfully for 20 miles. At Lohr, the task force met a small German tank unit moving westward. Baum's men destroyed 12 German tanks and rushed on. A few miles beyond, they knocked out an antiaircraft train. At Gemunden, they shot up a dozen locomotives in the railroad yard. There too was a bridge defended and wired for demolition, and the small German unit guarding it blew the structure in Baum's face.

This required a detour to Burgsinn, 6 miles to the north. Baum's troops liberated 700 Russians, who raided the town and broke into food dumps and liquor warehouses. Baum turned over to them the 200 German prisoners he had taken. In the early afternoon, as the Americans were nearing Hammelburg, they drove off with machine gun fire a small German plane that had been looking them over.

Frantic messages had been arriving in the German area command headquarters to tell of Baum's incursion, and the reports exaggerated his strength, some saying that a division was on the move. The pilot of the small plane verified the size and location of Baum's task force, and the Germans set about to destroy it.

Yet it was pure coincidence that a German assault gun battalion entered Hammelburg from the east as Baum came in from the west. A firefight broke out and lasted more than two hours. The Americans finally smashed through and headed for the prison.

There the German commander decided to surrender, and he asked the senior American to carry the word to Baum. One of the four Americans volunteering for this mission was Waters. In the process of walking out under a flag of truce with a small group of Americans, Waters was shot and severely wounded by a German guard.

The task force knocked down part of the barbed wire enclosure, and several thousand liberated prisoners of war swarmed around the vehicles in a pandemonium of joy. There were almost 5000 men in the camp, among them about 1500 Americans.

A few hours later, after order had been restored, Baum loaded as many Americans as possible on his tanks and personnel carriers, then started to return to Aschaffenburg. The German assault-gun battalion was lying in wait, knocked out Baum's lead tank, and barred the way home. Most of the prisoners silently returned to the camp.

To escape the ambush, Baum turned south to Hessdorf, which he reached close to midnight. There he and his men encountered other German units that had moved to intercept them. Withdrawing to the top of a hill, Baum discovered that his force was surrounded. His men siphoned gasoline out of the half-tracks, divided the fuel among the remaining tanks, then burned the personnel carriers. As day started to break, they tried to ram through the encircling Germans. The ensuing firefight only showed how hopeless the situation was. The Americans were well outnumbered. Baum called his men together and told them to try to slip back to the American lines in small groups.

Only a few made it. Most were taken prisoner. Some were sent to Hammelburg, among them Baum, who had been wounded three times that day. Some were marched off toward Nuremburg, among them Stiller.

*Gay's Journal, April 4, 1945*

Two officers who had been at Hammelburg and liberated by Task Force Baum entered Third Army lines and told what happened. This narrative is of particular interest to the Army Commander because this was the first time he had news that his son-in-law, Colonel Waters, was one of the prisoners in the camp.

*Diary, April 4*

Patch called . . . Three other officers who had escaped [from Hammelburg] had reported to his Army and stated that Johnny Waters . . . had been badly wounded and recaptured. Apparently the wound is serious but not dangerous, as it is in the leg.

I believe that the Seventh Army will probably relieve [capture] the camp today or tomorrow.

I felt very gloomy over the fact that I may have caused Waters' death, but I believe that I did the right thing, and I certainly could never have lived with myself had I known that I was within 40 miles of 900 Americans and not made an attempt to rescue them.

*Letter, GSP, Jr., to Beatrice, April 5, 1945*

My first thought was to send a combat command, but I was talked out of it by Omar and others . . .

The force started on March 26. I got the rest from two lieutenants who escaped . . . They both knew and admired J. They said he was the best looking and most military man in camp.

Last night Gen. Patch called to say that the column had been attacked . . . J was hit through the leg and recaptured and is back at H.

I feel terribly. I tried hard to save him and may be the cause of his death. Al Stiller was in the column and I fear he is dead. I don't know what you and [little] B will think. Don't tell her yet . . .

We have liberated a lot of PW camps but not the one I wanted.

*Letter, GSP, Jr., to sister Nita, April 5, 1945*

An expedition I sent out actually rescued Johnny and then got recaptured itself. When I sent it out, I did not know that Johnny was in the camp but did know that there were 900 American officers there. Actually, there were 1200. I am hoping that some of them got away.

To Beatrice on April 6: "The XV Corps, Haislip, is 4 kilometers from where J. probably is."

*Diary, April 6*

The Seventh Army telephoned that the 14th Armored Division had recaptured the American prisoner of war camp at Hammelburg and found only a few [American] prisoners, about 70, among them being Lt. Col. Waters, who was seriously but not dangerously wounded . . .

Colonel Odom left . . . for Hammelburg to look into the case of Colonel Waters.

*Gay's Journal, April 7*

Col. Odom returned with two cub planes, bringing Waters, shot through leg, bullet coming up through his buttocks and injuring his spine. Condition good, will live and probably not be paralyzed. In 34th Evacuation Hospital at Frankfurt.

*Letter, GSP, Jr., to daughter Beatrice, April 7, 1945*

I called General Eisenhower . . . and requested him to notify you that Lt. Colonel John K. Waters was safe . . . I will now recount the sequence of events which led to this . . .

I learned through various sources that an estimated 900 American officer prisoners of war were in a prison camp in the vicinity of Hammelburg . . .

It was important to deceive the enemy as to the direction of the attack, and also I did not wish to miss the chance of rescuing Americans. I therefore decided to send a task force . . . to release the prisoners and transport back as many as they could carry. I had no trucks available to send with this column as I was using them all to move up infantry and supplies . . .

Sometime before our tanks entered the camp, the Germans decided to surrender. They sent a German captain, Johnny, and an American lieutenant and captain to arrange with the Americans to cease firing. They walked out of the main gate of the camp with an American flag and a white flag.

When they had gone a little way, Johnny saw three soldiers – who turned out to be Germans – behind a picket fence. Suddenly one of these thrust his rifle through the fence and at a range of 15 yards fired at Johnny, striking him in the left groin but below the peritoneal cavity. The bullet went through the rectum, knocked the end off his coccyx, and came out his left hip, and naturally at that range knocked him down. He was taken by the two Americans to the Serbian Hospital which was in the prison camp where he was treated, allegedly, with considerable skill by a Serbian Colonel doctor.

While this was going on, the German general in command of the camp surrendered to Colonel Goode [the senior American prisoner], and about the same time, somewhere around 7:30, our tanks knocked the fence down and the prisoners walked out.

Two hundred and fifty were loaded on the vehicles and the rest were told which direction to go, which was straight west, and advised to pull out.

The column then started back . . . They fought until all the ammunition and gasoline was exhausted and the casualties had amounted to about 50 men, including the officer commanding the column . . . They apparently then surrendered . . .

Yesterday . . . the 14th Armored Division of the XV Corps, got to Hammelburg . . . where they recaptured the sick and wounded, including Waters.

This was telephoned to me from the Seventh Army, and then Colonel Odom, who is assistant Army Surgeon and who lives at my mess, flew down to the XV Corps and from there proceeded by peep to the vicinity of Hammelburg where a battle was still going on. He was supposed to take a tank there, but being unable to find one, he continued in a peep and got to the hospital, saw Johnny, and noted his condition.

He then telephoned about midnight, and we sent two cub planes, one fixed to carry a litter, which lit in the vicinity of the hospital and picked up Johnny and flew him to . . . Frankfurt.

I visited him at 11:00 o'clock and found him just getting shaved. He looked thin but not as thin as I had anticipated and was perfectly coherent, and not in pain.

The first thing Waters did was ask his father-in-law whether he had known that he was at Hammelburg.

No, Patton replied, not for sure.

The wound has considerable nuisance value but is not dangerous. It will be necessary to do a colostomy, namely, to open his gut at the side and use this as an auxiliary exit while his lower gut in the vicinity of the rectum is sewn up and cured . . .

[After four months] he should be perfectly well and have no disabilities of any kind . . .

I am asking Colonel Cutler, who is the head Surgical Consultant in Europe, and also Dean of Medicine at Harvard, to come down and look Jonny over. I believe it preferable that he should be flown to Paris where they have an excellent hospital . . . Or it may be that Cutler will advocate his being flown direct to the U.S. I will let you know . . .

He has changed hardly at all, except that he is thin, his face is yellow, and his lips slightly blue. They cannot operate . . . until they have built him up, and since he cannot eat, this buildup has to be blood plasma and some kind of serum which they squirt into the veins.

He is very philosophical about his wound, as am I, for if he had not been wounded he would now be on his way to Nuremburg.

I think we should all be very thankful to God that after all these various tribulations, we have saved him and saved him so that he will be perfectly all right. It will simply be necessary to exercise patience until his various plumbing systems can be patched.

*Letter, GSP, Jr., to Beatrice, April 8, 1945*

Today Sgt Meeks, Willie, and I all went to see him. He is much better and had chicken and potatoes for lunch . . .

Al Stiller . . . will escape or be rescued soon.

*Diary, April 8*

Waters is much better, having had a blood transfusion and a hot meal.

*Diary, April 9*

Gave Waters his Silver Star with Oak Leaf Cluster, which he did not know he had gotten. It is very peculiar; he has actually missed about two years of his life, but his spirit is unbroken and he is in fine shape. He left by plane [for Paris].

*Letter, GSP, Jr., to Beatrice, April 9, 1945*

He kept saying how well he was being treated so I told him that it was not because of me but because of Ike's speech which made him a national hero. I think that made him feel better. He looks fine but smells awful as he leaks all the time. Cutler took him to Paris where they will make a better examination and either operate there or send him to Washington by air.

On that day, Baum was being treated at the Evacuation Hospital at Frankfurt. Four days later Codman officially reported Stiller missing in action.

*GSP, Jr., Press Conference, Herzfeld, Germany, April 13, 1945*

The force which we sent over . . . was for the purpose of misleading the Germans and make them think we were going to Nuremburg, but actually [it] went to rescue the 900 American prisoners there, got to its objective. They met the 2d Panzer Division and two other divisions, which showed that our effort to mislead the enemy had its effect, because [had] he [the enemy] put these divisions up north, our efforts there would have been much slower.

*Letter, GSP, Jr., to Beatrice, April 13, 1945*

At the moment they are trying to make an incident out of my attempt to rescue John . . . How I hate the press.

They were saying that Patton needlessly sacrificed men and tanks merely to rescue his son-in-law.

He maintained that the Hammelburg mission was a routine reconnaissance and that Waters' whereabouts was uncertain and incidental.

There was much talk among the soldiers in the theater.

Col. Cutler thinks John may not have to have the hole cut in his side. He is . . . in Paris having the best possible care. I will fly up and see him when I have a little leasure.

He flew to Paris four days later and had a long talk with Waters, "also saw several repatriated American officers, all of whom thanked me for the efforts I had put out in their behalf."

*Message, Eisenhower to Marshall, April 15, 1945*

He sent off a little expedition on a wild goose chase in an effort

> to liberate some American prisoners. The upshot was that he got 25 prisoners back and lost a full company of medium tanks and a platoon of light tanks. Foolishly, he then imposed censorship on the movement, meaning to lift it later, which he forgot to do. The story has now been released, and I hope the newspapers do not make too much of it. One bad, though Patton says accidental, feature of the affair was that his own son-in-law was one of the 25 released. Patton is a problem child, but he is a great fighting leader in pursuit and exploitation.

On April 29, the 14th Armored Division liberated the Moosburg German prisoner of war camp containing almost 30,000 Allied troops, of whom about 14,000 were American. Stiller was in the camp, and on the following day reported to Third Army headquarters in good condition, although he had lost about 30 pounds.

Early in May, Eisenhower awarded the Distinguished Service Cross to Waters for his exploit in Tunisia. About the time the war was coming to an end in Europe, Waters was flown to Walter Reed Hospital in Washington. He would recover completely, continue his military career, and eventually be promoted to full general.

Most of the commanders involved in the Hammelburg operation, and particularly Hoge, remained convinced that Patton knew his son-in-law had been at the camp.

Task Force Baum disrupted the Aschaffenburg-Hammelburg area, damaged military trains, destroyed antiaircraft guns, upset troop schedules, disabled assault-gun units, provoked general uncertainty and confusion among the Germans, and showed how close the end of the war had come. But would Patton have sent a force to Hammelburg – whether to make a feint or to liberate the prisoners – if he had not thought that Waters was likely to be there?

Despite rumors and press reports, talk and speculation, all to the effect that the Hammelburg mission was a personal diversion of troops in the interest of family, the incident disappeared in the euphoria that came with the end of the war in Europe.

CHAPTER 37

# The Last Offensive

*"The war looks over to me."*

WHEN SAMPLERS OF PUBLIC OPINION asked, "What commander serving under Eisenhower do you admire most?" the replies invariably named Patton. The Navy too was impressed by Patton's exploits, and the naval detachments ferrying Third Army troops and supplies across the Rhine called themselves "U.S.S. Blood and Guts."

Giraud came for a visit, and Patton told him,

> Our success has been chiefly due to luck. He replied, "No, to audacity," and I believe he was right.

To Beatrice:

> The war looks over to me. We seem to be able to go anywhere, though "The enemy is still resisting fiercely in front of the British Second Army." We went 29 miles to day and took another 8,000 [prisoners] while doing it. They went 2 miles.

*Interview, GSP, Jr., with Brigadier General Bolzen, 18th Panzer Grenadier Division, March 30, 1945*

Patton: Tell the general that . . . he does not have to answer any questions that I ask . . . I am wondering how long this unnecessary killing will have to go on . . . Are they going to keep on getting killed to no purpose?

Bolzen: The ordinary fighting man and the professional soldier have long seen the unnecessary continuance of fighting and recognize this, but the honor to which they are bound as soldiers makes them continue to fight, especially the professional soldier. As long as the country is at war, they are honor-bound to fight . . .

Patton: How is the war going to end, and do we have to kill them all?

Bolzen: I believe that the speedy advances of your forces will end it. Large groups will be captured as you go on . . .

Patton: Do you think that there will be any underground movement, fighting from ambushes, etc.?

Bolzen: The population in general, no . . . The average run of the population . . . wants to be spared any further war . . .

Patton: It seems foolish [for the Germans] to [continue to] fight.

*GSP, Jr., Press Conference, Oberstein, Germany, March 30, 1945*

Patton: I first want to thank all of you for helping me out with those remarks I asked you to make about weapons. I read several editorials from home and while I was not quoted, it was damn well said. I also wish to thank the members of the British press for the very fine write-ups we have received in England . . .

Our losses in this operation have been extremely small. We have been trading about 12 to 1 . . . and it is all made possible by speed.

I hope that you will continue as you have so nicely done, giving these officers and men the credit . . . I think if the Germans could all read what you wrote, they would surrender quicker . . .

Question: Could you say which way we are going?

Patton: I don't know, and I'm sure nobody else knows. It has gotten to the point where you go where you damn well please . . .

Question: Is there any American Army slated to go to Berlin?

Patton: . . . I don't get much interested in what is more than ten miles further ahead. I don't know where I am going – I hope I can get to China.

Bradley telephoned that the Third Army could move to the Werra and Weser Rivers rapidly and then toward the Elbe River, but more slowly. "I told him that I considered any slowing up extremely dangerous, as we have the enemy on the run and should keep him that way."

But there appeared to be good and sufficient reason for the advancing Armies to be generally parallel, and Patton explained to his corps commanders that they had to confine themselves to moving ahead approximately 15 miles per day.

In his diary, Patton noted that Eisenhower and Bradley felt it would be risky to go faster.

Whenever those two get together, they get timid. I am sure that had a bold policy throughout been used in this war, it would have long since been over.

There had been talk in the United States of making some public acknowledgment to Patton for his successes. On March 30, the House of Representatives responded to this feeling and unanimously adopted a motion to express — through Eisenhower — "our congratulations and sincere thanks for the magnificent victories" to Devers, Spaatz, Bradley, Hodges, Patton, Simpson, Doolittle, Brereton, Patch, and Gerow.

*Letter, GSP, Jr., to Beatrice, April 1, 1945*

There seems to be an attempt to keep all at the same level. Congress voted to thank me and me only, and ended up by thanking everyone . . .

Just this second persuaded the tent maker to let me keep on. What a war.

*Letter, GSP, Jr., to Arvin H. Brown, April 1, 1945*

I agree with you that the difficulty in war is the fact that it imposes the loss of life to back one's decisions. On the other hand, you cannot command successfully if you let this interfere with what you conceive to be your duty.

Writing to Marshall to ask whether he — or anyone else — would like to have a handsome bust of Hitler that Patton's men had just captured, Patton suggested that if a hole were carved out of the top, it would make an excellent spittoon.

*Diary, April 3*

The roads here are in extremely good condition, and all the Germans were working violently, cleaning up their towns. Mainz is the first very large city I have seen so completely destroyed, and it certainly is, I would say, two-thirds ruins . . .

We are ordered to practically stop and wait for the arrival of the First and Ninth Armies.

*Letter, GSP, Jr., to Beatrice, April 5, 1945*

We never met any opposition because the bigger and better Germans fight Monty – he says so. Also he advertises so much that they know where he is coming. I fool them.

Now I am waiting for Courtney and Charley so we will end the war in line. I could join the Russians in a week if I were turned loose. Damn equality.

He had his three corps commanders in for lunch to work out the new boundaries among them. There

is always a bitter fight as to roads, so I let them settle it amongst themselves, merely retaining for myself the office of umpire. After a long and acrimonious debate, they went away happy.

*Gay's Journal, April 5*

General Walker is always the most willing and cooperative. He apparently will fight any time, any place, with anything that the Army commander desires to give him. General Middleton is the most methodical, probably the best tactician, very firm in his relations with the other corps commanders . . . General Eddy is very nervous, very much inclined to be grasping, and always worrying that some other corps commander is getting a better deal than he is, but when the decision is made, he always does as he is told.

Reflecting on the decision to restrain the advance, Patton thought it a mistake, at least "from a merely military standpoint," because there was hardly any opposition. "However," he admitted,

there may be reasons beyond my knowledge which make it desirable to advance [the Armies] abreast. By so doing, no one gets undue credit.

This was Eisenhower's implicit policy throughout the European campaigns. No single commander, no single nation was going to win the war alone. Victory had to be shared and shared equally.

Because of the need to regroup, "which is the first time the Third Army has ever indulged in this sport," Patton had to halt his offensive temporarily. But he told his corps commanders "to keep pushing along so as to prevent the enemy from getting set."

*Letter, GSP, Jr., to Beatrice, April 6, 1945*

Just got back from decorating a medic with the Medal of Honor. A boat full of wounded was caught under machine gun fire on the Saar. The crew was killed or jumped. This man swam out under fire and toed it to safety. He said, "I don't know why I did it; some one had to."

*Diary, April 6*

The XII Corps telephoned . . . that they had overrun and captured the German gold reserve, or at least part of it. We decided not to notify higher headquarters until we had better information, as it would be stupid to claim we had found the gold reserve and then not have done so.

*Diary, April 7*

Eddy stated that he had entered the gold reserve vault and had found over a billion dollars in paper money, but that the gold part was sealed in a safe behind a steel door . . . I directed him to blow the vault and definitely determine what was in it.

McCloy came to visit, and Patton took him driving to show him the sights. While going through Frankfurt, he

called Mr. McCloy's attention to the wanton and unnecessary bombing of civilian cities. He agreed with me and later stated that he had mentioned this to Generals Devers and Patch, who had the same opinion. We all feel that indiscriminate bombing has no military value and is cruel and wasteful, and that all such efforts should always be on purely military targets and on selected commodities which are scarce. In the case of Germany, it would be on oil.

*Diary, April 9*

McCloy . . . said that he intended to make a public statement to the effect that I am not only a great military commander but probably the best instructor general in the army. He said that there had been efforts to make it appear that I could do nothing but attack in a heedless manner.

*Letter, GSP, Jr., to Beatrice, April 9, 1945*

We have over 400,000 prisoners of war since August 1 . . . No one is now in our class.

We start attacking in the morning but will go slow so the others can catch up.

*Letter, GSP, Jr., to Beatrice, April 10, 1945*

We started an operation to day to gain about six miles and made from 10 to 15. All of us attack officially in the morning. We move our CP forward 95 miles, and it will still be too far back.

Mr. [Bernard] Baruch came to lunch. He is 75 and just as keen as can be.

*Diary, April 10*

Mr. Baruch . . . was most amusing. After lunch he had a meeting with the correspondents, at which he told them nothing for a long time.

*Gay's Journal, April 10*

The situation reference displaced persons continues to be aggravated. There is not in the possession of the Armies a definite policy emanating from higher headquarters, or perhaps there are no definite instructions as to how to handle these people. Most of them are like animals, or worse, and unless force can be used on them to insure reasonable sanitary measures, it would appear that disease, perhaps something bordering on a plague, is in the offing.

*Diary, April 11*

I was particularly impressed with the number of empty gasoline cans which had not been collected, so I directed . . . the Assistant Chief Quartermaster of the Army to take a trip over the road followed by two trucks and pick up every can he found.

I also issued orders that all civilian-impressed or looted autos, bicycles, or motorcycles would be apprehended and turned in to ordnance. It will be impossible to supply gasoline for this Army if every soldier in this Army has an automobile, which seems to be the present ambition. Furthermore, the bicycles are used for one day and they then tire of them, and the same thing applies to motorcycles. The German, whether we like him or not, has to live and has no transportation.

I issued an order on hats. As summer approaches, there is no reason for the sloppy appearance of this Army, which, however, Mr. McCloy says is the best looking Army he has seen.

There is a persistent rumor of a German attempt to murder somebody, possibly myself, by a small glider-borne operation. Everybody but Willie and me is nervous about this. However, I do take my carbine to my truck at night now.

First on Eisenhower's list "for immediate promotion to four star rank" was Patton, who, he told Marshall, was

> resourceful, courageous, and determined. In Sicily his drive and initiative contributed markedly to the speed with which that stronghold was reduced. In this theater he . . . conducted a magnificent pursuit and exploitation directly across France . . . including the occupation of the Brittany peninsula. In later operations, including the battle of Ardennes, of the Eifel, of the Saar, and of the later thrusts into Germany, his leadership has been characterized by boldness and skillful fighting ability.

Eisenhower, Bradley, and Patton drove to the mine containing the German gold reserve. Walker and Middleton met them, then all motored to Ohrdruf Nord, a camp for military and civilian prisoners. Patton's reaction to this "prison camp for slave labor, who had been employed in a munitions factory in the vicinity" was pure shock.

> This was one of the most appalling sights I have ever seen. One of the former inmates acted as impressario and showed us first a gallows where men were hanged for attempting to escape. The hanging was done with a piece of piano wire, and the man being hanged was not dropped far enough to break his neck but simply strangled by the piano wire . . .
>
> The wire is so adjusted that after a drop of about two feet, the man's toes can just touch the ground so that death takes some time. Two prisoners next to be hanged are required to kick the plank from under him.
>
> The impressario . . . was such a well fed looking man that I had an idea he may have been one of the executioners.

Two days later, this guide was torn limb from limb by returning inmates.

Just beyond . . . was a pile of about 40 bodies, more or less naked, all of whom had been shot through the head at short range. The ground was covered with dried blood. These men had become so exhausted as to be useless for labor and were disposed of in this humane (?) manner.

In a shed near this place was a pile of about 40 completely naked human bodies in the last stages of emaciation. These bodies were lightly sprinkled with lime, not for the purpose of destroying them, but for the purpose of removing the stench.

When the shed was full — I presume its capacity to be about 200, the bodies were taken to a pit a mile from the camp where they were buried . . .

When we began to approach with our troops, the Germans thought it expedient to remove the evidence of their crime. Therefore, they had some of the slaves exhume the bodies and place them on a mammoth griddle composed of 60-centimeter railway tracks laid on brick foundations. They poured pitch on the bodies and then built a fire of pinewood and coal under them. They were not very successful in their operation because there was a pile of human bones, skulls, charred torsos on or under the griddle which must have accounted for many hundreds. In the pit there were arms, legs, and bodies sticking out of the green water which partially filled it.

Walker and Middleton had very wisely decided to have as many soldiers as possible visit the scene, which I believe will teach our men to look out for the Germans. The mayor of the town, together with his wife, when confronted with the spectacle, went home and hanged themselves. There are several others in the vicinity who I think will be found dead.

Eisenhower's remarks, as noted by Gay:

The evidence of inhuman treatment, starvation, beating, and killing of these prisoners . . . by the Germans was beyond the American mind to comprehend. Hundreds and hundreds of bodies were left around the area. Some 200 or more had been dug up, apparently with the idea of burning them so that there would not be evidence of their inhuman treatment, but the advance had been so rapid that they had to leave them on the burning pyre.

Eisenhower and Bradley returned to Patton's headquarters and spent the night. They had a very pleasant evening, in the course of which General Eisenhower gave me a proposed stop line and explained his reasons, which it is not expedient at this time to set down.

Gay had no such objections, and he recorded Eisenhower's views:

From a tactical point of view, it was highly inadvisable for the American Army to take Berlin, and he hoped political influence would not cause him to take the city. It had no tactical or strategical value, and would place upon American forces the burden of caring for thousands and thousands of Germans, displaced persons, Allied prisoners of war, etc.

General Patton replied, "Ike, I don't see how you figure that one. We had better take Berlin and quick, and [then go eastward] on to the Oder [River]."

But this was not to be.

*Diary, April 12*

I went to bed rather late and noted that I had failed to wind my watch, so turned on the radio to see if I could get the time. Just as I turned it on, the announcer reported the death of the President. I immediately informed Generals Eisenhower and Bradley, and we had quite a discussion as to what might happen. It seems very unfortunate that in order to secure political preference, people are made Vice Presidents who were never intended, neither by Party nor by the Lord to be Presidents.

How Truman could replace and measure up to Roosevelt was difficult to see.

*Letter, GSP, Jr., to McCloy, April 13, 1945*

Yesterday, I saw the most horrible sight I have ever seen. It was a German slave camp . . .

We took all the soldiers we could to see it, as I believe it is one of the best arguments against fraternization that I know.

*GSP, Jr., Press Conference, Herzfeld, Germany, April 13, 1945*

Patton: If any of you haven't visited the charnel house near here, you should go. It is the most horrible sight I have ever seen. We had as many soldiers as possible . . . visit it so as to know that kind of people they are fighting. I think they were duly impressed, and I told them to tell their friends . . .

Question: What is holding the Germans together?

Patton: Fear of "They." Everybody is afraid of everybody else. They say if we surrender they will raise hell with Willie or Charlie. I do not believe there will be much underground stuff.

Attending a ceremony at Mainz to open a bridge,

I was requested to cut the ribbon across the bridge and was handed a pair of scissors for the purpose. I made the statement that I am not a tailor and asked for a bayonet, with which I cut the ribbon.

*Letter, GSP, Jr., to Scott, April 15, 1945*

We have lately been liberating the slave camps, and honestly, words are inadequate to express the horror of those institutions.

*Letter, GSP, Jr., to Eisenhower, April 15, 1945*

We have found at a place four miles north of Weimar a similar camp only much worse . . .

I told the press to go up and . . . build up another page of the necessary evidence as to the brutality of the Germans.

This was Buchenwald, one of the most notorious of the concentration camps, and Patton called Bradley to suggest that Eisenhower send photographers and senior representatives of the press to get "the horror details."

*Diary, April 15*

The political prisoners who were sent here to die were fed 800 calories a day and died on the average — so it is said — of 100 a night.

I went through two of the buildings. On each side were four tiers of bunks in which the inmates lay at right angles to the wall. They looked exactly like animated mummies and seemed to me on about the same level of intelligence. When we went through they attempted to cheer but were too feeble.

We then went to the place where they had apparently put the finishing touches on those who had died or were about to die. In a basement which was entered by a chute, they had a number of iron hooks on the wall like those you hang the side of a beef on. To these hooks they had a short piece of stout cord with a loop spliced on each end. This was put around a man's neck. Two men then lifted him and the loops were placed over the hook. If anyone showed signs of life, they had a club like a potato masher with which they bashed in the brains.

Upstairs there were six furnaces much like a baker's oven, connected with the basement by an elevator. Apparently they put six bodies on the elevator at a time, hoisted them up to the furnaces, and put them in.

Gay's impressions:

The scenes witnessed there are beyond the normal mind to believe. No race except a people dominated by an ideology of sadism could have committed such gruesome crimes . . . inmates, all in a bad stage of starvation . . . even those who lived, in my opinion, will never recover mentally . . .

On a paved courtyard were said to be 170 bodies, all dead of starvation. They were naked. The bodies were wasted away, the legs the size of an ordinary man's arm or smaller . . . These dead bodies were apparently shoveled into incinerators or crematories in which there were some eight or ten ovens . . . In them were bones and parts of the bodies that had been burned there. Beneath this was the torture chamber in which some of the prisoners were hung . . .

The sight and the stench of these living dead . . . was entirely too much . . . It is a shame that more people cannot see these things, particularly politicians, who, after all, bring on wars, and doubly a shame that they cannot be seen by those people back in our own country . . . who have criticized minor events of alleged cruelty on the part of American soldiers and will frantically preach to the people that the Germans are grand people, and that they should be given our love and munificent gratitude.

No race and no people other than those which are strictly sadists could commit crimes like these. To take prisoners out and shoot them is kind, but to deliberately starve them to death is an atrocity. I doubt if the world will ever know how many were starved to death, as no records were kept and the bodies burned.

According to Patton's diary, when he asked where he was

to go after getting to the present stop line, Bradley stated he did not consider my supplies adequate to go anywhere. I stated that he was in error.

I believe that this is simply an excuse for lack of any ideas as to what to do next, for which he is probably not wholly responsible, as it is presumable that the Combined Chiefs of Staff had not yet told Eisenhower.

I sometimes get very disgusted at the lack of initiative and drive on the part of the 12th Army Group. They now seem convinced that there are some bogies east of the Elbe River which are apt to jump up and destroy us. Personally, I believe that continued vigorous advance would completely destroy what little German resistance now exists.

There was, as a matter of fact, some intelligence information that Hitler was planning to leave Berlin for a National Redoubt area in the mountains of Germany and Austria, there to defend to the last; also that young German boys called "Werewolves" had been specially trained in sabotage and demolitions to harass the advancing Armies and later the occupation forces.

Writing to Marshall on April 15, Eisenhower said he intended, now that Germany was split into two parts, to send the 21 Army Group to Lübeck in the north and the 12th Army Group to the so-called Redoubt area in the south, both objectives being "vastly more important than the capture of Berlin."

Eisenhower also described his visit to Buchenwald:

> The visual evidence and the verbal testimony of starvation, cruelty, and bestiality were so overpowering as to leave me a bit sick. In one room where there were piled up twenty or thirty naked men, killed by starvation, George Patton would not even enter. He said he would get sick if he did so. I made the visit deliberately, in order to be in a position to give *first-hand* evidence of these things if ever, in the future, there develops a tendency to charge these allegations merely to "propaganda."

He urged Marshall to fly to Europe in the very near future, for Marshall "would be proud of the army you have produced," particularly the higher commanders.

> There is no weakness except for the one feature of Patton's unpredictability so far as his judgment (usually in small things) is concerned . . . Patton's latest crackpot actions may possibly get some publicity . . . Three or four newspapers have written very bitter articles about Patton, on this [Hammelburg] incident, and to my disgust they call it another example of "Army Blundering." I took Patton's hide off.

Baruch sent his thanks for Patton's courtesies, said that all Americans were proud of Patton, and assured him that "I have not forgotten what you said about your desire to tank around in China."

Patton replied:

> Meeting you was a very great pleasure because, when one meets famous men, one is sometimes let down. In other words, they do not live up to their reputations. In meeting you, this was certainly not the case. You were just as great as I had always pictured you.

Meeting with Bradley at Wiesbaden, Patton was glad to learn that he was to get three brand-new armored divisions, which would have "an opportunity of fighting in what I consider to be the last stages of the war." His Third Army was to attack from Wuerzburg to Linz in a southeasterly direction, while the Seventh Army turned due south, and the First and Ninth Armies remained on the defensive.

> *Letter, GSP, Jr., to Beatrice, April 17, 1945*
> There was a big meeting yesterday and we got the ball for what looks like the final play . . .
> Some times I feel that I may be nearing the end of this life. I have liberated J. [John Waters] and licked the Germans, so what else is there to do?
> Well, if I do get it, remember that I love you.

He had his four corps commanders in and explained "the new setup," then flew to Paris, where he and Hughes "sat up too late, as usual, talking."

At 11 P.M., Gay heard over the radio that President Harry S. Truman had nominated Patton for promotion to full general.

*Letter, Hughes to Beatrice Patton, April 18, 1945*

I have just put George on his plane for return to the wars . . .

When we went to the plane, Codman, the plane crew, and about ten others were all lined up stiff as ram-rods and grinning from ear to ear. They had just finished putting an extra star on George's plane.

At breakfast with George the waiter handed me a Stars and Stripes and pointed to the announcement of George's promotion. I read it and passed the paper to George without comment. He read the headlines and threw the paper back on the table. I picked it up and passed it to him again. He glanced at it the second time and discarded it. I picked it up the third time and said "read that," pointing to the announcement. He did and then leaned back in the chair and amused everybody who had been hovering in the vicinity by saying, "Well, I'll be ——."

He was looking fine and is still carrying on, trying to kill Germans and get this war over with.

*Diary, April 18*

While I am glad to be a full General, I would have appreciated it more had I been in the initial group [promoted – along with Bradley, Devers, and Clark], as I have never had an ambition to be an also-ran.

Codman secured for me the last two 4-star pins in existence in Paris and also a 4-star flag.

His date of rank was April 14. Hodges, also promoted, had his four stars from the following day.

*Diary, April 19*

Eisenhower explained that he was anxious to have us start our attack in the direction of Linz, but that due to the failure of the British to make sufficient progress, it might be necessary for him to send a corps up there, and he did not want to become overextended until that situation was cleared up. The situation as far as the Third Army goes is very satisfactory.

*GSP, Jr., Press Conference, Herzfeld, Germany, April 20, 1945*

Patton: I want to thank you for the publicity on that camp which is having a very good effect . . . This new direction of attack . . . We don't want to spill the beans as to where we are going to meet the Russians . . .

Question: When do you expect to meet the Russians?

Patton: Just as fast as God will let me. It depends how fast I can go . . .

Question: We would like to congratulate you on your four stars.

Patton: Thank you . . . One more thing, I think we had an all time low in casualties yesterday, 111 for the whole Army.

*Diary, April 20*

Flew to Headquarters XX Corps at Schloss Wiessenstein, which is the most magnificent and most hideous building I have ever seen. It was built around 1700. It is full of murals and also has a very fine art collection with a number of very bad statues all over it — mostly plaster. The stable, which is directly across from the main building, has a saddle-room full of murals much better than most drawing rooms in America . . .

We flew from there to the Headquarters of the III Corps [in an L-5 cub] . . . Just before we got there, a plane which looked like a Spitfire made three passes at us, but was unsuccessful. On the third pass, it flew so close to the ground that it could not pull out and crashed. The planes in this group had RAF markings on them, and I believe they were probably a Polish unit flying for the RAF. Why they were out of their area, I don't know.

The incident was disturbing but inexplicable. Had the Polish flyer misread the markings on Patton's plane?

I told the corps commanders to move out from the [jumpoff] line and make from three to four miles a day until we get the go signal. On getting back to headquarters, I found that Bradley had already telephoned that we could go.

"If the question of somebody going to China to fight the Japanese comes up," he wrote McCarthy, Secretary of the War Department General Staff, "please count me in."

*Letter, GSP, Jr., to Beatrice, April 21, 1945*

We go all out in the morning for a junction with the Russians near Linz.

Willie ate something and got paralized but is now better. I would have felt terrible had he died. To him I am always right . . .

The country here is the most beautiful I have ever seen. All the trees are in bloom and there are yellow fields of mustard.

There is a big green house where we have our mess. All the plants were dying for water, so I personally watered them. I am not as hard as painted.

As usual, the day before an attack there is nothing to do.

He sent photos of Buchenwald to Marshall and wrote:

I was so deeply moved by this thing that I had the leading citizens of Weimar, to the extent of some 1,500, marched through the camp and made to look at the horrid spectacle. I do not believe that even the Germans realized to what depths they had sunk.

The Third Army is attacking in what I trust will be the last act of this war, but as I wrote you, I am still hoping to do some fighting in China should you see fit to let me.

Patton was pleased to hear that Beatrice made a further gift to the Richard Jenson Memorial Fund in the form of 125 shares of Deere and Company stock, equivalent to the original gift of $5000. According to Harbord, letters would soon go to the headmasters of the leading private schools to ask for nominations of students qualified to go to West Point as recipients of the fund – "A worthy and fine type American boy [who] must have an American name."

When his classmate Robert H. Fletcher asked what effect education had in producing successful generals, Patton reminded him that according to "old Colonel Feberger," the qualities of generalship were a desire to fight, good health, historical knowledge, and intelligence. Patton could "claim some eminence in the first three" but was "not so outstanding" in the fourth. The Command and General Staff College at Leavenworth and the Army War College gave officers familiarity with a body of definite rules, and this education stood to war as spelling to literature. Schooling produced no combat leaders but improved men who naturally possessed the peculiar qualities of combat leadership. What Patton had was self-confidence and "a sixth sence by which I can always know to a moral certainty what the enemy is going to do."

I agree with you that peace will be much more difficult than war. In fact, war for me has not been difficult, but has been a pleasant adventure . . . The best thing . . . would be to get a clean hit in the last minute of the last fight and then flit around on a cloud and watch you all tear my reputation to pieces or get yourselves torn to pieces defending me.

Marshall offered Hodges and his First Army headquarters to MacArthur, who was glad to have them.

Patton was no doubt aware of this development. He had probably always thought that MacArthur would be far from happy to have him. Two prima donnas, two colorful personalities in a single theater were one too many. Perhaps for this reason, Patton always spoke of going to China rather than to the Pacific. In China, Stilwell was the theater commander before he was replaced by Wedemeyer, and both were friends of Patton's. In addition, Marshall intimated that an expeditionary force might be sent to China if the Chinese army could open a suitable port; and, further, that he had Patton in mind as the commander of that force.

*Diary, April 27*

I flew over Nuremburg, which is the most completely destroyed place I have ever seen. It is really rather pathetic to see such a historical monument so completely removed.

On that day, the Third Army processed the 600,000th prisoner of war.

*GSP, Jr., Press Conference, Erlangen, Germany, April 27, 1945*

Patton: I appreciate your staying mum on the change of direction . . . I am very much obliged. That was a very nice operation for which the staff gets the praise. We sideslipped two corps and continued to attack . . .

Question: Do you expect the Germans to try to hold . . ?

Patton: I hope they do . . . I really don't know . . . I don't see what the fools are fighting for . . . There is nothing of interest happening. I was down there today and crossed the [Danube] river, and it wasn't even worth pissing in.

There is a sign down there, "Danube River, just another Damn River." . . . The river doesn't even look blue there; it looked very muddy . . .

Question: Can you say anything about the Redoubt?

Patton: I think it is a figment of the imagination. It is just a good word . . .

Question: How much longer do you think the war will last here?

Patton: The 10th of May is when I lose my bet.

*Letter, GSP, Jr., to son George, April 28, 1945*

The war is sort of petering out. We go anywhere we want to with very limited opposition. Personally I cannot see why the Germans keep on fighting . . .

If you succeed in graduating a year from now, you will be able to join the Third Army in China.

*Letter, GSP, Jr., to Beatrice, April 28, 1945*

I have not heard from any of you since John was rescued so I suppose that having done that, my usefulness is ended.

This part of the war is rather dull, a sort of "Last roundup" . . .

There is a rumor that the Germans are trying to surrender so I am pushing harder.

*Diary, April 28*

Personally I cannot see that there is very much more glory in this war, and I am afraid it will end on an anti-climax.

*Letter, GSP, Jr., to Beatrice, April 30, 1945*

The [fourth] star is as much yours as mine, and I am glad you like it.

We move Wednesday to an Arch Ducal palace at Regensburg . . . never beheld so much gaudy junk. Each room, and there were at least a hundred, had three times too much stuff in it . . .

The war is very dull . . .

I wish we could take a drive in this country in peace. It is full of beauty and ruins – not the ones I have made but old ones too.

I always think of interesting things to tell you while I am driving or flying and then when I get time to write I forget them.

*Diary, April 30*

Just finished recording speech to be delivered on a national hookup in conjunction with other Army commanders on V-E day . . .

There was a rumor . . . that Hitler was dead and that Himmler was about to surrender. Personally I do not put any credence in it, but I believe that most of the German troops will surrender because they had nothing but defeat since the initial landing in Normandy.

*Diary, May 1*

Noticed that all the tanks [in the 14th Armored Division] were covered with sandbags, which in no way afforded any further protection and greatly increased the load on springs and engines. I ordered these removed . . .

Visited a prison camp of some 30,000 Allied prisoners . . . I gave them a few minutes' talk on the fact that under difficult conditions they had maintained their prestige as officers and soldiers. There was considerable cheering, clapping, and pictures taken.

*Letter, GSP, Jr., to Frederick Ayer, May 2, 1945*

The war is sort of dragging its end out to a non-spectacular termination . . .

Judging from the last war, when one gets to the point where the enemy starts making rumors of peace, his fighting value completely disappears. We have been taking tremendous numbers of prisoners.

Headquarters Third Army moved from Erlangen to Regensburg, "which in French is Ratisbon. This is where Napoleon fought a battle in one of his advances on Vienna and about which a poem is written."

*Diary, May 3*

Information was obtained over the radio last night of the unconditional surrender of all troops in Italy and southern Austria. This will probably be contagious, and the war may end any minute . . .

[Was] nearly killed by a bull cart coming out of a side street. We missed the end of the pole by a few inches.

*Letter, GSP, Jr., to Beatrice [May 3, 1945]*

Last night the German Armies in Italy surrendered . . . Those in front of me will quit to day or tomorrow, and I will be out of a job. I feel lower than whale tracks on the bottom of the ocean. I love war and responsibility and excitement. Peace is going to be hell on me. I will probably be a great nusance . . .

I would like to come home for at least a few days. I miss you.

*Diary, May 4*

The V Corps . . . was put in this Army today. This gives us the biggest Army we have had, 18 divisions in all and over 500,000 men . . .

At 7:30, Bradley called up and said the green light was on for the attack on Czechoslovakia. We immediately called the V Corps and told them to get going . . .

Things like this are what is going to make the peace so terrible, because nothing exciting will ever happen.

*Diary, May 5*

It will be necessary for them [V Corps] to halt on the stop line through Pilsen, but they could send reconnaissance to Prague . . .

In view of the radio report about the Patriots having taken Prague, it seems desirable to me to push on and help them.

Apparently the Third Army is doing the last offensive of the war.

"If I am fortunate enough to get to China," he wrote a friend, "I shall certainly do my best to see that you come along."

*Letter, GSP, Jr., to Charles F. Ayer, May 6, 1945*

I certainly hope to be in the U.S. for awhile before going to China. However, I may be kept over here commanding an Army, or I may be sent God knows where, or – and this is off-the-record – I may ask for retirement and go sailing . . .

This morning the Third Army is the only one left attacking; the enemy has surrendered everywhere else, and the resistance in front of us is not serious.

*Diary, May 6*

The halt line through Pilsen is mandatory . . . Eisenhower does not wish at this late date to have any international complications. It seems to me that as great a nation as America should let the other people worry about the complications. Personally I would go to the line of the Moldau River and tell the Russians that is where I intended to stop.

Bradley also directed us to discontinue our advance east along the Danube to make contact with the Russians, and let them make contact with us . . . I doubt the wisdom of this.

An alleged 100,000 White Russians are attempting to surrender to us. These people have fought for the Germans against the Russians and are in a pitiable state. However, they will have to be treated as displaced persons. I am having them moved west of the Czechoslovakian border [to save them] . . .

We have moved the III Corps to the vicinity of Nurnburg to start in occupying Bavaria.

*Diary, May 7*

Mr. Patterson, Under Secretary of War, spent the night, and we left by cub to visit the XX Corps . . . We found that the Imperial Spanish Riding Academy, which has been teaching high school riding in Vienna since the time of Charles V, had been moved to the vicinity of the XX Corps headquarters. After lunch they gave us an exhibition of riding and made an address.

*Translation of address made by Mr. Podhajsky in the horse stables of Schloss Arco at St. Martin/Innkreis, Austria, May 7, 1945*

General Patton, I am announcing the end of the performance and I thank you and the Honorable Mr. Patterson . . . as well as all generals for the great honor you have paid this Spanish Imperial Riding Academy by your gracious visit . . .

I ask you, General Patton, and the representatives of the US government to take under your protecting hand this old Austrian Academy, a cultural institution of the noble art of riding, unique in Europe, and perhaps unique in the world. This school demonstrates the development of culture of the 16th century and it represents the era of the Baroque almost kept intact.

*Diary*

It was rather peculiar to realize that with a world tearing itself apart in war, about twenty middle-aged men in perfect physical condition, and about an equal number of grooms, had spent their time teaching horses tricks. As much as I like horses, it seems to me there is a place for everything . . .

The Secretary was extremely cordial and had a wonderful memory for names and could state where he had formerly met each officer. We had a very pleasant evening and I found him extremely talkative and had the good sense to let him do the talking.

Stiller was present and according to his recollections, Patton said to Secretary Patterson,

"Mr. Secretary, for God's sake, when you go home, stop this point system; stop breaking up these Armies; give us an opportunity to keep 30% of our battlewise troops home on leave if you wish, etc. – send us replacements and let us start training here, keeping our forces intact. Let's keep our boots polished, bayonets sharpened, and present a picture of force and strength to these people [the Russians]. This is the only language they understand and respect. If you fail to do this, then I would like to say to you that we have had a victory over the Germans and have disarmed them, but have lost the war."

The Secretary replied, "Oh, George, you have been so close to this thing so long, you have lost sight of the big picture. You don't realize the strength of these people."

Gen. P. said, "Mr. Secretary, it is your privilege to say 'Oh, George,' if you wish, but for God's sake listen to what I am trying to tell you."

Mr. P. said, "What would you have us do, George?"

Gen. P. said, "I would have you keep these Armies intact. I would have your State Department, or the people in charge, tell the people concerned where their border is, and give them a limited time to get back across. Warn them that if they fail to do so, we will push them back across it."

The Secretary said, "You don't realize the strength of these people."

Gen. P. said, "Yes, I have seen them. I understand the situation. Their supply system is inadequate to maintain them in a serious action such as I could put to them. They have chickens in their coops and cattle on the hoof – that's their supply system. They could probably maintain themselves in the type of fighting I could give them for five days. After that it would make no difference how many million men they have, and if you wanted Moscow, I could give it to you.

"They lived on the land coming down. There is insufficient left for them to maintain themselves going back! Let's not give them time to build up their supplies. If we do, then I repeat, we have had a victory over the Germans and disarmed them; we have failed in the liberation of Europe; we have lost the war!

"There is nothing democratic about war. It's a straight dictatorship. The use of force to attain the end desired. We the Armed Forces of the U.S.A. have put our government in the position to dictate the peace. We did not come over here to acquire jurisdiction over either the people or their countries. We came to give them back the right to govern themselves. We must either finish the job now — while we are here and ready — or later under less favorable circumstances."

Even as the war was coming to an end, Patton was forecasting the cold war of the postwar period. In part his estimate was a realistic appreciation of power politics, his recognition that the United States and the Soviet Union were emerging as the leading nations in the world. They had opposing interests, and in that context he believed that conflict was inevitable. He was sure that redeployment and demobilization would weaken the United States and strengthen the Russians, who would threaten to overrun all of Europe.

In part, no doubt, his bellicose attitude was nurtured by his reluctance to see the war come to an end. The excitement and the glory were already fading, and if an armed conflict was inevitable, as he believed, why not at once when the Americans still had combat-effective forces in being?

His view of the Soviet danger would color his attitude during the occupation.

Germany officially surrendered, the capitulation taking effect in the first minute of May 9.

*Letter, GSP, Jr., to Beatrice, May 8, 1945*

Two and a half years ago to day we landed in Africa and now it is all over . . .

We will move . . . near Munich soon and take up the governing of this part of Germany. I hope I don't stay there long. I want to go home for a while on my way to China.

*Letter, GSP, Jr., to Eisenhower, May 8, 1945*

My dear Ike: Please accept my most sincere congratulations on the accomplishment of probably the most difficult job in the history of the world under the most difficult conditions. No one is happier than I at your magnificent success. Devotedly yours,

*Diary, May 8*

This morning at the regular briefing I spoke to the assembled officers . . . I added that I hope we will have other similar briefings in China. I thanked them for what they had done . . .

There is going to be a tremendous let down unless we watch ourselves . . .

I said goodby to the war correspondents and was excessively photographed by them and with them. I also signed a large number of short snorters and handed out a general letter of thanks, which I had personally signed . . .

I also received today a very fine letter of congratulations from the Secretary of War which reads as follows: "I congratulate you and your heroic soldiers of the Third Army. I commend you for the dashing and spectacular victories which have played a great part in bringing about this glorious day. The exploits of the Third Army have been in the highest traditions of the armies that have defended America throughout its history. You and your gallant forces well deserve the nation's homage."

*GSP, Jr., Press Conference, Regensburg, May 8, 1945*

Patton: I certainly appreciate your efforts in informing the people back home of the various units composing this Army and their whereabouts. I have personally received hundreds of letters from parents of soldiers I don't know emphasizing that point, and I want to thank you for it . . .

Are there any questions?

Gay: General, I had a telephone message . . . Colonel Polk found the worst concentration camp yet . . .

Patton: . . . Two or three of you people can use my plane to get up there and take pictures. You can drive up if you want to, but I thought several of you would like to go by plane.

Question: Would you explain why we didn't go into Prague?

Patton: I can tell you exactly – we were told not to. I don't know the exact reasons but those were orders. Of course there are probably many reasons which we don't know which would explain this, as there may be cause of international incidents up there we don't know anything about . . .

Question: Do you have any objection about releasing the story on the gold?

Patton: I have no objection to anything.

Question: There is a question as to who owns this gold.

Patton: I don't give a damn . . .

Question: Are SS troops [taken prisoner] to be handled any differently?

Patton: No. SS means no more in Germany than being a Democrat in America – that is not to be quoted. I mean by that that initially the SS people were special sons-of-bitches, but as the war progressed, they ran out of sons-of-bitches and then they put anybody in there. Some of the top SS men will be treated as criminals, but there is no reason for trying someone who was drafted into this outfit . . .

Question: Is there any time limit for the return of prisoners to their homes?

Patton: I think that is in the terms of surrender. I haven't read the terms of the surrender. I catch them and somebody else can cook them . . .

Well, I wish you goodby and all the best of luck.

*GSP, Jr., Radio Speech (prerecorded) delivered in the United States, May 8, 1945*

Now that victory in Europe has been achieved, let us review the Third Army's part in this epic struggle . . .

To those at home we promise that with their unremitting assistance we shall continue, so that with the help of Almighty God, and through the inspired leadership of our President and the High Command, we shall conquer not only Germany but also Japan until the last danger to life, liberty, and the pursuit of happiness shall perish from the earth.

*Letter, GSP, Jr., to Beatrice, May 9, 1945*

Your telegram . . . [and your] modest estimate of me means more than the opinion of the rest of the world . . .

All the Germans are trying to surrender to us so that the Russians wont get them. It is realy a serious problem. There are hundreds of thousands of them, all with out food.

*Letter, GSP, Jr., to Hull, May 9, 1945*

I will even be more your debtor if you can get me sent to China, so please don't forget.

*Diary, May 9*

Inspected the Skoda Munitions Plant . . . and I found a new form of bogie suspension for tanks, of which I took some pictures. I believe that for light tanks it is very satisfactory . . .

We issued orders . . . to take over control of Czechoslovakia up to the stop line and to prevent, so far as possible, German units from crossing. However, Bradley indicated that it was permissable for German civilians to cross.

*Letter, GSP, Jr., to Handy, May 10, 1945*

Please don't forget that I still am very anxious to fight in China.

*Diary, May 10*

I issued General Orders No. 98, terminating the war today . . .

Lunched with the Supreme Commander and four Army commanders and their air officers. After lunch General Eisenhower talked to us very confidentially on the necessity for solidarity in the event that any of us are called before a Congressional Committee. He outlined what he thought was the proper form of organization [for the occupation]. While none of us exactly agreed with it, it was not sufficiently contrary to our views to prevent our supporting it in general.

He then made a speech which had to me the symptoms of political aspirations, on cooperation with the British, Russians, and the Chinese, but particularly with the British.

It is my opinion that this talking cooperation is for the purpose of covering up probable criticism of strategical blunders which he unquestionably committed during the campaign. Whether or not these were his own or due to too much cooperation with the British, I don't know. I am inclined to think that he over-cooperated.

So ended the war for George Patton, not with a bang but a whimper. He could hardly know that ahead of him lay further battles of another sort.

# VIII

# Germany: The Occupation

*"I am still confused asto just what one has to do."*

## CHAPTER 38

# Postwar Europe: The New Look

*"They are a scurvy race and simply savages. We could beat hell out of them."*

THE WAR IN EUROPE merged almost imperceptibly into peace, and the victory that had promised so much – to return the world instantly to virtue, innocence, and amity – uncovered further problems, additional troubles, continuing international frictions. Victory, it turned out, was anything but a panacea, hardly a final settlement of the world's ills. If it solved the fate of Nazi Germany, it brought in its wake a host of complications.

The key features seemed obvious. The Soviet Union appeared to be strong and intransigent. American units had to be redeployed to the United States for eventual transfer to the Pacific theater and the war against Japan. And Germany was a shambles.

Hundreds of thousands of soldiers populated prisoner-of-war cages. An equal number of homeless displaced persons wandered through the land in search of children, parents, brothers, sisters, and other relatives who had disappeared, victims of chaos and concentration camps. The German government had vanished, the economy was at a standstill, and the people were on the verge of starvation.

The missions of the occupation, in broad terms, were to provide subsistence for the Germans, to eliminate the Nazi ideology, and to render the Germans capable of self-government; to demilitarize, denazify, and deindustrialize Germany and make the nation incapable of war; to enforce nonfraternization, which prohibited normal social intercourse with Germans; to care for and eventually to repatriate the displaced persons; and to make disposition of prisoners of war and civilian internees, some of whom were charged with being war criminals.

On May 10, the U.S. Joint Chiefs of Staff appointed Eisenhower Commander in Chief, U.S. Forces, European Theater (USFET), named him the American member of the four-power Allied Control Council responsible for the occupation of Germany, and placed him at the head of the military government in the American zone, with duties that included the surveillance of economic, industrial, financial, social, and political conditions.

Under the American occupation plan known as Eclipse, issued on April 24, the Third Army was to administer the American zone, which was virtually synonymous with Bavaria. But the Seventh Army was also there, and Eisenhower soon regularized the situation by creating two occupation authorities. He put the Seventh in charge of the Western Military District, the Third in the Eastern.

Patton's region encompassed an area of 25,000 square miles containing more than 7 million Germans, an additional 2 million homeless persons, and, of course, his Third Army of more than half a million troops.

As Colonel George Fisher, Third Army Chemical Officer, later said, "Instead of killing Germans, the job was now to govern them," and Patton "was expected henceforth to guide his late enemies into paths of sweetness and light."

Like many military men, Patton was temperamentally and intellectually little fitted for the task of supervising the restoration of a bankrupt nation and grappling with political, social, and economic matters of enormous complexity. Familiar with war and the training and employment of units, he lacked the specialized knowledge, the technical expertise required to deal with such matters as banking or education. Brought up to make decisions quickly and lacking detailed appreciation of postwar problems that frequently had no swift and sure remedies, he sought the simplistic rather than the realistic. He knew little and cared less of the programs he was expected to implement.

His life style, his ruthless drive, his entire military experience militated against the role he was expected to assume. He felt distinctly out of place. He was, in addition, tired, exhausted, ready for honors and applause, anxious for reward and recreation. Instead, all sorts of problems clamored for attention and solution, and he resented these demands on his now ebbing energy and vitality.

Staff officers, experts in various fields of human endeavor, administered the occupation under the rather loose supervision of military commanders who, like Patton, preferred the troop duties they were comfortable with.

Since he was a fighter rather than a manager or administrator, Patton turned his immediate efforts to being transferred to the Pacific. Unless he could get to the Far East, he had participated in his last war. Had he then fulfilled his fate? He hoped not. And thus his letter to a classmate was only one of many he wrote in the weeks following the German surrender.

*Letter, GSP, Jr., to Lt. Gen. Robert L. Eichelberger, Eighth Army, Pacific, May 25, 1945*

You have certainly been doing a great job, and I should think by now you practically have webbed feet. In my limited experience with amphibious attacks, I found them the most dangerous form of sport yet devised.

I would like nothing better than to have a chance of fighting somewhere in the East against the Japanese. If I should be so fortunate, I am going to sit at your feet and learn how to do it.

As he thought about the postwar world and specifically Germany, he felt increasingly out of sympathy with his milieu and particularly with the aims of nonfraternization and denazification. No one had been more zealous than he in working for the defeat of the German military forces. In the process, he came to have great, if grudging, admiration for the German military men who had fought bravely, if foolishly, who had maintained the honor of the military profession. Why oppress them? Surely, he began to believe, only a handful had been dyed-in-the-wool Nazis. Party membership, he was certain, had been required in order to survive in Hitler's Germany, and those who had joined had done so to retain their jobs so they could support their families. What, he asked, was wrong with that?

He disagreed "with some of the foolish ideas about non-fraternization with the Germans. All Nazis are bad, but all Germans are not Nazis."

Later in May, he told his brother-in-law:

Germany is really a very depressing place . . . I think that this non-fraternization is very stupid. If we are going to keep American soldiers in a country, they have to have some civilians to talk to.

> Furthermore, I think we could do a lot for the German civilians by letting our soldiers talk to their young people.

The ruined German cities were indeed depressing. During the war, most Americans, upon seeing the demolished buildings for the first time, had an immediate thrill of exultation – it served the Germans right. But this soon gave way to compassion. In the rubble, in the cellars of the houses torn apart by bombs and shells lived human beings, mostly women, children, and old men.

Responding to a request from a man in London for news of his in-laws in Munich, Patton asked Brigadier General Walter J. Muller, the G–4, to have a look. Accompanied by the Provost Marshal and an interpreter, Muller investigated. His report touched and moved Patton:

> The home of this old couple has been practically destroyed. They live in extreme poverty, probably in about two rooms as they cook and eat in one little kitchen. They stated that their home was an English home at one time. While [we were] there, the old gentleman tried to do his best by putting on his one celluloid collar and his coat. The home had an atmosphere of extreme poverty and had an odor which comes from people living, eating, and sleeping in about two rooms.

This was the real Germany, Patton believed, not the war-making and inhuman Nazis, who had been defeated and laid to rest.

Patton's West Point roommate, Brigadier General Philip S. Gage, wrote late in April, mainly to congratulate him:

> It would seem superfluous to tell you how mighty proud we all are over the stupendous things you have done in this war. Having known you of old, I am, of course, not surprised . . . Even though we lived together for two years at West Point, I would be quite overawed to be in your presence. Few men of our time have seen so much, done so much, and for such a length of time occupied the headlines of every paper and magazine in this broad land.

Gage went on to talk about the Germans. His attitude was one that many Americans shared:

> Tonight I read in the paper of how you required the civil population of Weimar to visit the Buchenwald prison camp and see for themselves the horrors of the Nazi regime. Little enough! Of course I know even your extensive powers are limited, but I *do* hope that wherever and whenever you can, you will do what you can to make the German populace suffer. For God's sake, please don't ever go soft in regard to them. Nothing could ever be too bad for them.

When Patton replied on May 15, he made no reference to Gage's concern over punishing the Germans for misdeeds and crimes against humanity. His thoughts were elsewhere:

> At present I seem destined to sit around here and do some housekeeping, but there may be a chance of my going to China, which is of course what I should prefer to do.

With the war in Europe over, Patton apparently felt it was time to bind up the wounds as after the American Civil War, forget the horrors, and re-establish Germany as a respectable entity among the nations of the world. Not so much to live in peace and charity, but rather to help the United States fulfill its role as an international power of the first order. It was important, he believed, to build up the Germans to the point where they could become American allies. The British were exhausted by the war, the French debilitated and disillusioned by it. Only the Germans, it seemed to him, could emerge from the ashes of defeat and contribute to the stability of Europe. Only they could stand as a bulwark against the Russians and Communism.

The regret and the pity he expressed on occasion during the war over the devastation, both human and material, caused by combat carried over into the postwar period. The Germans were an Anglo-Saxon people, with proud military traditions. They were adept in the art of war. They resembled Americans. They should, he was certain, be rehabilitated quickly.

This was linked in his mind to the exciting prospect of meeting the Russians in battle. In March, a member of the Russian Trade Delegation in London had complimented the Americans on their progress in the campaign and mentioned Patton by name with warm admiration. The comment was passed along to Patton:

> He said that you were showing everyone how the Germans should be fought, and that you had made a greater advance in one day than the Red Army had ever done. You seem to be the kind of General that the Russians like.

"I am particularly happy to have met the approbation of the Russians," Patton replied, "because I like the way they fight too."

Would it not be sporting if the two best armies in the world had a go at it? Perhaps his destiny had yet to be altogether fulfilled.

But more than his personal destiny was at stake. He understood that the destruction of Germany had upset the balance of power in Europe. He saw clearly the political realities of the times.

Thus, he objected, privately and among his friends, to demilitarizing Germany, to dismantling the German economic structure. On the contrary, the Western Allies should strengthen, restore, and welcome Germany as a force against the rising threat of Bolshevism.

Little matter that Patton's prediction eventually prevailed – nonfraternization relaxed and then abolished, western Germany rehabilitated and made part of the democratic West, the cold war between the superpowers a postwar fact of life.

The Berlin blockade and the hostile confrontation between the North Atlantic and Warsaw Pact nations, as well as the other events of the cold war, belonged to the future. For the moment, Nazis had to be punished, purgatory passed. And in that intermediate period, a potent if unorganized force played its role – the press.

Most newspapermen in Germany were knowledgeable, perceptive, and articulate. Trained to be inquisitive, they were alert for news that made headlines. They had a sixth sense that told them where the sensational was to be found and uncovered. Many were liberal and democratic in their outlook and sympathy; they were what was called at the time "socially conscious." They were concerned that the war have meaning, and meaning to them was, above all, the extirpation of Nazism.

They admired Patton for his wartime exploits and wondered whether he could handle his peacetime duties. They suspected that his patrician background and status made him comfortable not only with the rich and the powerful, but also with those on the political right. They felt intuitively that, except for the soldiers, he had little patience with the common man. In their private conversations, some of them loosely called

Patton a proto-fascist, a would-be demagogue, a right-winger. If the wartime expenditure in blood and materiel was to have any lasting significance, they believed fervently, the postwar world would have to be different.

Patton's news value and quotability, the natural hostility between the press and the military in peacetime, the function of news as sensation, the statement Patton had made during the war that Nazis could hardly be distinguished from Democrats and Republicans, his identification with the upper class — all this made it inevitable that some reporters in Germany would keep a sharp eye on him. Because of Patton's proclivities and because of the traditional role of the American press as investigators as well as reporters, he was already a marked man.

Meanwhile, certain other missions had to be accomplished.

*Diary, May 12*

To Linz where, by my invitation, we met the Commanding General of the 4th Russian Guards Army . . . I felt it was more correct for him to call on me than for me to call on him.

The 65th Division provided a guard of honor. We then decorated the General and 12 other members of his party with different types of Legion of Merit.

In a short address, Patton emphasized the "cordiality" of Russo-American relations.

After the ceremony . . . we went to the officers' club . . . and had lunch, which consisted mostly of whiskey. The Russians tried to drink American whiskey without water with very bad results. I unquestionably drank the Russian commander under the table and walked out under my own steam.

We are going to pay back a call on the 14th, prior to which date I will drink quite a lot of mineral oil, as they will unquestionably try to get us drunk.

*Letter, GSP, Jr., to Beatrice, May 13, 1945*

Every one wanted me to get vodka for them to drink but I decided they could drink whiskey or nothing. The results were great. The [Russian] general went out cold and I . . . did not even have a head ake. I kept putting water in my bourbon and he did not.

When I toasted Stalin and the 4th Guards Army, I did a school [skoal] with him and then broke the glass. I think I will get a good medal as his aid said that I was the only man he had met with feeling (and an iron stomach).

When I broke the glass he imbrased me.

They are a scurvy race and simply savages. We could beat hell out of them.

*Diary, May 14*

Received by Marshal Tolbukhim, Commander of the Third Ukrainian Front . . . to present me with the Medal, the Order of Kutuzov (First Degree) . . . He was a very inferior man and sweated profusely at all time.

They certainly put on a tremendous show. The whole road, which I should think was 15 miles from the bridge where we met them till we reached the chateau formerly belonging to the Emperor Francis Joseph of Austria, had actually been swept. There were soldiers about every hundred yards along the road, standing at present arms, and also extremely buxom female MP's.

When we got to the chateau, they had soldiers with a sort of shoe blackening arrangement to clean our boots. They had a great many women retainers who did everything except wipe your face. They did go to the extent of spraying your head with perfume.

No Russian could sit down or get up without asking the Marshal's permission.

After lunch they had a very splendid show which unquestionably had been flown in from Moscow. They did their best to get us drunk, but we had taken the precaution of drinking two ounces of mineral oil before starting on the expedition. We were also very careful of what we drank.

The medal given me is No. 58, which indicates that it is quite highly considered.

I have never seen in any army at any time, including the German Imperial Army of 1912, as severe discipline as exists in the Russian army. The officers with few exceptions give the appearance of recently civilized Mongolian bandits. The men passed in review with a very good imitation of the goose step. They give me the impression of something that is to be feared in future world political reorganization.

*Gay's Journal, May 14*

Everything they did impressed one with the idea of virility and cruelty.

Not only because of his feelings about the Russians but also because it was his habit to do so, Patton forwarded ideas for improving military equipment. To General Motors War Products Division in Detroit, he forwarded photographs

> of a new form of suspension which I saw on a German tank and which may be of interest . . . I have never seen the thing in operation, but it struck me as a good idea.

To Lieutenant General Levin H. Campbell, Jr., Chief of Ordnance, he sent a tank sight captured from the Germans – "The finest optical instrument I have ever seen" – and suggested developing an identical device for the war against Japan.

He was happy to learn that he was a hero at home. Lieutenant Colonel Brenton G. Wallace, on three weeks' leave in the United States, wrote that everyone wanted to hear about Patton and his famous Third Army. When his picture appeared in the newsreels, audiences applauded and cheered – more for Patton than for anyone else.

Jennie Mears wrote from South Hamilton to express "pride and gratitude for the seemingly impossible things" Patton had done. He symbolized everything that was noble in the American soldier. In the eyes of his neighbors, he was "a truly great man." More than 250 people in the community signed the letter.

John Bryson of the American Broadcasting Corporation said it was his greatest privilege to report on the Third Army during the war and to be close to "the greatest military genius since Lee and Jackson." He honestly believed that the war would be still in progress if Patton had not been there. Patton was without doubt the "greatest front line general in the world" and his Army was the best. He had heard somewhere, Bryson added, that there had been other American Armies engaged, but for him that would always be a rumor.

Patton was unhappy to hear from Gilbert Cook who said that some people in Washington doubted whether Patton's sweeping rather than methodical method of fighting Germans was applicable to the Japanese. Hurt and enraged, Patton replied, "Such criticism is only another example of the great brevity of human memory." What about Tunisia, where he attacked continually for 23 days against dug-in supermen? What about Sicily, where his Army made five miles each day? What about the fighting in November and December, when the Third Army on an 80-mile front advanced 65 miles through defended country, crossed six large rivers, broke through the Siegfried Line, and was in position to advance on Worms when it was required to turn north to "deflate the Bulge"? What about the fighting at Bastogne, "the most violent which I have ever encountered"? What about the offensive from January 13 to March 13, when the Third Army penetrated the Siegfried Line at three different points? What about the Palatinate campaign? Everyone forgot. All they remembered were the exploitation across France and the final pursuit through Germany.

Patton must certainly have smiled sourly at the irony of turning his greatest successes against him. He was, they said, too good for the Japanese.

*Letter, GSP, Jr., to Beatrice, May 15, 1945*

If the little launch I built is stall extant, get her painted and fixed up as we may be able to take a short cruise together very soon.

They are sending groups of generals home to make talks . . . I will go around the end of May or the first part of June. I tour the Pacific coast and then get several weeks leave. Hot Dog. Get the horses shod too . . .

Some PDF's [poor damn fools] say that my style of fighting is too fast for the Japs . . .

I am going to England on leave in the morning and will visit the Leicester-Warrens and the Stockdales.

He hoped also to have ribbons of his decorations made in London so he could wear them on his uniform during his trip to the United States:

Distinguished Service Cross, with Oak Leaf Cluster
Distinguished Service Medal, with two Oak Leaf Clusters
Silver Star, with Oak Leaf Cluster
Legion of Merit
Bronze Star
Congressional Medal of Honor for Life Saving, 2d Class
Mexican Medal
World War I, with 4 stars
World War II, with 7 stars and 1 arrowhead
American Defense Medal

Knight of the British Empire
Companion of the Bath
Grand Cross of the Ouissam Alaouite
Order of Kutuzov, 1st Degree
French Legion of Honor, Grand Officer
Croix de Guerre, with Palm (French)
Croix de Guerre (Luxembourg)

*Diary, May 16*

Hughes and I, Codman . . . Sgt. Mims, and Sgt. Meeks left by plane first for Paris and then for London, where I am going to take leave in Manchester and visit my friends in that vicinity.

Before we left, General Frederick Osborn, in charge of morale, came to see me and made some of the profoundest remarks, indicating utter lack of knowledge of Americans and American soldiers that I have ever heard. The idea which has suddenly impinged on his brain is that officers and soldiers should talk more freely [together]. I know of no army in the world where it is done more than in this army, and I told Osborn I had known that for some forty years. He said he had studied this for four years and felt that I was wrong. I think he is a man whose education has surpassed his mental capacity . . .

We were billeted at Claridge's and by telephoning to the Lunts, I had a chance to get two tickets and see their play, which was most amusing. During the show numerous reporters came and took pictures of me . . . We stopped to speak to the Lunts in their dressing room, then we got into the car. The whole street for about three blocks was a solid mass of people waiting to see me, and there was much yelling, handshaking, etc.

*Diary, May 17*

The telephone started ringing early in the morning, with members of the press requesting interviews. I dodged most of these, but had to talk to some. I simply stated that I was very glad to be in England because it felt like home to me, which is a mild remark, well swallowed by the English . . .

Lady Astor asked me to lunch at the House of Commons, but I told her that people stared at me too much and invited her to have lunch with me at Claridge's. She accepted and we had a very pleasant time together. She is a very smart old lady.

Just after lunch the telephone rang. It was General Bull calling up from Reims, requesting me to come back at once. This put an end to my proposed leave . . .

I arrived at Reims at 5:30, and went to see General Eisenhower, where I found that my recall was due to the fact that Tito is raising hell at the northern end of the Adriatic, and General Marshall had telegraphed . . . that it was necessary to use the prestige of my name and the Third Army and at least five armored divisions to bluff him. I went over the proposed arrangements with Bull, and we arrived at the very simple solution of turning over the XV Corps to me and turning over our III Corps, which is on occupation duty, to the Seventh Army.

Eisenhower, Bradley, and I had dinner together and talked until about 1:30.

*Letter, GSP, Jr., to Beatrice, May 18, 1945*

My leave went out the window . . . [I am] to bluff Tito and some of his Mongolian friends.

We are doing it now and will either quiet them or start a new war in a few days . . .

I am scheduled to leave Paris [for home] on June 7, and will tour the west coast and then get a two weeks leave – provided Tito behaves . . .

If we must fight, the sooner we start the better.

It looks as if I were not going to China for a while – if at all. But things are so confused that no one can tell from one day to the next. If we stay in Germany, families are to be allowed to come, so you may see the sights after all.

The inclosed pictures are of me and the Mongols.

Tito was making trouble over Trieste.

*Diary, May 18*

The idea is to make a strong bluff along the Enns River and if offensive action becomes necessary, to cross it . . .

The question at issue is not so much Tito but as to whether or not he is the pawn of the Russians and, if so, whether he is being used as a red herring to pull us to the south so that the Russians may resume an offensive in central Germany; or whether the Russians are actually backing Tito with the idea of getting a port, or ports, on the northern end of the Adriatic.

GSP, Jr., in the United Kingdom before the Normandy invasion, April 1944

GSP, Jr., in light plane

GSP, Jr., and Gaffey

Left: Eisenhower, GSP, Jr., Bradley, Hodges

Lower left: Patch, Eisenhower, GSP, Jr., Devers

Below: GSP, Jr., and Marshall

GSP, Jr., and Averell Harriman

Upper right: GSP, Jr., and the Russians, May 1945

Lower right: Willie with GSP, Jr.

CG
CS

GSP, Jr., wearing four stars for the first time, April 1945

Upper right: Patton family, June 1945

Lower right: GSP, Jr., and grandchildren, June 1945

GSP, Jr., and Truscott at farewell ceremony, Third Army Headquarters, Bad Tolz, October 1945

Sergeant William G. Meeks at Patton's funeral, December 1945

Grave at Hamm, Luxembourg, 1946

MP

Patton at peace with himself and the world, April 1942

The situation should clarify itself within a few days. If it does not, considerable complication will arise on deployment.

In my opinion, the American Army as it now exists could beat the Russians with the greatest of ease, because while the Russians have good infantry, they are lacking in artillery, air, tanks, and in the knowledge of the use of the combined arms; whereas we excel in all three of these. If it should be necessary to fight the Russians, the sooner we do it the better.

Eisenhower and Bradley were somewhat worried about the attitude of the [American] soldiers. Personally, I don't think the soldier cares . . . so well disciplined and so patriotic he will fight anywhere he is told to fight, and do a good job. I believe that by taking a strong attitude [on our side], the Russians will back down. So far we have yielded too much to their Mongolian nature.

*Letter, GSP, Jr., to Beatrice, May 20, 1945*

It is the prettiest country . . . with snow mountains, forests of all shades of green, and green fields. War has not touched it to any extent. It is full of pretty girls, all of whom say they are Czechs.

The desire to fight is evaporating, and these soldiers will not be much good unless they get in soon.

I doubt if I go to China unless something happens to Doug[las MacArthur] . . .

I hope that Tito does not keep me from coming home . . . If he does, I am going to give him a special licking.

"Tito is still making a fool of him self," he wrote Beatrice, "and no one knows whether or not the Mongols are backing him. If we have to fight them, now is the time. From now on we will get weaker and they stronger." He hoped to get to the United Kingdom before going home, "so I wish Tito would put up or shut up." He was shocked to hear that people were already "thinking that rules and votes can end wars. One has only to see the Russians to know how stupid such talk is."

He told his sister Nita:

I am personally sorry for Mussolini, because I had a great admiration for a man who could do so much with so little, and it was a typically Italian stunt to murder him. I think he should have been properly hanged.

Of course, any fool idea that you can have a league for security [like the United Nations Organization] is nuts, and all people who favor it are potential murderers . . . As long as man is man, there will be war, and the only way to avoid trouble is to have the best Army and Navy, which we now have.

*Letter, GSP, Jr., to Beatrice, May 23, 1945*

Tito is, I think, behaving but SHAEF is as usual 48 hours behind time so does not know it.

*Letter, GSP, Jr., to Lt. Gen. Daniel Van Voorhis (Ret.), May 24, 1945*

This business of not having to fight and having about 17 divisions to look after is rather an inglorious ending for a great experience. However I happen to be doing it in a very pleasant place, and I am still hopeful of having a chance to fight the Japanese.

*Letter, GSP, Jr., to Maj. Gen. LeRoy Lutes, Washington, May 24, 1945*

I trust that we will meet each other again shortly in China where it is my ambition to go.

Patton was right about Tito, who retreated. With the situation around Trieste calm, Patton went to England for four days. He left no record of his activities.

Meanwhile, the Third Army headquarters moved to Bad Tolz and into a 900-room building on a 40-acre site, formerly an SS officers' training school. It was, he told his brother-in-law, "the best laid out building I have ever seen. If I were planning a headquarters building for an Army, I would copy it."

*Letter, GSP, Jr., to Frederick Ayer, May 24, 1945*

We live in a house about fifteen minutes from here on a lake. It belonged to . . . Mr. Emman, who is alleged to have been Hitler's First Sergeant in the last war and who made his money by publishing Mein Kampf. Also Hitler confiscated a Jewish newspaper and sold it to Emman for a 100,000 marks when it was worth about a million marks. As a result, he has one of the best houses I have ever seen. It has a bowling alley, a swimming pool, a large number of rooms, a boat house and two boats, the latter are not very good. If one has to occupy Germany, this is a good place to do it from.

*Letter, GSP, Jr., to Edward Weeks,* Atlantic Monthly, *Boston, May 25, 1945*

The villa is the handsomest house I have ever seen except the one I had in Morocco, which also belonged to a publisher . . . who had also gotten his money in peculiar ways. Don't gather from this that I am opposed to publishers.

The people of this country are in a sort of daze, there being no newspapers, no telephones, no telegrams, no automobiles, no railways. They are just as isolated as if they were on a desert island. I am not sure that it is the best thing for them.

More interested in the military aspect of his duties, Patton issued on June 1 a letter of instructions to his corps, division, and separate unit commanders:

Unless we exert ourselves, much of the greatness and efficiency which has marked this Army will be lost. You will therefore pay particular attention to the following:

1. Discipline . . . If you, their commander, cannot enforce discipline in peace, you are useless in war . . .

2. Sense of Obligation: Everything in the Army belongs to the United States — you are part of the United States — the things which you waste, spoil, and destroy are things for which you and your children and your children's children will be paying for years to come . . .

3. Deportment and Carriage: I am tremendously proud of your deportment; the way you carry out orders with regards to non-fraternization; the way you behave towards private property. But the way you carry yourself is shockingly bad. You, the soldiers of the greatest Army of the greatest nation in the world, wander about like furtive pickpockets with your shoulders slipping, your stomachs sticking out, and your heads hanging down . . . Show the world how great you are. Look like soldiers!

4. Maneuvers . . . You will immediately initiate and continue a series of maneuvers from the squad to include the reinforced battalion — battles are just a number of battalion fights . . .

5. Ceremonies . . . are important as a means of impressing our enemies, our allies, and our own troops . . .

I will personally inspect the administrative, tactical, and ceremonial activities listed above.

*Letter, GSP, Jr., to Keyes, June 2, 1945*

The other day when I was still optimistic about going to China, I said . . . the three corps I would like to take would be yours, Van Fleet's, and Walker's, because all of you like to fight.

I am leaving . . . on a bond selling tour [in the United States] which I look forward to with no pleasure at all.

*Letter, GSP, Jr., to Handy, June 2, 1945*

I am naturally somewhat interested in my own future and hate to see all these other Armies going to the Pacific and me staying here. I am not asking any favors, but I am curious to know the reason, so if it is a proper question, please tell me.

On June 4, Patton, Codman, and Meeks departed for Paris, where, together with a group of officers and enlisted men, they boarded a plane. Patton was ill with a strep throat but insisted on going. They arrived at the Bedford Airport near Boston three days later.

When the plane stopped and the door was opened, Patton jumped the few feet to the unloading platform and walked briskly across the runway to where Beatrice waited. Doffing his helmet, he kissed her.

With one hand on his shoulder and the other stroking his cheek, she said, "Oh, I'm so glad to have you back."

Patton embraced his son and daughters.

Mrs. Patton told reporters, "When he left me two years and seven months ago, he told me he expected to die fighting. It seems like a miracle that he has come back."

He said that he wanted to return to his boyhood church in San Gabriel, California, and give thanks to God. "I sincerely hope I fight the Japanese," but he indicated he might not have the chance.

Then commenced a 25-mile drive to the city, where an estimated million people gave him a hero's welcome, one of the most tumultuous receptions in Boston's history. He was saluted everywhere by shouting throngs downtown, around the Common, near the State House, and on the route to the Hatch Shell on the Charles River Esplanade, where 20,000 people awaited him.

After he was greeted by city and state officials, Patton spoke briefly. About 400 wounded veterans of the Third Army sat in a reserved section in front of the shell, and throughout his address Patton looked directly at the men who had fought with him.

"With your blood and bonds," he said, "we crushed the Germans before they got here. This ovation is not for me, George S. Patton — George S. Patton is simply a hook on which to hang the Third Army."

He went on to say something which came out all wrong. He certainly had no intention of having it sound the way it did.

It was a popular idea, he said, that a man was a hero when he was killed in action. Rather, he thought, a man was frequently a fool when he got killed. "These men are the heroes," he said, pointing toward the wounded soldiers. Dramatically drawing himself even more erect and standing at attention, he saluted them, then walked to his seat on the platform.

In the evening he attended a state dinner at the Copley Plaza Hotel, where he spoke again to an enthusiastic audience. At the end of his address, he was overwhelmed by emotion. The applause was thunderous.

He spent the night at home with his family, spoke to the townspeople of Hamilton on the following morning, and, accompanied by Beatrice, departed for Denver, where similar ceremonies and ovations awaited him.

On to Los Angeles for more welcomes, speeches, and celebrations. At the Coliseum where 100,000 persons had gathered to listen to him, he wept, swore, and roared for the defeat of Japan. He stayed with his sister Nita, visited Pasadena and the Army Regional Hospital, participated in a ceremony at the Rose Bowl, attended the Church of Our Saviour, stopped in at the Huntington Library, and placed a wreath of roses on the graves of his parents.

On his return to the East Coast, he halted briefly at Fort Riley before going on to Washington where he saw his daughters and grandchildren, talked with army officials in the Pentagon, and chatted with the President.

He also went to the Walter Reed Hospital, where his daughter Ruth Ellen was a volunteer worker in the double amputation ward. The men had begged her to ask him to come so they could see him. When he entered the room, he stopped and looked around at the men lacking arms and legs. He burst into tears. As he dried his eyes with his handkerchief, he said, "God damn it, if I had been a better general, most of you wouldn't be here."

Meanwhile, an adverse reaction, provoked by his remark in Boston, was building up. In a letter to Marshall, Alfred C. Stoddard of Phoenix, Arizona, said it was heartbreaking for his son to lie in his grave in France and for Patton to be alive and telling who the heroes were. G. W. Nicholson of Michigan, whose only son was killed while a member of the Third Army, wrote Senator Arthur H. Vandenberg that he thought the face-slapping, gun-toting general owed American gold-star fathers and mothers an apology.

There were many letters to newspapers from Americans who abhorred the image he presented and the remarks he made.

Stimson tried to explain in a press conference. He noted that Patton had expressed deep concern over the misinterpretation of his statement. What he had said or meant to say was not that a man was frequently a fool to be killed but rather that men were frequently killed under foolish circumstances. As illustration, he cited a personal friend of Patton's who served in all the campaigns from Sicily through Normandy with no wound greater than the pinpricks he received when being decorated; he was killed by a stray shell while eating lunch 16 miles behind the front. Patton, Stimson emphasized, had deep respect for the nation's honored dead.

Ulio, The Adjutant General, wrote the official replies to persons complaining to the War Department about Patton's language and comments. What Patton had meant to say, Ulio explained, was that some men were killed by the tragic mischances of war.

Despite his faux pas, people everywhere clamored to see and hear him. Many wrote laudatory letters that appeared in the press.

In general, newspapers and radio commentators mentioned Patton favorably, and this he loved, along with the cheering crowds. He was glad to see Beatrice and the children, but he was happy to leave the United States.

On July 3, Patton and Meeks — Codman remained in Boston because his wife was ill — departed Washington by air for Europe.

*Diary, July 4*

Shortly after daylight we flew over Le Havre, and Sgt. Meeks said to me, "General, that is France, we have sure done our thirty days [in jail]!"

In a sense I had a similar feeling because with the exception of my own immediate family the whole attitude of the people in America is quite inimical to that which exists in Europe. None of them realizes that one cannot fight for two and a half years and be the same. Yet you are expected to get back into the identical groove from which you departed and from which your non-warlike compatriots have never moved.

He had experienced what the great majority of soldiers returning from overseas service felt, the sense of personal dislocation during a period of transition, as it was called, which would last anywhere from weeks to months, when it was necessary to discard attitudes and habits which were out of place in a civilian world.

He also had a premonition of death. When Beatrice was out of the room, Patton said to his daughters, "Well, goodbye girls. I won't be seeing you again. Take care of George. I'll be seeing your mother, but I won't be seeing you."

One of them said that he was being silly; the war was over.

"No," he said, "I mean it. I have a feeling that my luck has run out at last."

A man, he said, was born with a certain amount of luck, like money in the bank. A front-line infantryman spent his luck faster than a rear-echelon cook. His own reservoir was going dry. The last few shells that had struck near him in the final months of the war seemed to land closer to him. He had narrowly escaped death twice – when a Polish pilot flying an RAF plane had mistakenly tried to attack him, and when his automobile barely avoided a long pole in a German ox-cart. He was sure that the end of his life was fast approaching.

It was hardly like him to say something like that. He had always insisted that luck was the subconscious recognition and solution of a problem before the conscious mind was aware even that a problem existed. Luck, he had said many times, was the "still, small voice."

Yet it was obvious now that he was tired, exhausted by his efforts during the war, his fight to keep his war mask from slipping, his struggle for recognition and fame.

Hazen Ayer, who with Patton's brother-in-law was a cotrustee of the family finances, thought that Patton "had changed and changed notably. Naturally, he was older and grayer, but he was also more mature and quieter . . . I even sensed a new element of grandeur about him."

But Patton was disappointed. He had learned in the Pentagon that he would go to the Pacific if the Chinese opened a port, which seemed unlikely, or if MacArthur became incapacitated. He had therefore probably fought his last war — unless, of course, the Russians acted up. But even that seemed hopeless, given the self-satisfaction and apathy in the United States.

> I was particularly depressed with the attitude in the War Department where everyone seems to place emphasis on what they call "planning" and no emphasis at all on fighting . . .
>
> The last day I was in Washington I was talking with Cook, and he made the remark, "George, you are to be congratulated because Courtney Hodges has gone to China . . . Courtney will get himself in trouble over there and you will have to go and get him out."
>
> As I did in the Bulge, I suppose. Speaking of which reminds me that Courtney Hodges and Omar Bradley got a DSM for their unsuccessful defense of the Bulge, and I did not get one for successfully defending it.

In his fatigue he particularly resented all the slights, real and imagined, he had endured. He had won the greatest victories on the battlefield, and the recognition of his accomplishments, the applause for his achievements somehow failed to measure up to the exhilaration he expected.

> Hughes met me at the airport, and I went to his apartment at the Georges V Hotel and was surprised to find it was already after lunch time, so we had some sandwiches. He then asked me if I wanted to go to the reception of the American Ambassador [at the traditional July 4th celebration party], so we went, and it was somewhat reassuring to find that I was still a fairly good sized [social] lion.
>
> Aside from this interlude, Paris was a gloomy and uninteresting place.

On the following day his spirits were lifted. The Third Army had planned a magnificent welcome home for him that started while he was flying from Paris to Germany. Over Strasbourg, three fighter groups from the XIX TAC met this plane and escorted it to Holzkirchen Field. The 24 P-51s, he told Beatrice, "played around our nose like porpoises." At the airfield, an armored infantry battalion and a division band comprised the guard of honor. Motorcycles to the front and rear escorted his car to Bad Tolz. Along the way tanks were parked close to the road, and tank commanders saluted as his car passed. An antiaircraft battalion was formed along the route of march and presented arms. A company of armored infantry and a company of colored soldiers were stationed along the road, with individuals placed alternately on each side at 50-yard intervals. Meanwhile, some 50 planes provided a "continuous and nerve-wracking protection – nerve-wracking in that they very seldom missed the tops of the pine trees along the road by more than ten feet." At the casern, Patton's car halted at the commanding general's sally-port entrance, where the corps commanders awaited him, then escorted him to the reviewing position in the quadrangle for a guard of honor and a review.

He loved it all. He was home, back with the troops, where he belonged. Overcome with emotion, "I said a few well chosen words to the assembled officers and enlisted men" over the loudspeaker. Then he and the high-ranking officers went to the Officers' Mess lounge for cocktails and lunch.

It was a beautiful ceremony, exactly what Patton liked. He felt much more comfortable than he had in the civilianized United States. "It gave me a very warm feeling in my heart to be back among soldiers."

Although "it seemed to me that there was nothing more of interest in the world now that the war was over," Patton summoned his staff for a report of the events during his absence. Everything seemed to be going well, and Patton decided to give his personal attention to a vigorous program of troop-unit inspection, not only "more to his liking," according to George Fisher, "than groping among the papers on his desk," but also more in accord with his sense of the priorities.

Bradley rated him "Superior," placed him Number 1 as a commander in combat and Number 5 of 10 generals he knew with comparable experience for all around duty –

> colorful, courageous, energetic, pleasing personality, impetuous. Possesses high degree of leadership, bold in operations, has fine sense of feeling of enemy and own capabilities. An outstanding combat leader.

*Letter, GSP, Jr., to Brig. Gen. Bruce C. Clarke, July 6, 1945*

On returning from Washington, I fear that at the moment there is very little chance of my going to the Pacific theater of operations.

*Letter, GSP, Jr., to Lt. Gen. A. C. Wedemeyer, Commanding General, China Theater, July 6, 1945*

I do not believe that I will get to the Pacific theater, at least not immediately. If the war should end before I do, I would like very much to take advantage of your invitation and visit you in your theater.

*Letter, GSP, Jr., to Maj. Gen. John K. Herr (Ret.), former Chief of Cavalry, July 7, 1945*

The future of the cavalry depends on Gay, Truscott, and myself . . . Had you accepted the command of the armored corps [Armored Force?] when I tried to make you do it, the cavalry would now be in a much better position than it is.

Patton was delighted to hear from John L. Hines, Jr., and to know that his father had presented him with the Oak Leaf Cluster to the DSC at Walter Reed Hospital, that young Hines was in the Valley Forge Hospital, the best in the country for treating the blind and for plastic work, that he had had an operation, the first of a series, to clear the debris from his face, after which he would have his face rebuilt. Meanwhile, he was learning to get around by himself, to read Braille, and to type. And, finally, Hines wrote,

> I wish to express to you the satisfaction that I felt in finally achieving my aim in serving in combat . . . under the command of our greatest soldier and leader. This feeling of your greatness as a leader and of the superiority of the Third Army seems to me to be one generally felt by most combat officers.

*Letter, GSP, Jr., to Beatrice, July 7, 1945*

I am still confused asto just what one has to do. I have five corps and some 30 divisions. I will know more in a day or two. I love and miss you.

Several USFET officers came to Bad Tolz to try to answer confusing questions on redeployment policy, but that hardly seemed to help.

*Letter, GSP, Jr., to Beatrice, July 8, 1945*

This so called re-deployment [is] realy [a] vote catching program. Ike's people were here to help explain the in-explainable.

From Philadelphia came a dignified request for reassurance. Senator Eastland of Mississippi was making "terrible accusations" against the "American Negro soldier . . . I am a Negro. I was deeply shocked and hurt." Was it true that black troops had been an "utter and abysmal failure" during the war?

Patton made no reply. He marked on the letter simply that it was to be filed.

*Letter, GSP, Jr., to Beatrice, July 11, 1945*

Inspite of no war I am terribly busy inspecting four divisions this week. But it is better than just waiting quietly for dear Doug. to die.

You are a great sport and I love you.

*GSP, Jr., General Notes on Remarks to be Made to Divisions, July 13, 1945*

Now that all or nearly all of you are returning to civil life, I believe that I should continue to do my best to instruct you how to save your lives and the lives of your children. I realize that in doing this I shall be criticized, but my conscience will be much clearer in the knowledge that I have done my duty as I see it . . .

It is certain that the two World Wars in which I have participated would not have occurred had we been prepared . . .

The progress made in airplanes and self-propelled missiles is such that the possibility of an early knockout cannot be discounted . . .

You have found out that discipline, self-reliance, and mutual responsibility and faith are necessary in the Army. These traits are just as necessary in civil life . . .

I have been speaking to you not as your commanding general, but rather as an old man to young men. I am in no way trying to propagandize you . . .

In closing, let me say that it is my profound hope that we shall never again be engaged in war, but also let me remind you of the words attributed to George Washington: "In time of peace, prepare for war." That advice is still good.

*Letter, GSP, Jr., to Beatrice, July 13, 1945*

I am like a rat with out a tale doing and doing.

On July 14, because of the rapid progress of denazification, Eisenhower relaxed the ban on fraternization. American military personnel could now engage in conversation with adult Germans on the streets and in other public places.

Patton congratulated Devers upon being named head of the Army Ground Forces in Washington. He hoped that Devers could save armor and mechanized cavalry while still retaining some horses in the army. The war records of polo players, steeplechase riders, and other horsemen, he thought, justified retaining the horse, particularly since "two full Generals of the Class of 1909 were both eminent polo players." Otherwise,

> we will have nobody in the next war who knows anything about an animal. You will remember what happened in Italy, and I had a similar experience in Sicily, in trying to improvise mounted troops out of Ford-minded young men.

A few days later, Colonel Thomas J. Johnson of the American Remount Association made known his concern over "the present, thoughtless discrimination against animals in the Army" and "the actual need of horses and mules . . . in a modern, mechanized Army." Would Patton care to dictate a long letter on the subject and reinforce these views? "Your opinions on this subject," he said, "will have more effect than those of anyone living."

Patton obliged:

> Nearly every boy in America understands how to run an automobile or a tractor. Fewer and fewer American boys understand anything about horses. Owing to shipping difficulties, I think we will never be able to move large bodies of horse cavalry to a foreign theater of war . . . but we should maintain at home horse cavalry, pack artillery, pack trains, horse-drawn artillery, and wagons, so that we would have a group of officers and enlisted men capable of organizing such units overseas from local horses or mules, using equipment, both riding and pack, transported from America . . .
>
> Hap Gay and myself go riding here every day on two captured animals, whose only virtue is that they do not run on gasoline.

*Letter, GSP, Jr., to Colonel Charles B. Odom, New Orleans, July 16, 1945*

As you know, I was disappointed in not going to the Orient, but

I believe that my luck or destiny, or whatever it is, will get me there if there is need for my services. Personally, I do not concur with the rumors current in Washington that the Japs are about to quit. I certainly hope they don't because I think they should be utterly destroyed.

*Letter, GSP, Jr., to Codman, July 18, 1945*

I am more occupied than during combat, as I have to, or feel that I have to, visit all the divisions, inspect them administratively and tactically, and also again visit them when they leave, to say good bye. The result is that I spend a great deal of time flying . . . There is no probability, although there is always a possibility, of a flare-up on the continent.

He was tired, discouraged, burned out, and apparently of little use to anyone. The world had gone to hell. Redeployment and demobilization were dissipating the immense force that the United States had acquired during the war, the Russians seemed about to win the peace, and no one cared – no one except him.

## CHAPTER 39

# The Growing Bitterness

*"One cannot help but feel that Berlin marks the final epitaph of what should have been a great race."*

UNUSUALLY DEPRESSED, his joie de vivre having temporarily abandoned him, Patton tried to settle down to live with the grim fact that he had fought his last campaign. Was then his destiny fulfilled? Had he accomplished all that had been reserved for him? Or would there be one last battle still, one last meeting of arms to decide the fate of civilization?

The Potsdam Conference was in session, and Harry Truman, Clement Attlee, and Joseph Stalin were trying to remake and reorder the new world. But Patton suspected that the results they accomplished would be different from and much less perfect than those he wished to see.

As he told Beatrice later:

> At Potsdam I was just a visitor but later had long talks with George [Marshall] and Harry [Stimson]. Hap Arnold is the only one who understands the Mongols except me. But the rest are waking up.

Major General Floyd Parks, who commanded the U.S. troops in the Berlin Military District, telephoned during the evening of July 19. The Secretary of War, he said, was to review the 2d Armored Division and wanted very much to have Patton with him.

*Letter, GSP, Jr., to Beatrice, July 21, 1945*

I left here at 0630 and got there in two hours and a half. We could have gone faster but for the fact that if one flies over Russian occupied territory, they shoot at you – nice friends. The review was great . . .

Drove to Potsdam and saw the palace you, Nita, my self, and the family visited in 1912 . . .

The place was not hurt but all the furniture and rugs have been taken by the Mongols.

We also saw Berlin which is not nearly as much bashed in as represented.

The Mongols are a bad lot, even the U.S. sector has their guards in it, and I had to have a pass. However, I did not need it. I just pointed to my [Russian] medal and the world was mine . . .

Berlin gave me the blues. We have destroyed what could have been a good race and we [are] about to replace them with Mongolian savages. And all Europe will be communist.

It's said that for the first week after they took it, all women who ran were shot and those who did not were raped. I could have taken it had I been allowed.

Harry [Stimson] looks tired . . .

George [Marshall] was most friendly, almost gushing.

I also saw the President who was nice.

We now have Wacks. Mine is a secretary.

*Letter, GSP, Jr., to sister Nita, July 21, 1945*

I am very much afraid that Europe is going to go Bolshevik, which, if it does, may eventually spread to our country.

*Letter, GSP, Jr., to Codman, July 21, 1945*

One cannot help but feel that Berlin marks the final epitaph of what should have been a great race. I really do not see how they can recover, particularly in view of the activities of some of our Allies, and I am not at all sure that we are not stepping out of the frying pan into the fire by concurring in what is going on. However, this is a personal opinion which probably nobody else shares.

*Letter, GSP, Jr., to Beatrice, July 24, 1945*

Felix [of Luxembourg] spent the night. He is very gloomy over the future of Europe. So are all thinking men who are not running for office.

Patton was happy to go to Prague to receive a decoration from the Czech government at the hands of President Beneš.

A young officer being tried for killing prisoners of war cited Patton's instructions in his defense. Queried by the theater Judge Advocate, Patton replied:

> I made it a habit to talk to every division prior to its going into battle. In all these talks, I emphasized the necessity for violent offensive action, and also the necessity for the proper treatment of prisoners of war, both as to their lives and property. My usual statement was . . . "Kill all the Germans you can, but do not put them up against a wall and kill them. Do your killing while they are still fighting. After a man has surrendered, he should be treated exactly in accordance with the Rules of Land Warfare, and just as you would hope to be treated if you were foolish enough to surrender . . . Americans do not kick people in the teeth after they are down." . . . I have no apologies or excuses to make for any statement which I have made to troops in combat.

To the editors of a division history, he wrote:

> Divisions have souls which they inherit. They have characteristics which they pass on . . . [I] urge you to transmit to future members, those magnificent fighting qualities which you have ever demonstrated.

He flew to Frankfurt on August 1 to accept Eisenhower's invitation to dinner. They dined alone,

> and I learned some interesting facts, particularly what impelled him to order us to halt short of the Moldau River when we could so easily have advanced that far . . . The same hold order of course applied also to the Ninth and First Armies.
>
> It seems that when Churchill, Roosevelt, and Stalin were in Teheran in the fall of 1943, Churchill was convinced that even in the unlikely event of the Allies being able to make a landing on the Continent, they would never be able to cross the Rhine River, and he therefore persuaded FDR to go along with him in asking Stalin to have the Russians capture Berlin and Vienna and gave the Russians a line about a hundred miles west of Berlin. Later when we were going along well and could easily have taken Berlin, Churchill asked Ike to do it, and Ike replied by stating that it was Churchill's fault that the line had been established where it was. I believe this was a great

mistake on his part because, had we taken the country to the Moldau River and Berlin, we would have saved a great deal of agricultural Germany and prevented what I believe historians will consider a horrid crime and great loss of prestige in letting the Russians take the two leading capitals of Europe.

Telling Beatrice of his evening with Eisenhower, Patton said he "learned the inwardness of quite a few things. He did not have a bed of roses either."

*Letter, GSP, Jr., to Beatrice, August 6, 1945*

I am much upset about [opposition at home to] universal service. If we don't have it, we are sunk and soon too. The President now talks of doing it [being prepared] with the N. [National] G. [Guard] – will we never learn?

If there ever was a war breeder, it is the Europe of today. Russia is just like the French Republic of 1870. Germany is out. The Checks hate every one. The French are communistic. The British fools. And we, God knows.

*Diary, August 8*

Gay and I flew to Hanau to inspect and say goodbye to the 6th Armored Division . . . Only 2,500 of the original . . . men were present. In spite of this, the soldiers, more than 12,000, put on a really good show, which proves that the spirit of a unit is something beyond and outside the personnel composing it. Also, that troops who are veterans are good in any unit. However, this virtue of being a veteran does not last after the man has got soft and forgotten his military training, so we cannot base our trust in any future army on the fact that we have some eleven or twelve million veterans to call upon.

At the close of the ride around and before the march past, the massed colors of the division were brought to the front, and I had an opportunity to decorate them and also some officers and men. The ceremony was new to me and very pretty. I will try to have it repeated in other units.

At the close of the Sicilian Campaign I talked to a group of officers from each division . . . to obtain from the men who did it, the means they used to fight, because having studied war since I was about sixteen years old, I have only come across some twelve books which deal with fighting, although there are many hundreds which deal with war. This is because the people who fight either are killed or are inarticulate.

With this end in view, I talked to a selected group . . . and intend to repeat it . . .

Of course, the horrid thought obtrudes itself that, in spite of my efforts – which will probably be filed and forgotten – the tactics of the next war will be written by someone who never fought and who acquired his knowledge by a meticulous study of the regulations of this and the last World War, none of which were ever put into practice in battle. However, I console myself with the thought that I have, in so far as the ability within me lay, done my damndest.

But it seems very queer that we invariably entrust the writing of our regulations for the next war to men totally devoid of any but theoretical knowledge. In this war we were also unfortunate in that our high command in the main consisted of staff officers who, like Marshall, Eisenhower, and McNarney, had practically never exercised command. I think it was this lack of experience which induced them to think of and treat units such as divisions, corps, and Armies as animated tables of organization rather than as living entities.

Lieut. General Bishop Gowlina of the Polish Army came to see me and stayed to lunch. He is a very bright man, speaks perfect English, and hates the Russians with reason. He told me some of their methods . . .

According to the Bishop, more than two million Poles have been taken to Russia for slave labor. In every case . . . they split families . . .

The difficulty in understanding the Russian is that we do not take cognizance of the fact that he is not a European but an Asiatic and therefore thinks deviously. We can no more understand a Russian than a Chinaman or a Japanese and, from what I have seen of them, I have no particular desire to understand them except to ascertain how much lead or iron it takes to kill them. In addition to his other amiable characteristics, the Russian has no regard for human life and is an all out son of a bitch, a barbarian, and a chronic drunk.

Strange to say, I had a letter from General Sibert [12th Army Group G–2] on the question of the Russians, so that apparently for the first time in his career, he is on a good scent.

After the Bishop left, a Mr. G. A. Kemper whom I used to know in Hawaii . . . called. He is now mayor of a town in the British zone and states . . . that he came to Germany in 1936 as a representative of Woolworth . . . Being not a Nazi, according to himself, he was run out of business but was not jailed. He made some remarks which to me sounded sensible to the effect that our military government is handicapped by the necessity of using dug-out Germans – that is, Germans who are so definitely anti-Nazi that they have not held any office since 1933, and are therefore not only inexperienced in current methods of government but are more or less old, whereas the whole cry is for youth.

Under our rules, which demand the total deNazification of Germany, we have to remove everyone who has ever expressed himself in any way as a Nazi or who has paid party dues. It is very evident that anybody who was in business, irrespective of his real sentiments, had to say he was a Nazi and pay dues. The only young people who were not Nazis came out of the internment camps and are therefore either Jews or Communists. We are certainly in a hard position as far as procuring civil servants is concerned.

These were the themes that would occupy his thoughts, poison his mind, and increasingly embitter his outlook during the remaining few months of his life: the managers like Eisenhower and Bedell Smith had been and still were the prominent and powerful persons, and they no longer needed the fighters like Patton; the Russians were unscrupulous beasts who would dominate Europe because they knew what they wanted and because the United States, the only nation strong enough to oppose them, was uninterested, even unaware of their purpose and methods; and denazification was wrong.

Eventually he would come to abhor the American immediate postwar policies, which he believed were the result of a conspiracy of international bankers and labor leaders and Jews and Communists, all of whom were working for the downfall of the United States. Too many changes, it seemed to him, were transforming the world into something alien to his upbringing and social outlook.

*Letter, GSP, Jr., to Beatrice, August 10, 1945*

Well the war is over. We just heard that Japan had quit. Now the horrors of peace, pacafism, and unions will have unlimited sway. I wish I were young enough to fight in the next one. It would be . . . [great] killing Mongols.

I suppose poor George [his son] is all broken up. I would be in his case. Tell him that if I am here in June [when he graduated] I will get a special dispensation and have you and he over for ten days and we will drive all over the campaigns. It would be fun . . .

Last time a war stopped I wrote a poem . . . Now I feel too low. It is hell to be old and passé and know it.

*Diary, August 10*

Another war has ended and with it my usefulness to the world. It is for me personally a very sad thought. Now all that is left to do is to sit around and await the arrival of the undertaker and posthumous immortality. Fortunately, I also have to occupy myself with the de-Nazification and government of Bavaria . . .

I have arranged to have wood cut by the Germans and by prisoners of war so that all the cities of Bavaria will have sufficient wood to heat at least one room for every family. This project is proceeding quite well except in the case of the Displaced Persons who are too worthless to even cut wood to keep themselves warm.

We have also started, by the use of German prisoner of war Signal personnel, to restore German commercial telephone lines. In addition to this, we are working to re-establish railway, canal, and road communications – primarily as a means of redeploying our own troops . . .

I have to occupy myself with inspecting every division, particularly those ordered to the United States . . . I have inspected some ten or twelve divisions at the rate of approximately three a week. In every case, I make a speech along . . . [the same] lines.

It often appeared to be an empty exercise, for even here the old magic was gone. According to George Fisher, who accompanied Patton on one of these trips, the division was lined up and waiting at the airfield when Patton's plane landed.

With the precision of a familiar maneuver the General hit the ground, strode a few paces, and mounted a platform that had been set up for the purpose . . . Patton, resplendent as always, proceeded to give the troops the works.

He never talked very long and he certainly followed no conventions of finished oratory. He would start off rather slowly, and his squeaky, high-pitched voice did not carry very well . . .

I had the personal feeling that the General regularly got himself punch-drunk with profanity. His sulphurous son-of-a-bitching, I thought, was a habit he had permitted himself to form in days when there might have been some reason for him to strike a pose . . .

The reaction of the troops was somewhat mixed. There were many, of course, to whom roughness of oral intercourse was normal and habitual, and it was Patton's habit to act as if this were true of every man in uniform . . .

Stripped of bitching and damning, Patton's farewell to the troops came down to something like this: You have served with the greatest group of soldiers ever assembled anywhere at any time . . . Never forget that you are heroes. And if any civilian – here one must fall back into Pattonese – and if any goddamned civilian ever tries to make fun of your uniform, you are to knock the son of a bitch down . . .

Patton was eternally ready to fight; and if there was no enemy in front of him, there were still some lily-livered civilians back home to be attended to.

But . . . these men who were on their way back home had their own notions about how the civilian situation in the States should be handled. They were willing enough to have their Army commander remind them of the glories of their service under him, but as for the future – well, they had come to a parting of the ways with Patton and all that he stood for . . .

Patton was forever preaching a gospel of warfare that was somehow alien and antipathetic to young Americans who had reluctantly and only temporarily suffered themselves to become soldiers. If in North Africa and Sicily they had listened gravely to his words, it was because they had to . . . [Later] they began to see that Patton was a consistent winner. That was the true basis of Patton's esteem among the rank and file of Third Army. As the war progressed, he was . . . an eagerly followed commander – not because of his theatrics but simply because he had demonstrated beyond question that he knew how to lick Germans better than anybody else.

• • •

Denazification was proceeding satisfactorily. All the clergymen in the American zone had been screened by mid-July, and those without Nazi affiliations were cleared. The work of eradicating Nazi street names and memorials was practically complete. Former Nazis had been excluded from industrial concerns and businesses, as well as removed from the professions. By early August, telephone, telegraph, and radio workers were almost all checked. Soon the German financial institutions would be similarly purged.

On October 11, Stimson was quoted in the Paris edition of the *Herald Tribune* as saying that the Nazi party in the American zone had been eradicated and that German administrators, "purged of Nazi membership and influence," were gradually superseding American military administrators.

On the same day, Patton was suggesting that Eisenhower pass "a word to the people responsible for civil government" to go more slowly on denazification. Too many trained administrators, Patton said, were being removed and too many inexperienced and inefficient officials were being put into office. As for Nazism, he repeated his observation:

> It is no more possible for a man to be a civil servant in Germany and not have paid lip service to Naziism than it is for a man to be a postmaster in America and not have paid at least lip service to the Democratic Party or Republican Party when it is in power.

His refusal to distinguish between Democrats and Republicans on the one hand and Nazis on the other — to say nothing of his slander of the American civil-service system — indicated that he had missed the whole point of the struggle insofar as American public opinion was concerned. His failure to understand a large part of the moral foundation underlying the American support of the war effort would lead to his downfall and disgrace.

All he could see was the little German, the man in the street, whose only responsibility for Nazism was his unwillingness to comprehend its evil.

"I am raising the devil," he wrote Beatrice, "to get enough wood cut to keep the people from freezing this winter."

Four days later, Eisenhower reminded the Third and Seventh Armies that "Nazis should not be allowed to retain wealth, power, or influence merely because they do not hold public office."

*Diary, August 18*

In a letter from Beatrice today she stated that Gerow is to get [that is, to be Commandant of] the [Army] War College. This is too bad, as he was one of the leading mediocre corps commanders in Europe and only got the Fifteenth Army because he was General Eisenhower's personal friend. With the War College gone, there is nothing open to me so far as now seems available. However, things have looked gloomy before and something has always turned up.

At the request of General Juin, I flew to Paris and today returned to the French at the Invalides six sets of colors taken from the French in the war of 1870. It was quite a colorful ceremony . . . There was a crowd of several thousand people and much cheering for Patton. On the way back, Charles de Vaux, the son of Mme. de Vaux, my old friend at Langres, was very nearly shot by the escort when he rushed out to shake my hand.

At dinner with General Juin the remarkable statement was made by him to me that, "It is indeed unfortunate, my General, that the English and the Americans have destroyed in Europe the only sound country — and I do not mean France — therefore the road is now open for the advent of Russian Communism."

The use of the atomic bomb against Japan was most unfortunate because now it gives a lot of vocal but ill-informed people — mostly fascists, communists, and s.o.b.'s assorted — an opportunity to state that the Army, Navy, and Air Forces are no longer necessary as this bomb will either prevent war or destroy the human race. Actually, the bomb is no more revolutionary than the first throwing-stick or javelin or the first cannon or the first submarine. It is simply, as I have often written, a new instrument added to the orchestra of death which is war.

*Letter, GSP, Jr., to Beatrice, August 18, 1945*

I was particularly sorry you were not around yesterday. Juan asked me to come to Paris to hand back some French flags we had taken from the Germans . . .

Yesterday he and I drove to the Invalides in an open car with much screaming of sirens . . .

We then drove to the Arch de Triumph where there was a large crowd, quite a few thousand . . . After playing both national anthems, I took a wreath which cost me $100.00 and kneeling on one knee put it on the tank. Then they played "to the dead." Then I signed the Golden Book – France is full of them.

I think giving Gerow the W. C. [War College] is a joke. He was the poorest corps commander in France . . . I guess there is nothing left for me but the undertaker. However, after when the future seemed bleak I have lit on my feet – heres hoping. I can always resign.

General Herr, former Chief of Cavalry, replied to Patton's letter:

Reference your Parthian shot about my not accepting command of the Armored Corps, I will counter by saying the Cavalry might also be in better position than it now is if you had not refused command of the 1st Cavalry Division. Anyway Marshall would never have given me the power that was essential to command, and am sure that I could never have tolerated him and his evasive methods.

*Letter, GSP, Jr., to Frederick Ayer, August 21, 1945*

The advent of the atomic bomb was no more startling than was the act of the first man who picked up a rock and bashed out the brains of another man, thereby spoiling the age-old method of fighting with teeth and toe-nails. Certainly the atomic bomb was not as startling as the first cannon or the first gasoline motor or the first submarine. I am not decrying the intelligence of those who devised it, but I am decrying the lack of intelligence of those who will use it as a means of making our country defenseless. The only way to stop atomic bombing of a country by self-propelled bombs, which is what we will get at the beginning of the next war, is to be able to invade the country sending the bombs and destroy their place of construction. We have proved definitely that you cannot put factories out from the air. As a matter of fact, I know considerably more about the bomb than I am at liberty to state, but . . . the Germans had not progressed anywhere with theirs and they were using a different atom; namely, hydrogen.

He went to Salzburg as the guest of Clark and Keyes, then at St. Martin witnessed a demonstration by the dressage team from Vienna's Spanish Riding School and their famous Lipizzaner horses.

On the same day that Bedell Smith telephoned to congratulate the

Third Army on the progress of its denazification program, Patton's chief of staff, Gay, was issuing a somewhat ambiguous memorandum to the Third Army G-5, the staff officer concerned most directly with the occupation and government of Germany. Gay told him to be sure to comply with the regulations and with the established policies but to use care and discretion; borderline cases who were good administrators or good technicians, he seemed to be saying, were to be given a break.

On August 22, Eisenhower reminded the Eastern and Western Military Districts to provide stateless persons with high standards of accommodations and to care for Jews in special Jewish centers. "Wherever necessary," he said, "suitable accommodations will be requisitioned from the German population."

More specifically on August 23, Eisenhower advised Patton that "obliteration" of Nazism was a major United States war aim and that a Joint Chiefs of Staff directive, which he cited, clearly prohibited the retention of Nazis for administrative necessity, convenience, or expediency. Denazification, he warned Patton, was "a most delicate subject both here and at home" which "our governmental representatives as well as newspapers have been quick to seize upon."

*Letter, GSP, Jr., to Col. Hugh H. McGee, New York, August 23, 1945*

In my opinion and strictly for your private ear, we never had a better chance of producing another war than we have in Europe now. I have never seen so much vitriolic hatred, mistrust, and avarice as exists here today. Furthermore, as you know, a certain proportion of the people with whom we are dealing do not have Occidental minds which makes it even more difficult if not impossible to come to an understanding with them. I doubt if the top blows off very soon, but unless something very radical happens and happens within a reasonable time, the top will blow off, probably after we have redeployed our army.

*Letter, GSP, Jr., to Beatrice, August 23, 1945*

I feel very let down but am still very busy and will be for a month or two more . . .

The atomic bomb was most unfortunate and may be the means of destroying our country. Also the radio said this morning that C.I.O. Murray [the labor leader] wants a bigger "New Deal" — where in

> Hell do they think money comes from? or do they simply want to destroy our form of government and go communist? If they knew as much about Russia as I do, they would not be so crazy to be communists.

On the following day he wrote Beatrice that a man who said he knew William Wood, the husband of Beatrice's eldest half sister,

> came to see me to day with the most fantastic stories about the Mongols. The trouble is I am inclined to believe them. He is very anti-Jew. Is he a Jew? Can he be trusted?

Later that day he wrote again to Beatrice:

> I heard a lot more about those unmitigated bastards the Mongols . . . No one takes the least interest except that the Germans and the Poles hope to fight on our side and soon. The M's will not take over all Europe until we have reduced [our military forces] to about 6 divisions, then they will.

On August 26, the Third Army requested permission to discontinue arrests of Nazis in the lowest category of party officials coming under the regulation that required automatic detention; and to release those being held in prison awaiting trial — or as the letter said, "without trial," which implied an un-American procedure.

> *Diary, August 27*
>
> I attended the Military Government meeting at Frankfurt. There were a number of speeches by General Eisenhower and his various assistants, all of which were unrealistic and in every case the chief interest of the speaker was to say nothing which could be used against him. It is very patent that what the Military Government is trying to do is undemocratic and follows practically Gestapo methods. It is very probable, to me it seems evident, that the doctrines being executed or attempted are those promulgated by Morgenthau at the Quebec Conference which were not approved by either the Secretary of War or the Secretary of State. It was the meeting in which Morgenthau and later Roosevelt, copying him, stated that Germany was to be [de-industrialized and demilitarized and] made into an agricultural

state. It is patently impossible for Germany to be an agricultural state. First, because there is not enough in Germany for the country to feed itself on such a basis, and, second, because if Germany has no purchasing power, we will not be able to sell our goods to her and, therefore, our markets will be very considerably restricted.

If any [news]paper opposed to the Democrats should get hold of the stuff that is being put out by those in charge of the Military Government of Germany, it could produce very bad results for the Democratic government [in Washington].

I stated that in my opinion Germany was so completely blacked out that so far as military resistance was concerned they were not a menace and that what we had to look out for was Russia. This caused considerable furore.

Referring to the Third Army letter mailed on the previous day, Patton proposed releasing some of the interned Nazis, "many of whom," he said, "were either aged or pregnant." Whether this was a joke or merely his extravagant language, it made a poor impression on his colleagues.

*Letter, GSP, Jr., to Beatrice, August 27, 1945*

I have been at Frankfurt for a civil government conference. If what we are doing is "Liberty, then give me death."

I can't see how Americans can sink so low. It is semitic, and I am sure of it.

*Diary, August 29*

Today we received a letter . . . in which we were told to give the Jews special accommodations. If for Jews, why not Catholics, Mormons, etc? I called up General Bull, Deputy Chief of Staff for Eisenhower, and called his attention to possible repercussions but got nowhere. He simply stated that he had investigated it and that the letter had considerable background. Naturally I intend to carry out the instructions to the limit of my capacity in spite of my personal feelings against them and in spite of my fear that in doing such things we will lay ourselves open to just criticism.

We are also turning over to the French several hundred thousand prisoners of war to be used as slave labor in France. It is amusing to recall that we fought the Revolution in defense of the rights of man and the Civil War to abolish slavery and have now gone back on both principles.

In a letter of instructions to the Third and Seventh Armies dated August 31, USFET warned that the care of displaced persons remained a major military objective. In many instances, Germans living near the DP camps were immeasurably better off. "Where this is so, military government is not doing its job." No DPs were to be lodged in tents after September 15, even if German civilians had to be moved from their homes in order to make them available to the DPs.

On the same day, the Third Army issued a bulletin stating that denazification was causing hardships by paralyzing essential services. The removal of so many laboratory technicians from their jobs was provoking the spread of typhoid; the exclusion of so many forestry experts from employment was leading to a fuel shortage.

Something was obviously out of kilter. USFET and the Third Army seemed to be operating on different wavelengths.

*Letter, GSP, Jr., to Beatrice, August 31, 1945*

I am going to quit the army when I leave here or so I think now . . .

Ike and George [Marshall] and some others of the union know where people are going but they never tell me. I see no job that I could take. But I have been at a dead end before and have gotten out O.K. Something may turn up. Any how we have the boat and the new horses . . .

The stuff in the papers about fraternization is all wet . . . All that sort of writing is done by Jews to get revenge. Actually the Germans are the only decent people left in Europe. It's a choice between them and the Russians. I prefer the Germans. So do our cousins . . .

I got Van S. Merle Smith for ADC. He plays squash and badminton and is a gentleman.

*Diary, August 31*

Today we received an order to investigate the possibilities of destroying the Eagle's Nest, Hitler's special home at Berchtesgaden, so that it would not become a Nazi shrine . . . If anything could make it a Nazi shrine, it would be to destroy it. Furthermore, the first thing our soldiers like to visit when on pass is this lookout. To date some 40,000 have seen it. I wrote a letter to General Eisenhower pointing out these facts and trust the order will not be enforced.

I also wrote a letter to the Secretary of War, Mr. Stimson, on the question of the pro-Jewish influence in the Military Government of Germany. I dared do this because when I was in Washington, he showed me a great deal of correspondence he had had with the Secretary of State and Mr. Morgenthau prior to the Quebec Conference.

*Diary, September 1, 1945*

Father Bernard Hubbard, SJ, "The Glacier Priest," spent last night with us and showed us his movies. He is very anti-Russian and anti-Semitic and talks very well when he forgets to advertise himself.

I decided to rewrite the letter to Mr. Stimson as I think that even when writing to him, I stuck my neck too far out.

CHAPTER 40

# The Approaching Showdown

*"I am frankly opposed to this war criminal stuff. It is not cricket and is semitic."*

*Letter, GSP, Jr., to Beatrice, September 2, 1945*

Every thing I say is not only misquoted but also put out of context . . .

I can't see what future I have but I am certainly getting a great education in S.O.B's . . .

I had never heard that we fought to de-natzify Germany — live and learn. What we are doing is to utterly destroy the only semi-modern state in Europe so that Russia can swallow the whole.

HE MAY NEVER HAVE SEEN Eisenhower's directive of June 29, for he was then in the United Sates. This was a major document. Drawing on the official communiqué of the Crimea or Yalta Conference, it set forth the policy governing the removal and exclusion of Nazis and German militarists from public office and from positions of importance in quasi-public and private enterprises.

"One of the principal objectives of the war," the directive stated categorically, "is 'to destroy German militarism and Nazism' and 'to remove all Nazi and militarist influences' . . . from the cultural and economic life of the German people." Nominal members of the Nazi party could be retained for administrative purposes, but the question was, who was nominal?

As Lieutenant General Lucius D. Clay, Deputy Military Governor, U.S. Group, Control Council in Berlin, explained to Patton, everyone realized that removing Nazis from governmental positions resulted in less effective administrative machinery. The President's orders permitted the retention of "nominal Nazis," but defined them in such a way as to make the number that could be retained for administrative convenience quite small.

Many Germans had told Clay they could not understand why any Nazi was kept in office. It was perhaps true that many Nazis joined the party for the same reason that some Americans became Democrats or Republicans — in order to gain public office. But the Nazis were "part and parcel" of the group being charged with starting the war. Policies from home rigidly excluded Nazis from government office and particularly from places of prominence.

In other words, there was little ambiguity about certain high party officials and those charged with crimes against humanity, who were in the mandatory arrest category. It was the smaller men who caused the confusion, and four months after the end of the war, in September, the Third Army headquarters was still grappling with the problem, admitting not only considerable inconsistency in the practices carried out but also clear cases where policy had been misinterpreted and misapplied.

An example of the difficulty involved came to light when the XX Corps chief of staff phoned Gay for help. Under the current regulations, he said, it was necessary to remove from important positions and to place under arrest all Germans in the automatic arrest category. But what about a certain mine director who was the most capable engineer in Bavaria? No one could replace him, and to remove him would decrease the production of coal. Gay authorized — subject, of course, to approval by higher authority — placing the man in house arrest and keeping him at work.

At this time, a telegram from Eisenhower questioned the Third Army on alleged mistreatment of Jewish displaced persons. Brigadier General Mickelsen, Chief of the Displaced Persons Branch of G-5, USFET, would soon make a formal inspection of the Jewish camps in the Eastern Military District. Eisenhower specified that stateless Jews who had yet to be moved to special Jewish camps be so transferred before the inspection.

If Patton paid any attention to — or was even aware of — these matters, he made no mention of them. He was engaged in a far more fascinating activity.

In order to amuse himself and also to instruct coming generations of soldiers, he was writing a book entitled "War as I Saw It," soon to be renamed "War as I Knew It." It was a compendium of observations, lessons learned, strictures, and the like, all derived from his experience, all set forth with the usual Patton verve, clarity, and bravura.

He sent chapters to friends at home, Harbord, Summerall, Codman, and others, asking them to consider the manuscript confidential. One of the recipients was Under Secretary of War Patterson, soon to become Secretary, whom Patton characterized in a letter to Beatrice as "quite a nice man . . . He is a military historian and got a DSC in the infantry in the last war. He may lack moral guts."

The manuscript provided the basis for a much edited – or, in Pentagon terminology, "sanitized" – version that Mrs. Patton published after the general's death.

On September 6, he went to Berlin to represent Eisenhower at an inter-Allied military parade.

*Letter, GSP, Jr., to Beatrice, September 11, 1945*

I think I was never so tired and stiff as I was yesterday. I did not realize how much out of condition I was.

I left here after lunch on the 6th and flew to Berlin where there was a guard [of honor] from the 82d Airborne. It was realy very nice in a tin soldier sort of way. Then I went to Ike's villa which was turned over to me – very nice.

I went for a sail in an 8-meter which is realy a nice boat and sleeps four, but is pretty . . .

On the 7th there was an inter-allied review to celebrate V-J day. U.S., English, French, and Russians each had 1,000 men and 50 vehicles in the parade. Marshall Sukov [Zhukov] was senior, I was next. He was in full dress uniform much like comic opera and covered with medals. He is short, rather fat and has a prehensile chin like an ape but good blue eyes. He was in the cavalry. Our troops looked the best, the Russians next.

The R's had a lot of new heavy tanks of which they are very proud. The Marshall asked me how I liked them. I said I did not, and we had quite an argument. Apparently I was the first person ever to disagree with him.

From the parade I flew to Pilsen and reviewed the 16th Armored Division.

On the 8th we went to Brow in Sudeten land and went on a duck shoot . . . This lasted till about 3 PM and then we started walking through potato patches after Hungarian partridges. We walked till 6 PM so were on our feet about ten hours.

Then we had a dance till 10 – at least I went to bed then. We got up at 4:30 and went deer hunting, walking over mountains for two hours. I did not see a deer. But all the mushrooms, shown in the colored plates [in the encyclopedia], red with yellow spots, yellow with red spots . . . red, green, pink, and yellow, hundreds of them.

*Letter, GSP, Jr., to Beatrice, September 11, 1945*

I just won another battle – only this time it was against me. Hap and I have a little course of jumps which we have been working on for a couple of weeks. There was one red and white pole not over 3–6 [three feet, six inches] but the highest we had so that I have been making all sorts of excuses to my self for not jumping. I just jumped it.

Remember after the last war I got timid too, but beat it down . . .

Count von Luckner called on me to day. He wants a job teaching the Germans democracy.

*Letter, Eisenhower to GSP, Jr., September 11, 1945*

As you know, I have announced a firm policy of uprooting the whole Nazi organization regardless of the fact that we may sometimes suffer from local administrative inefficiency. Reduced to its fundamentals, the United States entered this war as a foe of Naziism; victory is not complete until we have eliminated from positions of responsibility and, in appropriate cases properly punished, every active adherent to the Nazi party.

I know that certain field commanders have felt that some modifications to this policy should be made. That question has long since been decided. We will not compromise with Naziism in any way.

I wish you would make sure that all your subordinate commanders realize that the discussional stage of this question is long past and any expressed opposition to the faithful execution of this order cannot be regarded leniently by me. I expect just as loyal service in execution of this and other policies applying to the German occupation as I received during the war.

More important seemed a letter from Maxwell Taylor, Superintendent of the Military Academy, who solicited Patton's views on what changes he would suggest at West Point. More weight, Patton replied, should be given to the Tactical Department and less to the academic aptitudes.

I say this as a goat but without bitterness because although I was turned back I outrank all members of my initial class.

I am convinced that nothing I learned in electricty or hydraulics or in higher mathematics or in drawing in any way contributed to my military career. Therefore I would markedly reduce or wholly jetison the above subjects.

I am convinced that much more emphasis should be placed on history . . . The purpose of history . . . is to learn how human beings react when exposed to the danger of wounds or death, and how high ranking individuals react when submittted to the onerous responsibility of conducting war or the preparations for war. The acquisition of knowledge concerning the dates or places on which certain events transpired is immaterial . . .

I have regretted all my life that I did not know more languages . . .

I believe that gallantry and a desire to attain military prestige can be cultivated . . .

The greatest thing you and I got out of it was our profound belief in the greatness of our motto [Duty, Honor, Country].

*Letter, GSP, Jr., to Beatrice, September 14, 1945*

I was going to Nancy in the morning to become a [honorary] citizen but Ike phoned he is coming here so I had best stay and see him. Perhaps I can make him see the menace of the M's. They have 300,000 troops in Checo. now and are running 200,000 more in, and we are pulling out – getting the boys home by Xmas. It may well result in getting them back in the trenches by spring . . .

I am frankly opposed to this war criminal stuff. It is not cricket and is semitic. I am also opposed to sending PW's to work as slaves in foreign lands [in particular, to France] where many will be starved to death . . .

Some times I think I will simply resign and not be a further party to the degradation of my country.

*Diary, September 15*

Late yesterday afternoon I was notified that General Eisenhower would arrive . . . near Munich at 0930 this morning, having flown from the Riviera . . .

I later found out that the purpose of his visit was to inspect the DP camps, particularly at least one occupied by Jews, to determine the condition of these Jews in order that he may write a letter to Mr. Truman.

Harkins and I went there to greet him in spite of the fact he had suggested that I not put myself out. I have always felt that an officer should be present to meet in person an officer of the next higher grade and in this case, General Eisenhower was also my friend.

Harkins and I waited until 12.00 o'clock, at which time we heard that General Eisenhower had been unable to land and had had to go to Paris to get down, using the beam at the field there.

While waiting, I talked to Brigadier General Mickelsen who is G–5 for Eisenhower's headquarters [in charge of DP affairs], and he showed me a letter from President Truman to General Eisenhower which was unnecessarily harsh and in much less considerate language than I would have used in cussing out a 2nd Lieutenant.

Mickelsen also showed me the report of a man named Harrison (which report was inclosed in the President's letter) on the condition of Displaced Persons in Europe, particularly Jews. Harrison is a member of the State Department. The report contained many allegations against General Eisenhower, the Army, and the various commanders.

One of the chief complaints is that the DP's are kept in camps under guard. Of course, Harrison is ignorant of the fact that if they were not kept under guard they would not stay in the camps, would spread over the country like locusts, and would eventually have to be rounded up after quite a few of them had been shot and quite a few Germans murdered and pillaged.

The brilliant Mr. Harrison further objected to the sanitary conditions, again being ignorant of the fact that we frequently have to use force in order to prevent the inmates, Germans, Jews, and other people, from defecating on the floor when ample facilities are provided outside.

Evidently the virus started by Morgenthau and Baruch of a Semitic revenge against all Germans is still working. Harrison and his associates indicate that they feel German civilians should be removed from houses for the purpose of housing Displaced Persons.

There are two errors in this assumption. First, when we remove an individual German, we punish an individual German while the punishment is not intended for the individual but for the race. Furthermore, it is against my Anglo-Saxon conscience to remove a person from a house, which is a punishment, without due process of law. In the second place, Harrison and his ilk believe that the Displaced Person is a human being, which he is not, and this applies particularly to the Jews who are lower than animals. I remember once at Troina in Sicily, General Gay said that it wasn't a question of the people living with the dirty animals but of the animals living with the dirty people. At that time he had never seen a Displaced Jew.

Furthermore, I do not see why Jews should be treated any better or any worse than Catholics, Protestants, Mohammedans, or Mormons. However, it seems apparent that we will have to do this, and I am going to do it as painlessly as possible by taking a certain group of buildings in several cities and placing the Jews, who do not exceed 20,000, in sort of improved ghettos.

To put the Jews on farms would be disastrous because it would break up the agricultural economy of Bavaria on which we depend for providing what food is provided which is not paid for by American taxpayers.

We arranged a good itinerary for General Eisenhower which we will put into effect when he comes. Unquestionably he is just as much under fire as is anyone else and in this particular case, very unjustly so.

If the people in Washington would stop trying to find fault with others and wake up to the extent of making the Russians take back the Poles and other people whom they have not permitted to return, the situation in Displaced Persons would be much ameliorated . . .

It seems to be quite a hell of a mess.

*Letter, GSP, Jr., to Keith Merrill, Washington, D.C., September 16, 1945*

I have just been handed a Mr. Parker W. Buhrman as an advisor on political affairs. He was sent to me by [Robert] Murphy and is alleged to have been a member of the Foreign Service.

Please let me know what you know about him and, if you know nothing, speak to someone who does, as it is always a good idea to get the dope on one's assistants. Particularly – does he belong to the chosen people?

*Diary, September 16*

General Eisenhower . . . arrived at 2000, and we had supper and spent the evening talking over the situation. In fact we talked until 3.00 o'clock in the morning.

General Eisenhower felt at that time that he would undoubtedly become [U.S. Army] Chief of Staff and that McNarney was slated to take over his job in Europe. He asked me, in view of that situation, what I wanted to do.

I told him I did not care to serve under General McNarney, not because I had anything personal against him but because I thought it unseemly for a man with my combat record to serve under a man who had never heard a gun go off.

I stated there were only two jobs in the United States which I felt I could take. One was President of the Army War College, which I believed was taken, and the other was Commanding General of the Army Ground Forces.

General Eisenhower stated that the Army War College would probably be a combined institution with the Army, Navy, and Air Force [eventually the National War College], and that in that event, the first President would be a naval officer since the former president had been General DeWitt, an Army officer. This seems to put the War College out of the running.

With reference to the . . . Army Ground Forces, Eisenhower stated he saw no reason why he as Chief of Staff could not remove Devers and put me in. However, he stated he felt that the Army Air Force would become The Air Force with a Chief of Staff of its own and a promotion system of its own, in which case he could see no reason for having an Army Ground Force.

I agreed with him. Therefore, at the present writing, it would seem the only thing I can do is go home and retire. However, Eisenhower asked me to remain at least three months after he left so as to get things running quietly. I tentatively agreed to this.

He did so because he was a good soldier and because he owed so much to Eisenhower.

*Diary, September 17*

Eisenhower and I drove to Munich where we inspected a Baltic Displaced Persons camp. The Baltic people are the best of the Displaced Persons and the camp was extremely clean in all respects . . . We were both, I think, very much pleased with the conditions here . . .

We drove for about 45 minutes to a Jewish camp . . . established in what had been a German hospital. The buildings were therefore in a good state of repair when the Jews arrived but were in a bad state of repair when we arrived, because these Jewish DP's, or at least a majority of them, have no sense of human relationships. They decline, where practicable, to use latrines, preferring to relieve themselves on the floor . . .

This happened to be the feast of Yom Kippur, so they were all collected in a large wooden building which they called a synogogue. It behooved General Eisenhower to make a speech to them. We entered the synagogue which was packed with the greatest stinking bunch of humanity I have ever seen. When we got about half way up, the head rabbi, who was dressed in a fur hat similar to that worn by Henry VIII of England and in a surplice heavily embroidered and very filthy, came down and met the General. Also a copy of the Talmud, I think it is called, written on a sheet and rolled around a stick, was carried by one of the attending physicians.

First, a Jewish civilian made a very long speech which nobody seemed inclined to translate. Then General Eisenhower mounted the platform and I went up behind him, and he made a short and excellent speech, which was translated paragraph by paragraph.

However, the smell was so terrible that I almost fainted and actually about three hours later lost my lunch as the result of remembering it.

From here we went to the Headquarters of the XX Corps, where General Craig gave us an excellent lunch which I, however, was unable to partake of owing to my nausea.

After lunch we visited a . . . model German workers' village . . . It was my purpose to turn this over into a Jewish concentration camp. Here we met the most talkative Jewish female, an American who was running the UNRRA part of the camp . . .

After inspecting this and making another speech, which I avoided, General Eisenhower directed that sufficient Germans be evicted from houses contiguous to the concentration camp so that the density per capita of DP's and Germans should be approximately the same. Also that the American guards be removed from the camp except for a standby guard in case of a riot, and that guards composed of unarmed inmates take over the police of the camp proper . . .

After this we returned home and went for a fishing trip on the lake which, while not successful, at least removed from our minds the nauseous odors and aspects of the camps we had inspected.

We then took as long and as hot a bath as we could stand to remove from our persons the germs which must have accumulated during the day.

I believe this was the first time General Eisenhower had inspected or seen much of Displaced Persons. Of course, I have seen them since the beginning and marvelled that beings alleged to be made in the form of God can look the way they do or act the way they act.

*Diary, September 18*

Ike and I drove to the airfield . . . I took off for Pilsen . . . to carry out an invitation extended to me by General Harmon to go on a shoot.

Harmon met me at Pilsen airport and we immediately took off by motor, preceded by a Czech army car, to the chateau of the Prince Schwartzenburg family. Schwartzenburg was the only general who actually ever defeated Napoleon on the field of battle before Waterloo . . .

The chateau which is extremely large, having 140 rooms, was built around 1700, and is therefore not a sensible building but a show-off place . . .

As usual in Europe, the first thing to do was to eat. This meal consisted of salad, soup, three kinds of meat, four or five kinds of wine, and an unlimited quantity of beer.

After this was taken aboard we went through the chateau which reminded me very much of Bannerman's [store near West Point, an emporium]. I have never seen so much armor and weapons assembled in one place with total disregard of historical sequence. That is, you would find a weapon of late 1400 crossed over one of early 1800. There were four complete suits of plate [armor]. One of these was a working suit of about 1500, which was a good one. The rest were fluted and fixed up, really tin dress clothes of a later date. In the armory proper there was a tremendous collection of 1600 steel helmets and earlier morions of the Spanish type, also a number of pikes of the Gustavus Adolphus period which, however, had been sawed off. There were two or three wheel-lock guns which were priceless. We were also shown a great deal of what I believe is called Boule furniture — that is, furniture composed of ebony, tortoise shell, and ivory. The whole tour of the chateau proper took about two hours.

Then we were taken to a sporting museum which was another chateau built prior to the first one we visited. Here they had every animal ever killed on the estate stuffed . . .

Behind this museum was a zoo containing a bunch of very dejected animals with a sign on it in Russian . . . saying they were not to kill or tease the animals . . .

About an hour before dark we drove into the woods where we met some more game-keepers and were placed on stands. The stand I was on was an elevated tower about thirty feet high camouflaged in the trees with a couple of peep holes. There was a bench up there, and all one had to do was sit down and wait until the keeper, who stood guard with a pair of binoculars, announced that the deer had arrived. Unfortunately for me these deer did not arrive until it was practically dark. I got one shot at 138 paces and luckily got a hit. However, since I was using a carbine, the animal did not go down, so we had to sit and wait for him to die and listen to his mournful coughing.

When it was quite dark, we went to get him and heard him in the woods about fifty feet from us, but it was decided that the best thing to do was to wait until morning. I believe this was correct, for had we pursued him, it might have been difficult to find him. As it was, he was very easily located in the morning.

Unquestionably the peep-sight on the American carbine and M-1 rifle is not suitable for fighting in a bad light.

*Diary, September 19*

When I woke up in the morning and looked out, the stag had already arrived and was being properly arranged in the center of the courtyard where they had made a bed of green leaves for him and laid him down with his head propped up with a stick. It was amusing to note that where he had first been laid on the stone and bled a little, three old women were scrubbing on their knees.

We went down and had some pictures taken, then had breakfast at which they served cognac which nobody drank. Then, having thanked our friends for their courtesy, we departed for another shooting place belonging to a prince whose name I do not know.

We were met by the heir apparent who took us to a wood road where his father, mother, and wife, riding in a carriage, met us. Here we dismounted and walked through the woods for a considerable distance. I at once shot a fallow deer at about 200 yards standing. I think I probably hit him as he went down and the other two deer who were with him ran in the opposite direction. We walked after these and came upon them in about half an hour. I gave Harmon the shot, but he did not kill the deer; apparently he shot high.

We then returned to the hunting lodge where the ladies and the older prince met us and we had sandwiches and a bottle of white wine. From there we drove back to Pilsen and took the airplane for Bad Tolz, which we reached about 3:15.

Stimson had submitted his resignation, and on that day, September 19, it took effect and Patterson, the Undersecretary, became Secretary of War. For Patton's future, Stimson's departure was unfortunate. No one had supported and protected Patton during trying times as had Stimson. In all the incidents that had occurred during the war, Stimson's understanding had been critical in saving Patton from relief and figurative exile.

Now another incident was about to take place and Patton would miss Stimson's backing. Codman too was gone, as was Bradley, who had returned to head the Veterans' Administration in Washington, and these men who had contributed stability and judgment might have helped save Patton from himself.

During the past few months, Gay had been Patton's closest adviser. Gay was as uninterested in the occupation and as unqualified to deal with it as the boss himself. Perhaps more so. Inclined to joking and jesting — his nickname was Happy, shortened to Hap — he was essentially a plain man. He was utterly devoted and completely loyal to Patton, "dumb loyal," someone said, followed orders faithfully, did what he was told to do without pointing out that there might be other sides to the question. And thus he failed to provide diverging points of view that needed consideration before decisions were made. A splendid companion who liked to ride and to hunt, a superb staff officer who ran the military details of the headquarters with exceptional efficiency, he lacked breadth and depth of intellectual capacity. His prejudices and politics paralleled Patton's, and as a consequence reinforced instead of correcting them. If Gay's journal accurately reflected his concerns, he — much like the Old Man — closely followed the movements and the activities of the troop units and little else. He failed to understand the profound issues of his time and the serious nature of the human problems involved, and in Patton's hour of need, through no deliberate fault of his own, Gay let Patton down.

Unfortunately for Patton, even Gay, who might at least have helped keep up his spirits, was away. Along with Muller and Koch, he was on leave in the United States at the moment of the showdown which was about to occur.

Eisenhower's visit to the displaced persons' camps on September 15 foreshadowed the showdown, but the opening gun in what some described as a campaign to "get" Patton, sounded in a story that appeared in the New York *Times* on September 19. It was by Raymond Daniell who reported that "Nazis still hold some of the best jobs in commerce and industry" because military government was more concerned with preserving German industrial efficiency than with fulfilling the objectives for which the war had been fought.

This general accusation became explicitly directed against Patton when Daniell further reported overhearing a remark by the Third Army commander. Patton had asked a military government fiscal officer who was investigating bankers "if he did not think it 'silly' to try to get rid of 'the most intelligent' people in Germany."

Patton's concerns remained essentially military, and his focus stayed on the Third Army.

*Letter, GSP, Jr., to Graves, September 21, 1945*

Over here we are sloughing away, the Third Army being very much like a person with leprosy, dropping off an arm or a leg or a toe practically every day, while the displaced sons-of-bitches in the various camps are blooming like green trees.

He was terribly depressed and terribly angry. Everyone was hurrying to get home, military discipline was vanishing, and the wrong people were benefiting from everything.

Yet he had a premonition of what was to come.

*Letter, GSP, Jr., to Beatrice, September 21, 1945*

I think that leaving here sooner than I had intended is perhaps fortunate, as this radical political emphasis on redeployment (spelled votes) is likely to undoe all we have done. I think it is the most utterly unpatriotic thing imaginable. No one will say a word — no one! ! ! . . .

I told all of them [Gay, Muller, Koch] that if they get a chance to catch a good job, they had better take it as we are just a corpse loosing a toe one day and a finger the next.

Well the squash court is working so I get some exercise . . .

As I may be home by Xmas don't send me any presents here. If I am not relieved by that time, I shall try and get a leave.

*Diary, September 21*

General Louis Craig came in to see me this morning to explain how he had arranged for taking care of the Jews. It has been necessary for him, against his and my instincts, to move twenty-two rich German families from their houses in order to put the animals in them. I told Craig to take pictures of the houses before they were occupied by the Jews and then subsequently. I also told him to move the Germans with as much consideration as possible and to give them transportation to move as much of their decent property out as they could.

Craig . . . told me he had inspected another Jewish camp yesterday in which he found men and women using adjacent toilets which were not covered in any way although screens were available to make the toilets individually isolated, which the Jews were too lazy to put up.

He said the conditions and filth were unspeakable. In one room he found ten people, six men and four women, occupying four double beds. Either the Displaced Persons never had any sense of decency or else they lost it all during their period of internment by the Germans. My personal opinion is that no people could have sunk to the level of degradation these have reached in the short space of four years.

It sounded very much like what he had said about the Arabs, the Egyptians, and the Sicilians, all of whom he had classified as subhuman. Now it was the eastern Europeans, whose appearance, dress, manner, language, customs, beliefs, behavior, and condition he was unable to fathom. They were poverty-stricken, not always clean, coming from a primitive culture and society without such amenities as toilets, and their manners, according to Anglo-Saxon standards, were frequently less than exquisite. Many of them had been compelled to divest themselves of some human qualities in order to survive the war and the holocaust.

His lack of understanding of these odd and apparently inferior persons was the logical extension of his boyhood in southern California, which gave him a special view of Mexicans and Indians; and of his southern heritage, which shaped his outlook toward blacks. In part he simply reflected a parochial interpretation of the non-American world, a vision that was middle-American, populist, and the essence of Babbittry and conformity, where anyone who was different was undoubtedly bad. His snobbery based on wealth, breeding, social advantage, and privilege, together with his father's insistence on being a gentleman in the stereotyped country-club image, also played a role.

Lehman, Morgenthau, Baruch, when Patton entertained them during the war, were perfectly acceptable, as was Rabbi Brickner; they were cultured, moneyed, dignified, clean, and therefore gentlemen despite their Jewish faith. They were Jewish Wasps. In contrast, Patton characterized the wife of a man prominent in government as "a very Jewy Jewess," and he meant it to be a double pejorative.

He shared whatever endemic anti-Semitism existed in America, in the U.S. Army, and among the rich and fashionable during the early and middle years of the twentieth century. He had listened with interest and sympathy to Beatrice's half brother Charles, who believed passionately in the reality of the long-discredited Protocols of Zion.

Now, although he kept his feelings private and discreet, confined to his diary, his personal letters, and his conversation with friends, his emotions seemed on the verge of going out of control.

CHAPTER 41

# The Showdown

*"The more I see of people the more I regret that I survived the war."*

WHEN SEVERAL NEWSPAPER CORRESPONDENTS at Third Army headquarters asked Patton's press officer, Major Ernest C. Deane, whether they could meet with Patton, Deane passed their request to the chief of staff. Patton agreed to talk with the reporters, and the conference was scheduled for September 22, immediately after the normal Saturday morning briefing, which had replaced the daily wartime sessions. The journalists could attend the briefing, and at the end of the staff reports, they could interview Patton. Several days beforehand, Deane had a notice of the event posted on the bulletin board of the nearby Bad Wiessee press camp.

Only eleven newspapermen attended the staff briefing that day. Most were Third Army regulars – among them, Kathleen McLaughlin of the New York *Times,* Nora Waln of the *Atlantic Monthly,* and Pierre J. Huss of the International News Service. There were also four newcomers, Ray Daniell of the New York *Times,* Carl Levin of the New York *Herald Tribune,* Edward P. Morgan of the Chicago *Daily News,* and Daniell's wife, Tania Long of the New York *Times.* McLaughlin had informed them by telephone of the conference, and they drove from Nuremburg the previous evening, spent the night at Bad Wiessee, and accompanied the others to the headquarters.

As soon as the staff meeting was over, Patton, who seemed irritable and on edge, started to leave. He apparently assumed that the correspondents were interested primarily in occupation matters, and he expected his staff officer in charge, Colonel Dalferes, his G–5, to answer their questions. Daniell, Levin, and Morgan asked whether Patton himself would give them a few minutes. He consented.

No stenographic notes were made, but according to Gay's journal, the questions put to Patton seemed to suggest that denazification was proceeding too slowly. The reporters said that Dr. Friedrich Schaeffer, President-Minister of Bavaria, ought to be removed from office because he disagreed with the denazification program.

Patton replied that all the Germans appointed to office did as they were told or were dismissed. They followed Third Army instructions, which were based on directives from higher headquarters. No known Nazis, he asserted, held government posts.

He then brought up the analogy he had used before. Suppose, he said, America had lost the war. If the conquering nation removed persons in political power from office, it would have to exclude all the Republicans and Democrats who held government posts. If Patton indiscriminately turned efficient people out of their jobs, he would create an administrative turmoil that would very likely cause the deaths of many innocent persons.

Repeating that denazification was being carried out in an orderly manner, Patton said that further screenings of Germans to discover Nazis would continue. But what he thought was more essential was to get the Germans back on an economic basis comparable with that of the surrounding countries. That would save the American taxpayers, who could not bear to see people starve, from an inordinate drain on their resources for the purpose of supporting Germany. At the moment, he said, he was trying to get enough wood cut and enough stoves provided so that the displaced persons and the German people would not freeze to death that winter.

Reduced to these terms, the exchange seemed harmless. But it was not so much what was said as how the interview was conducted. Gay stated categorically that when Daniell, Levin, and Morgan were dissatisfied with Patton's answers, they tried to put words into his mouth. According to another recollection, these three reporters,

> making use of only partial truths, construed the answers to their questions to suit their own purposes and . . . tried to bring discredit upon General Patton.

Deane recalled that things went wrong from the start. As early as the staff briefing, the general was made upset and angry by the report of an officer who talked too long and too loudly. Then,

> Daniell, Levin, and Morgan moved right in, and Tania too. Nothing went right with us from that moment.
>
> Just what was said back and forth nobody could say for certain, even an hour after it was all over . . .
>
> Was there actually a frameup . . . against General Patton? A . . . correspondent . . . later said he overheard the three of them plotting at breakfast that morning before the press conference, to needle the General and make him lose his temper.

Concurring in this point of view was Frank E. Mason, who was in Europe at the time. With credentials as a correspondent of the North American Newspaper Alliance, he was on a confidential mission for former President Herbert Hoover. Mason had been president of the International News Service, had a distinguished career in broadcasting, and was prominent in public affairs. He was a neighbor in Leesburg, Virginia, of Marshall and other influential men, including Fletcher, Patton's West Point classmate and Marshall's close friend.

Concerned over the evident strength of the Russians, Mason wrote on September 26, to Roy W. Howard, president of the Scripps-Howard newspapers, with copies to Hoover, Harbord, and Fletcher, that

> The New York Times and the New York Herald Tribune have come to the aid of PM [the liberal New York newspaper]'s campaign to run interference for a Red government in Germany. I am sure that this is innocent as far as the Times and Trib are concerned at home. But I don't ascribe any innocence to their correspondents over here who are provoking the story.

Mason believed that a conspiracy existed to make sure that only those Germans who were acceptable to the Russians and to the German Communists were appointed to local government posts in the American zone. To this end, he felt, radical journalists attacked general officers who named anti-Communist German officials. If these newspapermen succeeded in their campaign, the governments in the American zone, and the British as well, would be Russian puppets.

Only two forces, Mason said, stood in the way of complete Soviet domination of Germany: "the dominant Catholic Centrum party" in Bavaria, supported by "Cardinal Faulhaber of Munich [who for] long had an overt record of defying Hitler and the Nazis"; and the U.S. Army. The attack against these forces could be seen in PM reporter Victor Bernstein's attempt to assassinate the Cardinal's reputation and in the vilification by

> the team of Levin, Daniell, and Morgan [who] started to work out on Patton. Morgan's part was to stand close to Patton with a pipe in his mouth and insolently puff smoke into Patton's face . . .
>
> Levin and Daniell, using a sneering tone, with the attitude of a criminal prosecutor interrogating a hardened criminal, and both talking at once at times, went after Patton for permitting a German named Schaeffer to hold public office in Munich. The Schaeffer case is confused. He was once in a concentration camp and in wrong with the Germans and at other times held municipal jobs under them. I can't say whether or not he was a member of the [Nazi] party.
>
> The other correspondents stood back and not one of them got into the crossfire of Levin and Daniell attacking Patton . . .
>
> Remarks were made by Levin and Daniell in a condescending tone . . .
>
> Levin was so disagreeable . . . that Patton once said, "You are so smart. You know everything. Why do you ask me?"
>
> Obviously they were trying to get Patton to lose his temper . . .
>
> Colonel Dalferes, Patton's G–5, answered the questions for about five minutes as they were so technical about government situation that in fairness Patton could not be expected to know the details . . .
>
> One of the regular correspondents here at Bad Wiessee . . . told me that he had heard the three . . . plotting at the breakfast table how they would get Patton.

No doubt the conversation at the breakfast table turned on how best to get at Patton's basic feelings. The reporters wanted a significant story, and they suspected strongly, in the light of previous Patton statements, that he had little sympathy with the denazification policies. If they could get him to say so, that was news.

Deane later said,

> There is no denying that General Patton lost his temper on that awful morning and put himself into the hands of his enemies, but God knows he was provoked into it deliberately. I'll never believe otherwise.

George Fisher, who was there, had another impression:

> There was to be the regular, fast-moving review of the weekend situation for the orientation of section chiefs. This would then be followed by a second briefing for the special edification of certain representatives of the American press who had come to Bad Tolz to obtain enlightenment on some matters pertaining to the occupation of the liberated territories . . .
>
> [Patton] decided he would have none of it. He was in a hurry, he said, and hadn't time to wait through a double briefing. So the press parties were ushered into the operations room [for the regular review].
>
> These particular men were unknown to most of us, yet it seemed fairly obvious that in their field they were men of distinction . . .
>
> With the end of the last [staff] presentation, Patton jumped to his feet and made as if to dash off. At the same instant, up popped the journalists with a few questions.
>
> It did seem that what they wanted to know was reasonable enough. And they wanted the information from the Army commander himself instead of from his staff. And they bore credentials from Washington as well as from Frankfurt. And they did evidence a degree of deference toward the Old Man that was notable.
>
> But Patton was just not in the mood. Something was gnawing his guts that morning. His own people knew enough to let him alone at such moments. But of course the press could not wait . . . Patton . . . barked out the first things that happened to come into his head.
>
> Lunch that noon was a serious affair. Everyone had a notion that the fat was now in the fire.

In his diary entry of September 22, Patton recorded his own reaction:

> This morning we had the ragtag and bobtail remnants of the great U.S. press present . . . [I] always had them on my side. Today there was very apparent hostility, not against me personally, but against the Army in general. The special gripe seems to be that we are backing the wrong horse in the choice of the Governor or President of Bavaria. The temerity of the newspaper man in suggesting that he knew more about who we should have than I do, although I know nothing, made me mad which I think is what they wanted.

To admit, even privately in his diary, that he knew "nothing" was a remarkable statement. Or was he joking with himself?

> There is a very apparent Semitic influence in the press. They are trying to do two things: First, implement Communism, and second, see that all business men of German ancestry and non-Jewish antecedents are thrown out of their jobs. They have utterly lost the Anglo-Saxon conception of justice and feel that a man can be kicked out because somebody else says he is a Nazi. They were evidently quite shocked when I told them I would kick nobody out without the successful proof of guilt before a court of law.
>
> If people have time to read anything besides the number of points which will get a soldier home, I will probably make the front page but, frankly, do not give a damn.
>
> The attitude of the American people as evinced by the press and the radio is such [that] I am inclined to think I made a great mistake in serving them for nearly forty years, although I had a very good time doing it.
>
> Another point which the press harped on was the fact that we were doing too much for the Germans to the detriment of the DP's, most of whom are Jews. I could not give the answer to that one because the answer is that in my opinion and that of most non-political officers, it is vitally necessary for us to build Germany up now as a buffer state against Russia. In fact, I am afraid we have waited too long. If we let Germany and the German people be completely disintegrated and starved, they will certainly fall for Communism and the fall of Germany for Communism will write the epitaph of Democracy in the United States.
>
> The more I see of people I regret that I survived the war.

*Letter, GSP, Jr., to Gaffey, Armored School, Fort Knox, September 22, 1945*

When I was in the States, I sensed that things were pretty tumultuous, but you have no idea how tumultuous they have gotten here. All the correspondents who have nothing better to do go around and attempt to form political parties and then accuse me of being either pro-Fascist, pro-Republican, or pro-Communist, according to their desires.

*Letter, GSP, Jr., to Beatrice, September 22, 1945*

I will probably be in the headlines before you get this. As the press is trying to quote me as being more interested in restoring order in Germany than in catching Natzies. I can't tell them the truth that unless we restore Germany we will insure that Communism takes America.

The New York *Times* of September 23, quoted Patton as having said, "The Nazi thing is just like a Democrat-Republican election fight," and the story appeared in papers across the country. Accompanying the account was a great deal of editorial comment, which questioned not only Patton's understanding of what the war had been about, but also the army's ability to conduct the occupation and run military government.

One of Schaeffer's ministers, it turned out, had been in the military forces as a general staff officer in German-occupied Poland, France, and Italy; two others were also in a mandatory removal category because of their wartime careers; and another had falsified his *Fragebogen,* the questionnaire that all Germans seeking employment had to fill in. Schaeffer was forced to dismiss them, but he entered a formal protest against the "hardship and injustice" of denazification.

By then the Third Army had discharged from internment camps about 8000 Germans in the lowest mandatory arrest category. Probably stirred by the story in the New York *Times,* Eisenhower telegraphed instructions to stop the practice. Patton agreed to halt further action but ordered his own military government detachments not to re-arrest those already released.

*Letter, GSP, Jr., to Mrs. M. B. Horan, New York, September 24, 1945*

When General Gay cannot go [riding with him], I take my stable sergeant who is a paroled German Colonel of Cavalry, and former Captain of the German Olympic team and a very good man. I have never had any animus against the professional soldiers who fought against me. That was what they were hired to do.

Patton would soon receive remarkably good advice that reached him too late. An American who had been born and educated in Germany before coming to the United States and who served in the U.S. Army, for a time under Patton's command, wrote to make known his distress over "the progress of our policy" in Germany. Newspapers at home indicated that Patton had "an entirely disinterested attitude toward that program," that Patton knew and cared little about political parties in Bavaria, that Patton failed to sponsor "liberal elements" in German government. Many American soldiers learned at Malmédy, Buchenwald, Dachau, and Belsen about "the Nazis and their inhuman, fiendish methods." All Germans "were guilty to a degree but not equally guilty," and the paramount task of the Occupation was to find those Germans who were worthier than others of American support. "In the name of the common man, in the name of Justice, and those millions who perished in these death factories of Oswiecim," the writer pleaded, "COME HOME. Come home quickly and leave the job to rule our sector of Germany to a man who will see our interests through to a successful end."

Unfortunately, there was no place for Patton to go, no proper assignment, no place in the United States for him. And he could hardly bear to think of retiring because destiny or fate might be saving him for the coming struggle with the Bolsheviks.

There was no reply to the letter. Marked at the top was the word "File."

*Diary, September 25*

I have just finished reading a resume of the Potsdam Conference as set out in "Army Talks."

If Mars and the Devil had gotten together with the intention of producing a violent and prompt war, they could not have written a greater document. As is always the case with Allies, it is a compromise, but it is a compromise in which one of the high contracting parties was uncompromising, namely Russia. Russia knows what she wants (domination of the world) and is laying her plans accordingly. We, on the other hand, and England and France to a lesser extent, don't know what we want and get less than nothing as the result . . . Under the present system all that has been produced is a hot bed of anarchy and hopelessness which is an ideal germinating ground for Communism.

Just before lunch Beedle Smith called and said that because I was one of his best friends, I caused him more trouble than any other man. He then read me extracts from headlines in the United States covering the remarks I was alleged to have made on Saturday.

I told him now that the war was over, I did not propose to be jumped on any more by the press, and if they did not like what I

> said, I would resign so I could be in a position to talk back. He urged me not to do this and said there were going to be many changes soon and that both he and I might be out of jobs. He then suggested I have a press conference this afternoon and clarify my statements.
>
> I did this and wrote out a statement . . . [and had a] stenographic report of remarks made during the conference.
>
> From what two of the old correspondents told me, the whole thing was the result of the unlucky presence of two itinerant correspondents . . . both pink.
>
> A Mr. Mason who used to be in the I.N.S. and who alleges he is a friend of Colonel Rob Fletcher's, came in with a long story about the attempt on the part of Jewish and Communist elements to put the bug on people like myself. While his story sounded plausible, I have developed such a low opinion of all newspaper people that I think he is probably a liar.

"Fate gave me a ticket for the bleachers for the second half of the great Levin-Patton bout," Frank Mason wrote.

> I was here by accident for the second press conference which was supposed to straighten out the first one. I had phoned Patton's headquarters from Munich, and much to my surprise when I asked for the General's aide, Patton himself came on the phone.

Patton asked Mason to identify himself, and Mason said he had last seen Patton right after World War I, when Mason was an officer at Trier in the headquarters of General Preston Brown, Pershing's deputy chief of staff for the Occupation. Patton had been "very kind to me when I was a young instructor at the Army Intelligence School at Langres, where he had his Tank Center," and Patton insisted that Mason come to visit him and sent a staff car to bring him to Bad Tolz.

In the presence of Harkins, Patton and Mason talked for 35 minutes. "What do you think of the progress we are making denazifying Germany?" Patton asked. "We are doing pretty well, aren't we?"

Mason replied, "General, I think the so-called denazification of Germany is a lot of B.S."

"There is no dictaphone here," Patton responded, " — so do I."

Mason said that the Allied failure to take Berlin, Vienna, and Prague provided the foundation for the next war.

Patton nodded. "I could have taken two of them," he said.

Mason then mentioned the prisoner-of-war-camp scandals.

"What scandals?" Patton asked.

"Arresting people, holding them incommunicado for five months."

"Yes, yes," Patton said. "I know."

At 4 P.M., as Mason went out of Patton's office, he found the press outside and waiting to meet with Patton. Deane asked Mason to stay, "so I went back in."

*Transcript of Press Conference, Bad Tolz, Germany, 1615, September 25, 1945*

Patton: I am sorry I haven't got anything exciting for you this afternoon. Owing to some difficulties which we sometimes incur, I am going to become extremely like most other generals and read a statement . . .

As the direct result of our last talk together, apparently some startling headlines appeared in the home papers. I say "apparently" because I only know of them through hearsay. Of course, I understand that the reports you all send in do not contain headlines, and that these headlines are written afterwards at home.

My point . . . is that some of these things alleged to have been said by me might possibly reflect on my commanding officer, General Eisenhower. That would be very unjust. His policy and orders exactly reflect the terms of the Potsdam Conference . . .

General Eisenhower reiterated these instructions in a personal letter to both District Commanders; that is, to both myself and General Keyes, which I quote as follows . . .

It is my considered opinion that I am carrying out these directives with the same vigor and loyalty as I carried out those which resulted in the victories at Casablanca, El Guettar, Sicily, and here. I am convinced that as the result of my efforts I shall be just as successful here as I was in those other places. God knows, I was pretty successful. However, you must remember that results cannot be obtained overnight . . . It will certainly take a reasonable time to de-Nazify and reorganize our portion of Germany.

Unquestionably when I made the comparison of so vile a thing as Nazism with political parties, I was unfortunate in the selection of analogies. The point I was and am trying to bring out is that in Germany practically all or at least a very large percentage of tradespeople, small businessmen, and even professional men such as doctors and lawyers were beholden to the Nazi party, particularly for the patronage which permitted them to carry on their businesses and professions, and that therefore many of them had to give lip service, but lip service only, and I would extend this to mean that paying dues was nothing but a form of black mail and holding their jobes. If we kick them out, all this bunch, we will so retard the reorganization of Bavaria . . . that we will certainly be guilty of the death by starvation or freezing of women, children, and old men this winter.

To do so, he repeated, would be un-American.

I will now give you seven minutes in which to ask whatever questions you may want to.

Question: General, if you recall, what was that direct quote about political parties?

Patton: I said that Naziism might well be compared to any of the parties at home, either Republican or Democrat. I also referred to my cousin who remained a postmaster for years by judicious flip-flops, and I don't consider him a son of a gun either.

He went on to amplify this, much as he had before.

Question: Will there be removals in the future?

Patton: Yes.

Again he talked of the administrative vacuum that might be created by denazifying too quickly.

Deane: Would it be appropriate to give the official figure on how many Nazis have been taken out so far? I have heard the figure 47,000 from G–5 –

Patton: Yes. I believe the figure 47,000 sticks in my mind . . .

Question: General . . . aren't there some who consider Friedrich Schaeffer was a Nazi?

Patton: He was in an internment camp and so far as I know has not been proved to be a Nazi . . . Schaeffer was, as a matter of fact, picked out before I got here. So far, we have not definitely proved he is a misfit, but we have no brief for him or against him. What we are trying to do is to provide a governing body for Bavaria.

Question: Some American paper on Monday said that USFET wanted this man removed.

Patton: I have no knowledge of any such request, but you can be sure that if USFET wanted a man removed, he would go and go promptly.

Mason's impression of the meeting:

There is not much to report about this conference except that . . . [it] was decent and courteous in tone . . .

He [Patton] is sound. He is American. He is getting hell for daring to block the radicals in running interference for a red government in Germany.

Mason then drove all night in the rain from Bad Tolz to Wiesbaden to discuss the entire matter at breakfast with Eisenhower's chief of public relations, Colonel Fitzgerald, whom Mason had known in Washington when Mason was a Special Assistant to Secretary of the Navy Frank Knox. Fitzgerald was flying to Berlin that morning for a meeting which Eisenhower would attend, and Mason felt that if Fitzgerald told Eisenhower about the plot against Patton, Eisenhower would better be able to resist pressure from the "small but vociferous group of newspapermen led by PM with the Stars and Stripes echo." He gave Fitzgerald copies of his letter to Howard, with the other addresses listed, and of an unaddressed memorandum he had written and checked for accuracy with Deane, Huss, and Deane's assistant, Lieutenant Paul S. Gauthier. At lunch Mason saw Brigadier General R. B. Lovett, Eisenhower's adjutant general, and handed him copies of the same documents.

*Letter, GSP, Jr., to Codman, September 25, 1945*

I am again at one of those critical periods when I may be sent home in a hurry at any moment.

You certainly aren't missing much by not being here.

*Letter, GSP, Jr., to Beatrice, September 25, 1945*

If the Devil and Moses had gotten together to plan for an early and certain resumption of hostilities, they could not have produced a finer document than the attached ["Army Talks"].

As always among allies, it is a compromise but Russia did the least compromising since Russia knows what she wants (world conquest) and the rest don't.

[Son] George need not worry about missing a war. The next is on the way.

*Diary, September 25*

After supper I received a telegram from General Eisenhower stating that I had been accused of differing with him in the conduct of the de-Nazification of Bavaria and asking me to fly up either Wednesday or Thursday, whenever the weather permitted.

It may well be that the Philistines have at last got me. On the other hand, every time I have been in serious trouble or thought I was, it has turned out to my advantage. At least, this time I do not have to go on the defensive.

*Telegram, Eisenhower to GSP, Jr., September 25, 1945*

Press reports make it appear that you and I are of opposite conviction concerning method to be pursued in denazification of Germany and that in spite of repeated orders, you have given public expression to your own views on the matter. I simply cannot believe that these reports are accurate, and Smith tells me that in a telephone conversation with you he understood, in spite of the poor connection, that you stated you were incorrectly quoted. He tells me also that you are holding a press conference immediately to straighten out the matter. I hope you are completely successful because this question is a very serious one . . . Please take the first opportunity to fly up here on a good weather day and see me for an hour.

*Letter, GSP, Jr., to Beatrice, September 26, 1945*

It may be that I will get home as soon as this. You are even now probably being bothered by reporters.

The whole thing is a deliberate mis-quote with the intent of getting me in trouble because I am not "pink." . . .

If Ike etc. don't like what I do, they can relieve me. Then I will resign, not retire, and can tell the world a few truths which will be worth having.

DD asked me to see him to day but I said it would have to be tomorrow. I am going shooting to day with Betois [Bethouard]. Must start now.

*Diary, September 26*

Weather conditions prevented my flying to Frankfurt, and I was very glad of this as I had three times refused General Beth[o]uard's invitation to go chamois hunting.

Major Merle-Smith and I left by car . . . crossed the border . . . and were met . . . We transferred into peeps . . . My guide had remarkable eyes and could see chamois where I could find them with high powered field glasses. I had one shot at about three hundred yards with the Springfield .06 with the sniper's sight. I was all right for windage but about a foot low.

We . . . stopped in a native's house to let a snow storm pass. I noticed the man was limping and asked what was the matter. Since I do not know German I had to guess at his reply but it seemed to me that he had cut his foot with an axe and that it was nearly rotted off. We got the first-aid kit out of the peep and repaired his foot.

We then walked for about two hours and a half in the snow and rain but saw no chamois . . .

We then drove to a swiss chalet which I have a sneaking suspicion belonged to the former Emperor of Austria, and had a very good French dinner, including oysters which I had to eat without dressing — not me, the oysters.

After dinner General Beth[o]uard presented me with a really extremely handsome 8 mm. Mauser rifle with set trigger and telescopic sight. Unquestionably he had stolen it but he must have stolen it from a gun store as it was perfectly new.

On that day, September 26, USFET promulgated Military Law Number 8. It read: "In order further to diminish the influence of Nazism in Germany," there was to be no employment for members of the Nazi party or affiliate organizations except as ordinary laborers.

On the same day, at 11 A.M., Bedell Smith met with reporters at Frankfurt-am-Main. Among them were Daniell, Levin, and Morgan.

Smith opened with a brief statement of Eisenhower's occupation policies. No subordinate, Smith added, would dare "ignore or vitiate" Eisenhower's orders or subvert his program.

"Tell us, General," a reporter said, "whether you think that program can be carried out by people who are temperamentally and emotionally in disagreement with it."

"I don't think," Smith replied, "we have anybody who is temperamentally or emotionally in disagreement with it."

> Question: Wouldn't General Patton's statement indicate that . . . ?
>
> Smith: No.
>
> Question: General Smith, are you familiar with General Patton's statement on Saturday?
>
> Smith: I am familiar only with the press reports . . .
>
> Question: . . . He said that this Nazi thing is just like a Democratic Republican election fight. For this reason, he said, he personally never has seen the necessity for the de-Nazification program . . .
>
> He said he didn't know what reactionaries were, but he did ask, "What do you want — a lot of Communists?" . . .
>
> And then he said that Germans are innocent of Nazism until proven guilty, and then the fragebogens . . . he said, "What the hell is a fragebogen? I don't know what that means." . .
>
> He said that 98% of the Nazis were only pushed into it anyway.
>
> Smith: . . . General Patton is a soldier and will carry out his orders.
>
> Question: . . . There are still a few Nazis carrying on a deliberate program of sabotage, withholding fragebogen, slowing them up —
>
> Smith: Are you sure of that — I mean, can you support that statement? Because if you can, it is very interesting, it will be helpful to us. I count on you to help us in what goes on here and I act on things that you tell me.
>
> Question: I would be in a pretty weak position to support it, frankly, but —
>
> Smith: Now, I act on things like that that you tell me . . .
>
> General Patton will be up here sometime next week to give an account of his stewardship with General Eisenhower.
>
> Question: Is that on the record?
>
> Smith: You may say he is making a report to General Eisenhower as to the present state of Bavaria . . .

A reporter pointed out that families of high-ranking Nazis were still living in luxurious homes, that the daughter of Frank, the notorious governor of Poland, was occupying a large house containing much loot and even working for the U.S. Army, and that other such instances existed.

"When you run into things like that," Smith said, "slip it to me, will you?"

The point was, a reporter said, Patton had expressed "views in direct contradiction to everything he was asked to carry out."

It was "quite wrong," Smith admitted, for a subordinate of Eisenhower's to do that.

More to the point, a reporter said, Patton's "political opinions have filtered down to his junior officers."

"That is the great danger," Smith said.

It was Patton's "incompatibility" with Eisenhower's directives that bothered the newspapermen.

"Well, what you say," Smith admitted, "is very interesting."

Smith himself, he went on to say, was not nearly so concerned about political parties or institutions with Nazi antecedents in Bavaria – they were "easy to eliminate." He was concerned with the "very strong ultra conservative party in Bavaria, and I say that advisedly, being a Catholic myself." That group was no "excrescence like the Nazi party," but it was deeply rooted in the region. Schaeffer, the Minister-President of Bavaria, was no Nazi; he was "ultra conservative."

Schaeffer, a reporter suggested, had offered to resign "because his Nazis were kicked out."

"Has he really offered to resign?" Smith asked.

"We were told he had."

"Well," Smith said, Schaeffer had talked about resigning but never had.

According to Colonel Dalferes, Patton's G–5, a reporter said, Dalferes had Schaeffer's resignation in writing and could use it any time he wished.

Getting back to the main point, wasn't it true that Patton's statements on denazification were "in direct contradiction" to those of Eisenhower?

"It depends, fellows," Smith replied, "on how you read it and how you interpret the intentions in the ideas of the individual . . . Possibly I have been naive, but . . . Patton will carry out his orders . . ."

The reporters said they doubted that Patton knew "anything about politics" and they objected to his "double talks." In conferences with the press, Patton said he supported Eisenhower's instructions "to the fullest extent"; then he reverted to a completely different point of view.

"Well," Smith said, "let's . . . see what his actions are."

The "smart Nazis," the reporters suggested, were "playing a clever game by allying themselves with the Bavarians," the ultra-conservatives, and this discouraged the "social democratic and left wing parties," particularly since "we" – the Americans – "are doing everything that we can to make the Bavarian Peoples Party as strong as it can be."

"Well," Smith said, "we shouldn't do that. That is the reactionary party."

Question: . . . how will that affect our relationship with Cardinal Faulhaber? . . .

Smith: I don't know. I don't have any idea.

Question: . . . The Cardinal . . . didn't want any playing with the Social Democrats.

Smith: Well, it's entirely within his prerogative, of course.

Question: But it's defeating our purpose . . .

Smith: . . . We are not going to interfere with the freedom of religious worship . . .

Question: I think the discussion is confused.

Taking another tack, the questioner asked whether it would be healthy if the Americans could accomplish all their occupation aims by using Nazis "who very subtly had played along with you" and remained in the background but in actual control.

Smith: Well, the statement you make is completely incompatible. If I say that you have accomplished the orientation . . . toward Western ideals and democracy, it's inconceivable with Nazis in the saddle. Can you reconcile that?

Question: Well, no, except, General, that what you have down there is exactly that . . . What you have is a lot of machinery that is working, but it is working with Nazis.

Smith: I don't quite understand you. I'm afraid I'm obtuse.

But he was sure that Bavaria would become democratized and that that could not be done with Nazis remaining in control. In any event, it was clear that "we are in the process of de-Nazifying." The real argument, he continued, was over "how effectively it is being carried forward." Smith's answer to his own question was that "I am not prepared to state that it has been carried out effectively in every case." What he suggested was that everyone wait a week and see whether there wasn't a "marked improvement."

"Has the War Department asked General Eisenhower for a report on this question?"

"No," Smith said, "they have a great deal of confidence in General Eisenhower, I think."

Smith was somewhat shaken. And on that note the conference ended. It was hardly one of Bedell Smith's best performances.

According to an unsigned memorandum among the papers of Frederick Ayer, the transcript of Bedell Smith's press conference clearly showed that Daniell, Levin, and Morgan put into effect

> a definite scheme to undermine and discredit General Patton. Their method was to sow seeds of doubt as to whether or not General Patton was loyal to General Eisenhower . . .
>
> Many influential United States citizens feel that there exists today a well organized group with definitely laid plans to bring discredit upon the Army and Navy; and that General Patton having news value, like General M[a]cArthur, was one of the first to feel the effect of their venom, and that later this group will attack others, for instance General Bradley, General Eisenhower, and perhaps certain high ranking Naval officers. It is highly probable that Mr. Levin, Mr. Morgan, and Mr. Daniels are tools of this group but definite proof of this is at present lacking.

Mason had no doubts. In a letter to Frederick Ayer, he later wrote:

> The Daniell-Levin-Morgan plot to destroy Patton . . . was successful [because] Bernstein of PM was the most powerful force in Germany in 1945 because he had the support of Harry Dexter White and Henry Morgenthau . . . Laughlin Curry, David K. Niles, and Alger Hiss.

*Edward P. Morgan, "Patton is Called on Carpet," Des Moines* Tribune, *September 26, 1945, page 1*

General Eisenhower has summoned Gen. George S. Patton, Jr., to Frankfurt to give an accounting of his "stewardship" as military governor of Bavaria.

This action follows Patton's statement . . . that he saw no need for

> a sweeping de-Nazification program in Germany . . . The famous combat soldier is being called on the carpet to explain the situation in Bavaria, where a German political scandal of major proportions is brewing . . .
>
> Some leading American newspapers have demanded Patton's removal on the basis of his now celebrated Saturday interview at which he revealed that many of his views clashed with the declared American policy of ruthlessly purging Nazis from any and all important positions in Germany, either public or private . . .
>
> Patton's remarkable comment to reporters that the Nazi question was as simple as a Democratic-Republican election scrap at home . . . may be enough to detonate an explosion in Bavarian politics, which, many observers think, already has been too long delayed — due to the general's own "reactionary" attitude . . .
>
> The original American military government teams . . . were primarily concerned with getting some semblance of normalcy established; firing Nazis was a secondary consideration.
>
> Since Bavaria is predominantly Catholic, they, not unsurprisingly, contacted individuals in the traditionally Bavaria's People's party.
>
> But, while not out and out Nazis, a lot of these people including Schaeffer had managed to play along with them during Hitler's regime without suffering much personal damage . . .
>
> They were far more afraid now that Bavaria would go left politically than they were of playing with individual Nazis . . .
>
> Although this pattern was drawn before General Patton moved into the area as commander, his critics charge that he and his officers not only condoned but encouraged this state of affairs, which systematically and deliberately excluded Communists and Social Democrats from a large measure of Bavarian political life.
>
> General Patton himself said . . . that "anarchy" might well be the alternative to the current regime and left no doubt that he had no use for "radicals" . . .
>
> General Patton Tuesday indorsed [Eisenhower's] sentiments, but no sooner had he done so than he contradicted them . . .
>
> It is such a policy of so-called expediency that the latest Eisenhower directives say clearly will not be permitted.

When Mason returned to the United States in November, he learned from Fletcher that Marshall wished to see him. On the following morning, "in order to serve the ends of truth and justice," Mason spent 90 minutes with Marshall discussing the whole affair. He left with Marshall a letter, dated November 4. In it he said that the service of the church in Leesburg that Marshall usually attended had as the scriptural lesson that morning, "Then went the Pharisees and took counsel how they might entangle him in his talk." (Matthew XXII-15.) That sentence, Mason said, covered the Patton incident.

Three men and a woman, Mason continued,

> came down to stage the Patton attack . . .
>
> Then they went back to General Eisenhower's headquarters to entangle W. Bedell Smith . . . I would say that they succeeded with Bedell just about as well as they did with Patton, except that the press was asleep at the switch and apparently did not get the significance of the words finessed into Bedell's mouth. I say finessed because it is inconceivable that an officer of W.B. Smith's unusual intelligence and keen mind should have wittingly laid himself so wide open . . .
>
> The remarks attributed to Bedell Smith that the Catholic conservatives . . . are of more concern and more troublesome than Nazis is about on a par with the remarks attributed to George Patton comparing Republicans and Democrats with the Nazis.
>
> For surely Bedell Smith isn't setting the United States Army against Catholicism or conservatism per se in order to run interference, in a Kerensky role, for the Sovietizing of the American zone in Germany . . .
>
> The United States Army is now building a record which will lay itself open to charges of having created such chaos as to make it appear that some of our representatives and officials deliberately desired to throw the American zone into ultimate Russian control.
>
> In the meantime, while the Frankfurt high command seems to be immersed with and worried about political trends toward conservatism . . . the American forces in Germany have deteriorated as combat outfits far below any acceptable ordinary peace-time standards . . .
>
> The Stars and Stripes is generally credited with much of the responsibility for bad morale . . .
>
> The pressures on commanding officers are to coddle displaced persons, inspect Jewish camps and keep them happy, to explain soldiers' gripes to the B Bag column in Stars and Stripes, everything apparently except to reactivate quickly into first class fighting units the remnants of their outfits shattered by re-deployment . . .

With such a large number of the interpreter activities in the hands of German, Austrian, and Polish Jewish refugees, it is questionable whether adequate checks have been established to protect these refugees now in American uniforms, many as U.S. Army officers, from indulging in natural revenge for what they have suffered. Unfortunately, some of these recent refugees, who are now U.S. Army officers, are more versed in Gestapo methods than they are in American traditions.

In the mountains of the French zone of occupation, Patton was having a thoroughly enjoyable time.

*Diary, September 27*

We had breakfast at 0430 and, with a new guide, proceeded up a new canyon. We saw two groups of chamois which the guide determined by the use of a telescope contained no warrantable heads . . . driving down the valley when we saw a chamois . . . at a range of about 1,000 yards. We made a long stalk and when we got within 100 yards he saw us and ran away . . . Sgt. Terill pointed out another chamois on the opposite side. We made a quick stalk on him and fired from behind a rock at a range of 350 meters. I was very lucky in hitting him with the first shot of my new rifle . . .

The assault on me in the papers is still going on but is losing its steam.

Murphy had dinner with Patton and advised relieving Schaeffer as Minister-President but keeping him as Minister of Finance. He thought that the "setup in Bavaria" might be changed "from rightest leanings to more Social Democrats with a little lean to the left."

Patton said he had no brief for any of the Germans. They did what they were told to do. If anyone above Patton ordered anybody removed, Patton would see that he was "removed pronto."

He was talking big. For he knew he was out of his depth, and he felt vaguely that he was being victimized by those on the political right as well as by those on the political left. He also had a distinct impression that something important was going to happen on the following day when he went to see Eisenhower.

# CHAPTER 42

# The Relief

*"Am I weak or a coward? Am I putting my posthumous reputation above my present honor? God how I wish I knew."*

*Diary, September 29*

Yesterday the weather was unflyable so Merle-Smith and I left by car for Frankfurt . . .

As we drove along, I was following my practice of forty years in deciding how I would attack various positions that presented themselves in the changing landscape or how I would emplace troops for rear guard action in the same country when suddenly I realized that I had fought my last war and other people would have to be picking positions . . .

The ride reminded me of a similar one Codman and I took from Knutsford to London . . . when I was strongly of the impression I was going to be relieved and sent home – if not tried. I did not believe yesterday I would be tried, but I thought I might be relieved of command.

After a drive of seven and a half hours, we reached General Eisenhower's headquarters. Ike was quite friendly and gave me a long oration on my inability to keep my mouth shut. I told him that in this particular case the words I was said to have said had been deliberately altered.

It was strange, Patton's inability or unwillingness to hear and understand what he had said.

One curious thing came up in the course of the conversation. I was thinking yesterday that perhaps my greatest virtue and my greatest fault was my honesty and lack of ulterior motive. Ike said my greatest virtue and my greatest fault was my audacity.

He stated he was certainly at fault as much as I was in that, knowing my strength and weakness as he did, he should not have put me in as Military Governor. I told him it was my considered opinion that Bavaria was the best governed state in Germany . . . We had probably removed and de-Nazified better than any other state . . .

Ike said that had he possessed any adequate command for me at the time, he would have given it to me rather than have me act as Military Governor of Bavaria. He then was apparently struck with an idea, which probably was acting on his part, that since Gerow was going home, it might be a good idea to transfer me to the Fifteenth Army whose mission it is to write the account of the history and tactics of the war.

He talked about this . . . and said I might be criticized because I would be taking the place of a three-star General, although he too had been an Army commander.

I told him in my opinion I should be simply relieved, but he said he did not intend to do that and had had no pressure from the States to that effect.

I said then I thought I should be allowed to continue the command of the Third Army and the government of Bavaria.

He said he felt on mature thought I should certainly continue for ten days or two weeks and then he thought I should take command of the Fifteenth Army because, while he had complete confidence I would do my full duty as I understood it, I did not, in his opinion, believe in the policies being put into effect and that, while I would not have ever expressed these views to my staff, they had all absorbed them from me in the same way they absorbed my battle system.

At the present moment I am of two minds. If I am kicked upstairs to the Fifteenth Army, should I accept or should I ask for relief and put in my resignation? By adopting the latter course, I would save my self-respect at the expense of my reputation but, on the other hand, would become a martyr too soon. It is my belief that when the catchword "de-Nazification" has worn itself out and when people see it is merely a form of stimulating Bolshevism, there will be a flop of the pendulum in the opposite direction.

When that occurs, I can state that I accepted the job with the Fifteenth Army because I was reluctant, in fact unwilling, to be a party to the destruction of Germany under the pretense of de-Nazification. Further, that the utterly un-American and almost Gestapo methods of de-Nazification were so abhorrent to my Anglo-Saxon mind as to be practically indigestible. Further, that I believe Germany should not be destroyed but rather rebuilt as a buffer against the real danger, which is Bolsheivsm from Russia.

These were illusions of grandeur and glory.

During the course of the interview, General Eisenhower brought in General Adcock, his G-5, and a Professor Dorn. Apparently the Professor is the person who provides Adcock with all his information. He is a very slick individual – I think a pure German, and very probably a Communist in disguise. I had great difficulty in not losing my temper with him, but knew that if I did, I would simply get more adverse reports than I already had.

Eisenhower also said during the conversation that several of his staff officers had reported to him that I had told them that I believed we should strengthen Germany because we were going to fight Russia in five years. The two staff officers who told him that were unquestionably Adcock and Bull, as I never made the statement to anyone else and only made it to them under the erroneous assumption that they were my friends.

Ike made the sensational statement that while hostilities were in progress, the one important thing was order and discipline, but now that hostilities were over, the important thing was to stay in with world public opinion – apparently whether it was right or wrong; I suppose on the same basis as Dacatur's famous remark: "My country, may she ever be right, but, right or wrong, my country." We could paraphrase that to "My public, may it ever be right but, right or wrong, my public."

Apparently Ike has to a high degree got the Messiah complex for which he can't be blamed as everybody bootlicks him except myself.

I asked the Professor what was the particular gripe on Fritz Schaeffer and found out he . . . had kept in his cabinet, in minor positions it is true, some twenty people (16 in Agriculture and 4 in Finance) who were mandatory cases for removal under our instructions.

General Eisenhower said he felt that no matter how much immediate removal of all Nazis from office adversely affected the administration of Bavaria, they should be removed because it was his experience that there was always some subordinate to take over the job of a superior. In battle I believe this is true and it is probably true in Military Government. It is a strange thing that in battle I am perfectly willing to chop off heads but in peacetime my Anglo-Saxon ancestry makes me reluctant to remove people without due process of law. However, I shall carry out General Eisenhower's wishes to the letter and in the spirit also.

Since it was very evident from General Eisenhower's demeanor that we had to relieve Fritz Schaeffer, I asked him who he wanted for President. He said, "Ask Dorn," which I did and Dorn recommended a man named Dr. Wilhelm Hoegner. So I called Harkins at 6.30 and told him to remove Schaeffer, Lange, and Rattenhuber and all members of their ministries in any way tainted with Nazism regardless of the setback it would give to the administration of Bavaria and the resultant cold and hunger it would produce – not only for the Germans but also for the DP's. This seemed to make everyone happy except myself.

Ike was apparently very anxious that he should not seem too friendly with me because almost the first word he said was, "If you are spending the night, of course you will stay with me, but since I feel you should get back to Bad Tolz as rapidly as possible, I have my train set up to take you, and it leaves at 7.00 o'clock." It was then 6.30. I took the train.

When we left, we met in the hall the same group of correspondents who caused the trouble . . . Eisenhower asked them what they wanted, and they said they wanted a statement from him as to what we had been talking about. He said, "I have conferences with my Army commanders whenever I feel like it – period," and went by.

During the whole of the preceding interview Eisenhower was more excited than I have ever seen him, and I believe this can be traced to the fact that he is very much worried about the delay in getting appointed as Chief of Staff at home, and fears that if he stays here, he will lose some of his prestige. I think this fear is well grounded, but I do not believe that a fear psychosis should make him so utterly regardless of his better nature as to make him practically unmoral in his treatment of the Germans.

Harkins carried out Patton's order, and, on September 29, the Third Army announced that Hoegner had replaced Schaeffer. For many years no one knew for sure whether Schaeffer resigned or was dismissed.

*Letter, GSP, Jr., to Beatrice, September 29, 1945*

Your radio about asking for an official investigation . . . felt just like a look out of your brave loyal eyes.

At this time it is my belief that an investigation would be futile.

The noise against me is only the means by which the Jews and Communists are attempting and with good success to implement a further dismemberment of Germany. I think that if I resigned as I threatened to do yesterday, it would simply discredit me to no purpose . . .

This august lady [Fifteenth Army] . . . has the job of reviewing the strategy and tactics of the war to see how the former conformed to the unit plans and how the tactics changed. Were it not for the fact that it will be, so far as I am concerned, a kick up stairs, I would like it much better than being a sort of executioner to the best race in Europe.

Later, when people wake up to what is going on here, I can admit why I took the job.

Am I weak and a coward? Am I putting my posthumous reputation above my present honor? God how I wish I knew . . .

P.S. No one gives a damn how well Bavaria is run. All they are interested in now is how well it is ruined.

The newspapers in the United States at the end of September were full of stories about Patton's being in the doghouse again. According to many press accounts, the displaced persons in the Third Army area, many of them Polish Jews, were overcrowded, underfed, and underprivileged in the concentration camps until Eisenhower personally traveled to see them, read the riot act to Patton, and emphasized he meant what he said about ousting Germans from their homes if necessary to make victims of the war comfortable. Yet Germans, some of them Nazis, still entertained American officers in fine houses they were permitted to occupy. No German, it was alleged, could be kicked out of his house without the personal approval of Patton's chief of staff.

Eisenhower wrote Patton on September 29, and made known his decision to transfer Patton to head the Fifteenth Army, which was studying the lessons of the European campaigns. Truscott was to have the Third Army. Eisenhower planned to make no advance announcement of the change. Insisting that he continued to admire Patton's loyalty, ability, and soldierly qualities, Eisenhower said he believed simply that Patton's particular talents were more suited to the new job.

Truscott, on his way home from Italy, had stopped in Frankfurt briefly to pay his respects to Eisenhower, and when Truscott reached Paris, he found a message from Eisenhower calling him back to Germany.

*Diary, September 30*

Beedle Smith called up about 1:30 yesterday and read me a letter from General Eisenhower which he said General Eisenhower had directed him to read.

It told of Patton's replacement by Truscott.

So, another die has been cast and probably for the best, as I am sure that hell is going to pop soon in this government business and trust I can avoid detection until [his relief] on the 8th.

Lucian Truscott . . . I am sure will do as good a job as he can in an impossible situation.

*Letter, GSP, Jr., to Beatrice, October 1, 1945*

In my present frame of mind, the outstanding thing is the difference between Harry [Stimson]'s attitude in instantly backing George [Marshall] and the lobster like agility with which the high command over here backs water when any of us are attacked.

In a sense I am glad to get out, as I hate the roll we are forced to play and the inethical means we are required to use.

All the troops are going down hill at a wonderful rate and are practically all recruits.

All military governments are going to be targets from now on for every sort of Jewish and Communistic attack from the press.

My self esteem would be better had I simply asked for immediate retirement but then any thing I said in the future could be attributed to revenge . . .

At the moment I feel pretty mad.

*Diary, October 1*

I left the office at 1330 for the purpose of visiting the DP camps . . . At Feldafing . . . we inspected the camp and found material improvement since I visited it with General Eisenhower . . .

However, considerable remains to be done, primarily because the Jewish type of DP is, in the majority of cases, a sub-human species without any of the cultural or social refinements of our time. They prefer to live in densely populated buildings, the sexes indiscriminately mixed. In consonance with the wishes of General Eisenhower, we had removed German families . . . and on last Friday directed the transfer of the DP's into these houses. Here we met with two peculiar resistance movements. First, in the majority of cases, they preferred to stay where they were. Second, Saturday and Sunday were the dates of a Jewish festival for taking in the harvest. Why this festival is celebrated by a group of persons who, so far as I know, have never engaged in agricultural pursuits, I do not know. However, in view of the festival, they flatly refused to move, unless we used force, prior to Monday because they had to get ready for the celebration on Friday . . .

Again we ran into the sub-human characteristics of these people in that they do not understand toilets and refuse to use them except as repositories for tin cans, garbage, and refuse . . .

We drove to Welfratshausen . . .

The UNRRA woman in charge of the local UNRRA group there has done an excellent job, but called my attention to the fact that the portion of the camp still occupied by Estonians was far better policed than that occupied by the Jews. I instructed the camp commander that the Jewish inhabitants were to be made responsible not only for the houses in which they live but also for the ground adjacent which, at the time of my visit, was covered with trash. I further stated that if they failed to comply, their rations would be stopped until they had done so.

The UNRRA woman informed me without solicitation that the Estonians detailed to cut wood for the camp cut four times as much wood per day as did the Jews. She believes, and I think with some show of veracity, that the Jews are in a psychopathic condition which may be materially improved, although personally I doubt it. I have never looked at a group of people who seem to be more lacking in intelligence and spirit. Practically all of them had the flat brownish gray eye common among the Hawaiians which, to my mind, indicates very low intelligence.

The cooking and hospital facilities in the village were of a superior character and the Jewish doctors in charge seemed to be men of very high personal and technical capacity . . .

Owing to the cooler weather, the smell of the inhabitants was below average but still extremely nauseating to western nostrils. It is an unfortunate fact that the people at home who are so vociferous in their demands for the betterment of the Displaced Jews have no conception of the low mental, moral, and physical standards of the objects of their solicitude . . .

So far as it is humanly possible, it is my purpose, and I shall strongly recommend it to General Truscott, to see that the density of population per house among the DP's and the German inhabitants is comparable. The result of this policy will be that should the German people ever rise from the state of utter degradation to which they have now been reduced, there will be the greatest pogrom of the Jews in the history of the world.

I believe the Jews realize this and probably for that reason are reluctant to move out of the camps . . .

In thinking over the situation, I could not but be impressed with the belief that at the present moment the unblemished record of the American Army for non-political activities is about to be lost. Everyone seems to be more interested in the effects which his actions will have on his political future than in carrying out the motto of the United States Military Academy, "Duty, Honor, Country."

I hope that after the current crop of political aspirants has been gathered, our former tradition will be restored.

*Letter, GSP, Jr., to Handy, October 2, 1945*

From a personal standpoint the new assignment is more in keeping with my natural academic tendencies than is that of governing Bavaria, but I naturally regret being relieved, however graciously, under circumstances which will be considered detrimental to my reputation.

*Diary, October 2*

The portrait [of himself] has at last been finished . . .

Just as I was about to go home at five o'clock, the telephone rang and General Eisenhower told me . . . that information of the ensuing change in command had leaked in Berlin and that therefore it might be necessary for him to make the announcement at noon tomorrow . . .

I said I could not see that that made any difference . . .

After the conversation terminated, Colonel Harkins, who had listened to it, said the only person who could have let it spill in Berlin was Mr. Murphy. I said no, Mr. Murphy I would trust, but I did not trust Beedle Smith. This is interesting as showing how guileless I still am because on the way home the truth suddenly dawned on me that Eisenhower is scared to death, which I already knew, and believes that a more prompt announcement of my relief than the one he had originally planned will be beneficial to him. The alleged leak is nothing but a figment of the imagination which is a euphemism for a damned lie.

On the advice of Major Deane, we are going to have the INS and UP correspondents in at eleven o'clock as they are probably the only loyal ones we have left, if any correspondents can be so termed.

His statement to the press was tame. He repeated that he was as responsible for the deaths in battle of as many Germans as "almost anyone," but he would be un-American if he did not try to prevent unnecessary deaths after the war was over.

I called up General McBride . . . [on] the density of population. He said the chief difficulty of carrying out my instructions would be the fact that it would be necessary to use force in order to get the Jews to separate themselves.

He also told me he had visited another camp which he thanked God the correspondents had not seen, where, although room existed, the Jews were crowded together to an appalling extent and in practically every room there was a pile of garbage in one corner which was also used as a latrine. The Jews were only forced to desist from their nastiness and clean up the mess by the threat of the butt ends of rifles.

Of course I know the expression "Lost tribes of Israel" applied to the tribes which disappeared — not to the tribe of Judah from which the current sons of bitches are descended. However, it is my personal opinion that this too is a lost tribe — lost to all decency.

*Editorial, "The Punishment of Gen. Patton," Cincinnati* Times-Star, *October 3, 1945*

The drastic penalty inflicted upon Gen. Patton . . . will shock most Americans, though it will probably delight those leftist commentators who have lately been hounding the great tank commander with all the venom of a Goebbels.

Patton was admittedly indiscreet in making his "unfortunate analogy" . . . But it should have been obvious that Patton did not mean what he seemed to say . . .

Without blaming Eisenhower, it must be said that the drastic punishment of Patton, in view of the occupation mess in Germany, has the effect of making the man a scapegoat.

On the same day John O'Donnell in his column "Capitol Stuff" carried by the New York *Daily News* published a rumor that purported to tell why Patton was a "scapegoat." Drew Pearson's report of the slapping incident had failed to reveal that the soldier slapped was of Jewish descent and that Patton called him a yellow-bellied or yellow-streaked Jew. Thus, behind the drive to disgrace Patton was a cabal, the members of which included Felix Frankfurter, David Niles, Sidney Hillman, Henry Morgenthau, and others, who never forgave Patton for making derogatory references to his victim's Jewish origins. Patton's mishandling of the occupation in Germany gave his enemies the opportunity to have Patton removed.

Repeating his accusations on the following day, O'Donnell added that Patton's dismissal showed how powerful "this republic's foreign-born political leaders" were.

Two weeks later, on October 19, O'Donnell published an apology for his statements and a retraction. Although he mentioned only Kuhl and not Bennett, the two soldiers whom Patton slapped on different occasions, O'Donnell admitted that Kuhl was not Jewish but a member of the Nazarene Church. He also publicly regretted having said that Jewish leaders were behind Patton's removal.

*Letter, GSP, Jr., to Codman, October 4, 1945*

I presume that . . . you have . . . been considerably perturbed by the scurrilous attacks made on me by the non-Aryan press . . .

However, that too will pass, and I think probably the reaction will be as beneficial as was that following our friend Drew Pearson's asseverations . . .

Today I am performing with my usual efficiency my duties as undertaker at my own funeral and am at the moment sitting at a perfectly cleaned up desk . . . Actually, while I regret being relieved for what amounts to cause or rather, perhaps, to a lack of guts – not on my part though – from the Third Army, it may all work out for the best . . .

So far as the Jews are concerned, they do not want to be placed in comfortable buildings . . .

I am really very fearful of repercussions . . . and I am certain we are being completely hood-winked by the degenerate descendants of Ghengis Khan . . . The envy, hatred, malice, and uncharitableness in Europe passes belief.

*Letter, GSP, Jr., to Beatrice, October 5, 1945*

Like William Jennings Bryan, "My head is bloody but unbowed." All I regret is that I have again worried you.

I have been helping Lucien to get the hang of the show and he feels rather depressed. I don't blame him.

I was terribly hurt for a few days but am normal again.

*Diary, October 7*

Owing to the rain, we decided to have the transfer of command ceremony in the gymnasium. The four corps commanders, Robertson, Harmon, McBride, and Prickett, assembled on the stage before we got there. On the right were the national colors, on the left the colors of the Third Army, while behind in the middle were the General's and Lieutenant General's flags.

At exactly noon Truscott and I, followed by Brigadier General Carleton [Truscott's chief of staff] and Colonel Harkins, entered and marched on the platform. The command, consisting of a company of MP's, most of the clerks, and all of the officers of both Forward and Rear Headquarters, was then presented and four ruffles and four flourishes were played.

I then made a speech . . .

*GSP, Jr., Speech to the Officers and Men of the Third Army on the Occasion of his Leaving*

General Truscott, Officers, and Men: All good things must come to an end. The best thing that has ever come to me thus far is the honor and privilege of having commanded the Third Army.

The great successes we have achieved together have been due primarily to the fighting heart of America, but without the coordinating and supply activities of the General and Special Staffs, even American valor would have been impotent.

You officers and men here represent the fighting, the administrative, and the supply elements of this Army. Please accept my heartfelt congratulations on your valor and devotion to duty, and my fervent gratitude for your unwavering loyalty.

When I said that all good things come to an end, I was referring to myself and not to you because you will find in General Truscott every characteristic which will inspire in you the same loyalty and devotion which you have so generously afforded me.

A man of General Truscott's achievements needs no introduction. His deeds speak for themselves. I know that you will not fail him.

Goodbye and God bless you.

Auld Lang Syne was [then] played. At the termination of this piece, the Color Bearer with the Colors of the Third Army approached me. I took the Colors from him and handed them to General Truscott, saying I could think of no more worthy recipient. General Truscott took them and handed them back to the Color Sergeant who withdrew to his former post.

The Command was again presented, and three ruffles and three flourishes were played in honor of General Truscott. Following this, he made a short speech, which I could not hear as he was very emotional and shouted too loud into the machine. I think he was very much perturbed at taking over the command. Of course, he had nothing to do with this and was simply carrying out orders.

After this, the band played the Third Army March.

We then left the gymnasium together and while we walked out the band played "For He's a Jolly Good Fellow."

All the Generals and the heads of General and Special Staff Sections assembled in the Officers Dining Room, where we had some cocktails and highballs. After this the Senior Officers had place cards at a table where we had a lunch and quite a few speeches.

I left at exactly 2.30 and was accompanied to the Third Army train by General Truscott. We pulled out at 3.00 o'clock.

There was an escort in the headquarters quadrangle. Troops lined the road all the way to the railroad station.

George Fisher's recollection:

The skies were dripping . . . when Patton officially turned over the command, so the formal ceremony was staged in the spacious Bad Tolz gymnasium. The General attended religious services that morning, as usual, after which he went directly to the gym. Nothing in his dress or bearing reflected the torture of his soul as he stepped forward to hand over the symbol of his command. "All good things must come to an end" was the burden of his brief remarks.

The luncheon that the headquarters mess officer spread out that noon really deserved a better appetite than most of us could muster. All the old corps and division commanders who could be found were there. Their testimonies varied in length but no wise in sincerity. Some thoughts strayed to George Washington and [his farewell address at] Fraunces' Tavern. [Chaplain] O'Neill may have remembered the Last Supper.

Along about midafternoon Patton had had enough. He arose, squared his shoulders, and moved resolutely off to his waiting car.

A week later, in his first press conference, Truscott said:

> I have left too many white crosses across North Africa, Italy, and France, and I have seen too many young men wounded and maimed not to be in complete sympathy with any policy that designs to eradicate, root and branch, the evil force, Nazism, that loosed this holocaust on the world.

CHAPTER 43

# Fifteenth Army

*"I hate to think of leaving the Army but what is there?"*

*Diary, October 8*

The train reached Bad Nauheim around 5.30 this morning. After breakfast General [Leven] Allen came to pick me up at 8.30 as had been arranged, and we drove at once to the office of the Fifteenth Army.

Allen gave me a good orientation [on the mission of the headquarters]...

I spoke to the Chiefs of the various sections telling them I proposed to make no changes for one week and that the best is the enemy of the good, by which I mean that something now will be better than perfection when it is too late to have any influence.

Mr. McDermott of the AP called, and I talked to him in the presence of General Allen and Lt. Lynch and, most of the time, Major Merle-Smith.

A stenographer took notes of the interview and recorded that Patton said:

My friend, I know nothing in a big way . . . I got here this morning . . . and at present I am completely bemused. There is an awful lot [of headquarters reports and studies] to be read [by me]. I have got to get some eyedrops. It is the most essential piece of equipment. This [assignment] is right down my alley because I have been a student of war since I was about seven years old . . .

(Off the record) I felt that perhaps I had not had quite a square deal because I believe it will be proven that Bavaria is more de-Nazified and more reorganized than any section of Germany . . .

I had the same sentimental attachment to the I Armored Corps and the Seventh Army [as to the Third Army] . . .

If a man has done his best, what the hell [more] is there? I consider that I have always done my best . . . [My] conscience is clear . . .

Anyone who says there won't be a future war is a God damned fool . . .

I won't discuss American-Russian relations.

*Letter, GSP, Jr., to Truscott, October 8, 1945*

Please let me thank you very much for your nice remarks yesterday and for all the arrangements for my departure. I sent the train back this morning.

So far, I have just got to the point of being wholly confused as to what is going on in this job.

*Letter, GSP, Jr., to Beatrice, October 10, 1945*

This is very much like . . . the old Historical section in Washington. We are writing a lot of stuff which no one will ever read.

The Fifteenth Army was a paper organization in more than one sense. The headquarters controlled no troop units except those necessary for its own housekeeping. And it had as its sole mission the preparation of historical and analytical studies on the tactics, techniques, organization, and administration of the war in Europe. Committees of officers wrote Theater or General Board Reports, as they were known, on a variety of subjects. Some were excellent. But the typed and mimeographed pages inevitably grew into mountains of paper.

*Letter, GSP, Jr., to Beatrice, October 11, 1945*

I hate to have you feel so badly about this last incident.

The whole thing is utterly unjust and the result of poor "Fear of They" . . .

Thanks for the clippings but I don't read them. It does no good and keeps me awake at night.

The thing will change and I will be away out in front.

*Letter, GSP, Jr., to Beatrice, October 12, 1945*

DDE is full of friendship. We are dining ensemble this evening.

*Diary, October 13*

John Eisenhower told his father yesterday that since I had taken over the Fifteenth Army, people had begun to work.

During the course of the dinner which I had with Eisenhower on a purely social basis, I stated to him that I could not hereafter eat at the same table with General Bedell Smith. Eisenhower said that Smith said he had been misquoted and wished to apologize. Eisenhower was also quite anxious for me to run for Congress — I presume in the belief that I might help him.

To avoid having correspondents constantly telephoning about his feelings toward future wars and to prevent his being misquoted, Patton sent a statement to Eisenhower's public relations officer:

I have studied and practised war all my life. Therefore I am utterly opposed to it but I am not an ostrich . . .

I am firmly convinced that we must have a universal training because the one hope for a peaceful world is a powerful America [with] . . . adequate means to instantly check aggressors.

Unless we are so armed and prepared, the next war will probably destroy us. No one who has lived in a destroyed country can view such a possibility with anything but horror.

To scotch a rumor that Patton might run for Congress, he sent another statement for release to the newspapers:

I am a soldier, have always been a soldier, belong to no political party, and have never even voted. I am not interested.

He was avidly reading anti-Russian literature, including letters from witnesses who described the horrors of life in the Soviet Union as well as various Communist plots and conspiracies designed to overwhelm the decent people of the world. Patton was fascinated.

*Letter, GSP, Jr., to Beatrice, October 15, 1945*

People don't work here on Sundays so Saturday late I went to spend the night with Everett . . . Sunday we went to a football game . . . Ike was there and they put me right next to him. As usual a lot of soldiers with cameras, several hundreds, came and wanted to take pictures but the MP's would not let them get close, so Hughes suggested that Ike let them come up. Instead he decided to go down in front near them. He waved his hand and "grinned" and they took a few pictures and he came back but the soldiers did not leave and presently they began to shout we want Patton, so I went down and there was realy an ovation. Lots of film was used up.

Then Ike came down a second time and we posed together . . .

Ike is bitten with the presidential bug and is also yellow. He has convinced him self that he did me a favor by getting me out of the realy grave risks entailed by being a governor.

He will never be president! . . .

I will resign when I have finished this job which will be not later than Dec. 26. I hate to do it but I have been gagged all my life, and whether they are appreciated or not, America needs some honest men who dare to say what they think, not what they think people want them to think.

Joseph Wilner of Washington, D.C., who had lost two sons in the war, one a captain in Patton's command, telegraphed to make known his distress over the effect of O'Donnell's allegations on Patton's reputation. From his son's correspondence, he was certain that Patton had never made derogatory remarks about Jewish soldiers. Would Patton please reassure him on what could only be O'Donnell's misrepresentation of Patton's attitude?

Patton's response was rather stiff and official.

*Letter, GSP, Jr., to Wilner, October 15, 1945*

I am glad to have the opportunity of categorically denying that I have ever made any statement contrary to the Jewish or any other religious faith. I am a sincere believer in the Supreme Being and have never interfered with or even examined into the religious or racial antecedents of the men I have the honor to command. My sole effort has been to provide victorious soldiers who can serve their country and defeat the enemy with the minimum loss to themselves. With appreciation of and thanks for your interest, I am, Truly yours,

*Diary, October 16*

General Keyes flew up from Heidelberg to see me. I think his sole reason was to express in a very refined manner, as is always the case with him, sympathy. I was delighted to see him as I think he is one of the pleasantest companions and most loyal friends I have ever known.

*Letter, GSP, Jr., to Beatrice, October 17, 1945*

I read against my better judgment the clippings Codman sent. I got physically sick. But cheer up. The reaction has started. I will come out on top sooner than people think.

*Letter, GSP, Jr., to Beatrice, October 19, 1945*

Fan mail has just started, also telegrams. I think things will come out for the best and may result in my getting lined up with the Anti-Communists because it is they and the Jews who are back of it and successful due to the lack of spine of DD.

*Letter, GSP, Jr., to Codman, October 18, 1945*

My present plan is to finish this job, which is a purely academic one, about the first of the year and then submit my resignation after which I can do all the talking I feel like . . .

My private opinion is that practically everyone but myself is a pusillanimous son of a bitch and that by continued association with them I may develop the same attributes.

*Letter, GSP, Jr., to Beatrice, October 20, 1945*

I know I am right and the rest can go to Hell or I hope they can but it is going to be very crowded.

*Letter, GSP, Jr., to Harbord, October 22, 1945*

I have been just as furious as you at the compilation of lies which the communist and semitic elements of our government have levelled against me and practically every other commander. In my opinion it is a deliberate attempt to alienate the soldier vote from the commanders because the communists know that soldiers are not communistic and they fear what eleven million votes [of veterans] would do.

It is owing to this fact that I have failed to raise any stink because, while I think General Eisenhower is most pusillanimous in yielding to the outcry of three very low correspondents, I feel that as an American it will ill become me to discredit him yet — that is, until I shall prove even more conclusively that he lacks moral fortitude. This lack has been evident to us since the first landing in Africa but now that he has been bitten with the presidential bee, it is becoming even more pronounced.

It is interesting to note that everything for which I have been criticized in the handling of Germans had been subsequently adopted:

to wit – I stated that if we took all small Nazis out of every job, chaos would result. Military Government the other day announced that from two to five per cent of Nazis would be kept in.

He cited other facts, for example, that he "had removed from or deprived of office 49,088 Nazis."

All the general officers in the higher brackets receive each morning from the War Department a set of American headlines and, with the sole exception of myself, they guide themselves during the ensuing day by what they have read in the papers. Personally I never read these headlines because I have perfect confidence that I do my duty as I see it and I do not need to be told how to do it by a number of very low type individuals.

It is my present thought . . . that when I finish this job, which will be around the first of the year, I shall resign, not retire, because if I retire I will still have a gag in my mouth . . . I should not start a limited counter-attack, which would be contrary to my military theories, but should wait until I can start an all out offensive . . .

The great tragedy of my life was that I survived the last battle. It had always been my plan to be killed in this war, and I damned near accomplished it, but one cannot resort to suicide . . .

The study [here] was progressing with remarkable exactitude and no speed until I assumed charge . . .

I am convinced we should avoid the error we made at the end of the last war of taking this war as an approved solution for future unpleasantnesses. We must use this factual account simply as a datum plane from which to annually build a new set of jiggs and dies.

*Letter, GSP, Jr., to Beatrice, October 22, 1945*

Did I tell you that on the 25 Du Gall is giving me a medal of some sort. General Giraud came to see me to say that France was shocked to the heart at the treatment accorded the greatest soldier since Napoleon . . .

How can one expect any backbone in a man [already] running for President.

*Diary, October 23*

Tomorrow . . . flying to Paris for the purpose of lunching with de Gaulle . . . and being decorated . . . A letter from General Juin . . .

stated that France had always desired and that General de Gaulle, who represented France, also desired to decorate me for my preeminent part in the liberation of France but that, as a result of my recent change in command status, France was more than twice as anxious as before to do me honor.

*Diary, October 25*

To the Ministry of War . . . for a special luncheon given in my honor . . . by General de Gaulle . . . There were about 35 guests . . .

At the end of the luncheon . . . he compared me to everybody from Napoleon up and down. I replied . . . that the history of France's great leaders had always been an inspiration to American soldiers and that in the room there were the busts of two such leaders and also the living presence of two others. The busts were those of Turenne and Conde, and the soldiers were de Gaulle and Juin. Apparently this did a good deal to impress the President-General.

After lunch we went to the Invalides and . . . to the tomb of Napoleon, and . . . downstairs where people are not normally allowed. It was very impressive, and we all enjoyed it.

At 8.00 o'clock Merle-Smith and I dined with Juin . . . As usual Juin got on the question of the Russians whom he distrusts and fears as much as I do.

Nothing was scheduled for the following day, so he and Merle-Smith visited Notre Dame and Sainte Chapelle, "then drove to Versailles and had a quick look around. I had not been there since 1912, but it has not changed."

On the 27th, he went to Rennes, where he met with dignitaries, drank champagne, attended a luncheon in his honor, and watched Breton folk dancing that ended with "a very fat and sweaty young girl [who] presented me with a large bouquet of flowers and then she demanded that I kiss her, and I found that she had certainly bathed recently because she tasted soapy." With large crowds in attendance, he reviewed troops, listened to speeches by mayors who made him an honorary citizen of their towns, and gave a short address himself.

On to Angers for more champagne, an appearance on a balcony to wave to a "tremendous crowd," and "the distinguished privilege of becoming a Citizen of Honor." At the Franco-American Union, a woman talked exactly like the voice on his French-lesson phonograph records.

He met the daughter of his old friend General Houdemon, Madame Becourt Foch whose husband, the marshal's grandson, had been killed, he thought, "by my troops in Africa. Aside from mentioning this fact, she did not bring the question up." He must have misunderstood, for actually Becourt Foch had been in London with De Gaulle, flew with the RAF and later with the Free French, and was killed in a plane crash in 1944.

The ceremonies continued on the following day at Chartres, where Patton was welcomed at the city hall, taken on a tour of the city, and escorted to the cathedral for a mass attended by "at least 5000 people" and "many more outside yelling 'Vive Patton' – and some of them, to the scandal and disgrace of religion, started yelling in the Church." After lunch and a parade, Patton and his party returned to Paris.

> I collected ten Citizen of Honor certificates, two plaques, and a tremendous case of indigestion . . . Went to the Folies Bergeres, which has gone steadily down hill since 1912.

"The whole damned world is going Communist," he wrote Beatrice. "The last US troops to leave Europe will be fighting a rear guard action." He thought it possible that "this last attack on me is another act of God definately lining me up against the Reds." He had been in an automobile accident that had been reported in the press, but it "was nothing – just a bent fender, so your dream did not work."

Beatrice's dream, whatever it was, was premonitory but premature.

Patton too had dreamed that "when I got home you met me with your hair all shaved off but a scalp lock and your scalp painted white." He had to read so many Theater Board reports "that I am almost nuts." He mentioned the pleasant prospect of shooting grouse with Gay. "Destiny relieved me simply in a state of funk and because he has no moral courage."

"The staff is having a big party for me on the eleventh – what a sad day [to be sixty years old]."

*Diary, November 2*

> In the Russian occupied zone the Russians materially augment the food allowances to all Germans who become Communists. This is reminiscent of Mohammed's method of securing Mohammedans . . . There is very little new under the sun . . .

The utter folly of the Potsdam Convention which contemplated the ability of four antagonistic nations, one of which is not even civilized, to govern by unanimous consent is . . . being admirably justified [in Berlin].

*Letter, GSP, Jr., to son George, November 3, 1945*

It is quite natural that my speeches should sound like Napoleon's because, as you know, I have studied him all my life. You are wrong in saying he fought a different type of war – he and I fought the same way but my means of progress were better than his.

On November 4, Patton issued what would be his final "Notes on Combat," ten single-spaced typed pages devoted to divisions and their organizations, formations, and tactics. Among his comments:

Violent and rapid attack with the marching fire is the surest means of success in the use of armor . . .

The length of a command is measured in time, not in miles . . .

A great deal has been written and a great many maps have been drawn to show where various units have gone during a war or a battle, but there is very little information available as to how they went or what formations were employed . . .

A cursory glance at the foregoing recommendations may lead to the belief that there is practically no difference between an infantry division and an armored division. The difference is very real and two fold. First, the purpose of the tanks in an infantry division is to get the infantry forward, while the purpose of the infantry in an armored division is to break the tanks loose.

Second, the mental characteristics of the commander of an infantry division who has to conduct the slow bitter slugging tactics essential to that arm may not, and probably will not, have the attributes essential to the commander of an armored division where rapidity of movement and reckless operation are the criteria of success . . .

In considering the foregoing or any other organizational scheme we must remember that it is simply the datum plane from which new ideas and new formations must be developed. The primary function of war has not within historic time been materially changed by the advent of new weapons. The unchanging principle of combat is to inflict on the enemy the maximum amount of wounds and death in a minimum of time and as cheaply as possible. If future leaders will remember that nothing is impossible, that casualties received from enemy action in battle are a function of time and effective enemy fire, and that any type of troops can fight any place, they will not go wrong.

*Letter, GSP, Jr., to Beatrice, November 5, 1945*

I doubt that I will be home for Xmas but I fully intend to leave here shortly after the 1st of Jan. and we can have a belated celebration . . .

As everything I do gets in the press I had better tell you that I had a wart or some such thing cut out of my belly – the outside skin – this morning. It was done with a local [anesthetic] and only needed two stitches.

*Diary, November 5*

Yesterday while driving to Mannheim for a shoot and looking over the utter devastation of Frankfurt and Mannheim, it occurred to me that the only possible salvation for a country so completely destroyed as Germany is another Messiah – whether he serves God or the devil. Nothing conceivable could be more apt to bring back a Hitler than what we are doing.

*Letter, GSP, Jr., to Gerow, November 6, 1945*

Owing to the rapid reduction of personnel due to redeployment and owing to the fact that the majority of people with adequate information are in America, we have decided that this Board's Report should be and probably will be completed by 1 January.

To receive a decoration, Patton drove to Brussels via Cologne, Aachen, and Liège, which he had never seen. Cologne and Aachen were badly destroyed, and he "kept wondering how Charlemagne would have felt about his former capital [Aachen], could he see it today, which he probably can." At the outskirts of Brussels, a motorcycle escort took him to the Embassy, where many Belgians were waiting "for the ecstatic privilege of seeing me."

We were met by a full Colonel wearing a DSM, who was nothing but a God damned interpreter in the last war and probably never heard a gun go off in anger.

The ceremony was very simple. I walked into a room where the

Ambassador and His Royal Highness were standing. HRH spoke excellent English and said he wanted to give me a medal, which he proceeded to pin on – namely, Grand Officer of the Order of Leopold and the Croix de Guerre of the same Order with Palm; also a Belgian 1940 Croix de Guerre with Palm. Either the Belgian protocol on decorations is wrong or the Prince is ignorant, because he pinned the sunburst on my left breast where, according to my understanding, only Grand Cross sunbursts should go.

"Well now I am a Grand Officier of the Order of Leopold," he wrote Beatrice, "one more sun burst. Also I got a bad cold."

Bernard Baruch wrote Patton that he resented the unfair criticisms being made against "a great soldier." He was sorry he had been unable to persuade the authorities to send Patton to the Pacific to fight the Japanese. He particularly regretted not having seen Patton during his visit to the United States, for he had wanted to warn Patton of some of the dangers of the occupation. He enclosed a newspaper clipping, which quoted Lieutenant K. E. Wallach of Galesburg, Illinois, who was recuperating from wounds in a hospital:

The attacks on General Patton as an anti-Semite sound strange to a Third Army soldier. Our general was on the record as knowing only good soldiers or bad soldiers and not soldiers of different religious preference...

It will be the pride of my life that I had the honor to serve under a man like General Patton.

*Letter, GSP, Jr., to Baruch, December 3, 1945*

My sincere thanks for your nice letter...

I was particularly interested in the clipping . . . which is exactly in accordance with the facts. I cannot understand who had the presumption to attribute to me anti-Semitic ideas which I certainly do not possess.

With warm personal regards, and looking forward to the pleasure of seeing you on my return to America,

*Adolph Goldsmith, "Old Blood and Guts Idol of his Men," Arkansas Democrat* Sunday Magazine, *Little Rock, November 16, 1945*

Patton is a soldier's general. He did not ask his men to fight for him; he asked them to fight with him..

Much has been written about Patton's ruthlessness and disregard for the individual. True, he was daring, rough, and brutal, but so were his soldiers. They would not have defeated the Nazis if they had been otherwise. He expected the impossible from the Third Army — and got it.

You probably have read the incident when a higher general sent a message to Patton to bypass Trier, since it would require four divisions to take it. Patton answered, "Have taken Trier with two divisions. Do you want me to give it back?"

As for Patton's most recent transfer to the doghouse, we are as much confused as the American public. He certainly has no love for the Nazis . . .

The soldiers of the Third Army are practically unanimous in their belief that "their boss" got a d——ed rotten deal.

*Letter, GSP, Jr., to Goldsmith, December 4, 1945*

I am deeply moved by the fact that one of my soldiers who, so far as I know, I did not have the pleasure of meeting personally should take this much interest in my career.

Kent Hunter, former public relations officer, wrote to say that he had talked with hundreds of Third Army soldiers since returning to civilian life. Their reaction to Patton was always the same: "Goddam that old sonofabitch! Wasn't he swell?"

On his birthday Patton wrote Beatrice: "For a man of my advanced age I feel fine and every one says I look the same way." He was sixty years old.

Several days earlier he had written to Beatrice:

In a day or so, Ike leaves and I command [the theater] — some joke — if he comes back I will just sit, if he don't I will have a grand house cleaning.

Beadle and I will have some fun any how. He has never apologized but sent word he had been misquoted. I have never seen him. In my hope he will be investigated by Congress.

*Diary, November 13*

In my capacity as Acting Theater Commander, I visited USFET Headquarters at Frankfurt and was present at the morning staff conference . . . The gentleman representing the President on behalf of the Jews is apparently using grapevine methods to induce a large number of Polish Jews to migrate from Poland into Bavaria. Since these Jews have to cross two frontiers, it is very evident that they are being assisted by the Russians and Poles and Czechs who are probably as anxious to get rid of them as the Jews are to change domicile. It seems possible that the New Jerusalem may occur in Bavaria rather than in Palestine.

However, since I am simply pinch-hitting during the brief absence of General Eisenhower, I do not conceive it to be my duty to make any radical changes pending his return.

After the meeting I signed a number of court-martial cases and discovered that it is the policy of the Theater commander not to give death sentences to any American soldier accused of raping a German woman. This seemed somewhat at variance with Anglo-Saxon customs.

*Letter, GSP, Jr., to Beatrice, November 15, 1945*

It is very evident that Beadle realy runs the show in so far as it can be said to be run . . . The chief interest seems to center on doing nothing positive and never going counter to what the papers say.

Some one proposes something and Beadle makes a speech against it and ends up by saying that while he is against it in principle he will go along with it just this once.

Of course since we don't get on and are pretty nearly on official terms, it is not very plesant. But since Ike will be back — so it is said . . . I am not being much worse than a rubber stamp. If I had the job permanently — which God forbid — I would certainly drive things. It is not a Headquarters, just a chatequa. I go down there about three times a week mostly to sign court martial sentences.

*Diary, November 16*

I again visited USFET Headquarters at Frankfurt and at the Staff Conference brought up the point that in view of the critical housing shortage existing in Germany, which will unquestionably get worse, I doubted the expediency of blowing up factories, because the ends for which the factories are being blown up — that is, preventing Germany from preparing for war — can be equally well attained through the destruction of their machinery, while the buildings can be used to house thousands of homeless persons. I therefore directed that inquiry be made to see if the machinery could not be removed and destroyed and the buildings made available for housing – the buildings to be destroyed in the spring, should it be found that the Control Commission believed such action necessary.

*Letter, GSP, Jr., to Frederick Ayer, November 17, 1945*

I quite agree with you that we are getting not older but damned old in spite of the fact that I do not feel that way. It is therefore my firm determination to spend all the money which you can provide or which I can borrow, beg, or steal on a life of continued amusement as soon as I can get rid of my present job . . .

I further suggest that you look into the possibility of hiring, buying, or otherwise securing a quail shooting preserve in either Florida, Georgia, or the Carolinas . . .

I do propose to hunt six days a week in Virginia whenever I am not engaged in shooting or sailing.

*Letter, GSP, Jr., to George Murnane, Jr., Syosset, New York, November 17, 1945*

I do not consider the episode leading to my transfer to Fifteenth Army so much an attack on me as a lack of intestinal fortitude on the part of others. However, I feel that I have obligations to my profession which, for the time being at least, outweigh personal emotions and I therefore do not propose to take any personal action because I am convinced that just as in the case of the slapping incident and the Knutsford affair, the final reaction is more favorable to me than to the other parties.

Furthermore, and this is very frank and personal, there is one job which would cause me to contemplate remaining in the Army. This job would be President of the War College . . . Therefore, it would be inexpedient for me to start throwing my weight around until I find out.

I trust this does not shock your opinions of my high motives which, after all, are not too high.

*Diary, November 17*

The other day Beedle Smith brought up the fact that General Eisenhower will take a final farewell of his troops . . . The question of a proper farewell entertainment was discussed . . . I stated that we should go all out to make a very appropriate and solemn ceremony in order to honor the greatest General who had ever lived.

To day I have been working on my thoughts as to how to reduce the human expense of war by a judicious increase in mechanization. Americans, as a race, are adept in the use of machines, and also in the construction of machines. The people whom they will have to fight will be the Russians and the Japanese, neither of whom are adept . . . but both have a large manpower which they are willing to expend recklessly. It therefore behooves us to devise military formations which will exploit our natural aptitude for machines and at the same time save our somewhat limited and very valuable manpower.

*Letter, GSP, Jr., to Beatrice, November 18, 1945*

I hope to leave here by boat around the 1st of the year. I am going by boat so I can keep my numerous boxes of papers with me in my state room and not have them lost in transit . . .

At the moment retirement seems the only solution but we can never tell . . .

I realy shudder for the future of our country.

*Letter, GSP, Jr., to Handy, November 23, 1945*

I would like to ask some advice . . . What is your suggestion as to my personal course? . . It would seem to me that the best thing I could do is ask for retirement. I am sincere in asking your advice because, as you know, I have a very high opinion of your ability.

What he was really asking Handy was, how good were his chances for becoming Commandant of the Army War College or of the new National War College?

*Diary, November 23*

Attended the meeting at USFET . . . was handed a telegram stating that General Eisenhower, owing to a cold, will not be able to return [from the United States] and that General McNarney was coming to the ETO to take command . . .

Prince Bernhard of Holland decorated a number of USFET officers, including . . . Lieutenant Summersby. The last was in a high state of nerves as a result of hearing that General Eisenhower is not returning.

*Diary, November 25*

To Metz . . . first to the house of General Dody, the Governor, where we had champagne. We then went to the Mairie and from there walked to the Cathedral through quite a large crowd . . .

The service lasted a long time in a zero temperature, which gives some reason for the upper bracket clergymen wearing ermine capes . . .

We drove to the Town Square . . . walked around the troops . . . participated as a decoratee and decorator in a ceremony . . . a march past and then a luncheon which lasted four hours, with much oratory . . .

I was made a Citizen of Honor of . . . Metz, Toul, Reims, Luxembourg, Chateau Thierry, Saargeumines, Thionville, Eperney, and Verdun.

At the Mairie I met General Houdemon, and after the luncheon I drove him back to Pont-a-Mousson, where I met his wife and was presented by them with two much treasured porcellain figurines of the Grenadiers of Napoleon's Army, in which Houdemon's grandfather was a general. I tried to persuade them not to give them to me, but had no success.

*Letter, Weyland to GSP, Jr., November 26, 1945*

I feel that the Third Army has died. To me, the Third Army meant Patton. When you left it, it ceased to be a thing alive. In a way I'm glad — a fighting Army and a peacetime Army are two different things.

Harbord replied to Patton's request for advice by saying that he would feel bad if Patton resigned from the army, especially if he announced that he was doing so in order to be able to speak freely. The public would expect and listen for something sensational and, no matter how true the allegations that Patton might express, would be disappointed. The reaction was sure to be unfavorable to Patton in the long run. Besides, why would Patton, at that stage in his life, want to start a "backfire" against Eisenhower? Harbord thought that Patton should defer his decision until he came home and discovered what job he would have in the postwar Regular Army.

*Letter, GSP, Jr., to Harbord, November 26, 1945*

Your advice is very good and, having gotten over my rage, I had almost reached the same conclusion myself . . .

> I am not at all discouraged about the treatment I personally have received but I am terribly worried about the situation in America and in Europe . . . It may well be that V-E Day is misnamed and simply marked the beginning of a relatively short armistice. I bet Monty a hundred pounds to that effect and he gave me a ten-year limit, so I fear that his Scotch soul is worrying. I hope it is . . .
>
> This afternoon I am leaving for Copenhagen and then Stockholm and then probably to a coffin as a result of acute indigestion from overeating.

Patton, Merle-Smith, Meeks, and Duncan departed Frankfurt on a special six-car train that he "considered quite unnecessary for four people." But he learned that it cost no more to move six cars than the two – formerly Hindenburg's – they actually occupied.

After a short stop in Copenhagen for a cocktail party at the American Embassy, he traveled to Stockholm, where he called on the King, had an audience with the Crown Prince, and lunched with Count Bernadotte. At the Olympic stadium he watched a special ice carnival and hockey game put on for him. Then with eight men who had competed with him in the 1912 Pentathlon events, the pistol shoot was re-enacted; Patton came in second.

There were ceremonies, visits, and dinners, and several times Patton noted in his diary that he "ate and drank steadily for some two hours." At various military installations he was impressed by a Swedish submachine gun, a field stove that had a combination chimney and tent pole, and an 81-mm. mortar. He would later recommend that the Ordnance Department in Washington look into these items.

At a banquet given by the Swedish-American Society, "which was the ostensible reason for my going to Stockholm," he addressed the 500 guests. He was distressed to receive

> three telegrams and a letter from interned Baltics and Germans requesting my intervention to prevent their return to the Russians, where they very rightly anticipated elimination. I could do nothing about this.

Having returned to Copenhagen, where he had an audience with the King, Patton flew to Frankfurt. "It is my considered opinion," he later wrote in his diary, "that anyone who can survive a trip to Metz and one to Sweden within a week is apt to live forever or die of a stroke." He loved it all.

*Letter, GSP, Jr., to Frederick Ayer, December 3, 1945*

The main thing is that I wish to have sufficient money to be very extravagant for the next fifteen years because, as I told you, it is my intention to do that.

*Diary, December 3*

General Smith gave a luncheon for General McNarney, the new Theater Commander, at which were present all the youth and beauty of the ETO. With the exception of Generals Keyes, Truscott, Allen, Gay, and myself, and a limited number of others, I have rarely seen assembled a greater bunch of sons-of-bitches . . .

I had a good deal of fun at luncheon quoting from recent articles on the Military Government of Germany, which I had the forethought to take with me, and which removed the appetite from Bob Murphy and the new Commanding General . . . The trouble with both of them is that their answer is that they could not do anything about it as they were carrying out orders. My answer is that a man who receives a foolish order should not carry it out – but such is not the breed of cats in authority. It is certainly quite a criticism of our form of Military Government to find that the Deputy Theater Commander, General Clay, and the Theater Commander, General McNarney, have never commanded anything, including their own self-respect, or if that, certainly not the respect of anyone else.

The whole luncheon party reminded me of a meeting of the Rotary Club in Hawaii where everyone slaps every one else's back while looking for an appropriate place to thrust the knife. I admit I was guilty of this practice, although at the moment I have no appropriate weapon.

Had he known that this was to be his last entry in his diary, would he have ended thus in such bitterness and resentment?

*Letter, GSP, Jr., to Cook, December 4, 1945*

God willing, I shall leave this Theater sometime around the first of the year and I look forward to seeing you and having many long arguments.

*Letter, GSP, Jr., to Truscott, December 5, 1945*

I expect to leave here on the 12th for a month's leave and therefore take this opportunity of bidding you goodbye and wishing you and all your staff a very merry Xmas.

*Letter, GSP, Jr., to Col. Harry Whitfield, Middleburg, Va., December 5, 1945*

Your munificent present of cigars which I have stopped smoking arrived a few moments ago with the result that I have resumed smoking.

Please accept my sincere thanks and also look up a few reliable foxes because I expect to go hunting around the first of January.

*Letter, GSP, Jr., to Beatrice, December 5, 1945*

I just sent you a paragraph on the daily radio that I leave South Hampton on the USS New York, 45,000 ton battle ship on December 14 and should arrive where ever it lands on December 19. I have a months leave but don't intend to go back to Europe. If I get a realy good job I will stay in [the army], otherwise I will retire . . .

I hate to think of leaving the Army but what is there?

We can get a chance at the visiting foxes any how . . .

I was going to shoot pigs to day but it was too snowy . . .

I may see you before you see this.

That was his last letter to Beatrice.

A USFET Order dated December 7, 1945, directed Patton to proceed on or about December 14 to Paris for subsequent air travel to the United States and a leave of absence of 30 days. He was authorized a baggage allowance of 165 pounds.

On December 8, Patton wrote his last letters — to Miss Coughlin of Brewer, Maine, and Miss Mary Jane Krieger of Harrisburg, Pennsylvania, thanking them for their "constant support," clippings, and Christmas boxes; to Ed Fansler saying that he was "leaving in a day or two for thirty days leave in America"; and to Emil Ludwig of Switzerland thanking him for sending Patton Ludwig's article about him "which I very much enjoyed reading."

A prolific writer who had produced several best sellers, including a biography of Napoleon, Ludwig had come to visit Patton late in April, when the war was nearing its end. They talked, of course, and Ludwig spent the night at the headquarters. Enchanted by Patton, he put his impressions into a short article that was beautifully done, perceptive, and gracious.

Ludwig found Patton "slim and elegant, the born gentleman in every movement, 'Grandseigneur' at his table, sportsman as he walks with a whip in his hand." His face was full of contradictions and as complex as his character. His eyes were critical. His mouth sometimes smiled, then suddenly became hard. He seemed to Ludwig like a gallant and high-strung horse at the gallop, unwilling to be reined. He was a poet, a Lord Byron, with imagination and pride "the governing traits of his nature." Above all, he was an artist of war, "a sort of genius."

"What made a great general?" Ludwig asked.

"Not to be beaten," Patton replied.

Great decisions, Patton said, were improvised. There was no strategy, only inspiration. Yet, inconsistently, he revealed that his plans for crossing the Danube had been made long in advance of the actual event.

Ludwig's sharp eyes photographed Patton during the war, during his glory, and no doubt this was the best time to see the general at his best.

# IX

# Death and Transfiguration

*"This is an ironical thing to have to happen to me."*

## CHAPTER 44

# The Last Fight

*"What chance have I to ride a horse again?"*

GEOFFREY KEYES, who commanded the Seventh Army and the Western Military District, wrote to his wife Leila on Friday, December 7:

> Gen Patton called this morning to say he is leaving for home in a short while so I think I'll go up and spend the night with him to-morrow. I shall hate to see him go, but I'm glad he will soon get out of all the controversy.

*Letter, Keyes to his wife, December 10, 1945*

He was leaving Monday (to-day) on his way home for Christmas, so I drove up to Bad Nauheim Sat. to spend the night and say good bye. Had a fine visit with him, and yesterday morning after breakfast I started home, and he and Hap Gay were to start for Mannheim . . . in a few minutes to go hunting. They also planned to stop along the way to visit some old Roman ruins.

Well about 5 miles out, my car died out, and the driver couldn't start it, so I thumbed a ride back to Bad Nauheim to get a mechanic or another car. I passed Gen P and Hap but didn't stop them. They saw my car, stopped, and when they found I had gone for help, they continued . . .

It took some time to round up help and then the darned car broke down twice more, so to make a long story short, I didn't get home until after 1 PM, when I should have been here by 11 AM. As soon as I arrived, I was told of the accident.

*Statement, Horace L. Woodring, no date*

I was stationed at Bad Nauheim, Germany with the Fifteenth Army as a Private First Class driving for General George S. Patton.

On a Sunday morning, 9 December 1945, General Patton went pheasant hunting with Major General Gay. I was driving for them at the time in a 1938 Cadillac, 75 Special Limousine. I had driven for General Patton for four months . . .

This trip was strictly a pleasure trip for the General. He was leaving on the following day, Monday morning, for the States in General Eisenhower's plane. His equipment had already been stored on the plane, and this was to be his last hunting trip. He went hunting every Sunday morning and on this morning he offered me a position as a civilian driver.

We left his headquarters and on the way to where he was to hunt he visited a castle high in the hills. The weather was clear and cold, and we encountered snow up in the hills which we didn't have below. The General had gotten his feet wet.

From the castle we rode on the auto-bahn and before turning into road N-38 on the outskirts of Mannheim we stopped at an MP check point. There the General got into the right rear seat. (He had been riding in the front with me.) General Gay was in the left rear, and at the check point their hunting dog, which had been in the jeep ahead of the General's car, was moved into the limousine, since he was very cold, and they thought he wouldn't hunt well if he was too cold.

On N-38, we stopped at a railroad crossing for a train to pass.

We had just crossed the Polish DP camp on our left.

When the train got by, we passed the Quartermaster Depot which the General was looking at and commenting on. About 600 yards beyond the railroad track, I noticed two 6 x 6 trucks ahead.

When I first started up, one of these also pulled away from the curb and approached in our direction. General Patton made a comment on the depot just as I noticed a GMC [truck] coming close from the opposite direction.

The driver made no hand signal. He just turned into my car. Both generals made the remark . . .

I saw him in time to hit my brakes but not in time to do any thing [else]. I was approximately not more than twenty feet away from him. The GMC [2½-ton truck] barely hit with its right front fender and hit us solid with the right side of the bed.

The General was thrown forward and hit his head on the railing above the rear of the driver's seat. The partition glass at the time was in a lowered position. It took all the skin from the General's forehead for approximately three inches above his eyebrows and three inches across, partially scalping him and completely separating his spinal column.

The car was knocked back approximately ten feet.

It was approximately 11:45 in the morning . . .

The General was conscious at the time and swore a little.

Within five minutes the MPs were there.

The left front end of Cadillac was crushed and demolished, but when the military police learned that the truck was traveling at 10 miles per hour, the car at 30, they placed no charges against Woodring or T/5 Robert L. Thompson, who was driving the truck. In letters Gay later wrote to both drivers, he absolved them of any blame. The accident apparently just happened.

No one was injured except Patton, who said he could not move and had pain in his neck. Most of his scalp was peeled from his head and hanging in a loop. Across the middle of his forehead was a ragged, deep laceration, leaving the bone bare. He was bleeding moderately.

Someone called the 130th Station Hospital near Heidelberg for an ambulance and a doctor – probably by radio from a military police vehicle or from the jeep that preceded the Cadillac to carry weapons and other equipment. It was not long before the general was being taken to the hospital, about 25 miles from the scene of the accident.

The doctor in the ambulance put adhesive tape on Patton's skull to hold the scalp down temporarily.

Woodring thought that Patton had struck the railing above the rear of the driver's seat. Gay believed that Patton hit the partition between the front and back. Captain William Duane, Jr., a medical officer who examined Patton later, concluded that he had come into contact with the strut of the car roof.

Whatever it was that received the blow of Patton's nose and forehead, he sustained a severe smash that injured the spinal cord in his back. The Cadillac was a large roomy, seven-passenger automobile, with jump seats that were folded down and closed at the time. The distance from the partition behind the front seat to the rear of the back seat was at least six feet, perhaps as much as eight. The impact of the collision sent Patton hurtling through the air. His head brushed the interior light on the ceiling of the vehicle, a diamond-shaped fixture with sharp points and edges that protruded dangerously. It was probably this that ripped the skin from his head just before he landed with a crash on the rail or partition.

Admitted to the hospital at 12:45, about an hour after the accident, he lay fully clothed on a litter. He was conscious, oriented, in mild shock, and aware of his serious predicament. He was unable to move his arms or legs. He had no sensation below his neck except at the tips of his shoulders.

In the outpatient room, after they cut his clothing away, they gave him blood plasma for shock. He showed improvement at once. Later they gave him a tetanus shot and penicillin.

Remarking that Patton opened his eyes and grumbled something, Dr. Frank S. Yordy leaned over him and asked what he wanted.

Patton said, "Relax, gentlemen, I'm in no condition to be a terror now." He chuckled.

A few minutes afterward he said, "Jesus Christ, what a way to start a leave."

The hospital chaplain came in, and Patton said, "Well, let him get started; I guess I need it."

The chaplain said a few prayers, and Patton thanked him.

Within two hours, Yordy recalled, eleven generals had come to the hospital.

As soon as Keyes heard the news,

> I went at once to the hospital and spent the rest of the day there. Hap was there of course and later Kenner and another specialist arrived.
>
> Well it was a bad accident, and the remarkable part about it is that neither Hap nor the driver were hurt at all.
>
> General P sustained a severe dislocation of a vertebra and a bad scalp wound as well as a bang on the nose . . .
>
> The big question is of course the extent of damage to the spinal cord.

Patton's old friend Kenner, now a major general and the chief surgeon of the theater, Colonel Earl E. Lowry, the chief surgical consultant in the theater, and Duane, chief of neurosurgery at a nearby general hospital, were there soon after the accident.

The doctors x-rayed Patton and gave him more plasma. After suturing the scalp wound, Lowry inserted Crutchfield tongs into the skull to apply traction to Patton's neck. They catheterized him and moved him to a private room.

As soon as Kenner realized the gravity of Patton's injury, he telephoned Washington. The Surgeon General advised him to get in touch with Brigadier Hugh Cairns, Professor of Neurosurgery at the Oxford University School of Medicine and a consultant to the British Army. When Cairns agreed to come to Heidelberg, Kenner had a military plane dispatched to London for him.

The Surgeon General notified Beatrice Patton of her husband's serious condition. She asked whether she could go to him. Eisenhower, now the Army Chief of Staff, made a plane available to her. The State Department worked at record speed to issue her a passport. On the evening of December 10, the day after the accident, she was at the Washington airport.

In Heidelberg, Patton spent his first night sleeping in short naps. He was restless and complained to the nurse of severe pain in the back of his neck. Awakening at 5 A.M., he talked with her for more than two hours. He tried to be cheerful, but she noted that he was "apprehensive about his condition."

Late that morning Cairns, accompanied by Colonel Gilbert Phillips, another British neurosurgeon, arrived. They examined Patton and approved what had been done.

*Letter, Keyes to his wife, December 10, 1945*

Gen Patton's condition is still very serious but he has made some remarkable strides toward recovery. The doctors say it will be another 48 hours before they can make a definite prognosis . . .

The x rays today show the dislocation almost reduced but the swelling and inflammation as yet makes it difficult to assess final damage.

To day a couple of British specialists arrived, and to-morrow Mrs. Patton arrives. She will stay at my quarters at least initially.

The General's spirits yesterday were fine, and he sounded like his old self, but to-day, although actually better, he was uncomfortable and sore — principally I believe because of his nose which is difficult to breathe through.

Think of all he has been through and then to meet with such an accident. Had he spent another 10 seconds inspecting the Roman ruins or had he started 10 seconds earlier, he would have missed the truck completely! . . .

It is about closing time, and I want to run out to the hospital again before I go home. Heaps of love, sweetheart. I know how hard you are praying for him [to] get well, and I sure have put in my best efforts along that line.

Patton was very cooperative and in good spirits that evening, although the nurse thought he sometimes confused the time of day. He drank a cup of coffee, which he said – apparently trying to make a joke – was the worst he ever tasted, then added that he enjoyed it.

Duane noted at midnight:

Although the nurse believes the general is slightly confused, I do not believe he is, so much as that he is despairing of recovery. This fact will play considerable part in the prognosis. His mental attitude is *not good.* He is greatly concerned about being permanently paralyzed.

They gave him glucose intravenously. Although Patton seemed to be resting well, the bottle of fluid, which he could see, bothered him. When the nurse removed the needle from his arm and the bottle from his sight, he said good night and ten minutes later fell asleep.

In the morning he said he felt much better. He thought he could move his right index finger ever so slightly. Shortly after lunch he said he had a queer sensation in his hands, as though the skin was falling away from the bone. He was suddenly depressed.

About thirty reporters had come to the hospital, many of them having left the Nuremberg trials, to cover the Patton story. Keyes authorized the hospital to issue periodic press releases.

That afternoon Mrs. Patton arrived in Heidelberg. With her was an American specialist, Colonel R. Glen Spurling.

Spurling had been the chief neurosurgical consultant in the European Theater, then had gone to Washington to be senior consultant in neurosurgery to the Surgeon General. On the afternoon of December 10, he was returning to Washington after a three-day leave in Louisville, Kentucky. He was traveling by train instead of by air because the weather was bad and unpredictable. The conductor came through the car paging him, and Spurling learned that an urgent message awaited him at Cincinnati. On the platform there, the station master handed him a telegram from the Adjutant General: "You will . . . proceed to the airport . . . where an army plane will fly you to Washington, thence Germany."

A waiting army car took Spurling to the airport, where he was hustled to a plane that was warming up. In Washington, in a small room at the air terminal, he met Mrs. Patton and Lieutenant Colonel Walter J. Kerwin, Eisenhower's representative. After being assured that the Surgeon General knew of Spurling's whereabouts and would cancel his appointments, he, together with Mrs. Patton and Kerwin, boarded a C-54 aircraft that had bucket seats, about 7000 pounds of mail, and a small curtained room arranged for Mrs. Patton.

When she noticed how inadequately Spurling was clothed for the flight in an unheated plane, she insisted that he take a pair of ski pajamas to wear and a sweater.

To Spurling, Mrs. Patton had a personality that radiated "like a brilliant gem." Within a few minutes of meeting her, he felt they were old friends.

They flew to Stevensville, Newfoundland, and after refueling and breakfast, to the Azores, where they learned that severe storms covered Europe. All airports on the continent were closed. A news bulletin informed Spurling that Patton "had sustained a fracture of his cervical spine, with paralysis," which was a "bad outlook under any circumstances." After dinner the pilot decided to chance the weather and continue. At Paris both airports were closed because of fog and rain. They proceeded to Marseilles, where General J. C. H. Lee and his personal plane were waiting to take them to Germany. After they landed near Heidelberg, Spurling went directly to the hospital where "the doctors were waiting for me."

Keyes took Mrs. Patton to his headquarters, where Gay and Kenner were waiting. "After we brought her up to date," Keyes later wrote his wife,

> we went to the hospital. She and he were fine — of course they would be. She is staying at my place and so is the WAC Capt. we've detailed as a sort of aide. Also Gen P's aide Merle-Smith.

Spurling learned that Patton had a fracture-dislocation of the third and fourth cervical vertebrae.

> He was paralyzed from the neck downward. There was complete paralysis of both legs and all of the abdominal muscles and the muscles of respiration. He was incompletely paralyzed in both arms. He was breathing with only one side of his diaphragm. His bladder and bowels were paralyzed. The only ray of hope was that the tendon reflexes, which are so commonly abolished after an acute injury of the spine, were still active. It was hoped that perhaps the spinal cord had just been shaken — a concussion, as we call it — rather than completely destroyed.
>
> His medical condition was therefore precarious. In the first place, there was serious doubt that he could live very long with so much restriction of breathing. The chances of his ever regaining complete control of his musculature, even under the most favorable circumstances, were very slight. All medical experience indicates that patients who have sustained spinal cord injuries at this high level seldom recover.

After conferring with the doctors, Spurling went to Patton's bedside. Patton was cheerful. He apologized "for getting you out on this wild goose chase" and taking him away from his family at Christmas.

Spurling checked the patient and found the reports "accurate in all details."

Patton's only comment during the examination was, "This is an ironical thing to have to happen to me."

Asked whether he was comfortable, Patton said he was in no pain except for "the rather persistent drag" of the skeletal traction.

The doctors then conferred again and

> decided that nothing further could be done. Certainly an operation was out of the question . . . The spinal cord had undoubtedly been damaged the instant the accident had occurred, and no surgical effort could hope to restore it. In the second place . . . an operation . . . would have been an almost impossible task because the patient was barely able to breathe under normal conditions, much less anesthesia.

The consultation was interrupted by a message from Patton asking Spurling alone to come to his room.

When Spurling entered, Mrs. Patton was gone, and the nurse left soon afterward. He was sure he knew what was coming – "the General wanted the truth."

After some small talk about Spurling's trip, Patton said, "Now, Colonel, we've known each other during the fighting, and I want you to talk to me as man to man. What chance have I to recover?"

Spurling said that Patton was doing so much better than the usual patient with a cervical cord injury that it was impossible to give a forthright answer at the moment. If the cord was severed or severely damaged, his chance of recovery was very slight. But if the cord had been only shaken up, there might be rather drastic improvements in the next 48 to 72 hours.

"What chance have I to ride a horse again?" Patton asked.

Spurling answered directly. "None."

"In other words," Patton said, "the best that I could hope for would be semi-invalidism."

"Yes."

Patton thought a moment, then said gravely, "Thank you, Colonel, for being honest."

In a flash he became jovial. "Colonel," he said, "you're surrounded by an awful lot of brass around here. There are more generals than privates, so far as I can gather from the nurses and the doctors. I just want you to know that you're the boss. Whatever you say goes."

Spurling then told him that many of Patton's friends were clamoring to see him.

"It's your decision," Patton said.

"All right, no one is to see you except Mrs. Patton, General Keyes, General Gay, the doctors and the nurses on duty."

"I think that's a good decision, irrespective of the medical point of view. After all, it's kind of hard for me to see my old friends when I'm lying here paralyzed all over."

Spurling asked him to save his strength. He explained the medical problems in his case, and Patton grasped them at once and accepted them without question.

"I'll try to be a good patient," he said.

At midnight when he awakened, the nurse read him a get-well message from President Truman.

"That was nice, wasn't it?" he said.

The newspapers and radio broadcasts were full of reports of the accident and of Patton's condition, and a host of telegrams, letters, and cards poured in from well-wishers, individuals, and organizations, who hoped for his speedy recovery. "Best of luck from an American among the millions," wrote one. "Just one of the great many persons who are deeply distressed to hear of your unfortunate accident," wrote another. "A grateful America prays for the recovery of her greatest war hero." Communications came from the Jewish War Veterans, the Irish War Veterans, the Veterans of Foreign Wars, the American Legion, mayors of villages in France, a nun who offered to send a sacred healing badge, a physiotherapist who promised his services in Germany or anywhere "(without charge)," Ira F. Lewis, President of the Pittsburgh *Courier* who wired "the hope and prayers of every Negro GI who served in the war and of 15 million Negroes throughout the nation in wishing you our heartfelt desire for complete recovery. America and the world needs men who practice the democracy they preach."

There was a letter from Eisenhower, and Beatrice read it to her husband:

> You can imagine what a shock it was to me to hear of your serious accident. At first I heard it on the basis of rumor and simply did not believe, thinking it only a story . . . I immediately wired Frankfurt and learned to my great distress that it was true . . . By coincidence, only the day before yesterday, I had directed that you be contacted to determine whether you wanted a particular job that appeared to be opening up here in the States. The real purpose of this note is simply to assure you that you will always have a job and not to worry about this accident closing out any of them for your selection . . . It is always difficult for me to express my true sentiments when I am deeply moved . . . You are never out of my thoughts and . . . my hopes and prayers are tied up in your speedy recovery.

When she was not with her husband, Beatrice was answering the messages that stacked up in piles. Throughout her stay at the hospital she kept her equanimity. Nothing seemed to ruffle her. Spurling thought that her devotion to her husband was evidence of an exceptionally beautiful human relationship. "She had lived her life for him."

In the middle of the morning of December 12, when Spurling and

Kenner examined Patton, they found no voluntary motion, no sensation, more labored breathing. Their impression was that the patient had failed to maintain the progress noted the day before. Recovery became more doubtful.

Since the Crutchfield tongs tended to slip because of the shape of his skull, the doctors put Patton under local anesthesia and Cairns inserted large-caliber fishhooks beneath his cheekbones.

Examination afterward revealed no fracture of the nasal bones and almost perfect reduction of the vertebral dislocations. The paralysis remained unchanged. The general's attitude was deemed good.

That evening Patton said he had no appetite. He felt fatigued. He had pain in his neck.

Fred Ayer departed New York for London on a commercial flight en route to Heidelberg. With Spurling on hand to take charge of the case, Cairns and Phillips left for England.

At 1.30 A.M., December 13, Patton awakened and showed great apprehension over his condition. He told the nurse he wanted to sleep and "forget it all."

He seemed alert at breakfast. His disposition became cheerful. At midnight he complained of neck pains.

According to Spurling,

> Twenty-four hours after my arrival, there had seemed to be a distinct improvement in the General's condition. He regained a little more power in one arm and a very minute amount of power in one leg. Also the muscles of respiration began to function feebly. This gave us high hopes that the cord was not as seriously damaged as we had had every reason to believe in the beginning. In addition to these favorable neurological signs, his general condition remained remarkably good. He was cheerful and took a well balanced diet freely. His temperature and pulse remained normal, and his elimination was highly satisfactory.
>
> At the end of 48 hours, while improvement still was noticeable, it was not nearly so rapid as it had been . . . By the end of the third day the improvement ceased and there was no further return of spinal cord function. Yet in spite of this grim outlook, General Patton's general condition held up remarkably well.

*Letter, Keyes to his wife, December 14, 1945*

Things have gone along with satisfactory progress as to general condition but the final outcome is still in doubt. Day before yesterday was the only day so far that some progress wasn't noted. But yesterday and to-day he has really picked up and everyone is pleased. I wish you could see the telegrams that come in from over the world.

Patton was wide awake during most of the night and the early morning hours of December 14. He talked a great deal, and cheerfully, with his nurse. He had a good breakfast and a good lunch, but wanted no supper, preferring to sleep. Several hours later he said he was cold. Throughout the night he tried to raise phlegm by coughing.

Spurling found slight reflexes in both arms and the right leg on December 15. Patton was sweating, and his sensory level was down to just above the nipple line. He said that the traction hooks were painful.

On December 16, Patton had breakfast, refused lunch, and reluctantly had grapefruit juice and beet juice for supper. He was coughing much of the time. He was, Spurling noted,

> undoubtedly aware of extent of paralysis and is always subtlely testing out the doctors' statements. Occasionally on awakening he is confused mentally for a few minutes, otherwise normally alert.

*Letter, Keyes to his wife, December 16, 1945*

Well it [is] just a week ago to-day . . , that the accident occurred and it really seems ages in view of all that has happened. However, things look much brighter this Sunday than they did last Sunday. The doctors are very optimistic now and say, barring unforseen complications, Gen Patton is out of danger as far as saving his life is concerned, but the degree of recovery is still unsettled, although each day now there is improvement and real cause for encouragement.

Mrs. P is just as cheerful and lively as ever and of course has won everybody from MPs to nurses to doctors etc. Last night her brother Mr. Fred Ayer arrived, and he too is a real addition to the party. I don't know how long he will remain but with the progress being made by the Gen I don't imagine he will remain long.

On December 17, Patton said all he wanted to do was sleep. Reluctantly he swallowed some juice and soup during the day. He was still trying to cough to raise mucus.

The doctors applied a plaster neck-and-shoulder cast and removed the traction fishhooks. "Once the General was out of traction," Spurling noted, "he was much happier." He said he thought he had a tingling in his hands and feet or in his arms and legs, but he could not be sure.

Since he took insufficient nourishment and drank liquids only when urged, Spurling prescribed eggnog and whiskey before supper to stimulate his appetite. Although Patton drank only part of his allotted ounce and a half of whiskey, he was cheerful that evening and alert. He said that eating tired him.

When a reporter learned that Patton had liquor, he filed a story that the general was following his usual custom of taking his whiskey straight. Screaming headlines followed.

*Letter, Keyes to his wife, December 18, 1945*

I think I wrote you that Mrs. Patton's brother (Mr. Fred Ayer) was arriving. Well he did and is still with us. They are certainly nice and it is a treat having them in the house.

The Gen. still improves and now . . . he seems much better.

Alone with his nurse, Patton was depressed. With visitors, he tried to keep up appearances and be cheerful, jovial, and joking.

*Telegram, Spurling to Lieut. Col. Michel de Bakey, Office of Surgeon General, Washington, D.C., December 19, 1945*

Arrangements being made air evacuation General Patton, 30 December [to the United States]. Family desires that I wait and accompany him. While unnecessary, this course appears desirable.

Blood chemistry studies revealed a marked protein disbalance, so the doctors gave Patton plasma and albumin. They remarked a few slight rales – rattles or bubbles in his breathing; otherwise his lungs were clear.

"From the beginning," Spurling recalled,

Mrs. Patton had been concerned about the possibility of an embolism. When he had had a broken leg 15 or 20 years previously, he had almost died of a pulmonary embolism. She kept saying to me every night, "If he just doesn't get an embolism, I think he may pull through."

On the afternoon of December 20th, it happened. Mrs. Patton was reading to him at the time, and he was perfectly quiet and under no emotional strain. All of a sudden he said, "I feel like I can't get my breath –" A doctor was called and, sure enough, he was cyanotic. Oxygen was started and he rallied very fast, but he raised a little blood-tinged sputum – unmistakable evidence of a small infarction of the lung.

The next morning a bedside x-ray showed that he had an embolism involving the right upper lung; but that morning he was feeling fine again and was as cheerful as ever. There was no predicting where the embolism might have formed. There was certainly no external evidence of phlebitis in any part of the body.

*Letter, Keyes to his wife, December 21, 1945*

We are all in a pretty low state, sweetheart. Gen Patton took a sudden turn for the worse last night, and he is again very critically ill. In fact the doctors hold out very little hope. Of course we haven't given up, and Mrs. Patton is as plucky and courageous as five ordinary people.

I have just come back from the hospital where I had lunch with her. She spent the night there and will probably stay there to-night. Fortunately her brother is still here, and he is a great help in these times . . .

Well everyone is getting ready for the holidays and if I have to attend all the troop and Red Cross and private parties, I think I'll have to get a week's leave to recover! Of course the condition of Gen Patton has changed things as far as my own plans are concerned . . .

Sure hope I have better news when I next write, sweetheart, but the chances are mighty slim.

An oxygen mask was being held to Patton's nose and mouth most of the time. His pulse was weak. He slept or rested quietly almost constantly. He roused himself to have eggnog at noon. He told his nurse several times during the day that he was going to die.

At 4 P.M., he was very drowsy.

The hospital press release stated that his condition was considered serious. An accumulation of secretions in the lungs embarrassed respiration and the heart.

The doctors thought that Patton probably had a small collection of fluid in the pleural cavity of the right chest. His heart showed cardiac dullness, but no aortic examination was possible because of the cast.

He fell asleep shortly after 4 o'clock, although his breathing was irregular. At 5:30, he was still sleeping. His breathing was better.

*Letter, Keyes to his wife, December 23, 1945*

It looked pretty bad for the General, but the doctors thought it was a matter of 48 hours or more. However that evening he was sleeping, and Mrs. P. went to supper there in the hospital, and as I left her, she told me to tell her brother not to bother about coming back to the hospital after supper as everything was OK, and she was going [to] sleep there.

Spurling remembered that "the day of December 21st went along smoothly enough. Mrs. Patton spent most of the afternoon reading to him." Since Patton was asleep, she and Spurling went to the hospital dining room for dinner. They were

half-way through the meal when a messenger appeared, asking that we come immediately. When we got there, he was dead. Death was undoubtedly due to a large pulmonary embolism.

He had simply expired at five minutes to six. The cause was "pulmonary edema and congestive heart failure."

*Letter, Keyes to his wife, December 23, 1945*

The minute I got home the phone rang and it was the Gen's aide at the hospital asking me to come right back. The General had dozed off and never woke up. Mrs. Patton was just wonderful.

Spurling:

Patton died as he had lived – bravely. Throughout his illness there was never one word of complaint regarding a nurse or doctor or orderly. Each and every one was treated with the kindest consideration. He took orders without question – in fact, he was a model patient.

Heidelberg was unusually quiet. All the service clubs were closed. A plain Christmas tree in a square near the university seemed almost a discordant note in the hushed city.

*Seventh Army General Orders 635, December 22, 1945, signed Keyes*

With deep regret, announcement is made of the death of General George S. Patton, Jr. . .

Probably no soldier has had a greater compliment paid him than that given General Patton by his most powerful and skillful opponents. He was termed the ablest American field commander faced by the German Army on any front.

The entire Allied World now pays tribute to the man who deserves more than a lion's share of the credit for the victories of our arms in the bitter European struggle just ended.

Seventh Army has lost a great friend, a gallant warrior, and inspiring leader. Our country has lost a great and fearless citizen. May we comfort ourselves with the thought that he died as he loved to live – ever fighting!

*Letter, Williston B. Palmer to Ruth Ellen Totten, December 22, 1945*

For him I think it is seemly that he rode out on the storm, and escaped the dullness of old age, while he was at the height of his fame. Surely no man ever held the attention of the entire world more completely by sheer force of his own personality and achievements, without the brilliance of a sovereign position to draw attention to him.

Lieutenant Colonel Montgomery C. Jackson was in London, and more than fifty British officers and men had anxiously inquired of Patton's condition before his death. Jackson had never realized the hold that Patton exerted on the hearts of the British who regarded him as their favorite American general.

*Letter, a soldier ("in mourning") stationed in Germany to his parents, December 22, 1945*

Last night one of the greatest men that ever lived died. That was Patton. The rest of the world thinks of him as just another guy with stars on his shoulders. The men that served under him know him as a soldier's leader. I am proud to say that I have served under him in the Third Army.

It sure looks different here. All the flags are at half-mast. We are making every Heinie that passes stop and take off his hat. They can't understand our feelings for him. I don't know whether or not you can understand them either.

*Letter, Capt. Charles W. Clark, Jr., Clarksdale, Miss., to Beatrice Patton, December 22, 1945*

He was the greatest soldier of them all.

Spurling requested permission to undertake an autopsy, but Mrs. Patton refused. Not only was a fully qualified pathologist unavailable, but "Mrs. Patton felt that under the circumstances she would prefer not to have one performed."

While communications between Washington and Heidelberg were arranging the return of the body to the United States for burial, Keyes took Spurling aside and said that no deceased American soldier had been sent home since the beginning of the war. An exception in Patton's case, Keyes feared, would have an adverse effect on American mothers whose sons had been interred overseas. Yet he hesitated to put the matter to Mrs. Patton because of his long friendship with the family.

So Spurling talked to Mrs. Patton.

She said, "Of course he must be buried here. Why didn't I think of it? Furthermore, I know George would want to lie beside the men of his Army who have fallen."

Certainly in his letters he had made this wish known.

From among three large American military cemeteries which held most of the Third Army casualties, Mrs. Patton selected the one at Hamm, Luxembourg.

*Seventh Army Memo, December 22, 1945*

Mrs. Patton wishes to present a case of wine to Hospital Mess in appreciation of kindness and best wishes for Merry Christmas and Happy New Year.

Later she would write to Cairns, offering payment for his services. He said he would cheerfully accept a donation to his hospital for the purchase of medical equipment.

*Letter, Keyes to his wife, December 23, 1945*

Yesterday Hap took her and her brother to Bad Nauheim to see the General's last CP and house. They spent the night there and will be back [today] about noon.

The funeral services at the church will be at 3 PM and then we go by train to Luxembourg where he will be buried at 10 AM tomorrow.

The arrangements have been enormous. Troops from all over had to be assembled. Dignitaries invited and cared for. Transportation. Flowers from Paris, the Riviera, and every other place as there are none locally at this time of year. Planes for the return trip. As the burden of arrangements and coordination fell on us, you can imagine how busy we've been. . .

If I go to Paris to see Mrs. P and her brother off [for home], I probably won't get back till late Xmas.

Someone gathered up Patton's belongings for shipment to Green Meadows — official papers, stag horns, footlockers, a big wardrobe, two steamer trunks, several canes, a sword (which the family gave to Sergeant Meeks), books, a portable typewriter, his portrait (his Christmas present for Beatrice), helmets, dictaphones, scrapbooks, suitcases — Willie too.

On Saturday, December 22, the day after Patton's death, his body was placed in state at the Villa Reiner, a lovely house on a mountain overlooking Heidelberg. On Sunday, December 23, the casket was closed, then escorted by a platoon of cavalry and the pallbearers to the Protestant Church in Heidelberg for the Episcopal funeral service. Flowers surrounded the coffin — camellias from Keyes, white lilacs from Clark, cut flowers, plants, lilacs, pussy willows from friends and organizations, including a large spray from the 130th Station Hospital. Present were official delegations from Britain, France, the Soviet Union, Sweden, Belgium, and Luxembourg, as well as from the major American commands in Europe.

After the service, the body was solemnly escorted the mile to the railroad station. As the train started to leave, an artillery battery fired a 17-gun salute. When the train was gone, the band played a lively tune.

*Letter, Keyes to his wife, December 26, 1945*

The honorary pall bearers assembled about noon and after greeting them I came home and had lunch with Mrs. Patton and Mr.

Ayer and of course Hap and the aides. Then we drove to the church and the services there were very impressive. Hap and I sat with and accompanied Mrs. Patton throughout. From the church we drove to the RR station, and the streets were lined with troops and civilians. It was really a great tribute . . .

On our train was of course the casket with all the flowers, the color guard, the pall bearers (NCOs), several honorary pall bearers, and the family party. Commencing at about 7 PM as we crossed into the French sector, and continuing until after 11 PM, we stopped 6 times for honor guards at stations. Each time Mrs. Patton would get off and inspect the guard, and the commander would make a very appropriate little speech, which she answered just as appropriately in French. At the last stop the Division Commander Gen Caille was there with a beautiful wreath which he placed at the casket.

When we got up at Luxembourg it was raining and dreary looking. There was first the ceremony of placing the casket on the half track with the guard of honor formed of Lux-troops. Then the procession through the city with the streets lined with troops and civilians. It took about half an hour to reach the cemetery and again the services and ceremony was awfully impressive. Afterwards Mrs. P sat in the car and the various dignitaries and representatives came up and paid their respects.

Patton's marker would be a white cross, like every other, bearing his name, rank, and serial number. In 1948, his body would be moved to a more central place in the cemetery, with five surrounding graves left vacant, for the convenience of the thousands who came to visit him.

We then drove back to the train and found the weather reports favorable for flying, so drove to Metz and flew to Paris. There another lucky break occurred, and they took off at 3 PM headed home via Iceland with great hopes of getting home before noon Xmas. I haven't heard yet of their arrival . . .

I couldn't get a plane back from Paris, so Seignious and I took an afternoon train and arrived at Frankfort at 8 AM Xmas. I got back to Heidelberg just in time for 9:30 Mass and then rushed home, changed my clothes, and started out on inspections of mess halls and hospitals.

## CHAPTER 45

# The Legend and the Man

*"I can't decide logically if I am a man of destiny or a lucky fool, but I think I am destined . . . I feel that my claim to greatness hangs on an ability to lead and inspire . . . I am a genius—I think I am."*

—November 3, 1942

IF FROM SOME UNEARTHLY PLACE George S. Patton, Jr., observed the human scene after his death, he no doubt smiled cynically. He had been removed from the post he cherished above all, command of his beloved Third Army, and banished in disgrace to the lowest depth of the dungeon. Then in a single bound he regained his fame and surpassed it. How quickly after his fall from grace had his achievements been resurrected and acclaimed!

In large measure the timing of his death determined the status accorded him. It was too soon after the war for him to be forgotten, too soon for him to spoil irretrievably the reputation he had earned. He was lucky in this too, for he had ever been alternately the hero and the goat.

After his accident had he died at once, the upsurge of emotion would probably have dissipated. He would, very likely, have shot up like a rocket and, to use his phrase, come down like a stick.

But he lingered as he fought for his life in the hospital at Heidelberg, and the sympathy swelled. The long waiting gave people pause, provided them perspective on his accomplishments, and permitted them to reconsider his importance.

Who else could have whipped the prewar army into fighting shape as he did? Or won so convincingly at Casablanca? Restored the American soldier in Tunisia? Triumphed so handsomely in Sicily? Exploded the breakthrough into the pursuit to the German border? Saved Bastogne? Who else?

Even his protest over the Occupation now seemed warranted, for after his departure from the scene, as the lines of the cold war began to be drawn, the policies changed.

Americans came to believe that Patton had been badly used. And when he died, there was a sudden and sincere grief. From all over the world came characterizations of his greatness.

"He inscribed his name in the annals of military history by bold and brilliant leadership."

"Our most gallant soldier."

"The greatest general America has known."

"The greatest soldier of this terrible war."

"The greatest general of all times."

"Essential to the nation."

"There will never be another like him."

"No man ever meant so much to me."

A staff sergeant struggling with the English language and with the unfamiliar task of setting down his thoughts, after writing a hopelessly inarticulate letter, signed his name and added quite simply, "I love him."

From London: "His personality is more firmly fixed in our minds than any other military commander of the late war, and therefore his memory will remain with us and our children for generations."

"He came to us fellows in the 12th Evac. Hospital and he told me in plain words, 'Don't you loose that leg, I need you.' But I left him down. I had to loose it. I did love him as a leader, and I believe that every man under him did."

"I will never forget the feelings of the men in my battery when, after reaching the Rhine, we were informed the division was being transferred to another Army. They were afraid the General thought they were not good enough for him."

"The fondest memory I have of the war just finished is the thought that I was a member of the Third Army. In the earliest days of the Ardennes, we green troops were fighting with desperation, and in the darkest moments of the worst hours, the news came that we were in the Third Army and that help was coming. It would have warmed your heart to see the hope that came with that simple announcement. The Third Army meant the 'old man,' and he meant hope, success, and victory . . . I feel that I am a better man because of the General, and . . . he will be a source of strength for the rest of my life."

"[He] held . . . all the lore and wisdom of America's past and stood face forward. Germany never terrified him, Russia never mystified him, the future came to him as nothing strange . . . Out of the mud of vilification a great man and soldier has arisen. It's a shame that death should have been necessary to clarify his true value and virtue."

Brigadier General B. G. Chynoweth, a friend of 37 years, to the Editor of the Washington *Post:*

> I have never known a man more single-minded in preparing himself for battle leadership . . . He experimented with and cultivated the art of the spectacular just as earnestly and purposefully as he developed his mastery of weapons, tactics, military history, and battle psychology.
>
> You state that "Patton the man never lived up to Patton the soldier." I fear that it was not your privilege to know Patton the man. The man who deliberately and continually courted every form of personal danger, in peace and in war, in order to crush out of his own heart any vestige of the fear which he knew to be the greatest of all enemies in war . . .
>
> You state that he "was made for no other purpose than for war." Please let me inform you that he was also made for friendship, for kindly affection, and for sympathy with the underdog. I have never known a friend upon whom one could count more surely for disinterested help in time of trouble . . .
>
> This soldier and man has passed on, leaving in the lives of his friends and in the service of the nation a vacancy that cannot be filled except through a reflection upon his heroic example.

On Sunday, December 30, at a memorial service in the Church of Our Saviour, San Gabriel, California, Bishop W. B. Stevens said something that many had failed to notice:

> General Patton was at heart a child, like most great men. His impetuousness and his occasional impatience were manifestations of a childlike character.

On the same day, the Reverend W. F. A. Stride spoke at a service of remembrance in St. John's Church, Beverly Farms, Massachusetts:

> "Those whom the gods love die young." And that is applicable to

> George S. Patton. For he had in him a quality of intrinsic youth, despite his more than sixty years . . .
>
> We know and have smiled over his habit of carrying two revolvers, of swearing and swashbuckling. All this flamboyance of his . . . was in fact a token of his unfaded youthfulness. And he used it all, and perhaps developed and exaggerated it . . . to be a better leader of men.

"I have never heard such singing by choir and congregation," the Reverend A. Abbott Hastings wrote Beatrice; "it was most triumphant and convincing."

On Sunday, January 20, 1946, at the Cathedral Church of St. Peter and St. Paul on Mount Alban, in Washington, D.C., the George S. Patton, Jr., Tank Corps Post Number 19 of the American Legion held a memorial service. Colonel Harry H. Semmes delivered the address:

> We . . . are here to lay our modest sheaf of green bay and yellow broom upon the tomb of the man who was our comrade and friend through many years . . . I see him riding the outside of a tank into battle at San Mihiel . . . He lies next to me in a cot in an evacuation hospital in a roofless church near the Argonne forest . . .
>
> George Patton, your old comrades-in-arms and friends, both living and dead, salute you. A thousand years of unborn Americans will look down on what you have done and find it good.

The tributes continued long after his death — bills in the Congress to award him posthumously the Medal of Honor, to promote him to five-star rank, to provide a Patton national monument; measures in state legislatures to authorize suitable memorials; innumerable avenues, public squares, and buildings named for him all over the world; statues erected, plaques placed, poems written. As late as 1972, a new Patton Museum was dedicated at Fort Knox.

All this made evident the persistent and tenacious hold he exerted over the imagination.

Someone had written to Beatrice in December 1945: "Great persons never really die." And in 1972, Livorno M. Ruberto, former army mess sergeant who cooked for generals in Europe during the war, confessed, "I still can't think of Patton as being dead, a man like that. I expect to turn around and still see him standing there."

Why did his reputation continue to grow and elicit increasing respect over the years? He had become a myth and had entered into American folklore. Like Davy Crockett, he was half real, half god. An entire subculture arose about him, spreading invented and exaggerated tales of his fabulous feats and incomparable courage.

Max Lerner once wrote during the war:

> I suspect that what we ask of our commanders is that they live up to the image we have formed of them – which means, I suppose, the picture we have of ourselves in their places.

Patton filled the bill. First and foremost, he conformed to one of the most persistent traits of American national character, an identification with the man of the West. From Daniel Boone to Wyatt Earp, from the Virginian to Matt Dillon, Americans cherished the self-reliant fighter handy with a gun. Two-gun Patton, wearing his .45 Long Colt Single Action revolver and his .357 Magnum Smith & Wesson revolver in matching holsters, personified the image to perfection. In the American mind he was a throwback to the cowboy folk hero.

Hardly less important was his childlike nature. In his attitudes and appearance he seemed to be a perpetual adolescent, an eternal juvenile, rash, impetuous, boyish. "He is so *very* young in spirit," Codman remarked. He was

> a real and literal *enfant terrible – enfant* . . . in his candor, intuitiveness, shrewdness, and unawareness; *terrible* in the intensity of his convictions, his self-discipline, and all the Spartan virtues. And a marvelous Thespian gift.

This too Americans understood and admired. He was always, no matter his age, the figure of youth.

He was also a winner, and his single-minded obession with victory thrilled and reassured Americans who had been disillusioned at the end of the last war. Triumph in World War I had slipped away and somehow been betrayed, no one quite knew how. This time, with Patton exerting the will to win, things would be different. The belief in Patton's invincibility continued long after the war was over, even when the United States became involved in southeast Asia. If only we had Patton, they said.

And so he was idealized and idolized. The characteristics he displayed to the public fitted the American preconception of the dashing military leader. He made his countrymen glad that he existed. He was unique.

"Most generals are just names-in-the-paper to most civilians," Mrs. Edgar M. Whiting of Winchester, Virginia, wrote him in April 1945, "but you seem to stand out from them as a very real and heroic person — which you are."

The postmaster of the municipality of Patton, in Cambria County, Pennsylvania — the only place so called in the United States — received thousands of letters during the war from people all over the country who asked to have a postmark of his name.

All his life he worked to attain and project the picture of the fighter. His aide Codman related that on their first morning in Normandy he knocked on the door of Patton's trailer. Pattan had just finished shaving and was standing before the mirror.

"Codman," he said, "I wish to hell I had a real fighting face."

"I should have thought it was a reasonable facsimile," Codman replied.

"No, no, no," he said impatiently, "you are either born with a fighting face or you are not. There are a lot of them in Third Army, Paddy Flint, Stiller, and many others. Having practiced for hours in front of the mirror, I can work up a fairly ferocious expression, but I have not got, and never will have, a natural-born fighting face."

The posturing and swaggering, all the things that Patton did to enhance his public image, were efficacious, and the press portrayed him, according to Codman, as "a kind of two-dimensional colored cartoon of a swashbuckling, sulfur-breathing, pearl-handled 'superman' packaged in tinsel and labeled Old Blood-and-Guts." Even the term Blood and Guts was his own coinage, struck off in the 1930s, when he described his qualifications for the post of Commandant of Cadets at West Point, an appointment he wanted and never received.

Yet "the much advertised exterior trappings — themselves quite good" were, Codman thought, relatively minor characteristics.

Once after Patton watched a group of soldiers at bayonet practice, he gave his approval but thought the men could do better. Pointing to a shredded dummy, he said,

> That's a German. You don't hate him enough. You're all too gentlemanly. Just because you've been brought up not to kick your

> grandmother in the ass, don't think he hasn't, because he has – they all have. They are the lowest so-and-so's and so-and-so's that crawl the earth, except perhaps the Japs, but we won't have to worry about them until next year. For the present just keep hating Germans. They are —— and damn fine soldiers. Get mad and keep mad all the time. After all, your outfit comes from a part of the country that has produced fighters.

Where did the outfit come from? Codman later asked.

"I haven't the slightest idea," Patton said. "That was just Speech Thirty-three."

The language was fine and in character, but the admission at the end indicated his occasional boredom with the role of the tough guy he had assumed.

One night when Patton was unable to sleep, he wrote to Dr. P. P. Johnson of Beverly, who had saved his life in the 1930's. In the course of his rather long letter, he described the landscape in North Africa to the doctor who was an amateur photographer.

> Next to Hawaii, this is the most vividly colored country I have ever seen. In flying over it the contrasts between the vivid greens of the grass fields and the bright red of the plow fields is almost startling. Then, too, at this time of the year, the almond trees add a touch of almost fairy-like loveliness to the whole scene.

Patton then went on to say: "This sounds like very poor writing for a soldier, so I will change." It was unseemly to him for a fighter to have thoughts so unmasculine as those. So he continued in a vein he believed to be more representative of the fighting spirit, better barracks talk.

> The other day, I went on a pig hunt with a gentleman called "The Glaoui," who rules some 3,000,000 other gentlemen of color in this vicinity. He is sixty-eight years old and still supports four wives and twenty concubines with considerable success . . .
>
> On the hunt upon which he took me and on which we killed 14 wild boar . . . we passed over about a hundred miles of country where he had fought as a young man . . . One place he showed me an olive orchard where, as the results of his efforts, the dead were so thick the jackals got sick.

This was much more like the warrior he was supposed to be.

Patton's cousin and boyhood friend, Arvin H. Brown, once wrote to him:

> Your poem, A Soldier's Burial, is a beautiful thing. It reflects the depth of your feeling and understanding, that you so often try to conceal by a studied pretence of being something other than your own great self — or so it seems to me.

He yearned to be tough and made himself so against his inner reality. That long struggle had its costs. Not only did he succeed in making himself a caricature of the image he wished to project, an exaggerated version of what he aspired to be, but in the process he came close to killing the gentle soul within himself. Toward the end of his life, little remained except the violence. He was emotionally drained by the lifelong struggle to make himself into something fundamentally alien to his being.

If Patton had, as doctors later suspected, a subdural haematoma, a phenomenon that exerts subtle physiological changes affecting personality, temperament, outlook, and behavior, he probably also benefited from it, for it produced on occasion a hardness of attitude, a coldness of spirit, a ruthlessness of will. Aside from his mastery of the military skills of his time, Patton's unique strengths — his driving energy, unconquerable will power, obsession to attack — were, in some part at least, probably attributable to his likely medical condition.

His insatiable ambition contributed. Always an overachiever, he overextended his physical, mental, and emotional capacities. In the relaxation that came with the end of the war in Europe, he felt that few appreciated his accomplishments. Bitterness, resentment, and jealousy marred the latter months of his life. This was in part a consequence of the waning of his own powers and, as Father Stride noted, "the disillusion and reaction that follow a supreme effort."

Ultimately Patton came close to collapse because of his internal dilemma. He loved the solitary pursuits rather than team play, and he could take part in polo and in war only by putting on an ardor, recklessness, and brutality that were fundamentally false to him. His profanity on the polo field was legendary, but it took that to make him play.

In the end he paid a price. His inner turmoil eventually distorted his balance and his view of the world. Thus, a strange and fulminating Patton emerged during the Occupation, a disturbed and at times near-paranoid man who was dreadful in the private thoughts he committed to paper.

Why did he drive himself with such unflagging intensity? Apart from those impulses from the recesses of his libido, some of the pressures no doubt originated in his childhood and came from his parents, who overwhelmed him with love but also with subtle yet iron expectations of his future. His father's letters, overflowing with devotion, irresistibly urged him to conquer himself and the world.

Patton probably suffered in his childhood from a mild form of dyslexia, a reading disability that transposed letters of words and accounted for his erratic spelling. No doubt for that reason he stayed home longer than most children, went to school only when he was eleven years old. During his preschool years, his father read to him, taught him numbers, and inculcated in him a sense of history and a love of literature. And perhaps Mr. Patton compensated for his own feelings of inadequacy — after all, what had he done compared to his own father, the first George Smith Patton, who fought and died gloriously in the Civil War? — by planting in his son the seeds of obligation to perform and excel, to be great in the mold of the classical heroes of antiquity.

Thus Codman could note about Patton:

> His standards, values, and preoccupations antedate the technique of present-day publicity. For what seems to have escaped most contemporary journalists is the fact that General Patton is not a contemporary figure.
>
> To be sure, he has contributed to the science of warfare professional proficiency of the highest modern order. More significant, however . . . he brings to the art of command in this day and age the norms and antique virtues of the classic warrior. To him the concepts of duty, patriotism, fame, honor, glory are not mere abstractions, nor the shopworn ingredients of Memorial Day speeches. They are basic realities — self-evident, controlling . . . In the time of Roger the Norman or in ancient Rome, General Patton would have felt completely at home.

Sitting in his father's lap and listening to his father declaim Homer's

*Iliad* and *Odyssey*, Patton learned the ancient and noble virtues. These he was brought up with, and these he had to live up to. Nor did he escape when he went off to college. The brooding presence of anticipated glory on the part of his family during his early boyhood accompanied him. Throughout most of the time he was at VMI and West Point, Aunt Nannie or Mama was staying, boarding, nearby.

His failure at the end of his first year at West Point only stung him to greater effort. Forty years later Fletcher still remembered "that disconsolate caydet" – Patton – "crushed by the news of being turned back; and I can feel again my sympathy and sorrow for the sensitive spirit so rebuffed."

Patton gritted his teeth and determined to show them that he was and could be, in fact as well as in fantasy, better than they. The notion that he was destined to be great, implanted at an early age, had to come true or his life would be meaningless and a disappointment to those who loved him. So he became the unconscious extension of their desires and unknowingly a victim of their innocent pressures.

He thus forced himself into an image that became second nature and was nevertheless false to his basic disposition.

It was exactly that which tickled the fancy of the public. Behind the supposedly perfect exterior, everyone suspected there was more. As Harold V. Boyle said, the public was familiar with the dominating figure with the high-pitched voice who used profane language unmatched anywhere in the army. This blood-and-guts figure was presented to the world with tongue in cheek, while he tried to conceal the military scholar, philosopher, and poet.

"What kind of man was George?" Hazen H. Ayer asked: he was tough, demanding, and rough, frequently unreasonable, often emotional, sometimes volatile and capricious. Critical, he was more than sensitive to criticism. He was vain, even childish. Yet so thoroughly was he an actor that one never knew for certain whether a statement or an act was genuine or for effect. The revolvers and helmet were trademarks and part of the show. But under that brash exterior was a soft-hearted, sensitive man, a profound student of history, an intelligent mind, a dedicated professional soldier, brave, generous, and religious.

If indeed he bore a cross passed to him by his parents, he carried another in the form of his marriage to a rich, talented, and adoring woman. She devoted her life to him. Until her death in 1953, when she fell from a horse as the result of an aneurysm, she nourished and enhanced his career and his legend, supporting him in private as in public, collecting his papers, lecturing on his achievements.

Precisely because she did all this, he was impelled to excellence. He had to prove that she had been right to marry him, right to overcome her father's initial reluctance to let her give up her mansions for army quarters. He had even to show that he was as good as her father, a great captain of industry who had amassed enormous wealth and power by his own endeavors.

This too drove him to dreams of personal glory. His complete conformity to the system — he was never a rebel — argued for his thorough identification with his country and its armed forces. Honor, duty, country in the West Point motto were more than words to him, and patriotism, as Codman noted, was more than an abstraction.

As a matter of fact, Patton was an incurable Romantic in the nineteenth-century sense, and therefore a figure out of the past. Despite his love for the heroes of antiquity, his immersion in the sentimental chivalry of Walter Scott — what Codman called "the straight *moyen-age* quality which permeates every thought and action" — he was more truly imbedded in Kipling, in the historical period between the French Revolution and the atomic bomb, when nations using citizen soldiers fought total wars for total victories.

Napoleon was the first of the great national leaders. Born in Corsica on the fringe of metropolitan France, rising to power through his own efforts, he dominated his contemporaries. A dashing, charismatic leader, he was an individual, never a team player submerging his personal aspirations in favor of the organization. He used the new conditions of his time, applied them to the art of war, and crushed his enemies on the battlefield. As emperor he personified France, a solitary figure at the head of the nation which fought the impersonal coalition of states under Britain. He was defeated only when he met Wellington who was endowed with much the same Romantic qualities of leadership.

It was no accident that Patton sought to emulate Napoleon, adopted his aphorisms of warfare, and tried, like Napoleon, to gain total victory. Born in the far west, in California, rising to prominence through his own sustained efforts, Patton stood out from his contemporaries. He was always an individual, frustrated by the exigencies of team play, and he came to embody the colorful, charismatic qualities of the lonely leader. He too became the hero figure, the Romantic *Geist,* the superman, the splendid soldier who single-handedly conquered.

The era of warfare inaugurated by Napoleon came to an end with Patton. He was the last of the Romantic warriors. He was the final nineteenth-century figure in military history.

If he had a single overriding disappointment, it was his failure to attain political preferment like Napoleon, to grasp political power as an adjunct of military success. Early in his life Patton spoke of winning in war so that a grateful people would elevate him to dictatorship. In his later years he realized, although he was at a loss to explain it, his unsuitability for a political post. He was aware of vague deficiencies on his part that made high public office unlikely for him. He understood that Eisenhower was more in tune with the times and had a much better chance to be catapulted from the military to the Presidency.

Younger than Patton, charismatic in his own right, Eisenhower grasped the passing of the old order, recognized the rightness of his role as supreme manager of a coalition effort. Unlike Patton and MacArthur, who represented the earlier tradition of Pershing, Eisenhower personified the new type of leadership required in the twentieth century.

During the 1920s and 1930s, the Army War College course of instruction followed the Pershing precept. Pershing had resisted adamantly what he saw as attempts on the part of his allies to submerge American aspirations and interests. And his message to those who followed him was: for God's sake, don't fight alongside allies.

Ironically, in World War II the United States found itself a member of a coalition, a partnership that sometimes required America to put aside temporarily its own national aims in the greater interest of winning the war and, it was hoped, the peace.

Eisenhower was brought up in the same Pershing outlook, yet was flexible enough to understand that it was outmoded; he accommodated to the new conditions. Patton, like MacArthur, resented the need for a new tradition in World War II. Eisenhower, Patton felt, always overcooperated with the British, but MacArthur never even tried — his headquarters in the Pacific was thoroughly an American organization in the older fashion.

It was significant, but no accident, that a group of younger commanders came to outrank Patton. Eisenhower, Bradley, Clark, Handy, all received four stars before he did.

Yet Patton emerged supreme, not in the manner of Marshall who put his stamp on the strategy and conduct of the global struggle; not like Eisenhower who superbly managed coalition forces; nor like Bradley who was balanced and calm in his management of American forces; nor like Stilwell who gained the sympathy of his countrymen because his mission was doomed from the start; not like Clark who became enmeshed in and associated with a secondary theater; and certainly not like MacArthur who remained an austere and awesome figure, somewhat remote and appearing sometimes to be hardly human.

Among Americans, Patton probably most resembled Admiral William Halsey, who was impetuous, colorful, and difficult to keep in check.

Among his contemporaries, Patton probably came closest to Rommel, who led his troops in combat and shared their dangers and who in the end seemed to repudiate Hitler, not because the Fuehrer was evil but because he was losing the war.

Patton sought instruction from Alexander the Great, Scipio, Caesar, Saxe, Murat, and a host of others, but most of all from Napoleon. Like Nathanael Greene in his military intuition, like Winfield Scott in his flamboyance, like Sherman in his tenacious focus on the objective, like Grant in his stubborn dedication to fighting, Patton once said:

> It seems to me that the hardest thing a general has to do is to make up his mind and then be undeterred from the accomplishment of his fixed purpose by any gruesome rumors that less stouthearted people thrust upon him.

He modeled himself on Pershing, who always remained in his mind his principal mentor. In appearance and manner, in his insistence on discipline, in his method of judging individual and unit performance, in his expectations of loyalty, he tried to be like Pershing. Harbord, Hines, Summerall, and Malin Craig were also his teachers, and Fox Conner, Paul Malone, and André Brewster contributed to his formation as a military man.

Like Pershing, Patton was a cavalryman in his military origins. He believed fiercely in the mobility that characterized the operations of this branch of service. He used the tank in both World Wars like the horse, stressing reconnaissance and movement, the envelopment and the pursuit, all based on the advantage of speed.

But he went beyond. In the Second World War he admitted the efficacy of other virtues. He adopted the concentrated strength of fire provided by the artillery, the capacity for sustained action provided by the infantry, and the wide-ranging, yet close support provided by airplanes. He fused these combat arms — armor, motorized infantry, self-propelled artillery, and tactical air — into a fighting organization that fundamentally incorporated the mobility of the cavalry. Swift, surprising thrusts and long, lightning strikes, reinforced and backed by power, became his battlefield trademark.

In conception this was no more than the blitzkrieg instrument fashioned by the Germans. Yet no one used this combination more effectively than Patton. What enabled him to do so was his proficiency in handling large units. He had schooled himself to a thorough knowledge of the elements of war.

Quite apart from his understanding of soldiers, he knew intimately the weapons and equipment at his disposal, what they could do and how they were best employed. He estimated terrain and area, distances and road-nets at a glance. He could place in his mind's eye without effort the ground accommodations needed by troop units. He could tell whether troops were well trained and ready for combat. The sureness with which he grasped a tactical situation and the deftness with which he moved to handle it were like a fine surgeon's diagnostic perception and instant action.

Yet he fumed too over shortages of men and materiel that plagued him in Europe. It was inconceivable to him that in a war largely determined by logistics, the greatest industrial nation in the world had to deny him the necessary means — gasoline and ammunition, as well as manpower — to triumph rapidly.

He was a doer rather than a thinker. Although he devoted much thought to his profession, he was a field soldier, a man of execution. He delighted in the work of training, practicing, and perfecting troop units and formations. He loved to employ all that was available to him in a practical manner for concrete results. A craftsman, an artisan, he shaped his materials superbly to his tasks and to the exigencies of an ever-shifting battle scene. He refined and improved processes and methods, adapted and fashioned doctrine, but contributed nothing to military theory or philosophy. He was a tactician rather than a strategist, and he was interested always in the immediate problem at hand.

If he was somewhat cavalier about the details of what the engineers or signalmen were up to, he could be so because he was always attuned to the qualifications of his subordinates. A large part of his success in the exercise of command came from judging constantly, if subconsciously, the performance of those under him. He was an expert evaluator of individuals — his corps commanders, his staff officers, all who served him. If on occasion he tolerated mediocrity, it was because, pragmatically, he had no other choice. Or because he felt that he could inspire the mediocre to perform above their capacities.

To everything and everyone he touched, he imparted his burning impatience to attack, his blazing desire to overwhelm the enemy. This was the essence of his generalship, and all that he did in study and preparation was for the supreme moment of meeting. Then his drive and his will, as well as his sixth sense of anticipation, triggered a near-faultless implementation of what his imagination and his mastery of the art of war had projected.

What Patton had above all as a military leader was, in Devers' words, "that power to make soldiers follow him anywhere." It was already manifest in the First World War, and it became legendary in the Second.

According to Codman:

> I have seen or heard of none . . . who can even remotely compare with General Patton in respect to his uncanny gift for sweeping men into doing things which they do not believe they are capable of doing, which they do not really want to do, and which, in fact, they would not do, unless directly exposed to the personality, the genius . . . of this unique soldier who not only knows his extraordinary job but loves it. Here in France, as in Sicily, an entire Army, from corps commander to rifleman, is galvanized into action by the dynamism of one man.

That was the essential quality of his greatness. And everyone had his own personal testimony on how Patton did it.

Hal C. Pattison:

> I well remember the day at Arracourt in September 1944, when the German attacks started against us, and we of CCA [4th Armored Division] were in a nip and tuck situation. For at least six hours that day the Army Commander was there, not interfering, just there "to hearten the driver."

William H. Wolfe: "When I left your organization, I left something behind I've never been able to replace."

John M. Devine:

> Like everybody else who has served under you, I feel that working for you is enough of a reward in itself. To get a citation . . . from you is almost too much. Whether or not I get the medal is immaterial.

Codman:

> I know of no one living who equals the boss in one respect, namely, as regards that amazing capacity for instant rightness and lucid anger. It's a rare and invaluable quality . . . You can't fake it. You either have it or you haven't.

Master Sergeant John L. Mims, Patton's personal driver from September 1940 to May 1945, marveled at the alternating periods of commotion and calm. He knew well the intensity of Patton's anger. How anyone could raise so much hell and then be so nice immediately afterward remained a mystery to Mims, and he wondered whether Patton rehearsed the screaming in order to have his troops more scared of him than of the enemy.

What endeared Patton to his men above all, Mims thought, was that he was fair and square. If he made a mistake or if he discovered that he had treated someone unjustly, he apologized — no matter what the man's rank or station. Patton never used his stars to cover his errors.

His flair endowed the frequent monotony and discomfort of military duties with excitement, glamour, and magic. Major General I. D. White, in command of the 2d Armored Division in the latter part of the war, wrote:

The training which the division received and the esprit which was built up in it while under your command has endured and will continue as long as it remains a unit. Over half of us have been with the division since its days at Benning, and you may be sure that the maneuvers, the parades, and the other events of those times bulk as large in our memory as do our travels and campaigns since coming overseas. They are a proud part of the division history, and every new man learns of Louisiana, Carolina, Benning, and the Pee Dee [River] as quickly as he learns of Morocco, Sicily, the St. Lo breakthrough, and the Siegfried Line.

Brigadier Charles Dunphie joined the II Corps in Tunisia as assistant chief of staff and liaison officer between Alexander's and Patton's headquarters. "My first meeting with Patton," he recalled,

on arrival, was typical. He said that so far he'd only met one British officer that he really liked, and he wasn't wholly British, but that he hoped I would change his views; that I had his full authority as a member of the staff to "call anyone a son of a bitch" if I wanted. I became very fond of him indeed, and I know that it was mutual . . .

He was, of course, a born leader, a great personality, and surprisingly, a very tender hearted man . . .

Although he gave his chief of staff and me the shortest orders I've ever heard on which to work out a plan, he gave out the plan superbly well at a conference and answered all the questions.

I have no doubt that he personally made II Corps into a first-class formation in an amazingly short time.

He was in all respects an extraordinary man, Betty South found. The captain of the Red Cross Clubmobile crew of about 25 girls attached to the Third Army headquarters, she recorded her impressions of Patton as follows:

I looked at the great Third Army field commander proposing the toast. His magnificent, tall figure . . . excited my admiration, but I was surprised at the thin, high-pitched voice that so poorly matched his striking looks and impressive bearing. The brick-red face, with its round, receding forehead sparsely framed by silvery-white hair, magnetized me chiefly because of the eyes. For in those blue eyes there was an intensity that burned with white-hot heat. There was arrogance unspeakable there, authority unrelinquished even to his superior officer, the Supreme Allied Commander, whom he was toasting.

In the depth of those eyes there was breath-taking boldness, utter fearlessness, naked daring, headlong defiance, proud contempt. Sparks of haughty aloofness, rude scornfulness, indomitable willfulness flew from his eyes to sear all about him in the room. Stark egotism and love of glory leapt out from behind the thin lashes, mixed with the immeasurable assurance and unshaken confidence in his own ability that unceasing hard work, personal fortune, and social position bestowed upon him. Belief in himself, proved by his superb feats of generalship, was supreme in George Patton's eyes. While he was speaking, his eyes were keen and shrewd, so telescopic it required no small amount of courage to stand his gaze. The tremendous surge of vitality and life that came from him exhilarated everyone present.

Yet . . . while we were still in the drawing room, I had furtively watched this great general, fascinated to be so near him, and I saw a tired, aging man, a sorrowful, solitary man, a lonely man, with veiled eyes behind which there was going on a torment of brooding and introspection. I saw a showman, aware of the necessity of drama. That General Patton battled with many different conceptions of himself I was sure.

And then when I met him and had my turn of conversation with him, I sensed the sandy, shallow places of his being, as well as the stormy depths. I tried earnestly to grasp the meaning of a man who could knock the camera from the hands of an accredited reporter and kick it to pieces, and the man who had picked up a GI in his arms and wept over him because he had fallen from a pole while doing his job of stringing wire to the general's mobile war van.

I was not altogether successful in keeping my poise as I watched the general's gentle, twinkling eyes, full of infectious humor when something amused him, change abruptly to flashing, angry blazes at something else which displeased him, and back again as quickly to frank, guileless, simple honesty. His agility in leaping back and forth between vulgar and shocking profanity and cultured, gentlemanly speech bewildered me. I was particularly hard-pressed to know what to do or say when he turned tearful eyes to me and spoke about God and prayer.

That evening at Patton's house in Luxembourg City, where Eisenhower was a guest, Betty South found Patton's conversation "a marvelous display of tact, diplomacy, and flattery."

When Eisenhower said he was surprised to learn that American troops were disappointed because he was unable to review their unit and had to cancel the scheduled inspection, he added, "Hell, George, I didn't think the American GI would give a damn even if the Lord Himself came to inspect them."

Patton immediately replied, "Well, I hesitate to say which of you would rank, sir."

All the Red Cross girls at the headquarters were close to Patton because his niece Jean Gordon was a member of the group.

The age of Patton's younger daughter and the child of Mrs. Patton's half sister, who was an invalid, Jean Gordon had lost her father at an early age and spent many of her school vacations with the Pattons. She was a bridesmaid in the weddings of both Patton girls.

Betty South said,

> Jean was a lovely young woman of great charm, intelligence, and sensitivity. I think it was a happiness for General Patton to have a member of the family with him. She understood and loved him. Although she was modest and unassuming, she had the same background of wealth, social position, and culture, as he did . . . She spoke fluent French and they often spoke it together. At home in any situation, she graced his table when he entertained important guests. She had a delightful sense of humor and was as witty as he was, and as interested in as many things, including horses, sailing, and history.
>
> In the rather austere and lonely life he led during the war, she was a bright, warm touch, a feminine touch I am sure he needed and appreciated . . .
>
> Our work of driving the doughnut and coffee trucks to Third Army units in combat was hard, rough, and dirty. General Patton's dinners were enjoyable affairs for us, a bit of glamor and elegance, excitement . . . We dressed in our Class A uniforms, wore white gloves, white scarves, dress pumps, and perfume (which he liked very much).

"Don't worry about Jean," Patton wrote to Beatrice in some exasperation on March 31, 1945. "I wrote you months ago that she was in this Army . . . I have seen her in the company of other Red Cross [girls], but I am not a fool, so quit worrying."

The girls had Patton to dinner several times – in Nancy, Luxembourg City, and on the shores of Tegernsee not far from Bad Tolz. Jean Gordon invariably called him "Uncle Georgie," but no one else dared.

According to Betty South:

> He was always easy with us, affable, charming, gracious, humorous, and witty, and friendly. He teased the girls about their various love-affairs. We respected and admired him and liked him. But we never forgot who he was. This was the result, I think, of two things: the general's own sense of dignity and decorum, and the fact that we were just a little bit afraid of him . . .
>
> We were cautious with him. We seldom saw the vulgar, tough aspect of the general, but we knew the famous temper (even experienced it a few times), and the aristocratic arrogance and disdainful manner in which he could behave, also the quick tongue that could cut you to pieces . . .
>
> His great ego sometimes repelled us but more often it amused us, for he was like a little boy boasting. However, we were never sure whether it was safe to laugh. Sometimes he purposely said or did things to confuse us, and we were uncertain as to whether we should agree with him, be impressed, or laugh . . .
>
> He was no "palsy-walsy" type of older man chucking the Red Cross girls under the chin or pinching our fannies. He was first, last, and always General Patton . . .
>
> The thing I liked best about him was his wonderful sense of humor, his great wit. He could laugh at himself and make all of us laugh. The thing I liked least was the arrogance . . . He was such a fine man and so accomplished, and was so often gentlemanly, gracious, warm-hearted and kind, that I was disappointed to find that streak of snobbishness and arrogance in him.

Once after dinner, they persuaded him to sing.

> To hear General Patton sing "Lily from Picadilly" was a treat no Broadway first-nighter ever has had. He beat time with the finger on which he wore a coiled-snake ring, and composed his own lyrics which

Tin Pan Alley probably would have found unusable. At these moments he was a very lovable elderly gentleman.

He could and did recite poetry by the hour, with exuberance or sadness, real or faked, not usually his own lines but rather those of the masters. Very often he embodied the charm and the humor of a lyric — perhaps of his own composition — that he had sent to some senior members of Pershing's headquarters in 1918:

You never can tell about a woman,
Perhaps that's why you think they are so nice
You never see two alike at any one time
And you never see one alike twice.

You are never very certain that they love you
You are often very certain that they don't,
For a man may argue still that he has the strongest will
But a woman has the strongest won't.

After the war was over, the girls became even more a part of his entourage. When Codman wrote to Patton in September 1945, he closed with: "Very best to yourself and to Gen. Gay, George [Murnane], Francis [Graves, his new aide] — in fact the whole household — not forgetting Sgt. Meeks, the ladies of the Croix Rouge, and Willie."

Betty South returned to the United States in October, Jean Gordon a month later. When Betty learned of Patton's death, she telephoned Jean to express her sorrow. Jean said, "I think it is better this way for Uncle Georgie. There is no place for him any more, and he would have been unhappy with nothing to do."

Jean took her own life in New York early in January 1946, little more than two weeks after Patton died. Some thought she did so in despair over her uncle's demise. Others believed she was hopelessly in love with a young married officer.

Whatever she had been to Patton before the war, during the conflict, and afterward, she helped to sustain and support him. Immediately after the war was over, when he had apparently achieved his destiny, and had no place to go in the army, he needed all the help he could get.

He wanted recognition and honors, applause and adulation, awards and decoration. He wanted to go fishing, hunting, to visit the commands, take part in ceremonies and reviews, to relax and enjoy himself. He felt he had earned all the tributes. Emotionally, mentally, and physically tired by his supreme effort during the war, as well as by the continual struggle with himself, he was on the verge of collapse. He was all used up, and his self-control was about to crack and come apart.

And instead of getting the things he wanted in the aftermath of the war, he entered a world he never understood, a place of continuing problems that refused to stand still and give him what he desired — comfort, a sense of well-being, contemplation of his successes, conversation with old friends.

During the immediate postwar months of the Occupation, he could see that transportation was restored, that water was available again, that sanitation was practiced, that food was distributed, that heat was provided, that housing was rehabilitated. But the subtle nuances of political dialogue were beyond him. What did he care about German political parties? Why couldn't everyone forget the war and Nazism, and settle down to building a Germany that resembled his conception of America?

The older and simpler precepts that applied to an innocent America in his early California years shaped his view of the cosmos and society. His outlook was essentially white and Protestant, and he saw no reason why the virtues of that ethic should not apply universally, even in Bavaria.

The world was supposed to be an ordered entity, where class, wealth, and breeding conferred special privileges automatically on certain favored individuals. As for the rest, so long as everyone was dignified, clean, neat, and did his job well, he was entitled to respect — like Sergeants Mims and Meeks, one white, the other black.

But the times had changed, and he was an anachronism.

Although combat soldiers usually shield their wives from knowledge of the dangers they face, Patton constantly noted — in his diary and in his letters to his wife — his brushes with death, the close calls, the falling of a shell nearby, the near accident. Was he boasting that he disdained the safety of a rear-echelon headquarters? Probably to some extent. His preoccupation with death was no doubt a manifestation of his childishness. But, more important, he was always searching for evidence of his destiny, marking, as it were, his viability. Would fate permit him to attain the destiny he hoped awaited him?

In the end he missed the top rank of five stars. He was never a field marshal or a general of the armies, like Marshall, MacArthur, and Eisenhower during the war, like Bradley who was promoted in 1950 after serving as U.S. Army Chief of Staff and then as the first Chairman of the Joint Chiefs of Staff.

But he gained something more than that, far more important to him — enduring fame as a fighter. Like Horatio Nelson, he was a hero in the grand manner.

Undoubtedly, as I. D. White remarked, he loved war. But not the death and destruction. The concentration camps and the ruined cities sickened him, and the losses of his soldiers hurt him. Even the bodies of the enemy, no longer an abstraction of warfare, saddened him.

He loved the excitement of war, the responsibility of war, the prerogatives of his position, and, most of all, the opportunity that war presented to use the skill, leadership, and courage required by his profession — in the same way that a surgeon loves his calling but not the disease, illness, and injury he treats.

"All his life," Codman said,

> General Patton has been obsessed with an almost neurotic aversion to suffering and cruelty in any and every form. It is this quality — so difficult, nay, impossible to square with the business of war makin — which sheds light upon some of the contradictions . . . of the General's character . . .
>
> When you come right down to it who, other than the enemy, *is* scared of him? Not his staff, nor his household, nor his drivers and orderlies. Not his dog, at whom in public he thunders and in private croons a kind of baby talk. Not the exhausted division commander whom the general has brought back to his own quarters, patted on the back, put to bed, and, a day or two later, sent off refreshed, rejuvenated, re-charged . . . Certainly not the tanker or the rifleman up front to whom the name of Patton means the captain of the winning team, a captain who demands much, but nothing that he himself has not done or is not prepared to do. No, other than the congenital shirker, the phony, and the misfit, I can think of no one under his command who has reason to be unduly scared of the General. His gift for leadership is based not on fear but rather upon a dynamism of total dedication and communicable humanity . . .

I have never heard the General tell a really sacrilegious or dirty story or encourage the telling of one. Alcoholic intake? Except on very rare occasions, an average of one whiskey-and-water before the evening meal, and possibly (when and if available) a glass of wine with it. The fair sex? Any serious interest on the General's part in any woman other than the members of his own family would be news to me.

A thoroughbred, Patton was high-strung. He often lost his temper but never harbored a vicious grudge and was immediately sorry for an unseemly outburst and more than willing to make amends. A bundle of conflicting tensions, he was always somewhat of a mystery. Whatever the paradoxes that surrounded him and were part of him, whether accidental or of his own making, there was one unresolved problem — as Codman said, "the reconciliation of the fighting soldier and the gentle man."

Most historic figures had a single great moment when they achieved what no one else was capable of.

Patton had several such moments, and thereby made himself indispensable to the Allied victory in World War II. No one else could have done so well, if at all, what he did during the training period in the United States, during the landings near Casablanca, during the aftermath of Kasserine Pass in Tunisia, during the invasion of Sicily and the subsequent drive to Messina, during the weeks when he catapulted the breakthrough in Normandy into the breakout and pursuit to the German border, during the days when he turned his Army toward Bastogne.

Those were his great moments, and they demonstrated his military genius. They would have been impossible without the force of the man himself. That is the legend of Patton.

# X

# Chronology
# Acknowledgments
# Index

# Chronology

| | | |
|---|---|---|
| 1940 | July | Colonel, assigned Commanding Officer, 2d Armored Brigade |
| | October 2 | Promoted to Brigadier General |
| | November | Assigned Acting Commanding General, 2d Armored Division |
| 1941 | April 4 | Promoted to Major General |
| | April 11 | Assigned Commanding General, 2d Armored Division |
| | June | Tennessee maneuvers |
| | Oct–Nov | Carolina maneuvers |
| | Aug–Sep | Louisiana-Texas maneuvers |
| | December 7 | Pearl Harbor |
| 1942 | Jan 15 | Assigned Commanding General, I Armored Corps |
| | Mar 26 | Designated to command the Desert Training Center |
| | April 10 | Arrived Desert Training Center |
| | July 30 | To Washington to prepare for Torch |
| | Aug 5–21 | To London for Torch planning |
| | Nov 8 | Torch landings in French North Africa |
| 1943 | Mar 6 | Assigned Commanding General, II Corps in Tunisia |
| | Mar 12 | Promoted to Lieutenant General |
| | April 15 | Relieved from command of II Corps |
| | July 10 | Invasion of Sicily; activation of Seventh Army; assigned Commanding General, Seventh Army |
| | Aug 17 | Capture of Messina |
| 1944 | Jan 22 | Ordered to United Kingdom |
| | Jan 26 | Appointed Commanding General, Third Army |
| | Feb 3 | Orders revoked; attached to Third Army as Acting Commanding General |

| | | |
|---|---|---|
| | March 26 | Assigned Commanding General, Third Army |
| | June 6 | Invasion of Normandy |
| | July 6 | Arrival in France |
| | Aug 1 | Third Army becomes operational in France |
| | Aug 16 | Appointed Brigadier General, Regular Army, with date of rank from September 1, 1943; appointed Major General, Regular Army, with date of rank from September 2, 1943 |
| | December 16 | German Ardennes counteroffensive |
| 1945 | April 14 | Promoted to General |
| | May 9 | End of war in Europe |
| | June 4–July 4 | Leave in the United States |
| | Oct 6 | Relieved of command of Third Army; assigned Commanding General, Fifteenth Army |
| | December 9 | Automobile accident near Mannheim; hospitalized in Heidelberg |
| | December 21 | Death |
| | December 24 | Interred at Hamm, Luxembourg |

# Acknowledgments

ONCE AGAIN I wish to record my thanks to the heirs of General Patton — his daughter Ruth Ellen, Mrs. James W. Totten; his son Major General George S. Patton; the children of his deceased daughter Beatrice, Mrs. John K. Waters — John Knight Waters, Jr., and George Patton Waters — who kindly gave me unlimited access to the papers and who were extremely helpful without interfering.

I shall always remember with pleasure and gratitude the warmth and directness with which Mrs. Totten answered my questions, even those that were unpleasant to consider. Her contribution to my understanding is immense, and I am happy to note particularly my debt to her.

The guidance, assistance, and support of Craig Wylie, Richard McAdoo, Austin Olney, Ruth Hapgood, and Sylvia Cleveland of Houghton Mifflin were invaluable. It is impossible for me to imagine a more competent and more sympathetic group of editors.

I am indebted to Blanche Gregory, Billy C. Mossman, and Sue Burt; Roy P. Basler, John C. Broderick, and Paul T. Heffron of the Library of Congress, and also Carolyn H. Sung, Charles F. Cooney, Marilyn Parr, and Mary Wolfskill of its Manuscript Reading Room; James L. Collins, Detmar Finke, Joseph R. Friedman, Edith Gibson, Charles B. MacDonald, and Hannah Zeidlik of the Army's Center of Military History; Earl Schwass and his staff at the Library of the Naval War College; L. James Binder of *Army* magazine.

Also Ruth Briggs, Mark W. Clark, Bruce C. Clarke, Hugh M. Cole, B. F. Cooling, Jacob L. Devers, Trevor N. Dupuy, Keith Eiler, Dominick S. Graham, Thomas Griese, Robert W. Grow, Thomas T. Handy, Frederick Hartmann, John Hattendorf, John E. Hull, Alfred Hurley, John Keeley, Robert Kelso, Carl F. King, Lyman Kirpatrick, Brooks Kleber, Lyman L. Lemnitzer, Carl Levin, Jay Luvaas, A. Laurie Jones,

G. Patrick Murray, George J. Nelson, Andrew P. O'Meara, George Pappas, Michael Pearlman, James H. Polk, Edwin Tribble, Thaddeus V. Tuleja, Francis J. West, and William Yates.

The following graciously gave permission to quote from published and private materials, and I am grateful to them: Stephen E. Ambrose, Ernie Deane, Jackie Keyes Desobry, Sir Charles Dunphie, John S. D. Eisenhower, Ernest M. Eller, Hobart R. Gay, Frank E. Mason, Troy H. Middleton, Hal C. Pattison, Forrest C. Pogue, Donald J. Smythe, Betty South, John Wickman, Edward C. Williamson, and the editors of *Army* magazine.

My wife has been my constant colleague in this endeavor as in all the others.

No one here listed is, of course, responsible for whatever errors may be found in the book.

—M. B.

# Index

# Other titles of interest

**MASTERS OF THE ART OF COMMAND**
Martin Blumenson and
James L. Stokebury
410 pp., 11 maps
80403-4 $14.95

**PANZER LEADER**
General Heinz Guderian
Foreword by B. H. Liddell Hart
New introd. by Kenneth Macksey
554 pp., 22 photos, 37 maps
80689-4 $17.95

**WAR IN ITALY, 1943–1945**
**A Brutal Story**
Richard Lamb
363 pp., 25 photos, 5 maps
80688-6 $14.95

**THE BITTER WOODS**
**The Battle of the Bulge**
John S. D. Eisenhower
New introduction by
Stephen E. Ambrose
550 pp., 46 photos, 27 maps
80652-5 $17.95

**THE FALL OF BERLIN**
Anthony Read and David Fisher
535 pp., 17 photos, 5 maps
80619-3 $16.95

**THE LUFTWAFFE WAR DIARIES**
**The German Air Force in World War II**
Cajus Bekker
447 pp., 119 photos, 20 maps
80604-5 $15.95

**RED STORM ON THE REICH**
**The Soviet March on Germany, 1945**
Christopher Duffy
415 pp., 14 maps
80505-7 $14.95

**THE SECOND WORLD WAR**
J. F. C. Fuller
431 pp., 61 maps & diagrams
80506-5 $14.95

**THE ROMMEL PAPERS**
Edited by B. H. Liddell Hart
544 pp., 17 photos
80157-4 $16.95

**MY RISE AND FALL**
Benito Mussolini
New introduction by Richard Lamb
590 pp., 8 photos, 1 map
80864-1 $18.95

**THE KILLING OF REINHARD HEYDRICH**
**The SS "Butcher of Prague"**
Callum MacDonald
272 pp., 33 photos
80860-9 $14.95

**TO THE BITTER END**
**An Insider's Account of the Plot to Kill Hitler, 1933–1944**
Hans B. Gisevius
Foreword by Allen W. Dulles
New introduction by Peter Hoffmann
648 pp.
80869-2 $18.95

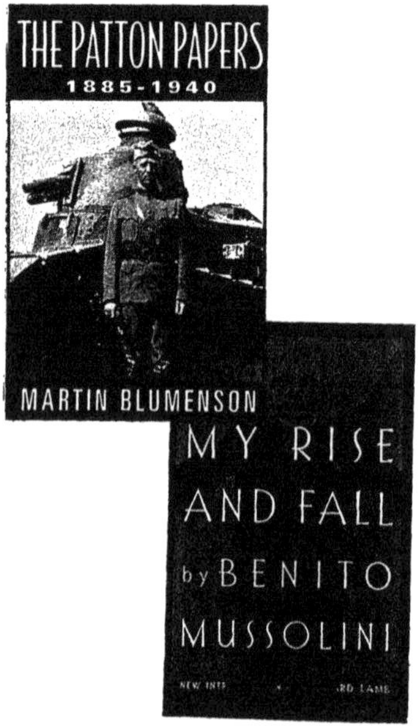

CPSIA information can be obtained
at www.ICGtesting.com
Printed in the USA
LVHW040732120223
739064LV00001B/1

9 780306 807176